HINDU POLITY

HINDU POLITY

A CONSTITUTIONAL HISTORY OF INDIA IN HINDU TIMES

[PARTS I AND II]

BY

K.P. JAYASWAL

M.A. (OXON.), PH.D. (HONS., PATNA UNIV.)

Of Lincoln's Inn, Barrister-at-Law;
Advocate, Patna High Court; Sometime Honorary Scholar, Jesus College, Oxford;
University Chinese Scholar, Oxford (1909); Tagore Professor of Law,
Calcutta (1917, 'Development of Law in Manu and Yajnavalkya');
Author of 'an Introduction to Hindu Polity'; Editor of
Chandesvara's Rajaniti-Ratnakara (Hindu Monarchy);
Editor, Journal of the Bihar and Orissa
Research Society; &c.

अथ धर्मार्थफलाय राज्याय नमः।

'And firstly, To STATE, the source of life and spirit.'

— *Nitivakyamrita.*

GYAN

Published by

GYAN

Gyan Publishing House
5, Ansari Road
Daryaganj, New Delhi-110002
Phone: 011-47034999, 9811692060
E-mail: books@gyanbooks.com

Distribution Network
gyanbooks.com
India, USA, Canada, UK, Australia, France

ISBN : 978-81-212-9923-7 (PB)
First Published, 1924

2nd Impression 2021

Printed at: Gyan Press, Delhi.

HINDU POLITY
Author: K.P. JAYASWAL

To

THE MEMORY OF

THE REPUBLICAN

VRISHṆIS, KAṬHAS, VAIŚĀLAS, AND ŚĀKYAS

WHO ANNOUNCED

PHILOSOPHIES OF FREEDOM

FROM

DEVAS, DEATH, CRUELTY, AND CASTE

मज्जेत्त्रयी दण्डनीतौ हतायां सर्वे धर्माः प्रक्षयेयुर्विवृद्धाः ।
सर्वे धर्माश्चाश्रमाणां हताः स्युः क्षात्रे त्यक्ते राजधर्मे पुराणे ॥
सर्वे त्यागा राजधर्मेषु दृष्टा सर्वाः दीक्षा राजधर्मेषु युक्ताः ।
सर्वा विद्या राजधर्मेषु चोक्ताः सर्वे लोका राजधर्मे प्रविष्टाः ॥

म. भा. शा. ६३. २८. २९.

"When Politics becomes lifeless, the triple Veda sinks, all the *dharmas* [i.e., *the bases of civilization*] (howsoever) developed, completely decay. When traditional State-Ethics are departed from, all the bases of the divisions of individual life are shattered.

"In Politics are realised all the forms of renunciation, in Politics are united all the sacraments, in Politics are combined all knowledge: in Politics are centred all the Worlds."

—*Mahābhārata, Sānti*—63.28.29.

Publishers' Note

THIS, the second edition of Mr. K. P. Jayaswal's well-known work, *Hindu Polity*, appears without his final personal revision, owing to the sudden and premature demise of the versatile author. It had been, however, carefully revised by him for the Press.

We are thankful to many learned scholars for the co-operation they have extended by enriching it with their valued Appreciations of the learned Author and his splendid work in the field of Oriental learning. We thank all of them most cordially for their valued help.

BANGALORE PRESS,
BANGALORE CITY,
10th August 1943.

C. HAYAVADANA RAO.

Preface to the Second Edition

SOON after its publication (end of 1924) 'Hindu Polity' was put on the syllabus of almost every University in India. The first edition having been long exhausted, I have been pressed by the need of the students to print the book again. In doing so I have availed myself of the suggestion and offer of Rao Sahib C. Hayavadana Rao to bring out a cheap edition in view of the demand for the book both from the students and the general public.

Apart from a general revision and verbal changes which are few, new matters and proofs brought to light have been added in their proper places. The original scheme, however, has been preserved. It may be noticed that there arose a controversy as to my interpretation of the *paura* (पौर) and *jānapada* (जानपद) terms as corporate bodies of the citizens and the country-people. By the discovery of a large number of seals at Nālandā—seals of the local jānapadas, *e.g. Purikā-grāma-jānapadasya*—the corporate character of the term is now put beyond controversy. On the evidence of these seals the jānapada institution existed down to the late Gupta times. I must note here that in the past controversy Professor Vanamali Bhattacharya was the only critic whose view coincided with truth.

October, 1936.

K. P. J.

Preface to the First Edition

'HINDU POLITY,' in two volumes (Parts)—the first on Vedic Assemblies and Republics, the second on Monarchy and Imperial Systems—is a sketch of the constitutional life of the Hindus. The subject is great but its treatment has to be modest. The works of *pūrva-sūris* had long been hidden ; the path opened by them had long been lost. It had to be researched. In 1911–13 a probable line was laid to dig and discover the Ancients' highway in the field of Polity. In these pages that line has been deepened and widened. And the way of the Fathers is in sight.

Subject and Difficulty

The author made a special study to find out what constitional progress, if any, Ancient Indians had achieved. In 1911 and 1912 some results of the study were published in the legal journal the *Calcutta Weekly Notes* and the Calcutta monthly the *Modern Review*. A connected paper was read to the Hindi Literary Conference in 1912 and its translation published in the *Modern Review*, 1913, under the title, '*An Introduction to Hindu Polity*'.

Pioneer Work

Before the publication of the *Introduction* there had been no work in any modern language on the subject. The *Introduction* fulfilled its purpose. To-day the subject finds place in University teaching. And the author has had the satisfaction of seeing his results quoted and reiterated, with or without acknowledgement, almost every year; the subject has become popular ; the truth has been recognized, accepted and adopted : it has rightly ceased to be his.[1]

---

[1] Mr. B. K. Sarkar, however, thinks otherwise—'But all the references in Jayaswal's studies, have been appropriated by subsequent writers.' (*Political Institutions*, etc., Leipzig, 1922, p. xvi), Can they not retort, '*ayaṃ nijaḥ paro veti gaṇanā laghuchetasām*' ?

Vincent Smith suggested to the author to treat the subject of Hindu republics in detail, and several friends insisted on having the *Introduction* in book-form. About the same time, Sir Asutosh Mookerjee, President of the Council of Post-Graduate Teaching, Calcutta University, asked him to prepare a curriculum of ancient Indian History. Need at that time was badly felt for a somewhat comprehensive book on ancient Hindu Polity. The author towards the close of 1917, undertook to revise the *Introduction* with a view both to carry out the suggestion of Dr. Smith and to supply the want. The present work was the outcome. In April, 1918, the revision was complete and the manuscript ready. The book was made over to Sir Asutosh Mookerjee who kindly took upon himself the publication of the work, placing it on the University syllabus.

Preparation of the Present Work

When a few chapters had been in type, the author was informed that scientific plagiarism was at work. Then, the manuscript was stolen from Sir Asutosh, no other belonging out of the group from which the box of manuscript was missing, was touched by the critical though secret admirer. Sir Asutosh informed the police, with the result that a professor who claimed to have recovered the manuscript made it over to Sir Asutosh. After three days' confinement the book obtained liberation. Having no other copy of the book, the Calcuta University Press being too slow, and the desire to publish "original researches" in certain quarters in Calcutta being great, the author brought back the manuscript to Patna. Engagement was then concluded to print the book at Allahabad. In the meantime the book was cited by Sir Sankaran Nair from the manuscript in his Note to the Government of India's *First Despatch on Constitutional Reforms* (dated 5th March, 1919), and chapters were printed in the *Modern Review* (Feb., 1920). When the whole of Part I was in type the English Section of the Press at Allahabad was sold away and the book once more came back home. Until this autumn, owing to the difficulties of getting a suitable press from a 'mofussil' town, and owing to professional

Why delay in publication

duties, no fresh arrangement could be made for the publication of the work.

The Present Work

The lines laid down in the *Introduction* (1913) have been closely followed in the present work. Except the chapter on Paura-Jānapada there has been no addition to those broad lines. The whole work otherwise is only a commentary on the *Introduction.*

Date of Kautilīya *Artha-Śāstra*

The book is presented in the form and substance just as it was completed in April, 1918, but for the amalgamation of the matter published by the author in the *Modern Review* in April, 1920, on Paura Jānapada, and the addition of one passage (§ 27) on a datum from the *Abhidhāna Rājendra* (1919), of the last line of the footnote at p. 33, and of Appendices C and D. The date of the Kautilīya (*Artha-Śāstra*) has been retained as originally given, although Dr. Jolly has recently revived the controversy through his edition of the *Artha-Śāstra.* On account of the importance of the subject the present writer has re-considered it here.[2] He is unable to agree with Dr. Jolly's conclusions.

Acknowledgements

The author's thanks are due to his kind friends Dr. A. Banerji-Sastri and Dr. Suniti K. Chatterji for reading the proofs and valuable suggestions, to Mr. H. Chakladar and Mr. Bata K. Ghosh for verifying references, and Dr. Kālidās Nāg and Prof. Arun Sen for doing the index. His friend the late Mr. H. Panday had helped him in the preparation of the MS.

PATNA, K. P. J.
November, 1924.

See Appendix C: '*Additional Notes on Part I.*'

SCHEME OF THE WORK

DETAILED CONTENTS

APPRECIATIONS

Dr. K. P. JAYASWAL—A MEMOIR

Kashi Prasad Jayaswal was born on the 27th November, 1881, at Mirzapur, a district town on the south bank of the Ganges between Benares and Allahabad. His father Sahu Mahadeva Prasad came of a very poor family, but by the dint of his industry built up a fortune in the shellac trade. He took keen interest in the education of his children. The early education of Kashi Prasad was begun under a private tutor and continued at the local London Mission High School. Besides, he studied Sanskrit at home under a *Sādhu* known by the pet name Handiābābā—because he cooked his meals in a *handiā* or earthen pot. The learning and character of this *Sādhu* and the depth and precision of his knowledge made such an impression upon young Kashi Prasad that he continued to remember him with reverence to the last of his days. Mr. Jayaswal always recalled with pride and gratefulness the debt he owed to Handiābābā, and how it stood him well in his whole career as an Indologist, making him feel much surer of his ground in Sanskrit than many a scholar who had got all his Sanskrit from the usual run of colleges.

After passing the Entrance Examination, Kashi Prasad joined the Queen's College, Benares, but soon gave up his studies and entered his father's trade, which he carried on with zest and remarkable success. His public spirit at this stage found three different outlets. He organised a Chaprā Sabhā (Shellac Association) and a Kalwār Sabhā or an association of his caste for the purpose of social reform. Besides, he began writing articles in Hindi journals in the wake of the school of Hindi litterateurs founded by Pt. Mahavir Prasad Dwivedi. This last activity at once brought him to the notice of the nationally inclined intelligentia of Northern India.

In August 1906, at the age of 25, when he was already father of two children, Mr. Jayaswal proceeded to England for higher studies. In those days, orthodoxy still ruled in the society of Northern India, and foreign travel was looked upon with disfavour. However, Mr. Jayaswal was permitted to go to England on condition that he would not take food touched by anyone there, except his Brahmin cook who accompanied him, and that he remained a vegetarian. And with his cook went all sorts of food-stuffs and even charcoal! Arrangements were made thereafter to send weekly consignments of these precious articles regularly for the duration of his stay in Europe!

In England, Mr. Jayaswal joined and graduated from Jesus College, Oxford, where he was awarded the Davis Chinese Scholarship for 1909. He was also called to the Bar at Lincoln's Inn.

While in England, Mr. Jayaswal came under the influence of two new forces which gave a definite turn to his life and determined its future course. His intelligence and sincerity brought him to the notice of the Indian revolutionary exiles in Europe, who had just then formed a centre in England for recruitment from amongst their countrymen who went to that country for higher studies. They included such brilliant personalities amongst them as Shyamji Krishna Varma, S. R. Rana, Har Dayal and V. D. Savarkar. Mr. Jayaswal did not join their party, but felt a warm sympathy for them, which developed into life-long friendship. In fact, it was the nationalistic fervour kindled by contact with these gentlemen that drove Mr. Jayaswal into the study of his country's past and sustained him in his efforts throughout life. A still more potent factor which left its impress upon Mr. Jayaswal's mind was his contact in England with Don Martino De Zilva Wickremsinghe. Mr. Jayaswal received his first lessons in Indian epigraphy and archæology from him. He accepted him as his *guru* and he felt the same reverence for him as he felt for Handiābābā. Indeed, it was Wickremsinghe who turned Jayaswal's mind from Hindi journalism to the study of his country's past, and it would be no exaggeration to say that the Jayaswal whom we know, the Jayaswal of *Hindu Polity* and Indian History generally, is one of the gifts of that Simhalese savant to modern India.

Mr. Jayaswal returned from England overland, passing through Turkey, Egypt and Arabia and reached home in July 1910. He settled down in Calcutta as a Barrister of the High Court. From 1911 onwards, he began to contribute to research journals devoted to Indology. Even while in England, he had come in contact with scholars like George A. Grierson. His new contributions brought him into touch with Wilfred Schoff, A. J. Edmund, V. A. Smith, F. W. Thomas and others.

In 1912–13, Sir Ashutosh Mukerji, then Vice-Chancellor of the Calcutta University, induced Mr. Jayaswal to join the post-graduate teaching department of the University. Jayaswal worked there for sometime, but had soon to resign that post as the University was directed by the authorities to remove him from the staff, solely for his alleged political opinions. With him had to resign two of his colleagues, *viz.*, Dr. A. Suhrawardy and Mr. Abdul Rasool, the President of the historic Barisal Conference of 1906, which inaugurated the anti-partition movement in Bengal.

The resignation, however, did not in the least affect Mr. Jayaswal's cordial relations with Sir Ashutosh. It rather raised him in the eyes of that nation-builder, who, as the sequel will show, invited him again as Tagore Law Lecturer in 1917. When the Carmichael Chair for Ancient Indian History was founded in the Calcutta University, Sir Ashutosh offered it to Jayaswal, who however did not accept it as he had a lucrative legal practice at Patna by that time and had given up entirely the idea of being a poor professor again.

After the separation of Bihar and Orissa from Bengal, Mr. Jayaswal migrated to Patna in 1914 and remained there permanently. He was on the roll of the Patna High Court since its inception. His practice at the Bar was large and distinguished. He easily won for himself a position as an authority on Hindu Law, and was often consulted by eminent lawyers and judges. He also came to be considered a specialist in Income-Tax Law and a *facile princeps* in that line at the Patna Bar.

But though a lawyer of high standing, Mr. Jayaswal never took the practice of law as the mission of his life. As Dr. Rajendra Prasad has observed, " he was a historian by choice and instinct and a lawyer by compulsion. His own inclinations and talents attracted him towards History but the demands of the flesh dragged him towards law courts and law reports. .... He was more at home in the archæological museum and the library than in the High Court and if India were a free country his talents would have borne greater fruit than they did on account of his professional preoccupation ". He often used to carry in his pocket, while going to the court, undeciphered ancient coins and utilised his leisure moments there in trying to read them !

Apart from his early contributions to journals specializing in Indic studies, Mr. Jayaswal contributed from 1911 to 1913 a series of articles on Hindu Law to the *Calcutta Weekly Notes*. Hindu Law was till then considered to be something fixed and immutable, something based on revealed or ancient books. It referred to personal law only. Mr. Jayaswal took a historical view of Hindu Law and tried to reconstruct it as a complete system. This method found approval from Prof. J. Kohler of the University of Berlin, who during his life-time was considered to be the leading comparative jurist in Europe. Prof. Kohler observed that the articles marked a new stage in the history of the study of Hindu Law. Besides Prof. Kohler, Sir Lawrence Jenkins, Sir Ashutosh Mukerji and Sir Rashbehari Ghosh also encouraged Mr. Jayaswal to continue his line of enquiry on historical lines and to prepare an account of the whole system of

Hindu Law. The University of Calcutta elected him as Tagore Law Lecturer for 1917. In that capacity, he delivered in 1919 a series of twelve lectures on Manu and Yājñavalkya which were printed ten years later.

Recognition of the historical development of Hindu Law naturally led to the search for the constitutional agency or agencies to whom that development was due in different periods. With this started a new line of enquiry, the final outcome of which was *Hindu Polity*, the subject of this work. Mr. Jayaswal's first articles on the subject appeared early in 1912 in the *Modern Review*, and he read a connected paper on it to the All-India Hindi Sahitya Sammelan (Hindi Literary Conference) at Bhagalpur held in the same year under the presidentship of Mahatma Munshi Ram (later Swami Shraddhanand). The rest of the story is told in the author's *Preface* to this work and need not be repeated here. The study of ancient Indian political institutions has since been taken up by a number of other scholars. But it will be agreed that the credit of first opening this line of research belongs to Mr. Jayaswal.

When Mr. Jayaswal came to Patna in 1914, Sir Edward Gait was the administrative head of the newly formed Province. He was himself a scholar and interested in India's past. Mr. Jayaswal found a ready friend in him for his historical studies and with his help and the support of the leaders in the Province, he was able to organise a number of activities. In 1915 were founded the Bihar and Orissa Research Society, its *Journal* and the Patna Museum. Mr. Jayaswal was closely associated with all these institutions from their very start. He felt a paternal affection for these institutions and devoted a good deal of his time in directing their various activities. In a letter to him dated London, the 14th April, 1937, Sir E. A. Gait wrote: "I may have had a hand in forming the Bihar and Orissa Research Society, but it was you who have been its mainstay from the beginning up to the present time." Mr. Jayaswal was the editor of the *Journal* of the Society from its start in 1915 to the last days of his life and he made it one of the leading research journals of the world. Mr. Jayaswal was also editor for sometime after his arrival at Patna, of a Hindi weekly, *Pātaliputra*, which was published from there.

With Mr. Jayaswal's arrival at Patna and with the foundation of the Bihar and Orissa Research Society, started the second period of his research contributions. It is not intended to enumerate all of them here, but a brief reference may be made to the most important of them. He contributed an article entitled the *Brahmin Empire* to the Patna periodical the *Express*. The Śuṅga and Sātavāhana empires which arose after the fall of the Mauryas were claimed to be actuated by a movement for the revival of Brahminism. The whole thesis was revised in 1930 when he contributed a comprehensive article on the *Śaka-Sātavāhana Problems*.

From 1917 onwards, he was engaged, in collaboration with Mr. Rakhal Das Banerji, in reading the difficult Hātigumphā inscription of Khāravela. The study was continued by the two eminent scholars for fourteen years until they were able in 1930 to publish their final reading and interpretation of the inscription in the *Epigraphia Indica*. Another interesting study started by Mr. Jayaswal in 1917 related to what he claimed to be Śaiśunāka statues. It gave birth to a lively controversy in which Hara Prasad Shastri, Gaurishankar Hirachand Ojha, R. D. Banerji, Rama Prasad Chanda, Chandra Dhar Guleri, L. D. Barnett, V. A. Smith, R. C. Majumdar, Arun Sen, O. C. Ganguli and others joined.

At the end of his article on the Problems of *Śaka-Sātavāhana History*, written in 1930, Mr. Jayaswal declared that a complete account of the sovereignties between the Sātavāhanas and Guptas was recoverable and " we have no right to own that we have still a dark period in the history of Hindu Times." He recovered this account, and in 1933 published his *History of India 150 A.D. to 350 A.D.* Before writing this book, he undertook a detailed tour of the places which had witnessed the scenes of that history. In 1933, Babu Durga Prasad of Benares published a remarkable paper on the most ancient punch-marked coins of India. As is well-known, these coins have no legends or human figures on them, but a number of symbols only. Babu Durga Prasad compared and classified these symbols and from such classification drew conclusions as to the respective sequence of their different classes. Mr. Jayaswal was struck by the ingenuity of his friend and eagerly joining in the research carried it some steps further, specially in respect of the Mauryan coins. In the summer of 1935, while he was in England, he was invited by the Royal Asiatic Society of London to deliver a lecture on the subject which was highly appreciated.

In 1934, Mr. Jayaswal published what he called *An Imperial History of India*. This was a history of the imperial dynasties of India as told in a Buddhist Chronicle of the 9th century A.D. *Ārya-Manjuśri-Mūlakalpa*. The Chronicle had been published sometime before, but its text was corrupt, and Mr. Jayaswal was encouraged to extend his study to it on the discovery by his friend, Rāhula Sānkṛityāyana, of a much better Tibetan translation. The interpretation of this text is in the nature of the decipherment of a code, as it is full of cryptic statements about historical personalities, whom it often refers to only by the first syllables of their names.

Mr. Jayaswal was invited by the Government of Nepal to visit that country in 1936. On his return from there, he wrote a *Chronology and History of Nepal from 600 B.C. to 800 A.D.*, which was destined to be the last important work of his life.

Mr. Jayaswal was elected President of the 6th Indian Oriental Conference held at Baroda in 1933. In the same year, he presided over the Bihar Provincial Hindi Sahitya Sammelan held at Bhagalpur. In 1935, he was elected President of the History section of the All-India Hindi Sahitya Sammelan held at Indore, and in the same year and in the next,

President of the Numismatic Society of India for its two consecutive sessions. In 1936, the Patna University conferred on him the honorary degree of Doctor of Philosophy, an honour which was long overdue.

During the last decade of his life, the association with two of his friends, Prof. Jayachandra Vidyalankar and Mahāpandita Rāhula Sānkrityāyana exerted a great influence on Mr. Jayaswal's views and activities. The former, a pupil of M. M. Gaurishankar Hirachand Ojha, came to Patna in 1927 as Lecturer in the Bihar Vidyapitha. His work (in Hindi) on the geographical background of Indian History had attracted Mr. Jayaswal's attention. Prof. Vidyalankar had undertaken another comprehensive work on the History of India and had begun to consult Mr. Jayaswal about its problems and difficulties. By and by, he became his regular apprentice and colleague and the two scholars consulted each other almost on every problem that either of them had to face for about ten years. Mr. Vidyalankar's work on Indian History was published in 1933 under the title *Bhāratīya Itihās kī Rūparēkhā*. It covers the period from the earliest times to *Circa* 200 A.D. Before its publication, the whole manuscript was read to Mr. Jayaswal in July 1931, and revised in the light of his criticism. While this was being done, Mr. Jayaswal felt uneasy from time to time over the fact that work of that type and of such national utility was not being done in an organised manner. He recorded the opinion that "such a synthetic work had not been attempted before," and remarked that he himself should have been engaged in it, but his life had been taken up by the Hātigumphā Inscription! He regretted he was wasting his time over his practice at the Bar, but there was no help for it. Now, however, he had almost fulfilled his family obligations; his son and daughter whom he had sent abroad for study were due to return soon. So he decided to renounce his practice at the Bar and devote himself exclusively to such work by joining some university which might undertake to help him in organising it. With this end in view, he made an offer to a well-known university of Northern India. But it met with little success. Mr. Jayaswal then broached the subject in his Presidential Address at the Indian Oriental Conference at Baroda and continued to canvass support for his scheme of a comprehensive history of India. He had good response from many different quarters as his correspondence shows, but he could not see what to do with those promises. He was a scholar and not a practical man of affairs. He realised this and approached Babu Rajendra Prasad to help him in organising the work. On the 31st of May 1936, Rajendra Babu came to his house and discussed the scheme with him and Mr. Jayachandra Vidyalankar. They decided to start what is now known as the *Bhāratīya Itihās Parishad.*

Mahāpandita Rāhula Sānkrityāyana, the other close friend of Mr. Jayaswal, was introduced to him in 1930, on his return from his first adventurous expedition to Tibet. A profound scholar of Sanskrit and Pali, he had gone to Tibet to study Tibetan Buddhism at first hand and returned after performing his mission under the greatest hardships. He engaged himself in restoring from Tibetan the lost work of the Buddhist philosopher Dharmakīrti, and undertook three more journeys to Tibet, with the result that he was successful in securing not only the original text of Dharmakīrti but more than a hundred texts of Buddhist philosophers, hitherto considered as lost. Mr. Jayaswal took a keen interest in the work of his friend. His views and feelings about him may be known from his recorded appreciation in the *Modern Review* for February 1937.

Mr. Jayaswal was a diabetic and had to be careful about his diet and exercise. He walked two miles daily to take an early morning bath in the Ganges. This he did throughout the year and this was the only physical exercise he took. He could not, however, get rid of his disease, and passed away from this world on the 4th of August, 1937, after an illness of two months, due to a virulent type of carbuncle. During his last illness, there appeared a remarkable equanimity and contentment on his face, which was doubtless due to his feeling that he had done his best in his life and that his mission had been taken up by his successors.

Benares,
1-6-1941. GADADHAR PRASAD AMBASTHA.

* * *

DR. K. P. JAYASWAL — *A Tribute*

DR. KASHI PRASAD JAYASWAL was one of the Foundation Members of the Bihar and Orissa Research Society and the Editor of its *Journal* for the greater part of its existence. He died at Patna on 4th August, nearly twenty-six years after his call to the cause of Indology by Sir Ashutosh Mukherji.

Born at Jhalda in Manbhum (Bihar) in 1881, Jayaswal would have been 56 on 27th November 1937, the year of his lamented death. The London Mission School at Mirzapur, where his father was a big merchant, and Oxford were mainly responsible for his education. At Oxford, he obtained the Davis Scholarship in Chinese and took his M.A. in History. He was called to the Bar from the Middle Temple and was enrolled as a Barrister in the Calcutta High Court in 1909. About 1910, at the instance of Sir Ashutosh Mukherji, the Senate of Calcutta University recommended Jayaswal for appointment as a Lecturer in Ancient Indian History. Under the convention then obtaining in academic circles at Calcutta, active participation in current and controversial politics was considered undesirable and Jayaswal was asked to give up his appointment. Since then, Jayaswal eschewed politics and instead enriched Indology with a sustained devotion equalled by few of his contemporaries. His contributions embrace Indian epigraphy and numismatics, Hindu History and polity, Sanskrit texts and Hindi literature: they are valuable and varied, and all imprinted with his personality and predilection.

Jayaswal first came to prominence with his articles on 'An Introduction to Hindu Polity' in *the Modern Review* in 1913. These articles were later developed and appeared as *Hindu Polity* in 1924. In 1917, he was appointed Tagore Professor of Law at Calcutta and delivered lectures on the *Development of Law in Manu and Yāgñavalkya*, published in 1934. It was this combination of a trained legal practitioner and theorist that makes his comparison of political Saṃghas with Buddhist ecclesiastical organisations so attractive. He edited the well-known Sanskrit text on politics *Rājanītiratnākara, Circa* A.D. 1300–25, in 1925, a second edition of which appeared in *JBORS*, 1936, Vol. XXII, Pt. IV. This acquaintance with most of the original sources Jayaswal made full use of in his writings on ancient and mediæval systems of Government in India.

When in 1914, that scholar-administrator Sir Edward Gait founded the Bihar and Orissa Research Society at Patna, Jayaswal's literary activities multiplied. Since then, till the day of his death, he was a constant contributor to the pages of its *Journal* with only occasional publications in the *Indian Antiquary*, *Journal of the Bengal Asiatic Society*, *Journal of the Royal Asiatic Society of London*, *the Kāshī Nāgarī Prachāriṇī Patrikā* and a few other journals. His writings on the Pātaliputra statues, Hāthigumphā inscription, the Nāga-Vākāṭaka history and pre-Mauryan and Mauryan coins in *JBORS* evoked wide interest. This interest, whether of warm appreciation or of acute controversy, was due essentially to an unusual vigour of mind and an alluring gift of expression. In 1934, he revisited London and placed his conclusions regarding Mauryan coins before the Royal Asiatic Society of London. The President summed up by saying that like the theories of Sir Alexander Cunningham, those of Jayaswal would be criticised by his contemporaries, but would find acceptance afterwards. The available data are admittedly inadequate. In awaiting fresh discoveries, Jayaswal's work has been most useful in provoking discussion where formerly there was either indifference or neglect.

Besides editing the *Pratipadapaṃcikā*, commentary on the *Arthaśāstra*, and some volumes of the Mithilā MSS. with the present writer, Jayaswal edited the *Manjuśrīmūlakalpa* in collaboration with Rev. Rāhula Sānkṛityāyāna. His last important work was on *Nepal Chronology*, published in *JBORS* (1936).

Jayaswal's services were recognised by Government and learned institutions in India. Government appointed him first a member and then the President of the Managing Committee of the Patna Museum. It was mainly due to the efforts of his predecessor as President, Mr. Manuk, and of Jayaswal that the Patna Museum has within a short time become a storehouse of the ancient relics of Bihar and Orissa. He received the Honorary Doctorate of Philosophy, from the Patna University in 1936. He was twice elected President of the Numismatic Society of India and was awarded their special medal. He was also awarded the Gaekwad Golden Jubilee Medal in 1930. He presided over the Sixth All-India Oriental Conference in 1932 and continued to be a member of its Council to the end of his life.

Both in India and Europe, Jayaswal was well known to a wide circle of friends and admirers who will lament the passing of a fine scholar and a warm-hearted friend.

Patna,
31-7-1941. A. BANERJI-SASTRI.

* * *

DR. K. P. JAYASWAL—*An Appreciation*

IN response to a request from my friend Rao Sahib C. Hayavadana Rao, I have great pleasure in paying my tribute to the late lamented scholar Dr. K. P. Jayaswal, whom I had the honour and privilege of knowing intimately for over a decade. In his death the world of Indian History and Culture has suffered a great loss. By profession a distinguished and successful Barrister, Dr. Jayaswal took to Oriental Studies early in his life. A good student of Sanskrit literature, Vedic and Epic, Dr. Jayaswal carefully studied original texts, and put forward the results of his investigations which were new and original interpretations of the Vedic and Epic texts, especially those dealing with Hindu administrative institutions. His frequent contributions to learned journals in India and abroad soon won for him a name for real scholarship and mature judgment; so much so that the late V. A. Smith quoted him as an authority in his writings. Dr. Jayaswal revised his numerous articles and published them in a book entitled *The Hindu Polity*. In this book, Dr. Jayaswal endeavoured to establish the thesis that parliamentary and democratic governments were in vogue in ancient India with representative assemblies such as the *Paura* and *Jānapada* functioning in the royal capital. This well-written book attracted the serious attention of Oriental scholars, East and West, and he soon got an unique place in the international world of Orientalists.

Dr. Jayaswal was primarily a Historian and then a Barrister. Yet he was a successful Barrister. Side by side with his professional activities, Dr. Jayaswal devoted all his spare hours to the field of Indology. He was a trained investigator and scientific method was his chief plank. What he began as a hobby became an all-absorbing life-work. His activity in this direction was many-sided. He was an archæologist of great enthusiasm. He undertook in his private capacity the further work of excavating the ancient Pataliputra sites and he had a number of discoveries to his credit. His interest in Indian architecture was exceedingly great. He was, perhaps, the first to take the origins of the *sikhara* style of architecture to pre-Gupta times. His work in the field of sculpture too is well known. He was, again, a born numismatist. He had the keen eye to discover many new coins and to decipher them. His reading of legends on the coins was generally correct, and won often the approval of experts in numismatics. As the President of the Numismatic Society of India, he did much to strengthen that

Society and to popularise it by bringing his weighty influence to bear on it.

Above all, Dr. Jayaswal was the life and soul of the Bihar and Orissa Research Society. He was the distinguished Editor of the *Journal of the Bihar and Orissa Research Society* for years together, maintaining a high standard of excellence. His articles were always a contribution to knowledge. In this Journal, he published the *Rājanītiratnākara*, a valuable work to students of Indian polity. His other publications, equally valuable, are the *Imperial History of India* and *History of India from* 150 *to* 350 *A.D.*, both of which show much painstaking research. His wide knowledge, pleasing manners and exceeding generosity endeared him to every well-wisher of Indian civilization and culture. The All-India Oriental Conference honoured itself by asking him to preside over its sessions at Baroda. The address he then delivered is a masterly piece of education by itself. He took abiding interest in the promotion of the objects and aims of the All-India Oriental Conference. But Mysore was the last Conference which he attended. In recognition of his well-merited scholarship, the University of Patna rightly conferred on him the Degree of Doctor of Philosophy, an honour long overdue in his case.

One can conclusively say that what he accomplished has helped much to enlarge the sphere of Indian History. He would have done much more had he been spared for some years to come. By dint of selfless research work to which he dedicated his entire life, Dr. Jayaswal takes a legitimate place in the front rank of India's historians.

The University,
MADRAS,
12-8-1941.

V. R. RAMACHANDRA DIKSHITAR.

OPINIONS

Late Dr. K. P. Jayaswal

Tribute paid by the Patna University Senate

We are indebted to the "*Indian Nation*", Patna, dated Friday, August 6, 1937, for the following account:—

The following speeches were made in the Patna University Senate on March 28, 1936, when it was decided to confer the degree of Doctor of Philosophy on Mr. K. P. Jayaswal.

It was on the 28th March 1936 that the Vice-Chancellor of the Patna University moved in the Senate, on behalf of the Syndicate, recommending to H. E. the Chancellor that the honorary degree of Doctor of Philosophy be conferred on Mr. K. P. Jayaswal on the ground that he is, by reason of his eminent position and attainments, a fit and proper person to receive such a degree.

VICE-CHANCELLOR'S SPEECH

In moving the resolution, the Vice-Chancellor delivered the following speech:—

" Mr. K. P. Jayaswal has a record of 25 years of original research in the field of Indian History in its widest significance. His contributions have shed light on Hindu Law and Constitution, Political History, Chronology, Epigraphy, Sanskrit Literature, Prakritic Vernaculars, Indian Art and Indian Numismatics. When his constitutional history of Hindu Period entitled "Hindu Polity" was published, Professor F. W. Thomas, Boden Professor of Oxford, the leading authority in England on Indian History and Culture, prefaced his review in the *Journal of the Royal Asiatic Society of London* (1925) with these remarks:—

'Mr. Jayaswal is to be congratulated upon the publication of a long meditated work. We may also congratulate the students of ancient Indian institutions: for in addition to an unusual vigour of mind Mr. Jayaswal, as a trained legal practitioner and theorist, brings to bear upon the history of the Indian state a more concrete realization of the vale-in-use of terms than is natural to a scholar as such. It was this that enabled him in his first publication to direct upon the political Samghas (aristocratic or republican governments) of ancient India the light obtainable from the procedure of the Buddhist ecclesiastical organisation. In more recent years, he has delivered, as Professor at Calcutta (1917), the Tagore Law Lectures on the 'Development of Law in Manu and Yajnavalkya' (the appearance of which is awaited with interest); while in the sphere of pure scholarship he has found time amid his professional occupations to publish many striking articles, and also a new Sanskrit text on politics (the *Rājanītiratnākara* of Chandesvara, *Circa* A.D. 1300–25), and to lend powerful support, as Honorary Secretary and Editor of an exceptionally valuable journal, to the work of the Bihar and Orissa Research Society.'

Another competent critic, namely Dr. D. R. Bhandarkar, Carmichael Professor of Indian History and Culture of the Calcutta University, in his Manindra Chandra Nandy Lectures, says:

"The importance of the subject was first perceived with prophetic vision by K. P. Jayaswal, Esq., M.A. (Oxon.), Barrister-at-Law, who began by contributing thought-provoking articles in the *Modern Review* in 1913. His mature views will now be found enshrined in his classical book entitled "Hindu Polity".

Mr. Jayaswal is regarded as the founder of this branch of study and his book "Hindu Polity", which covers some 600 pages, is lectured upon in almost every University of India, in the University of London and in foreign Universities where Indian History is studied.

Equally, if not more, important work is his Tagore Law Lectures on Manu and Yājñāvalkya dealing with the growth of basic Hindu Law. Dr. Fitz Gerald, I.C.S., Lecturer to the Inns of Courts on Hindu Law, described this work in the *English Law Quarterly Review* in these terms:—

'Hindu Law', said J. D. Mayne, 'has the oldest pedigree of any known system of Jurisprudence.' Yet its ascertained history has hitherto been a miscellaneous collection of dry bones without flesh or blood and with even the position of the bones in the skeleton disputed by the anatomists. Generalizations of the widest type—for instance, that the age of the Dharmasūtras preceded that of the Dharmashāstras; dates which were seldom within half a millennium of certainty: these were all that the scholar had to offer a lawyer anxious to understand the growth of the system which he has been called upon to administer. Max Muller and Bühler destroyed the Anglo-Brahminical legend (enshrined in Majne's *Ancient Law* and in the Holman Hunt fresco at Lincoln's Inn) of the Manudharma-shāstra as a code of laws claiming obedience in the same manner as *e.g.*, the XII Tables or the 'Corpus Juris': but they put nothing in its place. Little or no attempt was made to connect the history of thought with the political history of India; though it must be obvious that, however detached from the world's affairs the Rishis might be, great kingdoms could not rise and fall nor great religious systems strive for acceptance without some effect on the jurisprudence and ethics of the schools. It is to the credit of Mr. Jayaswal that he makes a real constructive attempt to bridge this gap. Sanskritist and lawyer, he adds to those qualifications a rare independence of judgment."

The book is studied not only in Indian Universities but also in Continental Universities and is recognized as a standard work on Ancient Law.

The early papers of Mr. Jayaswal on Hindu Law were translated in German by no less an authority than Professor Kohler whom the *Encyclopædia Britannica* describes as the foremost comparative jurist in Europe. Professor Kohler announced that Mr. Jayaswal's contributions marked a new stage in the study of Hindu Law (17 *C.W.N.*, 227: *Notes*).

Mr. Jayaswal's work on Political History based on inscriptions and Sanskrit Texts have even overshadowed his legal and constitutional contributions in the popular view. The late Mr. E. Edwards of the Indian Civil Service, who revised the standard book of Vincent Smith on " Early History of India ", conspicuously acknowledged in his preface that new knowledge gained from Mr. Jayaswal's researches necessitated a revision of the book. Readers of Vincent Smith's two histories find numerous references to Mr. Jayaswal's results on various periods and topics.

In 1933, Mr. Jayaswal published his " History of India, 150 A.D. to 350 A.D.", that is, the period which had been blank and had been called the Dark Period in Indian History and the next year saw the publication of his commentary on a Buddhist Sanskrit Text on Indian History, under the title " An Imperial History of India ". The Sanskrit text has also been published by him after comparison with its Tibetan translation made in the eleventh century of the Christian Era. This supplied an original source of the Indian History of the period subsequent to 320 A.D., that is, where Purāna Chronicles stop.

The long inscription at Hāthigumphā, near Bhubaneshwar, which in importance ranks only next to the inscriptions of Emperor Asoka, has been solved by Mr. Jayaswal after a labour extending over ten years. This document is invaluable for the political history of India of the second century B.C. and will always be referred to as a primary source.

On Indian coinage, his contribution is no less remarkable. Last June when he was invited to lecture before the Royal Asiatic Society of London, and it may be added that he was the first Indian scholar to receive the honour of an invitation to lecture before that learned Society, he placed discovery of the coinage of Mauryas before the Society, whereon he was hailed as a second Sir Alexander Cunningham. Mr. Jayaswal has been twice elected President of the Numismatic Society of India and has been awarded their special medal for conspicuous original work on the science of Indian coins.

Mr. Jayaswal was elected President of the All-India Oriental Conference, an honour which has not been conferred on any scholar at comparatively such an early age, Mr. Jayaswal's predecessors and successors in this high office being all older than him by twenty years and more.

Mr. Jayaswal has supervised the search for Sanksrit manuscripts in the province, instituted by the local Government, and has edited *Catalogue of Manuscripts on Hindu Law and Sanskrit Literature*. He has edited the *Journal of the Bihar and Orissa Research Society* for over 15 years. The Journal is honoured and read all over the learned world."

Mr. Sachidananda Sinha's Tribute

Mr. Sachidananda Sinha said:—

"I second the proposal which you have been good enough to place before the Senate on behalf of the Syndicate. You have said everything which should have been said on an occasion like this. There can be no doubt that Mr. Jayaswal is a distinguished scholar and an eminent historian of Ancient India. He has rendered very valuable services to the cause of scholarship and it is only right and proper that the Patna University should confer a degree of Doctor of Philosophy upon an eminent scholar like Mr. Jayaswal. He fully deserves it and I entirely agree with your observations that in honouring a scholar of Mr. Jayaswal's position and eminence the University will really be honouring itself."

Mr. S. M. Hafeez

Mr. S. M. Hafeez said:—

"Mr. Jayaswal is a man of such deep erudition in Oriental learning and ancient culture that he has made the land of Asoka and Chandragupta his home. He has come to live with us and he is one of us and in conferring this degree on Mr. Jayaswal I may say that we have delayed it too long. We ought to have conferred it upon him much earlier. Apart from what you have said about his work and worth I call to my memory the recent Convocation Address delivered by him at the Ayurvedic School at Kadamkuan and those who were present on that occasion would agree with me that his contributions towards that branch of Oriental learning were as deep and thorough as of any experienced Ayurvedic physician. If I may be permitted to disclose a secret of what transpired in the Syndicate meeting, we all agreed that a degree should be conferred on Mr. Jayaswal but we were differing whether we should confer upon him the degree of Doctor of Law or Doctor of Philosophy, and after a careful consideration we decided that considering his services towards Oriental learning we should confer upon him the degree of Doctor of Philosophy. This, however, does not mean that he is not good enough for the degree of Doctor of Law. He is a fit person on whom both the degrees can be conferred."

Mr. Rai Brij Raj Krishna

Mr. Rai Brij Raj Krishna said:—

"I deem it a privilege to associate myself with the resolution which you, sir, have placed before the Senate on behalf of the Syndicate. Whenever the University confers an honorary degree on a person, it is always conferred on one who by reason of his eminent position and attainments is considered a fit and proper person for the same. The attainments of different persons may be of different character, but it may be said that on the present occasion the person on whom the University proposes to confer this honour is one who has extracted admiration from all and sundry by sheer dint of his merit in the field of genuine scholarship. Mr. Jayaswal, though born in the United Provinces, is a

Bihari by domicile. He is universally respected not only in India but in the whole of Europe, for his high scholarship. It would not be out of place to mention that Mr. Jayaswal is one of the three persons so far invited by His Highness the Gaekwar of Baroda for the Baroda Golden Jubilee Prize which was inaugurated by His Highness ten years ago. That prize is considered to be the Nobel Prize of the Baroda State. The condition attached to the prize is that His Highness, himself a most enlightened ruler, invites persons of established reputation in the field of scholarship to go to Baroda and lecture before His Highness. Mr. Jayaswal was the second out of the three persons so far invited, the other two being Dr. Rabindra Nath Tagore and Dr. C. V. Raman. So we see that Mr. Jayaswal has been honoured everywhere and we would be failing in our duty if we did not confer on him this degree even at this late stage."

R. B. Dwaraknath

Rai Bahadur Dwaraknath said:—

"As one of the oldest members of the Senate, it is my duty to associate myself wholeheartedly with the resolution moved from the Chair. I remember with pleasure my association with Mr. Jayaswal as a distinguished member of the Senate, who rendered strenuous and admirable services to the cause of vernacularisation which we are now going to adopt. I very well remember his powerful advocacy for adopting vernaculars as the medium of instruction, and the great learning which he brought to bear on the cause of vernaculars. The speech delivered by him in that connection at the Senate meeting which was presided over by the late Mr. Jackson, will always be remembered by us. I do not think that in honouring Mr. Jayaswal, we are honouring not only his distinguished scholarship and eminence in the field of research only, but we are also honouring a member of the Senate of this University, who, though not a sitting member, had rendered distinguished services to the Senate in that capacity. The University has always been very careful and cautious in honouring people and they have only honoured such people who by their distinguished services to the University and by their scholarship and eminent position have adorned the public life of the province."

Sir Stewart Macpherson

The Hon'ble Sir Stewart Macpherson said:—

"It is very satisfactory that when the University makes a new departure and honours a person of eminent position and attainments in the field of scholarship, there should be outstanding reasons to recommend for the Doctorate a native of Bihar (Mr. Jayaswal was, I believe, born in Jhalda, in this province) whose reputation in the world of scholarship extends not only over India and over Europe but throughout the whole learned world. I would congratulate the University in having on the roll of its Doctors a scholar of the eminence and position of Mr. K. P. Jayaswal."

Mr. Nirsu Narain Sinha

(Hon'ble) Mr. Nirsu Narain Sinha said:—

"I associate myself with the resolution which you have placed before the meeting. I do not propose to traverse the grounds which other Hon'ble members have already set out by reiterating the services which Mr. Jayaswal has rendered towards the cause of learning not only in this Province but throughout the whole of India and Europe. He has almost attained world-wide reputation. But what I feel is that the Patna University has not utilised the services of such a great man as it ought to have done. I should have expected that a man of his vast learning and reputation should have been utilised at least to train some of our post-graduate students in the same field of learning in which Mr. Jayaswal has attained world-wide reputation. I hope, however, that it is not yet too late and the Patna University will utilise his services to train young men under him so that Mr. Jayaswal may be able to train and produce a future Mr. Jayaswal."

Mr. G. P. Das

Mr. Gajendra Prasad Das said:—

"On behalf of Orissa, I beg to associate myself with every word that has fallen from the lips of my predecessors. The motion was moved by the Vice-Chancellor and there have been so many speeches that it is hardly necessary for me to speak anything on this motion. But I feel I shall be failing in my duty if on behalf of Orissa I did not associate myself with the feelings that have been expressed here. Mr. Jayaswal by his scholarship has attained such an eminence that every Indian, wherever he may reside, feels it a proud privilege to call him his own and there is a special pleasure in feeling that he is one of every one of us. The Vice-Chancellor in his able speech has told you of the activities of Mr. Jayaswal and they were connected with the Hāthigumphā inscriptions of Bhubaneshwar in Orissa. Mr. Jayaswal has thrown lustre on the ancient history of India and thereby he has also thrown lustre on the obscure history of Orissa, because in Orissa you will find an unbroken record of the Hindu culture which has not been influenced by any other culture like other parts of India. He lived in Orissa practically in thought and mind for 10 years. He paid many visits to Orissa and studied the language, the habits and custom of its people. Therefore, I can call him to be an Oriya and I have special pleasure in seeing Mr. Jayaswal honoured."

Mr. S. Mahmud Shere

Mr. S. Mahmud Shere said:—

"It is with a sense of pride that I rise to support this resolution. Every Indian has shared the pride when he has found the name of Mr. K. P. Jayaswal becoming famous in the domain of Constitutional Law and Constitutional History. It is he, who has by his original research on a track untrodden by others, given us the constitutional and political history of Ancient India, chiefly between 1400 B.C. and 700 A.D. Before him Maine, Max Muller and Bühler had only succeeded in proving that Hindu Law had the oldest pedigree of any known system of Jurisprudence, but all the great historians and research scholars were roaming in the desert to find out innumerable missing links. It was left to Mr. Jayaswal not only to find out most of the missing links but also to give flesh and blood to the skeleton pedigree and introduce life and vitality and the result is that now Hindu Polity is one living constitutional history wherein we can visualise for ourselves how our ancestors ruled and lived in their own land and how they developed their municipal and social laws from stage to stage. He has added laurels to the great name of India.

I am representative of a Muslim organisation but my community takes equal share of pride, because the recipient of the honour is popular in our community for his great qualities of head and heart and for his personal associations. He has depicted the glory of ancient India and ancient India was the home of our ancestors—Hindus and Muslims. At the conclusion of his *Hindu Polity*, as pointed out by Dr. Fitz Gerald in the *Quarterly Review* of England, he writes that 'conquest is only a method of receiving new thought and new life.' He has not shut his eyes to truth when he declares that the coming of Muslims saved India from senile decay. It is refreshing to read that the modern History of the Hindus begins with the 17th Century 'when Vaishnava preached the equality of all men, when the Sudras, the helots of ancient Hindus, preached shoulder to shoulder with Brahmins.' The Muslim thought contributed its little mite to the period of Renaissance."

The Vice-Chancellor's Final Words

The Vice-Chancellor said:—

"It is a matter of gratification to me personally that I have been a party to the conferment of this degree on

Mr. Jayaswal, who is a personal friend, to the Syndicate that its proposal has been so well received. I should say one word. It must be very pleasing to the members of the Senate to have from the Hon'ble the Finance Member the suggestion for the creation of a scholarship for research work under Mr. Jayaswal. I hope Hon'ble the Finance Member will remember this when preparing the Provincial Budget."

PART I

CHAPTER I

Scope and Sources

It is proposed to outline here certain chief features of Hindu Polity. The Hindu race has experimented in great and various systems of state and political machinery. We are not yet in a position to reconstruct a complete history of the constitutional development of the race. Nevertheless some outstanding facts and the principles underlying them may be noticed with profit.

Scope of the book

The topics to be discussed here[1] are:

(1) the Sovereign Assembly of the Vedic times,
(2) the Judicial Assembly of the Vedic times,
(3) Hindu Republics (1000 B.C.—600 A.C.),
(4) Hindu Kingship (from the Vedic times to 600 A.C.),
(5) the Jānapada or Realm Diet, and the Paura Assembly of the Capital (600 B.C.—600 A.C.),
(6) the Council of Ministers under Hindu Monarchy (1000 B.C.—600 A.C.),
(7) Judiciary under Hindu Monarchy (700 B.C.—600 A.C.),
(8) Taxation (1000 B.C.—600 A.C.),
(9) The Hindu Imperial Systems (1000 B.C.—600 A.C.), and
(10) Decay and Revival of Hindu constitutional traditions (650 A.C.—1650 A.C.).

The sources of our information extend over the vast field of Hindu literature—Vedic, Classical and Prākṛita, and also the inscriptional and numismatic records of the country. We are fortunate in having also a few technical treatises on Hindu Politics left to us in the original. They are, however, mere remains of a considerable library, contributed to by a long series of political thinkers and statesmen of Hindu India. The *Artha-Śāstra*

Our sources

Technical literature

---

[1] In some cases, very briefly.

of Kauṭilya[2] (300 B.C.), which may be called the Imperial Code of Governance of the Early Mauryas, is such a remnant. It is avowedly based on previous authorities. Such authorities, cited by name in Kauṭilya's Code, number eighteen or nineteen. There are some others mentioned elsewhere. For instance, the *Mahābhārata*, which gives a brief history of Hindu Political Science,[3] mentions, in addition, Gaura-Śiras. The *Āśvalāyana Gṛihya-Sūtra* mentions one more, Āditya.[4] The catalogue of this large number of writers shows that politics had been studied for centuries before Kauṭilya's time, and had become a recognised subject when the *Kalpa-Sūtras* were still being completed.[5] If we allow an interval of even twenty years for each of these known authorities, we shall have to date the literature of Hindu Politics as far back as *circa* 650 B.C. This date is corroborated by the *Jātakas*, which are regarded as pre-Buddhan (*i.e.*, anterior to 600 B.C.): they recognise *Artha*, that is, *Artha-Śāstra*, as a chief science for the guidance of successful ministers.[6]

Its early date

---

[2] *Mysore State's Bibliotheca Sanskrita*, No. 37, edited by Dr. Shama Sastry, 1909. Translation by Dr. Shama Sastry, 1915, Mysore, is not quite satisfactory. The text in places is not beyond doubt: compare the quotations in the commentary on the *Kāmandakīya Nīti-sāra* published by the Travancore Government which at times differ greatly from the published text. See also Dr. Sorabji Tarapurwala's *Notes on the Adhyakshaprachāra* (1914).

The name of the author should be 'the Kauṭilya,' it being his *gotra* name (*J.B.O.R.S.*, II. 80, also Śaṅkarārya on *Kāmandaka*, I. 6), but to avoid heaviness, *the* has been omitted here throughout.

[3] *Śānti-Parvan*, LVIII, LIX. It is possible that Gaura-Śiras is later than Kauṭilya. The point in favour of the antiquity of Gaura-Śiras is that he is placed in a group of ancient writers. The *Śānti-Parvan*, in its present shape, is later than the *Kāmandakīya* whose author it seems to know. See Ch. CXXIII. See also p. 5, n. 11.

[4] *Āśvalāyana Gṛihya-Sūtra*, III. 12. 16.

[5] The *Artha-Śāstra* literature had existed before the earliest *Dharma-Sūtras* were compiled. See *Āpastamba Dh.-S.*, II. 5. 10. 14, 'राजा पुरोहितं धर्मार्थकुशलम्'। Haradatta 'धर्मशास्त्रेष्वर्थशास्त्रेषु च कुशलं पुरोहितं ....'

[6] *Cf.* Fausböll, *J.*, II. 30, 74.

The treatises on political theories and practical governance were originally called DANDA-NITI or the 'Principles of Government'[7] and ARTHA-ŚASTRA or the 'Code of Common-wealth'. Kauṭilya defines the latter: "ARTHA is *human population*, that is to say, *territory with human population*. The Code of *Artha* (Common-wealth) is a code dealing with the means (art, *upāya*) of acquisition and growth of that territory".[8] *Daṇḍa-Nīti* was the title adopted by Uśanas,[9] and *Artha-Śāstra*, by Bṛihaspati,[10] for their respective works which were very famous in Hindu Classical times. A book, rather an encyclopædia, under the title *Daṇḍa-Nīti*, ascribed to Prajāpati, is mentioned in the *Mahābhārata*.[11] The subject is also called *Rāja-Śāstra*[12] or the 'Code for the Rulers,' and *Rāja-Dharma* or the 'Law for the Rulers'. Under the latter term, it has been treated in the *Śānti-Parvan* of the *Mahābhārata*. The *Mahābhārata* draws on materials generally old, but handled as late as the fifth century after Christ, with an earlier systematization, *cir.* 150 B.C.[13]

Terms

The Book on Politics in the *Mahābhārata*: 400 B.C.–500 A.C.

---

[7] *Śānti-Parvan*, LVIII. 77–78 [Kumbakonam (80–81)].

[8] मनुष्याणां वृत्तिरर्थः मनुष्यवतो भूमिरित्यर्थः, तस्याः पृथिव्या लाभपालनोपायः शास्त्रमर्थशास्त्रमिति । Bk. XV, p. 424. वृत्तिः here is explained by the following मनुष्यवतो. It has therefore to be taken as वृत्तिर्वर्त्तनम् (भविक्तिन्). *Pālana* has the sense of *growth*, not mere *maintenance*. This is borne out by the description of *Daṇḍa-Nīti* given by Kauṭilya (I. 4, p. 9): दण्डनीतिः अलब्धलाभार्था, लब्धपरिरक्षणे, रक्षितविवर्धने, etc.; and also by "अलब्धलाभो लब्धपरिरक्षणं रक्षितविवर्धनं चेत्यर्थानुबन्धः ।" *Nītivākyāmṛita*, II.

[9] *Mudrā-Rākshasa*, I.

[10] Vātsyāyana, *Kāma-Sūtra*, I.

[11] *Śānti-P.*, C. 59 (Bengal) (58, Kumb.). *Cf. Kāma-S.*, I.

[12] *Śānti-P.*, C. 58 (Bengal) (57, Kumb.).

[13] For the date of the *Śānti-Parvan* see my *Tagore Lectures*, I. The authors who are treated as historical persons in Kauṭilya's *Artha-Śāstra* have been taken to be divine and mythological in the *Śānti-Parvan*. The Śakas and the Tokharis are mentioned as having come under Hindu kings (Ch. LXV)—a fact of the early fifth century A.C. It should be also noticed that the political science book of the 'Great Ṛishis' which had been current in the time of Kāmandaka (VIII. 23) disappeared when the *Śānti-Parvan* was completed (c. 343, 52, Kumb.).

Works of the 4th and 5th centuries A.C.

Later, the terms *Nīti* ('Policy' or 'Principles') and *Naya* ('Leading,' 'Principles') seem to have superseded the old words *Artha* and *Daṇḍa*. Kāmandaka calls his metrical treatise a *Nīti-sāra*. The book ascribed to Śukra, which, in its present shape is a revised edition of an earlier well-known work, probably based on the ancient Uśanas' *Daṇḍa-Nīti*, is also called a *Nīti-sāra* (*Śukra-Nīti-sāra*).[14] The *Pañcha-Tantra*, which is a book on politics put into fables for the early education of princes and would-be statesmen, adopts the term *Naya-Śāstra* to denote the literature.[15]

Complications by Hindu Lawyers of 14th to 18th Centuries A.C.

It is interesting to note that the study of Hindu Politics was continued like the study of Hindu Law, during Muhammadan times.[16] I was agreeably surprised to find that the famous lawyers, the Nibandhakāras Chaṇḍeśvara, Mitra-Miśra and Nīlakaṇṭha, have compiled works on Hindu Politics. There is a *Rāja-Nīti-Ratnākara*, and there is a *Vīra-Mitrodaya Rāja-Nīti*; similarly, there is also a Mayūkha, called *Rāja-Nīti-Mayūkha*.[17] As to the value of these latter-day works, they, of course, are products of the

---

[14] This work is quoted by law-commentators of the Middle Ages and later. I could not find the quotation in the text of the current *ŚNS*. It must have been, therefore, revised about the 17th century. It, however, embodies mostly ancient doctrines.

[15] 'नय-शास्त्र-कर्तृभ्यः' । *Pañcha-Tantra*, Ch. I.

[16] See Addendum I at the end of this chapter, on the growth of the literature in the earlier period.

[17] An old copy of this is in the library of the well-known Sanskritist, Mr. Govinda Das of Benares. The *Vīra-Mitrodaya Rāja-Nīti* has been published in the Chaukhamba Sanskrit Series. Chaṇḍeśvara's *RN.-Ratnākara* I am editing for the Bihar and Orissa Research Society.

Before Chaṇḍeśvara, two other digest-writers had composed Digests of Hindu Politics: one was Lakshmīdhara, the well-known author of the law-digest *Kalpataru*, and the other was the author of the *Kāmadhenu*. These scholars compiled *Rāja-Nīti-Kalpataru* and *Rāja-Nīti-Kāmadhenu*, respectively. They have been quoted by Chaṇḍeśvara.

Politics in the Purāṇas, 6th and 7th centuries A.C.

decadent period. They may be classed together with the political science portions of the Purāṇas. The Nibandhakāras and the Purāṇas have no originality. The Purāṇas merely copy some chapters from some well-known authors, *e.g.*, the *Agni-Purāṇa* borrows from an author called Pushkara.[18] The Hindu jurists of Muhammadan times, however, evince a strong desire for collecting materials, and the great value of their work consists in the extracts from authorities which are otherwise unknown. They are, moreover, witnesses to living tradition in ceremonial matters. Better materials, next in value only to regular treatises, are to be found in the Aphorisms and Codes of *Dharma* under the chapter styled the 'Laws for the King,' which represent the constitutional laws as defined by *Dharma*-writers.

Politics in the books of Dharma (Law): 400 B.C.-500 A.C.

Works of early Middle Ages

We must not lose sight of another class of mediæval productions. The little book *Bṛihaspati-Sūtra*, recently edited by Dr. F. W. Thomas (*Le Muséon*), is one of them. It is a piece of *Artha-Śāstra* literature in *Sūtras*. But in its present shape, it is a product of the Middle Ages, though portions therein are undoubtedly based on ancient materials. It gives, as we shall see, some very valuable information. Similarly, the *Nitivākyāmṛita* by Somadeva who flourished in the tenth century A.C., is in *Sūtras*. It is an eclectic work based generally on old authorities.[19] The *Sūtras* are generally quotations which the Jaina author calls, not altogether without justification, 'immortal essence' ' (*amṛita*) of 'political maxims'.

---

[18] *Cf.* also *Matsya*, Chs. CCXV-XXVII.

[19] Somadeva quotes a *Sūtra* from Manu, indicating that his was not the Svāyambhuva M., *i.e.*, the author of the *Dharma Ś*. In other words, he quotes from the *Mānava Artha-Śāstra* :—

यदाह वैवस्वतो मनुः । उञ्छषड्भागप्रदानेन वनस्था अपि तपस्विनो राजानं सम्भावयन्ति । तस्यैव तद्भूयात् यस्तान् गोपायति । इति । *N.V.* 6.

See Addendum I below.

Political-ethical and politico-religious books

Ethico-political writings are kept out of our scope. Opinion, for instance, would be divided as to the true character of certain works in our vernaculars, like the *Dāsa-Bodha* ('Address to the Enslaved') by the Teacher Rāma-Dāsa, the great text-book of the time of Śivāji Chhatrapati, and the Hindi books of Guru Govinda-Siṃha. Mystic and non-political interpretations would be given by religious enthusiasts to many views apparently political. It is therefore better to leave them out in our present studies.

ADDENDUM I

On the Growth of Political Science Literature after the Third Century

(A critique on a Jaina Commentary to the *Nītivākyāmṛita*, published by me in the *Journal of the Bihar and Orissa Research Society* (Vol. XI, 1925, pp. 66–70) under the title *New Light on Hindu Political Science Literature*, is reproduced here as dealing with the history of the science after the third century A.D.)

The work which opens up for us a catalogue of hitherto sealed literature on the subject is a commentary on the Jaina author Somadeva Sūri's *Nītivākyāmṛita*. The *Nītivākyāmṛita* is a well-known little book written for the education of young princes in the tenth century of the Christian era. It is a mixture of ethics and politics, in short *Sūtras* or aphorisms. The commentary under discussion is by an author whose name is yet unknown. A manuscript of the work discovered is dated the 4th of Kārtika Sudi, Vikrama Saṃvat 1541 (= 1463 A.C.) in the reign of Sultān Bahalola Sāhi, *i.e.*, Bahlol Lodi. The manuscript was presented by a pious Jaina lady to a Jaina scholar, Paṇḍita Medhāvi, of Hisār, where it was placed in a Jaina library. From there it was transferred to a Jaina library at Āmer. Paṇḍita Nāthūrāma Premin of Bombay obtained this manuscript through some Jaipur friends and has printed the commentary as a volume in the *Manikachandra Digambara Jaina Series*. It discloses a welcome mass of information, and we are thankful to Paṇḍita Nāthūrāma for the publication. Unfortunately folios 51 to 75 of the manuscript are missing, the matter available in 133 folios (11½" × 5½", 20 lines to each page) alone could be published. The missing portion covers parts of Chapters 11 and 19 and the whole of Chapters 12 to 18. The gap could not be filled in as no other manuscript has been traced. The editing is not, as Paṇḍita Nāthūrāma himself points out, very good. The editor is not acquainted with the *Artha-Śāstra* literature. His notes, where he attempts to give his own opinion, may be omitted by the reader with advantage.

The chief value of the commentary lies in the method of the commentator. His method is to find out and give the authority on which Somadeva drew, and in most cases we get the original authority of Somadeva almost verbatim. It should be noted that Somadeva has given no reference to his original sources. The commentator following his method has had to cite various and numerous authorities. The result is that we come to know of authors whose works are now lost and whose names we had not heard before in connection with our political science. We not only now know their names but also a few fragments of their writings. Out of them about thirty we can take, with almost certainty, to have been *Artha-Śāstra* writers. In a Hindu Political Science Digest it is at times uncertain as to whether a passage comes from a *Dharma-Śāstra* (Law) book or an *Artha-Śāstra* (Political Science) book, for the *Dharma-Śāstra* authors have also their views on politics and they generally give a chapter on constitutional laws. A quotation taken from the latter may be hardly distinguishable from an *Artha-Śāstra* opinion. Yet when we get a passage on a point which is exclusively dealt with by *Artha-Śāstra* writers, we can conclude with some degree of certainty that the writer is an *Artha-Śāsrta* authority and that the passage comes from an *Artha-Śāstra* book. Judged in this manner out of thirty or thirty-one authors culled from the quotations of the commentator we get about twenty writers on *Artha-Śāstra* whose names are not to be found in other places and which are new to us. Probably they are all later than Kauṭilya and Kāmandaka as they do not figure either in the Code or the Epitome. This is significant for it shows that the tradition of authorship and original thinking went on in the study of Political Science in the country for centuries even after the third century of the Christian era.

It seems, as already pointed out in the introduction to the *Rāja-Nīti-Ratnākara*, that the study of politics had a similar history as the study of law in the country.[20] When we find a secondary stage in the study of law we find a similar new stage in the study of Hindu Politics. A little before the Muhammadans came into the country Digests of Hindu Law began to be composed by Hindu writers. Similarly, Digests of Politics marked a new stage about the same time in the *Artha-Śāstra* literature.[20] The earliest of these Political Digests is, as far as I have been able to trace them up to this time, the *Rajā-Nīti-Kalpataru* by Lakshmīdhara Bhaṭṭa who was the Foreign Minister of King Govinda Chandra Gāhaḍavāla of Kānyakubja and Kāśī. Now it is important to note that Somadeva who lived about two hundred years before Lakshmīdhara Bhaṭṭa does not compose a Digest but an original book to which he gives the authority of his own name. Yet in the opinion of the commentator, Somadeva's *Nītivākyāmṛita* was a mere Digest. Somadeva lived at a time when tradition of original writing had not ceased; the commentator lived at a time when the Hindu mind had ceased to venture originality and when it had to fall back upon authority. The change was complete within two or three hundred years after Somadeva.

To show the value of the book I have been discussing, let us take the *Sūtra* which is the first in the *Nītivākyāmṛita* :— अथ धर्म्मार्थफलाय राज्याय नमः[21] "To begin, Salutation to the State, the tree of *Dharma* and *Artha*."

This idealization of the State is remarkable. I selected it as the motto for my *Hindu Polity* and considered it to be a conception of Somadeva Sūri. But we are indebted to the commentator for carrying the idea back to one of the first thinkers of Hindu Political Science. It goes back to Śukra. The commentator raises the question—*How is it that the author who is a Jaina* (Somadeva) *does not salute the Tīrtha[ṅ]kara but salutes the State which is composed of ordinary humanity?* ननु कस्मादाचार्य्येण क्षपणक-व्रत-धारिणा सता तीर्थङ्करान् परित्यज्य[22] मनुष्य-मात्रस्य

[20] The December number of 1924, of *J.B.O.R.S.*, Introduction, p.4.

[21] As in the Bombay edition and in Madras MSS. The present work reads धर्मार्थकामफलाय ।

[22] The printed matter before me reads: "परित्यज्य मुनेर्मनुष्य-मात्रस्य राज्यस्य च". In Gopāla Nārāyaṇa Janatā's (Bombay) edition of the *N.V.* there is no salutation to any Muni. The preceding verse

राज्यस्य नमस्कृतिः कृता । The commentator replies that the *Bārhaspatya* and the *Auśanasa Śāstras* are the main authorities of Somadeva, and Bṛihaspati has saluted the Muni (author) and Śukra has saluted the State :—" नमोस्तु राज्यवृक्षाय षाड्गुण्याय प्रशाखिने । सामादि-चारु-पुष्पाय त्रिवर्गफलदायिने (Śukra)." This is the original verse of the famous *Auśanasa Artha-Śāstra* now lost.

The verse quoted from the *Bārhaspatya*, as its opening line, has no great direct bearing on the point, yet we are thankful to get the opening line of the most famous book of the *Artha-Śāstra* literature which is now lost to us.[23] The verse shows that the book *Bārhaspatya* was in its claim a mere human work where the author expresses his gratitude to his original authority Aṅgiras and avowedly writes his Code for the benefit of kings. In other words, there is no pretension for a mythical origin.

An author called Varga is largely quoted by our commentator. As the Hindu Law literature is fairly well known by references in commentaries and digests and as Varga is unknown to the law literature, it seems almost certain that Varga's work was on politics. Similar is the case of Bhāguri. The passages of Bhāguri and Varga probably have a tendency to the ethical side. And this tendency is a distinguishing feature which separates them from earlier writers on pure politics. Bhāradvāja, one of the severest writers of the early political school, is also largely quoted. Those quotations are in verse. Probably we will have to revise our view that the early writers had their works wholly in *Sūtras* (prose).

Amongst the other authors whose names we now know from the commentary, the following may be mentioned :—Bhṛigu, Rājaputra, Raibhya, Jaimini, Nārada, Gautama, Garga, Kauśika, Ṛishiputra and Hārita. Amongst ancient names already known I may draw attention to the quotations from Chārāyaṇa, Pāraskara, Bhāradvāja, Manu, Bṛihaspati and Śukra.

---

in the present edition where Muni Somadeva is saluted could not be by Somadeva himself.

[23] वाचा कायेन मनसा प्रणम्याङ्गिरसं मुनिम् ।
नीतिशास्त्रं प्रवक्ष्यामि भूपतीनां सुखावहम् ॥ (Bṛihaspati).

CHAPTER II

Samiti

The Sovereign Assembly of Vedic Times

Samiti represented the whole people

Going back to the oldest literature of the race, we find from the Vedas that national life and activities in the earliest times on record were expressed through popular assemblies and institutions. The greatest institution of this nature was the *Samiti* of our Vedic fore-fathers. The word *Samiti* (*sam* + *iti*) means 'meeting together,' *i.e.*, an assembly. The Samiti was the national assembly of the whole people or *Viśaḥ* (विशः);[1] for we find 'the whole people' or *Samiti*, in the alternative, electing and re-electing the *Rājan* (राजा) or '*King*'.[2] The whole people were supposed to be present in the Assembly.

Its functions

The functions of the *Samiti* may be gathered from different references. We have already noticed the most important business of the *Samiti*, to wit, electing the *Rājan*.[3] It could also

---

[1] In Vedic times, Hindu Society was divided into *Janas*, tribes or nations, *e.g.*, Anus, Yadus, Kurus. But, at the same time, they were conscious of the fact that they all belonged to one common race, for all of them called themselves "*Āryas*," आर्याः The people or the tribe were called *Viśaḥ* (विशः), from which the word *Vaiśya* ('one of the people'—'the commoner') is derived. On Vedic Society, consult Zimmer, *Altindisches Leben*. See also Macdonell and Keith, *Vedic Index*, sub. *Arya*, *Jana*, etc.

[2] विशस्त्वा सर्वा वाञ्छन्तु ; *Ṛig-Veda*, X. 173. 1. *Atharva-Veda*, VI. 87-1.

ध्रुवाय ते समितिः कल्पतामिह ; *A.V.*, VI. 88. 3.

त्वां विशो वृणतां राज्याय ; *A.V.*, III. 4. 2.

Also *A.V.*, III. 345. See Chap. XXIII, on Vedic Kingship.

[3] *Cf.* नास्मै समितिः कल्पते ; *A.V.*, V. 19. 15.

re-elect a king who had been banished.[4] They were thus a sovereign body from the constitutional point of view. In the *Atharva-Veda*, VI. 64, which is a prayer-hymn for union and concord, and also in the *Ṛig-Veda* (X. 191. 3), we have a prayer for a 'common Samiti' and 'common policy of State' (समानो मन्त्रः समितिः समानी), a 'common aim and a common mind' (समानं व्रतं सह चित्तमेषाम्).[5] This indicates that matters of state ('*mantra*') were discussed in the Samiti.

The King and *Samiti*

The king attended the *Samiti*, and it was thought necessary that he should do so. The *Ṛig-Veda* has 'like a true king going to the *Samiti*' (राजा न सत्यः समितीरियानः).[6] The inference is that it was the king's duty to attend the *Samiti*, and that if he did not attend it, he would be considered 'untrue,' the significance of which we shall see when we come to the ceremony of Vedic Coronation. The practice of the king presenting himself before the *Samiti* continued probably as long as the *Samiti* existed. The *Chhāndogya Upanishad*, one of the youngest Vedic works, relating the visit of Śvetaketu Āruṇeya Gautama to the Samiti of the Pañchālas, mentions the King (Pravāhaṇa Jaivala) as present in the *Samiti*.[7]

Deliberations

In deliberations, speakers were anxious to make speeches agreeable to the assembled *Samiti* (ये संग्रामाः समितयस्तेषु चारु वदेम ते).[8] The speaker wanted to prove himself 'brilliant, not to be contra-

---

[4] See Ch. XXIII on Vedic Kingship.

[5] "Same be their counsel, same their assembly, same their aim, in common their thought"—Bloomfield, *S.B.E.*, XLII. 136. [Some texts read *manaḥ* for *vrata*.—*Ed.*]

[6] *Ṛ.V.*, IX. 92. 6; *cf.* यत्रौषधीः समग्मत राजानः समिताविव, *Ṛ.V.*, X. 97. 6.

[7] *Chh. Up.*, V. 3. *Cf. Bṛ. Ār. Up.*, VI. 2. See p. 19.

[8] *A.V.*, VII. 12. 1; XII. 1. 56.

dicted,' in the *Samiti*.[9] To these deliberations would also refer the prayer in the *Atharva-Veda*, II. 27:

"May the enemy not win the debate.... Overcome the debate of those that debate against us, render them devoid of force!

"Overcome thou the debate of him that is hostile to us, O Indra! Encourage us with thy might! Render me superior in debate."[10]

Non-political business of the *Samiti*

That questions other than political were also occasionally discussed in the *Samiti*, is borne out by the above-mentioned record about Śvetaketu. Śvetaketu was a young man of great learning who, as the *Chhāndogya* says,[11] claimed complete knowledge of the sacred and philosophic literature at the age of twenty-four. In the *Chhāndogya* and *Bṛihadāraṇyaka Upanishads*, we see the young man who had just completed his education, presenting himself before the *Samiti*, also called the *Parishad* of the Pañchālas (पञ्चालानां समितिमेयाय, पञ्चालानां परिषदमाजगाम). The Kshatriya (Rājanya) king in the Assembly of the Pañchāla nation, Pravāhaṇa Jaivali (or Jaivala), put to him five philosophic questions, none of which the presumptuous young man (Kumāra) could answer, and he had to go away with the remark of Jaivali: 'How could anybody who did not know these things say that he had been educated?'[12] Here we find the Samiti acting as a sort of national academy.

Samiti, an institution of developed society

It is noticeable that references to the *Samiti* in the *Ṛig-Veda* are to be found only in portions which are considered to be the latest. We may, therefore, conclude that the *Samiti* was a product of the developed, not early, Vedic age. The developed stage of debate, evidently a free right of

---

[9] "When he has arrived at the *Samiti*, he should murmur 'Superior (to my adversaries) I have come hither, brilliant, not to be contradicted!' अभिभूरहमागमविराडप्रतिवाश्या:—a Vedic text quoted in *Pāraskara-Gṛihya-Sūtra*, III. 13. 4. See *S.B.E.*, XXIX, p. 363.

[10] *S.B.E.*, XLII, 137–38.

[11] *Chhāndogya Up.*, VI (Prapāthaka), 1. *Cf. Apastamba Dharma-Sūtra*, I. 2. 5–6.

[12] *Chh. Up.*, V. 3; *Bṛi. Ār. Up.*, VI. 2.

discussion, the anxiety of the debater to win over the opinion of others, all point to a culture of considerable degree. In the Germanic folk-assembly, we have some nobleman speaking and the ordinary people present merely expressing inarticulate approval, conveyed by noise of arms[13]: the stage of debate is not yet known to them. It is therefore not accurate to compare the *Samiti* (as some European scholars have done) with the early folk-assemblies of Western Europe.

President of the *Samiti*

Another index of the developed stage of the Samiti is that the *Samiti*, like the *Sabhā* (which we shall presently discuss) had its Pati or Īśāna, President. For instance, see the *mantra* cited in *Pāraskara-Gṛihya-Sūtra*, III. 13. 4: 'the lord (Īśāna) of this assembly is a man insuperable in his power.'[14]

Constitution of the *Samiti*

It is clear, as observed above, that the whole people were considered to be present in the Samiti. But when, for instance, Śvetaketu goes to the Samiti of the Pañchālas where philosophers and statesmen were sitting, it would be hardly probable that the whole nation, without any principle of representation, would be actually present. We already find in the Vedic period the principle of representation appreciated and variously acted upon: we have the *Grāmaṇī* or the 'leader' of the town or village, as a representative *persona* in the coronation ceremony;[15] representatives of trade also are seen at the ceremony. From a passage in the 'Hymn to the Land' of the *Atharva-Veda*, where the Samitis (XII. 1. 56, ये संग्रामा समितयः[16] '*the assembled Samitis*') of the whole land are referred to, it seems that those who were

---

[13] Tacitus, *Moribus et Populis Germaniæ*, c. ii.

[14] *S.B.E.*, XXIX. 362. Original: अस्याः पर्षद ईशानः सहसा सुदुष्टरो जन इति.

[15] See Ch. XXIII.

[16] ये ग्रामा यदरण्यं या सभा अधि भूम्याम् ।
ये संग्रामाः समितयस्तेषु चारु वदेम ते ॥

assembled (*saṃgrāmāḥ*) were the 'villages together' (*saṃgrāma*). The village, as a collective unit, is well known: Śaryāta Mānava 'wandered about' with his *grāma* (*Śatapatha*, IV. 1, 5, 2, 7).[17] In later times in law-books, 'the village' fights out legal disputes; 'the village' is even fined. The *Grāmaṇī* was the key-stone of the village-constitution. The village even took to themselves the name of their leader (*Grāmaṇī*).[18] We have the 'village-together' meeting (*saṃgrāma*) 'desirous of agreement' in the *Taittirīya Saṃhitā* संग्रामे संयन्ते समयकामः).[19] It seems that the village formed the basis of the constitution of the *Samiti*, if not originally, certainly, in later times.

Historical career of the *Samiti*

The *Samiti* had a very long life. We find it in the Vedic age itself regarded as eternal, called 'a daughter of Prajāpati,'[20] the Creator. It must have been, therefore, an ancient institution even then. Its continuous existence is attested by the *Ṛig-Veda* and the *Atharva-Veda*, and later, by the *Chhāndogya Upanishad* (800 or 700 B.C.) which nearly marks the end of the later Vedic period. The period covered by these records extends over several centuries. That the institution did not far outlive the later Vedic age and did not come down to the epoch which, in its latest phase, saw the rise of empires, is borne out by the *Pāraskara-Gṛihya-Sūtra* (*c.* 500 B.C.) which treats the Samiti (called by the other name, *Parishat*, or rather *Parshat*)[21] evidently as a reminiscence

---

[17] *Cf.* "In several passages, the word (*grāma*) occurs with what appears to be the derivative sense of 'body of men'." Macdonell and Keith, *Vedic Index*, I. 245.

[18] See Kāśikā on *P.*, V. 3. 112, 'देवदत्तो ग्रामणीरेषां त इमे देवदत्तकाः'.

[19] II. 1. 8. 451. *Cf.* आर्थायैस्सुहृद्भिरैकमत्यं समयः। शत्रुभिः सन्धिरित्यन्ये। Bhaṭṭa Bhāskara Miśra on *TS.*

Inter-village gathering for war purposes gave the secondary meaning of 'war' to the expression *saṃgrāma*.

[20] *A.V.*, VII. 12.

[21] *Parishat*, lit. means the 'great session'. The *meeting* of the *Samiti* came to denote the *Samiti* itself. The form *parshat* is also occasionally found. (*Cf. Baudhāyana Dh.-S.*, I. 1. 9.)

(*Pār. G.*, III. 13. 4). In *Pāraskara* the ancient tradition of *Samiti* is merely applied to the *Sabhā*, as the opening sentence indicates (अथातः सभाप्रवेशनम्). The Samiti disappears before the time of the *Jātakas* (600 B.C.) We have thus the age-history of the *Samiti* from the latter part of the millennium of the *Ṛig-Veda* down to about 700 B.C., a life extending certainly over a thousand years, and very likely longer. In the imperial epoch, we naturally do not find the *Samiti*, but we find another institution which, as we shall see (Ch. XXVII), was a phœnix, risen out of the ashes of the *Samiti*.

CHAPTER III

The Sabhā

Sabhā a distinguished popular body

There was another noteworthy constitutional organism in the Vedic Age and later. It was the Sabhā. It is described as a sister of the *Samiti*, one of the two daughters of Prajāpati.[1] This also was a popular body. Prayer for co-operation in the *Sabhā* shows that discord in the *Sabhā* assembly was as much disliked and dreaded as in the *Samiti*.

---

[1] *Atharva-Veda*, 7. 13.

सभा च मा समितिश्चावतां प्रजापतेर्दुहितरौ संविदाने ।

येना संगच्छा उप मा स शिक्षाच्चारु वदानि पितरः संगतेषु ॥ १ ॥

विद्म ते सभे नाम नरिष्टा नाम वा असि ।

ये ते के च सभासदस्ते मे सन्तु सवाचसः ॥ २ ॥

एषामहं समासीनानां वर्चो विज्ञानमा ददे ।

अस्याः सर्वस्याः संसदो मामिन्द्र भगिनं कृणु ॥ ३ ॥

यद्वो मनः परागतं यद्बद्धमिह वेह वा

तद्व आ वर्तयामसि मयि वो रमतां मनः ॥ ४ ॥

Translation :—

(1) "May the *Samiti* and the *Sabhā*, the two daughters of Prajāpati, concurrently aid me. May he with whom I shall meet co-operate with me; may I, O Ye Fathers, speak agreeably to those assembled."

(2) "We know thy name, O Assembly: *Narishṭā* verily is thy name. May all those that sit assembled in thee utter speech in harmony with me."

(3) "Of them that are sitting together I take to myself the power and the understanding in this entire gathering, O Indra, render me successful."

The *Sābha* called *narishṭā* which Sāyaṇa explains as a *resolution* of 'many' that cannot be broken or violated (नरिष्टा ; अहिंसिता परैरनभिभाव्या. . . . बहवः संभूय यद्येकं वाक्यं वदेयुस्तर्हि न परैरतिलङ्घ्यम् अतः अनतिलङ्घ्यवाक्यत्वात् नरिष्टेति नाम ।). 'Hence from the inviolability the name is derived.' With reference to this name, the speaker wishes that '*all those that sit assembled in Thee, utter speech in harmony with me.*' Free discussion was thus held in the *Sabhā*, and a resolution of the *Sabhā* was considered binding on all and inviolable. Evidently, the *Sabhā* was almost as important as the *Samiti*.

Its resolutions

It was certainly related to the *Samiti*, but its exact relationship is not deducible from the data available. Probably it was a standing and stationary body of selected men working under the authority of the *Samiti*. *Sabhā* means, *lit.*, 'a body of men shining together'.[2] Those entitled to a seat therein were invested, so to say, with lustre. They are pointedly alluded to.[3] They were objects of special respect.[4] The *Sabhā* had its president, called *Sabhā-pati*.[5] It seems there were 'Elders' in the *Sabhā*. We meet with Elders and 'Fathers' of councils in other ancient bodies holding executive authority (Ch. VI). Reference to the "Fathers" in the above-quoted hymn is probably to the Fathers or Elders in the *Sabhā*, a view which Sāyaṇa alternatively puts forward (हे पितरः पालकाः. . . . पितृभूता वा हे सभासदो जनाः).

Composition of the *Sabhā*

---

(4) "If your mind has wandered to a distance, or has been enchained here or there, then do we turn it hither: May your mind take delight in me!"

[I have adopted the translation of the hymn as proposed in the *Sacred Books of the East* volume on the *Atharva-Veda* (XLII. 138), with the exception of the rendering of *narishṭā* which has been translated there as 'mirth,' and, alternatively, as 'most favourable to men' (p. 544).]

[2] *Cf.* Jayarāma: सह धर्मेण सद्भिर्वा भातीति सभा । *Pārasakara-Gṛihya*, III. 13. 1.

[3] *A.V.*, VII. 12; *White Yajur-Veda*, XVI. 28.

[4] *Cf. White Yajur-Veda*, XVI. 24: नमः सभाभ्यः सभापतिभ्यश्च ।

[5] See p. 20.

Judicial function of the Sabhā

One function of the *Sabhā* is definitely clear. The *Sabhā* acted as the national judicature. The *Sabhā* is called '*Trouble*' and '*Vehemence*' in the *Pāraskara-Gṛihya.*[6] As 'trouble' and 'vehemence' were in store there for the culprit, the *Sabhā* seems to have acquired those names, like the present-day appellation "Criminal" of our Criminal Courts. In the Purushamedha of the *Śukla Yajur-Veda*, *Sabhā-chara*, 'one going to the *Sabhā*,' is dedicated as a victim to justice (धर्माय सभाचरम्, 30. 6). Again, the *Ṛig-Veda* (X. 71. 10) describes the friends of one who has come back successful from the *Sabhā* 'joyful' and 'delighted' and the man himself as 'free from blame':

सर्वे नन्दन्ति यशसागतेन सभासाहेन सख्या सखायः ।

किल्बिषस्पृत्पितुषणिर्ह्येषामरं हितो भवति वाजिनाय ॥

The *White Yajur-Veda* mentions also people repenting of the sins committed in the *Sabhā.*[7]

The *Jātakas* preserve an old memorial verse, which says that the *Sabhā* which has no good people (संतो) is no *Sabhā*, that the people who do not speak out the *Dhamma* (justice) are not good people, that those who avoid personal sentiments and speak out justice are called the 'good people':

---

[6] III. 13, नादिर्नामासि त्विषिर्नामासि । Jayarāma renders them as 'sounding' and 'shining' (नदनशोला दीप्ता) because of performance of justice (धर्मनिरूपणात्). 'Trouble' and 'Vehemence' are Oldenberg's rendering in *S.B.E.*, XXIX, 362. If Jayarāma's view be right, त्विषि would refer to the fire which, according to the law-books, was kept in the court-house and which is probably also indicated by the Vedic term *sabhya* for fire (*Atharva-V.*, VIII, 10, 5). See p. 26, fire was kept also in the Vidatha. नादि as 'sounding,' may point to the feature contributed by discussions.

[7] यद्ग्रामे यदरण्ये यत्सभायां यदिन्द्रिये ।

यच्छूद्रे यदर्ये यदेनश्चकृमा वयं यदेकस्याधि धर्माणि तस्यावयजनमसि ॥

XX. 17.

न सा सभा यत्थ न संति संतो न ते संतो ये न भणन्ति धंमं ।
रागं च दोसं च पहाय मोहं धंमं भणन्ता व भवन्ति संतो ॥[8]

Sabhā, a later Rig-Vedic institution

In Vedic literature, the expression *Sabhā* is used in several senses, for instance, to denote a hall, a house, the gambling hall, and the royal court. In our constitutional sense, there is only one late reference in the *Ṛig-Veda*, *viz.*, in X. 71. 10, noticed above. The rise of the *Sabhā*, therefore, is to be dated like that of the *Samiti* in the latest period of the *Ṛig-Veda*. Its career is co-extensive with that of the Samiti. Even during royal and imperial centralisation, as we shall see, the judicial *Sabhā* of the king preserved traces of its popular origin and retained some important popular features in its administration of justice.

Vidatha and Senā

The Samiti and *Sabhā* were not the only popular institutions of the Vedic times. The religious life was organised through the 'Vidatha' assembly,[9] which had existed even earlier[10] than the *Samiti*. It seems to have been the parent folk-assembly from which the *Sabhā*, *Samiti* and *Senā* differentiated, for we find the Vidatha associated with civil, military and religious functions (Roth).[11] The *Senā* or the Army, which was in early times the nation-in-arms, was regarded as a body by itself and evidently as a constitutional unit:

तं सभा च समितिश्च सेना च (*A.V.*, XV. 9. 2)[12]

---

[8] *Jātaka*, v. 509. The first half of the verse is given by Vyāsa in his law-book in the description of the legal *Sabhā* (*Aparārka V.*, II. 4). Instead of *santo* ('the good') Vyāsa has *vṛiddhāḥ* or Elders which shows that probably the *Sabhā* was originally composed of Elders.

[9] *A.V.*, I. 13. 4. (Whitney translates it by 'council'.)

[10] *Ṛ.V.*, I. 60 [where fire is called the flag (*Ketu*) of Vidatha]. Zimmer (p. 177) thinks, probably not correctly, that it was a smaller body of the Samiti (M. & K.).

[11] विदथस्य धीभिः क्षत्रं राजाना प्रदिवो दधांथे, *Ṛ.V.*, III. 38. 5; II. 1. 4; III. 26. 6. See also M. & K., *V.I.* on Vidatha.

[12] This and the reference in the *Pṛithivī-Sūkta* (*A.V.*, XII. 1. 56) conclusively prove that the *Sabhā* was a distinct institution like the *Senā* and that it was not the building where the *Samiti* met, as taken by some scholars.

Much information about the *Senā* is not yet available, and we are here more concerned with the civil aspect of our Hindu Polity.

Post-Vedic tendency

In later times, education was separately organised in *Charaṇas*, which were a species of Vedic Faculties. The *Parishat* or Convocation of learning had evidently separated from the general national *Parishat* or *Samiti*. Economic life, similarly, was crystallised in trade-guilds and guilds merchant whose existence is traced in the *Jātakas* and *Dharma-Sūtras*. In post-Vedic times, national life thus expresses itself into various self-governing institutions, and, in doing so, it really carries forward the Vedic traditions of communal institutions.

CHAPTER IV

Rise of Hindu Republics and Hindu Terms for Republics

Republics, generally post-Vedic institutions

Hindu Republics are another illustration of the communal self-governing habits of the post-Vedic age, referred to in our last paragraph. The early Vedas know only monarchy. Departure from this normal constitution was made in post-Vedic times, and, as Megasthenes also records the tradition, '*sovereignty (kingship) was dissolved and democratic governments set up*' in various places.[1] The *Mahābhārata*, similarly, as we shall see in our discussion on Hindu Monarchy, considers monarchy alone as the Vedic form of government. The hymns of the *Ṛik* and *Atharvan*, the view of the *Mahābhārata* and the tradition which Megasthenes heard in India in the fourth century B.C., all point to the fact that republican form of government in India came long after monarchy, and after the early Vedic age. It appears in the later Vedic literature : in the *Ṛig-Vedic Brāhmaṇa* the *Aitareya*, and in the *Yajur-Veda* and its *Brāhmaṇa* the *Taittirīya*. The republican constitutions mentioned in these documents will be discussed, for the sake of convenience and clearness, after the better known cases of later history.[2]

The account of Hindu States of non-kingly forms of government presents a great chapter in the constitutional history of the race. We will therefore pay particular attention to it in these studies.

Ancient terms for Hindu Republics

Prof. Rhys Davids, in his *Buddhist India*, showed that republican form of government obtained in the country of the Buddha and his neighbours. But it had not been pointed out that our literature preserves technical names for Hindu Republics. One of these terms which first attracted my attention was the word *Gaṇa*. In the *Ācārāṅga-Sūtra* of the Jaina

---

[1] *Epitomé of Megasthenes*, Diod. II. 38 ; Mc Crindle, *Megasthenes*, pp. 38, 40.

[2] See Ch. X.

branch of Hindu literature, I came across the terms *Do-rajjāṇi* and *Gaṇa-rāyāṇi* (II. 3. 1. 10)[3] which struck me as defining constitutions. *Do-rajjāṇi* were states ruled by two rulers; similarly, *Gaṇa-rāyāṇi* would be states where *Gaṇa* or 'numbers' ruled. In other places, I found the word *Gaṇa* alone standing for a *Gaṇa*-state. Further enquiry supplied evidence to confirm my belief that *Gaṇa* denoted a republic and that its interpretation as then current ('tribe,' by Fleet and others; 'corporation of tradesmen or workmen,' by Bühler) was wrong. I further noticed that *Saṃgha* was another term in the same sense. Some of the data on which my conclusions were based were set forth in the original essay published under the title *An Introduction to Hindu Polity*.[4] Now I am in possession of new materials which throw further light on the significance of the two terms.

Significance of '*Gaṇa*'

It is necessary to ascertain what was exactly meant by *gaṇa*. It means 'numbers': *gaṇa-rājya* will therefore mean the rule of 'numbers', 'the rule by many'. Here the Buddhist Canon comes to our assistance. The Buddha was asked as to how the number of the monks was to be made out[5] :—

"At that time the people asked the Bhikkhus who went about for alms: 'How many Bhikkhus are there, Reverend Sirs?' The Bhikkhus replied, 'We do not know, friends!'

The people were annoyed....They told this thing to the Blessed One."

The Buddha prescribed that the brethren should be counted on the *Uposatha* day by the system employed in a *gaṇa* or by collecting voting tickets :—

"I prescribe, O Bhikkhus, that you count (the Bhikkhus) on the day of *Uposatha* by the method of gaṇas (*gaṇamaggena gaṇetuṁ*) or that you take the voting tickets (*salākā*)."

---

[3] अरायाणि वा गणरायाणि वा जुबरायाणि वा दोरज्जाणि वा वेरज्जाणि वा विरुद्धरज्जाणि वा—See on the significance of these terms Ch. X. *Gaṇa-rājya* is given by Varāha-mihira also—*Br. S.*, VI. 14.

[4] The *Modern Review*, Calcutta, 1913.

[5] *Mahāvagga*, II. 18. See Translation by Rhys Davids and Oldenberg in *S.B.E.*, XIII, p. 269.

The Bhikkhus were to be counted in an assembly by the method of counting votes as done in a *gaṇa*, or by the method of ballot-voting[6] where tickets were collected. In this connection, let us also take the term *gaṇa-pūraka* of the Pali Canon.[7] The *gaṇa-pūraka* was an officer who saw whether the lawful quorum of the assembly was formed before it transacted official business. It literally means "the Completer of the *Gaṇa*". *Gaṇa* thus was the *assembly* or *parliament*, so called because of the 'number' or 'numbering' of the members present. *Gaṇa-rājya*, consequently, denoted *government by assembly* or *parliament*. The secondary meaning of *gaṇa* came to be 'parliament' or 'senate', and as republics were governed by them, *gaṇa* came to mean a republic itself.

Pāṇini, dealing with the formation of the word *Saṃgha*, in III. 3. 86 (संघोद्घौ गण प्रशंसयोः ।), says that the word *Saṃgha* (as against the regular *saṃghāta*,[8] derived from *han*, III. 3. 76) is in the meaning of *gaṇa*. When Pāṇini has occasion to mention individual *Saṃghas*, he names communities which are known from monumental and other evidence to have been republican. In his time *Saṃgha* denoted *Gaṇa*, and the religious *Saṃgha* does not appear to have come into prominence. In fact, as we shall see, the latter was a copy of the political *Saṃgha*. Known republican bodies are called by Kauṭilya *Saṃghas*.[9] There is thus not much room to doubt that *Saṃgha* originally meant a republic. The most ancient work of the Buddhists, the Pāli, Pitaka itself confirms this. The *Majjhima Nikāya* (I. 4. 5. 35) uses the terms *saṃgha* and *gaṇa* side by side, taking them to mean, without the fear of the least confusion, the republics of the time of the Buddha: "*imesam pi hi bho Gotama saṃghānaṃ, gaṇānaṃ seyathīdam Vajjinaṃ Mallānaṃ*" "and this is so, O Gotama, in respect of the *Saṃghas*, *Gaṇas*, for instance, the Vajjis, Mallas". Thus *Saṃgha* and also *Gaṇa*, which are used here as in Pāṇini, synonymously, signified, *par excellence*, the republics. The republics

---

[6] See Ch. XI, on Procedure of Deliberations.

[7] गणपूरको वा भविस्सामीति, *Mahāvagga*, III. 6. 6; *cf. S.B.E.*, XIII, p. 307.

[8] गणप्रशंसयोः किम् । संघातः । *Kāśikā*, p. 214 (Benares, 1898).

[9] See Ch. VII.

were the *Saṃghas* and the *Gaṇas* at the time. Their secondary use, adoption by religious communities of the time, was just taking shape.[10]

The term *gaṇa* signified the form of *government*. *Saṃgha*, on the other hand, signified the *state*. As Patañjali says, *Saṃgha* is so called because it is one body, a unity (*saṃhanana*).[11] As we shall see presently, the *Saṃgha*, as a unit, a *body politic*, had its 'arms'[12] like a king or a corporation aggregate.

Controversy on *Gaṇa* in England

A wrong value to *gaṇa* has been assigned in the Dictionary of Monier-Williams which has misled many modern students of Sanskrit literature. Monier-Williams translated the word by the English word *tribe*. This meaning was adopted by the late Dr. Fleet in his translation of the Gupta Inscriptions in connection with the *Mālava-gaṇa* of those records. When my interpretation was published, Dr. F. W. Thomas, the foremost Indianist scholar in England, pointed out that the 'tribe' meaning was to be given up. And when Dr. Fleet insisted on the correctness of his rendering—'tribe'—Dr. Thomas challenged him to show that meaning from Sanskrit literature. Dr. Fleet found no authority except that of modern English translations of the *Raghuvaṃśa* and the *Mahābhārata*. Dr. Thomas drew attention to the fact that the St. Petersburg Dictionary and some later dictionaries never authorised and accepted the 'tribe' interpretation.[13] Further data collected by me on the point leave no room for controversy.

Pāṇini on *Gaṇa*

Pāṇini, as we have seen, equates *gaṇa* with *saṃgha*. No one would say that the word *saṃgha* can in any way be connected with 'tribe' there. Again, new *gaṇas* were founded.[14] Would that mean

---

[10] See the use of *saṃghī* and *gaṇī* in *M.N.*, I. 4. 5.

[11] संहनने वृत्तः, on Pāṇini, V. 1. 59; Kielhorn, II, p. 356 (2nd Ed.).

[12] See Ch. V.

[13] *J.R.A.S.*, 1914, pp. 413, 1010; 1915, p. 533; 1916, p. 162.

[14] See Ch. XV. See *Sāmaññaphala Sutta* (2–7); where Teachers, as founders of new schools, are called "*Saṃghī* cheva *gaṇi* cha,"—'Founder of *Saṃgha* and Founder of *gaṇa*'. This also displaces the 'tribe' theory.

that *new* 'tribes' were founded? Such a meaning would hardly deserve consideration.

The Jātakas on Gaṇa

The *Jātakas*, Vols. I and II, have two passages which help us considerably in appraising the value of *gaṇa*. They describe how families in Śrāvasti managed to entertain the Bhikkhus of the Buddha's Order. Some households combined into threes and fours, in some cases the whole quarter combined together, and jointly provided for the feast of the Bhikkhus, while in some cases 'many' people managed the entertainment by 'combining' according to the '*gaṇa-binding*' (*gaṇa-bandhana*).[15] Here the real sense of *gaṇa* becomes apparent: *assembly* or *association*. The word *bandhana* (the *binding*, Ger. '*bund*') shows the artificial nature of the *gaṇa*-organization, as opposed to the tribal and primitive.

The Mahābhārata on Gaṇa

The best discussion on the subject is Ch. 107 of the *Śanti-Parvan* of the *Mahābhārata* which tells us in the clearest possible terms what *gaṇa* was. I give the whole chapter with translation in Chapter XIV. *Gaṇas* were noted according to that, for their successful foreign policy, for their full treasury, for their ready army, for their skill in war, for their good laws, for their discipline. *Mantra* or policy of state and the discussion of that policy by the large number of the *gaṇa* are alluded to. These characteristics, among others, cannot refer to a tribe as such or to a corporation of traders; they refer to *gaṇa* as an organization of assembly-government or republic. Its general meaning is assembly[16] and technical, assembly-government or a republic.

Hindu Law and Amarakośa on Gaṇa

In the time of the legal commentators, *gaṇas* as political institutions had long ceased to exist. But the commentators never fell into the error of taking them as 'tribes'. They treat them as artificial associations or assemblies, *e.g.*, take

---

[15] *Jātaka*, I. 422: *Kadāchi tini-chattāri ekato hutvā, kadāchi gaṇa-bandhanena, kadāchi vīthi-sabhāgena, kadāchi sakala-nagaram chhandakam samharitvā*. *Jātaka*, II. 45, *gaṇa-bandhanena bahû ekato hutva*.

[16] In that meaning it is used also in the *Divyavādāna* which calls the body of ministers the *gaṇa* of ministers, pp. 404, 429.

the view cited by Dr. Jolly in his translation of Nārada (*S.B.E.*, XXXIII, p. 6, *n.*), "*gaṇa*, an assembly of co-habitants".[17] Dr. Jolly, in fact, translates *gaṇa* in verse 7 of Nārada as 'assembly,' and *gaṇārtham*[18] as 'on behalf of Society'. Though it is not strictly the technical sense of Nārada, yet it is very near the original sense and it follows the spirit.

Amarasiṃha, an author of the early Gupta time (very probably, under Chandra Gupta *Vikramāditya*), explains in his lexicon the constitutional terms *Rājaka* and *Rājanyaka* as a *gaṇa* of kings and a *gaṇa* of Kshatriyas (ordinary rulers) respectively (···· अथ राजकम् । राजन्यकं च नृपतिक्षत्रियाणां गणे क्रमात् । II. 8. xi. 3–4).

The *Avadāna-Śataka* on *Gaṇa*

In the *Avadāna-Śataka*, *gaṇa*-rule is opposed to royal rule. Merchants from the Middle Country of Northern India had gone to the Deccan in the time of the Buddha. When questioned by the King of the Deccan, 'Gentlemen Merchants, who is the king there (in Northern India)?' they replied:

> "Your Majesty, some countries are under *gaṇas* and some are under kings."[19]

Here the royal form of government is contrasted with the *gaṇa*-form; these were the two divisions. And the only form of government which can be contra-distinguished from the royal is republican.

Jaina definition

A Jaina text in explaining *gaṇa* says that with reference to human society *gaṇa* is a group with the main characteristic of 'possessing a mind,' of being conscious. According to the text there is also an abuse of the term. The examples given of its right

---

[17] *Cf.* Jagannātha, "आदिशब्दो गणसंघादिसमूह विवक्षया," Jolly, *Nārada-Smriti* (text), p. 163 *n.* Nilakaṇṭha in his *Vyavahāra-Mayūkha* (Chapter on Saṃvid-vyatikrama), equates *gaṇa* with *Saṃgha*.

[18] *S.B.E.*, XXXIII, p. 349, verse 24.

[19] Ed. Speyer, Petrograd, 1902, II, p. 103, "अथ मध्यदेशाद्वणिजो दक्षिणापथं गताः । तैः राज्ञो महाकप्रफिणस्य प्राभृतमुपनीतम् । राज्ञा उक्तं भो वणिजः कस्तत्र राजेति । वणिजः कथयन्ति । देव केचिद्देशा गणाधीनाः केचिद्राजाधीना इति ।" I am thankful to Mr. Ramaprasad Chanda for this reference.

use are: 'the *gaṇa* of the Mallas' (a known republican community, as we shall presently see[20], and 'the *gaṇa* of the *Pura*,' *i.e.*, the *Pura* assembly (see Ch. XXVIII, on the Paura). As an example of its abuse, 'the *gaṇa* of Vasus (Vasu gods) is given by the commentator. Its non-social use is pointed out in music (*bhāva-gaṇa*). Non-constitutional *gaṇas*, according to the commentary, lack mentality or purpose (in making up the group),' *e.g.*, 'Vasugaṇa' (the Vasu gods).[21] In other words, the application of the word to a non-constitutional body is distinguished. The constitutional *gaṇa* is the real *gaṇa*, and in the eye of the Jaina authority, it has a mind: it is an organised conscious body of men like the political assembly of the Mallas or the assembly of the corporate *Paura*. It is a corporate assembly, as opposed to a mere multitude or chance collection.

This passage, along with the discourse in the *Mahābhārata* on *Gaṇas*, the *Jātaka* and the *Avadāna* references, and Pāṇini's equation of *saṃgha* with *gaṇa* leave no doubt as to the real significance of *gaṇa*.

Now we may pass on from the terms to the republics themselves.

---

[20] See Ch. VII.

[21] सचित्तादि समूहो लोगम्मि गणो उ मल्लपूरादी।
कुप्पावयणम्मी लोउत्तर ओसन्नगोयाणां ॥—Text quoted in the Jaina Prākṛita Encyclopædia, *Abhidhāna-Rājendra* (Rutlam, 1919), Vol. III, p. 813, comments: सचित्तसमूहो यथा मल्लगणः. . . .अचित्तसमूहो यथा वसुगणः कुप्रवचने द्रव्यगणो यथा चरकादिगणः। चरकः परिव्राजकः (p. 814).

Cf. on अचित्त Pāṇini, IV. 2. 47; and IV. 3. 96 where political loyalty is implied to be स-चित्त, 'with mentality,' 'thought'; and see Ch. XII.

CHAPTER V

Republics in Pāṇini

Pāṇini on *Saṃgha*

Pāṇini gives most valuable information about Hindu Republics of his time which I take to be about 500 B.C.[1] He gives several rules about the formation of words connected with *Saṃghas*. The large number of the rules impresses one with the importance which the contemporaries of Pāṇini attached to the existing republics. Like any other important, orthodox institution the Republics engaged the attention of the orthodox grammarians. Further, Pāṇini gives an indication as to the part of the country and area covered by the republics in his days.

With Pāṇini, as we have seen above, the word *Saṃgha* is a technical term which denoted the political *Saṃgha*, or, as he calls it, the *Gaṇa* or Republic. He does not know the religious *Saṃgha*, which, as we shall presently see (Ch. VI), was a copy of the political *Saṃgha*. In the days of Pāṇini, Buddhist and Jaina *Saṃghas* either did not exist (and in that case Pāṇini's date would be about 600 B.C.), or they had not become important. It is to be noticed that Kātyāyana (*c.* 400 B.C.)[2] found *Saṃgha* in the same technical sense as Pāṇini, for he gives no *vārttika* to Pāṇini, III. 3. 86, in dissent. Kauṭilya (*c.* 300 B.C.) too has the same use but with the

---

[1] This date is based on political data in Pāṇini which may be discussed in detail in a separate paper. Here, however, attention may be drawn to the fact that Pāṇini knew the Order of Makkhalī Wanderers (=*Maskarin*, VI. 1. 154; *M.V.*, I, p. 256, '*Maskarin*'; see the remark of Patañjali on the word). The Makkhalīs merged into the Ājīvakas in the time of Makkhalī Gosāla, contemporary of the Buddha, from whose time they acquired the latter designation. Aṅga had evidently ceased to be a separate kingdom, while Kosala was still independent (IV. 1. 170–175). Again, Pāṇini knew *Saṃgha*, as discussed above, only in the sense of a republic. The mention of the script of the *Yavanas* can now be easily explained, in view of their identification proposed here below with the Hellenic City State of Nysa on the Kabul River, which had existed long before Alexander. See also Greek letters on Persian coins struck in India, Rapson, *IC.*, pl. I.

[2] *J. Bors.*, I, pp. 82, 116.

difference that he employs it in a general sense as well (pp. 36, 49, 407), *viz.*, that of a corporate association.

Castes in a *Saṃgha*

Pāṇini in V. 3. 114 to 117 gives *taddhita* rules with regard to the *Saṃghas* of the Vāhika country. By those rules, the members of a particular *Saṃgha*, when mentioned, could be distinguished, whether they were Brahmins, Kshatriyas, or of castes other than those. For instance, take the well-known example of the Mālavas, called Malloi by Alexander's historians.[3] A non-Brāhmin and a non-Kshatriya of the Mālava *Saṃgha* would be called Mālavyaḥ; while a Kshatriya would be Mālavaḥ, the plural in each case being Mālavāḥ.[4] This points to the stage of a developed, the familiar, Hindu society as opposed to a tribal stage.

Kātyāyana on *Saṃgha*

Kātyāyana, commenting on Pāṇini, IV. 1. 168, says that the rule (of the *añ pratyaya*) in making a derivative from the national designation of a Kshatriya will hold good only if the Kshatriya is not a member of a *Saṃgha*, for the rule is limited to the case of a monarchy.[5]

---

[3] The credit of identifying the *Oxydrakai* and *Malloi* of the Greek writers with the *Kshudrakas* and *Mālavas* of the grammar belongs to Sir Rāmakrishna Gopāla Bhandarkar, who was the first to correct the mistaken identification put forward by scholars. They had taken the former to stand for the śūdras. See *Ind. Ant.*, Vol. I, p. 23.

[4] आयुधजीविसंघाञ्ञ्यड्वाहीकेष्वब्राह्मणराजन्यात् ॥ ५ ॥ ३ ॥ ११४ ॥

Kāśikā. .वहीकेषु य आयुधजीविसंघस्तद्वाचिनः प्रातिपदिकादब्राह्मण-राजन्य-वर्जितात्स्वार्थे ञ्यट् प्रत्ययो भवति । ब्राह्मणे तद्विशेषग्रहणम् । राजन्ये तु स्वरूप-ग्रहणमेव....क्षौद्रक्यः क्षौद्रक्यौ क्षुद्रकाः । मालव्यः । मालव्यौः । मालव्य.... pp. 455–456.

[5] जनपदशब्दात् क्षत्रियादञ् ॥ ४ ॥ १ ॥ १६७ ॥ Kātyāyana :—क्षत्रिया-देकराजात्संघप्रतिषेधार्थम् ।

[*Ekarāja* is a technical term for monarch in Hindu politics. The term is explained in coronation rituals in Vedic literature. Its interpretation as 'monarch' is now accepted (see Macdonell and Keith, *Vedic Index*, Vol. I, p. 119). Literally, it means the 'sole sovereign'. (See *Artha-Śāstra*, Bk. XI, Ch. I, p. 379.)]

Patañjali on the above says :— क्षत्रियादेकराजादिति वक्तव्यम् । किं प्रयोजनम् । संघप्रतिषेधार्थम् । संघान्माभूत् । पञ्चालानामपत्यम् विदेहानाम-

The results of the above discussion are that *Saṃgha* is contrasted with monarchy, and that a *Saṃgha* or a Hindu Republic had Brahmin members, Kshatriya members and other castes, *i.e.*, the personnel of the *Saṃghas* was not composed of one caste or tribe.

Āyudhajīvin Saṃghas named in Pāṇini

Pāṇini mentions the following *Saṃghas* or Republics by name :—

1. the Vṛika,[6]
2. the Dāmani ('and others'),[7]

3 to 8. the Trigartta-Shashtha[7] or the League of the Six Trigarttas whose names are given in the *Kāśikā* on the authority of an ancient verse as follows[8] :—

(*a*) the Kauṇḍoparatha :

(*b*) the Dāṇḍaki ;

(*c*) the Kaushṭaki ;

(*d*) the Jālamāni ;

(*e*) the Brāhmagupta ;

(*f*) the Jānaki [or Jālaki] ;

पत्यमिति ॥ तत्तर्हि वक्तव्यम् । न वक्तव्यम् । न ह्यन्तरेण बहुषु लुकं पश्चाला इत्येतद्भवति । यस्तस्मादुत्पद्येत युवप्रत्ययः स स्यात् । युवप्रत्ययश्चेत्तस्य लुक्कस्मिंश्चाल्लुग्-भविष्यति ॥ इदं तर्हि क्षौद्रकाणामपत्यम् मालवानामपत्यमिति ॥ अत्रापि क्षौद्रक्यः मालव्य इति, नैतत्तेषां दासे वा भवति कर्मकरे वा । किं तर्हि । तेषामेव कस्मिंश्चित् । यावता तेषामेव कस्मिंश्चिद्यस्तस्मादुत्पद्येत युवप्रत्ययः स स्यात् । युवप्रत्ययश्चेत्तस्य लुक्कस्मिंश्चाल्लुग् भविष्यति ॥

अथ क्षत्रियग्रहणं किमर्थम् । इह मा भूत् । विदेहो नाम ब्राह्मणस्तस्यापत्यं वैदेहिः ।

—Kielhorn, Vol. II, pp. 268–69.

[6] वृकट्टेण्यण् ॥ ५ ॥ ३ ॥ ११५ ॥ The connexion of this *Sūtra* is with the previous one, which is already quoted above.

[7] दामन्यादित्रिगर्तषष्ठाच्छः ॥ ५ ॥ ३ ॥ ११६ ॥

[8] आहुस्त्रिगर्त्तषष्ठांस्तु कौण्डोपरथदण्डकौ ।
क्रौष्टुकिर्जालमानिश्च ब्राह्मगुप्तोऽथजानकिः ॥ p. 456. On their probable coins see *J.B.O.R.S.*, XX. 289. Bhaṭṭoji Dīkshit reads *Jālaki*.

9. the Yaudheya, 'and others';[9] and
10. the Parśva, 'and others'.[9]

Pāṇini calls these *Saṃghas Āyudhajīvins*. Kauṭilya has in its place *Śastropajīvins*. Now, what is the meaning of this? The first impression will be to interpret it as 'those who live by the profession of arms', as I took it myself in my essay in the *Modern Review*. But this meaning is not maintainable for two reasons. The *Artha-Śāstra* contrasts the *Śastropajīvin Saṃghas* with *Rājaśabdopajīvin Saṃghas*, which means according to Kauṭilya's further discussion (p. 377)[10] the *Saṃghas* whose rulers assume the 'title' (*Śabda*) of *rājan*. We know from inscriptions, coins and literature that elected or appointed rulers in some Indian republics did assume that title.[11] Now, here '*upajīvin*' cannot mean 'living by' as a republic cannot *live* by the title *rāja*. The meaning which would suit both classes of Kauṭilya's republics is the other known meaning of the verb *upajīv*, 'to observe', *e.g.*, in *Manu*, X. 74, where a Brahmin is asked to *upajīv* the six duties, which include making gifts.[12] *Upajīvin* in that sense would mean that the *Saṃghas* called '*Śastropajīvins*' *observed* the practice of arms or military art, and that the *Saṃghas* called '*Rājaśabdopajīvins*' *observed* the practice of assuming the title *rājan*. In other words, their respective

Interpretation of *Āyudhajīvin*

---

[9] पर्श्वादियोधेयादिभ्यामणञौ ॥ ५ ॥ ३ ॥ ११७ ॥ (as read by the *Kāśikā*).

The *Kāśikā*, after this *Sūtra*, says that with 117, the *āyudhajīvi-saṃgha* description ends. By IV. 1, 178 (to be read with *Sūtra* 168 *supra*) Pāṇini calls the Yaudheyas a *janapada*, a nation or country, *i.e.*, political community.

The Parśvas of Pāṇini were in the Vāhīka country (see p. 50), and there were Brahmins and Rājanyas amongst them. The Parśvas are mentioned in the Vedas also. VI. I. pp. 504–05.

[10] राजशब्दिभिरवरुद्धमवक्षिप्तं वा . . *AŚ.*, XIX, p. 377.

[11] *Cf.* Ch. XVIII; also p. 50.

[12] ब्राह्मणा ब्रह्मयोनिस्था ये स्वकर्म्मण्यवस्थिताः ।
ते सम्यगुपजीवेयुः षट्कर्म्माणि यथाक्रमम् ॥ ७४ ॥
अध्यापनमध्ययनं यजनं याजनं तथा ।
दानं प्रतिग्रहश्चैव षट्कर्म्माण्यग्रजन्मनः ॥ ७५ ॥ *Manu*, X.

Kullūka, उपजीवेयुः=अनुतिष्ठेयुः

constitutions enjoined on the members to be skilled in military art in the former, and on the rulers or every privileged member to bear the title in the latter (p. 56).

The Macedonian writers[13] describe many of these republics, two of which are the grammarians' 'military' (*āyudhajīvin* or *śastropajīvin*) *Saṃghas*: the Kshudrakas and the Mālavas. Their terrritories and populations were large. Their state comprised several cities. They were very rich. Any idea of mercenary life is excluded by the Greek description. They were large sovereign states, with noted wealth, prosperity and civil organisation. Do these writers notice any characteristics which may correspond to the *āyudhajīvin*? They do; and their datum agrees with the interpretation which we have offered above. They say that these free communities were the most famous for their *military skill*.[13] The Greek writers further describe one constitution, the law of which made the citizens devote only limited attention to military matters, implying thereby that others did the opposite.[14] *Upajīv* thus has a reference to their conventional or constitutional practice. The *āyudhajīvins* of Pāṇini are to be taken as denoting those republics which considered military art as the vital principle of their constitution. That was the chief feature of their constitution in the eyes of their contemporaries, as the chief feature in the other class of republics was the law which allowed the elected president to be called *rāja* or 'king'.[15]

Identification of the Vāhīka-land

Further Pāṇini says that these republics were situated in the Vāhīka Country. Now, what was the Vāhīka Country? It has been already realized that the people

[13] See Chapter VIII, on Hindu Republics in Greek Writers.

[14] See Strabo, XV. 34, on Mousikanos; (p. 50).

[15] I take this opportunity to correct the interpretation which I put on the expression *rajaśabdopajivins* formerly. I thought that it referred to all the citizens of a republic being called *rājans*. But now I find that no such constitution existed. The republics mentioned in Buddhist documents, which we shall discuss presently, allowed the title only to the elected president, although the citizens in general are alluded to as *rājans*, in the sense that they composed the sovereign body, and also that every one had the possibility of being elected *Rājan*.

Vāhīkas mentioned in the *Mahābhārata* were in the Punjab.[16] But the significance of the word *Vāhīka* has not yet been considered. I think, the word *Vāhīka* means 'the country of the rivers,'[17] and as such, the Vāhīka-land would comprise the Sind valley and the Punjab. These are exactly the limits given in the *Mahābhārata*: '(the Vāhīkas) that live in the valleys of the five rivers and in that of the Sindhu as the sixth'.[18] From the known history of some of the Vāhīka republics of the grammar, we can say that the Vāhīka-land did include Sind. For instance, the Kshudrakas and the Mālavas were partially in Sind.[19] The *Kāśikā* puts them amongst the illustrations of the Vāhīka-*Saṃghas*.[20] The Vāhīka Country was 'away from the Himalayas', *i.e.*, it did not include the mountain districts.[21] (The Six Trigarttas were at the foot of the Himalayas in the Punjab, about Jammu or Kangra.)

Other republics in Pāṇini

Besides these martial republics, Pāṇini gives us the names of six other communities which from independent sources[22] are known to have been republican about that period.

---

[16] See Sylvain Levi, *Ind. Ant.*, Vol. XXXV (1906), p. 18.

[17] From the verb वह् to *flow*, *cf.* वाहिनी—a river.

[18] पञ्चानां सिन्धुषष्ठानां नदीनां येऽन्तराश्रिताः । *Karṇa-Parvan*, XLIV. 7.

Nāgeśa Pradipoddyota on Pāṇini, एङ् प्राचां देशे, I. 1. 75,

" शतद्रुर्विपाशैरावती वितस्ता चन्द्रभागेति पञ्चनद्यः सिन्धुः

षष्ठस्तन्मध्यदेशो वाहीक इति तद्व्याख्यातारः " ।

The whole of the Punjab, according to the *Mahābhārata*, was under one ruler, who was at Śākala, and the people had become heterodox. This indicates the time of Menander and later.

[19] See also *Karṇa-Parvan*, *Mahābhārata*, Ch. XL. 41 where the Madras and Sindhu-Sauvīras are grouped together. *Cf.* V. Smith, *J.R.A.S.*, 1903, 685.

[20] वाहीकेषु य आयुधजीविसंघस्तद्वाचिनं. . . . कौण्डीबृस्यः । क्षौद्रक्यः । मालव्यः pp. 455–56.

[21] The *Mahābhārata* describes the Vāhīka Country away from the Himalayas (*Karṇa-Parvan*, XLIV. 6). Pāṇini also treats the mountaineers as distinct (IV. 3. 91).

[22] See subsequent chapters for the account of the republics named here.

These are :—

(1) the Madra ;[23]
(2) the Vṛiji ;[23]
(3) the Rājanya ;[24]
(4) the Andhaka-Vṛishṇi ;[25]
(5) the Mahārāja ;[26] and
(6) the Bharga.[27]

Although Pāṇini had no occasion to call them *Saṃghas* yet the rules show that he knew them as republican. As we shall have opportunity to discuss these states in sequence, it is not necessary to go into details here.

The Andhaka-Vṛishṇi *Saṃgha*

Pāṇini's Andhaka-Vṛishṇis have to be noted separately. They, in the Purāṇas, are identical with the Sātvats. The Sātvats, according to the *Aitareya Brāhmaṇa*, had the *Bhaujya* constitution, and their rulers were called *Bhojas*.[28] In the *Mahābhārata*, the Andhaka rulers are called *Bhojas*, and a subdivision of the Yādavas itself is latterly called Bhojas.[29] The fact that the Vṛishṇis had no *rājan* in their constitution,

---

[23] मद्रवृज्योः कन् ॥ ४ ॥ २ ॥ १३१ ॥

[24] राजन्यादिभ्यो वुञ् ॥ ४ ॥ २ ॥ ५३ ॥ See also the *Gaṇapāṭha* on this for names of some other communities which are known to be republican.

[25] राजन्यबहुवचन-द्वन्द्वेऽन्धकवृष्णिषु ॥ ६ ॥ २ ॥ ३४ ॥

[26] महाराजाट्ठञ् ॥ ४ ॥ ३ ॥ ६७ ॥ See discussion below on the Mahārāja ' nation '. (Chs. XII and XV).

[27] न प्राच्यभर्गादि-यौधेयादिभ्यः ॥ ४ ॥ १ ॥ १७८ ॥

The Bhargas are called here ' Easterners '. According to the *Mahābhārata* (*Sabhā-Parvan*, XXX. 10. 14), they were between the Vatsa territory and the Southern Mallas, who were not very far from the Videhas. Pāṇini finds them a political community like the Yaudheyas, with whom he groups them (IV. 1. 168–78). The Buddhist records mention the Bhargas in the republican groups extending from Kosala and Kauśāmbī eastwards, and place the Bhargas next to the Vatsas (*Buddhist India*, p. 22 ; *Jātaka*, III. 157). See p. 44 on their location. The other Bhargas whom Pāṇini notes were amongst the Traigarttas (भर्गात्त्रैगर्ते, IV. 1. 111).

[28] *Aitareya Brāhmaṇa*, Bk. VIII, 14.

[29] *Sabhā-Parvan*, Ch. XIV ; *Śānti-Parvan*, Ch. LXXXI.

is expressed in folklore and legend in that they had been cursed not to be crowned kings. The *Mahābhārata*, in *Sabhā-Parvan* (XXXVII. 5), says that the Daśārṇas (Vṛishṇis) were 'kingless'. That they were a *Saṃgha*, is attested by Kauṭilya who mentions the Vṛishṇi *Saṃgha* as having come to grief by offending Dvaipāyana in olden days.[30] The *Mahābhārata* gives an 'ancient' discourse on the Andhaka-Vṛishṇi *Saṃgha*.[31] That they had no republican '*rājan*,' is proved by their coin which, in the scripts of the first century B.C., is struck in the name of their *Gaṇa*.[32]

The Vṛishṇi coin has a peculiarity which distinguishes it from the coins of other republics. Coins of republics where there was no 'king'-consul, were struck in the name of the *Gaṇa*,[33] *e.g.*, "Victory to the *Gaṇa* of the Ārjunāyanas," "Of the Mālava-*Gaṇa*," "Victory of the Yaudheya-*Gaṇa*". There is one exception to this in the case of one type of the Yaudheya coins which is struck both in the name of the Executive Council (*Mantra-dharas*) and the *Gaṇa*.[34] The Vṛishṇi coin resembles none of these varieties. It is struck in the name of the *Rājanya* and *Gaṇa* of the Vṛishṇis: "*Vṛishṇi-rājañña-gaṇasya*."[35] The constitutional significance of the word, *Rājanya*, has to be ascertained. There is evidence to hold that in the case of the Vṛishṇis it had a definite constitutional meaning. Let us examine it.

Constitutional significance of '*Rājanya*'

We gather from Pāṇini that there were two *Rājanyas* amongst the Andhaka-Vṛishṇis.[36] He gives a special rule how

---

30 *AŚ.*, I. 6, 3, p. 11.

31 See Appendix A, where the whole discourse has been translated.

32 Cunningham, *Coins of Ancient India*, p. 70, pl. IV; *J.R.A.S.*, 1900, pp. 416, 420, 424 (Rapson).

33 Cunningham, *Ibid.*, pp. 77, 89, pl. VI, VII; V. Smith, *Catalogue of Coins in the Indian Museum, Calcutta*, pp. 166, 170.

34 Hoernle, *Proc. A.S.B.*, 1884, pp. 138–40.

On *mantra-dharas*, consult discussion below on ministers, under Monarchy, Ch. XXX.

35 Read *ññ* instead of *jñ*; *cf.* Kharoshṭhī *rājaṇṇa* (*J.R.A.S.*, 1900, p. 416).

36 राजन्यबहुवचन-द्वन्द्वेऽन्धकवृष्णिषु ॥ ६ ॥ २ ॥ ३४ ॥

to mention them (VI. 2. 34). The *Kāśikā*,[37] commenting on that says that the rule does not apply to the members of the Andhakas and Vṛishṇis as such, but to their *Rājanyas* only, the '*Rājanyas* being leaders of families consecrated to rulership'. The names of several of these 'dual' groups of rulers are preserved in literature: the *Rājanyas* of the groups of Śini and Vāsudeva, Śvāphalka and Chaitraka are cited in the *Kāśikā*,[38] the Party (*varga*) of Akrūra and the Party of Vāsudeva are alluded to by Kātyāyana,[39] Vāsudeva and Ugrasena Babhrū are mentioned as leading their parties in the *Mahābhārata* (Appendix A).

Apparently, the Vṛishṇi-Andhaka league had a joint federal constitution where executive power was vested in two *rājanyas*, with their respective *vargas*, representing each division; and this was probably the *Rājanyaka* of Amara.[39] Kātyāyana mentioning 'the Party (*varga*) of Akrūra' and the 'Party of Vāsudeva,' undoubtedly draws on old literature. Akrūra was an Andhaka leader; and it seems that at one time he was one of the two presidents of the Federal Council. This explains Kṛishṇa's saying in the *Mahābhārata*[40] that he

---

[37] *Kāśikā,* राजन्यवाचिनां बहुवचनान्तानां यो द्वन्द्वेऽन्धकवृष्णिषु वर्त्तते तत् पूर्वपदं प्रकृतिस्वरं भवति । श्वाफल्कचैत्रकाः (after Dikshita), शिनि-वासुदेवाः । ....अन्धकवृष्ण्य एते न तु राजन्याः । राजन्यग्रहणमिहाभिषिक्तवंश्यानां क्षत्रियाणां ग्रहणार्थम् । एते च नाभिषिक्तवंश्याः । ....बहुवचनग्रहणं किम् । संकर्षण-वासुदेवौ । ...." pp. 546–47.

[38] *Kāśikā*, p. 546. *Chaitraka-rodhaka* was probably the full name. The *Kāśikā* treats it as such; Dīkshita omits *rodhaka* as does the *Kāśikā* later on.

[39] On Pāṇini, IV. 2. 104 :—अक्रूरवर्ग्यः । अक्रूरवर्गीणः । वासुदेववर्गीणः । On the word वर्ग, see discussion below, under *Jānapada*, Ch. XXVII. It really means an assembly or council. Bṛihaspati (*Vivāda-Ratnākara*, p. 569) calls *gaṇa*, *pūga* (guild) and similar bodies '*vargas*'. Mitramiśra explains a *vargin* body as a *gaṇa* (*Vīramitrodaya*, p. 12); see also Nīlakaṇṭha, *Mayūkha*, I, on *varga* as a corporate body, and Pāṇini (V. 1. 60), in the sense of assembly whose members were counted. A Senate or Council (*gaṇa*) of Kshatriyas is called *Rājanyaka*, and a council of 'Kings'. *Rājaka* by Amara (II. 8. 4), p. 27 above. See also below on *Arājaka*, Ch. X.

[40] See Appendix A.

holds authority or *Aiśvarya* to the extent of one-half only (*ardhabhoktā*). In the tradition quoted in the *Mahābhārata* the Party of Akrūra is bitterly complained against by Kṛishṇa. Probably it is to a constitution like that of the Andhaka-Vṛishṇis that the Jaina *Sūtra* refers as the rule of opposing parties.[41]

Changing dual groups—Vāsudeva and Ugrasena, Akrūra and Vāsudeva, Śini and Vāsudeva—suggest that the Andhaka *Rājanya* and the Vṛishṇi *Rājanya* were elected rulers. The coins were struck in the name of the *Rājanya* and in the name of the *Gaṇa*, jointly. Other coins struck in the name of *Rājanyas* without the mention of the name of the states, have been found.[42] In view of our interpretation of the term *Rājanya*, in all probability, they are republican coins.

State arms of the republics

Pāṇini implies by his rule IV. 3. 127 that a *Saṃgha* had its *aṅka* and *lakshaṇa*.[43] *Aṅka* means a mark, and *lakshaṇa* also has a similar significance. I propose to identify this '*lakshaṇa*' of Pāṇini with the '*lāñchana*' or heraldic crest of later Sanskrit. The *lakshaṇa* was the permanent heraldic mark of a *Saṃgha*-state which they employed on their seales, and probably also on their coins and standards. The *Artha-Śāstra* of Kauṭilya (II. 12, p. 84), in laying down rules for the manufacture of silver and copper coins, calls the Mint-Master '*Lakshaṇa-adhyaksha*' or the 'Director of *Lakshaṇas*'. The Mint-Master appears to have acquired this official designation on account of the *lakshaṇa* he stamped on the coins. Evidently this refers to a coinage when no name, far less the figure, of the ruler was struck. The *lakshaṇa*, therefore, in Kauṭilya, is the 'royal' or 'state' mark. The *aṅka*, it seems to me, refers to symbols adopted by changing governments. An elected ruler or body of rulers adopted their own special *aṅka* which was given up when those officers went out of

---

41 *Achārāṅga-Sūtra*, II. 3. 10 : *Viruddha-rājya.*

42 *E.g.* See Cunningham, *Coins of Ancient India*, p. 69, pl. IV.

43 संघाङ्कलक्षणेष्वञ्यञिञामण् ॥ ४ ॥ ७ ॥ १२७ ॥ See *Kāśikā*, p. 350, गार्गः संघः । गार्गोङ्कः । गार्गं लक्षणम ।

office. In Hindu Law-books we get *hastāṅka* for signature.[44] Kālidāsa uses the term *gotrāṅka* in connection with a song, that is, a signed song.[45] The verb *aṅk* is used from the time of Kauṭilya[46] (and evidently earlier) up to Kālidāsa,[47] and even later, in the sense of 'marking with letters or figures'. We have the term *Rājāṅka*, in Kauṭilya, with which the bulls of the royal stable were marked or branded. *Aṅka* thus signifies an individual mark. It may mean even the legend or the motto adopted by a ruler. Reference may be made to the legends *Mānāṅka* and *Guṇāṅka* (*aṅka* of King Māna, *aṅka* of King Guṇa) of Nepal coins, 576–600 A.C.[48] This interpreration would explain the permanent and the changing symbols and legends on republican coins. In the case of punch-marked coins with legends, a *Saṃgha* probably employed its special *aṅka* in initial letters or fuller legends[49] and its *lakshaṇa* in the figure of an animal or river, town or the like. The figure most likely is the *lakshaṇa*, and the legend. *aṅka*. The constitutional point is that the corporate character of the *Saṃgha* is emphasised by the corporate crest and symbols.[50]

---

[44] प्राड्विवाकादि-हस्ताङ्कं मुद्रितं राजमुद्रया। Vṛiddha Vasishṭah quoted in the *Vīramitrodaya*, p. 195 (ed. Jīvānanda).

[45] उत्सङ्गे वा मलिनवसने सौम्य निक्षिप्य वीणां
मद्गोत्राङ्कं विरचितपदं गेयमुद्गातुकामा।
—*Meghadūta*, II. 85.

[46] *Artha-Śāstra*, II. 29, p. 129.

[47] णामाङ्किदं (*Śakuntalā*). But *cf. Garutmad-aṅka* in Samudra Gupta's inscription (*GI.*, p. 8).

[48] Jayaswal, *Chronology and History of Nepal*, IV, VIII; *J.B.O.R.S.*, XXII (1936).

The *Kāśikā* (p. 304) gives *nānā* as an example of *aṅka*. We know that some of the Kushān coins bore the lenged NANA. The *Kāśikā* is evidently referring to that legend.

[49] For such coins see *J.B.O.R.S.*, XXII. 63, 65.

[50] Kātyāyana points out that Pāṇini's IV. 3. 127 will apply to township called *Ghosha* also, घोषग्रहणमपि कर्त्तव्य (Bhattoji Dīkshita). This leads us to the inference that townships or municipalities also had their corporate symbols or arms. Such arms have been recognised, *e.g.*, in the Sohgaúra plate. (Fleet, *J.R.A.S.*, 1907, p. 528.) Now their technical name, *lakshaṇa*, is disclosed by the grammar. See also numerous Jānapada seals dug out at Nālandā, *E.I.*, XXI. 72 and *Memoir* by Dr. Hirananda Sastri on Nālandā seals.

Political Nikāyas: a species of Saṃgha

Again by *Sūtra* III. 3. 42, Pāṇini indicates a division of republics into two classes: (1) Where no 'Upper-and-lower condition' exists, and (2) where that condition does exist.[51] By the first we may understand a one-chamber constitution and by the second a double-chamber constitution. The word used by Pāṇini for (1) is "*anauttarādharya*," and he lays down the rule that a *Saṃgha* to which this characteristic attached, was designated *Kāya* or *Nikāya*, meaning one 'body'.[52] In Pālī, *Nikāya* has got the same primary meaning, a 'fraternity' (Childers). The Buddhist fraternity was composed of only one house. Apparently the term was borrowed by the Buddhists from political phraseology. Three political *Nikāyas* are named in grammatical literature: *Śāpiṇḍi-Nikāya*, *Mauṇḍi-Nikāya* and *Chikkali-Nikāya*.[53]

As we shall see now (p. 42), *Nikāya* was not the only constitutional designation for the community borrowed by Buddhism. *Saṃgha* itself was borrowed.

---

[51] संघेचानौत्तराधर्ये ॥ ३ ॥ ३ ॥ ४२ ॥ With this *S*. III. 3. 8, 6 should be read. The latter refers to *Saṃgha* as Pāṇini understood and defined it, a political *Saṃgha*, a *gaṇa*.

[52] See the previous *Sūtra*, III. 3. 41: निवासचितिशरीरोपसमाधाने-ष्वादेश्च कः ॥

[53] *Kāśikā* on Pāṇini, VI. 2. 94 (p. 559). Pāṇini's rule is about the proper names of *Nikāyas*, संज्ञायां गिरिनिकाययोः ।

F

CHAPTER VI

Republican Origin of Buddhist Saṃgha and Republics in Buddhist Literature (500–400 B.C.)

Buddhist *Saṃgha* borrowed from Political *Saṃgha*

The Buddha was born in a republican people. He had *Saṃgha* neighbours around him, and he grew up amongst them. He called the community which he founded "Bhikkhu-*Saṃgha*," or 'the Republic of Bhikshus'. He, following his contemporary teachers, adopted the name as well as the constitution of the political *Saṃgha* in founding his religious *Saṃgha*; and this was a reason why his religion and monastic organisation lasted so long. From the words of the Buddha himself, as reported in the Pālī *Sūtras*,[1] the historical connection between the political and religious *Saṃgha*-constitutions can be demonstrated. When the Chancellor of Magadha, deputed by the King of Magadha, wanted to know the opinion of the Buddha, on behalf of his master, as to the advisability of invading the Vajjis (the Vṛijis of Pāṇini)—the Lichchhavis and Videhas[2]—the Buddha addressed his reply (not to the Chancellor, but to his foremost disciple) in these words :—

> "Have you heard, Ānanda, that the Vajjians often hold *full* and *frequent assemblies*."

To this, Ānanda replied in the affirmative. The Buddha put such seven questions relating to the Constitution of the Vajjians, intended to be heard by the Chancellor. The verdict of the Buddha may be summed up in his own words as follows :—

(1) "So long, Ānanda, as the Vajjians hold *full* and *frequent assemblies* :

(2) "So long as they *meet together in concord* and *rise in concord* and *carry out Vajjian business in concord* (Vajjī-karaṇīyāni—Vajjian acts of state) :

---

[1] *Dīghanikāya*, *Mahāparinibbāna Suttanta* Trans. adopted from Rhys Davids, *Dialogues of the Buddha*, Pt. II, pp. 79–85. *Cf. S.B.E.*, Vol. XI, pp. 3–6.

[2] For details regarding them, see below.

(3) "So long as they *enact nothing not already established, abrogate nothing that has been already enacted* and *act in accordance with the ancient institutions* of the Vajjians, as established in former days:

(4) "So long as they honour and esteem and revere and support the Vajji Elders, and *hold it a point of duty to hearken to their words*:

(5) "So long as no women or girls belonging to them are detained among them by force or abduction (*i.e.*, law and not force reigns):

(6) "So long as they honour and esteem and revere and support the Vajjian Chaityas (sacred monuments) (*i.e., follow the religion established*):

(7) "So long as the rightful protection, defence and support shall be fully provided for the Arhants amongst them (*i.e.*, follow the established practice and keep out Brahminic religious systems):

"*So long may the Vajjians be expected not to decline but to prosper.*"

Hearing this, the Chancellor murmured 'the Vajjians cannot be overcome by the King of Magadha.' The only possible policy was to create disunion (*mithubheda*).

As soon as the Chancellor had taken leave of the Buddha, the Teacher called a meeting of the Bhikshu *Saṃgha* in the Hall, and addressed them:

"I will teach you, O Mendicants, the *seven conditions of the welfare (of a community)*."

And he repeated the very seven conditions (with necessary modifications) which were the features of the practice of the Vajjians and which were well-known, as testified to by Ānanda:

(1) "So long as the Bhikkhus meet together in full and frequent assemblies:

(2) "So long as they meet together in concord and rise in concord and carry out in concord the duties of the order (*Saṃgha*):

(3) "So long as the Bhikkhus shall establish nothing that has not already been prescribed, and

abrogate nothing that has already been established and act in accordance with the rules of the *Saṃgha* now laid down :

(4) " So long as the brethren honour and esteem and revere and support the Elders, the Fathers and the Leaders of the *Saṃgha*, and hold it a point of duty to hearken to their words :

(5) " So long as the brethren fall not under the influence of that craving..........:

(6) " So long as the brethren delight in a life of solitude :

(7) " So long as the brethren so train their minds ....:

" *So long the Bhikkhus may not be expected to decline but to prosper.* "

The history of the birth of the Buddhist *Saṃgha* is a history of the birth of the Monastic Order in the world. This history, therefore, of the birth of the religious brotherhood of the Buddha from the constitutional womb of the Indian Republic is of interest not only to this country, but to the world at large.

It was a case of borrowing, no doubt, but, at the same time, there was an original idea behind it which only a great mind could conceive. The originality consisted in transferring the constituiton of a political corporation to religion, and conjuring up an organisation to perpetuate the being of that religion.

Recorded republics

The republics which engage the attention of the Buddhist Literature were the states amongst whom the Buddha arose and lived. They covered the land to the east of the kingdoms of Kosala and Kauśāmbī and to the west of Aṅga, from the districts of Gorakhpur and Ballia to the district of Bhagalpur, to the north of Magadha and the south of the Himalayas. They were the States of :—

(*a*) the Śākyas, with their capital at Kapilavastu in the district of Gorakhpur including their close neighbours ;

(*b*) the Koliyas of Rāmagrāma ;

(*c*) the Lichchhavis, with their capital at Vaiśālī, modern Basāḍh, in the district of Muzaffarpur ;

(*d*) the Videhas, with their capital at Mithilā (in the district of Darbhanga) (the last two were conjointly called the Vṛijis or Vajjis[3]);

(*e*) the Mallas, who covered a large area to the south of the Śākyas and east of the Vṛjis, from the district of Gorakhpur to that of Champaran, divided into two units, with their capitals at Kuśinagara (Kusinārā) and at Pāvā;

(*f*) 'the Moriyas of Pippalīvana'; and

(*g*) 'the Bulis of Allakappa' who were minor communities[4] (they played no important part in the history of Buddhism; they were neighbours of the Mallas of Kuśinagara but their exact territories are not known[5]); and

(*h*) the Bhaggas (Bhargas) who were neighbours of the kingdom of the Vatsas of Kauśāmbī.[6]

Politically, the most important of the group were the Vṛijis and the Mallas. The former are noticed both by Pāṇini and Kauṭilya. The Bhargas were next-door neighbours of the Vatsas to the east, both according to the *Mahābhārata* and the Pāli records (p. 35). Their seat was evidently a hill fortress (Siṃsumāra Hill), somewhere in or about the district of Mirzapur. Pāṇini found them an independent *Janapada* or a political 'nation', important enough to be placed at the head of the eastern communities as the Yaudheyas headed the Punjab list. It seems that in the latter days of the Buddha, they passed under the sway of their neighbour, the king of the Vatsas, whose son Bodhi was ruling over them according to the *Jātaka* and the *Vinaya*.[7] They were yet a separate unit.

---

[3] Mr. H. Panday tells me that the Thārūs call the Āryan population of Champaran 'Bajis'. (See now *J.B.O.R.S.*, VI, p. 261.)

[4] For (*a*) to (*g*), see *Mahāparinibbāna Suttanta*, VI. 21–27; Rhys Davids, *Dialogues of the Buddha*, pp. ii, 179–90.

[5] *Buddhist India*, pp. 22–23; *Jātaka*, III. 157.

[6] *B.I.*, pp. 8, 9, 22.

[7] *J.*, III. 157; V. 2. 127, 4, 198–99; *B.I.*, p. 8. [According to *Rāhula Sāṅkṛityāyana*, the Siṃsumāra Hill fortress is to be identified with *Chunār* (Fort) (Mirzapur District)—*Buddhacharyyā*, p. 412.]

The Śākyas were the community wherein the Buddha was born, being the son of the President of the Śākya *gaṇa*. They were under the suzerainty of the king of Kosala, and their independence was destroyed in the life-time of the Buddha by the king of Kosala. Their council seems to have been composed of 500 members. The Śākyas are said to have had a law that each citizen could have only one wife.[8]

Their administrative-procedure

I cannot do better than quote here the description of the administrative procedure of these republics as typified by that of the Śākyan, so well summed up by Rhys Davids, the foremost authority on Buddhist literature. In view of the results of a special study of the republican organisation, I differ from that great scholar when he calls them 'clans'. The evidence does not warrant our calling them 'clans'. Indian republics of the seventh and sixth centuries B.C., as we shall see in sequence, had long passed the tribal stage of society. They were states, *Gaṇas* and *Saṃghas*, though many of them very likely had a national or tribal basis, as every state, ancient or modern, must necessarily have.

"The administration and judicial business" says Prof. Rhys Davids[9] "of the clan (correctly speaking, 'the state') was carried out in public assembly, at which young and old were alike present, in their common Mote Hall (*Santhāgāra*[10]) at Kapilavastu. It was at such a parliament, or palaver, that King Pasenadi's proposition (*B.I.*, p. 11) was discussed. When Ambaṭṭha goes to Kapilavastu on business, he goes to the Mote Hall where the Śākyas were then in session.[11] And it is

---

[8] Rockhill, *Life of the Buddha*, Ch. II, pp. 14–15.

[9] *B.I.*, p. 19.

[10] [Skt. *Saṃsthāgāra*, lit., the House of Communal Law.]

[11] *Ambaṭṭha Suttanta*, translated in *Dialogues of the Buddha*, I. 113. [I may quote the passage—" Once, Gotama, I had to go to Kapilavatthu on some business or other of Pokkharasādi's, and went into the Śākya's Congress Hall. Now at that time there were a number of Śākyas, old and young, seated in the hall on grand seats." The *Lalita-vistara*, mentioning similar sessions of the Śākyas, 'has the Śākya-*gaṇa* in session':—सर्वं शाक्यगणं सन्निपत्यैव मीमांसते राजा शुद्धोदनः ....शाक्यगणेन सार्धं संस्थागारे निषण्णोऽभूत् (XII. p. 115, *Bib. Ind.* ed.)

to the Mote Hall of the Mallas that Ānanda goes to announce the death of the Buddha, they being then in session there to consider that very matter.[12]

"A single chief—how, and for what period chosen, we do not know—was elected as office-holder, presiding over the sessions, and, if no sessions were sitting, over the State. He bore the title of *rāja*, which must have meant something like the Roman consul, or the Greek archôn. We hear nowhere of such a *triumvirate* as bore corresponding office among the Licchavis, nor of such acts of kingly sovereignty as are ascribed to the real kings mentioned above. But we hear at one time[13] that Bhaddiya, a young cousin of the Buddha's, was the *rāja*; and in another passage, Suddhodana, the Buddha's father (who is elsewhere spoken of as a simple citizen, Suddhodana Sākiyan), is called the *rāja*."

Lichchhavi constitution

The *Jātaka* calls the Lichchhavi rulers '*gaṇa*-rulers' or republican rulers.[14] The constitution of the Lichchiavis to which Professor Rhys Davids has alluded is detailed in a later document, the *Aṭṭha-kathā*.[15] It mentions three highest officers, the President (*Rajā*), the Vice-President (*Upa-Rājā*) and the Generalissimo (*Senā-pati*). An early authority (*Jātaka*, I, p. 504) adds a fourth officer: the Chancellor of the Exchequer (*Bhaṇḍāgārika*). There is no doubt that these were the four highest administrative officers and that they composed the cabinet or executive authority. The *Jātaka* says that the government was located in the city of Vaiśālî which had a system of triple fortifications. The rule (*rajjaṃ*) vested in the inhabitants (*vasantānaṃ*), 7707 in number, all of whom were entitled to rule (*rājūnaṃ*, 'kings').

The Śākya-*gaṇa* probably had 500 members (XII). The significance of "Old and Young" members probably is that the Elders and Ordinary members were both present.]

[12] *M.P.S.*, 6. 23.

[13] *Vin.*, 2. 181.

[14] *Jātaka*, IV. 148: '*Vesālinagare gaṇa-rājakulānaṃ abhiṣeka-pokkharaṇiṃ*'.

[15] Turnour, *Journal of the Asiatic Society of Bengal*, VII (1838), p. 993, *et seq*.

They became Presidents (*Rājāno*), Vice-Presidents (*Upa-rājāno*), Commanders-in-Chief (*Senā-patino*) and Chancellors of the Exchequer.[16] What the *Jātaka* means to say is that the 7707 of the inhabitants, probably the foundation families, were the ruling class, that it is they who became (*honti*, 'become') the executive office-holders. The total population was much larger, divided in outer and inner citizens ('Vaiśālians'), 1,68,000 in number,[17] The rulers (*gaṇa-rājās*) underwent the ceremony of consecretion by anointing.[14]

According to the *Aṭṭha-kathā* when the Vaiśālians came to their House of Law (parliament), the tocsin used to be sounded at their House of Law.[18] In the parliament of these rulers, they discussed not only matters political and military, but also agricultural and commercial.

A Buddhist book describes the Lechchhavi *gaṇa* in session appointing a *Mahattaka* or a distinguished member to be the envoy, charging him to deliver a message "on behalf ('by the word') of the Lechchhavis of Vaiśālī," *i.e.*, the *gaṇa* transacted business on behalf of the whole people.[19]

A parody of their constitution is thus given in another Buddhist book: "amongst them (the Vaiśālians) the rule of having respect for the high, the middle ones, the oldest, the elders is not observed; every one considers himself to be the *rājā*, 'I am the *rājā*, I am the *rājā*'. No one becomes a follower of another."[20] Evidently in their council every member had an equal right of speech and voting; and every one wanted to be the next president.

---

[16] तत्थ निच्चकालं रज्जं कारेत्वा वसंतानं येव राजूनं सत्तसहस्सानि सत्तसतानि सत्त च [.] राजानो होंति तत्तका; ये व उपराजानो तत्तका, सेनापतिनो तत्तका, तत्तका भंडागारिका. *J.*, I. 504.

[17] *Mahāvastu*, *Triśakuniya J.*, ed. Senart, I, pp. 256, 271 (*MV.* and *LV.* being works of *cir.* 100 *B.C.*, are not so old as the Pāli cannon, but their tradition is old.)

[18] Turnour, *J.A.S.B.*, VII, pp. 994–95.

[19] *MV.*, I. 254. वैशालकानां लिच्छिवीनां वचनेन.

[20] *Lalita-vistara*, Ch. III. p. 21. नोच्च-मध्य-वृद्ध-ज्येष्ठानुपालिता, एकैक एव मन्यते अहंराजा अहं राजेति। न च कस्यचिच्छिष्यत्वमुपगच्छति....

The President was also the highest judicial authority. There was a Judicial Minister who could be even an outsider, a paid officer.[21] Liberty of the citizen was most jealously guarded. A citizen could not be held guilty unless he was considered so by the *Senāpti*, the *Upa-rāja* and the *Rājā*, separately and without dissent.

Lichchhavi safeguards for liberty of the citizen

A careful record was kept of the decisions of the President on the 'rolls' ('*Paveni-patthakān*') in which the particulars of crime and punishment awarded to the citizens, found guilty, were entered. Preliminary enquiry into the case was held in the Court of the Justices (*Vinichchaya-Mahāmāttas*), who evidently were the regular court for civil causes and ordinary offences. The Court of Appeal was presided over by "*Vohārikas*"—'Lawyer-Judges'. The High Court had its Judges called the *Sūtra-dharas* or 'Doctors of Law'. There was yet a Council of Final Appeal, called the Court of the Eight: *Ashṭa-kulaka*. Any of these successive Courts could pronounce a citizen innocent and acquit him.[22] And if all the Courts held him guilty, the matter was still subject to the decision of the members of the Executive Cabinet mentioned above.

This description of criminal procedure of *Aṭṭha-kathā* is in keeping with the general procedure of republican system of justice as preserved in Sanskrit literature. In the opinion of the author of the *Mahābhārata*, criminal justice in a republic should be administered by experts through the President (निग्रहः पण्डितैः कार्यः क्षिप्रमेव प्रधानतः),[23] that the Elders of the Kula Court (= *Kulaka*) were not expected to connive at an offence. Bhṛigu, enumerating different judicial authorities, implies that in the case of a *gaṇa* the deciding body was called *Kulika* and also *Kula*.[24] Kātyāyana uses *Kula* in the sense of a jury.[25] The *Ashṭa-Kulaka* thus would signify a judicial

---

[21] Turnour, *J.A.S.B.*, VII, pp. 994-95.

[22] Turnour, *ibid.*, VII, pp. 993–94.

[23] *Śānti-P.*, Ch. 107, 27. See Ch. XVII.

[24] *Vīramitrodaya*, p. 11. See quotation in chapter on *Paura* (Ch. XXVIII).

[25] वणिग्भिः स्यात् कतिपयैः कुलभूतैरधिष्ठितम्, quoted in *V.M.*, p. 41.

council of eight members, and not, as heretofore interpreted 'Representatives of eight clans'.[26]

Federal Council

The Videhas and the Lichchhavis were, according to Buddhist documents, united in a league and they were together called the *Saṃvajjis* (*lit.*, 'the Vajjians *together*').[27] The two Vajji republics, however, were not confined to their own federation. The Lichchhavis once had formed a federation with their neighbours, the Mallas, according to a Jaina Sūtra.[28] The confederacy existed in the year when the Mahāvīra died (*c.* 545[29] or 527 B.C.). The Federal Council was composed of eighteen members, nine 'Lechchhakis' and nine 'Mallakis'.[30] The members of the Federal Council are designated '*Gaṇa Rājās*'. Probably it was to a federal council of this class that the technical term *Rājaka* of Amarasiṃha (25, 47) originally applied. These 'eighteen confederate kings' as Dr. Jacobi makes them, are placed by the Jaina Sūtra, in the Kāśi-Kosala area. At the time of the death of the Mahāvīra, the empire of Kosala was called the Kāśi-Kosala.[31] The Jaina Sūtra is much younger in date than the Pāli Canon, and if the Jaina book has not made a mistake in its location, its description would imply that the Federal Council was in some sort of political alliance with the Kosalan monarchy, if not a Kosalan suzerainty. The republics were certainly on bad terms with Magadha, and Magadha was the deadly rival of Kosala: according to the *Aṭṭha-kathā*, the Vaiśālians lost one great battle with Ajātaśatru, Emperor of Magadha. The leagues naturally were formed to oppose the great powers between whom they were situated.

The composition of the Federal Council shows that the federal states had equal votes, that the federation was based on terms of equality. The Mallas were not so great a political power as the Lichchhavis, yet in the Federal Council both had equal number of members, that is equal voice.

---

[26] *Cf.* Rhys Davids, *Buddhist India*, p. 22; Turnour, *J.A.S.B.*, VII. 993 n.

[27] *Buddhist India*, p. 22.

[28] *Kalpa-Sūtra*, 128.

[29] *J.B.O.R.S.*, I. 103.

[30] *S.B.E.*, XXII, p. 266.

[31] *Cf. Kāśi-Kosala*, Patañjali (Keilhorn), II, p. 280 (2nd ed.).

The Lichchhavis owing to their political importance and connection with the Buddha figure largely in Buddhist literature.[32] There are indications that the general description in the *Mahābhārata* and elsewhere applied to them as much as to others. Their constitution was only a type, not an exception.

---

[32] See p. 53.

CHAPTER VII

Republics in the Artha-Śāstra (325–300 B.C.)

King-Consul Republics

The *Artha-Śāstra* of Kauṭilya deals with the characteristics of *Saṃghas* and the Imperial policy towards them.[1] They were still important although a decline had set in owing to the rise of large monarchies and Alexander's invasion, the latter having discredited small sovereignties and emphasized the importance of large States (p. 61). Kauṭilya divides *Saṃghas*, as we have already seen, into two classes. One of them was the class whose Consuls bore the title of *Rājā* or 'king'. As he contrasts them with the other class, he implies that the latter had no provision for this title and did not allow it. Such constitutions are known to have existed from the evidence of coins.[2] Amongst the former class whose rulers bore the title, Kauṭilya enumerates—

(1) the Lichchhavikas,
(2) the Vṛijikas,
(3) the Mallakas,
(4) The Madrakas,
(5) the Kukaras,
(6) the Kurus,
(7) the Pāñchālas, and 'others'.

Changes from Monarchy to Republic

The *Kāsikā*, in connection with rule V. 3. 114 of Pāṇini, points out that Mallas are not subject to the rule because they are not 'military'.[3] There is therefore agreement between Kauṭilya and grammatical literature with regard to the character of the Mallas. As to the Lichchhavis, we know from Buddhist sources[4] that they called their Consul 'the *Rājā*'. Apparently, Kauṭilya, by mentioning the Lichchhavis

---

[1] Ch. XI. 376–79.

[2] See discussion in Ch. XVII, on the coins of the Rājanyas, the Yaudheyas, the Mālavas, the Ārjunāyanas, etc.

[3] आयुधजीविग्रहणं किम् । मल्लाः । p. 456.

[4] See p. 47.

separately, means by the term Vṛijis the Videhas only. Pāṇini gives a special rule for the formation of Madraka and Vṛijika[5], which forms we find in the *Artha-Śāstra*. The Kurus, according to Buddhist records,[6] had become weak as a kingdom, in the time of the Buddha. According to the *Mahābhārata*, the *Purāṇas* and the earlier authorities[7], the Kurus had been in earlier times under monarchy. Their adoption ot republican constitution must, therefore, be dated after the Buddha and before Kauṭilya. The Videhas also had been in early (Vedic) times a monarchy. In the time of the Buddha, however, the Videhas had adopted a republican constitution. The Videhas are treated as a republic by Patañjali also.[8] The Pāñchālas in Buddhist books are found divided into two kingdoms. But Kauṭilya mentions them as a republic. Patañjali also finds them a republic.[8] The change in their constitution must have come after the death of the Buddha. The *Uttara* (Northern) Madras, according to the *Aitareya Brāhmaṇa*, originally had a constitution where the whole country, as opposed to a king, was solemnized as the sovereign.[9] The other portion of the Madras, or the Madras proper in the time of Kauṭilya, if not earlier, had the 'king'-consul constitution.

The political history of the Lichchhavis is tco well known to be repeated here.[10] They were very powerful. They survived the Saiśunāka and the Maurya empires and helped in building up the Gupta empire. They founded a curious constitution in Nepal which we shall have occasion to discuss later.

The Mallas do not live so long. They disappear in the time of the Mauryas, or a little later,[11] as a republican community,

---

[5] IV. 2. 131, मद्रवृज्योः कन् ॥

[6] Rhys Davids, *Buddhist India*, p. 27.

[7] The *Aitareya Brāhmaṇa*, in giving illustrations of monarchical nations, cites the Kurus and the Pāñchālas, Ch. VIII. 14.

[8] See p. 31.

[9] Bk. VIII. जनपदा उत्तरकुरव उत्तरमद्रा इति....तेऽभिषिच्यन्ते ॥ १४ ॥ See Ch. X.

[10] As to their alleged foreign origin, the theories are hopelessly untenable : see discussion in Ch. XXI.

[11] They do not figure in Kātyāyana or Patañjali.

though individual Malla families rise up now and then, in Tirhut and Nepal, up to the eleventh century and even later.[12] The modern representatives of the Mallas are the Malla caste in the districts of Gorakhpur and Azamgarh,[13] generally given to trade. It is a common phenomenon in the career of Indian republics that when the republicans lost their political power they still retained their commercial intelligence and turned into traders.[14] The Pāñchālas survived the Mauryas, for they are mentioned by Pātañjali. But the Kurus as a state succumbed. The Kukuras, according to the *Mahābhārata*, were a member of the Andhaka-Vṛishṇi league. Some of the members of the league apparently observed the 'king'-consul constitution, while others did not. The Kukuras are mentioned in inscriptions of Western India towards the close of the first century B.C.[15]

Nation-in-arms Republics

The other class of Kauṭilya's[16] republics is illustrated by—

(1) the Kāmbhojas,
(2) the Surāshṭras,
(3) the Kshatriyas,
(4) the Śreṇis, and 'others'.

This class, by implication, had no king-consul. The other chief feature of their constitution was that they emphasized on their citizens the duty to acquire military skill. In other words, they had a citizen army. Each state was a nation-in-arms. Conversely, the other class, where the 'king'-consul constitution obtained, probably had, like monarchs, a regular or hired (standing) army. The nation-in-arms class, however, did not become purely military, for their

---

[12] See Lévi, *Le Nepal*, II, pp. 210–13.

[13] *Cf.* H. Panday, *J.B.O.R.S.*, 1920, pp. 262–65, on modern Mallas.

[14] Other examples are the Khatris of Sind and the Punjab (the Xathroi of the Greeks), and the Aroḍas of the Punjab who very likely represent the ancient Āraṭṭas.

[15] *Ep. Ind.*, VIII, pp. 44, 60 ; see p. 55.

[16] काम्भोज-सुराष्ट्र-क्षत्रिय श्रेण्यादयो वार्त्ताशस्त्रोपजीविनः (*A.S.*, XI. 1. 160, p. 376). One of this group of republics seems to bear the name *Vaṭa* (= *varta*) Aśvakas, the Aśvakas following *vārttā*. See *J.B.O.R.S.*, XX. 289 on their coins.

constitution also required their citizens to devote attention to industry and agriculture (*vārttāśastropajīvinaḥ*).[16] Hence they were found rich as well as strong.

The Kshudrakas and the Mālavas, who were the most prominent amongst these martial republics, are not mentioned by Kauṭilya. Probably they had already come under the imperial sway. The martial republics named in the *Artha-Śāstra* are headed by the Kāmbhojas. They were in eastern Afghanistan. They are mentioned in Aśoka's inscriptions as a community next to the Gandhāras.[17] According to Yāska, their mother-tongue was Sanskrit with certain bases which seem to have been imported from the Iranian neighbours.[18] They are known to Pāṇini, for he gives a rule[19] for the derivative to denote their king. This would indicate that Pāṇini is referring to a monarchy. But the special rule and the exceptional form of the derivative raise a doubt as to whether the '*rājā*' of the Kāmbhojas was a monarch or a consul. In the time of Kauṭilya, their constitution certainly did not admit of even a titular 'king'. The Bhojas, as we shall see hereafter, were a class of non-monarchical rulers. 'Kambhojas' would literally mean 'Inferior Bhojas'.[20]

The Surāshṭras (Su-rāshṭra, *lit.* 'good realm') were in Kathiawar. Their name still lives in modern Soraṭha. They seem to have survived the Mauryan imperialism, as they figure in the inscriptions of Bala-Śrī (about 58 B.C.[21]) and

---

[17] See Ch. XVII.

[18] II. i. 3, 4, शवतिर्गतिकर्मा कम्बोजेष्वेव भाष्यते, काम्बोजाः कम्बलभोजाः कमनीयभोजा वा कम्बलः कमनीयो भवति विकारमस्यार्येषु भाषन्ते शव इति. *Cf.* The Persian root *shūdan*, 'to go'. See *J.R.A.S.*, 1911, 801.

[19] IV. 1. 175.

[20] Pāṇini spells it as Kamboja, so does Yāska. But Yāska derives it from *bhuj*. The *Rāmāyaṇa* (I. 55. 2) and the *Artha-Śāstra* have Kāmboja and Kāmbhoja, respectively. The former indicates Iranian or Paiśāchī influence.

[21] *Ep. Ind.*, VIII, p. 60. The date is based on my own theory of chronology and identification of Vikrama with Gotamīputra Śātakarṇi Sātavāhana (*J.B.O.R.S.*, I. 101 ; *Brahmin Empire* (' Express,' Patna, 1914) ; *Modern Review*, 1914. The date assigned by other scholars to this inscription is over a century later.

in the Junagadh inscription of Rudradāman (second century A.C.[22]).

The other two states—the Kshatriyas[23] and the Śreṇīs—appear as neighbours in Sind in the records of the Macedonian writers.[23] The Kshatriyas are called by them Xathroi. European scholars have taken it as a caste denomination; that it is a proper name of a political body is now disclosed by the *Artha-Śāstra*. Ptolemy also mentions the nation or community Xathroi. Various terms have been used by classical writers to denote what seems to be *Agra-Śreṇis* or the First-*Śreṇis*.[24] Apparently, the *Śreṇis* were subdivided into internal units, and the one which came in contact with Alexander was that of the "First-*Śreṇīs*".[25] Such divisions seem to have existed among the Yaudheyas, whose coins, marked "2" and "3", have been found.[26]

The Xathroi or the Kshatriyas seem to survive in the numerous caste called the *Sindhī Khatrīs* (the Khattris of Sindh), a handsome race occupying the neighbourhood of the site indicated in the Greek writers as the territory of the Xathroi. The *Khattrīs* of the Punjab may also represent them.

I may here point out that the translator of the *Artha-Śāstra* has fallen into an error in translating the passage '*Kāmbhoja-Surāshṭra-Kshatriya-Śreṇy-ādayaḥ*' as "the corporations of warriors (Kshatriya *Śreṇi*) of Kāmbhoja and Surāshṭra and other countries".[27] The rendering is against grammar; '*ādayaḥ*,' 'and others', excludes the possibility of a description coming in the group just preceding. If Kāmbhoja is a proper name, the rest, up to '*adāyaḥ*,' must be proper names. The description really comes after the enumeration closed with '*ādayah*,' in *vārttā-śastropajīvinaḥ*. Both in

---

[22] *Ep. Ind.*, VIII, p. 44.

[23] Arrian, Bk. VI, Ch. XV.

[24] See McCrindle, *Ancient India, Its Invasion by Alexander the Great*, p. 367. The forms are: Agalassi, Agesinæ, Acensoni, Argesinæ, etc.

[25] It is, however, not impossible that *Agra-Śreṇi* of Alexander has been abbreviated as *Śreṇī* by Kauṭilya.

[26] Cunningham, *Coins of Ancient India*, p. 78.

[27] Shama Sastry, Kauṭilya's *Artha-Śāsrta*, p. 455.

view of our identification and grammatical considerations, the translation is unacceptable. There is yet another error to be avoided, *viz.*, taking '*Śreṇī*' here to mean a guild. If ***vārttā*** (industry and agriculture) refers to alleged guilds (***Śreṇīs***) it ought to have been placed after, not before, ***śastra***, as *Śreṇī* is the last, coming after *Kshatriya*, in the group.[28]

---

[28] *Cf.* the expression *śastra-vārttāḥ* used by Varāha Mihira (मल्लान् मत्स्यकुरूञ्छकानपि काम्बोजोड्-किरात-शस्त्रवार्त्ताः, *Bṛi. S.*, V. 39) where the two characteristics have to be taken as applying to the same communities. See pp. 33 and 34.

CHAPTER VIII

Hindu Republics in Greek Writers (C. 325 B.C.)

The historians of Alexander's campaign have described a number of states as 'free', 'autonomous', or 'independent', by which they mean republican. McCrindle recognises the significance of the expression 'independent' but as he was ignorant of the fact of Indian republics, he thought that it referred to 'the Indian village system': "*Each of its rural units they (Greeks) took to be an independent republic.*"[1] But the Greeks never mistook a village *panchayat* for a republic; they treat the communities they met as states and not as village-units. They fought them, they negotiated treaties with them, they recorded details of their constitutions: the Greeks knew them too well to make a mistake of the sort suggested by McCrindle. The Greeks may be trusted for their description in matters constitutional. There cannot be any room for doubt or controversy if we see what Megasthenes, the Greek envoy at the Court of Chandragupta Maurya, has to say. He was not a passing raider like Alexander's companions but an observer for several years. He divides the country into two forms of government—monarchical and republican:—

> "*They···report every thing to the king where the people have a king, and to the magistrates where the people are self-governed.*"[2]

The republican states noted by the Greek historians may be briefly surveyed here.

Kathaians

The Greek writers describe the Kathaians as one of the most powerful 'nations' of India. They were to the east of the Hydraotes or Ravi, in the area now covered by the districts of Lahore and Amritsar.

---

[1] *Invasion of India by Alexander*, p. 115, *n.*

[2] McCrindle, *Megasthenes*, Arr. XII. *Cf.* also: "The councillors of state....who advise the king, or the magistrates of self-governed cities, in the management of public affairs....", *ibid.*, p. 212.

Their capital was Saṅkala. "*The Kathaians themselves enjoyed the highest reputation for courage and skill in the art of war.*"[3] They along with some other republican Indians had shortly before their battle with Alexander defeated both King Poros and the King of the Abhisāras. The Kathaians are described to have formed what in Hindu tactics is called a *śakaṭa-vyūha* or 'waggon formation' against Alexander, which presented a great difficulty to his soldiers. They fought very bravely and did not submit, although they were tremendously outnumbered.[4] Their men and women married by choice, and their women observed the practice of *Satī*. According to Strabo, amongst them "*the handsomest man is chosen as king*".[5]

The 'Kathaians' have been restored by some scholars into the Sanskrit 'Kshatriyas'.[6] This restoration is untenable. First of all the forms of words which the Greek writers give are based on Sanskrit pronunciation, and Katha would be a Prakritic form, and, therefore, an exception. When the whole country (Punjab) used Sanskrit forms, it is unreasonable to take Kathai as based on a Prākrita form. Then it is questionable whether even from the Prākrita of Kshatriya we would get Kathai : we would get some word like *Khattiya*, not Kathai. Again, we must not forget that for *Kshatriya* the very writers give *Xathroi*. Kathaia stands for the country of the Kaṭhas and the Kathaioi for the Kaṭha people, as already suggested by Dr. Jolly.[7]

Un-named Republics

Before reaching the Kathaians, Alexander had already encountered several independent Indian nations or republics, on the banks of the Ravi (Arrian, V. 21).[8]

---

[3] See Arrian, *Anabasis*, V. 22. II A. p. 115.

[4] Arrian has a tendency to exaggerate the number of the Indians and their casualties, to glorify Alexander. His figures should be always compared with those given by Curtius and Diodorus.

[5] Strabo, XV. 30. See McCrindle, *Ancient India as described by Classical Writers*, p. 38.

[6] McCrindle, *Invasion of India by Alexander the Great*, p. 347.

[7] *S.B.E.*, VII, p. 15 (Intro.). See p. 60 and Chs. IX and XX on Kaṭhas.

[8] McCrindle, *Invasion of India by Alexander the Great*, p. 116, *n*.

Adrestai

A little away from the Ravi with their capital at what the Greeks called Pimprama were the community spelt as *Adraistai*, *Adrestai*, and *Adrestae*. European scholars have proposed to identify them with the famous *Āraṭṭas*. But philologically the equation is impossible. They may be identified with the *Arishṭas* of Pāṇini (VI. 2. 100) and the *Gaṇa-pāṭha* (on P. IV. 2, 80).[9]

Saubhūti

Adjoining the territory of the Kathaians there was the state of the Sophytes which M. Sylvain Lévi has correctly identified with Saubhūti.[10] But it is not clear whether its ruler was an elected 'king' or a regular monarch.[11] It seems more probable that it was republican.[12] It is found in a republican area with republican associations and characteristics. The *Gaṇa-pāṭha* mentions Subhūta in the company of the people of Saṅkala.[13] Saṅkala, as we have seen above, was the capital of the republic of the Kaṭhas. The Saubhūti State extended up to the Salt-Range. Diodorus (XVII, 91) says that the cities subject to the sway of the Sopeithes "*were governed by laws in the highest degree salutary*" and "*their political system was one to admire*". "*Beauty was held among them in the highest estimation.*" Further, "*it follows that the inhabitants of these cities are generally held in higher estimation than the rest of their countrymen.*" As amongst the Kathaians so amongst the Saubhūtis men and women selected their own consort without reference to dowry. They attached great importance to good looks. This practice was not peculiar to the constituion of the Kaṭhas and the Saubhūtis only. We find the republican Vṛishṇis also giving great importance to handsome presence in a republican leader.[14]

---

[9] अरिष्टगौडपूर्वे च ॥ ६ ॥ २ ॥ १०० ॥ which alludes to the Capital of the Arishṭas.

[10] *Journal Asiatique*, VIII. 15, p. 237 ff.

[11] *Cf.* pp. 71 and 72.

[12] The coin of the State struck after Alexander's invasion with a Greek head, probably meant to be that of Alexander or his representative, is struck in the national name *Sophytes*. McCrindle, *Alexander*, II A, 280 ; Rapson, *I.C.*, 3, pl. I. 8.

[13] *Gaṇa-pāṭha* on Pāṇini, IV. 2. 75.

[14] See Appendix A.

Amongst the Saubhūtis and the Kaṭhas there was yet another reason for the observance of this rule. "*In contracting marriage they do not seek an alliance with high birth, but make their choice by the looks, for beauty in the children is a quality highly appreciated,*" because in the Saubhūti and Kaṭha States, public authority claimed the right to determine which of the babies born in the State were physically fit to be allowed to grow into citizens.[15] We need hardly recall here that this was also enjoined by the Spartan constitution. This examination amongst the Kaṭhas was made in the second month of the child (Strabo).

Two city-states are further mentioned as republics by Arrian (V. 24) but their names are not given.

A great Republic on the Beas

When Alexander reached the Hyphasis or Beas, he heard that beyond that river the country was "*exceedingly fertile and the inhabitants were good agriculturists, brave in war and living under an excellent system of internal government; for the multitude was governed by the aristocracy, who exercised their authority with justice and moderation.*" (Arrian, Bk. V. 25.)[16] The description tallies with Kauṭilya's *Vārttā-śastropajīvinaḥ*. They were prosperous by agriculture and kept themselves ready for war, fully depending on their own sword. It is unfortunate that the state has been left unnamed. Actual government vested in what the Greeks called an aristocracy. But their parliament consisted of five thousand representatives.[17] The find-spot of Yaudheya coins

---

[15] "Here they do not acknowledge and rear children according to the will of parents but as the officers entrusted with the medical inspection of infants may direct, for if they have remarked anything deformed or defective in the limbs of the child they order it to be killed."—McCrindle, *Invasion of India by Alexandar the Great*, p. 219. *Cf.* Dio. (p. 280). See Strabo, XV. 30, for the law of the Kathaians, according to which the final order was pronounced by a magistrate.

[16] McCrindle, *I. I. by Alexander*, p. 121.

[17] "All the country beyond Hupanis is allowed to be very fertile ....They mention also an aristocratical form of government consisting of five thousand Councillors each of whom furnishes the State with an elephant." Strabo, XV. 37 (McCrindle, *Ancient India as described in Classical Literature*, p. 45).

suggests that this unnamed state on the Beas was probably of the Yaudheyas.[18] Each member of parliament supplied one elephant to the state army. These Indians according to Arrian (V. 25), had elephants in greater number and of superior size and courage. As Alexander himself put it, the Macedonians had been "wont to fight only against small numbers,"[19] "now for the first time" they had to face really large armies. And they refused to move an inch forward amongst the nations whose very name, according to Alexander, filled his soldiers with terror.[20] There was this unnamed Republic which covered the land on the other side of the Beas. There was also the great army of the Nanda waiting to give reception to the Macedonian, but the immediate cause of alarm was the prospect of meeting the republic beyond the river. Alexander's army "now began to lose heart" and "they began to hold conferences" where people "positively asserted that they would follow no further".[21] It was from the doors of the unnamed republic that the campaign of Alexander assumed the form of retreat.

The large number of the members of their council is comparable with the number of the Lichchhavi-*gaṇa* (p. 47).

Kshudrakas and Mālavas, and Śibis

During this retreat Alexander came across a number of republics. In fact, all the States he met on his way back, down the Indus and up to the Indian frontier in Baluchistan, were republican. The most powerful amongst them were the Kshudrakas and the Mālavas. They are spelt by the Greeks as Oxydrakai and Malloi respectively. They were on the Hydaspes, by which the Greeks apparently mean the passage of the Jhelum after its union with the Chenab. The two states formed one league.[22] Arrian (VI. 4) says that they were the most numerous and war-like of the Indian

---

[18] Their dominions extended upto Saharanpur (Behat) where their coins were current; that is, they extended eastwards upto the frontiers of the Magadha empire. On their coins see *J.B.O.R.S.*, XXII, 59.

[19] *I.I.A.*, p. 224.

[20] McCrindle, *ibid.*, p. 226.

[21] Arrian, V. 25. See McCrindle, *I. I. by Alexander*, p. 121.

[22] *Cf.* the *Kshatriya-dvandva of the Kāsikā* on *P.*, IV. 2, 45.

'nations' in those parts. "Alexander first reached the nation called the Malloi." Near the Malloi there were their republican friends called the Siboi,[23] whom the *Jātakas* and Patañjali know as the Sivis and the Śaibyas.[24] The Malloi are called a race of independent Indians (Arrian, VI. 6); their cities were along the Chenab and their capital was near the Ravi. It was in the siege of the capital or one of the cities of the Malloi that Alexander nearly lost his life. Owing to the unity of the league, the Greek writers could not decide whether Alexander's narrow escape relates to the city of the Malloi or to that of the Oxydrakai. The strength of the army as given by Curtius, was 1,00,000. "*The Macedonians lost their heart at the prospect of meeting this army.*" "*When the Macedonians found that they had still on hand a fresh war in which the most war-like nations in all India would be their antagonists, they were struck with an unexpected terror, and began again to upbraid the king in the language of sedition.*"[25] These Indians were regarded by the soldiers as "fierce nations" who would not let them proceed without drawing their blood. The fear of the Macedonians was well justified and is attested by the account of the personal calamity of Alexander and the lamentations which followed (II A, pp. 241–42).

The Greek writers with their palpable desire to magnify the glory of Alexander[26] would make us believe that the

---

[23] Curtius, IX. 4. There was no king amongst them, only the citizens filled the highest offices (Diodorus, XVII. 96).

[24] *J.*, VI. 480; Kielhorn, II. 282. The *Jātakas* find them connected with Sovīra (IV. 401), *i.e.*, they then occupied the same locality where the Greeks encountered them. In the age of the *Jātakas* they had been monarchical. For their republican coin, and subsequent migration, see Ch. XVIII. Patañjali treats *Śibi* as the name of a country or state (*vishaya*).

[25] Curtius, Bk. IX, Ch. IV; McCrindle, *I. I. by Alexander*, p. 234.

[26] "*Many fictions also have been recorded by historians concerning this accident, and Fame, receiving them from the original inventors, has preserved them to our own day, nor will she cease to transmit the falsehoods to one generation after another.*" Arrian, Bk. VI, Ch. 11.

"*Fame is never brought to a clearness in which facts can be seen as they are. They are all magnified when she transmits them. Even our* (Alexander's) *own glory though resting on a solid basis, is more indebted for its greatness to rumour than to reality.*" McCrindle, *I. I. by Alexander*, p. 223.

Kshudrakas and the Mālavas were crushed and annihilated by Alexander. But Patañjali discloses a different story. The former mentions the league as living, and one of them, the Kshudrakas, being victorious.[27] The Macedonian writers themselves describe and admit their existing importance after the war. The two 'nations' sent "*hundred ambassadors*" who "*all rode in chariots and were men of uncommon stature and of a very dignified bearing. Their robes were of linen embroidered with in-wrought gold and purple.*" "*The gods, they said, were the authors of their submission and not fear.*" They were proud of their "liberty which for so many ages they had preserved inviolate". Alexander, who was very vindictive against all those who had opposed him, in spite of the personal suffering to which he had been subjected by these opponents, treated the ambassadors with uncommon hospitality. "He gave orders for the preparation of a splendid banquet to which he invited the ambassadors." . . . "Here a hundred couches of gold had been placed at a small distance of each other, and these were hung round with tapestry curtains which glittered with gold and purple" (Curtius, Bk. IX, Ch. 7).[28] Alexander entertained them with shows at which wine flowed. And the "ambassadors were dismissed to their several homes" (Ch. 8).[28] All this does not read like the description of a crushed enemy, but rather of one whose subordinate alliance was welcomed by Alexander after he had tested their valour. Alexander had not only to secure his rear in his retreat but had also to pacify and render confident the '*seditious*' Macedonians.

That they existed before the time of Kātyāyana as a league is proved by his *vārttika* and the comments of Patañjali on Pāṇini *Khaṇḍikādibhyaścha* (IV. 2. 45). The league did not exist in the time of Pāṇini as he does not provide a form for their united army. Kātyāyana supplied this, and removed what he found in his time a deficiency.[29]

---

[27] एकाकिभिः क्षुद्रकैर्जितम्, Patañjali on *P.*, V. 3, 52 ; Kielhorn, II, p. 412.

[28] McCrindle, *I.I. by Alexander*, pp. 248–51.

[29] Weber (*H.I.L.*, p. 222, *n.*) misunderstood the whole discussion and puts the cart before the horse when he says that Āpiśali regarded their armies as united and that therefore his successor Pāṇini lived after the union, *i.e.*, after Alexander. But both Kātyāyana and

Curtius says that to lead the united army a brave warrior of the Kshudrakas was selected, and that he was an experienced general (Bk. IX, Ch. 4).

It is important to notice the composition of the so-called ambassadors who had come to conclude peace with Alexander

---

Patañjali are supplying the very want which arises on account of Pāṇini's rule—a rule composed at a time when there was no such union. Āpiśali gives no rule for the special case and the grammarian who composed the verses quoted by Patañjali is applying a rule of Āpiśali which had no reference to the Kshudraka-Mālavas. The rule of Āpiśali (along with his examples धैनुकम् *versus* स्प्राधेनवत्) is cited on the *tadanta* formula, which did not provide for the exclusive formation क्षौद्रक-मालव [क्षौद्रकमालवीसेना]. The author of the verse, by his process, was showing the want for the *vārttika* of Kātyāyana which he finally summarizes in the last line of the second verse. This is made perfectly clear by the comments of Patañjali and his own summary in introducing the *vārttika.* If this exceptional rule had been anticipated before Kātyāyana's time either by Āpiśali or any one else, Kātyāyana would not have claimed the correction, as he does by his *vārttika.* The whole passage in quoted here for the convenience of those who may care to follow the discussion in the original.* The net result is that the league of the Kshudraka-Mālavas did not exist in the time of Pāṇini, though they themselves evidently existed, and that the league was a living institution in the time of Kātyāyana and that of Patañjali. The organization thus evidently outlived the Mauryan empire.

* खण्डिकादिभ्यश्च ॥ ४ ॥ १ ॥ ४५ ॥

"अञ्सिद्धिरनुदात्तादेःकोऽर्थः क्षुद्रकमालवात् ।"

अनुदात्तादेरित्येवाञ्सिद्धः किमर्थं क्षुद्रकमालवशब्दः खण्डिकादिषु पठ्यते गोत्राश्रयो वुञ्प्राप्तस्तद्बाधनार्थम् ।—[अनुदात्तादेरञ् । *P.*, IV. 2. 44.]

"गोत्राद्वुञ्न च तद्गोत्रं ।"—[*P.*, IV. 2. 39.]

गोत्राद्वुञ्भवतीत्युच्यते न च क्षुद्रकमालवशब्दो गोत्रम् । न च गोत्रसमुदायो गोत्रग्रहणेन गृह्यते । तद्यथा । जनपदसमुदायो जनपदग्रहणेन न गृह्यते । काशि-कोसलीया इति वुञ्न भवति ॥ तदन्तविधिना प्राप्नोति ।

"तदन्ताच्च स सर्वतः ॥ १ ॥"—[*P.*, I. 1. 72.]

परिगणितेषु कार्येषु तदन्तविधिर्न चेदं तत्र परिगण्यते ॥

"ज्ञापकं स्यात्तदन्तत्वे"

एवं तर्हि ज्ञापयत्याचार्यो भवतीह तदन्तविधिरिति ॥

"तथा चापिशलेर्विधिः ।"

from the two republics. These were the leading men represent ing their cities and provinces. "*From the Oxydrakai came the leading men of their cities and their provincial governors.*"[30] They were " entrusted with full powers to conclude a treaty ". The representatives of the Malloi are reported to have said that "*they were attached more than others to freedom and autonomy, and their freedom had been preserved intact from the time of Dionysius*"[31] (by whom the Greeks probably meant Balarāma).

It may be noted that the good features and fine, tall physique of these free Indians are particularly noticed by the Macedonian writers. The point is important on the question of the ethnology of Indian republics which we shall consider later (Ch. XXI).

The Mālavas were apparently on the lower course of the Jhelum after its union with the Chenab, while the Kshudrakas occupied the higher regions.[32]

एवं च कृत्वापिशलेराचार्यस्य विधिरुपपन्नो भवति ।
धेनुरनञि कमुत्पादयति । धेनूनां समूहो धैनुकम् ।
अनञीति किमर्थम् । अधेनूनां समूह आधेनवम् ।

" सेनायां नियमार्थं वा "

अथवा नियमार्थोऽयमारम्भः । क्षुद्रकमालवशब्दात्सेनायामेव । क्व मा भूत् क्षौद्रकमालवकमन्यदिति ॥

" यथाबाध्येत वाञ्वुञा ॥ २ ॥"

अथवा ज्ञापयत्याचार्यः पूर्वोऽपि वुञ्परमञं बाधत इति । ननु चोक्तं गोत्राद्वुञ्न च तद्गोत्रमिति । तदन्तविधिना प्राप्नोति । ननु चोक्तं तदन्ताश्च स सर्वत इति । ज्ञापकं स्यात्तदन्तत्वे । एवं तर्हि ज्ञापयत्याचार्यो भवतीह तदन्तविधिरिति । कथं पुनरेतदुभयं शक्यं ज्ञापयितुं भवति च तदन्तविधिः पूर्वश्च वुञ्परमञं बाधत इति । उभयं ज्ञाप्यते ॥

अञ्प्रकरणे क्षुद्रकमालवात्सेनासंज्ञायाम् ॥ १ ॥

अञ्प्रकरणे क्षुद्रकमालवात्सेनासंज्ञायामितिवक्तव्यम् । क्षौद्रकमालवी सेना चेत् । क्व मा भूत् । क्षौद्रकमालवकमन्यदिति ॥

—Kielhorn, Vol. II, pp. 280–81.

[30] Arrian, Bk. VI., Ch. 14 ; McCrindle, *Alexander*, p. 154.

[31] *Ibid.*

[32] See the view of V. Smith on the location, *J.R.A.S.*, 1903, p. 685.

Alexander met in the neighbourhood of the last two republics the Agsinae,[33] who had mustered an army, if we believe Diodorus, of 40,000 foot and 3,000 horse. "They barricaded their narrow streets, fought with great vigour, so that Alexander in pressing the attack lost a few Macedonians."[34]

The *Agra-Śreṇis*

According to Curtius when those brave fellows could not further resist the odds, they made, what we know now as Rājput,*Jauhar* of their wives and children into the flames by setting fire to their houses.[35]

European scholars have proposed their identification with the Ārjunāyanas.[36] But this is unacceptable on philological grounds. The name is a composite of two words, *Agra* and *Śreṇi*. And the main word is found in Kauṭilya in the list of republics which did not call their president *Rājan* and which were martial.[37] There the form *Śreṇi* only appears; the member *Agra* shows that there were probably more than one unit in the *Śreṇi* (p. 56).

The next republic mentioned by the Greeks was that of the Ambashṭhas, spelt as *Sambastai* and *Abastanoi*.[38] "*They were a people inferior to none in India, either for numbers or for bravery.*" Their form of government was "*democratic*".[39] Their army consisted of 60,000 foot, 6,000 cavalry and 500 chariots. "They had elected three generals renowned for their valour and military skill."[39]

Ambashṭhas

Alexander made peace with them having received fifty of the foremost citizens who had come as ambassadors "under the belief that they would be treated with all proper courtesy". It is stated by Diodorus that the embassy was sent on the

---

[33] On the identification of this name see p. 56 above.

[34] Diodorus, Bk. XVII, Ch. 96; McCrindle, *Alexander*, p. 285.

[35] Curtius, Bk. IX, Ch. 4; McCrindle, *Alexander*, p. 232.

[36] *Ibid.*, p. 367. At that time the Ārjunāyana State does not appear to have existed. It is unknown up to Patañjali, and to the *Mahābhārata* which notices all other republican peoples of the locality we have been dealing with (see *Sabhā-Parvan*, LII. 14–15).

[37] See discussion above (p. 53).

[38] Diod., XVII. 102; McCrindle, *Alexander*, p. 292.

[39] Curtius, Bk. IX, Ch. 8; McCrindle, *Alexander*, p. 252.

Ambashṭhas' having "adopted the advice of their elders 'not to fight'". This probably indicates that their democratic constitution allowed an Upper House of Elders.

The Ambashṭhas as a political community are mentioned by Patañjali and the *Mahābhārata*.[40] The Purāṇas say that Ambashṭha of the House of Aila founded a dynasty in the Punjab.[41] The Purāṇas in giving the early account know them as a monarchical people. The change in their constitution thus was from monarchy to republic like the change in that of the Śibis (p. 62). The Purāṇas say the same about the Yaudheyas, that they too, along with the Ambashṭhas, were monarchical. But the later monumental history of the Yaudheyas is the history of a republican people. The Purāṇic data therefore must refer to the origins.[42]

The next "independent nation" was the Xathroi. This, restored into Sanskrit, will be *Kshattriya*. As I have said above, they are identical with the republic which bore the proper name '*Kshattriya*' as in the *Artha-Śāstra*. Kauṭilya places them together with the *Śreṇis* and here also we find the *Śreṇis* as neighbours to the Kshattriyas. As already suggested, the *Sindhī Khattri* caste seems to be their modern representative. According to the division of Kautilya they did not have a king-consul.[43]

Kshattriyas

The Ossadioi were also an 'independent nation' according to Arrian.[44] No other writer mentions them. Their proposed identification with the Yaudheyas (by Cunningham)[45] is untenable on philological

Ossadioi

---

[40] On Pāṇini, IV. 1. 170; *cf. Kāsikā*, pp. 292–93. Patañjali treats *Ambashṭha* as the name of a country or state, and its inhabitants he calls *Ambashṭhyas*.

Sabhā-Parvan, Ch. XXXII, verses 7–9, where they are placed along with the Mālavas. See also Pāṇini, VIII. 3. 97.

[41] Pargiter, *J.R.A.S.*, 1914, p. 277.

[42] The people who were to the south of the Ambashṭhas are called *Sodrai* by the Greek writers (McCrindle, *Alexander*, p. 293). These Sindhī people are identified by Lassen (*Ind. Alt.*, II. 144, 177) with Śūdras. But the form brings it nearer the *Śaudras* (Saudrāyaṇas) of the *Gp.* on *P.*, IV. 2. 4.

[43] *A.Ś.*, XI, p. 376.

[44] Arrian, Bk. VI, Ch. 15; McCrindle, *Alexander*, p. 156; Strabo, Bk. XV, Ch. 34.

[45] Cunningham, *A.S.R.*, Vol. XIV, p. 140.

grounds. They seem to be, as suggested by V. de Saint-Martin (McCrindle, *Alexander*, p. 156, *n.*), identical with the Vasātis of the *Mahābhārata* (*Sabhā*, LII. 15) who appear there as neighbours of the Kshudrakas and the Mālavas and in a group commencing with the Ambashṭhas. Kātyāyana and Patañjali mention the 'country of the Vasātis' along with that of the Sibis (on *P.*, IV. 2. 52). The *Gaṇapāṭha* (on *P.*, IV. 2. 53) places them in the group commencing with the republican *Rājanyas* (Ch. XVIII).

Musicani

It is not certain whether the next state had a regal or popular constitution. Alexander's companions admired their constitution and laws. "They regard the excessive pursuit of any art, as war for instance and the like, as wickedness" (Strabo, XV. 34). The realm was reported to be the most opulent in India.[46] The citizens took their meals in common, a practice also mentioned in the *Atharva Veda*.[47] They did not recognise the institution of slavery (Strabo, XV. 34). It is possible to recover the name of this free people from our literature. The identification, proposed by Lassen,[48] with the Mushikas cannot stand. The Mushikas were below the Sahya or the Vindhyas.[49] *Mousikanos* seems to stand for what we have in the *Kāśikā* (p. 313, on *P.*, IV. 2. 80), as *Muchukarṇa* to denote the proper name of a country

---

[46] McCrindle, *Ancient India as described in Classical Literature*, p. 41.

[47] ज्यायस्वन्तश्चित्तिनो मा वि यौष्ट संराधयन्तः सधुराश्चरन्तः। अन्यो अन्यस्मै वल्गु वदन्तः एत सध्रीचीनान्वः संमनसस्कृणोमि ॥ ५ ॥ समानी प्रपा सहवोऽन्नभागः समाने योक्त्रे सहवो युनज्मि । ······ ॥ ३ । ३० । ५—६ ॥

"Following your leader, of (the same) mind, do ye not hold yourselves apart! Do ye come here, co-operating, going along the same wagon-pole, speaking agreeably to one another! I render you of the same aim, of the same mind.

"Identical shall be your drink, in common shall be your share of food! I yoke you together in the same traces...."

—Bloomfield, *S.B.E.*, Vol. XLII, p. 134.

[48] McCrindle, *IIA.*, p. 157 n.

[49] Jayaswal, *Hāthigumphā Inscription of the Emperor Khāravela*, *J.B.O.R.S.*, Vol. IV, p. 376; *E.I.*, XX. 71.

(*Mauchukarṇika*). The spelling of the word is corrupt in the printed *Gaṇapāṭha*, but the *Kāśikā* reading is supported by Vardhamāna in his *Gaṇa-Ratna-Mahodadhi*[50] (IV. 285) who gives it on the authority of Śakaṭāṅgaja. Another reading seems to have been *Muchikarṇa*[51] (corrupt *Śuchikarṇa*, *G.R.M.*, p. 174).

[The neighbouring states of Sambos and the Presti (probably the Prasthalas of the *Mahābhārata*[52]) are also described as kingdoms.]

Brachmanoi

The city of 'the nation called Brachmanoi' (Arrian, VI. 16; Diodorus, XVII, CII), also mentioned as the 'country of the Brachmans' (Dio., XVII, CIII) was next reduced by Alexander. This seems to have been identical with what Patañjali calls *Brāhmaṇako nāma Janapadaḥ* (II, p. 298) '*the country* (state) *called Brāhmaṇaka*'. *Janapada* here is in the same sense as in Pāṇini and on the coins, *i.e.*, a politically self-contained country or a state. The Greek idea of the identity of tribe and state is so strong that on account of the existence of a state the citizens are turned into a tribe as in the cases of all other independent cities and states in the Punjab and Sind, while Indian authorities, contemporary with the states in question, treat their names as derived from 'countries', *e.g.*, Pāṇini (IV. I. 168–77). In other words, the Indian view is territorial, not tribal.

This little republic showed great spirit and patriotism, and was especially marked down for revenge by Alexander. 'These philosophers,' says Plutarch in the biography of Alexander (LIX) referring to the city of the Brahmins (McCrindle, *IIA.*, p. 306) 'gave him no less trouble than the mercenaries, because they reviled the princes who declared for him and encouraged the free states to revolt from his authority. On this account he hanged many of them.'

Patala

To the south of the above there was the state of Patala in the delta of the Indus. Before Alexander arrived, the whole community had migrated to avoid submission. This preference for migration to submission

[50] Ed. by Bhīmasena, 1898 (Allahabad), p. 174.

[51] The Greeks were evidently rendering *Mauchikarṇi*. The change of *ch* into *s* is regular in their renderings.

[52] *Sabhā-Parvan*, Ch. XIV.

was a settled practice amongst smaller Indian republics. The Vṛishṇis, according to the *Jātakas* and the *Mahābhārata*, left Mathurā and went to Dvārakā when pressed by Jarāsandha. The movements of the Śibis from the Punjab to Rajputana and of the Mālavas from the Punjab to Mālwa were probably results of similar circumstances. In the constitution of Patala their ruler was called *Moeres*.[53] It is evidently identical with the derivative of *Mura* of the *Gaṇapāṭha* (*P.*, IV. 1. 151), which Vardhamāna in his *Gaṇa-Ratna-Mahodadhi* (III. 209,) takes as a ruler-designation. Curtius treats him as a monarch, a confusion which seems to have been occasionally made by these writers. Diodorus, on the other hand, gives the constitution of the state in these words : " *A city of great note with a political constitution drawn on the same line as the Spartan ; for in this community the command in war vested in two hereditary kings of two different houses while a Council of Elders ruled the whole state with Paramount authority.*"[54]

The Patala of the Macedonians has been identified with Haiderabad (Sind), whose ancient name is still remembered as *Potalpuri*.[55] It seems to be the Pātana of the *Gaṇapāṭha* (on *P.*, IV. 1. 14) and the Pātānaprastha 'a Vāhīka town' of Patañjali (*P.*, V. 2. 104).

With Patala the chapter of Hindu states closes in the history of Alexander. There were some minor communities on the frontier of Baluchistan which it would not be accurate to describe as Indian.

States ambiguously described

Some of the states treated ambiguously by the Greeks were very likely *Saṃghas*. We have already seen a few of this class. The state of *Phegelas* is probably another of them.[56] The name has been taken by scholars to be identical with the Sanskrit *Bhagala*, in view of the Gaṇapaṭha's *Bhagala*,[57] which comes along with the republican Traigartas. Alexander's *Phegelas* occupied the same region. Another such state was

---

[53] Curtius, Bk. IX, Ch. 8 ; McCrindle, *Alexander*, p. 256.

[54] McCrindle, *Alexander*, p. 296 ; Diodorus, Bk. XVII, Ch. CIV

[55] McCrindle, *Alexander*, p. 356.

[56] McCrindle, *Alexander*, pp. 121, 221, 281.

[57] On *P.*, IV. 2. 80.

that of the *Glausai* or *Glaukanikoi*[58] (Arrian), who appear to be republican. They are identical with the ***Glauchukāyanakas*** of the *Kāśikā*.[59]

The major portion of the Punjab and Sind which came under the survey of the Greek writers, shows only two or three monarchies, the important ones of which were the kingdoms of Poros and the Abhisāras. Otherwise the whole country was republican. This is also evident from Plutarch's (LX) account about Poros.[60] "Alexander then not only reinstated Poros in his kingdom with the title of Satrap, but added a large province to it, subduing the inhabitants whose form of government was the *republican*."[61]

Alexander's raid and retreat did not cover the whole of the Punjab. There was still the valley of the Sutlej and that of the Beas to be traversed. The republics in those regions are to be recovered only from Indian literature. The *Yaudheyas* and the *Ārattas* were in those regions, and so were also probably some of the republics mentioned in the *Kāśikā* which draws on ancient literature, *e.g.*, the *Śayaṇḍas*. the *Gopālavas*, the *Kauṇḍībṛisas* (*Kāśikā*, *P.*, V. 3. 114, p. 456).

---

[58] McCrindle, *Alexander*, p. 111. *Glaukanikoi* according to Aristoboulos, *Glausai*, according to Ptolemy.

[59] On *P.*, IV. 3. 99.

[60] Not to be identified with *Paurava*, but with the derivative of *Pura* of the *Gaṇapāṭha* on Pāṇini, IV. 1. 151 which is given in the list of the Punjab and Sind ruling designations. Consult also Vardhamāna (*G.R.M.*) on the word.

[61] McCrindle, *Alexander*, p. 308.

CHAPTER IX

Constitutional Survey of the Hindu Republics in Greek Writers

Democracy

In the above survey it would have been noticed that we have various constitutions. This shows that the constitutions were adjusted to the particular needs and circumstances of the people composing the states. We have for instance, the democracy of the Ambashṭhas. The democracy of the Ambhashṭhas had a Second House composed of elected elders. They elected their generals also. Apparently every man in the community had direct franchise, the Greeks calling the constitution a democracy.

Then we have the Kshudrakas and Mālavas who had no 'king' consul as they sent 100 or 150 representatives to negotiate the treaty of peace. Evidently their constitution would not allow power to vest in one man or a small body of men. It is noteworthy that the two armies elected a common general.

Elected 'king' President

Passing to the constitution of the Kathaians or the Kaṭhas we find an elected 'king'. In this state children were born to their parents as citizens first and individuals afterwards, the state deciding as to which of the prospective citizens were perfect in 'limbs and features' and which of them should be allowed to grow into manhood (Diodorus, XCI). The Saubhūta constitution was similar. In these states, man was really a political animal. The individual existed for the state. To secure the life of the group, the individual sacrificed himself and his sentiments as father and mother. Probably it was due to this law that the Kaṭha philosophers glorified a child (Nachiketas), offered to Death by his father, as attaining immortality.

The constitution, like that of Patala, which provided for the election of a 'king' consul, was what Kauṭlya calls a *Rāja-śabdin Saṃgha*, a republic which recognized the title of *Rājan*.[1] Such elected 'kings' also obtained amongst the

[1] It was probably a constitution of this sort which prevailed amongst the *Kuṇindas*, a state whose coins were struck in the name

Lichchhavis. The elected king was not necessarily the leader of the army. Amongst the Lichchhavis, the leadership of the army vested in another elected chief called *Senāpati* (General). An elected 'king' president was the feature of the Śākyan constitution as well.

Second Chamber

In the constitution of the Patalas the "Council of Elders" ruled. They had two so-called 'kings,' hereditary in two families, for the purposes of command in war only. Hereditary 'royal' families in republican bodies are also mentioned in the *Mahābhārata*.[2] The Patala 'kings' were responsible to the Council which in turn was probably elected by the whole community, it being a democracy. Here we have in the Patala constitution a mixture of aristocracy and democracy. The ultimate political authority in all these cases rested with the *Gaṇa* or *Saṃgha*.

Executive authority

As to the executive authority in these republics, it was in some constitutions delegated to a Second Chamber or the House of Elders, while in others there are indications that it remained with the general *Gaṇa* or Parliament. According to the Greek writers the Council of Elders at Patala had the supreme authority, and the Ambashṭhas listened to the advice of their Elders. The *Mahābhārata* says that the chief difficulty in the *Gaṇa* constitution is to keep a resolution of theirs secret, because their number is large. It is therefore urged that the matters of policy (*mantra*) should not be discussed by the whole *Gaṇa* and that the state policy should remain in the hands of the Leaders.[3]

---

of the king and the political community. Their king is always mentioned there as '*Amoghabhūti*,' '*Of unfailing prosperity*,' and the same appellation appears for centuries (150 B.C. to 100 A.C.). This was an official title, and not a personal name (as wrongly interpreted by numismatists. V. Smith, *C.C.I.M.*, Vol. I, pp. 161, 167). The leaders of the *Gaṇa* of the Kaulindas (spelt also as Kauṇinda) are mentioned by V. Mihira, *Br. S.*, IV. 24 (कौलिन्दान् गणपुङ्गवान्); XIV. 30, 33. Ptolemy has Kulindrine; the *Vishṇu P.*, Kuliṇḍa and the *Mārkandeya P.*, Kauliṇḍa. Cunningham, *C.A.I.*, 71. Their coins are found between Ambala and Saharanpur. Their proposed identification with '*Kunets*' (which ought to be *Kanets*) of the Simla hills (*A.S.R.*, XIV, p. 126) is doubtful.

[2] Ch. XIV below.

[3] Ch. XIV below.

One set of the coins of the Yaudheyas is struck in the name of the *Mantra-dharas*-and-the-*Gaṇa,* while other coins are struck simply in the name of the *Gaṇa*. *Mantra-dharas* mean the Council which was vested with the authority of *mantra* or policy. The officers called the chiefs or leaders of the *Gaṇa* thus formed the Executive Body or the Cabinet. The Elders formed another body. They were like a *Second House*. They had varying powers according to individual constitutions. Amongst the Patalas, they were for all purposes the *Government*. In the *Ambhashṭha Saṃgha* they were not so. They were like the Vṛiddhas mentioned in the *Mahābhārata* who advised on matters of mutual subordination and correct dealings, etc. (Ch. XIV). The *Vriddhas* or *Elders* were not necessarily people old in age, though primarily age might have been the qualification. The *Mahābhārata* has the expression '*Elders by knowledge*,' *i.e.*, by *merit*. Evidently one was elected an elder on merit.

The discussion in the *Mahābhārata* implies that some *Gaṇas* or Parliament did reserve in their own hands the executive policy and did not delegte it to their council or cabinet, as it says that the system is a weak point in the *Gaṇa* constitution. Probably non-delegation of executive power was more general a trait than delegation. The Ambashṭhas and the Kshudraka-Mālavas seem to have had such constitutions. The democracies seem to have followed the non-delegation system. The government of the *city-states* in the Punjab is taken by the Greek writers to have been as a rule democratic. "*At last after many generations had come and gone, the sovereignty, it is said, was dissolved and democratic governments were set up in the cities*" (Diodorus, III. 38).[4] "*Most of the cities adopted the democratic form of government, though some retained the kingly, until the invasion of the country by* '*Alexander*' (*ibid.*, 39).[5]

Aristocratic democracy

The states wherein the Greeks found Executive Power held by a few families on hereditary principle, although the rulers were subject to a *Gaṇa*, they have described as aristocratic. In fact they were a mixed constitution which may be called for want of a better term, aristocratic democracy.

---

[4] McCrindle, *Megasthenes*, p. 38. [5] *Ibid.*, p. 40.

Take for example, the state on the other side of the Hupanis (Beas). This had a *Gaṇa* or Parliament of 5,000 members. Yet it was called an aristocracy: "for the multitude was governed by the aristocracy, who exercised their authority with justice and moderation". It was according to the Greek view "*an excellent system of internal government*".[6] The *Gaṇa* of 5,000 was not a direct assembly, for only those were entitled to sit there who furnished the state with an elephant. This was the qualification, and a seat in the *Gaṇa* was based on qualification. The population was composed of 'good agriculturists, and men brave in war'. Every agriculturist and every fighter could not have afforded an elephant. But every agriculturist and fighter presumably must have been represented. Evidently the elephant men represented the 'no elephant' men. To the class of this mixed type belonged also the Patala constitution. The hereditary 'kings' were under the complete control of the House of Elders. It was an aristocracy in form but democracy in spirit.

Large Parliaments

The large number of the *Gaṇa* or Parliament of 5,000 noticed by the Greeks is not without parallel in Indian literature. The *Jātakas* describe Vaiśālī, the capital of the Lichchhavis, as having 7,707 kinglets (*rājūkas*). These rulers were composed of both rich and poor sorts who used to gather in the usual assembly in the House of Law on the call of tocsin. Probably all of them did not attend as they do not do in modern Parliaments.

Hindu term for aristocratic constitution

Hindu literature calls such aristocratic element of *Gaṇa*. a *Kula*[7] (literally, 'family'). The *Mahābhārata* treats 'the Kulas of rājās' as belonging to the class of *gaṇas*. The *Artha-Śāstra* refers to the rāja-kulas, 'ruling Kulas' or 'Kulas of rājās' as being of the nature of *Saṃghas* (*Saṃgha-dharmins*, p. 328). The hereditary 'kings' of the Pātalas would come under the description of the Kula-*Saṃgha*. The law-books always treat *Kulas* as distinct from *Gaṇas* and both come therein

---

[6] *IIA.*, p. 121; *Megasthenes*, p. 67.

[7] Asahāya commenting on *Nārada*, I. 7, defines *kula* as *controlled (or managed) by a few people* (कुलानि कतिचित्पुरुषप्रगृहीतानि). On *grihītāni* compare the verb *pra-grah*, 'to hold'.

side by side.[8] *Gaṇa*, therefore, pure and simple, had no hereditary principle and technically was of the nature of democracy. Often there was a mixture of the two, and pure Kulas were rare. The distinction was in later times ignored.[9] The Jainas who founded their religious *Gaṇas* also founded religious *Kulas*.[10] This *Kula* however was a misnomer, as the founders were celebates and no hereditary principle could be followed. In pure Kula States 'supreme rulership' went by turns to the few families (*Kuleṣu pachchekādhi-pachcham*).[11]

Culture in these Republics

We have concluded this brief constitutional survey of these Republics. But let us not part with this chapter of our republican polity without a few words on their general culture. Philostratus in the *Life of Appollonius of Tyana* gives the information that the *Sophoi* of Alexander were the Oxydracæ and that in the time of Appollonius (about 40 A.C.) they were regarded as 'rather dabblers in philosophy than philosophers'. It seems that the Kshudrakas in Alexander's time were noted for their philosophic wisdom and were called the wise, '*sharp-witted*' (Sophai). Similarly the Kaṭhas are famous in Indian literature for their Upanishadic philosophy and Vedic learning. They were followers of the *Krishṇa Yajurveda*, their edition of that Veda, the *Kāṭhaka Saṃhitā*, has come down to our times. In Patañjali's time, the Kaṭha recension was the ruling authority, it was recited in every town as he says in his *Mahābhāshya*.[12] Their law-book, the *Kāṭhaka-Dharma-Sūtra*, was also well known, and is believed to have been the basis of the *Vishṇu-smṛiti*. Their name in Hindu literature will live as long as the Upanishads live and the *Yajurveda* lives. Likewise the philosophy of the Vṛishṇi leader and that of his cousin Nemi are national beliefs to the present day. The Śākyas,

---

8 *Vīramitrodaya*, quotations at pp. 11 and 40.

9 Kātyāyana : कुलानां हि समूहस्तु गणः संपरिकीर्त्तितः। (*Vīramitrodaya*, p. 426). "The assembly (or body corporate) of Kulas is called Gaṇa."

10 See *Paṭṭāvalīs* edited by Dr. Hoernle in *Ind. Ant.*, Vol. XX, p. 347.

11 *Aṅguttara-Nikāya*, 58. 1 (Vol. III, p. 76). See discussion on p. 79.

12 On *P.*, IV. 3. 101.

although they ceased to exist by the fourth century B.C., had bequeathed the greatest religion to the world. Free constitutions seem to have given rise to free philosophies. Philosophy, politics and military training did not combine to develop a non-human type of humanity. The republics were noted for their love of music. Arrian (VI. 3) calls these Indians whom Alexander met, 'lovers of dance and song'.[13] The musical leanings of the Vṛishṇis are familiar to us from Sanskrit literature. The *Harivaṁśa* describes their ball and picnic (Chs. 146–47).[14] The *Artha-Śāstra* (XI, p. 376) supposes disputation (*kalaha*), on *Vidyā* and *Śilpa* ('science' and 'art') to be a well-known weakness in the republics.

It has been noticed as in the case of the Sikhs that belief and polity exercise a tremendous influence in moulding the physical features of man. The republican polity of this country is another illustration of this curious law of nature. The Greeks testify to the handsome looks and dignified bearing of the Kshudrakas and Mālavas, the Saubhūtas and the Kaṭhas. The remarks of the Buddha who compared the handsome Lichchhavis to a company of gods[15] go to prove the same. Kṛishṇa in the *Mahābhārata* is reported to have alluded to the handsome presence of certain Vṛishṇi leaders as a political asset.[16] It seems that the republicans consciously paid attention to physical culture. This the Saubhūtas and the Kaṭhas even enforced by the laws of their constitutions.[17] The disappearance of that physique in the land of the Lichchhavis which excited the admiration of the Buddha, is parallel to the decline of physique in modern Hellas. Features also seem to be amenable to what Aristotle called the Queen of Sciences.

---

[13] McCrindle, *I.I. by Alexander*, p. 136. (Every nation regards the singing of every foreign nation as 'wild'. It is true now; it was true 22 centuries ago.)

[14] R. Mitra, *Indo-Aryans*, Vol. I, pp. 430–42.

[15] "Let those of the Bhikkhus who have never seen the Tavatiṃsa gods, gaze upon this company of the Lichchhavis, behold this company of the Lichchhavis, compare this company of the Lichchhavis—even as the company of Tavatiṃsa gods." Oldenberg and Rhys Davids, *S.B.E.*, Vol. XI, p. 32.

[16] See Appendix A.

[17] See on the Madras, p. 82 n.

CHAPTER X

Technical Hindu Constitutions

(from c. 1000 B.C.)

Gaṇa and *Kula*, as seen above, were two main divisions of the *Saṃgha* states. Between them there were various technical classes of constitutions. Terms for them which have come down to us and their details, as far as I have been able to collect, I propose to set forth below. Let us take the oldest first.

Bhaujya constitution

The Bhaujya constitution is noticed by the *Aitereya Brāhmaṇa.*[1] We get some light on this constitution from an unexpected quarter. The Pāli Canon[2] enumerates careers open to a *Kulaputta.* Amongst these, next to the king-consul, we have *Raṭṭhika* and *Pettanika.* Aśoka in his inscriptions, equates Bhoja with Raṭhika or Rāshṭrika.[3] The commentary on the *Aṅguttara Nikāya* explains the Pettanika as being hereditary leadership (*Sāpateyya*), come down from forefathers.[4] The Rāshtrikas and Bhojakas or Bhojas as opposed to Pettanikas apparently meant non-hereditary leadership. *Sāpateyyam* leadership suggests that in each case there were more than one leader. The *Mahābhārata* also in its list of different classes of rulers mentions Bhoja as a class (*Sānti*, Ch. LXVII, *Śl.* 54).[5]

---

[1] *Ait. Br.*, VIII, 14.—दक्षिणास्यां दिशि ये के च सत्वतां राजानो भौज्यायैव तेऽभिषिच्यन्ते भोजेत्येनानभिषिक्तानाचक्षत.... ।

[2] यस्स कस्सचि महानाम, कुलपुत्तस्स पञ्चधम्मा संविज्जन्ति, यदि वा रञ्ञो खत्तियस्स मुद्धाभिसित्तस्स, यदि वा रट्ठिकस्स पेत्तनिकस्स, यदि वा सेनाय सेनापतिकस्स, यदि वा गामगामिणिकस्स, यदि वा पूगगामणिकस्स, ये वा पन कुलेसु पच्चेकाधिपच्चं कारेन्ति । *Aṅguttara Nikāya*, Pt. III, p. 76.

[3] Rock Series Proclamations V and XIII, गन्धारानं रिस्टिकपेतेनिकानं ये वापिअंजे अपराता (*Girnar*, V.); भोजपितिनिकेषु, *Shahbazgarhi*, XIII; see Jayaswal, "Places and Peoples in Aśoka's Inscriptions," *I.A.*, LXII, 1933, pp. 127–28.

[4] पितरादत्तं सापतेय्यं, *Aṅguttara*, III, Indices, p. 456; again भुत्तानुभुत्तं भुञ्जति, commentary at p. 300.

[5] राजा भोजो विराट् सम्राट्.

To this interpretation I am also led by Khāravela's inscription which describes the *Rāshṭrikas* and the *Bhojakas* as collective bodies with paraphernalia of sovereignty.[6] Later inscriptions have Bhojas and Mahā-Bhojas which signify higher and ordinary classes of leaders. Sovereignty rested in the Bhoja leaders. The constitution itself was called *Bhaujya* as in the *Aitareya Brāhmaṇa*. It is noteworthy that the *Bhojas* so called after their rulers, appear in later literature as a sub-division of the Yādavas whose earlier history we find as a league of two republics, called the *Andhaka-Vṛishṇis* (pp. 36–39). Now according to the *Aitareya Brāhmaṇa*, the Satvats, which is the ancient name for the Yādavas, were one of the peoples who observed the *Bhaujya* constitution.

That this constitution prevailed in Eastern India also is probable on account of the reference in the Pāli Canon, which as a rule, does not deal with institutions of Western India.

Owing to their special constitution a people in Western India acquired the name Bhojas. This is probably a case where a community is formed on account of its political constitution. The Andhaka-Vṛishṇis were in the Peninsula of Kathiawad. The name *Bhoja* still survives in modern caste-name *Bhojaka* who are found in the Indian state (Cutch) in the Kathiawad Agency.[7] Gujarat is one of the most ancient seats of Bhaujya; but it is likely that the Satvats had spread southwards, as the *Aitareya Brāhmaṇa* places them in the south.

Svārājya constitution

Svārājya is taken to be a peculiar constitution by the *Aitareya Brāhmaṇa* prevailing in Western India.[8] The ruler or President was called *Svarāṭ*. It literally means "self-ruler". The *Taittirīya Brāhmaṇa* in praising the Vājapeya royal consecration says that a wise man (*vidvān*) sacrifices by the Vājapeya and he obtains *Svārājya*, which it explains as 'becoming the leader of equals'. He attains 'eldership'

[6] Jayaswal, *Hāthigumphā Inscription*, *J.B.O.R.S.*, III, p. 455, revised in *E.I.*, XX. 71.

[7] See the discussion on their location by the writer in *I.A.*, LXII. 127-29; and Addendum (II) at the end of Ch. XVII below.

[8] एतस्यां प्रतीच्यां दिशि ये के च नीच्यानां राजानो येऽपाच्यानां स्वाराज्यायैव तेऽभिषिच्यन्ते स्वराडित्येनानभिषिक्तानाचक्षत...*Aitareya Brāhmaṇa*, VIII. 14.

(*jaishṭhya*).[9] This little information shows that the *Sva-rāṭ* ruler was taken from amongst equals, and was made President, and that the selection was based upon merit, for Indra who is said to have first obtained the *Svārājya* consecration (*abhisheka*) is described as having proved his merit. Evidently this refers to an election or selection to the presidentship amongst the members of a *gaṇa* or council. It should be noted that the members of the *gaṇa* according to the *Māhabhārata* were considered to be equals (*sadṛiśās sarve*).[10] According to the *Aitareya Brāhmaṇa* this form of government prevailed amongst the Nichyas and the Apāchyas of Western India. The Nichyas would have occupied, as their name signifies, the low lands bordering near the mouths of the Indus, and the Apāchyas, probably, the regions immediately above. In the time of the *Yajur Veda*, however, the *Svārājya* form had prevailed in Northern India.[11] Later reference than the *Aitareya Brāhmaṇa* for this form of constitution has not yet been met with.

Vairājya constitution

The *Aitareya Brāhmaṇa* describes the *Vairājya* as a national constitution of some of the 'nations' of the North. The locality is further defined by the words "by the side of the Himālayas". In the time of the *Yajur Veda* such constitution was followed in the South. This shows that this form of government was not confined only to the North but was adopted in widely different localities.[12]

---

[9] य एवं विद्वान् वाजपेयेन यजति । गच्छति स्वाराज्यम् । अग्रं समानानां पर्येति । तिष्ठन्तेऽस्मै ज्येष्ठ्याय । *T. Brāhmaṇa*, 1. 3. 2. 2 ; *cf.*, *e.g.*, Rapson (*Ancient India*, 1914, p. 55), who too takes *svarāj* to mean "self-ruling".

[10] See Ch. XIV below.

[11] स्वराडस्युदीची दिङ्मरुतस्ते देवा अधिपतयः etc., *Ś. Yajur-Veda*, XV. 13.

[12] एतेन च तृचेनैतेन त यजुषैताभिश्च व्याहृतिभिर्वैराज्याय तस्मादेतस्यामुदीच्यां दिशि ये के च परेण हिमवन्तं जनपदा उत्तरकुरव उत्तरमद्रा इति वैराज्यायैवतेऽभिषिच्यन्ते । विराडित्येनानभिषिक्तानाचक्षत.... *Aitareya Brāhmaṇa*, VIII, 14.

"विराडसि दक्षिणा दिग्रुद्रास्ते देवा अधिपतयः etc., *Yajur Veda*, XV. 11.

I have rendered the term, taking it literally, as "the king-less constitution".[13] According to the *Brāhmaṇa* the whole country or nation (*Janapada*) took the consecration of rulership. There is no doubt that this was a real democratic constitution. By way of example the Uttara-Madras and the Uttara-Kurus are given in the *Brāhmaṇa* as observing this constitution. The grammatical literature mentions the Madras defined according to *diś* or direction, which signifies that there were at least two Madras.[14] The Madras were republican in the time of Pāṇini and they were so up to the fourth century A.C. when the Guptas encountered them.[15] It seems that the Uttara-Madras or the Higher Madras had a somewhat different constitution from that of the Lower Madras. Now, the Uttara-Kurus in later literature have passed into the region of fable and mythology, where they are noted for prosperity and life of enjoyment.[16] In the *Aitareya Brāhmaṇa*

---

[13] *Cf.* "To this word two meanings can be given: (1) without king, (2) a very distinguished king. In this passage we must take it in the first meaning; for here are the *Janapadāh, i.e.*, people in opposition to the king mentioned as *abhishikta, i.e.*, anointed, whilst in all other passages of this chapter, we find instead of them, the *rājānaḥ* or kings." M. Haug, *Aitareya Brāhmaṇa*, Vol. II, p. 518, n.

[14] Pāṇini, IV. 2. 108. मद्रेभ्योऽञ्। See also the previous Sūtra, and VII. 3. 13. दिशोऽमद्राणाम्, where the janapadas of the North are treated.

[15] Fleet, *Gupta Inscriptions*, p. 8.

[16] *Cf. Milinda Panho*, Vol. I, pp. 2–3. The old Madra capital (p. 84 below) is thus described and compared with Uttara-Kuru about the beginning of the Christian era :—

"....a great centre of trade, a city that is called Sāgala, situated in a delightful country, well watered and hilly, abounding in parks and gardens and groves and lakes and tanks, a paradise of rivers and mountains and woods. Wise architects have laid it out, and its people know of no oppression since all their enemies and adversaries have been put down. Brave is its defence, with many and various strong towers and ramparts, with superb gates and entrance archways ; and with the royal citadel in its midst, white-walled and deeply moated. Well laid out are its streets, squares, cross roads, and market places. Well displayed are the innumerable sorts of costly merchandise with which its shops are filled. It is richly adorned with hundreds of alms-halls of various kinds ; and splendid with hundreds of thousands of magnificent mansions, which rise aloft like the mountain peaks of the Himalayas. Its streets are filled with

they are a historical people like the Madras. Apparently, they, as a separate people, disappeared in later times and the story of their material prosperity transferred them to the region of folklore, a fate very common in this country where history has been often converted into mythology.[17]

Hindu commentators failing to recognise the significance of the word *Vairājya* ('kinglessness') have fallen into the error of rendering it as '*shining condition*'. But there cannot be the slightest doubt as to the constitutional interpretation given here. Other terms of the same passage of the *Aitareya Brāhmaṇa* do bear constitutional interpretation; and if any additional evidence were necessary, I would refer to the term as used by Kauṭilya who treats it as a form of government and rejects it as a bad form.[18] He, like his contemporary Greek thinkers, held democracy in contempt. According to him,

> "no body feels in a Vairājya Government the feeling of 'mine' (with regard to the state); the aim of

elephants, horses, carriages, and foot-passengers, frequented by groups of handsome men and beautiful women, and crowded by men of all sorts and conditions, Brahmans, nobles, artificers, and servants. They resound with cries of welcome to the teachers of every creed, and the city is the resort of the leading men of each of the differing sects. Shops are there for the sale of Benares muslin, of Kutumbara stuffs, and of other clothes of various kinds; and sweet odours are exhaled from the bazaars, where all sorts of flowers and perfumes are tastefully set out. Jewels are there in plenty, such as men's hearts desire, and guilds of traders in all sorts of finery display their goods in the bazaars that face all quarters of the sky. So full is the city of money, and of gold and silver ware, of copper and stone ware, that it is a very mine of dazzling treasures. And there is laid up there much store of property and corn and things of value in warehouses—foods and drinks of every sort, syrups and sweetmeats of every kind. In wealth it rivals Uttara-Kuru, and in glory it is as Alakanandā, the city of the gods."

[17] *Cf. Sabhā-Parvan*, Ch. XXVIII. Also *Jātaka*, Vol. V, p. 316; Vol. VI, p. 100 where Uttara-Kuru is still a historical country located 'in the Himalayas'.

[18] वैराज्यां तु जीवतः परस्याच्छिद्य "नैतन्मम" इति मन्यमानः कर्शयत्यपवाहयति; पण्यं वा करोति विरक्तं वा परित्यज्य अपगच्छतीति।—*Artha-Śāstra*, VIII. 2, p. 323. Mr. Shama Shastry's translation is confused. He takes *Vairājya* to mean "foreign rule, which comes into existence by seizing the country from its king still alive", p. 395.

political organism is rejected ; any one can sell away (the country), no one feels responsible ; or one becoming indifferent leaves the state."

The Jaina *Achārāṅga Sūtra*[19] also mentions the *Vairājya* in giving different kinds of constitutions. And the *Mahābhārata*[20] notices *Virāj* as one of the official titles of ruler.

The 'capital' of the Madras is noted though not named by Pāṇini. We know from other sources[21] that it was Śākala which is supposed to be identical with modern Sialkot. If the identification is correct, the Śākala must have been originally the seat of the *Uttara-Madras*.

In the second century B.C. the capital was under Menander according to the *Milinda Pañho*. It seems that the Madras then left their original home and migrated to lower regions where they were found still flourishing in the Gupta age.[22]

Rāshṭrika constitution

It is evident that the *Rashṭrikās* of the West, who in Aśoka's incsriptions[23] are in the group of the Bhojas and Pitenikas, were a non-monarchical community. No king of theirs is noticed by Aśoka. Khāravela also mentions them in the plural, fighting him in league with the Bhojakas, and with paraphernalia of sovereignty.[24] No doubt now remains as to their republican character. As pointed out above the Pāli Canon knows and names the *Rāshṭrika* or *Raṭṭhika* class of rulers.[25]

According to the implication of the commentary, the *Rāshṭrika-Sāpatya* (*Sāpateyyam*) or 'board of leaders' were not hereditary.[26] They were therefore elected. The mention in the Pāli authority goes to indicate that the *Rāshṭrika* constitution was also very probably known to Eastern India. Like the *Bhaujya* this too gave a national name to the *Rāshṭrikas*

---

19 *Āyāraṅga Sutlaṃ* (Jacobi's edition), p. 83. *Verajjāni*, etc.

20 राजा भोजो विराट् सम्राट्. . . .*Śānti*., LXVIII. 54.

21 *Mahābhārata, Karṇa-Parvan*, Chs. XI, XLIV.

22 Fleet, *Gupta Inscriptions*, p. 8.

23 See p. 79 above.

24 See p. 79 above.

25 *Aṅguttara Nikāya*, Vol. III. LVIII. 1. See p. 79 above.

26 *Aṅguttara Nikāya*, Vol. III, p. 456, where the Pettanika, as opposed to Raṭṭhika, is hereditary.

of the West. They were in Gujarat[27] next to Saurashtra. In the *Artha-Śāstra*, the Su-rāshṭras also are a republic where no king consul was allowed.[28]

Pettanika

The passage in the Pāli Canon noticed above places the Pettanikas by the side of the Rāshṭrikas, and, as we have seen, the term denoted 'hereditary leaders'. Theirs appears to have been really a perverted form of the Rāshṭrika, or rather the Bhoja, form of government, where rulers or leaders had managed to become hereditary. In the *Aitareya Brāhmaṇa* itself, one class of Bhojas are distinguished from the other by the expression *Bhoja pitaram* (VIII. 12) or hereditary Bhoja (literally, who himself a Bhoja would also be the father of a Bhoja). The commentary to the *Aṅguttara Nikāya* has in one place[29] *bhuttānubhuttaṃ bhuṃjati* (= *Pettanika*) which would signify a Bhoja Pettanika. The Pettanika oligarchy, or probably aristocracy, was prevalent in Western India as evidenced by Aśoka's inscriptions. That it also existed in Eastern India is probable, coming as it does in the Pāli passage.

Dvairājya constitution

Kauṭilya discusses the constitution called *Dvairājya* in connection with the *Vairājya*. He characterises the *Dvairājya*, "the rule of two", as a constitution of rivalry and mutual conflict leading to final destruction.[30] It should be noticed that the *Āchārāṅga Sūtra* also refers to this constitution and treats it as distinct from the *Gaṇa* government. This 'rule of two' was neither a monarchy nor an aristocracy. It is a constitution peculiar to the history of India. Historical instances of this constitution are known to our literature and inscriptions. Avanti in some period of Hindu history was under this constitution, for the *Māhabhārata* relates that Avanti was under Vinda and Anuvinda, two kings ruling jointly.[31] The inscriptional instances have caused much

---

27 On the location of the Rāshtrikas, Pettanikas, and Bhojas see the writer's paper in the *Indian Antiquary*, Vol. LXII. 121, at p. 127, and extracts in Add. II at the end of Ch. XVII below.

28 *Artha-Śāstra*, p. 376 ; see pp. 54-55 above.

29 *Aṅguttara Nikāya*, Vol. III, Indices, p. 456. See note 27 above for their location.

30 द्वैराज्यवैराज्ययोः द्वैराज्यमन्योन्यपक्षद्वेषानुरागाभ्यां परस्परसङ्घर्षेण वा विनश्यति । —*Artha-Śāstra*, VIII. 1. 2, p. 323.

31 *Sabhā-Parvan*, Ch. 31 ; *Ud. P.*, 165, etc.

confusion to Indian epigraphists and they found no solution of the riddle. In the sixth and seventh centuries of the Christian era, Nepal was under such a constitution. Simultaneous inscriptions of the kings of the Lichchhavi family and the Thākurî family are found at Kāṭhmāṇḍu.[32] These are orders issued from two places in the same capital, and the dates prove that the two dynasties were ruling simultaneously. Epigraphists not knowing the *Dvairājya* form of government could not see the real significance. They were therefore forced to suppose an imaginary divided jurisdiction. It is, however, excusable, as the idea of *Dvairājya* is so foreign to modern mind. *Primâ facie* such a constitution is unthinkable and unworkable. Its working in India constitutes a unique constitutional experiment and success. The constitution in Nepal lasted for a long time. Hobbes' doctrine of indivisible sovereignty would not allow a foreign student to grasp the inscriptions of Nepal. But in India, where joint-family is a living doctrine, it is explicable. Such a constitution was feasible only in a country where the juristic notion of the Mitākshara family could develop into a practical principle. It seems that the legal principle of joint property and joint enjoyment was transferred to the region of politics and acted upon, whereby 'conflict', 'rivalry' and 'annihilation' could be avoided for centuries. The Nepal families were not collaterals. It was only the constitution which made them joint in sovereignty. The references in the *Artha-Śāstra* and the *Āchārāṅga Sūtra* indicate that the constitution was not a very rare thing in Hindu India.

The non-ruler state

The *Arājaka* or 'non-ruler'[33] was an idealistic constitution which came to be the object of derision of political writers of Hindu India. The ideal of this constitution was that Law was to be taken as the ruler and there should be no man-ruler. The basis of the state was considered to be mutual agreement or social contract between the citizens. This was an extreme

---

[32] Fleet, *Gupta Inscriptions*, App. IV; see discussion in this writer's *History and Chronology of Nepal* (1936).

[33] This technical *Arājaka* does not mean anarchy. For anarchy, Hindu politics uses a special term, *mātsya-nyāya*, *e.g.*, *A.Ś.*, I. 4, p. 9; Khālimpur copper-plate (*E.I.*, IV. 248); *Manu*, VII. 20.

democracy almost Tolstoïan in ideal. The *Māhabhārata*[34]

[34] *Sānti-Parvan*, Ch. LIX : In the beginning of the Current Cycle there was no monarchy and no monarch, and there was no man appointed to executive government. In fact, there was no executive power. The rule of law and government of law was established. This government of law did not last for want of mutual confidence. Hence monarchy was introduced.

In another place the same theory is expressed to this effect :

Subjects in the *Arājaka* state becoming anarchical formed resolutions in an assembly and made laws for control of violence and crime. All the castes for the sake of confidence entered into agreement to live by the contract. But when they were not satisfied with the working of the system they complained to the Creator who recommended them a sovereign, and a king was elected.

This occurs in Chapter LXVII. Both traditions relate to the same theory .—

नियतस्त्वं नरव्याघ्र शृणु सर्वमशेषतः ।
यथा राज्यं समुत्पन्नमादौ कृतयुगेऽभवत् ॥
नैव राज्यन्न राजसोन्न च दण्डो न दण्डिकः ।
धर्म्मेणैव प्रजाः सर्व्वा रक्षन्ति स्म परस्परम् ॥
पाल्यमानास्तथाऽन्योन्यं नरा धर्मेण भारत ।
दैन्यं परमुपाजग्मुस्ततस्तान्मोह आविशत् ॥
ते मोहवशमापन्ना मनुजा मनुजर्षभ ।
प्रतिपत्तिविमोहाच्च धर्म्मस्तेषामनोनशत् ॥
नष्टायां प्रतिपत्तौ च मोहवश्या नरास्तदा ।
लोभस्य वशमापन्नाः सर्व्वे भरतसत्तम ॥—Ch. LIX. Śl. 13–17.

In Śloka 22, they approach Brahman who writes a book on government and recommends a king (*passim*). Chapter LXVII—

इन्द्रमेव प्रणमते यद्राजानामिति श्रुतिः ।
यथैवेन्द्रस्तथा राजा संपूज्यो भूतिमिच्छता ॥ ४ ॥
अराजकाः प्रजाः सर्व्वा पूर्व्वं विनेशुरिति नः श्रुतम् ।
परस्परं भक्षयन्तो मत्स्या इव जले कृशान् ॥ १७ ॥
समेत्य तास्ततश्चक्रुः समयानिति नः श्रुतम् ।
वाक्शूरो दण्डपरुषो यश्च स्यात्पारदारिकः ॥ १८ ॥
यश्च नः समयं भिन्द्यात्त्याज्या नस्तादृशा इति ।
विश्वासार्थञ्च सर्वेषां वर्णानामविशेषतः ।
तास्तथा समयं कृत्वा समयेनावतास्थिरे ॥ ९ ॥
सहितास्तास्तदा जग्मुरसुखार्त्ताः पितामहम् ।
अनीश्वरा विनश्यामो भगवन्नीश्वरं दिश ॥ २० ॥

from which the above description is taken, ridicules the constitution and says that the framers of this legal state found out their mistake when the arrangement would work no more with the result that nobody obeyed the law-without-sanction; when the law would not rule, the citizens of this form of government took to monarchy. I was inclined to regard this "non-ruler" (*arājaka*) constitution as a mere fiction of Hindu politicians who, I thought, wanted to invent it as an argument against republican theories of social contract and rule-of-law. But the *Jaina Sūtra* compels me to take it as a constitutional experiment which had been tried more than once in this country. The Sūtra mentions the form as a living institution.[35] The group where this constitution occurs is composed of all real and historical forms of government. It gives:

(*a*) Non-ruler States,
(*b*) *Gaṇa*-ruled States,
(*c*) Yuvarāja-ruled States,
(*d*) Two-ruled States,
(*e*) *Vairājya* States,
(*f*) '*Viruddha-rajjāṇi*' or States ruled by parties.

The (*c*) class evidently refers to a government like the one over which Khāravela presided before his coronation (*Yovarājaṃ pasāsitaṃ*). Legally such a period of rule was considered as interregnum. Government was probably in the hands of some council of regency, the sovereign being too young. The (*f*) class seems to refer to the rule of parties as in the case of the Andhaka-Vṛishṇis.

The Jaina Sūtra says that all these states are unsafe for a monk or a nun to go to, as they are suspicious, prone to suspect strange ascetics as political spies. We know from the *Artha-Śāstra* that spies generally took the garb of sectarian ascetics.

Very small states on the doctrinaire principle of 'no man-ruler state' could have existed. There must have been

---

[35] Se bhikkhūvā 2 gāmāṇugāmaṃ dūijjamāṇe aṃtarā se arāyāṇi vā gaṇarāyāṇi vā juvarāyāṇi vā dorajjāṇi vā, verajjāṇi vā viruddharajjāṇi vā, sati lāḍhe vihārāe saṃtharamāṇehiṃ jaṇavaehiṃ, no vihāravattiyāe pavajjejjā gamaṇāe. kevalī būyā: āyāṇam eyaṃ; te ṇaṃ bālā: ayaṃ teṇe taṃ ceva jāva gamaṇāe, tato saṃjayām eva gāmāṇugāmaṃ dūijjejjā. *Ayāraṃgasuttaṃ* (ed. Jacobi), II. 3. 1. 10.

Hindu Mazzinis and Hindu Tolstois to found and work such glorious but well-nigh impossible constitutions.

Ugra and Rājanya forms of government

Another passage in the Jaina Sūtra[36] gives three classes of rulers: *Ugra* (*Ugga*), *Bhoga*, and *Rājanya*, (then follow the *Kshatriyas, Ikshvākus*, etc.). The technical, constitutional value of *Rajānya* we have already found out. *Bhoga* probably stands for *Bhoja*. *Ugra* we get from Vedic literature (Ch. XXIII).

Sacrament of rulership essential in every constitution

It should be borne in mind that in all these classes of constitutions, the ceremony of consecration was deemed essential. Without that there was no legal state. And why so? The rulers had to take the oath of good and honest government. The ceremony was so important that in democratic republics where the whole country was supposed to rule (*Vairājya*), the whole country took *abhisheka* consecration by a special ritual.[37] The Lichchhavis had their *abhisheka* (p. 47, *n*. 14), and the Mallas had their fixed place where their rulers in taking office went through 'coronation' ('*mukuṭa-bandhana*,') 'putting on the coronet,' *MPS*, 6. 15) which pre-supposes *abhisheka* (Ch. XXIII) 'Un-anointed' ruler is a term of contempt in Hindu politics. It is to denote an unlawful ruler. It is applied to foreign tribes in the Purāṇas.[38]

---

[36] उग्गकुलाणि वा भेागकुलाणि वा राइन्नकुलाणि वा खत्तियकुलाणि वा इक्खागकुलाणि • • • • *Ayāraṃgasuttaṃ* (ed. Jacobi), II. 1. 2. 2.

[37] *Aitareya Brāhmaṇa*, VIII. 14.

[38] *Vāyu Purāna*.—

भविष्यन्तीह यवना धर्म्मतः कामतोऽर्थतः ।

नैव मूर्द्धाभिषिक्तास्ते भविष्यन्ति नराधिपाः ॥

See Pargiter's *Purāṇa* (*Dynasties of Kaliyuga*), Text, p. 56.

CHAPTER XI

Procedure of Deliberation in Hindu Republics

To come nearer these republics, to come nearer their breathing life, let us try to steal a peep into their deliberations. If the curtain of the past be too heavy to be lifted, let us be satisfied only with an indirect view.

We know from the Buddhist Sūtras and the references noticed above that matters of state were discussed in the assembly of our republics. There is one single direct reference to the technical aspect of these deliberations. That one reference is of the highest importance, for it puts us on the right track. The capital of the Śākyas was besieged by the king of Kosala. It is recorded that while the question of surrender was being discussed, opinion was divided. The Śākyas therefore decided to find out the opinion of the majority. And voting was done on the subject.

> " So the king sent a messenger to the Śākyas, saying, ' Sirs, although I have no fondness for you, yet I have no hatred against you. It is all over ; so open your gates quickly '. Then the Śākyas said, ' Let us all assemble and deliberate whether we shall open the gates '. When they had assembled, some said, ' Open them,' others advised not doing so. Some said, ' As there are various opinions, we will find out the opinion of the majority '. So they set about voting on the subject."[1]

The voting resulted in favour of the proposed capitulation and the city capitulated. Now, where can we get greater details of this procedure of ' voting ' and ' majority ' ? We have seen that the Buddhist *Saṃgha* was copied from the political *Saṃgha*. We have also seen that the example of counting votes in the *Gaṇa* is directly cited by the Buddha as a guide. Therefore, if we can get at the procedure of either of the two, the political or the religious *Saṃgha*, we would be having a picture of the common type. The institutions were contemporary, and in ordinary course, technicalities of procedure of deliberations would be common to popular bodies. But in the case of the Buddhist *Saṃgha* its foundation is known and its borrowing from the political *Saṃgha* is clear.

---

[1] Rockhill, *The Life of the Buddha*, pp. 118–19.

The procedure of the Buddhist *Saṃgha* would be nearer the procedure of the parent *Saṃgha*, the Republic. If we eliminate the religious modifications, we can restore the common type. For this I reproduce the procedure of the religious *Saṃgha*, the very rules of which show that the terms and proceedings had already become technical before they were introduced by the Great Teacher into his Brotherhood. It will give us the details of the procedure of voting and majority.

Seats

All the members who had the right to be present, were present in the assembly on seats, placed under the direction of a special officer appointed for the purpose:

"Now at the time a Bhikkhu named Ajita, of ten years' standing, was the reciter of the Pātimokkha to the *Saṃgha*. Him did the *Saṃgha* appoint as seat-regulator (*āsanapaññā-paka, i.e., āsanaprajñāpaka*) to the Thera Bhikkhus."[2]

Motion

Deliberations were initiated with a motion in these terms:

Resolution

"Let the venerable *Saṃgha* hear me." "If the time seem meet to the *Saṃgha*, let the *Saṃgha* do···This is the motion (*ñatti, i.e., Jñapti*, 'notice')." After this the mover moved the matter in the form of a resolution (*Pratijñā*) to be adopted by the *Saṃgha*. All those who approved of the resolution were asked to remain silent, and those who would not approve were required to speak. In some cases the resolution was repeated thrice and then, if the assembly remained silent, it was declared as carried, and the party affected was formally informed of the resolution. I give below some instances from the *Vinaya Piṭaka* to illustrate the above description.

Here is a resolution moved at the instance of the Buddha himself:

"Let the venerable *Saṃgha* hear me. This Bhikkhu Uvāḷa being examined in the midst of the *Saṃgha* with an offence, when he has denied it then confesses it, when he has

---

[2] Account of the Congress of Vesāli, *Chullavagga*, XII. 2. 7. (*Vinaya, S.B.E.*, XX. 408.)

confessed it then denies it, makes countercharges, and speaks lies which he knows to be such. If the time seem meet to the *Saṃgha*, let the *Saṃgha* carry out the Tassa-pāpiyyasikā-kamma[3] against the Bhikkhu Uvāḷa. This is the motion."

"Let the venerable *Saṃgha* hear me. This Bhikkhu Uvāḷa (etc., *as before*). The *Saṃgha* carries out the Tassa-pāpiyyasikā-kamma against Uvāḷa the Bhikkhu. Whosoever of the venerable ones approves of the Tassa-pāpiyyasikā-kamma being carried out against Uvāḷa the Bhikkhu, let him keep silence. Whosoever approves not thereof, let him speak.

"A second time I say the same thing. This Bhikkhu Uvāḷa (etc., *as before, down to*) 'let him speak'.

"A third time I say the same thing (etc., *as before, down to*) 'let him speak'.

"The Tassa-pāpiyyasikā-kamma has been carried out by the *Saṃgha* against Uvāḷa the Bhikkhu. Therefore is it silent. Thus do I understand."[4]

"Then the *Saṃgha* carried out the Tassa-pāpiyyasikā-kamma against Uvāḷa the Bhikkhu (IV. 12. 4)."

The following is taken from the account of the Congress of Rājagṛiha, held after the death of the Buddha:

"Then the venerable Mahā-Kassapa laid the resolution before the *Saṃgha*: 'Let the venerable *Saṃgha* hear me. If the time seem meet to the *Saṃgha*, let the *Saṃgha* appoint that these five hundred Bhikkhus take up their residence during the rainy season at Rājagaha, to chant over together the Dhamma and the Vinaya, and that no other Bhikkhus go up to Rājagaha for the rainy season.' This is the resolution. Let the venerable *Saṃgha* hear. The *Saṃgha* appoints accordingly. Whosever of the venerable ones approves thereof, let him keep silence. Whosoever approves not thereof, let him speak. The *Saṃgha* has appointed accordingly. Therefore it is silent. Thus do I understand."[5]

---

[3] A punishment.

[4] *Chullavagga*, IV. 11. 2. Trans. by Oldenberg and Rhys Davids, *Sacred Books of the East*, XX. 29.

[5] *Chullavagga*, XI. 1. 4.

Again,

"And the venerable Mahā-Kassapa laid the resolution before the *Saṃgha*: 'If the time seem meet to the *Saṃgha*, I will question Upāli concerning the Vinaya.'"

"And the venerable Upāli laid the resolution before the *Saṃgha*: 'Let the venerable *Saṃgha* hear me. If the time seems meet to the *Saṃgha*, I, when questioned by the venerable Mahā-Kassapa, will give reply.'"[6]

Quorum

The rule of quorum was strictly observed. In small local societies of Buddhist monks a number of twenty formed the quorum to transact all kinds of formal acts.[7]

If any business was transacted without the required number of members being present, the act was regarded as invalid and inoperative:

"If an official act, O Bhikkhus, is performed unlawfully by an incomplete congregation, it is no real act and ought not to be performed."[8]

Gaṇa-pūraka or Whip

The duty of gathering the minimum number of members was undertaken by one of the members.[9]

"Or, I will act as the securer-of-the number (at the next meeting)." Oldenberg and Rhys Davids have translated the passage (*Sacred Books of the East*, XIII, p. 307) as follows:

"Or, I will help to complete the quorum."

The *Gaṇa-pūraka* was the 'whip' to the assembly for a particular sitting.

Consequence of disregarding procedure

The procedure of moving the *ñatti* (*jñapti*) once and the *pratijñā* once was called *ñatti-dutīya*, the Two-*ñatti* procedure; and when they had to be moved thrice, it was called *ñatti-chatuttha* (the Four-*ñatti*-procedure). Putting the resolution or *pratijñā* to the assembly was called

---

[6] *Ibid.*, XI. 1. 7.

[7] *Mahāvagga*, IX. 4. 1.

This corresponds to Patañjali's *Viṃśikaḥ Saṃgha* [*Mahā-bhāshya*, V. 1. 2, II, p. 355 (on *P.*, V. 1. 59).]

[8] *Vinaya, Mahāvagga*, IX. 3. 2.

अधम्मेन च भिक्खवे वग्गकम्म अकम्मं न च करणीयं ।

[9] *Mahāvagga*, III. 6. 6. गणपूरको वा भविस्सामीति ।

Kammavāchā (*Karmavāch*). Now if the *ñatti* was moved and no *Pratijñā* formally put, or if the resolution was proclaimed and no *ñatti* had been moved, the act would be considered invalid. Similarly, an act requiring a *ñatti-chatuttha* could not be lawful if the motion or the resolution was not moved for the prescribed number of times. Again, the order of the motion and resolution could not be subverted:

"If one performs, O Bhikkhus, a *ñatti-dutīya* act with one *ñatti* and does not proclaim a *kammavāchā* such an act is unlawful. If one performs, O Bhikkhus, a *ñattī-dutīya* act with two *ñattis* and does not proclaim a *kammavāchā* ···, with one *kammavāchā*, and does not propose a *ñatti*····, with two *kammavāchās* and does not propose a *ñatti*, such an act is unlawful. If one performs, O Bhikkhu, a *ñatti-chatuttha* act with one *ñatti* and does not proclaim a *kammavāchā*, such an act is unlawful. If one performs, O Bhikkhus, a *ñatti-chatuttha* act with two (etc.)[10]....... "

Votes

Vote was called *Chhanda*. *Chhanda* literally means 'wish', 'desire'. It connotes that in voting, a member was expressing his free will and choice.

Votes of absentees

Votes of the members, who were entitled to be present at the meeting but who owing to some illness or like disability could not attend, were scrupulously collected. An omission to do this vitiated the proceedings. But such votes were rejected if objected to by the assembled members. It was optional with the members to count them but they were expected to be collected usually:

"If, O Bhikkhus, at a *ñatti-dutīya* act not all the Bhikkhus, ...entitled to vote are present, but if the *chhanda* of those who have to declare their *chhanda* has not been conveyed (to the assembly), and if the Bhikkhus present protest, such an act is performed by an incomplete congregation.

"If, O Bhikkhus, at a *ñatti-dutīya* act as many Bhikkhus as are entitled to vote, are present, but if the *chhanda* of those who have to declare their *chhanda* has not been conveyed

[10] *Vinaya*, *Mahāvagga*, IX. 3. 4. 7. 8. Trans. by Rhys Davids and Oldenberg, *S.B.E.*, Vol. XVII, p. 265 ff.

(to the assembly), and if the Bhikkhus present protest, such an act is performed by an incomplete congregation."[11]

Ballot-voting: the Procedure-of-Majority

If the *Saṃgha* adopted a resolution unanimously, the question of voting did not arise; but if a matter entailed a division in the opinion of the members, speeches were made and the Procedure-of-Majority was observed. The opinion of the greater number (*bahutara*) decided the matter. The procedure is called *Ye-bhuyyasikaṃ* in Pāli. The Sanskrit restoration would be *Ye-bhūya siyakam*, the 'Those (who-were)-most-Procedure.' The voting was carried on with the help of voting-tickets which were coloured. The tickets were called *Śalākās* or pins[12] and the voting was called the pin-taking (*śalākāgrahaṇa*). There was a Teller, *Śalākā-grāhaka* ' taker of pins (tickets) appointed by the whole *Saṃgha* who explained the significance of the colours, and took the vote either secretly or openly.

"A Bhikkhu who shall be possessed of five qualifications shall be appointed as taker of the voting tickets, one who does not walk in partiality, one who does not walk in malice, one who does not walk in folly,....walk in fear, one who knows what (votes) have been taken and what have not been taken.

"And thus shall he be appointed.

"First the Bhikkhu is to be requested (whether he will undertake the office). Then some able and discreet Bhikkhu is to bring the matter before the *Saṃgha* saying:

"'Let the venerable *Saṃgha* hear me.

"'If the time seem meet to the *Saṃgha*, let the *Saṃgha* appoint a Bhikkhu of such a name as taker of the voting tickets (etc.)..........[13]

"By that Bhikkhu, the taker of the voting tickets, are the votes to be collected. And according as the larger number[14] of the Bhikkhus who are guided by the Dhamma shall speak, so shall the case be decided."

---

[11] *S.B.E.*, Vol. XVII, p. 266.

[12] We gather from a Chinese record that these tickets were of wood.

[13] *Chullavagga*, IV. 9. 5; *S.B.E.*, XX, p. 25.

[14] The odd number (3) of the *Sabhā* (jury) who are required to sit with the Judge under *Manu*, VIII. 10, points to the rule of

" I enjoin upon you, Bhikkhus, three ways of taking votes, in order to appease such Bhikkhus—the Secret method, *Gūlhakam*, the Whispering method, *Sakaṇṇa-jappakaṃ*, and the Open method, *Vivaṭakaṃ*. And how, O Bhikkhus, is the secret method of taking votes? The Bhikkhu who is the teller of the votes is to make the voting tickets of different colours, and as each Bhikkhu comes up to him he is to say to him thus: 'This is the ticket for the man of such an opinion, this the ticket for the man of such an opinion. Take whichever you like.' When he has chosen (he is to add), 'Do not show it to anybody.' "[15]

'Pointless speeches' and Delegation Committee

Sometime to escape many "pointless speeches" the right of deliberation on a matter was delegated to an appointed committee who decided the question amongst themselves and then communicated their decision to the *Saṃgha*. If the committee could not come to a decision, 'the custody of the case remained in the hands of the *Saṃgha*' who decided it according to the Procedure-of-Majority.

" If, O Bhikkhus, whilst the case is being enquired into by those Bhikkhus, pointless (*anaggāni*) speeches are brought forth, and the sense of any single utterance is not clear, I enjoin upon you, O Bhikkhus, to settle the case by referring it (to a jury or commission).[16]

" And thus, O Bhikkhus, is he to be appointed. First, the Bhikkhu should be asked (whether he be willing to undertake the office). Then some discreet and able Bhikkhu should address the *Saṃgha* thus:

" 'May the venerable *Saṃgha* hear me. Whilst this case was being enquired into, pointless speeches were brought

---

majority. It is clearly enjoined in the *Artha-Śāstra* (III. 9. 61) with regard to the decision of land disputes by a jury of neighbours. 'Land disputes are to be decided by village-elders of the neighbourhood. If there be a division of opinion among them, the decision to prevail is of the honest majority':

क्षेत्रविवादं सामन्तग्रामवृद्धाः कुर्युः । तेषां द्वैधीभावे यतो बहवः शुचयोऽनुमता वा ततो नियच्छेयुः ॥

Compare also the jury of 7, 5 or 3 in the *Sukra-nīti*, IV. 26.

[15] *Chullavagga*, IV. 14. 24; *S.B.E.*, XX, p. 54; XXVI, p. 56.

[16] *Ibid.*, IV. 4. 19 (*Ubbahikā* = Skt. *Udvāhikā*).

forth amongst us, and the sense of no single utterance was clear. If the time seem meet to the venerable *Saṃgha*, let it appoint Bhikkhus of such and such a name on a committee. This is the motion,' etc.[17]

"If those Bhikkhus, O Bhikkhus, are not able by the committee to settle that case, those Bhikkhus, O Bhikkhus, ought to hand over the case to the *Saṃgha*, saying, 'We, Sirs, are not able by a committee to settle this case, let the *Saṃgha* settle it.'

"I enjoin upon you, O Bhikkhus, to settle such a case by the vote of majority."[18]

The same principle operated when a matter was referred to a larger body:

"But if you, sirs, should not be able to do so, then will we ourselves retain the custody of the case."[19]

Again:

"Then the *Saṃgha* met together with the intention of enquiring into this legal question. But while they were enquiring into it, both was much pointless speaking brought forth and also the sense in no single speech was clear. Then the venerable Revata laid a resolution before the *Saṃgha*:

"...'If it seems meet to the *Saṃgha*, let the *Saṃgha* settle this legal question by referring (it to a jury).'

"And he chose four Bhikkhus of the East and four Bhikkhus of the West....'Let the venerable *Saṃgha* hear me. During the enquiry into this matter there has been much pointless talk among us. If it seem meet to the *Saṃgha*, let the *Saṃgha* delegate four Bhikkhus of the East and four Bhikkhus of the West to settle this question by reference.... The *Saṃgha* delegates four Bhikkhus of the East and four Bhikkhus of the West to settle this question by rèference. Whcsoever of the venerable ones...approves not thereof, let him speak. The delegation is made accordingly. The *Saṃgha* approves thereof. Therefore is it silent. Thus do I understand.'"[20]

A settlement by this procedure was called a "proceeding in presence" (*Sammukha-vinaya*). The delegates were regarded as lawfully representing the interests in the matter

[17] *Chullavagga*, IV. 4. 20.

[18] *Ibid.*, IV. 5. 24.

[19] *Ibid.*, IV. 4. 18.

[20] *Ibid.*, XII. 2. 7. 8.

and therefore the parties were considered to be present in the discussion.

Principle of representation

"If then, O Bhikkhus, those Bhikkhus are able on the reference (or on the committee) to settle the case, that, O Bhikkhus, is called a case that is settled. And how is it settled? By the Proceeding in Presence. And what therein is meant by the Proceeding in Presence? The Dhamma is represented, and the Vinaya is represented, and the particular person is represented."[21]

Res Judicata

If once a question was decided in accordance with a valid procedure it could not be re-opened[22] "Having been once settled, it is settled for good."

Procedures of Censure

It appears from *Chullavagga*, IV. 14. 9, that a member was liable to the 'Procedure-of-Censure', if he did not control himself in discussion and showed "contradiction, cantankerousness, and similar misdemeanours in speech".

Re-opening a settled question was also regarded as an offence. "When a legal question, O Bhikkhus, has been thus settled, if a disputant re-opens the question, such re-opening is a *Pachittiya*."

Act of Indemnity

An act of an assembly, inadequately constituted, could not be indemnified afterwards by a fuller assembly. A contrary opinion seems to have been entertained by some people. But the procedure-of-indemnity (*anumatikappo*) was altogether rejected by the followers of Buddhism.

Clerks of the House

There used to be Clerks or Recorders of the House, who without ever quitting their seats took down minutes of the deliberations and resolutions. A Buddhist suttanta, Mahā-Govinda, to which we shall have to refer again, describes a meeting of the Gods in their Hall the Sudhamma Sabhā ('the Hall of Good Law'). At the four angles just outside the rows of the celestial members of the assembly and in front of

[21] *Chullavagga*, V. 4. 14. 21; *S.B.E.*, XX, p. 52.

[22] *Chullavagga*, IV. 24. 25.

the demi-gods (spectators), four recorders, each with 'the title of the Great King' (*Mahārāja*), take their assigned seats. The four Kings became the receivers of the speeches and receivers of resolutions 'in respect of the matter,'

'for which the Tāvatiṃsa Gods having assembled and being seated in the Hall of Good Law, deliberated and took counsel together.'

'They the Four Lord Clerks of the House remaining the while in their places, not retiring.'[23]

The learned translator of the *Dīgha Nikāya* rightly saw in this that 'the Four Great Kings were looked upon as 'Recorders of what had been said. They kept the minutes of the meeting.'[24] Now as men attribute their own institutions to their Gods, it is a simple inference that the Indians in the days of the Buddha had such Clerks of the House in their parliaments or 'Mote Halls', as Prof. Rhys Davids has already pointed out.[25]

'Acts of indemnity' and other 'acts' and 'laws' passed must have been reduced into writing and we know that elaborate record of judicial business was kept by the Lichchhavis. The large body of the republican *gaṇas* necessitated the presence of more than one clerk. The members of the assembly made speeches from their seats and the Clerks near the section 'took down the words'. Evidently the Clerks of the House were men of position.

Historical significance of the terms and procedure

This view captured from the fleeting past, from the distant sixth century before Christ, shows clear features of a highly developed stage, marked with technicality and formalism in language, with underlying concepts of legalism and constitutionalism of a most advanced type.

---

[23] MG., *Dīgha Nikāya*, XIX. 14; Pāli Text Society's edition, Vol. II, pp. 220–25:

Yen' atthena devā Tāvatiṃsā Sudhāmmāya sabhayam sannisinnā honti sannipatitā, tam attham chintayitvā tam attham mantayitvā vutta-vachanā pi tam chattāro Mahārājā tasmin at the honti, pachchanusiṭṭha-vachanā pi tam chattāro Mahārājā tasmim at the honti sakesu āsanesu thitā avippakantā.

[24] Rhys Davids, *Dialogues of the Buddha*, Pt. II (*Sacred Books of the Buddhists*, Vol. III), pp. 263–64, *n*.

[25] *Ibid.*, 'There must have been such Recorders at the meetings in the Mote Hall'.

This pre-supposes a previous experience extending over centuries. The *Ñatpi*, the Pratijña, the Quorum, the Śalākā (ballot-voting), the Procedure of Majority, the Reference are all mentioned by the Buddha without any definition, that is, as terms already current.

Jātakas and Referendum

The *Jātakas*, which go back in date to pre-Buddhan times, do not let any doubt linger as to the existence of the procedure of voting and its use in political matters before the birth of the Śākya Muni. In *Jātaka* I[26] (p. 399) the election of a king to the vacant throne of a city is described. All the ministers and the Nāgaras (the members of the capital assembly or the citizens of the capital) having agreed unanimously by a common voting (*eka-chchhandā hutvā*) elected their new king. This was a *Referendum* of the whole city, and not the city assembly only, as the word for the city assembly in Pāli is Negama (see Ch. XXVII below). Referendum (**Chhandakā*) of the whole city (*Sakala-nagara*) was known to early Buddhist literature on which the author of the commentary on the *Jātakas* drew. *Chhanda*, according to the Pāli canon, is *voting*, and the **Chhandāka* of the whole city in a city-state would naturally mean a referendum. In any case, the reference to the election of king by a common voting is certainly pre-Buddhan in the text of the *Jātaka*.

There is another passage in the *Jātaka*, Vol. II, pp. 352–53, which proves that the procedure of moving a resolution three times in political matters obtained before the time of the Buddha. The procedure is mentioned in a humorous fable; it, therefore, must have been well known in actual life to be so mentioned. A bird is repeating a motion for the election of a *rājā*, evidently a republican *rājā*; he has done so twice and the motion was opposed by another member of the assembly: 'Wait please!' The opposer of the motion begged leave to make his speech which was granted on condition that the speaker should state his reasons on the principles of political science and law (*artha* and *dharma*). The speaker gave his reasons and he carried his opposition. The opposition was on the well-known republican ground: that the proposed king[27]

[26] Fausböll's ed.

[27] The owl.

had not a pleasant presence. Evidently, it is a mimicry of the republican principle of election on the ground (amongst others) of good looks and presence. But the procedure which comes out of the mimicry and ridicule establishes our thesis. The procedure was secular first and became Buddhistic afterwards.

The Buddha only adopts the procedure-rules for particular kinds of cases arising in his organization. He himself came from one of the republics and mostly lived amongst republican communities; he was perfectly familiar with their working system and adapted it to the benefit of his own Order. His ambition was to found a large state, an empire, of his religious system (*dharma-chakra*) but the organization he created to realise his aim was communal, fit to establish and hold only a city-state of *dharma* and not a *dharma-chakra*. The limitation was the result of early associations. Born in a republic, where political and public spirit was more intense than in contemporary kingdoms, he combined in him the capacity, the enthusiasm, and the ambition, not of a quiet recluse, but of a republican chief and of a conqueror.[28] Unlike the normal Hindu ascetic he would hold property for his *Saṃgha*, he would hold meetings and pass resolutions and punish offenders. Throughout his spiritual achievements, he is a republican Sākya, and his system is a constitutionalised spiritual propaganda, a Propaganda of Conquest. To achieve success in his spiritual designs, he had to perpetuate his Republic-of-*Dharma* (*Dharma-Saṃgha*), and to perpetuate the republic of *dharma*, he adopted the constitution and the constitutional procedure of the republic of politics.

---

[28] In personal matters also, the Buddha showed a conservativeness acquired from his early associations. He was proud of his Ikshvāku lineage even when a recluse. He asked the Brahmin Kṛishṇāyana, who had insulted him as a Śākya, was he (Kṛishṇāyana) not descended from one of the slave girls of the Ikshvākus? 'If you do not give a clear reply (to my charge), then your head will split in pieces on the spot.' *Ambaṭṭha Sutta*, *Sutta* 20, Rhys Davids, *Dialogues*, I. 114–16.

CHAPTER XII

Franchise and Citizenship

Basis of Franchise

In aristocratic republics the basis of franchise was the family, *i.e.*, the Hindu family. This is implied by the *Mahābhārata* when it says that there is equality in the *Gāṇa* by family (*kula*) and by birth (*jāti*).[1] Equality by birth and family made up the constitutional equality inside the Hindu republic. Every free man in a *Saṃgha* was equal by his birth and every family was equal, for political purposes. A passage in the Pāli Canon also takes the *Kula* as the basis of franchise.[2] The Buddha preaching to the sons of the Lichchhavis says that high careers open to a *Kula-putta* or cadet of a family were these: he might become consecrated to rulership, might become a Rāshṭrika, or Pettanika, or the Generalissimo, or the President of a Township (*gāmagāmaṇika*), or the President of an Industrial Guild (*pūgagāmaṇika*). It is meant that all these offices were elective and a *Kula-putta* was eligible to all these in a *Gaṇa*-state. A sixth career is added and it is with regard to a *Kula*-state which we have already noticed above: '*Supreme rulership (over other rulers) by turns*'.[3] Kātyāyana the law-giver says that *gaṇa* is the assembly of *Kulas*.[4] *Kula* or family was thus the basis of political right and power in aristocracies and in aristocratic democracies. But it could not have been the rule in what the Greeks called democracies. There everybody was equal by birth. Birth alone must have been the basis of franchise in constitutions like that of the Kaṭhas and the Saubhūtas, where even the selection of the 'king' depended upon personal qualification and no one attached any regard

---

1 See Ch. XIV below. *Jāti*, literally, 'birth,' is not caste. There were, as we have seen, all castes amongst the republics. Free birth as apposed to slave birth is probably meant by it. *Cf.* the Vedic *sajāta*, see below Ch. XXV.

2 See above, p. 78, *n*.

3 कुलेसु पच्चेकाधिपच्च । *Aṅguttara Nikāya*, Vol. III, p. 76.

4 कुलानां हि समूहस्तु गणः सम्परिकीर्त्तितः । *Vīramitrodaya*, p. 426.

to the family, and where the culture of the individual himself was the prime consideration of the State. We find in the Śākya Parliament both young and old assembled; in the Vṛishṇi *Saṃgha*, father, son, and younger brother (Kṛishṇa, Pradyumna, Gada) all possessing franchise (Appendix A).

Outsiders eligible to citizenship in republics

Pāṇini gives rules to form words denoting the country of origin of a man (IV. 3. 90),[5] or his present habitation (IV. 3. 89),[6] and also to denote *bhakti* which one bears to a particular country, tribe, ruler, or holders of a *janapada* (republican rulers).[7] One of the illustrations given by Patañjali is the community of *Glauchukāyanakas* whom we know to have been a political state from Macedonian writers.[8] As they owe *bhakti* to Gluchukāyana, they are called the 'Glauchukāyanakas'. Kātyāyana modifying one of the rules of Pāṇini introduces the republican illustrations of the Madras and Vṛijis.[9] One of Madra *bhakti* may be called Madraka and one of Vṛiji *bhakti*, Vṛijika. *Bhakti* in these cases means constitutional allegiance.

Bhakti literally means 'sharing,' 'exclusion', and secondarily 'attachment'. Separate rules to denote territorial and political *bhakti* over and above the rules to denote the country of origin or domicile of a man, suggest the idea of an artificial citizenship. By sharing Madra- or Vṛiji-*bhakti* one

---

[5] अभिजनश्च । ४ । ३ । ९० ॥

[6] सोऽस्य निवासः । ४ । ३ । ८९ ॥

[7] Pāṇini, IV. 3. 95–100: भक्तिः ॥ ९५ ॥ अचित्तादृदेशकालाट्ठक् ॥ ९६ ॥ महाराजाट्ठञ् ॥ ९७ ॥ वासुदेवार्जुनाभ्यां वुन् ॥ ९८ ॥ गोत्रक्षत्रियाख्येभ्यो बहुलं वुञ् ॥ ९९ ॥ जनपदिनां जनपदवत्सर्वं जनपदेन समानशब्दानां बहुवचने ॥ १०० ॥ Sūtra 96 distinguishes *loyalty* from *partiality* in the use of *bhakti*. *Cf. Kāsikā* (343); *achitta*, 'non-purpose' or 'non-thoughtfulness' is significant. One's weakness for milk is an '*achitta*' *bhakti*, *i.e.*, political *bhakti* is a considered and rational condition of mind.

[8] See above, p. 71.

[9] On Pāṇini, IV. 3. 100: सर्ववचनं प्रकृतिनिर्ह्रासार्थम् ॥ १ ॥ तच्च मद्रवृज्यर्थम् ॥ २ ॥ Patañjali: माद्रो भक्तिरस्य माद्रौ वा भक्तिरस्य मद्रक इत्येव यथा स्यात् वार्ज्यो भक्तिरस्य वार्ज्यौ वा भक्तिरस्य वृजिक इत्येव यथा स्यात्। *Mahābhāshya*, Vol. II. pp. 314–15.

would be called Madraka or Vṛijika. A Vṛijika therefore might not have been a born Vṛiji and a Madraka, a born Madra. It has to be noticed that Kauṭilya in mentioning the king-consul republics, uses the form Vṛijika and Madraka. The Jaina Sūtra also uses the form *Mallak(i)*. The 'Vṛijikas' included Vṛijis and non-Vṛijis owning a common Vṛiji allegiance, which would include people originally conquered by the Vṛijis or people voluntarily amalgamated with the Vṛijis.

It is thus evident that the republics extended citizenship to outsiders. This will explain the enormous territorial growth of the Mālavas and the Yaudheyas who covered vast expanses of land in early and later centuries.

Bhakti to Arjuna

Orientalists, both Indian and European, have based an argument on वासुदेवार्जुनाभ्यां वुन् (IV. 3. 98) of Pāṇini. It has been argued that the Sūtra establishes the worship of Vāsudeva in and before the time of Pāṇini. But the context shows that no religious *bhakti* is meant. Pāṇini uses the term in the sense of political or constitutional allegiance. Take for instance, the *bhakti* owed to the holders-of-*janapadas* in IV. 3. 100. These holders of *janapadas* were certainly not worshipped. Take again, the preceding Sūtra, IV. 3. 97, where *bhakti* to 'Mahārāja' is stated. Now nobody would contend that Mahārāja, either a man or a country, was worshipped. Then we have to take into consideration the previous Sūtras where place of origin (अभिजन) as opposed to domicile (निवास) in connection with the highlands, Sindhu and Takshaśilā and Śalātura, etc., is discussed. There is not a trace of religious *bhakti* (devotion) there. Again, scholars have taken note of Vāsudeva while Arjuna who is placed along with Vāsudeva in the same Sūtra has been ignored. There is no evidence that Arjuna was deified. *Bhakti* to those two Kshtriyas is the political *bhakti*. The party loyal to Vāsudeva and the party loyal to Arjuna must have been well known in literature like the *varga* of Vāsudeva mentioned by Kātyāyana (Kielhorn, Vol. II, p. 295).

CHAPTER XIII

Judicial Administration and Laws of Republics

The Hindu law books recognise the laws of *Kula* States as well as those of *Gaṇas.*[1] The *Kula*-Court was presided over by Kulikas or aristocrats.[2] In a mixed constitution of aristocracy and democracy we may find a Kulika-Court. Such a court, as a matter of fact, we do find amongst the Vṛijis, where there was a Board of Eight Kulikas to investigate into criminal cases.[3] The law books prescribe that an appeal should lie from the *Kula*-Court to the *Gaṇa*-Court.[4] We can understand this provision if we take into consideration a mixed constitution. There may be a Kulika-Court there, but then it would be subject to the higher jurisdiction of the *Gaṇa*. The Kulikas in the Vṛiji constitution were subject to the superior jurisdiction of the heads of the *Gaṇa*—Commander-in-Chief, Vice-King and 'King'. The *Mahābhārata* says

---

[1] Yājñavalkya, I. 360 ; II. 186 :

कुलानि जातीः श्रेणीश्च गणाञ्जानपदानपि ।
स्वधर्माच्चलितान्राजा विनीय स्थापयेत्पथि ॥ १ ॥ ३६० ॥
निजधर्माविरोधेन यस्तु सामयिको भवेत् ।
सोऽपि यत्नेन संरक्ष्यो धर्मो राजकृतश्च यः ॥ २ ॥ ४८६ ॥

See also, ग्रामश्रेणिगणानाञ्च सङ्केतः समयक्रिया । Bṛihaspati quoted in *Vīramitrodaya*, p. 424.

And Manu, VIII. 41 :—

जातिजानपदान्धर्मान् छ्रेणीधर्मांश्च धर्मवित् ।
समीक्ष्य कुलधर्मांश्च स्वधर्मं प्रतिपादयेत् ॥ ८ ॥ ४१ ॥

[2] Rāṭṭhapāla after whom a text is named in the Pāli Canon was a kula-putta and son of the *agga-kulika*. See also,

कुलिकास्मार्थमुख्याश्च पुरग्रामनिवासिनः ।
ग्रामपौरगणश्रेण्यश्चातुर्विद्यश्च वर्गिणः ।
कुलानि कुलिकाश्चैव नियुक्ता नृपतिस्तथा ॥

Vīramitrodaya, p. 11. Comm., कुलिकाः कुलश्रेष्ठाः ॥

[3] See p. 49 above. *Cf.* Kātyāyana (quoted in *Vīramitrodaya*, p. 41) :

वणिग्भिः स्यात्कतिपयैः कुलभूतैरधिष्ठितम्, where कुल = a court.

[4] See n. 7 at p. 106 below.

that it was the duty of the *Kula*-elders to take notice of criminal offences and that justice should be administered through the President, that is, punishment was given, in his name.[5] This seems to have been done amongst the Vṛijis. There were industrial organisations in a *Gaṇa*[6] as in a monarchy. These guilds (*pūgas*) had some judicial powers. But their decisions were appealable to the *Kula*- and *Gaṇa*-Courts.[7]

When the *Gaṇas* were conquered by, and became subject to, monarchs as in the days of the later law books (Nārada, Bṛihaspati and Kātyāyana) decision of *Gaṇa* was made subject to the appellate jurisdiction of the monarch or the royal Chief Justice.[8]

That the *Gaṇas* had their own laws is evident from the provision of the Hindu law-books which, as has been pointed out above, recognise their separate existence. It is also proved by the testimony of the Greek writers who praise the laws of Indian republics. The *Mahābhārata* also praises their good legal system. The Lichchhavis are recorded to have had a book of legal precedents.[9]

The laws of the *Gaṇas* are called by the law-books *Samaya*.[10] *Samaya*, literally, means a decision or a resolution arrived at in an *assembly* (from सम् + √ इ = '*to come together*'), that is, the laws of the *Gaṇas* were passed in their meetings.

---

[5] See Ch. XIV below.

[6] *Aṅguttara Nikāya*, Vol. III, p. 76. See p. 102 above.

[7] कुलश्रेणिगणाध्यक्षाः प्रोक्ता निर्णयकारिणः ।
येषामग्रे निश्चितस्य प्रतिष्ठानूत्तरोत्तरा ॥
विचार्य श्रेणिभिः कार्य्यं कुलैर्यन्न विचारितम् ।
गणैश्चश्रेण्यविख्यातं गणाज्ञातनियुक्तकैः ॥
कुलादिभ्योऽधिकाः सभ्यास्तेभ्योऽध्यक्षोऽधिकः कृतः ।
सर्वेषामधिको राजा धर्मं यत्तेन निश्चितम् ॥

—Bṛihaspati in *Vīramitrodaya*, p. 40.

All these quotations refer to a time when *gaṇas* had become subject to monarchies.

[8] See ns. at p. 106 and n. 7 above.

[9] Rhys Davids, *Buddhist India*, p. 22. Such books were kept in monarchies also. See *Jātaka*, Vol. III, p. 292. *Cf. J.*, Vol. V, p. 125.

[10] Nārada and Bṛihaspati quoted in *VM.*, pp. 423–25.

CHAPTER XIV

Characteristics of Republics according to the Mahābhārata

In *Śānti-Parvan*, Chapter 107 is devoted to the characteristics of the *gaṇas*. There are traces in the discussion which indicate that the characteristics given go back to fairly early times. It is nowhere contemplated that the *gaṇas* owed allegiance to monarchs, far less that they were conquered. This would relate to a period before the rise of empires.

As the discussion is of great importance, I give below the text and translation of the entire passage.[1] Former translations are hopelessly confused, the reason being that *gaṇas* had ceased to exist and their real significance was forgotten long before the time of commentators, who are followed by translators.

The disquisition in the *Mahābhārata* makes it clear that '*Gaṇa*' refers to the whole body politic, the entire Political Community, and, in the alternative, the Parliament, and not to the "governing body" only (a view to which Dr. Thomas inclines, *J.R.A.S.*, 1915, p. 534). The governing body was composed of the *Gaṇa-mukhyas* and *Pradhāna* (Chiefs and President) whose jurisdiction it was to conduct affairs of the community (verse 23).[2] Resolutions of State were matters which remained in their hands (verse 24); they held meetings and discussed those Resolutions (25). They also saw to the administration of justice (27). Thus the executive was a distinct body inside the *Gaṇa*.

It may also be noticed that the large number which composed the *Gaṇa* is alluded to in verse 8; and the *whole* body is mentioned in verse 24. It was impossible to keep matters of vital policy secret on account of the large number of the *Gaṇa*. This was in the opinion of the *Mahābhārata* writer a great defect in the *Gaṇa* constitution (8 and 24). It is thus apparent that a close body was not meant by '*Gaṇa*'.

---

[1] Asiatic Society of Bengal ed. of the *Mahābhārata, Śānti-Parvan*, Ch. 107.

[2] *Gaṇa-mukhyas = Saṃgha-mukhyas, Artha-Śāstra*, p. 377 (XI–i).

The *Gaṇas* generally formed *confederacies* (11 to 15). Learning in the *gaṇas* is alluded to in verse 21.

"*Of the Characteristics of the Gaṇas.*"

गणानां वृत्तिमिच्छामि श्रोतुं मतिमतां वर ॥ ६ ॥
यथा गणाः प्रवर्द्धन्ते न भिद्यन्ते च भारत ।
अरींश्च विजिगीषन्ते सुहृदः प्राप्नुवन्ति च ॥ ७ ॥
भेदमूलो विनाशो हि गणानामुपलक्षये ।
मन्त्रसंवरणं दुःखं बहूनामिति मे मतिः ॥ ८ ॥
एतदिच्छाम्यहं श्रोतुं निखिलेन परन्तप ।
यथा च ते न भिद्येरंस्तच्च मे वद पार्थिव ॥ ९ ॥

॥ भीष्म उवाच ॥

गणानाञ्च कुलानाञ्च राज्ञां भरतसत्तम ।
वैरसन्दीपनावेतौ लोभामर्षौ नराधिप ॥ १० ॥
लोभमेको हि वृणुते ततोऽमर्षमनन्तरम् ।
तौ क्षयव्ययसंयुक्तावन्योन्यञ्च विनाशिनौ ॥ ११ ॥
चारमन्त्रबलादानैः सामदानविभेदनैः ।
क्षयव्ययभयोपायैः कर्षयन्तीतरेतरम् ॥ १२ ॥
तत्रादानेन भिद्यन्ते गणाः संघातवृत्तयः ।
भिन्ना विमनसः सर्वे गच्छन्त्यरिवशं भयात् ॥ १३ ॥
भेदे गणा विनश्येयुर्भिन्नास्तु सुजयाः परैः ।
तस्मात् संघातयोगेन प्रयतेरन् गणाः सदा ॥ १४ ॥
अर्थाश्चैवाधिगम्यन्ते संघात-बल-पौरुषैः ।
वाह्याश्च मैत्रीं कुर्व्वन्ति तेषु संघातवृत्तिषु ॥ १५ ॥
ज्ञानवृद्धाः प्रशंसन्ति शुश्रूषन्तः परस्परम् ।
विनिवृत्ताभिसन्धानाः सुखमेधन्ति सर्व्वशः ॥ १६ ॥
धर्म्मिष्ठान् व्यवहारांश्च स्थापयन्तश्च शास्त्रतः
यथावत् प्रतिपश्यन्तो विवर्द्धन्ते गणोत्तमाः ॥ १७ ॥

पुत्रान् भ्रातॄन् विगृह्णन्तो विनयन्तश्च तान् सदा ।
विनीतांश्च प्रगृह्णन्तो विवर्द्धन्ते गणोत्तमाः ॥ १८ ॥
चारमन्त्रविधानेषु कोषसन्निचयेषु च ।
नित्ययुक्ता माहाबाहो वर्द्धन्ते सर्वतो गणाः ॥ १९ ॥
प्राज्ञान् शूरान्महोत्साहान् कर्म्मसु स्थिरपौरुषान् ।
मानयन्तः सदा युक्तान् विवर्द्धन्ते गणा नृप ॥ २० ॥
द्रव्यवन्तश्च शूराश्च शस्त्रज्ञाः शास्त्रपारगाः ।
कृच्छ्रास्वापत्सु संमूढान् गणाः सन्तारयन्ति ते ॥ २१ ॥
क्रोधो भेदो भयं दण्डः कर्षणं निग्रहो बधः ।
नयत्यरिवशं सद्यो गणान् भरतसत्तम ॥ २२ ॥
तस्मान्मानयितव्यास्ते, गणमुख्याः प्रधानतः ।
लोकयात्रा समायत्ता भूयसौ तेषु पार्थिव ॥ २३ ॥
मन्त्रगुप्तिः प्रधानेषु चारश्चामित्र-कर्षण ।
न गणाः कृत्स्नशो मन्त्रं श्रोतुमर्हन्ति भारत ॥ २४ ॥
गणमुख्यैस्तु सम्भूय कार्यं गणहितं मिथः ।
पृथग्गणस्य भिन्नस्य विततस्य ततोऽन्यथ ॥ २५ ॥
अर्थाः प्रत्यवसीदन्ति तथाऽनर्था भवन्ति च ।
तेषामन्योन्यभिन्नानां स्वशक्तिमनुतिष्ठताम् ॥ २६ ॥
निग्रहः पण्डितैः कार्य्यः क्षिप्रमेव प्रधानतः ।
कुलेषु कलहा जाताः कुलवृद्धैः रुपेक्षिताः ॥ २७ ॥
गोत्रस्य नाशं कुर्व्वन्ति गणभेदस्य कारकम् ।
अभ्यन्तरभयं रक्ष्यमसारं बाह्यतो भयम् ॥ २८ ॥
अभ्यन्तरं भयं राजन् सद्यो मूलानि कृन्तति ।
अकस्मात् क्रोधमोहाभ्यां लोभाद्वाऽपि स्वभावजात्॥२९॥
अन्योन्यं नाभिभाषन्ते तत् पराभव-लक्षणम् ।
जात्या च सदृशाः सर्व्वे कुलेन सदृशास्तथा ॥ ३० ॥

न चोद्योगेन बुध्या वा रूपद्रव्येण वा पुनः ।
भेदाच्चैव प्रदानाच्च भिन्द्यन्ते रिपुभिर्गणाः ॥ ३१ ॥
तस्मात् सङ्घातमेवाहुर्गणानां शरणं महत् ॥ ३२ ॥

TRANSLATION

(Yudhishṭhira said). "(6) I (now) desire to hear, O Leader of the Wise, of the nature of the *gaṇas*: (7) How the *gaṇas* prosper and how they avoid (the policy of) *Bheda* (disunion employed by the enemy), O Bhārata, and (why it is,) they aspire to conquer enemies, and also gain allies. (8) Disunion, it seems to me, is the root-cause of their destruction. (Again their) difficulty is, in my opinion, how to keep the resolutions of state secret on account of (their) large number. (9) I am desirous of listening to an exhaustive discourse on this subject, O Oppressor of Enemies. Tell me also, O Prince, how they might avert disintegration."

Leagues: their dangers

Bhīshma said: (10) "Greed and Jealousy, O King, are the two main provoking causes of enmity amongst the *gaṇas*, as well as amongst the *Kulas of Rājās*,[3] O Noblest of the Bhāratas. (11) One (of the *gaṇas* or *kulas*) yields to avarice, then follows jealousy, and the two entailing waste and decay lead to mutual destruction. (12) They oppress one another through spies, intrigues and military force, by employing the policy of conciliation, subsidy and division, and by applying other means of decay, waste and danger. (13) The *gaṇas* which form a confederacy are divided by those means; divided they become indifferent (to the common cause) and ultimately through fear they pass under the control of the enemy. (14) Thus, divided, the *gaṇas* would surely perish: separated, they fall an easy prey to the foe. *Gaṇas*, therefore, should always exert themselves

[3] Aristocracies like those of Patala: 'for in this community the command in war is vested in two *hereditary kings* of two different houses, while a Council of Elders ruled the whole State with paramount authority' (Diodorus); also *Artha-Śāstra*, p. 35: कुलस्य वा भवेद्राज्यं कुल-सङ्घो हि दुर्जयः ।

through the system of confederacy.[4] (15) Material prosperity is won by the prowess of the confederated army; outsiders also seek the alliance of confederate entities.

Good points in *gaṇas*

(16–17) "In good *gaṇas*, Elders-by-knowledge encourage mutual subordination; behaving with complete straight-forwardness (to one another), good *gaṇas* attain happiness all round. Good *gaṇas* prosper for they establish valid legal procedures according to the *Śāstras*, and they are fair to one another. (18) Good *gaṇas* prosper because they discipline their sons and brothers (members,[5] along with the younger generation) and always train them, and they accept (only) those who have been well trained.

(19) "*Gaṇas* prosper all-sidedly as they always attend. O thou of mighty arms, to the working of the espionage service, to the matters of policy, and to the collection of revenue to the Exchequer. (20) *Gaṇas* prosper because they always pay due honour to (their) officers who are wise, heroic, enthusiastic and persevering in the execution of their duties. (21) Wealthy, heroic, versed in the *Śāstras*,[6] and accomplished in the art of weapons, *gaṇas* help the help-less ones (= members) across miseries and calamities.

Weak points in *gaṇas* and how to avoid them

(22) "*Gaṇas* fall at once into the clutches of the enemy when driven by anger, division, absence of mutual confidence (lit. fear), military violence, tyranny, oppression and executions (amongst them). (23) Hence the Leaders-of-the-*gaṇas* are to be obeyed through the President. O King, the jurisdiction to conduct the community should be mainly vested in them. (24) O Reducer of enemies, (the department of) intelligence and the secret of the resolutions of state should remain in the hands of the Presidents. It is

---

[4] *Cf. Artha-Śāstra*, p. 376:—सङ्घाभिसंहतत्वादधृष्यान् परेषांताननुगुणान् भुञ्जीत सामदानाभ्याम् द्विगुणान् (read विगुणान्) भेददण्डाभ्याम् ।

[5] In Indian guild and caste associations even to this day, members address each other '*brother*!' which denotes equality.

[6] This is a clear reference to the learning and cultivation of thought amongst the *gaṇas*, an information which we have gathered from other sources as well.

not advisable that the whole body of the *gaṇas* should know those resolutions, O Bhārata. (25) The Leaders-of-the-*gaṇas* having assembled should adopt measures ensuring the welfare of the *Gaṇas*.

"The course is otherwise of a *Gaṇa* which remains aloof from others, has severed itself (from the confederacy), or which is (in) strained (relations with others). (26) Wealth dwindles down and misfortune follows on account of their division and on their falling back on their individual resources.

(27) "Criminal justice should be administered promptly and by men learned (in law), through the President. If disputes arise in the *Kulas* and the Elders of the *Kulas* remain indifferent, (28) they destroy the race (*gotra*) and dissolve the *Gaṇa*.

Internal danger

"The internal danger is to be guarded against, the external one is insignificant. (29) For the internal danger, O King, is destructive of the very foundations in no time. (30) When (the members of a *Gaṇa*) cease to discuss amongst them on account of uncalled-for anger, on account of foolishness, or on account of natural avarice, there is the symptom of discomfiture.

Equality in *gaṇas* and its effect

"There is universal equality by birth (in the *Gaṇas*) and also there is equality by *Kula*.[7] (31) They cannot be broken up by prowess or cleverness, nor again by temptations of beauty.[8] They can be broken up by enemies through the policy of division and subsidy only.

Confederacy recommended

(32) "The great safety of the *Gaṇas* therefore is considered to lie in (the maintenance of) a confederacy only."

---

[7] *Kula* = family of *rājās*, referred to above in verse 10, or, family as a unit, as opposed to individuals. The distinction is still maintained in our social phraseology *ghar pīchhe* and *pāgḍi pīchhe*, 'per household,' and 'per head' (lit. per turban = every male member). More likely it refers to equality amongst aristocrats, otherwise it would be illogical after the mention of the universal equality by birth.

[8] रूपद्रव्येण.

CHAPTER XV

Formation of New Republics

New Religious *Gaṇas*

Confining our attention to the period of the sixth and fifth centuries B.C., we not only find the Buddhists but also the Jains founding religious corporations in the very terms of politics. The Jaina-sūtras show individuals founding new *Gaṇas* and *Kulas* which sometimes take the name of the founder and sometimes that of the place, *e.g.*, *Godāsa Gaṇa* founded by Godāsa, the *Uttara Valissaha Gaṇa*, founded by Uttara and Valissaha conjointly, the *Uddeha Gaṇa* founded by Rohaṇa, the *Indrapūraka Kula* founded by Karmardhi.[1] Likewise we know of schisms in the Buddhist *Saṃgha*, and we know also of the formation of new *Saṃghas*. The phenomenon of new foundations is not confined to the history of our religious 'republics'. The *Māhabhārata* points out the great danger of disunion and schisms in republics. The authors of the *Mahābhārata* were probably aware of such political breaches. The two Mallas[2] and the two Madras were probably results of this propensity.

Historical instances of new republics

Apart from disruptive instances, we have instances of the formation of entirely new republics. The Kurus and the Pāñchālas who had been under monarchies according to Vedic literature[3] and the *Jātakas*, adopt republican form of government about the fifth or the fourth century B.C. As we have seen they are described as republics in the *Artha-Śāstra* of Kauṭilya. Another instance, which has been already pointed out by Prof. Rhys Davids, is the change of constitution of the Videhas.[4] They had been formerly under monarchy according to Vedic literature and the *Jātakas*. Megasthenes

---

[1] Hoernle, *Ind. Ant.*, XI. 246 ; XX. 347.

[2] The lower Mallas are called Dakshiṇa Mallas in the *Sabhā-Parvan* (Ch. XXXI. 12) which places the higher Mallas next to Kosala (XXX. 3).

[3] See Ch. XXII below.

[4] *Buddist India*, p. 26.

states that republican form of government was thrice established and thrice changed into monarchy.[5] This tradition would have been current in one of the principal seats of monarchy of the Doab where ancient chronicles had been kept.

Artificial stage

We have, though a little later in age yet certainly reflecting earlier established notions, republican coins struck either in the name of the *Gaṇa*, or of the country, and in one instance,[6] the *gaṇa* being described as the Protector (*trāta-sya*). We have thus reached the artificial country or territorial nation and abstract government. We find the Ārjunāyanas named after one man, the founder 'One of the family of Arjuna (*Ārjunāyana*)'.[7] The national or the tribal basis had thus ceased to work fairly early, a basis which every ancient republic in sister races outside India was built upon and which greatly operated in the establishment of the earliest republics in India as well, as implied by the references in the *Mahābhārata* to the Vṛishṇis and probably to the word *gotra* in Chapter 107 of the *Śānti-Parvan*.

The recognition of the system of naming a corporate association after the founder or president helps us in investigating the origins of our republics. The village corporation was named after the grāmaṇī,[8] Vedic charaṇas were named after founders, religious bodies took the names of their first organizers, and so did many of our republics.

Republican—a post-tribal period in India

As remarked above (IV. 2. 53), the constitution of the Vedic period was monarchical. Megasthenes also, as we have seen, notes the Hindu tradition current in the fourth century B.C. that after monarchy came the republican form. All these data indicate that the republican system is post-Vedic and artificial, that it is post-tribal and philosophic. Take also the names of technical constitutions: *Vairājya*, literally 'kingless (system),' *Svārājya*, 'self-ruling (system)', *Bhaujya*, 'temporary rulership (system)'. These names are not derived from tribes; it was not that the tribal names gave

[5] McCrindle, *Megasthenes*, p. 203.

[6] The Vṛishṇi Coin noticed above.

[7] See *Gp.* on Pāṇini, IV. 2. 53.

[8] See above, p. 16 *n*.

names to forms of government. The names of constitutions are artificial, philosophic. The tradition that there was first monarchy is supported by the Vedas, the tradition that monarchy was rejected and democratic forms of government set up is supported by the *Aiteraya Brāhmaṇa.*

Artificial political 'tribes,' not ethnic tribes

Again, in view of the above conclusion, take the tradition of the *Purāṇas* that Yaudheya and Madra, two cadets of a monarchical house in the Middle Country, went out to the Punjab and founded states called after their names. This Purāṇic history is in tull agreement with known facts : corpcrate institutions were named after founders. The Madras and the Yaudheyas thus were not tribes, but states and artificial 'political tribes', like the artificial, religious Śākya-putras. It was the state in these two cases which gave the name to the citizens, a name which was artificially tribal, or in modern phraseology a name which denoted Political Nationality as opposed to what we may call tribal nationality. The Kshudrakas and Mālavas, like the Madras and Yaudheyas, were political nations or states called after two personal names. We have the additional evidence of Pāṇini that martial states had men of all castes not one *gotra* or tribe. The Arājaka democracy also, according to the *Mahābhārata*, was not based on tribal but legal and communal basis. Many more of the republics had originated like the Yaudehya and Madra, Mālava and Kshudraka, under purely non-tribal conditions. The later states (Ch. XVIII) like Śālaṅkāyana, Ārjunāyana and Pushyamitra bearing personal names and names of recent origin further illustrate the practice.

Distinction between tribal and artificial organizations

At the same time it cannot be asserted, as already stated, that no tribal element is to be found in any of the Hindu republics. Basis of every state has been in all ages and in all climes, to a great degree ethnic—tribal or national. The real question is whether a state-organization is yet tribal—primitive, habitual and customary, or it is the outcome of intelligent thinking, of theories, of conscious experience and experiments. The stage when State is felt to be based on contract and the ruler is regarded to be a servant of the ruled and when political loyalty (pp. 103–104 above) is even open to strangers, is a high water-mark of constitutional development. Voting and ballot-voting, motion, resolution and legislation, legalism and formalism in procedure of deliberation, are other indicia of that stage.

Constitutions gave distinctive marks to individual political community and converted it, so to say, into artificial tribes. It, therefore, becomes very difficult to distinguish between real tribes and artificial tribes, the ethnic *gotra* and the political *gotra*. Probably the early Sātvats were originally a real tribe as the description of the Vṛshṇis and Andhakas in the *Māhabhārata* would indicate. But the 'Country of Rājanya (Elected Ruler),' Rājanya-Janapada, was evidently a political tribe, a political community, a creation of constitution. So was the 'Māharāja-Janapada'. *Janapada* in such cases becomes a political unit, probably a city-state. The Rāshṭrikas and Bhojas were, likewise, creations of constitution. The Kaṭhas, on the other hand, might have been originally a tribe, as Patañjali's[9] expression *Kaṭhajātīyāḥ* may denote. *Jāti*, however, may be a secondary character. Birth (*Jāti*) in a *gaṇa*-state was deemed to confer equality in citizenship on a free man. *Kaṭhajātīyas* and *Kaṭha-deśīyas* may thus signify only 'men born in the Kaṭha country,' 'men of the Kaṭha-country', and the Kaṭha-country and Kaṭha-state might have been called after one Kaṭha, the political founder. The other examples of Patañjali go to support this view, *viz.*, Karaka-jātīyas, Karaka-deśīyas, Sraughna-jātīyas, Sraughna-deśīyas. Sraughna and Karaka were both place-names, not tribe names. Karaka was evidently derived from a river, *e.g.*, in Pāras-kara (trans-Kara district). *Jāti*, here and in Pāṇini, VI. 3. 41, very likely means 'birth', not caste or nation. At the same time it is not incompatible with the advanced stage of constitution-making that a community which had been originally a tribal unit and still retained traces of its former organization, should adopt an advanced constitution. But to call these republics tribal organizations, or 'tribal republics' would be unscientific. Every state in ancient Rome and Greece was 'tribal' in the last analysis, but no constitutional historian would think of calling the republics of Rome and Greece mere tribal organizations.

---

[9] On *P.*, VI. 3. 42 ; Kielhorn, III, p. 157.

CHAPTER XVI

A Retrospect of the Period of Rise

Aitareya Brāhmaṇa to Kauṭilya

Thus we find Hindu republics existing and flourishing as early as the age of the *Aitereya Brāhmaṇa*. Ancient Hindus had already developed technical constitutions of various classes with special procedures of *abhisheka* for each class. They must have experimented in those systems for some centuries before the composition of the *Aitareya Brāhmaṇa*. The date of this Vedic work is to be regarded as *cir*. 1000 B.C. It knows King Janamejaya, son of Parikshit whom it mentions towards its end. The history of the *Uttara Kurus* also points to an early date of the *Brāhmaṇa*. The Uttara Kurus in later Vedic literature become a mythological people with a mythological country, while in the *Aitareya*, as we have already seen, they are a historical community. According to the *Brāhmaṇa*, the greater portion of Aryan India—North, West and South—was covered with republican constitutions. Only in the middle, in the Midland (the Madhyadeśa), monarchy prevailed. The Midland extended from the Kuru-land (the district of Delhi) up to Allahabad, the Doab between the Ganges and the Jumna.[1] Further east in the Prāchī (with its centre in or about Magadha), there was according to this *Brāhmaṇa* the constitution called *Sāmrājya* which literally means 'a combination of monarchies,' *i.e.*, a federal imperialism around one dominant member. Except the Doab and Magadha the whole country was republican. Such was nearly the case also in the time of the Buddha, as it appears from Pāli authorities. In his time states in Aryan India, according to the *Avadhāna-Śataka*, were divisible into the classes: 'those subject to *Gaṇa*-rule' or republican, and 'those subject to royal rule' or monarchical (*kechid deśā Gaṇādhīnāh, kechid Rājādhīnāh*).[2] This order, in which the republican countries are placed first, according to the well-known Sanskrit usage,

---

[1] The monarchies named there in the *Aitareya Brāhmaṇa* are the Kuru, Pāñchāla, Usinara and Vaśa.

[2] See p. 28 above.

connotes that preponderance in number rested with the republican form.

North and West and South-West were still mainly republican in the time of Alexander. Republics here, therefore, have had a career of about one thousand years at least when Chandragupta ascended the imperial throne.

This was the most flourishing period of the Hindu republics. For national prosperity the Uttara-Kurus become proverbial. For learning the Madras and the Kaṭhas, for bravery the Kshudrakas and the Mālavas, for political wisdom and valiant independence the Vṛishṇis and Andhakas, for power the Vṛijis, and for the philosophies of light and equality, for the emancipation of the low, the Śākyas and their neighbours, stamp their indelible marks on national life and national literature of Aryan India during that period.

CHAPTER XVII

Republics under the Mauryas

Policy of Maurya Imperialism towards Republics

The empire of the Mauryas included the republican areas. Greek writers say that Chandragupta won Arachosia and Aria from Seleucus.[1] Aśoka in his inscriptions tells us that Antiochus was his neighbour.[2] Antiochus held Seria and Persia. The Maurya empire thus extended up to Persia in the north-west. In the south it extended up to the Tamil country.[3] What was the fate of the republics under this gigantic monarchical system? To understand this, let us first examine the Maurya policy towards republics. Kauṭilya makes an excellent statement of that policy:—

'*Acquisition* (conquest) *of a Saṃgha*' says Kauṭilya, '*is more desirable than an alliance of goodwill or military aid. Those which are united (in a league) should be treated with the policy of subsidy and peace, for they are invincible. Those which are not united should be conquered by army and disunion.*' Then the policy of division is detailed ending with '*thus should the Monarch* (*Ekarāja*) *behave towards the Saṃghas*' etc.[4]

---

[1] See passages quoted by V. Smith, *Early History of India*, 3rd ed., pp. 149–51.

[2] Rock Series II.

[3] Proved by the site of the Miaski 'edict'. See Jayaswal, "Places and Peoples in Aśoka's Inscriptions," *I.A.*, LXII. 121; also "Proclamation of Aśoka and His Jambudvîpa", *ibid.*, p. 167.

सङ्घलाभो दण्डमित्रलाभानामुत्तमः । सङ्घाभिसंहतत्वादधृष्यान् परेषांताननुगुणान् भुञ्जीत सामदानाभ्याम् । द्विगुणान् (read विगुणान्) भेददण्डाभ्याम् । *Artha-Śūtra*, p. 376. अनुगुणान् will be opposed to विगुणान् । द्विगुण gives no satisfactory meaning. It can give the meaning 'league of two'; but they will be *Anuguṇas*. Hence I have proposed the above correction. The further use of विगुण in the same chapter, *e.g.*, at p. 379 and the total absence of द्विगुण in the discussion support my proposal. Mr. Shama Shastry's rendering of अनुगुणान् as those 'favourably disposed' is far wide off the mark. (*A.S.*, Ch. XI.) (This emendation is now confirmed by Gaṇapati Śâstrî's text, III. 144.)

[4] Details of the method of creating disunion are given in pp. 376–79 ending with सङ्घेष्वेवमेकराजो वर्त्तेत । see also 'Rājā' in कलहस्थानेषु हीनपक्षं राजा, etc., p. 379.

In other words, the Maurya policy was to allow honourable existence to those republics which were strong and united in leagues (for these were 'difficult to be conquered'). Those which were isolated were to be weakened by a policy of internal division and then reduced by force.

Evidently many of such isolated states had already come under the control of the Maurya empire when the *Artha-Śāstra* was composed. The status of the confederate republics varied according to their strength. Some of them were treated on terms of equality, while others were subsidized and probably expected to render military assistance, for 'acquisition of army' from them is a condition contemplated as against pure alliance (मित्रलाभ). The result of this policy was that the stronger republics survived the Maurya imperialism, while the weaker ones succumbed. The Kshudraka, the Mālava, and the Vṛiji states which appear in Kātyāyana and Patañjali as sovereign states and in flourishing condition,[5] lived on account of leagues, and so did the Rāshṭrikas and Bhojakas who fight jointly against Khāravela in the time of Patañjali.[6]

Republics under Aśoka

In the light of ascertained facts of the constitutional history of the time of Kauṭilya and Alexander we can now understand the inscriptions of Aśoka better on a point. We have to recognise the republican character of many of the political communities mentioned by Aśoka in his inscriptions.

In Rock series, section V, Aśoka enumerates :—

(1) the Yonas,
(2) the Kambojas,
(3) the Gandhāras,
(4) the Rāshṭrikas,
(5) the Pitinikas, and
(6) other *Āparāntas*[7] (Girnar version).

---

[5] *Mahābhāshya* on Pāṇini, IV. 2. 45 ; and on V. 3. 52.

[6] "Hāthigumphā Inscription of the Emperor Khāravela," *J.B.O.R.S.*, Vol. III, p. 455 ; revised in *E.I.*, XX. 71.

[7] See also *I.A.*, LXII. 121 ; Addendum II here below.

Against these in Rock series XIII we have :—

(1) the Yonas,
(2) the Kaṁbojas,
(3) the Nābhaka and the Nābha-paṅktis,
(4) the Bhojas,
(5) the Pitinikas,
(6) the Andhras, and
(7) the Pāradas (Pāladas).[8]

We know already that 2, 4 and 5 had non-monarchical constitutions. Now, two questions present themselves. What constitutional position do they occupy in the system of Aśoka's empire? Are these three the Kambojas, the Bhojas and the Pitinikas the only republican communities in the group?

Arāja-vishaya

The answer to the above questions is supplied by the latter inscription itself (Rock Proclamation XIII). The whole group (1–7) are predicated with the description—'*here, in the arāja-vishaya*'.[9] It means that they all were '*here*', *i.e.*, within the Maurya Empire, as opposed to Antiochus and others who were outside, *antas*, neighbours outside the frontiers of the Empire. The communities enumerated, all the same, were important enough to be noted by name, though they were within the Empire. They were, further, in the Province or administrative unit —*vishaya*—designated as *arāja* or '*non-monarchical*', *i.e.*, republican. In other words, they were important self-governing communities under the Maurya Emperor.

Āparāntas

Their location has been separately discussed in Addendum II below this chapter. The *Āparāṁtas* of Aśoka were not his 'Western neighbours' but communities within his empire (Rock Proclamation XIII). The *Rāshṭrikas*, the *Bhojas*, and the *Pitinikas* were Āparāntas, as they were in *Aparānta*, *i.e.*, Western India (see Addendum II). The Rāshṭrikas and Bhojas are almost interchangeable owing to their close unity; Rock Proclamation V has Rāshṭrikas while R.P. XIII has in its place Bhojas. The Rāshṭrikas, Bhojas and Pitinikas occupied what is called to-day

---

[8] See Addendum II below. Another spelling is *Pālidā*.

[9] इधाराजविसयम्हि । (Girnar). See Addendum II below.

Gujarat (including Cutch). The connected territory to the north had been also republican just before, in Alexander's time. The *Arāja-vishaya* thus extended from Afghanistan to Sindh and to Gujarat, and probably it had been a well-established term beginning with the reign of Chandragupta Maurya.

Andhras and Pāladas

The order of the republics as enumerated by Aśoka (Yonas to Pitinikas) is from Afghanistan to Gujarat (North-West), and then it goes out of the India proper of the Hindus, to the Oxus Province which is the region of the *Aṁdhras* (Northern Andhras) and *Pāladas* (Pāradas) (see Addendum II). The line of division is the Hindukush. The whole tract, however, seemed to be included in a Maurya administrative unit,—'the *Arāja-vishaya*'. The Purāṇic division *Bhārata-varsha* was bounded by the Oxus and the Pamirs which comprised many 'Kshatriya colonies' and Hindu population, according to the Purāṇas.[10] That population in the language of Herodotus (iii. 102), were the 'Indians settled northward of the other Indians, who resemble the Baktrians in the way they live. They are the most war-like of the Indians.' The Aṁdhras and Pālidas or Pāladas (Pāradas) who are noted in the Purāṇas to have been in that area[11] were amongst these Northern Indians.

Andhras

The Andhras of Aśoka could not be the southern Andhras. Two generations before, in the time of Chandragupta, the Andhras were a great kingdom, second in power only to Magadha.[12] It seems that the Andhra power was broken under the reign of Bindusāra, Aśoka's father, who is credited with having carried on the policy of his father, Chandragupta, of unifying India : 'between the eastern and western oceans' he is said to have annexed sixteen capitals.[13] This must point to the land of the Southern

---

[10] See "Aśoka's Jambudvîpa," *I.A.*, LXII. 169 ; *Matsya*, Ch. 113, pp. 40–43 [क्षत्रियोपनिवेश्याश्च वैश्याः शूद्रकुलानि च ॥ 42]

[11] See Addendum II below.

[12] See reference to Pliny in V. Smith's *Early History of India* (3rd edition), p. 206.

[13] Jayaswal, "The Empire of Bindusāra," *J.B.O.R.S.*, Vol. II, p. 82.

Deccan, as the area above it had already been under Chandragupta. Aśoka's inscriptions in the South prove the existence of a direct imperial government in the South.[14]

Constitution of the Nābha-paṅktis

The Gāndhāras had already separated before Alexander's time from Takshaśilā. In 326 B.C. they were monarchical. Young Porus, a nephew to the great Porus, was their king. But the question of the constitution of the Gāndhāras does not arise, although we have evidence of their being republican about 200 B.C.[15] In Section XIII of the Rock Proclamations in place of the Gāndhāras 'the *Nābhaka* and the *Nābha-paṅktis*' have been substituted. These were either neighbours of the Gāndhāras or some subdivisions thereof. The *Nābhapaṅktis* ('Nābha-lines') were like the *Agraśreṇis*, and the Three Yaudheyas or Three Śālaṇkāyanas, *i.e.*, a league of the Nābhas.[16]

Up to this time the Nābhaka has not been identified. I find the name in the *Gaṇapāṭha* on Pāṇini IV. 1. 112 as *Nabhāka*. The rule before IV. 1. 112 deals with derivatives from republican names, and, that after, from river-names. The *Gaṇapaṭha* on Pāṇini IV. 1. 112, gives an enumeration or group called 'Śiva and others' which contains names of *ṛishis* and founders of families (*e.g.*, Kakutstha, Kchaḍa, etc.), royal dynasties (*e.g.*, Haihaya), rivers (Gaṅgā, Vipāśa) and a lot of obscure proper names. Along with Piṭaka, Rikshāka, etc., are given Nābhaka and Ūrṇa-Nābha. The Ūrṇa-Nābhas appear also in the republican group of the Rājanyas, Ārjunāyanas, etc.[17] *Nābhaka* was probably a national title derived from the Nābha people. The "Nābha-lines" (*Nābha-paṅktis*[18]) which were evidently non-monarchical, were probably identical with the Ūrṇa-Nābhas, the Nābhas of the Ūrṇa, now called

---

14 The former reading *Pulindā* was a misreading for *Pālidā*.

15 The Gāndhāras instead of a king have *Mukhyas* in the *Mahābhārata*, *Udyoga-Parva*, Ch. 167. Patañjali (*P.*, IV. 2. 52) puts them along with the Vasātis and Śibis whom we know to be republican.

16 '*The Nābha-Paṁtis*,' another possible rendering, would suggest the Nābhas to belong to the Paktyes of Herodotus (see Addendum II below).

17 On Pāṇini, IV. 2. 53.

18 Compare '*śreni*' 'lines' or 'rows' and its interpretation in Ch. XXVII (Pt. II).

Ūṇa, a lofty range in eastern Swāt, recently identified with the Aornos of Alexander's campaign.[19]

The Yavanas of Aśoka

The identification of the *Yavanas* of Aśoka is necessary. It might incidentally settle a great controversy. The Yonas of Aśoka, the *arāja-vishaya* Yonas, were within the limits of the Maurya Empire. The grouping in Aśokan records is 'the Yonas and Kambojas,' while in Manu it is 'the Kambojas and Yavanas'. There is no doubt that these Yavanas were contiguous to the Kambojas.

The Kambojas are identified with the people on the Kabul river. Now, who were these Yavanas? They were the neighbours of the Kabulis. They were, therefore, on or near the Kabul river. Further, they were 'self-ruling' according to Aśoka, and according to Manu[20] they had lived along enough near the Aryan people to be regarded as occupying the position of a fallen caste though they had been a 'ruling people' (*Kshatriya-jātayaḥ*). According to the *Mahābhārata* they had ceased to be rulers and were living like Kambojas and others under Hindu kings.[21] All these descriptions refer to the same conditions. These Yavanas could not be referred to the town of Alexandria founded by Alexander in the Caucasus. That was never a self-governing unit, and the Macedonian element of invalid soldiers, who were anxious to leave the place, was too small and would have availed themselves of the death of Alexander to migrate. On the other hand we have positive evidence of the existence of a Greek community on the Kubhā or Kabul river who had been there for a long time before Alexander's invasion. It is strange that this fact has not been taken notice of. (It settles amongst other things, the vexed chronological question raised on the mention of Yavanānī in Pāṇini.)

The Kabul-Yavanas had been organised in a city-state of the Indian republican type in the time of Alexander—a fact which comes in perfect harmony with the description of Aśoka's *Arāja-vishaya*. These were probably Greeks or

---

19 See Mr. C. E. A. W. Oldham's note cited in Addendum II below.

20 With the Śakas, *i.e.*, the Śakas of Seistan. *Manu*, X. 44.

21 *Śānti-Parvan*, LXV. 13–15.

Ionians who had moved and immigrated under the suzerainty of the Persian Empire. The name of their city, Nysa, is a strong evidence of their origin. They had been Hinduised; Alexander's companions first regarded them as Indians. As stated by the Macedonian writers the Nysians claimed to have been Greek in origin; the claim was admitted. They knew Greek gods and Greek mythology and tradition.[22]

Their state was organised as an aristocracy and their President was called the *Akoubhi*. This word seems to be connected with *Kubhā*, the Vedic name for the Kabul river. It means ('the Leader) of the People by the Kubhā' (*Ā Kaubhi*). Alexander's companions were convinced of the ethnic claim of the Akoubhis and they passed ten days in Hellenic revels with them. Unless the Akoubhis had been Greek in origin they could not have been able to show such intimate familiarity with matters of Greek mythology as they did and could not have convinced the Macedonians of their claim of kinship.

From the treatment of Yavanas, the Kambojas, in *Manu* and the *Mahābhārata*, it appears that their republics soon lost their independence, and losing it they lost their social independence as well, and were absorbed into Brahmanism under a degraded caste-status—for the Hindu can visualise human organisations only in terms of caste. The result therefore was that these races were reduced into mere degraded castes living under Hindu rulers.

Republican coins of the Maurya period

Coins collected at Taxila by the late General Cunningham and published in his *Coins of Ancient India* (Pls. II and III) disclose names of some sovereign communities which struck their coins in the Early Maurya period. The *Vaṭa* (or, *Vāṭā*)-*Aśvakas*[23] were the *Aśvakas* who inhabited Eastern Afghanistan and who were included in the general term *Kaṁbojas* (see Addendum II). On their coin there is a Kābulī in long robes doing obeisance

[22] Arrian, Bk. V. Chap. I; Arrian, *Indika*, I, where Arrian without any doubt treats them as Greeks or Indo-Greeks. *Cf.* नैस्यो नाम जनपदः of Patañjali (on *P.*, IV. 1. 170).

[23] *J.B.O.R.S.*, XX. 290; correction of the foot-note in Vol. XXI. 191.

to the **Maurya** symbol, *Chandra*-on-hill (*J.R.A.S.*, 1936, 437); the inscription is in the old Sanskrit script (Brāhmī)—*V[ā]ṭāśvake*. Here *Vaṭa* probably stands for *varta* or *vārtā* (वार्ता) which reminds us of the *Vārṭāśastropajīvin* description of theirs in the *Artha-Śāstra*. Their coin (*kārshāpaṇa*) is of the old 100 ratti standard. The *Aṁta-Roh(a)takas*, that is, the *Rohatakas* or *Rohitakas of the end* (or *frontier*)[23] have also their coin with a Brāhmī inscription of the early Maurya period. They are the same as "*the Rohita-Mountaineers*" whom the Sanskrit Grammar cites as an *Āyudhajīvin Saṃgha* of the hills (Kāśikā on Pāṇini, IV. 3. 91, आयुधजीविभ्यश्च पर्वते । रोहितगिरीयाः ।). The *Roh* Rajputs survived down to Muhammadan times. The Afghans even to-day call their country *Roh*. These as well as some other subordinates whose coins have come down to us belonged to the *Arāja-vishaya* of Aśoka and his ancestors; while the Audumbaras who have on their earliest coin (*C.A.I.*, IV. 2) Maurya symbols and Dharmachakra—definitely pointing to Aśoka's suzerainty—[23], belonged to or the neighbourhood of Kangra (see Ch. XVIII).

ADDENDUM II

LOCATION OF HINDU REPUBLICS IN AŚOKA'S INSCRIPTIONS

The following extracts are given from a paper published by me in the *Indian Antiquary* (1933), Vol. LXII, pp. 121–33, entitled "Places and Peoples in Aśoka's Inscriptions," bearing on the identification and location of the republics mentioned in his proclamations.

I. *Aśoka's Pāladas, Aṁdhras, and the so-called Rāja-Viṣaya*

Rock Series Proclamations, Section XIII,[24] mention the (1) *Pāladas* and (2) *Aṁdhras* which have not been correctly identified. No definite proposal has been put forward about the *Pāladas*; and the *Aṁdhras* have been taken to be the Dakṣiṇāpatha Andhras. As I shall show below, the *Pāladas* were in Afghānistān and are well-known to Sanskrit geography as **Pāradas**, and there were their neighbours **Northern Andhras**, according to the *Purāṇas*.

[24] Hultzsch, *Inscriptions of Aśoka*, p. 211.

Pālada-Pālida

Aśoka's inscriptions have two main forms of the name of the *Pālada* community :

1. *P(ā)lada* (at Kālsī).
2. {*Pālida* (at Shāhbāzgaṛhī) ; *Pāriṁda* (at Girnār, which is only a dialectic variant of *Pālida*).

Curiously enough, the *Purāṇas* also have these two forms, as *Pārada* and *Parita.* The *Matsya* (Ch. 113, 40–43), describing the '*northern countries*' (*deśāḥ udīchyāḥ*), has :

गान्धारा यवनाश्चैव सिन्धुसौवीर-मद्रकाः ।
शका द्रुह्याः पुलिन्दाश्च पारदा हारमूर्त्तिकाः ॥ (41)[25]

The *Vāyu*, in the corresponding place (Ch. 45, *ś.* 116), gives :

गान्धारा यवनाश्चैव सिन्धुसौवीर-भ्रद्रकाः ।
शका ह्रदाः कुलिन्दाश्च परित्ता हार-पूरिकाः ॥[26]

Here *Paritā* has the hard form for the *Palidā* of Aśoka. *Pārada* is the general form in Sanskrit literature, as we shall see below. In the *Vāyu* text, भ्रद्रकाः is a mislection for मद्रकाः. On the *Pulindāḥ* (which occur in the same group in other authorities) we should recall here that Dr. Hall noted years back, in commenting on 'the Sindhu-Pulindas,' that there were northern Pulindas as well as southern Pulindas.[27] They are, I think, the modern *Povindah* clan of the Afghāns. The form *Kulinda* is also well-attested (see the citations on Khasas by Sir George Grierson in *L.S.I.*, IX, Pt. 4, pp. 3–5). It represents the *Kuṇinda* of the coins. In fact, one MS. of the *Vāyu* reads *Kuninda.*[28] Possibly at an early stage the Kunindas lived in the region of the present N.-W. Frontier Province. *Hārapūrika*, is a corruption of the well-known *Hāra-hūrika* which I would take as the Sanskrit name for Arachosia. The *Śakāḥ-Druhyāḥ* (= *Hradāḥ*, 'the lake people') of the texts evidently represents the people of Seistan-Drangiana.

---

[25] J. Vidyāsāgara's ed., Calcutta, 1876, p. 393.

[26] *Bibliotheca Indica* ed., Vol. I, p. 351.

[27] Wilson and Hall's *Vishṇu Purāṇa*, Vol. II, p. 159, notes, where he cites the *Rāmāyaṇa*, *Ki. Kāṇḍa*, XLIII.

[28] Ānandāśrama ed., p. 138, MS. ग.

Location of the Pāradas

Ptolemy's *Paryetæ* are our *Paritās-Pālidas.* Ptolemy's treatment shows that they were in Afghānistān.[29] It should be noted here that, in the previous verse, the *Vāyu* has *Aparitāḥ*[30] (= Afrīdīs), distinct from *Paritāḥ*.

Sanskrit authorities group these people along with communities most of whom are identical with those mentioned by Aśoka. They also afford data for their location. This will be better understood by comparing the following lists :—

Aśoka's inscriptions.[31]—Yona-Kaṁbojas (-Kaṁboyas); Nābhaka-Nābhapaṁtis (= Gaṁdharas of RP., V); Bhoja-Pitinikas (= Raṭhika-Pitinikas of RP., V); Aṁdhra (= Adha)-**Pāladas**.

Rāmāyaṇa (K. 43, 4–12).—Kāṁboja-Yavanas, Śakas, **Varadas** (= *Pāradas*).[32]

Manu (10, 44).—Kāṁbojas, Yavanas, Śakas, *Pāradas*, Pahnavas, Chīnas, Kirātas, Daradas, Khaśas.[33] (The

---

29 *Encyclopædia Brit.* (11th ed.), I, p. 315.

30 वाह्लीका वाटधानाश्च आभीराः कालतोयकाः ।

अपरीताश्च शूद्राश्च पह्[ह्ल]वाश्चर्मखण्डिकाः ॥ A., p. 138.

Their identification with the Afrīdīs is due to Mr. Jayachandra Vidyālaṅkāra (*J.B.O.R.S.*, XVIII, 99, 97). They are the same as the *Aparyatæ* of Darius and Herodotus (III, 91). I have heard Ghazni men pronouncing the name as '*aparīt*' and '*aparīt*'.

31 Jayaswal, *Hindu Polity* (first ed.), I, 142–45, stands modified by this paper.

32 The countries mentioned are expressly *northern* (verse 4) and in the Himālaya :

काम्बोज-यवनांश्चैव शकानां पत्तनानि च ।

अन्वीक्ष्य वरदांश्चैव हिमवन्तं विचिन्वथ ॥

In the previous verse, there are the Mlecchas, Pulindas, Śūrasenas, Prasthalas, Bhāratas, Kurus and Madrakas. These Kurus and Madras must be the Uttara-Kurus and Uttara-Madras. The former are located by Ptolemy in the Pāmirs. The Purāṇas mention the existence of 'colonies of Kshatriyas' in that region (*Matsya*, 113. 42).

33 पौण्ड्रकाश्चौड्र [चान्ध्र] – द्रविडाः काम्बोजा यवनाः शकाः ।

पारदा (:) पन्हवाश्चीनाः किराता दरदाः खशाः ॥

The *Chīnas* are the *Ṣiṇa* race of Gilgit (*L.S.I.*, IX, 4, p. 5, n. 5). The Daradas are the modern Dards; the Kirātas are the Kirantis of Nepal.

reading *Pahnava* interchanges with *Pahlava* in the MSS.)

Mahābhārata.—Śakas, Kāmbojas, Bāhlikas, Yavanas, **Pāradas**, Kuliṅgas, Taṅgaṇas.[34]

Harivaṁśa.—(Yavanas), Śakas, Tukhāras, Daradas, **Pāradas**, Taṅgaṇas, Khaśas, Pahlavas, and other 'barbarians' (Mlecchas) of the Himālaya.[35]

Here, in the *Harivaṁśa*, we have an express location in the Himālaya for the Pāradas.[36] A passage of the *Mahābhārata* (*Sabhā P.*, Ch. 52, 2–3) also locates them between Western Tibet (Mandāra) and evidently the Hindukush (Meru) range, on the river Śailodā,[37] which can only be the Kunār. I cite here the text:—

मेरुमन्दरयोर्मध्ये शैलोदामभितो नदीम् ।
ये ते कीचकवेणूनां छायां रम्यामुपासते ॥
खषा एकासनाग्र्यर्हाः प्रदरा दीर्घ-वेणवः ।
पारदाश्च कुलिन्दाश्च तङ्गणाः परतङ्गणाः ॥[38]

They dealt in 'ant-dug' gold (*cf. IA.*, 4, 225). There can be little doubt that the valley of the Kunār-Chitral river is meant here.[39] They seem to have been allied to the Aparītas, for the form Parītā is very near them.

The *Mahābhārata* (*Bhīṣma P.*) reads their corrupt variants *Aparāntāḥ* and *Parāntāḥ* together:

बाह्लीका वाटधानाश्च आभीराः कालतोयकाः ।
अपरान्ताः परान्ताश्च पह्वा [पह्नवा]श्चर्ममण्डलाः ॥

If this be compared with the *Vāyu* text quoted above, it will appear that the *Aparāntāḥ* and *Parāntāḥ* of the *Mahābhārata* stand for the *Aparītas* and *Śūdras* of the *Vāyu*.[40]

---

34 *L.S.I.*, IX, Pt. 4, p. 3. Taṅgaṇapura was near Badrināth (Gaṛhwāl), see *Ibid.*, IX, Pt. 4, p. 3, n. 6.

35 6440; *Ibid.*, IX, Pt. 4, p. 4.

36 *Ibid.*, IX, Pt. 4, p. 3.

37 Probably the origin of the classical stories of the river 'Silas'.

38 Southern text, Ch. 78, verses 78–79.

39 See below further data.

40 Wilson and Hall, *Vishṇu Purāṇa*, II. 16.

Northern Andhras

It seems certain that there was a community called Andhras in the North. The *Matsya*, in the opening verse on the enumeration of the *'northern countries,'* has *Pur Andhras* just in the place where *Aparītas* are given by the *Vāyu* :

बाह्लीका वाटधानाश्च आभीराः कालतोयकाः ।

पुरन्ध्राश्चैव शूद्राश्च पह्लवाश्चात्तखण्डिकाः ॥

The *Bhāgavata* (IX. 20, 30) includes Andhras in a list of northern peoples :—

किरात-हूणान् यवनानन्ध्रान् कङ्कान् खशान् शकान्

—Nirṇayasāgara ed. (1923), p. 414.

I am not in a position to ascertain whether any tribal name in Afghānistān at present corresponds with Andhra. It may, however, be pointed out that in the north of Afghānistān, about a hundred miles to the west of Balkh, there is the district of Andha-khui marked on the map; and according to the *Matsya* the *Pur Andhras* were in the Bālhīka group.[41]

The Aṁdhras of Aśoka seem to have been the northern Andhras, as he mentions allied and neighbouring units in pairs, *e.g.*, Yona-Kaṁboja, Bhoja-Pitinika, Raṭhika-Pitinika, Aṁdhra-Pālida. In the Hāthīgumphā inscription of Khāravela we have the Raṭhikas and Bhojakas fighting together (*E.I.*, XX, 87). Thus we may consider the Aṁdha-(Andhra-)Pālidas to have been neighbours.

These northern Andhras were self-governing (see below), while the Dakṣiṇāpatha Andhra, according to the evidence of the Aśokan inscriptions and of the Aśokan *stūpas* noticed by the Chinese pilgrims, seems to have been under the imperial government.

Location of Northern Andhras and Pāladas in Purāṇas

Fortunately we are not left merely to infer the situation of the Andhras and Pāladas from mere strings of names or from a reference to such a comprehensive term as Himavat,[42] which included the Hindukush, the Pāmīrs and Tibet. The

[41] I have ascertained since from Nazarkhan, an Afghān of Sarafza, Ghazni, that *Andherī* or *Andhrī* is a most warlike Gilzaī tribe in Afghānistān.

[42] *E.g.*, in the *Rāmāyaṇa*, *Ki.* 43. There is a distinction between our Himālaya and *Himavat*.

Purāṇas furnish data for a more definite location. There is a section in the Purāṇic geography of Bhāratavarṣa which deals with the watershed of a system of six rivers, three of which flow to the east, and three to the west. All these rivers had their sources in a lake system called *Bindu-sara*, situated in the region known as *Himavarṣa* (literally, 'the snow country').[43] The three rivers flowing westwards are the *Sītā* (spelt also *Śītā*), *Cakṣu* and *Sindhu* :—

सीता चक्षुश्च सिन्धुश्च तिस्रस्ता वै प्रतीच्यगा (:) ।

(See *Matsya*, ch. 120, 40 ; *Vāyu*, i. 47, 39 ; *Rāmāyaṇa*, *Bāla K.*, 43, 11–14.)

The countries by the side of each of these rivers are given in detail (*Matsya*, verses 40–49 ; *Brahmāṇḍa*, ii. 18, 41–49).[44] The *Sindhu* is undoubtedly the Indus. The *Cakṣu* is the Oxus, the *Fo-tsu* of Yuan Chwang.[45] It should be noted that the Chinese pilgrim describes the Oxus region and the countries lying between it and the Indus (on the Indian frontier) in Hindu terms, which tally with Hindu geography. The Bhāratavarṣa of the Purānas extended up to the southern bank of the Oxus, and was larger than the present-day India in that direction.

The name *Cakṣu* ('eye') is a sanskritisation of the original name of the Oxus, *viz.*, *Aksu*, which had been understood as *akṣu* (= Skt. *akṣi*, 'eye'). In Sanskrit literature we come across its other form, *Vakṣu* (also *Vaṅkṣu*), which is the origin of the Mongolian *Bakṣu*, Tibetan *Pakṣu*, and Chinese *Fo-tsu* or *Po-tsu* and is preserved in *Vakshan* (modern Wakhān). Its neighbour, mentioned several times by Yuan Chwang, is spelt both as *Śīta* and *Śīta* ('cold'). There is no room for doubting the identity of *Cakṣu* with *Aksu*, *i.e.*, the Oxus, supported, as this is, by the alternative and real form, *Vakṣu*. The countries on the *Cakṣu*, as named in the *Purāṇas* are :

---

[43] *Varṣa* is, literally, a tract of country subject to its own system of rainfall, *i.e.*, having a distinctive climate. The Purāṇas, however, base these divisions on culture, that is, on individual, characteristic civilisation.

[44] The *Brahmāṇḍa* text has become more corrupt.

[45] *Life*, p. 196 ; Beal's *Si-yu-ki*, ii, 289.

(1) Chīna-maru (*Vāyu*), Vīra-maru (*Matsya*); (2) Kālika[46] (*Vāyu*), Naṅgaṇa (*Matsya*); (3) Sarva-mūlika[47] (*Vāyu*), Śūlika (*Matsya*); (4) Tuṣāra (Tukhāra)-*cum*-Andhra (*Vāyu*), Tuṣāra (*Matsya*); (5) Tampāka[48] (*Vāyu*), Barbara-Aṅga (*Matsya*); (6) Balhava (*Brahmāṇḍa*), Pahnava (*Vāyu*), Yagṛhna (*Matsya*); (7) Pārada (*Matsya*), Pāraṭa (*Brahmāṇḍa*), Darada (*Vāyu*); (8) Śaka (*Vāyu*, *Matsya*); Khaśa (*Brahmāṇḍa*).[49]

Now, avoiding the question of the identification of each of these items, which is outside the scope of this paper, we are on firm ground in regard to Tuṣāra, which is a well-known spelling for Tukhāra (like Ṣasa for Khaśa). Tukhāra is sufficiently described by Yuan Chwang,[50] who visited all parts of the area that was included in ancient Tukhāra, *i.e.*, the districts of the present Afghānistān that go by the names of Tokhāristān and Badakhshān. The Tukhāra country does adjoin the Oxus, and does extend to the valley of the Chitral river, the country of the ancient Daradas and Chīnas (= Ṣīnas), on the east, and marches on the west with Balkh, which it once included within its limits. The Purāṇic description

---

46 *Tāla* in the *Brahmāṇḍa*.

47 *Masa-mūlika* in the *Brahmāṇḍa*.

48 *Lamyāka* in the *Brahmāṇḍa*.

49 The texts of the *Matsya* (*c.* 250 A.D.) and *Vāyu* (*c.* 350 A.D.) are given below :—

M. 120 :

अथ वीरमरूंश्चैव कालिकांश्चैव शूलिकान् ।
तुषारान् बर्बरानङ्गान् यगृह्वा[न्] पारदान् शकान् । 45
(बर्वराकारान् पह्लवान् पारदान् शकान्—*Ānand. ed.*)
एतान् जनपदांश्चक्षुः प्लावयित्वोदधिङ्गता । 46

V. i. 47 :

अथ चीनमरूंश्चैव नङ्गणान् सर्वमूलिकान् ।
सान्ध्रांस्तुषारांस्तंपाकान् पह्लवान् दरदान् शकान् ॥
एतान् जनपदान् चक्षुः प्लावयन्ती गतोदधिम् । 44

Cf. Br., II. 18 :

अथ चीनमरूंश्चैव तालांश्च मसमूलिकान् ।
भद्रांस्तुषारॉंल्लम्याकान् बाह्लवान पारटान् खशान् । 46
एतान् जनपदांश्चक्षुः प्लावयन्ती गतोदधिम् ॥ 47

50 *Life*, pp. 195–96.

would place Pārada (the Pālada of Aśoka) between Balhava (Balkh) and Darada and Khaśa (Dardistān), that is to say, the Pāradas would be located in what is now Badakhshān.[51] The Andhras were next to Tukhāra. They too were by the Oxus. In the time of Aśoka there were no Tokhāris there, and probably the Andhras and the Pāradas were neighbours, the two peoples occupying the area between And-khui (Afghān-Turkistān) and the frontier of Chitral. It seems that the Pāradas became insignificant in the early Gupta period, when the *Vāyu* was written in its present form, as it gives their neighbours, the Daradas, in their place, contrary to the *Matsya*, which was closed in the Kushāṇ-Andhra period (*c.* 250 A.D.). The neighbours of the Pāradas, called *Ambaṣṭhas* by Varāhamihira (अम्बष्ठ-पारता: XVI, 22), were not the *Ambaṣṭhas* of India proper, but the people whom Ptolemy (xviii, 3) calls Ambantai and places in the Paropanisadai, to the north of the Parietai (see his map in McCrindle, p. 8). Ptolemy gives the other Ambastai separately.

For our period, Manu is a good guide; and Manu's Code gives exactly the same situation as the *Matsya*, *viz.*,

Pāradas—Palhavas—Chīnas—Kirātas—Daradas—Khaśas (X, 44).

This means that in the time of the Code (*c.* 150 B.C.) the Pāradas and Palhavas extended up to the Chīnas (Ṣiṇas) and Daradas (Dards). Here **Palhava** seems to me to be a form of **Valhava** (Balkh), *v* changing to *p*, a change well known in Prakrit and in the area concerned. This *Palhava* of Manu has nothing to do with Parthia.

Evidence of Aśoka's Rule on the Oxus

Yuan Chwang includes the countries by the upper Oxus as well as the Pāmīrs in Jambudvīpa, just as the Purāṇas include them in Bhārata-varṣa. When Aśoka mentioned Jambu-dvīpa, he probably referred to a division greater than Bhārata-varṣa. The then All-India, *i.e.*, the India up to the Oxus

[51] We should, however, note that Yuan Chwang's Varadasthāna was probably somewhat farther south (see *Si-yu-ki*, ii. 285). *Varada-sthāna* would mean 'the land of the Varadas,' the form *Varada* being a softer development of *Pārada*. The form is met with as early as in the *Rāmāyaṇa*.

(his empire) was included in it : it was something like Asia.[52] That Aśoka ruled up to the Oxus is proved by his *stūpa* which Yuan Chwang saw in the Antarāpa, or Andarāb, country: "There is one *stūpa* built by Aśoka-rāja" (*Life*, p. 195).

Purāṇic Enumeration of Oxus Countries

The name *Vīra-maru* (*Matsya*) was changed into *Chīna-maru* (*Vāyu*) owing to Chinese political influence reaching up to Persia in the first century B.C., embracing the 'desert country' (Russian Turkistān). By this *maru* (*Chīna* or *Vīra*) were meant the waste lands of Turkistān commencing above And-khui on the Oxus. This is also suggested by Varāha-mihira's record :

Palhava-Śveta-Hūṇa (White Huns)—*Chola* (*i.e.*, northern[53]) —*Avagāṇa* (= *Apagāṇa* = *Afghān*)—*Maru*—*Chīna* (XVI, 38).

This *maru* was in Zend called *mouru*, which survives in the name Merv. The Purāṇic enumeration seems to run from west to east. Taking the tract between the Oxus and the Paropamisus-Hindukush, the Purāṇic names may be equated with the modern names thus :—

Desert	corresponding	to	Maru (China)
Kerki	,,	,,	Kālika ?
And(h)-khui	,,	,,	Andhras
Balkh	,,	,,	Valhava
Badakhshān	,,	,,	Pārada
Shighnān-Wakhān	,,	,,	Śaka
Pāmīrs	,,	,,	Khaśa

In the time of Aśoka, the districts of northern Afghānistān now known as And-khui, Mazār-i-Sharīf and Khulm seem

[52] Otherwise it would be identical with Bhāratavarṣa ; but it seems that a term was designedly adopted to indicate a wider area. In Hindu geography Jambūdvīpa is made up of several *varṣas*, including Bhāratavarṣa. I shall show in my note on the Āparāntas of Aśoka that he employed technical terms of Hindu geography. The wider significance of the name Jambūdvīpa dates from a time anterior to Aśoka, and the name is to be found used in that wider sense in the Buddhist canon as well as in the Epics. See "Proclamation of Aśoka as a Buddhist and his Jambūdvīpa," *I.A.*, LXII. 167–71.

[53] *Cf. Ency. Brit.* (11th ed.), XIII, 330.

to have been under the Andhras, and Badakhshān under the Pāradas.

Varada

The correct form of the name of the country is *Parada* (*Varada*), and of that of the people, Pārada, as Valhava would be the place name, and Vālhaveya and (Vālhīka) the name of the people. The present-day *Bāradzai*, a Durrānī tribe, allied to the *Yusuf-zai*, seems to be their representative.

The *a-Rāja-Viṣaya* of Aśoka

There has been a misreading and misappreciation of a term in Rock Series XIII. In connection with these self-governing communities, the emperor, after noting the success of his measures in the kingdoms of his foreign neighbours, outside his empire, records his success with regard to certain communities, 'here', *i.e.*, within his empire. To take the translation of Hultzsch :—

"And this (*dhaṁma-vijaya*, *i.e.*, 'conquest by morality') has been won repeatedly by Devānāṁpriya both (here) and among all his borderers, even as far as....where the Yōna king named Antiyoga..........

"Likewise here in the king's territory among the Yōnas and Kambōjas...."[54]

'*In the king's territory*' is a translation of *rāja-visayamhi* (Girnār). [The second member of the phrase had been misread by Bühler as *viśavaji* (Kālsī). I have compared the letters of the edition, and satisfied myself that Hultzsch's reading is correct. What Bühler read as *ji* is really *ṣi*; and it has to be read along with *viśava* as *viśavaṣi* (= Skt. *viṣaye*), corresponding with the Girnār *visayamhi*.]

But the grouping of the two words *hidā* and *lāja-(viśavaṣi)* is wrong. It should be *hidālājaviśavaṣi* (हिदालाजविशवषि), that is to say, it is '*hidā-*', or '*hida-*' [= *iha*], a-rāja-viṣaye (*i.e.*, 'here, in the non-monarchical tract'). The Girnār version has also *hidā*, not *hida* (see plate, p. 26).[55] At Kālsī we have both the forms, *hidā* and *hida*, but Girnār has only *hida* (for Skt. *iha*). It is thus clear that *hidārāja* (*hida a-rāja*, *hidā*

[54] *Inscriptions of Aśoka*, 1925, p. 48.

[55] The point has been missed by Hultzsch owing to the vowel sign not being prominent.

arāja) is engraved. This sort of *sandhi* is well known in Aśoka's inscriptions (*cf.* Hultzsch, pp. lviii, lxxiii).[56]

[In the term *a-rāja viṣaya*, *viṣaya* probably has a technical meaning. It was a part of the empire, a province or a governorship, an administrative unit, like the *viṣaya* of Antaravedī of the Guptas. There was probably a province of these republics, a separate imperial administrative unit, a protectorate province, like the Central Indian Agency of our day.]

II. *Āparāṁta, not Aparāṁta, and Aśokā's Āparāṁtas*

There is misapprehension with regard to another word. In Rock Series V, the text has been taken as *aparāṁtā*, and as meaning 'western neighbours', taking the word as made up of *apara* + *aṁta*. It might also be analysed as *a-para* + *aṁta*, *i.e.*, the 'home' or 'inside' neighbours; or possibly as *avara* + *aṁta*, the 'inferior' neighbours. But these interpretations must be given up as inadmissible, for the reading is *Āparāṁtā* (at Girnār, *Āparātā*; at Dhaulī, *Āpalaṁtā*), *i.e.*, 'the peoples belonging to Aparānta." The *Apalaṁta* of Kālsī is therefore to be taken as used just like the *Aparāntāḥ* of the Purāṇas. *Aparānta* is a term used by Hindu geographers: it means the division of India called 'Western India'. This Western India is thus described about 250 A.D. (*Matsya Purāṇa*, 113, 49–51):

कुलीयाश्च सिरालाश्च रूपसास्तापसैः सह ।
तथा तैत्तिरिकाश्चैव सर्वे [पा][57] रस्करास्तथा ॥
[ना][58] सिकाश्चैव ये चान्ये ये चैवान्तर-नर्म्मदाः ।
भारुकच्छाः स-माहेयाः सह सारस्वतैस्तथा ॥
काच्छीकाश्चैव सौराष्ट्रा आनर्त्ता अर्बुदैः सह ।
इत्येते अपरान्तास्तु

Cf. Brahmāṇḍa, ii, xvi, p. 27 (Veṅk. ed., verses 51–62).

× × × × × × × अपरांतान्[59] निबोधत ।

---

[56] Hultzsch translates as "western borderers," *Inscriptions of Aśoka*, 1925, p. 10. I had previously suggested this rendering (*Hindu Polity*, 1924, i. 43); but this is not maintainable, as we shall presently see.

[57] कां, corrected from the *Vāyu* text.

[58] कां, corrected from the *Vāyu* text.

[59] अपरांस्तान् in the printed text is an obvious misreading.

सूर्य्यारकाः कलिवना दुर्गला × कुन्तलैः सह ।
पौलेयाश्च किराताश्च रूपकांस्तापकैः सह ॥ 60 ॥
तथा करीतवश्चैव सर्वे चैव करंधराः ।
नासिकाश्चैव ये चान्ये ये चैवान्तर–नर्मदा ॥ 61 ॥
सह-कच्छाः स-माहेयाः सह सारस्वतैरपि ।
कच्छीयाश्च सुराष्ट्राश्च आनर्त्ताश्चार्बुदैः सह ॥ 62 ॥
इत्येते अपरान्ताश्च......

Cf. Vāyu, 45, 128–131.

............अपरांस्तान्निबोधत ।
सूर्पकाराः कोलवना दुर्गाः कालीतकैः सह ॥
पुलेयाश्च सुरालाश्च रूपसास्तापसैः सह ।
तथा तुरसिताश्चैव सर्वे चैव परक्षराः ॥
नासिक्याद्याश्च ये चान्ये ये चैवान्तरनर्मदाः ॥
भारु[60] कच्छाः समाहेयाः सहसा शाश्वतैरपि ।
कच्छीयाश्च सुराष्ट्राश्च अनर्त्ताश्चार्बुदैः सह ॥
इत्येते सम्परीताश्च [= अपरांताश्च][61]

The extra line in the *Vāyu* gives a definite datum in सूर्पारका (miscopied as सूर्पाकाराः), *i.e.*, from Śūrpāraka, the modern Sopārā, which is described as the capital of Aparāntā in *E.I.*, XI. The name probably owed its origin to Śūrpāraka having been the port for sailing to Assyria (*Śūra*). कच्छीयाः are the modern Kacchīs, the Gujarātī-speaking people living in Cutch (Kacch) *Samāheyāḥ* I have subdivided as *sa-Māheyāḥ*, 'with the people of the Māhi valley'. *Sārasvata* refers to the river Sarasvatī, still bearing its old name. It is to the west of the Māhi. *Cf*. Varāhamihira:

आनर्तार्बुद-पुष्कर-सौराष्ट्राभीर-शूद्र-रैवतकाः ।
नष्टा यस्मिन्देशे सरस्वती पश्चिमो देशः । (31)

According to the above text, Aparānta, lit., 'the western end,' extended from Nāsik to the Raṇ of Kacch, including the area now called Thar Pārkar on the northern edge of the Raṇ. It is for the most part identical with the Gujarāt country, with

---

[60] Ānandāśrama text: भारुं.

[61] सम्परिता is a misreading for the अपरांता of the *Matsya*.

probably a later extension beyond the Tāptī river (*Tāpakaiḥ saha*).[62]

Now, who were Aśoka's *Āparāṁtā*? The inscriptions are not very helpful here; in fact they are positively confusing, as will be seen from the extracts quoted below:—

Girnār—*Yoṇa-Kāṁboja-Gaṁdhārānaṁ* (1) *Ristika* (incorrect for *Rāṣṭika*)-*P(e)teṇikānaṁ ye vā pi aṁñe Āparātā* (2).

Mānsehrā—Practically the same as above, except that it reads *Raṭhika-Pitinikana*.

Kālsī—*Yona-Kaṁboja-Gaṁdhālānaṁ e vā pi aṁne Apalaṁtā*.

Shāhbāzgaṛhī—*Yona-Kaṁboya-Gaṁdharanaṁ Raṭhikanaṁ Pitinikanaṁ ye va pi Aparaṁtā*.

Dhaulī—*Yona-Kaṁbocha-Gaṁdhalesu Laṭhika-Pitenikesu e vā pi aṁne Āpalaṁtā*.

It will be noticed that Girnār, Mānsehrā and Dhauli would describe at least the second group (Rāṣṭrika-Pitinika) as Āparāntas, and would seem to indicate that there were other Āparāntas among whom Aśoka carried on his propaganda of positivism. Shāhbāzgaṛhī, on the other hand, would indicate both groups as non-Āparānta, while Kālsī knows only the first group, and will make them Āparaṁtas! The first group, we know from the *Rāmāyaṇa* downwards, to be *udīcyāḥ* (Northerners), and never Westerners. We have to regard Kālsī as defective, in omitting by mistake the mention of *Rāṣṭrika-Pitinikānam*. Similarly the Shāhbāzgaṛhī text is to be considered defective as omitting by mistake *añe* (other) before *Aparaṁta*. The mistake at Shāhbāzgaṛhī shows that in Gandhāra (Province) the engraver or writer on the rock did not know that Raṭhikas and Pitinikas were Āparaṁtās or that they were neighbours, for he makes them separate and does not group them. The mistake also shows that Yona-Kaṁboja-Gandhāra, which the writer knew well, were not

---

[62] Jayamaṅgala, commentator of the *Vātsyāyana Kāmasūtra*, similarly describes Āparānta as bordering on the Western Sea (पश्चिम-समुद्र-समीपेऽपरान्तदेशः) and (next to it) Lāṭa, 'which lies to the west of Western Mālava,' *i.e.*, the Ujjayanī country (अपरमालव-पश्चिमेन लाटविषयः).

Āparaṁtas. The writer at Kālsī, who does not use the form Āparaṁta but has Āpalaṁta, missed or omitted the real Āparāṅtas and employed the non-technical *apalaṁtā*, and writing as he was in the upper Siwāliks, he might correctly call the Peshāwarīs and Kābulīs 'the Westerners'. The true text is at Girnār, Mānsehrā and Dauli, according to which, read in the light of Shāhbāzgaṛhī, the peoples to whom *Āparāṁtā* applied were the *Raṭhika* (*Rāṣṭrika*)-*Pitinikas* (*Petenikas*).

Having Pitinikas as one of the Āparāṅta administrative units, we can safely infer that the next neighbours, the Bhojas (*Bhoja-Pitinika*, Rock XIII), were included in the 'other Āparāṅtas'. We have thus three communities who were Āparāntas :

Bhojas

Rāṣṭrikas

Pitinikas

The Rāṣṭrikas were the connecting link between the two, and must have been in a position from which they could link the Pitinikas and the Bhojas with themselves. Thus, if we can fix the localities of the other two, we can guess the position of the Pitinikas almost to a certainty.

For a period of less than a hundred years after Aśoka, we have the evidence of Khāravela (*E.I.*, XX. 79) that "all the Raṭhikas and Bhojakas" fought against him together. This shows that there was more than one Raṭhika republican chief and probably more than one Bhojaka republican chief, and that the two were distinct, though closely allied. They were probably, therefore, close neighbours : Bhoja-Rāṣṭrika-Pitinika made really one group.

Location of Rāṣṭrika, Pitinika and Bhoja States

According to a passage of the *Mahābhārata* one had to cross the Chambal to reach the Bhoja State and Nava-Rāṣṭras or Nine Rāṣṭras.[63] According to another passage, the Bhojas were between Karūṣa and Sindh (Sindhu-Pulindakas).[64] The Bhojas were allied to Kṛiṣṇa's kinsmen, the Andhaka-Vṛiṣṇis, and migrated with them to Western India from Śūrasena. They must have settled near them, that is near

[63] *Sabhā-Parvan*, Ch. 31 (1–7).

[64] *Bhīṣma-Parvan*, cited by Wilson and Hall; *V.P.*, ii, 158 (Ch. IX, 38–40).

Kāṭhiāwāṛ. The position suggested by the *Mahābhārata*[65] is below Sindh and to the west of the Mālavas, with whom are associated the Karūṣas (मालवाश्च करूषाश्च, *Matsya*, 113. 52). By crossing the Chambal one came into the Mālava country. The locality thus suggested is between Sindh and Mālava. The limit of the Mālavas in Western India was Mount Abu, Arbuda (*Arbuda-Mālavāḥ*), *i.e.*, the Aravali range. Leaving the Bhojas here, let us see if we can be more definite about the Rāṣṭrikas or Lāṭhikas.

Our best guide here is Ptolemy. He places Larikē between the mouth of the Māhi river and the peninsula of Kāṭhiāwāṛ (McCrindle, p. 38) and extends its dominions from the mouth of the Narmadā (Barygaza) to the east of Indo-Skythia or Sindh (McCrindle, p. 152). Ptolemy's *Poulindai*, whom Yule places to the NE. of the Raṇ of Kacch (McCrindle, p. 157), are the *Sindhu-Pulindas* of the Sanskrit texts. *Lārika* is an exact rendering of *Rāṣṭrika* in its Prakrit form.

We have thus on the authority of Ptolemy (c. 150 A.D.) Larikē extending from Bharoach to the Gulf of Kacch, *i.e.*, the modern Gujarāt (west of Western Mālwā). Larikē seems to have extended up to the river Sarasvatī—noted by Varāhamihira as the limit of Western India (नष्टा यस्मिन्देशे सरस्वती पश्चिमो देशः)—which rises from the Aravali hills and falls into the Gulf of Kacch. Ptolemy's limits of Larikē coincide with those of Lāṭa-deśa of Sanskrit writers (*Apara-Mālava-paścimena Lāṭa-deśa*). The names Lāṭhī, a State in Kāṭhiāwāṛ, and Rāṭhī, a caste name among Mārwāṛī (Mālav-wār) Vaiśyas preserve the ancient Rāṭhika.

The Pitinikas, for the reasons indicated above, should have lived somewhere between the lower courses of the Māhī and Sarasvatī rivers. Now, about 40 miles to the south-by-east of Ahmadabad lies the modern town of Petlād, in what is now part of the Baroda State. The old name of this place was Petila (see *A.S.R.W.C.*, 1920, pp. 47, 60). *Petila* = *Petina*. I think there can be little doubt that in this name we have a survival of the ancient Pitinika, Petinika, Petenika (omitting the suffix), and that it suits the location otherwise suggested.[65]

---

[65] For a *Pettaṇi* from Gujarāt in the seventh century see Moraes, *Kadambakula*, p. 65.

The Bhojas, who, according to the *Mahābhārata*, *Bhīṣma-P.* list, should have resided below the Raṇ of Kacch, must have occupied Kacch. The Rāṣṭrikas, in the middle, extended up to the frontiers of the Pitinikas and the Bhojas. The *Bhojakas*, a caste, are to-day mostly found in Cutch and Kāṭhiāwāṛ.[66]

Mahā-Rāṣṭra in Dakṣiṇāpatha

The Mahā-Rāṣṭras were, according to the Purāṇas, in the Dakṣiṇāpatha (*Vāyu*). They were thus not an Āparānta people. The Rāṣṭrikas should not, therefore, be identified with them. It is probable that some of the Raṭhikas and Bhojas moved down to the other side of the Satpura hills, and settled there. But their chief home, especially in Aśoka's time, was to the north of the Narmadā, in Gujarāt proper, from Kāṭhiāwāṛ to Kacch.

Rāṣṭrikas and 'Abiria'

In the time of the Periplus (*c*. 80 A.D.) the very area called by Ptolemy 'Larikē' was called 'Abiria'. It seems that the Ābhīras of Gujarāt were the Rāṣṭrikas of Aśoka and the Yādavas of the *Mahābhārata*. Again and again in that area we find republicans. In the time of the *Mahābhārata* there are Andhaka-Vṛṣṇis and Bhojas (Yādavas); in the time of Aśoka we have the Rāṣṭrikas and Bhojas; in the time of Khāravela we have the Raṭhikas and Bhojakas; in the time of Samudra Gupta we have the Ābhīras, while a contemporary Purāṇic

---

[66] Enthoven, in his *Tribes and Castes of Bombay* (I, 229) writes: "Bhojaks, also known as Magas, are found in considerable numbers in Kāthiāwār and Cutch. They were originally Shrīmāli Brāhmans who adopted the Jain faith for a living."

Rai Bahadur Hiralal, in a letter to me, notes their absence in the Central India States. In Rājpūtānā their number in 1931 was 2,754. In 1901 they were all returned from Mewāṛ, which is not far from Cutch. These facts point to Cutch being their original home.

I have ascertained at Konch, near Tekārī in the Gayā district, that Śākaldvīpī Brāhmaṇs are also called *Bhojakas*. In the Deobaraṇārk inscription of Jīvita Gupta II, *Bhojakas* appear as priests of the sun-god. The Śākal-dvīpa, or Śākadvīpa, from which they came to Bihar was evidently Indo-Scythia, which comprised Cutch and Sindh. In the time of Aśoka the Bhojakas, who survived till Khāravela's time as a political community, must be regarded as connected with the ancient Bhojas.

text designates the Saurāṣṭras and Āvantyas—'Ābhīras'[67] in the time of Kumāra Gupta I and Skanda Gupta we have the Puṣyamitras there. These were all one and the same or allied people, with different names at different times.

Rāṣṭrika-Bhojas

The treatment of these two in Aśoka's inscriptions shows that to some extent the Bhojas were identical with the Rāṣṭrikas, for in Rock P. V and Rock P. XIII they interchange like the Nābhakas and Gāndhāras. It seems that the Bhojas were amongst the Rāṣṭrikas, as the Nābhas were amongst the Gāndhāras.

III. *Aśoka's Republicans*

Pāradas and (Northern) Andhras are not in the list of *Saṃghas* (republics) of the *Artha-Śāstra*. But they are included in Aśoka's *a-rāja viṣaya* list which has the Kaṁbojas which is common to both.

The Sourāṣṭras, who had been a republic (*saṃgha*) at the time of Kauṭilya's *Artha-Śāstra*, soon ceased to be so in the very time of Chandragupta, who had a governor in Surāṣṭra (modern Soraṭh). Their political status was changed. Hence we do not find them in Aśoka's republican list. Kāmbhoja, which had been a republic in early Maurya times, was still so in Aśoka's time, but the Kṣatriya-Śreṇī ceased to be so. The enumeration in the *Artha-Śāstra* is followed in essence by Aśoka the *Artha-Śāstra's* list being:

> '*Kāṁbhoja—Surāṣṭra—Kṣatriya—Śreṇi* and others' (*Kauṭilya*, Bk. X.)

The Kāmbhoja of Kauṭilya probably included the Yavanas and the Nābhas, and his Surāṣṭra probably included the Rāṣṭrikas.

The second list of Kauṭilya is :—

(*a*) Licchavika—Vṛijika—Mallaka (Eastern India),

(*b*) Madraka — Kukura — Kuru — Pāñchāla and others (Eastern Panjāb to Madhyadeśa) who lost their political status by the time of Aśoka, though the Madrakas reappear in the succeeding centuries and continue up to 350 A.D. (*i.e.*, the time of Samudra Gupta) as republican.

---

[67] *Bhāgavata* (*cf.* Vishṇu) in Pargiter's *PT.*, p. 54; *J.B.O.R.S.*, XIX, 149–150.

The republics with political powers and full autonomy in the time of Aśoka are a limited list (Rock P. XIII): (*i*) the Yavanas, the Kāmbojas, the Nābhas and Nābha-Paṁtis, the Bhojas and the Rāṣṭrika-Pitinikas, and (*ii*) the Andhras (on the Oxus), with the Pāradas.

(The latter are found under a king, *Pāradān shāh,* in 293–294 A.D. (*Paikuli Inscription*, pp. 117–119, Berlin, 1924).

Aśoka's division

Aśoka's line of demarcation is Meru (Hindukush) with Nisadha (Paropa-Niṣad). Those to the south of the Meru-Niṣadha frontier are the above (*i*), and those to the north of them, in Himavarṣa (Imaus), are the (*ii*).[68] The territory commencing from the Hindukush is counted by Aśoka in his India, which was something like Bhāratavarṣa. The Greek writers have preserved the tradition that some reckoned India from the Hindukush, and some from the Indus or the Kōphen. The latter was what the Purāṇas call Kumārīdvīpa. Aśoka's Oxus Province was in his Jambudvīpa, which had been a well-established term before his time, as the Pāli canon shows. The Oxus Province we find included by the Purāṇas in Bhāratavarṣa and Jambūdvīpa —on the other side of the Jambū river. It seems that the Jambū river[69] and Meru (Hindukush) constituted the limits of Maurya India, otherwise Aśoka would have started his *arāja-viṣaya* enumeration with the Andhra-Pāladas. Up to the Hindukush we find an acutal Hindu population : Śaśi-gupta was a ruler there in the time of Alexander. Aśoka's dividing line has a geographical meaning, which is explained by the Greek authors writing on the limits of India, and the Hindu divisions of Bhāratavarsa and Himavarṣa.

Kaṁboja (Girnār, Kālsī and Mānsehrā, V and XIII), with its variants, *Kaṁboya* (Shāhbāzgaṛhī, V, XIII) and *Kaṁboca*

---

[68] It is definitely clear that the Hindus named the two ranges, and it was their nomenclature which the Greeks found in use. In the Purāṇic geography Meru and Niṣadha are adjoining, and between them the Jambū river flows (*Vāyu*). Their Jambū-tree was probably the blue plum, which is associated in India with Turkistān ('*ālū Bokhārā*,' 'the round fruit from Bokhārā') and which in shape appears like the *jāmun* fruit of India proper.

[69] Probably *Panjshīr*. See "Jambūdvīpa of Aśoka," *I.A.*, LXII. 168–69.

(Dhaulī, V), is the Kāmbhoja of the *Artha-Śāstra* (Bk. XI, c. 135). The regular form, however, in Sanskrit literature, from Yāska and the *Rāmāyaṇa* down to mediæval inscriptions, is Kaṁboja (country) and Kāṁboja (people).[70] The form Kaṁboya suggests that in Aśoka's time the name was pronounced thus in the country itself. From this, 'Kaṁboh,' the name of a numerous Hindu caste found in the Panjāb,[71] is derived. Their tradition is that they came from Gajni (*i.e.*, Ghazni), 'near Kambay'.[72]

Kābul seems to be connected with the ancient Kaṁboja. The capital of the latter, according to the Buddhist *sūtras*, was Dvārakā.[73]

The Kaṁbojas were between the Yavanas (Yonas of Aśoka) and the Gāndhāras. These **Yavanas** were pre-Alexander Yavanas, who are noted in the same position in the *Rāmāyaṇa* (*Kiṣkindhā*, 43, 11—*Kaṁboja-yavanānś caiva*) and in the Pāli canon (*Yona-Kaṁbojesu*).[74] These Yavana-Kaṁbojas of the Pāli texts had no Brāhmaṇas according to the Pāli canon and Aśoka (Rock P. XIII) : they had only free men and slaves, which is an accurate description of a Greek community. The Pāli form, Yona-Kaṁboja, here evidently refers to the Yonas who were in the Kaṁboja country and had become a part of it and were regarded more as Kaṁbojas than Yonas. In 1919 I had pointed out[75] that these were pre-Alexander Yavanas, the Yavanas of Pāṇini and Manu, for Manu treats them as a Hindu tribe; and I identified them with the community at Nysa, below the Hindukush (Meru), with their president Akoubi (Ā-Kaubhī). The latter official presided over the people who dwelt between the Hindukush and the Kubhā

---

[70] *Cf.* Wilson and Hall, *Vishṇu Purāṇa*, references in Index.

[71] Rose, *Glossary of Tribes and Castes of the Punjab and North-Western Frontier Province*, ii, 442 ff.

[72] *Ibid.*, p. 444.

[73] Rhys Davids, *Buddhist India*, pp. 23–28.

[74] *Majjhima*, ii. 149 (pointed out by Mr. C. D. Chatterji). These Yonas-Kaṁbojas had only two *varṇas* (castes), *viz.*, *ārya* (free men) and *dāsa* (slaves) ; and one could change to the other.

[75] While delivering my *Tagore Law Lectures* before the Calcutta University. See *Tagore Lectures*, 1919, p. 83 ; see pp. 124–25 above.

(Kābul) river, *i.e.*, to the north of that river. They claimed kinship with Alexander's Greeks, which was acknowledged. Patañjali notes their *janapada* : *Naiśyo nāma janapadaḥ* (*M.*, IV. 1. 4 on *P.*, 4. 1. 170).

Yona-Kaṁboja-Gaṁdhāras of Aśoka

From Arrian we get some light on the identification of Yona-Kaṁboja-Gaṁdhāras of Aśoka. In the edicts these are grouped together, which means, they were all neighbours situated in this order. The enumeration is scientific, being in geographical sequence, from west to east, which is confirmed by Arrian (I) :-

" The regions beyond the river Indus on the west are inhabited, up to the river Kōphen, by two Indian tribes, the Astakenoi and the Assakenoi, who are not men of great stature like the Indians on the other side of the Indus, nor so brave, nor yet so swarthy as most Indians....The Nysaioi, however, are not an Indian race, but descendants of those who came into India with Dionysos....The district in which he planted this colony he named Nysaia (= the *Naiśya janapada* of *Patañjali*)....and the city itself Nysa. But the mountain close by the city, and on the lower slopes of which it is built, is designated Mēros (Meru)....In the dominions of the Assakenoi there is a great city called Massaka, the seat of the sovereign power which controls the whole realm. And there is another city, Peukelaïtis (Puṣkalāvatī), which is also of great size and not far from the Indus. These settlements lie on the other side of the river Indus, and extend in a western direction as far as the Kōphen."

Arrian, in the above passage, indicates that Puṣkalāvatī was easternmost in this enumeration, and his Assakenoi, or the Aśvakas, were on the Kābul river and between the Nysa Yavanas and Puṣkalāvatī. Puṣkalāvatī was in Gandhāra. Aśoka's Kaṁbojas were between the Yavanas and Gandhāra. The Kaṁbojas of Aśoka and of the Sanskrit and Pāli texts thus occupy exactly the same position as Arrian's Assakenoi (Aśvakas). We thus get another name for the Kaṁbojas, *i.e.*, Aśvakas. The Kaṁbojas were famous for their horses, and as cavalry-men (*aśva-yuddha-kuśalāḥ*) ;[76] *Aśvakas*, 'horsemen,' was the term popularly applied to them.

Nābhaka

Arrian, starting his enumeration from the Indus westwards, mentions the Astakenoi first, which means that they were in Gandhāra. The Aṣṭakas are the well-known *Aṣṭaka-rājya*, 'the Confederacy

[76] *Mahābhārata*, *Śānti-P.*, 105. 5 (Kumbakonam ed.).

of Eight'.[77] They are now represented by Hashtnagar, the 'Eight Cities' tract on the lower Swāt in the neighbourhood of Puṣkalāvatī (Chārsaḍḍa). The Gandhāra of Aśoka was divided into two parts, (1) on the eastern side of the Indus, with Takṣaśilā as capital, which was an Imperial Province, and (2) the Bājaur and Swāt region under autonomous (city) states, with Puṣkalāvatī as the biggest town amongst them. They formed a league of eight city-states. Now, in Rock P. V. we have the Gaṁdharas, and in Rock P. XIII we have in their place (in the *arāja-viṣaya* group) the Nābhaka-Nābha-paṁtis (=*paṅkti*). Here the section of Gandhāra which was not under direct imperial rule was distinguished by these two names. Precisely in this region (Bājaur-Swāt) we have now the Nāhaka community and the Nāhakī Pass. Nāhaka is the exact equivalent of Nābhaka. I have already given other reasons[78] for placing the Nābhaka and the Nābha *paṅkti*, or 'Nābha lines,' in Gandhāra, on the authority of the grammatical literature, where they appear as *Nabhāka* and *Urṇa Nābha*. As Mr. C. E. A. W. Oldham points out, the name survives in *Ūṇa* in Swāt, identified by Sir Aurel Stein with Aornos.[79] *Paṅkti* is a synonym of *śreṇi*, 'line,' which is often used to denote a league of republicans. The Nābhakas and Nābha-paṁtis had their confederacy of eight city-states. If we take the second member as *Nābha Paṁti* (as we already have the Nābhakas), the **Paṁti** would be 'the Paṁtis' in league with the Nābhas, and would be identical with the **Paktyes** or people of the Paktyika or Paktyike country named by Herodotus.[80] The Nābhas occupied the country just to the south of the gold-trading Dardistānīs.

Nabhāka and Nābhāka occur as designations of Ṛishis in the *Ṛig Veda*. Nābha-nediṣṭha Mānava is well known as one who was left out in partition by his father, Manu. *Nābha-nediṣṭha*, 'nearest in descent,' has retained that meaning in

---

[77] *Cf. C.H.I.*, p. 355, n.

[78] P. 123 above.

[79] "Compare the modern name, Ūṇa (Pashtu, Uṇra) of the lofty ridge in eastern Swāt identified by Sir Aurel Stein with the Aornos of Alexander's campaign (*A.S.I. Mem.*, 42, pp. 89, 90".— C. E. A. W. O., Jt.-Editor, *I.A.*, LXII. 132.

[80] See Cary's trans., iii. 102; iv. 44.

the Avesta (*Vedic Index*, i. 442). The Nābhas appear to have been a Vedic community.

The Nābhas are now the Paṭhāns of the Swāt valley. '*City-states*' (*grāma-rāṣṭrāṇi*) were a tradition preserved and remembered down to the time of Varāhamihira :

> *Traigartta-Paurava-Ambaṣṭha-Pārata-Vaṭadhāna-Yaudheyāḥ,*
> *Sārasvata-Arjunāyana-Matsyārdha-grāmarāṣṭrāṇi.*
>
> —*Brihat-S.*, XVI. 22.

CHAPTER XVIII

Republics in Śuṅga Times and Later

In the Śuṅga period we have some of the old republics that survived the Mauryan policy. These, as observed above, were mostly powerful leagues. There were, however, some individual republican states also in the Śuṅga period. Most of these, now known from their coins, appear to be new states. The majority of the older states do not come on the stage again; and the necessary conclusion is that they were obliterated during the Maurya imperialism. Their next destroyer was the foreign rule of the Indo-Greeks and the Northern Satraps. The presence of these barbarians leads to a new phenomenon in the history of Hindu republics, namely, migration of the stronger republics to Rajputana.

Yaudheyas

The Yaudheyas were one of the older class. They not only survive the Mauryan empire and the Śuṅga empire[1] but also the Satraps and the Kushāns. There is evidence of their long life both in the coins struck by them and the inscriptions making adverse references to them. The atmosphere of the Second Century A.C. is full of their military glory. Rudradāman in the second century A.C. describes them as "*rendered proud, as they were, by having manifested their title of heroes among all Kshatriyas*" and "*who cannot be subjugated.*"[2]

They appear in the inscription of Samudra Gupta[3] amongst the group-setting limit to the Imperial Gupta Province (fourth century A.C.). There is a unique inscription of theirs in an ornate script discovered in the State of Bharatpur[4] mentioning

---

[1] For their coins and mint at Rohtak in the Śuṅga period, see *J.B.O.R.S.*, 1936, Vol. XXII, 59.

[2] सर्वक्षत्राविष्कृत-वीरशब्दजातोत्सेकाविधेयानां यौधेयानाम्—*Ep. Ind.*, VIII, p. 44.

[3] Fleet, *Gupta Inscriptions*, p. 8; नेपाल-कर्तृ पुरादिप्रत्यन्तनृपतिभिर्म्मा-लवार्ज्जुनायन-यौधेय-माद्रका....

[4] Fleet, *Ibid.*, p. 251, he bore the title of *Mahārāja, Mahā-Senāpati.*

the elected president ('who has been made the leader,' Fleet of the Yaudheya-gaṇa. This is taken to belong to the Gupta period.

Their coins which extend from the Śuṅga period to the fourth century of the Christian era, are found in the Eastern Punjab and all over the country between the Sutlej and Jumna rivers. Two large finds have been discovered at Sonpat between Delhi and Karnāl.[5]

It seems that before the second century A.C. they had already moved towards Western Rajputana as it is there that Rudradāman encountered them, his own dominions including *Maru*. Evidently the Yaudheya territory was very large.[6] They seem to have left their original seat in early Kushān times.

On one type of their coins (Śuṅga period) they stamp the figure of a moving elephant and that of a bull. And the coin is struck in the name of the Yaudheyas '*Yaudheyānam*', 'Of the Yaudheyas'. On the second type they give the representation of the God Kārttikeya,[6] the presiding deity of Heroism and War, and name him on the coin. In fact the coin itself is significantly dedicated to the Deity of Heroism. In other words, the figure is their *La Liberté*. The third type is purely constitutional. It is struck in the name of the Yaudheya-gaṇa or Yaudheya Parliament [or Republic] (*Yaudheya-Gaṇasya Jaya*: 'Victory of the Yaudheya Gaṇa'). The figure on it is a warrior with a spear in the pose of dignified '*tri-bhaṅga*'—representing the type of their citizen-soldier. Some coins bear '*dvi*' (two) and some '*tri*' (three).[7] These probably refer to their three sections, like Patañjali's trika Śālaṅkāyanas.[8]

---

[5] भगवतो स्वामिन ब्राह्मण्यदेवस्य । V. Smith, *Cat. of Coins in the Indian Museum*, Vol. I, 165, 181.

[6] The *Mahābhārata* divides their territory in *Bahudhānyaka* and *Maru-bhūmi*; Rohītaka (Rohtak) was the capital of the former, which was dear to Kārttikeya, *J.B.O.R.S.*, XXII, 60.

[7] Cunningham, *C.A.I.*, pp. 75–79; Cunningham, *A.S.R.*, Vol. XIV, pp. 141–42; *J. B. O. R. S.*, XXII. 59 on Rohtak finds.

[8] Patañjali on Pāṇini, V. 1. 58.

Yaudheya constitution from monumental records

The inscription of the Yaudheyas proves that they had an elected President. The order is issued by him describing himself as the 'President made by the *Gaṇa* of the Yaudheyas'.[9] It is not clear whether the records found in the district of Hoshyarpur are impressions of official seals or coins. In any case, the coin and the seal would bear the same lakshaṇas—the lakshaṇas of the *Saṃgha*. The constitutional significance of the records is of great value. They are in the name of the Yaudheyas and their cabinet or executive committee. The latter are called '*mantradharas*'—' those vested with the policy of state:' ('*Yodheyānaṃ jaya Mantradharāṇaṃ*).[10]

Their end

The Yaudheyas are lost to history some time before the seventh century. For Varāhamihira gives the traditional geography and has no living fact before him when he places them with the Gandhāras. The Johiyā Rajputs who are found on the banks of the Sutlej along the Bahawalpur Frontier have been identified as modern representatives of the ancient Yaudheyas.[11] This identification appears to be sound both on philological and territorial grounds.

Madras

The Madras who originally had their capital at Śākala (Sialkot) and who gave their name to the country around Śākala, also migrated downwards and became a neighbour of the Yaudheyas. They too are mentioned by Samudra Gupta. Their further history is lost and they disappear like their friends. The Madras seem to have been too conservative to take to the new system of issuing signed coins. They adhered to the old punch-marked : they have not left a single specimen of inscribed coins.

---

[9] Bijayagadh stone inscr. (C. Fleet, *G.I.*, p. 252) सिद्धम् । यौधेय-गण-पुरस्कृतस्य महाराज-महासेनापतेः पु......ब्राह्मण-पुरोगं चाधिष्ठानं शरीरादि-कुशलं पृष्ट्वा लिखत्यस्तिरस्मा........

" Success ! Of Mahārāja, mahā-senāpati...who has been made President (leader) by the Yaudheya Parliament................. (He) after wishing health to the Brahmin head-man and to the Settlement writes : " There is...."

[10] *Proceedings A.S.B.*, 1884, pp. 138–40.

[11] Cunningham, *A.S.R.*, Vol. XIV, p. 140.

The Mālavas and the Kshudrakas re-appear in the Śuṅga times. Patañjali knows them and mentions some victory of the Kshudrakas which they by themselves, alone, had won.[12] But in subsequent centuries they are no longer traceable. They were probably fully amalgamated with the Mālavas during their migration from the Punjab to eastern Rajputana. The Mālavas were in their new homes about 150–100 B.C., as evidenced by the earliest type of their coins found at Karkoṭa Nāgar (Jaipur State).[13] This was just the time of the inroad of the Parthian Śakas.[13a] The Mālavas seem to have migrated *via* Bhatinda (Patiala State) where they have left traces of their name (in 'Mālawāī' dialect extending from Ferozepore to Bhatinda, *L.S.I.*, IX. i, p. 709). Before 58 B.C. the Mālavas are found besieging the Uttamabhadras to the west of Ajmer which was relieved by the forces of Nahapāṇa.[14]

Mālavas and Kshudrakas

In 58 B.C.[14] Nahapāṇa is defeated and killed by Gautamīputra who re-struck Nahapāṇa's coins, and the *Gaṇa* of the Mālavas counted the beginning of Kṛita from that date.[15] Their *Gaṇa* adopted the date to measure future time (Kāla-jñānāya[16]). The era was 'made authoritative by their use'.[17] The authority of that Era of Prowess (*Vikrama*) still reigns: we use it to this day. The Mālavas subsequently covered the whole of the vast area to the south of Nāgar, which permanently bears their name. They are mentioned in the list of Samudra Gupta's subordinates along with other republicans,

---

[12] Not as a member of the League. Patañjali on Pāṇini, V. 3. 52: एकाकिभिः क्षुद्रकैर्जितम् ।

[12a] V. Smith, *Catalogue of Coins in the Indian Museum, Calcutta*, Vol. I, p. 161.

[13a] Cunningham, *A.S.R.*, Vol. XIV, p. 150.

[14] *Epigraphia Indica*, Vol. VIII, p. 44; Jayaswal, *Historical Position of Kalki*, etc., *I.A.*, 1917, pp. 151–52; on the date of Nahapāṇa and Gautamīputra, *J.B.O.R.S.*, I. 102.

[15] See references to *Kṛita* in *Gupta Inscriptions* having dates in Mālava years.

[16] Fleet, *Gupta Inscriptions*, p. 154.

[17] *Epigraphia Indica*, Vol. IX, p. 320. (श्री मालव-गणाम्नाते प्रशस्ते कृत-संज्ञके).

the Yaudheyas, the Madras, the Ārjunāyanas, etc. In the Gupta period they retire into the Unknown. Their era was used by great sovereigns of Mālava from the fourth to the sixth centuries. This would not have been done if the Mālava-gaṇa had been still subsisting, for that would have denoted subordination of the sovereigns using the era. They certainly did not exist in the time of Varāhamihira (who drawing on older materials) places them near the Himalayas. Varāhamihira himself was living in Mālava, and to use so antiquated a datum shows that the real Mālavas had for some centuries ceased to exist. The *Vishṇu Purāṇa*[18] gives their later habitation (Mewar-Jaipur) and gives it correctly.

The coins of the Mālavas[19] bear legends in Brāhmī: *Mālavānāṁ Jaya* ('Victory of the Mālavas') or, '*Malavā-Jaya*' ('the Mālava Victory'), '*Mālavahṇa Jaya*' ('Victory of the Mālavas', in Prākṛita), and '*Mālavagaṇasya*' (Of the 'Mālava-gaṇa').

The story of the name still survives in the close community of the Brahmins called 'Mālavī'—now Sanskritised as *Mālavīya*—a fair and handsome people with marked intellectuality and sharpness of business intelligence. They do not marry outside their own community. They had a colony as far removed as the vicinity of Allahabad and are now found in towns near about.

In the later Mālava area the Śibis also appear. The Śibis were associates of the Mālavas in the time of Alexander as a very rude people, or at least, wearing, very rude dress in war, on the authority of the Greek writers. They seem to have migrated with the Mālavas into Rajputana where at Nagarī near Chitor their coins are found. They are struck in the name of 'the Country (or Nation) of the Śibis of Madhyamikā' ('*Majhimikāya Śibi Janapadasa*').[20] No record of theirs of a period subsequent to the first century B.C. has yet been discovered.

Śibis

---

[18] *Vishṇu Purāṇa*, W. & H., II. 133.

[19] *C.C.I.M.*, pp. 170–74.

[20] Cunningham, *A.S.R.*, Vol. XIV, p. 146. Madhyamikā (known to Patañjali) was their Capital.

Ārjunāyanas

The Ārjunāyanas as a people do not appear in Pāṇini[21] or Patañjali, nor in the *Māhabhārata*.[22] But they are added to the Rājanya group of the *Gaṇapṇṭha*, palpably later as they come towards the end. The addition cannot be later than the time of Patañjali, for in 100 B.C. they are in Rajputana, away from the Rājanyas. There they figure with the Yaudheyas and others down to the time of Samudra Gupta. The Ārjunāyanas seem to be thus a younger political community founded about the Śuṅga times (200 B.C.), by, as the name implies, Ārjunāyana. Their coins are inscribed only in Brāhmī script, a fact excluding the idea of northern association about 100 B.C. They bear the legend '*Ārjunāyanāna*' 'Coin of the Ārjunāyanas' or '*Arjunayanana jaya*', ('Victory of the Ārjunāyana').[23] They are associates and friends of the valiant Yaudheyas, Madrakas and Mālavas in Rajputana with whom they migrated there.

The meaning of republican migration

This migration from the fertile lands of the Punjab to dreary Rajputana is the testimony to the love of liberty which these 'unconquerable' republicans bore 'more than others', as one of them put it in the time of Alexander.[24] They believed that the Yaudheya Country or the Mālava Country was wherever the Yaudheya or Mālava Gaṇa lived and lived as of yore in freedom. They would sacrifice paternal homes and lands to preserve their political self and soul. They would go to deserts but live in democratic glory and rule in parliament. It is a settled principle of Hindu politics that freedom is more important than home and is to be preserved at the cost of the latter.[25] The republics seem to have fully acted upon this principle.

---

[21] It is for the first time found in the *Gaṇapātha* on Pāṇini, IV. i. 112.

[22] See discussion in p. 154 on the *Mahābhārata* republics of Rajputana.

[23] V. Smith, *Catalogue of the Coins in the Indian Museum*, I, p. 166, Rapson, *I.C.*, Pl. III, 20.

[24] McCrindle, *Alexander*, p. 154. 'For they were attached more than others to freedom and autonomy', in the address of the Mālavas.

[25] *Ś.N.S.*

Rajputana republics in the *Mahābhārata*

In addition to the evidence of the coins and the inscriptions on the question of migration of these republics to Rajputana there is the evidence of the *Mahābhārata*. In the *Sabhā-Parvan* (Ch. XXXII), the Mālavas, the Śibis and the Trigartas are placed in Rajaputana (*Maru*), while in another place (Ch. LII) they are in the Punjab. Evidently Chapter LII (describing the Rājasūya) is based on earlier authorities. There the Śibis, Trigartas, Yaudheyas, Rājanyas and Madras are mentioned along with the people of Kaśmīra and Kekaya ; and the Ambashṭhas are placed in the same group as the Kshudrakas and Mālavas. In Chapter XXXII (in the (Digvijaya) the Śibis, Trigartas and Mālavas are given along with the Daśārṇas and Mādhyamakeyas. The Mādhyamakeyas were the people of the town Madhyamikā near Nagarī in the Udaipur State where Madhyamikā coins have been found in large numbers. Evidently Madhyamikā had not yet passed under the Śibis and was at the time the seat of a separate political community. In the route onwards the river Sarasvati and the Matsya Country (Alwar) are mentioned. All these *Gaṇas* then were in Rajputana extending from Sind to the Vindhyas. It is noticeable that though the Śibis, Trigartas and Ambashṭhas do appear with the Mālavas in Rajputana, the Kshudrakas do not.

The Mālavas in Chapter XXX, verse 8, are again mentioned with the Matsyas. The later data of the *Mahābhārata* evidently relate to the state of affairs about 150 B.C., while the earlier ones refer to the period of Kauṭilya or earlier, for like the *Artha-Śāstra* it places the Kukuras along with the Madrakas, Yaudheyas and others. The republics were still in the Punjab according to Ch. LII.

In the data of 100 B.C., *i.e.*, in Chapter XXXII, some republics are mentioned in the *Māhabharāta* which we have not met with in earlier literature. They are :—

(1) The *Gaṇas* of *Utsavasaṅketas*.

(2) The republic of the *Śūdras* and that of the *Ābhīras* who are placed in the Indus valley.

The Śūdra republic is evidently the same whom Alexander met in Lower Sind and whom we have identified[26] with the

[26] Pt. I, p. 74, *n*. 3.

Brahminical Śaudras or *Śaudrāyaṇas* of the *Gaṇapāṭha*. According to grammar it was based on the proper-name (of a man) *Śūdra*, not the caste name. The Five *Karpaṭas* and neighbours of the Utsavasaṅketas may have been republican although they are not described as such in the *Māhabhārata*. Samudra Gupta[27] places the Ābhīras next to the Mādrakas, and the Kharaparikas also in the same group, *i.e.*, the group of non-monarchical communities. Probably these Kharaparikas or Kharaparas are identical with the Five Karpaṭas of the *Mahabhārata*. The Utsavasaṅketas were republican, probably founded by two men Utsava and Saṅketa. We may, however, point out that Saṅketa is a technical term denoting an act or resolution passed by a republic (सङ्केतः समयक्रिया)[28] and it is just possible that 'saṅketa' here originally denoted a state 'founded' by a resolution of the Utsavas. The Utsava-Saṅketas are located in the *Māhabhārata* near Pushkara or Ajmer. They do not seem to come down to the time of the Guptas. Not only they are not mentioned in the Gupta records, they are treated as a semi-mythological people of the Himalayas by the Gupta poet, Kālidāsa. This would show that Utsava-Saṅketas had long ceased to exist. The *Mahabhārata* in the same passage mentions 'very powerful town-rulers' on the banks of the Indus.[29] They evidently are the city republics on the Indus as they had existed in the time of Alexander.

Considering the power and long career in their new homes, the period 150 B.C. to 350 A.C. may be still considered a living

---

[27] The other non-monarchical communities in Samudra Gupta's inscription are (1) the *Prārjunas*, (2) the *Kākas*, (3) the Ābhīras, (4) the Kharaparikas and (5) the *Sanakānīkas*. Kauṭilya in laying down punishment for defaming a country (*Janapadopavādāh*, III, 18) gives in illustration 'Prājjūṇāka', along with Gāndhāra, which is identical with (1). The (3) had been under monarchs according to inscriptions; having been broken down in power they seem to have copied the constitution of their neighbours. The name of the (4) has been traced in a later inscription by R. Br. Hira Lal (*EI.*, XII, 44). Nothing more is known of (5). See p. 162 below on Guptan republics (and Addendum III). On 'Five' Kh., *cf.* p. 158 below.

[28] *V.M.*, p. 424.

[29] See above. सिन्धुकूलाश्रिता ये च ग्रामणीया महाबलाः। *cf.* ग्रामराष्ट्राणि of Varāhamihira (Addendum II).

period of Hindu republican polity. It was the period of rise of the Rajputana republics.

At the same time that period was one of decay and decline of republican states in the Punjab and Western India. Parthian Śakas and the Śakas of Seistan who overran those parts destroyed their independence and dissolved their states there.

Kukuras

The Kukuras whom the *Artha-Śāstra* mentions were lost in the dominions of Rudradāman. After 150 B.C. they live only in the place-name which they bequeathed to the country they had lived in. The Pitinikas vanished probably in the Mauryan times.

The Saurāshṭras were also merged into common humanity about the second century A.C.

Vṛishṇis

The Vṛishṇis of classical glory fell under the Śaka barbarian leaving behind a couple of coins to tell the story. The orthodox Brāhmī and the republican legend, *Vṛishṇi-rājañña-gaṇasya trātasya* ('of the Vṛishṇi Rājanya (and) Gaṇa—the Protector of the country') yet remain. But at the same time the coin is obliged to bear the script of the invader, Kharoshṭhī, as well. The coin is marked with the state symbol the weapon *chakra* (discus), which was their symbol according to tradition as early as the time of Rājanya Kṛishṇa. The legend is in scripts of 100 B.C.[30]

It was the weakened condition of the country consequent on the Maurya policy of breaking up the republics that made the way easy for the foreign barbarians of the first century B.C. in Western India. There had been left no strong power to oppose them. But the case in other directions was not exactly the same. The barbarians proceed up to Mathurā, but beyond that they are checked, to the South-West by the old republicans. The foreigners could not join hands across their two seats at Mathurā and Ujjain.

The older republics in the Punjab, however, paid the price which nature decrees from freedom to force. The smaller

---

[30] See p. 37 above; Cunningham, *Coins of Ancient India*, p. 70, pl. IV, 15, has mistaken the disc for a wheel but the cutting edges and the projecting points on the rim are clear.

Punjab republics under the Mauryas had become mere constitutions; they had lost their biological constitution and retained the one of political phraseology: they were no more *Saṃghas*, but mere *Gaṇas*: self-governments without states, states without power.

Rājanyas

Such had become the ancient Rājanyas who come on the scene a second time 200–100 B.C. to appear no more. They struck their coins (200–100 B.C.) in the name of their country: '*Rājanya-Janapadasa*'.[31]

Numismatic scholars have taken this 'rājanya' as the 'well-known equivalent for Kshatriya' (see V. Smith, *Catalogue of the Coins in the Indian Museum*, Vol. I, p. 164). But this is a mistake. Rājanya is the proper name of a political people. It is clearly given as such by Pāṇini, Kātyāyana and Patañjali and also by the *Mahābhārata*. Their coins are still of the old class called *kāṃsika* (bronze) by Pāṇini (V. 1. 25), *i.e.*, cast. Their coin which is die-struck bears legend in Kharoshṭhī and is closely allied to the North Satrap coins, bearing the same figure as the latter. This tells the final tale—the tale of their absorption in the Punjab or the Mathurā Satrapy. Their coins are found in the Hoshyarpur District and Mathurā. The former region seems to have been their home.

Their constitution emphasised the 'Janapada', according to which the whole Janapada was consecrated to rulership. It should be noticed that Pāṇini's rule about the Rājanyas deals with '*Rājanya-Janapada*'. The Rājanyas were, therefore, a democracy.

Mahārāja-Janapada

Another old state which shared the fate of the Rājanya-janapada was the *Mahārāja-janapada*. Their coins originally bore legend in Brāhmī '*Mahārāja-Janapadasa*' ('Of the Mahārāja-Janapada') but latterly when they passed under the influence of the foreign rulers it was changed into Kharoshṭhī.[32]

---

[31] Cunningham, *C.A.I.*, p. 69.

[32] See Cunningham, *C.A.I.*, p. 69, where he classes them erroneously under the Audumbara coins. Princep's plate referred to by Cunningham should also be consulted.

The state was old as it is mentioned by Pāṇini in a rule which contemplates a man owing loyalty to it. It is not certain as to what form of government they followed in the time of Pāṇini, but their system is clearly republican of the democratic type in the Śuṅga period as evidenced by their coins. Their coins have been found in the Punjab. The bull with the crescent on the reverse of their coin shows that they were Śaiva.

Vāmarathas and Śālaṅkāyanas

Like the Ārjunāyanas some new republican states were founded in the closing and weak period of the Mauryas. To this class belong the *Vāmarathas* of Kātyāyana and Patañjali,[33] and the *Śālaṅkāyanas* of Patañjali.[34]

They are traced no further, nor are they found earlier. About the Śālaṅkāyanas we are told by the Kāśikā that they were in the Vāhīka country, a statement which is supported by the *Gaṇapāṭha* which places them along with the Rājanyas and Audumbaras.

They had the *Śastropajīvin* constitution. Patañjali furnishes the important detail that the Śālaṅkāyanas were composed of three sections. This datum helps us in understanding the coins of the Yaudheyas. It would not be correct to say that they were composed of three tribes. The state was founded, as the name signifies, by one Śālaṅkāyana, a descendant of Śalaṅka which is not even an ancient family name. The three members of the Śālaṅkāyana *Saṃgha* very likely represent an amalgamation of three small state-units.

No history of the Vāmarathas is yet available. According to Patañjali the republic was noted for the scholarship of their learned men. They in this respect resemble the Kaṭhas. They did not however seem to have any military glory like that of the Kaṭhas. Nothing is known about their seat. To this class of new growth and early death must be referred the

---

[33] On P., IV. 1. 151. The ' arms ' of the republic of the Vāmarathas (वामरथानि संघाङ्कलक्षणानि) are mentioned by the Kāśikā on P., IV. 1. 151.

[34] Patañjali on Pāṇini, V. 1. 58. त्रिकाः शालङ्कायनाः । Kāśikā, p. 456.

unnamed states of the Rājanya constitution whose coins are struck only in the name of their Rājanyas (Presidents), *e.g.*, *Rājanya-Mahamitasa* ('Of the Rājanya Mahā-mitra'). They bear legends both in Kharoshṭhī and Brāhmī and they are found in the hills.[35]

Audumbaras

The Audumbaras are not known to the early Pāṇinian literature; but they are mentioned in the *Gaṇapāṭha* in the Rājanya group of republics.[36] They are placed at the end of the Punjab republics in the earlier list of the *Sabhā-Parvan* of the *Mahābhārata* (Chapter LII). Probably they also were republican. Their coins of the first century B.C. are found in Northern Punjab and they bear legend in Kharoshṭhī as well as in Brāhmī. Varāhamihira places them in the company of the Kapisthalas who are a twin associate of the Kaṭhas in Patañjali. They were somewhere between Kangara and Ambala. A branch of theirs seems to have migrated to Cutch, as Pliny locates the *Odomboeres* there. Their coinage resembles that of the Ārjunāyanas in style. Their coins show that the Audumbaras (if a republic) had an elective king. They are struck in the name of the community and king, styled 'His Exalted Majesty' (*e.g.*, *Mahadevasa raña Dharaghoshasa Odumbarisa*). The coins bear the 'lakshaṇa' of a tree, the representation of a building with tall columns and a slanting roof which may be their mote-hall or some other public building, and the figure of their standard which Cunnigham mistook to be a *Dharmachakra*. Across the field *Viśvamitra* is written and a picture of the Rishi given. Probably Viśvāmitra was their national sage.[37]

The Kharoshṭhī script indicates that about 100 B.C. they came under the influence of the Satraps like their neighbours of the Punjab, and were finally absorbed. No later records of theirs is found. Their branch in Cutch appears to

---

[35] Cunningham, *C.A.I.*, p. 69.

[36] On Pāṇini, IV. 2. 53.

[37] Rapson, *I.C.*, pl. III, 8; Cunningham, *C.A.I.*, pp. 66–8; many of the coins grouped by him under Audumbara coins are not connected with the Audumbaras. Consult also the valuable note by him in *A.S.R.*, Vol. XIV, pp. 135–36.

have lived longer. They have left their descendants in the enjoyment of their name—the modern community of Gujarati Brahmins of the Audumbara caste.

Nāgas and Mālavas

On the position of the Hindu republics in the Nāga period (150 A.D.—284 A.D.) the situation is thus.[38] The Nāga performers of the ten *aśvamedhas*, or to put it in modern phraseology, the Nāga emperors, fostered the republics which covered the whole of (Eastern and Western) Malwā, and probably also Gujarat (Ābhīras), the whole of Rajputana (Yaudheyas and Mālavas), and probably also a portion of the Eastern Punjab (Madras)—all connected territory, to the west of the valley of the Ganges. These were certainly free in the next, the Vākāṭaka period, when Samudra Gupta emerges on the stage. The Malwā republics seem to have been formed by peoples and clans akin to the Nāgas. Those around Vidiśā were worshippers of Nāgas from early times, as the republican coins of Eran prove. Eran, the Airikiṇa town, is itself after the name Airaka, a Nāga, and the Eran coins bear a Nāga (serpent) figure. The Mālavas, near Jaipur, had founded their capital, Karkoṭa Nāgara, naming it after the Nāga Karkoṭa, which now lies within the territory of the Raja of Uniyāra—a feudatory of the Mahārāja of Jaipur, about 25 miles E.-S. from Ṭonk. The word *Nāgara* itself in the capital *Karkoṭa Nāgara* is connected with the word *Nāga*. It is important to recognise this fact that the Nāga monarchs and the republican Mālavas were, by their civilization and also probably ethnically, connected. Rājaśekhara says that the Ṭakkas and the people of Maru used *apabhraṁśa* idioms. The family of Gaṇapati Nāga of Padmāvatī was a *Ṭāka-vaṁśa*, which means that the family came from the Ṭakka-deśa. Thus we see that the Mālavas and the Nāgas spoke the same dialect. It seems that with the original migration of the republican Mālavas from the Punjab, the Ṭakka Nāgas had also migrated, and that the Nāgas themselves originally belonged to a republican community (the Five Karpaṭas ; *H.I.*, 150–350 A.D., p. 38) and that they were a Punjab people settled in Malwā.

---

[38] *History of India*, 150 A.D. to 350 A.D., pp. 53–54.

Other Republics

The Nāga emperors became the leaders of a movement for freedom from the Kushan rule. The Mālavas, the Yaudheyas, and the Kuṇindas (Madrakas) all re-strike their coins in the Nāga period. It may be possible to discern on a minute study their connection with the Nāga coinage disclosing the symbols of hegemony or suzerainty of the Nāgas.[39] Dr. Vincent Smith says, 'they (Nāga coins) are closely related to some of the later Mālava coins '[40]. The Mālava coins re-appear, after a break, about the same time as the Nāga coins of Padmāvatī, about the second century A.D.[41] The Yaudheya coinage revives about the second century A.D.[42] and the Kuṇinda coinage in the third century[43] who are, evidently, the last to be liberated. In other words, the re-rise of the Yaudheyas and the Mālavas is contemporaneous with the Nāgas.

---

39 The peculiar tree symbol with the side designs of the Bhāraśiva coins (*H.I.*, 150–350 A.D., pp. 19–24) is met with on several republican coins of the period.

40 *C.I.M.*, p. 164.

41 Rapson, *I.C.*, pp. 12–13 ; *cf. C.I.M.*, pp. 176–77.

42 *C.I.M.*, p. 165.

43 Rapson, *I.C.*, p. 12.

CHAPTER XIX

Disappearance

Guptas and Republics

The Gupta power struck the republican system in Rajaputana. The Guptas, however, rose to imperial position by their alliance with the republican Lichchhavis[1] who had survived the Maurya and Śuṅga times and had grown highly powerful. They had outlived their ancient contemporaries in power and glory and remained the single and sole representative of ancient republicanism.

Mitra Republics

Before the Gupta period there appeared in Malwā three new republics whose names ended in *Mitra*. The *Vishṇu Purāṇa* gives them as *Pushpamitra-Paḍhumitra-Padmamitrās trayaḥ*. The *Vāyu* and the *Brahmāṇḍa* name only two, *Pushpamitrāḥ* and *Paṭumitrāḥ*. But the *Brahmāṇḍa* adds *trimitrāḥ*. The *Bhāgavata* calls 'Pushyamitra' (*i.e.*, the President) a '*rājanya*', which is the technical term, as we have seen above, for a type of republican president. In view of the datum of the *Vishṇu Purāṇa*, naming the three communities and that of the *Brahmāṇḍa* mentioning *tri-mitras*,[2] we have to take that their state was divided into three sections, and that they had ten successions, and the expression *trayo daśa* of the *Vāyu* is to be taken as meaning that the three states had ten rulers or ten successions of presidents. The other reading in the manuscripts (in place of *trayo daśa*) *tathaiva cha*[3] would indicate that they were also given 30 years as given to the main rulers of Mahīshī.[4] They are assigned no separate location, and consequently I take that they were in Western Malwā. They.

---

[1] Their name is jointly inscribed with the name of the emperor Chandra Gupta I on the imperial coins.

[2] षट्त्रिमित्राः *Shaṭs trimitrāḥ* of the *Brahmāṇḍa* is to be taken as a misreading for पटु-त्रिमित्राः, *Patu-trimitrāḥ* (Patu, 'the Tri-Mitras,' the Three Mitras.)

[3] Wilson, *V.P.*, 4, 214 ; Pargiter, *P.T.*, 51, *n.* 14.

For references to Purāṇic texts, see Pargiter, *Purāṇā Texts*, p. 51, and notes.

[4] Jayaswal, *History of India*, 150 A.D. to 350 A.D., p. 85.

in the next period, *i.e.*, the Guptan, are described as 'Āvantyas' who were under or in the confederacy of the *Ābhīras*. It is well known that the Pushyamitras rose to such a height of power in the reign of Kumāra Gupta I that they nearly uprooted the Gupta dynasty.

The Pushyamitras 'developed great power and wealth'[5] to such an extent that they dealt a blow at the imperial throne from which it could not fully recover. The defeat inflicted by them on the imperial forces under Kumāra Gupta made the dynasty, to quote the language of his son Skanda Gupta, totter to its fall.[6] Evidently Kumāra Gupta himself was killed.[7] In the second war Skanda Gupta remained on the battlefield the whole night and slept on the bare ground. The next morning when the battle continued he succeeded in forcing a decision which entitled him, as the inscription says, to plant his foot on the royal footstool, *i.e.*, became entitled to sovereignty.[8] But it is not claimed that the Pushyamitras bent their head or became feudatory. It was therefore a military defeat at most, or rather if we take into consideration the site of the publication of this record of victory (Bhītari in Ghazipur District), it was the stemming back of the invading Pushyamitras. The subsequent history of Hindu India might have received a different turn had they reached Pāṭaliputra and made it the seat of their republican government. We might have seen a vast republic, vaster than the country had yet seen. But the issue was decided otherwise. The Pushyamitras retired, but the glory of the Guptas never returned. The course of their weakness and decline consequent on the Pushyamitra and Hun wars could not be checked. There seems to be a strange fatality in the history of the Guptas. They rose to power with the help of a republic, they abolished the ancient

---

[5] समुदितब[ल]कोशान् पुष्यमित्रान्........ Bhītarī Stone Pillar Inscription of Skanda Gupta, Fleet, *G.I.*, pp. 53–54.

[6] *Ibid.*, विचलितकुललक्ष्मी..*l.* 11; विप्लुतां वंशलक्ष्मीं..*l.* 13; प्रचलितं वंशम्.... *l.* 14.

[7] पितरि दिवमुपे[ति] etc.

[8] See lines 12–13. *Ibid.* The translation of this passage by Fleet is confused and does not reproduce the spirit of the text.

republicanism, and they in turn were shaken off their foundations by a republic. The Pushyamitras having executed this historical revenge withdrew in the mystic past.

(On other republics of the Gupta period see Addendum III below.)

Exit

By the end of the fifth century Republics disappear from Hindu India. The old Lichchhavis quit the political scene, a branch migrating into Nepal.[9] The young Pushyamitras vanish in the air. The following century saw the final exit of Hindu constitutionalism from the stage of History. All that was good, come down from the age of Vedic Forefathers, all that progress which had been achieved since the composition of the first Ṛik, all that gave life to the mechanism of State, bade good-bye to the Land. Republicanism was the first to begin the Great Departture, to lead the dirge of political *Nirvāṇa*. We have understood only one verse of that epilogue—the praise of the sword of destruction which nature gives into the hand of the barbarian. But the other verses are yet a riddle. The real causes of that Departure which the epilogue should disclose remain undeciphered.

From 550 A.C. onwards Hindu history melts into brilliant biographies—isolated gems without a common string of national and common life. We get men great in virtue or great in crime—we get Harsha and Śaśāṅka, Yaśodharman Kalki and Śankarāchārya—but they are so high above the common level that they are only helplessly admired and sacredly respected.[10] The community ceases to breathe freedom. The causes of this decay must be internal which have yet to be investigated. The Hun invasion alone cannot explain it. The Huns were fully crushed within a century by successive dynasts. Yet the old life refused to return.

---

[9] There is no trace of the Lichchhavis at Vaiśāli in the Gupta times after Chandra Gupta I; about his time the Nepal dynasty was founded. See my *Chronology and History of Nepal*, Part B.

[10] *E.g.*, see the biography of Harsha by Bāṇa. Kalki is deified in his life-time (*I.A.*, 1917, p. 145). Helpless admiration is an index of the great moral difference between the admirer and the admired.

ADDENDUM III

LOCATION OF THE GUPTAN REPUBLICS

On the Guptan republics the following extract from my *History of India*, 150 A.D. to 350 A.D. (pp. 147–49), may be consulted on their location.

Republics and Samudra Gupta

" The republics of the Mālavas, Āryunāyanas, Yaudheyas, Mādrakas, Ābhīras, Prārjunas, Sahasānīkas, Kākas, Kharparikas and others were not on the frontiers of Samudra Gupta's empire as wrongly supposed by Dr. Vincent Smith, for in line 22 (Allahabad Pillar Inscription) where 'the frontier kings' are mentioned, they are expressly excluded from that category. They were internal States and had become part of the Gupta empire by agreeing to pay all kinds of imperial taxes and obeying imperial orders. In the enumeration of the tributary republics there is a territorial scheme. The Mālavas, Āryunāyanas, Yaudheyas and Mādrakas are counted from the direct Gupta territory—say, from Mathurā. The first state is the Mālava. Nāgara or Karkoṭa-Nāgara which is situated in the modern state of Jaipur was the capital of the Mālavas whose thousands of republican coins—'*as thick as shells on the sea-shore*'—have been found there (*A.S.R.*, IV). The *Bhāgavata* calls them the Arbuda-Mālavas and the *Vishṇu* locates them in Rajputana (*Marubhūmi*). They were thus decidedly in Rajputana from Mount Abu up to Jaipur. The territorial designation Māḷwār (माळ्वार) seems to me to be based on their name.[11] To their south, there was the Nāga territory and with the Nāga coins their coinage bears affinity.[12] They were, like the Nāgas, followers of Nāga worship. Their capital was dedicated to Karkoṭa Nāga. Immediately north to them were the Yaudheyas, stretching from Bharatpur (where their repubiican inscription of a time anterior to Samudra Gupta has been found at Bijaygarh) right up to the

---

[11] *Mārwār* of our maps is pronounced in the Punjab as *Māḷwār* In Rajputana *ḷ* is pronounced as in the South. *Mālava* = *Māḷava* + *vāṭaka* will be the equivalent of *Mārwār*. For *Vāṭa* = *wār*, ' division,' see Hira Lal, *Inscriptions in C.P.*, pp. 24, 87 ; *E.I.*, VIII, 285. Both *Vāṭaka* and *Pāṭaka* occur with geographical names for ' division '.

[12] Rapson, *I.C.*, sec. 51 ; V. Smith, *C.I.M.*, 162.

lower course of the Sutlej on the border of the Bhawalpur State where Johiyāwār still bears the stamp of their name. This was the biggest republican state also in the time of Rudradāman (c. 150 A.D.); the Yaudheyas were his neighbours, that is, reaching Lower Sindh. Between the Mālava and the Yaudheya States there was the small state of the Āryunāyanas whose exact location is not known but whose coins indicate that they were near Alwar and Agra. The Mādrakas were immediately to the north of the Yaudheyas extending up to the foot of the Himalayas. Madra-deśa was the plain country between Jhelum and Ravi,[13] sometimes extending up to the Bias.[14] In the tract between the Bias and the Jumna lay the Vākāṭaka feudatories the Vermans of Siṁhapura and the Nāga king Nāgadatta. The other republican group of Samudra Gupta's inscription consists of the Ābhīras, Prārjunas, Sahasānīkas, Kākas and Kharparikas. None of these struck their coins before Samudra Gupta, and this for the simple reason that they had been under the Vākāṭaka governor of Western Malwā at Mandhātā (Māhishmatī) and under the Nāgas of Padmāvatī. Gaṇapati Nāga, in fact, is called the overlord of Dhāra (*Dhārādhīśa*). We know now that the Sahasānīkas and the Kākas were nearabout Bhilsa. The modern Kākpur was their town which is within 20 miles from Bhilsa[15]; the Sāñchi hill was called the *Kākanāda*. In the time of Chandra Gupta II a Sahasānika Mahāraja, probably a republican chief of the Sahasānikas, built the Chandra Gupta Temple in the Udayagiri rocks. About the Ābhīras, we get great help from the *Bhāgavata*. The *Bhāghavata* calls the Ābhīras, '*Saurāshṭra*' and '*Āvantya*' rulers (*Saurāshṭra-Āvanty Ābhīrāḥ*), and the *Vishṇu* treats the Ābhīras as occupying the Surāshṭra and Avanti provinces. We know from the Vākāṭaka history that in Westeren Malwā there were the Pushyamitras and two other republics with their names ending in Mitra. These were the Ābhīra republics and in their place in later Gupta history we find the Maitrakas rising as monarchs. This group beginning with the Ābhīras and ending with Kharaparikas is

[13] *A.S.R.*, Vol. II, p. 14.
[14] *J.R.A.S.*, 1897, p. 30.
[15] *J.B.O.R.S.*, XVIII, 213.

almost in a straight line from Kathiawar and Gujarat to Damoh, below the Māḷawa republic and above the Vākāṭaka kingdom. The Ābhīras in the time of the Periplus occupy Gujarat, and there is no justification in locating them in Bundelkhand as Dr. Vincent Smith did (*J.R.A.S.*, 1897, p. 30). He was led to do so on account of a mistaken notion that Kathiawar and Gujarat were at that time governed by the Western Satraps. Both the Purāṇas and Samudra Gupta's inscription leave no room for the Satraps in Kathiawar or Gujarat. The Western Satraps had been already dispossessed in the Nāga-Vākāṭaka period from Kathiawar. The Purāṇas here throw great light.

Purāṇic Evidence

"The *Bhāgavata* treats the Ābhīras of Surāshṭra and Avanti, the Śūras and the Mālavas of the Aravali as free republics. Their rulers are called *janādhipāḥ*, 'national' or 'popular' (*i.e.*, republican) 'rulers'. It does not mention the Mādrakas. It seems that the Mādrakas had already come within the Empire of Samudra Gupta as a sequene of the Āryāvarta wars and were probably the first amongst the republics to own allegiance to the Gupta Emperor when their overlord was conquered. The Śūras of the *Bhāgavata* are the famous Yaudheyas. The word *Śūra* ('*hero*') is a translation of the word '*Yaudheya*', their popular title. Rudradāman, 200 years earlier, recorded that the Yaudheyas were popularly known amongst the Kshatriyas by their title '*the heroes*'.[16] The Yaudheyas, according to the Purāṇas, were good and ancient Kshatriyas. They formerly lived, like the Mālavas, in the Punjab. It is they and the Mālavas who had kept the Kushan power in check, both at its western end on the Sindh borders and the eastern end at Mathurā. They were popularly known as '*Śūra*', '*Vīra*'. The *Bhāgavata* placing them next to the Ābhīras and before the Mālavas, puts them between the two, which indicates their position to the north of the Ābhīras and to the north-west of the Mālavas, *i.e.*, the western portion of Rajputana. The *Vishṇu* reads:—'*Saurāshṭra-Avanti-Śūrān*

[16] 'Sarvakshatrāvishkṛita-*vīra* śabda-jātotseka-avidheyānām' (*E.I.*, VIII, 44): "the Yaudheyas who were loath to submit, rendered proud as they were by having manifested their title of '*heroes*' among all Kshatriyas" (Kielhorn's translation).

Arbuda-Marubhūmi-vishayaṁś cha vrātyā dvijā Ābhīra-Śūdra read (*Śūra*)*-ādyāḥ bhokshyanti*'. Its reading *Śūdra* after *Avanti* has the variant reading—*Śūra* which is confirmed by the *Vishṇu Purāṇa* itself in another place[17] and the *Harivaṁśa*.[18] There was, however, a republic of the *Śaudrāyaṇas* whose name was derived from a proper-name *Śūdra*, not the caste-name but the personal name of the founder.[19] But the tests of the *Bhāgavata* and *Vishṇu* here evidently mean '*Śūras*' which stands for the *Yaudheyas*. The *Bhāgavata* and the *Vishṇu* do not mention at all the Prārjunas, Sahasānīkas, Kākas and Kharparikas. They had belonged to the Nāga group, being in Eastern Malwā."

---

[17] Wilson, *V.P.*, Vol. II, p. 133; *Śūra-Abhīrāḥ cf. Harivaṃśa*, 12, 837, *Śūra Abhīrāḥ*.

[18] See Hall's note in Wilson's *Viṣṇu*, II, 133.

[19] See p. 159 above.

CHAPTER XX

Criticism on Hindu Republican Systems

Moral assets

Before parting with the republics it is necessary to pass some general criticism on their systems. The *laws* and the administration of law, in the republican states of India are unanimously praised by the Greek observers and their praise is confirmed by the *Mahābhārata*. Some of them, at least, were careful to preserve precedents of decided cases in books. Even their sworn enemy Kauṭilya says that a republican chief in his state has the beneficial propensity of *justice*.[1] A high sense of justice was maintained. Without it no republic can last very long. *Discipline* was another virtue of theirs. Kauṭilya notices as a feature that the republican chief was a man accustomed to discipline.[2] The *Mahābhārata* points out, as we have seen, that discipline was maintained amongst members, both junior and senior, by responsible leaders. The leaders, further, made themselves and their actions popular.[3] Kṛishṇa in the *Māhabhārata* is reported as mentioning to his friend Nārada his difficulties in conducting his federal council. The latter rebukes Kṛishṇa for his want of control of his speech in public discussions. He advises the Vṛishṇi leader to cultivate the habit of bearing oratorical attacks with patience, and to sacrifice feeling of personal umbrage, to maintain the integrity of the *Saṃgha*.[4]

Likewise they were always ready to take the field. *Bravery* was a point of ambition and honour amongst the citizens.

Principle of equality

As the *Mahābhārata* says, *equality* prevailed in the *Gaṇa*. This was naturally necessary. The more democratic an institution, the greater must have been the emphasis laid on equality.

---

[1] सङ्घ्यमुख्यश्च सङ्घेषु न्यायवृत्तिहितःप्रियः । *Artha-Śāstra*, p. 379.

[2] दान्तो युक्तजनस्तिष्ठेत् । *Ibid.*

[3] सर्वचित्तानुवर्त्तकः । *Ibid.*

[4] See Appendix A.

In addition to moral virtues the republics had administrative virtues. They were specially successful, on the evidence of the *Mahābhārata*, in their financial administration. Their treasury remained always full.

Successful administration

A great reason of their political strength was that a republic was *nation-in-arms*. The whole community was their army. They were a citizen army and therefore immeasurably superior to the hired levies of monarchies. And when they formed an offensive and defensive league they were regarded, as Kauṭlya says, 'invincible'. Hindu Republics were prone to form leagues. The league of the Six-Trigartas of the grammarians, the league of the Kshudraka-Mālavas, the league of the Videhas and Lichchhavis (the federated Vajjis of the Pāli Canon), the league of the Andhaka-Vṛishṇis are examples in point. According to the *Mahābhārata* it was almost impossible for the enemy to crush federal republics. The Buddha as well gave his opinion to the Chancellor of Magadha that the federal Vajjis could not be conquered by the Magadha king.

Military system

The *wealth* of the Hindu republic is a matter of admiration both in home and foreign records. The Greeks noticed their riches and the *Mahābhārata* also bears testimony to it. A citizen had the ambition to be the leader of the trade association or of the guild-merchant, failing to be a political leader (p. 102 above). The art of peace and the art of war, discipline and perseverance, habits of ruling and being ruled, thought and action, home and state, went hand in hand. A highly practical and keen individual and citizen would have been the result of this life. With these virtues and this culture, there is no wonder that the *Mahābharata* says that their alliance was courted, and that they took delight in reducing their foes, and saw to their own material prosperity. This is explained by the fact that their training and genius were not one-sided. They were not solely political animals. They were economic animals equally. Kauṭilya characterises them as martial and industrial in the same breath ; they were forced to be industrial and martial by their laws. Attention paid to trade and agriculture kept their treasury and themselves rich.

Industrial system

On the evidence of the Greek witnesses they were not only good soldiers maintaining a very high tradition of bravery and skill in war, but also good agriculturists. The hand which weilded the sword successfully, was accustomed to use the scythe with equal facility. According to the *Artha-Śāstra* and Buddhist documents, they were both agricultural and industrial.

The type of citizen

Separation of powers and functions, which will be noticed in the data given above, for instance, command of the army and executive government amongst the Patalas, judiciary, military command, and executive authority amongst the Lichchhavis, similarly elective generalships in several states noticed by the Greeks, and complete absence of sacerdotal element in the chiefs, denote a highly developed sagacity and a vast constitutional experience in the republics.

Separation of powers

Technical books which have come down to us are of the monarchist school. If we recovered a book of the republican school, it would undoubtedly disclose the theories of state of Republican Polity. That there were such books is extremely probable. The chapters on *Gaṇa* and *Vṛishṇi Saṁgha* in the *Mahābhārata* indicate their past existence. So does the verse in Kauṭilya which is evidently quoted from another work, as the verse is the only matter in the chapter which has the republican point of view, the rest being all a monarchist look-out.[5] The discussion on the *Arājaka* state in the *Mahābhārata* also shows familiarity with a written theory of state of the Arājaka constitution. All these data indirectly prove the existence of well-considered philosophic bases on which republican constitutions were founded. They explain to a great extent the variety which we have noticed in republican constitutions. They were not unconscious, instinctive institutions. There could not have been a lack of philosophic thinking in the country of Kapila and the Kaṭhas who tackled much more abstruse problems of philosophy than that of state.

Philosophic basis

---

[5] *Artha-Śāstra*, p. 379.

Republican theories

The evidence of the *Chatuś-Śatikā* of Āryadeva, a fragmentary manuscript of which was discovered by Mahāmahopādhyāya Hara Prasad Shastri,[6] establishes that the elected ruler in a *Gaṇa* was regarded as a servant of the *Gaṇa* (*gaṇadāsa*). The same principle is declared by Kṛishṇa in the discussion cited in the *Mahābhārata*. 'It is the servant's duty (*dāsya*) which I have to perform under the name of rulership (*Aiśvarya-Vādena*)'.[7]

Individualism

It seems that the Kaṭhas and the Saubhūtas regarded the individual merely as a part of the state. By himself he did not exist. Hence they claimed an absolute right over the child born to individuals. It is evident that other republics did not subscribe to this view. They, as evidenced by coins, take *gaṇa*, the Government, as distinct from the community; the individual is not lost in the state. At the same time the unity between the two is so complete that the two are very nearly identical. The extreme case of individualism on the other hand, was the theory of the Arājaka state, the No-ruler-state[8]. Government itself was regarded by the theorists of that class of state as an evil. No one was vested with executive power. Only the law was to rule, and the only sanction they prescribed for one found guilty of crime was ostracism. The sovereignty of the individual was not to be delegated to any one man or a body of men. Of course, a state founded on such a basis, to be practical, must have been exceedingly small. Such states, however, did exist in Hindu India as noticed in the *Jaina Sūtra* referred to above. The monarchist may very well exclaim: 'No Government is more miserable than the Arājaka Government.[9] If a powerful citizen obeys the (law) it is all well, but if he rebels he can work total destruction.'[10] And

Social Contract

the monarchists may very well pick up the Arājaka theory from the republicans to justify their own theory of monarchy. But they could

[6] *J.A.S.B.*, 1911, 431. [7] See Appendix A. [8] See pp. 86-89 above.

[9] नहि राज्यात् पापतरमस्ति किञ्चिदराजकात्। *Śānti-Parvan*, LXVI. 7 (Kumb.).

[10] स चेत्समनुपश्येत समयं कुशलम्भवेत्। बलवान् हि प्रकुपितः कुर्य्यान्निःशेषतामपि॥ *Ibid.*, verse 8.

not ignore the Arājaka theory of Social Contract as the primary basis of state. On the basis of a mutual contract amongst the citizens, according to the Arājaka democrats, the state was founded.[11] This, of course, was true of the Arājaka state. When the monarchists postulate a contract between the king and the people (to take office on condition to rule honestly and to receive taxes in return)[12] they clearly say that this contract was resorted to when the contract of the Arājaka constitution failed in practical working. Here we find the monarchists really adopting the ***social contract theory*** originally formulated by the Arājakas. Probably a theory of social contract was common to all classes of republics. Its counterpart, applied to monarchy, was already known to Kauṭilya as an accepted truth.[13] Its origin in India is very ancient, evidently the most ancient in the world.[14] It is to be remembered

---

[11] संमेत्य तास्ततश्चक्रुः समयानिति नः श्रुतम् । *Ibid.*, verse 18.

विश्वासार्थञ्च सर्वेषां वर्णानामविशेषतः ।

तास्तथा समयङ्कृत्वा समग्रेनावतास्थिरे ॥ *Ibid.*, verse 19.

[12] See Chapters XXIV, XXV, XXXVI and XXXVII, on Monarchy, below.

[13] *Artha-Śāstra* (I. 14), pp. 22–23, मात्स्यन्यायाभिभूताः प्रजामनुं वैवस्वतं राजानं चक्रिरे । धान्यषड्भागं पण्यदशभागं हिरण्यं चास्य भागधेयं प्रकल्पयामासुः । तेन भृता राजानः प्रजानां योगक्षेमवहाः । 'People oppressed by anarchy made Manu, son of Vivasvat, their king. They settled one-sixth of agricultural produce, and one-tenth of merchandise, in cash, as his share. Kings salaried herewith carry on government (*yoga*) and well-being (*kshema*) of the people.' For the meaning of भृत see corresponding passages quoted under Monarchy, where king's 'wages' are mentioned. The meaning of भृत given here is in accordance with the sense of the word in *Manu*, XI. 62, and the Mitāksharā's definition of भृत्य. The meaning of Yoga becomes clear by the succeeding line, तेषां किल्विषमदण्डकरा हरन्ति where *adaṇḍakara* or 'king failing in government' is referred to in contrast. Compare also on *yoga*, युक्त 'member of executive service' in the *Artha-Śāstra*.

[14] Kauṭilya, 300 B.C., quotes it as a well-known theory. The Vedic hymns of election discloses clear germs of this theory. See Chapter XXV on Coronation for references in the *Brāhmaṇas*. The Buddhists have it in their old books. *Aggañña S.*, 21 (*Dīgha*) = *M.V.*, I. 347–48—शालिक्षेत्रेषु षष्ठ शालिभागं ददाम । महता जनकायेन सम्मतो ति महासम्मतो . . राजा ति संज्ञा उदपासि ।

that in its full exposition it was a republican theory. Such a theory was of immense value in its beneficial effect on the rulers in general.

Longevity

The best test of the success of a state system is the length of *life* which it can secure for the state. The republican system of India, as a class, proved very successful in securing longevity. As pointed out above, the system is mainly post-Vedic. Taking then the age of the *Aitareya Brāhmaṇa* as our earliest landmark, the Satvat Bhojas had a life of about 1,000 years. If the Uttara-Madras and Pāṇini's Madras were identical, they lived for about 1,300 years, otherwise for 800 years. The Kshudrakas and Mālavas had long existed free before 326 B.C. as they told Alexander. The Mālavas continued on in Rajputana up to *c.* 300 A.C. They thus enjoyed free life for about 1,000 years. And so did the Yaudheyas. The Lichchhavi record covers a full millennium. The principles regulating the life of Hindu republics thus stood well the test of time.

Weak points in Hindu Republics

But after all the Hindu republics, normally speaking, were not large units. Although they were larger in many cases than the ancient republics of Europe, they were, except for the Mālavas and the Yaudheyas and a few others, miniatures in comparison with the vast experiments of our own times, *e.g.*, the United States of America, France, and China.

This *smallness* was the very weakness of the polity. Nations and states, which remain small whatever their virtues, are not allowed to exist. Large states which developed greedy fangs, devoured up small sovereignties. The Mālavas and the Yaudheyas who survived mighty empires and great conquerors were large territorial units. They must have extended their laws and rights, like the Lichchhavis and Madras, to the arena of their expansion.[15] They, on account of their largeness, avoided the fate of their early contemporaries of smaller statures.

---

[15] The form *Mālavaka* in the *Mahābhāshya*, II. 296, points to that. See discussion on भाक्ति, *supra* p. 103. *A.-Ś.* gives *Lichchhivika* and *Madraka*; and Samudra Gupta, *Mādraka*.

The *Mahābhārata* says that Arājaka states could be easily conquered; that when an encounter took place between them and a strong foe, they broke like wood which does not know how to bend.[16] This was true of all democratic republics. Once conquered they ceased to exist as a community. Their life was so much bound up with their state that life proved only co-extensive with the state and no further.

In the time of Chandra Gupta, they were discredited by their not very successful opposition of Alexander. It is significant that young Porus, King or President of Gāndhāra, when faced with the foreign invaders, looked towards the imperial power of Magadha, and that Kauṭilya, a man of Taxila, should advocate their abolition in his Science of Commonwealth.

It appears that republics were liable to fall victims to intrigues. In aristocratic bodies *personal rivalry* and *greed of power* were marked out by statesmen like Kauṭilya, as the fit soil for sowing seeds of *dissension*. Varshakāra, a former Chancellor of Magadha, replied to the Buddha, who had said that the Vṛijis could not be broken, 'they can only be broken by mutual dissension'. Sources of dissension were not limited to enemy intrigues. As in popular forms of government in all ages, bitter hostilities arose out of discussions in the public assembly. Kṛishṇa in the *Mahābhārata* talking about his difficulties as leader of the republic says that his heart was roasted by terrible speeches. The *Mahābhārata* (in *Śānti-Parvan*, on *gaṇas* in general) alludes to this sort of unpleasantness and the consequent cessation of discussion on public affairs which lead to final disruption of the whole body.[17] The Buddhist tradition in describing the cause of the temporary discomfiture of the Lichchhavi, body-politic against Ajātaśatru,

---

16 अथचेदधिवर्त्तेत राज्यार्थी बलवत्तरः ।
अराजकाणि राष्ट्राणि हतवीराणि वा पुनः ।
प्रत्युद्गम्याभिपूज्यः स्यादेतदत्र सुमन्त्रितम् ।
—*Mahābhārata*, *Śānti-Parvan*, LXVI. 6–7 (Kumb.).
Cf. यत्स्वयं नमते दारु न तत्सन्नामयन्त्यपि । *Ibid.*, 10.
तस्माद्राजैव कर्त्तव्यः सततं भूतिमिच्छता । *Ibid.*, 12.

17 See Appendix A, and Chapter XIV above.

says that the Lichchhavis, owing to disagreement, had ceased to come to the Public Assembly when the tocsin sounded the call.[18] Then in some cases, the politicians were divided in opposing parties. This feature of the difficulty is put very graphically in the complaint of Kṛishṇa. 'As regard Āhuka and Akrūra, if they are in one's favour, there is no greater misery for that man; if they are not in one's favour, there is no greater misery for him either, I cannot elect the party of the either. Between the two I am like a mother of two gamblers, staking against each other, who cannot wish for the victory of one and the defeat of the other.'[19]

Internal dissension is said in the *Mahābhārata* to be the real danger to a republic. Fear from outside enemies as compared to that was 'nothing'.

Dissensions led to *breaking-up of gaṇas*. By this, as pointed out above, we should understand that sometimes schisms occurred and new states were formed. Thus small units to start with, and a tendency to become smaller, jealousy and rivalry amongst politicians, and license in public speaking seem to be the chief points of weakness of the Hindu Republican Polity.

---

[18] *J.A.S.B.*, 1838, 994–95.

[19] Appendix A.

CHAPTER XXI

Ethnology of the Republics

Mr. Vincent Smith in a letter[1] raises the question of the ethnology of the *gaṇas*. As the matter is put in issue by an authority of the position of Mr. Smith, I think it incumbent upon me, as the student of the *gaṇas* to discuss it.

Question raised by Mr. Smith

Mr. Smith is of opinion that they were of Mongolian origin like the Tibetans. "I believe" (he writes) "that as late as the early centuries A.C. the population of India was largely of Tibetan affinities, snub-nosed people—see the Bharhut and Sāñchī sculptures. The Lichchhavis certainly were such, and the customs of hill-men give the best clue to the working of the *gaṇas*. I think both Buddha and Mahāvīra were essentially hill-men of semi-Mongolian type, even if they did adopt Magian features into their teaching. You may, of course, quote me as you propose to do."

There are a few facts which are supposed to lend some strength to this view, and I should deal with them first. Some of the minor republics occupied valleys of the Himalayas. And in the Chumbi valley "an old form of elective government", as brought to light by Mr. E. H. Walsh, prevails. Mr. Smith has referred to Mr. Walsh's descriptions in the *Indian Antiquary* (1906, p. 290).[2] Once every three years, according to Mr. Walsh's description, the villagers assemble at a fixed meeting-place and present to the two *Kongdus*, who act jointly representing the two divisions of the valley as heads of the local administration, a list of their elected headmen of the villages. From the list the Kongdus select the names of four persons whom they consider to be the most suitable to be the next Kongdus. Then they throw with

Instance of Chumbi Government

[1] Dated the 25th November 1917.

[2] But the paper of Mr. Walsh was not before him, and the account in the *Indian Antiquary* may not be strictly accurate being based on a newspaper report.

three dice, in the name of each of the four persons they have selected, and the two who obtain the highest throw are chosen as the Kongdus for the coming term of three years. This ceremony takes place before an old stone altar sacred to the deity of the locality before which is placed the banner, the insignia of the Kongdu's office. The newly elected Kongdus do not enter on office at once. This is done in the eleventh month when another ceremony takes place and an *yak* is sacrificed at the stone altar. The new Kongdus place their hands on the bleeding skin and take an oath on the sacrificed *yak* that they will administer justice even between their own son and the enemy. The Kongdus say that they do not hold their power from the Tibetan government but the local deity; that they originally got the banner from him and have always held their power from him. "The administration," says Mr. Walsh, "is thus theocratic as well as elective."

Criticism

Mr. Vincent Smith, in his note in the *Indian Antiquary*, opines, "I have now come across an observation which suggests that tribal constitution like that of the Yaudheyas may have been of Tibetan origin." Again, "for the purpose of illustrating ancient Indian tribal constitutions this slight abstract of Mr. Walsh's paper suffices, because no record exists which gives any details of such constitutions." Nothing like proof on the identification of the Yaudheyas as Tibetans is suggested, and it is hard to see why the Tibetan illustration should serve to fill up the vacuum of Indian details. Because no detail of Indian constitutions was known in 1906, was the gap to be filled up from Tibet? Now as the details are forthcoming, it will be admitted that there is not the slightest resemblance between the ceremony of the Chumbi valley which takes place in the eleventh month of the election of the Kongdus and the republican consecrations given in the *Aitareya Brāhmaṇa*. Even the States which were near the Himalayas and which received the Vairājya consecration are poles apart from the Chumbi *yak*-sacrifice. The parliament or *gaṇa* of the Yaudheyas, their *Manthra-dharas*, their *elected President* have nothing corresponding to them in the theocratic government of the Chumbi valley.

Bharhut and Sāñchī Sculptures

As to the sculptures, it has never been claimed on behalf of the *gaṇas* that the *Sāñchī* and *Bharhut* monuments are the products of republican art. The question, therefore, strictly speaking is irrelevant. I may, however, express a fear that probably Mr. Smith's conclusion is based on misleading photographs of the reliefs of Sāñchī and Bharhut. The noses have been the pointed target of decay and iconoclasm. Further, many of the figures are meant to represent foreigners and barbarians and evil spirits, and their features have been deliberately made un-Hindu.[3] A good example of this is the representation of *Yakshas* and *Yakshiṇis* which occur again and again. The Yaksha and Yakshṇī have been the theme of Indian mythology and folk-lore, poetry and romance, throughout the literature. They are always connected with the Himalayas and treated not only as foreign but also mischievous. Now, if the Himalayan people are represented with snub-nose, credit is due to the artist, but no credit can be given to ethnology which makes the sculptor identical with the sculptured, the virtue with the dreaded evil. The point becomes clearer if we take the life-size female statue discovered at Patna. The Bharhut Yakshṇī is ugly, heavy and repulsive, while the statue lately discovered is as perfectly Aryan as it could be, with the poetic *tribhaṅga*, a beautiful nose, small chin, and the Aryan head.[4] This is the type which the *Jātaka* describes[5] as the statue of the Māṭrika which decorated royal courts and deceived people in darkness as a living figure. One is the representation of the home type and the other foreign. In Indian art there is a tendency to devote pointed attention to the foreign and queer, as the Hindus do to-day in their national pageants. The man which the Hindu saw every day, namely, one like himself, did not interest the artist and his public so much as the outlandish, the uncommon, the *dwarf*, the *lion-rider*, the *snake-man* and

Mr. Smith's error

---

[3] Consult *History of India,* 150–350 A.D., p. 215, pl. VI, on Bharhut features. (*J.B.O.R.S.*, XIX.) The features are probably local, Gond features.

[4] *J.B.O.R.S.*, 1919, p. 103.

[5] *J.*, VI. 432.

the *snake-woman*, the *Yaksha*, the *Abyssinian*,[6] the mischievous alien slave. Incidentally when the Sāñchī or Bharhut artist has come to deal with his own kings and queens, women and boys, ascetics and trees, the virtuous elephant, and the surgeon monkey, he has anticipated this ethnolcgical controversy. I venture to challenge any one to show the snub-nose or the high cheek bone or any outlandish element in those representations.

Alleged Mongolian basis of Indian population in early centuries

With regard to the general suggestion as to the Mongolian basis of India's population "as late as the early centuries," no amount of a "it is possible"[7] opining can satisfy me or one who reads in the *Mahā-Bhāshya* that the Brahmin still had fair eyes and fair hair (गोरः पिङ्गलः कपिलकेशः on P. V. 1. 115) and who reads in the *Gopatha Brāhmaṇa* that the Vaiśya was still Śukla or white and who reads in the *Dharma-Śāstras* that the Śudra woman was still the 'black

---

[6] Some of these reliefs were evidently prepared from designs executed by other hands and it is that what is implied by the expression rūpakaṁma prepared by the ivory carvers of Vidiśā (वेदिसकेहि दंतकारेहि रूपकंमं कतं). In such cases the word sculptors as used by me above is not quite suitable.

My friend, Mr. Panday, has drawn my attention to Prof. Grünwedel's conclusion on the subject which runs as follows :—

"The different peoples that lived side by side in India were distinguished from one another above all physically: contact with peoples of higher Asia in the time of Aśoka revealed new types, and thus we undoubtedly see an attempt, for instance, to represent foreign nations in the equestrian groups that adorn the Sāñchī gateways

"On the eastern gate, for example, besides mythical foreign peoples two figures are represented riding on horned lions. One of the heads is clearly not of the Aryan type; the woolly negro-like hair and the thick coarse shape of the whole head surprises one; this same figure holds a bunch of grapes in his hand....The whole series of these figures—those mounted on goats, on dromedaries, on lions—present a distinct contrast to the Hindus riding on elephants....

"The great majority of the other reliefs at Sāñchī present the Hindu type—a long head with full round face, large eyes, and thick lips. At Bharhut the same type appears but it is somewhat harsher." —*Buddhist Art in India*, Trans. by Burgess, pp. 33–34.

[7] *E.g.*, *Ind. Ant.*, 1906, p. 290.

beauty ' of the land. The republics, as we have seen, had Brahmins, Kshatriyas, Vaiśyas and Śūdras. The Greeks saw them and admired their physique from their point of view. They could not have praised snub-noses. An ounce of evidence is weightier than tons of theories.

Nationality of Lichchhavis

The Lichchhavis, whose form of republican government was noticed by orientalists in the first instance, attracted much attention and curiosity, and gave rise to various speculations. Mr. Vincent Smith wrote a short paper on "Tibetan Affinities of the Lichchhavis".[8] This paper is referred to in successive editions of Mr. V. Smith's History, and has been often taken by others as having established its thesis.

Mr. Smith bases his theory, firstly, on an alleged custom of exposure by the Lichchhavis of dead human bodies, a custom which he says also prevails in Tibet; and, secondly, on judicial procedure of the Lichchhavis which he thinks has a very close resemblance with the procedure followed in Tibet. An examination of the two data shows that the exposure of the dead as "the usage of the Lichchhavis of Vaiśālī" "in ancient times"[9] has existence only in a mistaken imagination; that there is not even a remote resemblance in the two judicial procedures.

Mr. Smith relies on a Chinese legend saying that the Buddha at Vaiśālī observed a Cemetery under a clump of trees and had the cemetery described to him by Ṛishis: "In that place, the corpses of men are exposed to be devoured by the birds; and there also they collect and pile up the white bones of dead persons, as you perceive; they burn corpses there also and preserve the bones in heaps. They hang dead bodies also from the trees; there are others buried there, such as have been slain and put to death by their relatives, dreading lest they should come to life again; whilst others are left there upon the ground that they may return, if possible, to their former homes."[10] Now this, is the passage (I have quoted it in full) upon which the whole theory of the exposure of the

[8] *Ind. Ant.*, 1903, pp. 233–35.

[9] *Early History of India*, 3rd ed., p. 155.

[10] Beal, *Romantic Legend of Sakya Buddha*, p. 159.

dead is based and on the basis of which Mr. Smith has considered the Lichchhavis to have been of Tibetan origin. The passage is from a legend in China of about 1,000 years later than the time of the Buddha, and as such it is worthless as a piece of historical evidence for contemporary details. But the passage, however, as it stands, is innocent. To one acquainted with the standard dramas of Sanskrit literature and the social and religious customs of the orthodox Hindus as they have prevailed, the passage connotes differently in its natural way. A typical *Smaśāna*, 'cremation ground,' is what is described. In some cases, as it is enjoined in the *Dharma-Śāstra* a dead body cannot be burnt but has to be either buried or exposed, or in the language of Manu, "to be thrown in the forest like a log of wood"[11] (and for that, it is hoped, no one would dare to call the author of the Mānava Code a Tibetan or Pārsī). Dramas and fictions in Sanskrit are full of allusions to men being executed at the *Smaśāna* and people hanging themselves by a tree in the *Smaśāna* grounds. The practice of laying the dead body in hope of recovery is observed even to-day.

As to the alleged '*close resemblance*' which according to Mr. Smith 'is impossible not to perceive in the matter of the two types of criminal procedure, I quote in the footnote[12] the

---

[11] *Manu*, Ch. V, verse 69.

[12] Turnour, the authority of Mr. Smith on the Lichchhavi procedure, says thus :—

" On this point, the *Atthakathā* contains this note :

" In aforetime, the *Wajjian* rulers on a person being brought and presented to them, thus charged ' this is a malefactor ' without at once deciding ' he is a malefactor,' dispose of him accordingly. They surrender him to the *Winichchhiya mahāmattā* (chief judicial officers). Having examined him, if they conceive ' this man is not a culprit,' they release him. If they decide ' this is a malefactor' without awarding any penalty, they transfer him to the *Wohārikā* (learned in the customs or laws). They also having investigated the matter, discharge him, if he be innocent ; but if he be guilty, there are certain officers called *Suttadharā* (maintainers of the *suttan*) to whom they transfer him. They also inquire into the matter and discharge him, if he be innocent ; but if guilty, they transfer him to the *Aṭṭhakulakā*. They also having observed the same procedure, transfer him to the *Senāpati* (chief minister), he again to the *Uparājā* (sub-king) ; the *Uparājā* to the *Rājā*. The *Rājā* enquiring into the

whole passage about the two procedures in Mr. Smith's own words. A mere comparison by both lawyers and laymen would show that it is impossible 'to perceive' the alleged 'resemblance'. I may here refer the reader to the interpretation of the Lichchhavi procedure given above and its comparison with

---

matter, if he be innocent, releases him, but if he be guilty, he causes the *Pavenipatthakān* (book of precedents or usages) to be propounded. There it is written, to him by whom such a crime is committed, such a punishment is awarded. The *Rājā* having measured the culprit's offence by that standard, pronounces a suitable sentence. —*J.A.S.B.*, 1838, I, 993–94.

On this Mr. V. Smith observes :

" The stages in this complicated procedure are eight in number, namely :—

1. Arrest and production of prisoner before the ' rulers ' ;
2. Enquiry by the *Winichchhiya mahāmattā* ;
3. ,, ,, *Wohārikā* ;
4. ,, ,, *Suttadharā* ;
5. ,, ,, *Aṭṭhakulakā* ;
6. Production before the *Senāpati* ;
7. ,, ,, *Uparājā* ;
8. Final judgment by the *Rājā*, who is bound to follow fixed written rules in awarding the penalty.

" The stages in the Tibetan procedure, as described by Babu Sarat Chandra Das (*Proc. A.S.B.*, 1894, p. 5), are exactly similar :—

1. The accused person is arrested, and sent to the lock-up ;
2. He is watched, treated kindly, and mildly interrogated ;
3. He is subjected to a mild but minute interrogation called *Jamli* and his answers are noted down ;
4. He is examined more strictly and whipped at intervals ; this is called *Tshan-di* ;
5. If he makes any kind of confession, true or false, he is subjected to further prolonged examination, repeated whippings, and cruel tortures of various kinds ;
6. If the case is serious and the Government becomes a party, he is taken to the Kalons or Ministers) Court ;
7. This Court suggests to the *Gyal-tshab* (Regent), which is the highest Court of the Country, that one of the three punishments mentioned in the decision may be approved ;
8. The sentence may be mitigated, commuted or revised by the *Dalai Lama* only.

The Regent has no power to do more than select one of the three punishments suggested by the Court of Ministers."—V. Smith, *Ind. Ant.*, 1903, p. 235.

the procedure of the *gaṇa* as mentioned in the *Mahābhārata*.[13] The Lichchhavi prodedure was based on rules which were normally common to all *gaṇas*.

Lichchhavi Criminal Procedure

There are circumstances which when taken into consideration leave no doubt as to the Hindu nationality of the Lichchhavis. Both the Videhas and the Lichchhavis had a common national designation 'the Vṛijis'. In other words, they were two branches of the same nation. No one responsible will venture to suggest that the Videhas were also Tibetans. The very colonization of Northern Bihar by the Vedic Videhas is recorded.[14] If the Videhas were pure Hindus, a centre of Upanishadic philosophy and orthodox theology, the Lichchhavis who were a ramification of the same nation could not have been barbarians. The Lichchhavis were at Vaiśālī. And the Purāṇas as we have seen connect the Vaiśālas like the Videhas with a well-known Aryan dynasty. They were not 'unanointed' rulers, a term applied by Hindu writers to barbarians settled in India. The *Aṅguttara-Nikāya* contemplates the Lichchhavi rulers to be 'anointed' rulers, *i.e.*, *abhishikta*; like any other Kshattriya rulers. The *Jātaka* mentions the celebrated lake which was jealously guarded and in which the *gaṇa* (republican) rulers obtained their *Abhisheka*.[15] The Buddhist literature unanimously treats them as good Kshattriyas. In the dynastic inscriptions of Nepal the Lichchhavis are said to have branched off from the Ikshavakus (*I.A.*, IX. 178); that is, they were allied to the Śākyas.

Their name according to the rules of grammar is a derivative of the word *Lichchhu*, *i.e.*, the followers or descendants of Lichchhu which in Sanskrit would be *Likshu*. *Liksha* means a mark and *Likshu* is connected with it. The name might have originated on account of some feature marks. The name Lakshmaṇa is a similar instance. *Lachchhu* in Bihar and the Doab is a very common name to-day denoting the same thing. A man born with some prominent black or blue mark on his person easily acquires the name.

---

[13] See above, Ch. XIII, Ch. XIV.

[14] *Śatapatha*, I. 4. 1. 10, ff.

[15] *Ante*, p. 47.

Mallas

The Mallas, neighbours of the Lichchhavis, are styled Vāsishṭhas in the *Mahāparinibbāna Sutta*,[16] and Vasishṭha is a well-known Aryan *gotra* name. The *Mahāparinibbāna Sutta* is not the work of crafty Brahmins of the type reputed to concoct Aryan genealogies for barbarian rulers.

Nationality of Śākyas

There is some discussion about the origin of the Śākyas also. Now the testimony of the Pāli authorities is unanimous that the Śākyas were a branch of the Aikshvākas. This is admitted by the adverse side, the Purāṇas, which place the Buddha, his father and his son, in the Ikshvāku house. Contemporaries of the Buddha amongst whom was Ajāta-śatru, king of Magadha, claim him as a Kshatriya.[17] As we have seen in the history of the formation of new republics and the Purāṇic detail about the Yaudheyas and Madras, the state-community was called after the leader. We find the same origin of the Śākya Community given by the Buddha himself.[18] That history of origin agrees with the ascertained history of similar republican foundations. That history—that a cadet of an Aikshvāka king founded the Śākyan republic christened after his name—therefore should be accepted.

The tradition of an ancient and obsolete custom of sister-marriage amongst the Śākyas had misled some scholars into wrong theories of race-origins. Such ancient and once living custom or law is accepted by the Vedic literature to have existed in the orthodox race. Buddhist tradition also does not limit to the Śākyas. It extends it to the Ikshvāku royal dynasty and the Ikshvākus were not new comers; they were never desacramented. They are as ancient as the Vedas. If the Ikshvākus were Aryan, their offshoot the Śākyas cannot be otherwise.

Evidence of the Greeks

The evidence of the Greeks who actually saw many Indian republicans is as decisive as any other fact. They describe the handsome looks and tall stature of the Punjab and Sind republicans. The snub-nose of the Ḥimalayan Mongoloid could

[16] *Mahāparinibbāna Sutta*, V. 19.

[17] *Ibid.*, V. 24.

[18] *Ambaṭṭha Sutta*, 16.

have never been described as a handsome feature by the Greeks, who must be taken as good judges in these matters. Nor could the stature of the Himalayan be mistaken by the Greeks to be majestic. The very discription proves perfect and pure Aryan type of the Republican Hindu. All these republicans are expressly mentioned by them as Indian.

Evidence of names and orthodox literature

The names of the republicans are an internal evidence of their Hindu origin. The Kathaians or the Kaṭhas are a Vedic people to whom the the Kaṭha recension of the *Yajur-Veda* and the *Kaṭha Upanishad* owed their origin. The Madras are not simply known to Vedic literature but are known as a home of orthodoxy where men like Śvetaketu went for post-graduate studies in sacrifices. There is a definite history of the origin of the Yaudheyas and Madras as noticed above. The 'Kshatriyas' were *par excellence* Kshatriyas. The Vṛishṇis are not only Kshatriyas but sacred Kshatriyas, the Vedic Satvat Yadus. As to the names like the Ārjunāyanas, and the Śālankāyanas, etc., the names are proof positive of their orthodox origins. The rules of Pāṇini stamp the formation with orthodoxy.

Orthodoxy has, so to say, anticipated the controversy and has already set its seal on the orthodox origin of these republics. The *Aitareya Brāhmaṇa* describes the Vedic rituals with which the republican Madras, the Satvats, the Kurus, and others were consecrated to political rule, and with which the constitutions *Bhaujya* and the *Svārājya* in the west and south-west and *Vairājya* by the side of the Himalayas received orthodox sanction.

Whatever the race-origins of a particular republican community, the system was Indian and orthodox Indian. It goes back to the time of the *Aitareya Brāhmaṇa* and earlier. That democratic and republican states were experiments of the Hindus themselves, who at times had been regal and in turn republican, is further proved by what Megasthenes saw and learnt in the country twenty-two centuries before (see p. 21 above).

PART II

CHAPTER XXII

Hindu Monarchy

Antiquity and Theory of Origin

Rājan or King

The word *Rājan* and its original *Rāṭ* literally mean a ruler. It is connected with the Latin *rex*. But Hindu political theorists have given it a philosophic derivation. King is called Rājā because his duty is 'to please' (*rañj*) the people by maintaining good government. This philosophic interpretation has been accepted as an axiom, throughout Sanskrit literature. The kings also acquiesced in and accepted this constitutional interpretation of the term. Emperor Khāravela of Kalinga, who was a Jaina, says in his inscription (*c.* 170 B.C.) that he did *please* his subjects, thirty-five hundred thousand in number. In the Buddhist Canon the same theoretic definition is found: *dammena pare rañjetīti kho, Vāseṭṭha, rājā.*[1] Both orthodox and heterodox branches of the race had adopted it. It was a national interpretation and a national theory of constitution.

Antiquity of Hindu Monarchy

Magasthenes, as observed before,[2] records the Hindu tradition current in his time that Monarchy was the earliest form of organised government in India. This is supported by the *Ṛig-Veda* where Monarchy is the normal and the only form of government known. Monarchist writers, as we have seen, utilised this fact as an argument against non-kingly forms of constitution.[3] After Monarchy, Megasthenes was told, republican experiments were made. As the *Aitareya Brāhmaṇa* puts it, it was in '*the firmly established* Mid-land' where monarchy held its own[4]; that is, the change from Monarchy to

---

[1] *Dīgha-Nikāya*, *Aggañña Suttanta*, III, p. 93.

[2] *Ibid.*, p. 25. See also McCrindle, *Megasthenes and Arrian*, p. 200.

[3] See pp. 86–89 and p. 17 above. *Cf.* नाराजकेषु राष्ट्रेषु वस्तव्यमिति वैदिकम् । *Mahābhārata, Śānti-P.*, 66. 5 (Kumb.).

[4] See *Aitareya Brāhmaṇa*, VIII. 14.—एतस्यां ध्रुवायां मध्यमायां प्रतिष्ठायां दिशि ये के च कुरुपञ्चालानां राजानः स-वशोशीनराणां राज्यायैव तेऽभिषिच्यन्ते । राजेत्येनानभिषिक्तानाचक्षते ।

republican form to which Magasthenes alludes, did not occur there. This Mid-land was the land from Kurukshetra to Prayāga—the valleys of the Jumna and the Ganges, which became the seat of the Aryan conquerors and Aryan monarchy. The Purāṇic history also confirms this. Its ruling houses cover the Middle Country, going beyond only in one direction—the East. The constitution of the East (*Prāchī*) according to the *Aitareya Brāhmaṇa*, was *Sāmrājya*,[5] which was a species of monarchies—meaning, literally, 'a collection of monarchies, *i.e.*, a Federal Imperialism.[6]

Hindu Theories on the origin of Kingship

There are several theories known to Hindu literature on the origin of Hindu Kingship. A brief notice of those theories is necessary to understand the constitutional effect which they produced on practical administration.

Vedic theory : origin in war

The Vedic theory is found in the *Aitereya Brāhmaṇa*. It asserts that the Devas, *i.e.*, their worshippers, the Hindus, originally had no king. In their struggle against the Asuras—when the Devas found that they were repeatedly defeated, they came to the conclusion that it was because the Asuras had a king to lead them, they were successful. Therefore they decided to try the same experiment. And they agreed to elect a king;

"*The Devas and Asuras were fighting* . . . . *the Asuras defeated the Devas* . . . . *The Devas said, 'It is on account of our having no king that the Asuras defeat us. Let us elect a king'. All consented.*"[7]

---

[5] See below, Ch. XXXVII. (Evidently at the time of the *Aitareya Brāhmaṇa* the North Bihar Republics had not come into existence.)

[6] Videha and Magadha. *Janaka* (probably a royal style and not a proper name), king of the Videhas, according to Vedic literature (*Śatapatha Br.*, XI. 3. 1. 2; see also उभयमेव सम्राट्, *Bri. Up.*, IV. 1. 1) and Jarāsandha, king of Magadha, according to the Purāṇas, were holders of the title Samrāt (*Mahābhārata*) (see Ch. XXXVII below).

[7] *Aitareya Brāhmaṇa*, I. 14—देवासुरा वा एषु लोकेषु समयतंत.... तांस्ततोऽसुरा अजयन्....देवा अब्रुवन्नराजतया वै नो जयंति राजानं करवामहा इति तथेति ॥

If it has a historical reference it would refer to the tribal stage of the Aryans in India and it would suggest that the Institution of kingship was borrowed from the Dravidians. Whatever the historical truth in the theory, the important point to note here is that kingship is contemplated to be elective in its origin.

Scientists' Theory of Contract

Political writers, however, had a theory of their own which is confined more to the abstract side of the question. They held that the first king was elected on certain conditions or on a contract, and that original contract was always enforced subsequently.[8] According to this view the election was necessitated for internal administration, the authority of law by itself, the people having refused to follow. This theory of contractual monarchy, which undoubtedly was a reflex of the express republican theory of contract,[9] found support in Vedic hymns and songs of royal election, in rituals of royal consecration which were based on elective principles, and in the Coronation oath which made the king swear that he should rule according to law.

Theory of elective kingship

These ceremonials were invariably observed even when succession to throne had become hereditary. In theory, according to these sacred ceremonies, the king, as we shall presently see, was always an elected officer holding office on conditions which he accepted in his Coronation oath. The contract theory of the politicians, as we shall see, was always believed in and accepted by both the ruler and the ruled.

Actual election at times did take place even in post-Vedic times.[10] Megasthenes notes that after Svayambhū, Buddha and Kratu, the succession was generally hereditary but that '*when a failure of heirs occurred in the royal house, the Indians*

---

[8] See the discussion in the *Artha-Śāstra*, 1, 9, pp. 22–23; also that in the *Mahābhārata* (see p. 225 below).

[9] See pp. 171–72 above.

[10] The following cases of election of king are found in the *History of Kashmir*: Baka '*was crowned king by the citizens*' (*R.T.*, I. 325); Yaśaskara was elected after great deliberations (*R.T.*, V, 445–77).

elected their sovereign on the principle of merit.'[11] The *Jātakas*[12] have stories of election of kings and even the fables[13] of the country made animals elect their king. They indicate that the theory of elective kingship was a national theory widely current. Let us now take the sacred hymns of royal election of the Vedas and the Vedic kingship.

---

[11] McCrindle, *Megasthenes and Arrian*, p. 200.
[12] The *Jātaka*, I, p. 399.
[13] See *Mahāvastu* (ed. Senart), II, p. 70.

CHAPTER XXIII

Vedic King and His Election

King's election and his position

The king was elected by the people assembled in the *Samiti*. The people assembled are said to elect him to rulership unanimously. The *Samiti* appoints him. He is asked to hold the state. *It is hoped that he would not fall from his office.* He is expected to crush the enemies.

Here is a complete Song of Election.[1]

आ त्वाहार्षमन्तरभूर्ध्रुवस्तिष्ठाविचाचलत् ।
विशस्त्वा सर्वा वान्छन्तु मा त्वद्राष्ट्रमधि भ्रशत् ॥ १ ॥
इहैवैधि माप च्योष्ठाः पर्वत इवाविचाचलत् ।
इन्द्रेहैव ध्रुवस्तिष्ठेह राष्ट्रमु धारया ॥ २ ॥
इन्द्र एतमदीधरद्ध्रुवं ध्रुवेण हविषा ।
तस्मै सोमो अधि ब्रवदयं च ब्रह्मणस्पतिः ॥ ३ ॥
ध्रुवा द्यौर्ध्रुवा पृथिवी ध्रुवं विश्वमिदं जगत् ।
ध्रुवासः पर्वता इमे ध्रुवो राजा विशामयम् ॥ १ ॥
ध्रुवं ते राजा वरुणो ध्रुवं देवो बृहस्पतिः ।
ध्रुवं त इन्द्रश्चाग्निश्च राष्ट्रं धारयतां ध्रुवम् ॥ २ ॥
ध्रुवोऽच्युतः प्रमृणीहि शत्रून्छत्रू यतोऽधरान् पादयस्व ।
सर्वा दिशः संमनसः सध्रीचीर्ध्रुवाय ते समितिः कल्पतामिह ॥ ३ ॥

---

[1] *Atharva-Veda*, VI. 87-88. This hymn occurs also in *Ṛig-Veda*, X. 173 with slight modification.

"Gladly you come among us; remain firmly without faltering; all the people want you; may you not fall off the State.

"Here be you firm like the mountain and may you not come down. Be you firm here like Indra; remain you here and hold the State.

"Indra has held it (the State) firm on account of the firm Havi offering; for it Soma as well as the Brahmaṇaspati has said the same.

"Firm (as) the heaven, firm (as) the earth, firm (as) the universe, firm (as) the mountains, let this *rājā* of the people be firm.

"Let the State be held by you, be made firm by the rājā Varuṇa, the God Brihaspati, Indra and also Agni.

"Vanquish you firmly, without falling, the enemies, and those behaving like enemies crush you under your feet. All the quarters unanimously honour you, and for firmness the assembly here creates (appoints) you."

Here is a passage employed at the re-election of a *Rājā* who had been apparently driven out :—

त्वां विशो वृणती राज्याय त्वामिमाः प्रदिशः पञ्च देवीः ।

वर्ष्मन् राष्ट्रस्य ककुदिश्रयस्व ततो न उग्रो वि भजा वसूनि ॥

"The people elect you to rulership, the wide[2] glorious quarters elect you. Be seated on this high point in the body of the state and from there vigorously[3] distribute the natural wealth."[4] *Kakud* literally means the "hump" of the bull. The allusion is to the throne which is regarded as the highest place in the body-politic. The previous verse in the Mantra shows that the reference is to *Ekarāt*, or monarch.

---

[2] The word पञ्च may mean either 'wide' or 'five'. Here the former meaning is more appropriate because the people assembled could be only confined to the four quarters and not the sky. Quarter comes in Election Hymns as a figurative use for the people assembled.

[3] Or 'like Ugra ruler' (न उग्रः). See p. 89 above.

[4] *Atharva-Veda*, III. 4. 2.

Sole taker of Taxes

According to the last verse of a hymn in the *Ṛig-Veda* corresponding to the song of election quoted above,[5] he becomes the sole taker of taxes from the people; he becomes the king of the people. The 'sole taker' signifies that the regular tax, as a royal due, had already developed. No one else but the king alone was entitled to it. The king is asked to ascend a raised seat which is significantly described as the highest point of the body of state. It shows that the idea of state as organism is realised as early as the Vedic kingship.

King-makers

The new king after ascending the throne received from the assembled people and the 'king-makers' who according to later authorities[6] were high functionaries or ministers,[7] a symbolic armlet called Maṇi. It was made of Palāśa wood. These high functionaries were the Treasurer, the Commander of the Army, the Grāmaṇī or the leader of the township, and some others. They are called 'kings' and 'king-makers' by the newly elected king. The 'king-makers' thus appear to be communal or popular officers of state who were regarded as rulers, amongst whom the king was the chief ruler. They are called latterly Ratnins or those in whom the Ratna or Maṇi is vested. For it was they who gave the king the symbolical jewel of royal authority. The king originally took the jewel of authority from all the folk present, including artizans and chariot-makers. This was the only symbolical ceremony which accompanied the Vedic election.

The king taking Parṇa or Maṇi says :—

ये धीवानो रथकाराः कर्मारा ये मनीषिणः ।

उपस्तीन् पर्ण मह्यं त्वं सर्वान् कृण्वभितो जनान् ॥ ६ ॥

---

5 ध्रुवं ध्रुवेण हविषाभि सोमं मृशामसि ।

अथो त इन्द्रः केवलीर्विशो बलिहृतस्करत् ॥ *Ṛ.V.*, X. 173. 6.

6 *Brāhmaṇas* and *Krishna Yajus*.

7 *Cf. Mahā Govinda Suttanta*, 32 ; *Dīgha N.*, II, 233, where the six great nobles of the state are called the King-makers, *Rāja-kattāro*.

ये राजानो राजकृतः सूता ग्रामण्यश्च ये ।

उपस्तीन् पर्ण मह्यं त्वं सर्वान् कृण्वभितो जनान् ॥ ७ ॥

"The skilful builders of chariots and the ingenious workers of metal, the folk about me all, do thou, O Parṇa, make my aids. The kings and king-makers, the charioteers and leaders of hosts, the folk about me do thou, O Parṇa, make my aids."[8]

Election for life-time

The king thus accepted his royal authority from the whole folk including equally the king-makers and the artisans. The king was elected for his whole life; "*Rule here a mighty benevolent* (king) *up to tenth decade of thy life.*"[9]

The throne was covered with the skin of a lion, tiger or leopard. This was done, as we shall see, even when the throne was made of precious materials. A particular symbolism was attached to the skin-cover. It was the emblem of prowess. "Thyself a tiger, do thou upon this tiger-skin stride through the great regions. All the clans shall wish for thee."[10] When seated on the throne he was sprinkled with water.[11]

Deposition and re-election

At times he was degraded and banished. After a period of exile an ex-king was sometimes re-elected.

"The eagle shall bring hither from a distance him that is fit to be called, wandering exiled in a strange land. The

---

[8] *Atharva-Veda*, III. 5. 6–7. Translation adopted from Bloomfield, *S.B.E.*, XLII. 114.

[9] *Atharva-Veda*, III. 4. 7.—दशमीमुग्रः सुमना वशेह ।

[10] *Ibid.*, IV. 8. 4.—व्याघ्रो अधि वैयाघ्रे विक्रमस्व दिशो महीः । विशस्त्वा सर्वा वाञ्छन्तु·· ॥

[11] *Ibid.*, IV. 8. 5–6.—तासां त्वा सर्वासामपामभि षिञ्चामि वर्चसा ॥ ५ ॥ अभि त्वा वर्चसासिचन्नापो दिव्याः पयस्वतीः ।..॥ ६ ॥ That the ceremony relates to monarchical Rājā (*Ekarājā*) is clear from the *Śrauta Sūtras* of the *Atharva-Veda*.

Aśvins shall prepare for thee a path, easy to travel! Do ye, his kinsfolk, gather close about him.

"Thy opponents shall call thee. Thy friends have chosen thee."[12]

He is said to have come to agreement with his electors.

"Come thou to the Viśes (the people), for thou hast agreed concordant with the electors."[13]

His duty

The king was expected to secure material prosperity to the people.[14]

"Fix thy mind upon the bestowal of wealth. Then do thou, mighty, distribute wealth amongst us."

In this connexion it would be interesting to quote here a poem from the *Atharva Veda* where the prosperity of the people is described. The song, evidently contemporary, praises the successful rule of king Parikshit of Kuru land.[15]

---

[12] *Atharva-Veda*, III. 3. 4.—

श्येनो हव्यं नयत्वा परस्मादन्यक्षेत्रे अपरुद्धं चरन्तम् ।

अश्विना पन्थां कृणुतां सुगं त इमं सजाता अभिसंविशध्वम् ॥

Was the *eagle* a mark of royalty? A recorded case of disposition is that of Dushṭaritu, king of the Sriñjayas (*Śatapatha Brāhmaṇa*, XII. 9. 3. 1; Weber, *I.S.*, I. 205). He was recalled.

[13] *Ibid.*, III. 4. 6.—

इन्द्रेन्द्र मनुष्या३ः परेहि सं ह्यज्ञास्था वरुणैः संविदानः ।

स त्वायमह्वत् स्वे सधस्थे स देवान् यक्षत् स उ कल्पयाद्विशः ॥

[14] *Ibid.*, III. 4. 4.—

अधा मनो वसुदेयाय कृणुष्व ततो न उग्रो वि भजा वसूनि ॥

S.B.E., XLII. 113.

[15] *Ibid.*, XX. 127. (3). 7–10.—

राज्ञो विश्वजनीनस्य यो देवोमर्त्यं अति ।

वैश्वानरस्य सुष्टुतिमां श्रणोता परिक्षितः ॥ ७ ॥

.. .. ..

कतरत् त आ हराणि दधिमन्थं परि श्रुतम् ।

जाया पतिं वि पृच्छति राष्ट्रे राज्ञः परिक्षितः ॥ ९ ॥ (Contd. on p. 198.)

"Listen ye to the high praise of the king who rules over all peoples. What may I bring to thee, curds, stirred drink, or liquor? (Thus) the wife asks her husband in the kingdom of King Parikshit."

In other words, in the Kuru land the wife never thinks of offering such a poor drink as water to the thirsty husband. And the barley beverage when brought 'overran the brim'. This shows "*the people thrive merrily in the kingdom of King Parikshit.*'

Germs of later political philosophy

The election in the Vedic age appears fairly simple and business-like. But it has a latent philosophy behind it. The king is elected by the people; he is expected to fulfil certain duties; and is invested with certain privileges. He accepts his office from the people and the 'king-makers'. He was in agreement with his electors. He could be removed from his office and could be brought back from exile. The germs of the political philosophy of kingship are all to be found in these Vedic mantras.

The fact, if not the theory, was clear that the office of the king was a creation of the People and was held conditionally. Above him there was always the National Assembly, the *Samiti* which was, as we have seen above, the real sovereign.[16]

अभीव स्व१ः प्रजिहीते यवः पक्वः परो बिलम् ।

जनः स भद्रमेधते राष्ट्रे राज्ञः परिक्षितः ॥ १० ॥

See *S.B.E.*, XLII, pp. 197–98.

[16] *Cf.* Macdonell, *History of Sanskrit Literature*, p. 158 : 'The king (*rājā*) was often hereditary....His power was by no means absolute, being limited by the will of the people expressed in the tribal assembly (*Samiti*)'. See also Zimmer, *Altindisches Leben*, 162 ff.; Weber, *Indische Studien*, XVII. 88; Geldner, *Vedische Studien*, II. 303.

CHAPTER XXIV

Coronation Ceremony of the Brāhmaṇa Period and Its Constitutional Significance

In the age of Brāhmaṇa literature, coronation becomes elaborate, ritualistic and very technical. Special royal ceremonies were invented. But they all retain the same constitutional characteristics as we find in the true Vedic period. In fact they are developments of the same underlying ideas.

Fixed formulæ

Sacred formulæ and rites for royal installation are formed and prescribed in this period. And they become prescribed once for all. Since that time every Hindu sovereign crowned in India has observed them, for according to the orthodox view of both law and ritual, no one could attain kingship without them. The same ceremonies, in essentials, came down and are prescribed by lawyers of the seventeenth century who wrote for Hindu kings in Muhammadan times.[1]

Rājasūya, Vājapeya and *Sarva-medha*

In the Śrutis there are three ceremonies for consecrating heads of society. There is the first and foremost, the *Rājasūya*, or the inauguration of a king, there is secondly, the *Vājapeya* used for consecrating a king or a high functionary as the royal priest, and thirdly, there is the *Sarva-medha*, 'a sacrifice for universal rule'. The *Vājapeya* probably did not partake of political nature in its origin, it being primarily designed to celebrate something like an Olympic victory.[2] It was, later on, adopted for royal and religious consecrations. The *Sarva-medha*[3] is an exceptional ceremony performed by emperors who are already consecrated to rulership. The ceremony proves the existence of the territorial ideal of a

---

[1] See Mitra Miśra, *Vīramitrodaya Rājanīti*, pp. 85–113.

[2] Cf. *Taittirīya Brāhmaṇa*, I. 3. 2. 2.
See *contra* Eggeling, *S.B.E.*, XLI, p. 24 (Introduction).

[3] See *Śatapatha Brāhmaṇa*, XIII. 7. 1.

one-state India.[4] The normal ceremony of Coronation, however, is the *Rājasūya*.

राज्ञ एव राजसूयम् । राजा वै राजसूयेनेष्ट्वा भवति...

"To the king doubtless belongs the *Rājasūya*, for by offering the *Rājasūya* he becomes king."[5]

We shall here mainly discuss the rituals of the latter and also of the *Vājapeya*. In fact they all have very many details in common, and they supplement each other. The *Vājapeya* came to be regarded as a preliminary to the *Rājasūya*.

The *Rājasūya* is comprised of three distinct parts; the first is a series of preliminary sacrifices, the second is the *Abhishechanīya*, 'the sprinkling', or 'the anointing', the third is a number of post-anointing ceremonies. Out of the three, the *Abhishechanīya* is the most important; and, perhaps, in practice the rites and formulæ of it alone were considered indispensable at normal coronations.

'He' the king-elect

One of the first things which strike the student of the ceremony is the pronoun "he" by which the king-elect is studiously designated. It is only after the sprinkling stage that he is called 'king'; that is, only when the ceremony is complete, he becomes invested with the royal office and powers; before that he is an ordinary citizen.

The Ratna-Havis

Among the preliminary offerings there are the eleven ratna-havis (the 'jewel'-offerings) which 'he' has to make to the eleven Ratnins or the 'Jewel-holders' at their respective houses. The recipients of the Ratna-havis are :—[6]

---

[4] Cf. *Aitareya Brāhmaṇa*, VIII. 15; Pāṇini, V. 1. 41–42 on *Sārva-bhauma*.

[5] *Śatapatha Brāhmaṇa*, V. 1. 1. 12.

[6] *Ibid.*, V. 3. 1. *Cf.* also *Taittirīya Brāhmaṇa*, 1. 7. 3 (Poona ed., I, pp. 308–10) and *Taittirīya Samhitā*, I. 8. 9 (Mysore ed., I, pp. 146-49).

The text says that the *ratnins* are eleven (एकादश रत्नानि). But the *havi* is offered at twelve places. Evidently the offering at his own house is not counted (the school of *Kṛishna Yajur-Veda* does not prescribe an offering at the king-elect's house).

(1) *Senānī* (the commander of the army).

(2) *Purohita* (the court chaplain); 'Brahmin' in the *Taittirīya* ritual.

(*a*) The King-elect himself as representing the Kshatra or 'rule'; in the *Taittirīya* we have '*Rājanya*' in the place of the king-elect.

(3) *Mahishī* (the queen). The Queen had an official character inasmuch as she appeared with the king on the throne on certain official occasions. It seems, however, the underlying principle here is the sacred theory that without the wife no sacrament could be performed, the sacrificer by himself being only one-half of his whole spiritual body, the other half being the wife. On this principle in the *Vājapeya*, she ascends the throne together with the husband.

"'Come wife, ascend we the sky'—'ascend we!' says the wife....She the wife in sooth is one half of his own self; hence as long as he does not obtain her, so long he is not regenerated for so long he is incomplete."[7]

In the *Rājasūya* ritual of the *Yajur-Veda* no direction is given as to the future Queen's ascending the throne. But the Epics prove the practice of joint coronation.[8] As the formulas are already prescribed in the preliminary *Vājapeya*, they have not been repeated in the *Rājasūya*. The same principle of completing the spiritual self of the king-elect is extended by other schools of the *Yajur-Veda* who make the king-elect do worship also to his other wives of lower castes, Vāvātā and Parivṛikti.[9] In the *Aśavamedha* ceremony even the wife of the lower Śūdra caste (*Pālāgalā*) takes part.[10]

---

[7] *Śatapatha Brāhmaṇa*, V. 2. 1. 10; *S.B.E.*, XLI, p. 32.

[8] *Rāmāyana, Yuddha Kāṇḍa*, 128, 59; *Mahābhārata, Śānti-Parvan* (Kumb.), 39, 14:—उपवेश्य महात्मानं कृष्णां च ।

[9] Cf. *Śatapatha*, XIII. 5. 2. 5–8.

परिवृक्ता राज्ञो मध्यमपत्न्याः Bhaṭṭa Bhāskara, *Taittirīya Saṁhitā* (Mysore), III, p. 146.

[10] *Śatapatha*, XIII. 5. 2. 8; *Rāmāyaṇa, Bāla Kāṇḍa*, 14, 35.

(4) *Sūta* (the court-minstrel and chronicler). Probably in early times he combined in him some important office other than that of the chronicler. In the Mauryan Civil List of the *Artha-Śāstra* (V. 3–91, p. 245), he is placed amongst minor officers (*Paurāṇika*, etc.) who got 1,000 (silver paṇas) a year. It seems that every provincial capital had its *sūta*, as *Bṛ. Up.*, IV. 4. 37, indicates. He is the later histriographer whom Yuwan Chwang (Hiuen Tsang) found in the empire of Harsha Vardhana, whose duty it was to register 'good and evil events, with calamities and fortunate occurrences' in every province. That the record of each year was kept is evidenced by inscriptions of Khāravela and others.

(5) *Grāmaṇī* (the head of the Township or the village corporation), "Vaiśya-Grāmaṇī"[11] in the Maitrāyaṇī edition of the *Yajur-Veda*.

(6) *Kshattri* (the Chamberlain).

(7) *Saṅgrahītṛi* (the master of the treasury). In later times he is called *Sannidhātri* (*e.g.*, in the *Artha-Śāstra*).[12]

(8) *Bhāgadugha* (the collector of revenue). In later times he is called *Samāhartṛi* (*e.g.*, in the *Artha-Śāstra*). The expression literally means 'milcher of the share' (of the king one-sixth, etc.). This shows that the amount of taxation had already become fixed.

(9) *Aksharāpa*—Commentators have explained it as the controller of gambling. Gambling, being under state-control, brought in revenue; but the prominence of the department is rather strange and one is inclined to doubt the meaning of the commentators. Among

---

[11] See p. 204, *n* 18.

[12] Bhaṭṭa Bhāskara (Mysore ed., *Taittirīya Saṁhitā*, III, p. 148) points out the primary meaning of *Saṅgrahītā*, the 'holder of the reins', lit. 'the driver' (संग्रहीतुः··रश्मिग्राहिणः) and then gives the secondary meaning (quoting opinion of others रज्जुभिर्नियन्ता कुमाराध्यक्ष इत्यन्ये 'he who leads (the administration) by holding the reins (of government), *i.e.*, Prince-minister'.—This has some bearing on Asoka's *rājūka*, if it is connected with *rajju*.

the Officers the one who comes after *Sannidhātri* and *Samāhartṛi* in the *Artha-Śāstra*, corresponding to Nos. 8 and 9 of our list, is the *Akshapaṭala* or (the Department of) the Accountant-General. Thus the corresponding *Akshavāpa* seems to be the officer in charge of State Accounts. The Gambling Officer will be quite out of place here. It seems that squares or *Akshas* were made on some board (*Paṭala* or *Adhidevana*) by the help of which accounts were in those days calculated. The *Akshaśāla* (*Artha-Śāstra*, p. 85) should also be considered in this connexion. The *Akshaśāla* department took charge of gold and silver and the mint. *Aksha* in these technical offices has no connexion whatsoever with gambling.

(10) *Govikartṛi* (master of forests, literally, destroyer of beasts). He was evidently the officer described by Magasthenes amongst the 'Great Officers of State'[13] having 'charge also of the huntsmen' who cleared the land of wild beasts and fowls which devoured the seeds.[14]

(11) *Pālāgala* (the Courier). His uniform was a red turban and leathern quivers.[15] He was of the Śūdra caste.[16] In his place the *Maitrāyaṇī Saṁhita*[17] of the *Yajur-Veda* gives the *Taksha* and *Rathakāra*, carpenter and chariot-builder.

The Ratnins

The Ratnins are a development of the Vedic 'bestowers of the (*palāśa*)*maṇi*'. The latter were the '*king-makers*' (राजकृत: = the ministers), the *Sūta* the head of the village community, the builders of chariots and the skilful in metals, 'sorrounded by the folk'.

Now the Ratnins tend to be high functionaries of the state. In the selection of the functionaries the principle of class and caste representation appears to have operated. The

---

13 McCrindle, *Megasthanes*, p. 86.
14 McCrindle, *Ibid.*, p. 84.
15 The last two not in the *Taittirīya* ritual.
16 *Cf.* XIII. 5. 2. 8.
17 *M.S.*, II. 6. 5.

Purohita is studiously referred to as 'Brahmin' only, in the majority of *Yajus* Schools. He symbolises the Brahmin. The Rājanya or the king-elect himself symbolises the *Rājanya* or Kshatriya class. The *Grāmaṇī*, called the 'Vaiśya-grāmaṇī' in the *Maitrāyaṇī*,[18] a *grāmaṇī*, or Township-President of the Vaiśya caste represented the Vaiśya class or the remnant of the original 'people', now the 'commoners'. The *Taksha* and *Rathakāra* correspond to the Veda's 'skilful workers in metals and builders of chariots'. Their place is supplied by the Pālāgala in the *Śukla* ritual; the class is replaced by caste. The *Senānī*, *Purohita*, *Kshattā*, *Saṅgrahīta*, *Bhāgadugha*, *Akshāvāpa* and *Gokartrā* are the High Ministers, the old *Rājakṛits*, the king-makers. The High Ministers were still called 'king-makers' in the *Rāmāyaṇa* (समेत्य राजकर्त्तारो भरतं वाक्यमब्रुवन्, *A.* 79. 1, Com. राजकर्त्तारः मन्त्रिणः).

When society grew, it was not possible for the whole Folk to assemble, the adoption of the representative principle was natural. The most noticeable feature in the change is the express recognition of the Śūdra as a part of Society. From the constitutional point of view it is a great change. The conquered helot is now worshipped by the man who is going to become king. He is as much an integral part of the polity as any one else. This recognition, as we shall see, becomes more and more emphatic as time goes on.

The offering to the 'jewel-holders' is explained by the set phrase in each case, '*for it is for him that he is thereby consecrated and him he makes his faithful follower*'. He treats with *Havi* the headman of the village corporation because 'he assuredly is one of his jewels and it is for him that ' he is therby consecrated, etc.'[19]

---

[18] मारुतः सप्तकपालो वैश्यस्य ग्रामण्यो गृहे । *Maitrāyaṇī Saṁhitā*, II. 6. 5; IV. 3. 8.

[19] ग्रामण्यो गृहान् परेत्य मारुतम् सप्तकपालं पुरोडाशं निर्वपति विशो वै मरुतो वैश्यो वै ग्रामणीस्तस्मान् मारुतो भवत्येतद्वाऽ अस्यैकम् रत्नं यद् ग्रामणीस्तस्माऽ एवैतेन सूयते तम् स्वमनपक्रमिणं कुरुते—*Śatapatha Brāhmana*, V. 3. 1. 6.

Origin of Hindu Ministers

The reason for the respect due to the High Functionaries or Ministers should be noted. The Ratnin Ministers existed before the king came to the throne. They had existed independently of him. *They were in origin part of the Samiti*, 'the folk around me'—the Vedic 'kings' and 'king-makers'. In later history, ministers still retain these designations of popular times; they still retain the privileges of the ritualistic period—they are worshipped before every coronation. Likewise they retain pronounced traces of independence throughout their history (Chs. XXX, XXXI). The latter we can understand only with reference to this history of origin.

Approval of the Land

The whole procedure symbolises the obtainment of the approval of the differentiated organs of government in his consecration to kingship. The seeking of approval does not rest here. Symbolic 'approval' (*Anumati*) of the Earth (Motherland) itself is requested and obtained. This is done before the estates of the Realm are approached.

"They then return (to the sacrificial ground) without looking backward. He now proceeds with the cake on eight potsherds for *Anumati*. For *Anumati* is this (Earth); and whosoever knows to do that work which he intends to do, for him indeed she approves (*anu-man*) thereof; hence it is her he thereby pleases, thinking 'May I be consecrated, approved by that (genius of) approval!' "—[20]

The idea underlying is altogether human; there is no divinity about the person or the office of the sovereign.

The idea underlying

"After the jewels he offers a pap to Soma and Rudra." That the great gods should come after the secular officers was unpalatable to theologians, and they therefore give a fanciful explanation by

[20] *Satapatha Brāhmaṇa*, V. 2. 3. 4.—अथानुमत्याऽष्टाकपालेन पुरोडाशेन प्रचरतीयं वा अनुमतिः स यस्तन् कर्म शक्नोति कर्तुम् यच्चिकीर्षतीय ँ हास्मै तदनुमन्यते तदिमामेवैतत् प्रीणात्यनयानुमत्यानुमतः सूयाऽइति ।

introducing a myth that as offerings had been rendered to some unworthy of sacrifice, it was necessary to sacrifice to gods 'for enlightenment' (expiation).[21]

Abhishechanīyam

The *Abhishechanīyam* or the Sprinkling Ceremony starts with sacrifices to a set of deities for instilling in the king-elect certain virtues necessary for his office. Savitā is prayed for energy, the family fire for family virtues, Soma for capacity to protect forests, Bṛihaspati for eloquence, Indra for the ruling capacity, Rudra for power to protect cattle-wealth, Mitra for truth, and lastly Varuṇa for the protection of law.

Protector of Law

Says the *Śatapatha Brāhmaṇa*:[22] "Thereby Varuṇa the protector of the law makes him the protector of the law, *and that truly is a supreme state when one is protector of the law*, for whosoever attains to the supreme state to him, they come in causes of law." Here is a new theory of the monarchical days when the *Brāhmaṇas* were written. The sacred fromula only contemplates the protection of the law as a necessary duty of the king, but the commentator takes it in the sense that one of the chief features of a 'full-fledged' state must be that the law should be administered by the king or his officers ('for him they come in causes of law'). The old theory had been that the law of the community was administered by the community. The new theory was operating in actual life in the time of the *Jātakas* and it was fully extended in the imperial days of the Mauryas, when salaried judges not only dispensed royal justice but also administered royal laws.

---

[21] *Śatapatha Brāhmaṇa*, V. 3. 2.

[22] *Ibid.*, V. 3. 3. 9.—अथ वरुणाय धर्मपतये । वारुणं यवमयं चरुं निर्वपति तदेनं वरुण एव धर्मपतिर्धर्मस्य पतिं करोति परमता वै सा यो धर्मस्य पतिरसद्यो हि परमतां गच्छति त ॐ हि धर्मऽउपयन्ति तस्माद्वरुणाय धर्मपतये ॥ Cf. *S.B.E.*, XLI, p. 71.

Collection of Waters

Waters are then collected from the sea and other reservoirs of the land, proclaiming in sacred formulas the name of the person for whose anointing they were gathered. The waters are taken in each case with a poetic formula; "*Self-ruling waters, ye are*" "*bestowers of kingship, bestow ye kingship on. N.N.*"[23]

In the description and details of the waters there is to be found a poetic finish to the symbolical constitutionalism. Waters are brought from the Sarasvatī of historic memories, from the mighty rivers of the land, from the great Ocean. The sum total of these waters is yet to be contributed to by a humble pool of the country. The latter is invoked with the lofty address: "*Pleasing ye are, Bestowers of kingship, bestow ye kingship on. N.N.*" The comment on the sacred address of the *Brāhmaṇa* is majestic and is reserved only for this insignificant reservoir; "*He thereby makes the people steady* (the water of the pool being steady) *and faithful to him.*"[24] A common pool of the country over which he is going to rule is made a sacred source of his sovereign powers.

The gods have been invoked to endow the potential king with ruling virtues 'for national rule,' *jānarājyāya*,[25] 'for the ruling of the folk', yet the rivers of the land, the waters of India are prayed as 'bestowers of state' to confer the actual status of kingship. Gods might give him virtues for 'national rule" but they could not give the kingship of the land; it was the right of the waters in the land to do it. And they too only when combined from the highest to the lowest, could do it; hence the flattering address to a common country pool. An important conception is crystallised in this sacerdotal procedure. It is on the whole a symbolism enshrining a great idea for all ages.

---

[23] स्वराजस्थ राष्ट्रदा राष्ट्र मनुष्मै दत्त, *Satapatha Brāhmaṇa*, V. 3. 4. 21.

वृषसेनोऽसि राष्ट्रदा राष्ट्र ममुष्मै देहीति, *Ibid.*, V. 3. 4. 6.

[24] मान्दा स्थ राष्ट्रदा राष्ट्रममुष्म दत्तेति ताभिरभिषिञ्चति . . . स्थावरामनपक्रमणीं करोति . . . *Ibid.*, V. 3. 4. 14. Cf. *Taittirīya Saṁhitā*, I. 8. 11.

[25] Cf. *Taittirīya Brāhmaṇa*, I. 7. 6. 7.

Abhishechana or Consecration

The *Abhishechana* (the anointing) is twofold, the first part is the sprinkling of waters by what may be described as different estates of the realm, and the second is the theological anointing on the head by the priest just before the king-elect ascends the throne (*āsandī*). A tiger skin is spread in front of the Mitrā-Varuṇa's hearth and the king-elect steps upon it. Four men, one after another sprinkle him—a Brahmin, a kinsman of the king-elect, a Rājanya, and a Vaiśya which literally means 'one of the people'.[26] The Śūdra is absent and the kinsman seems to be a tautology. The latter is not found in the corresponding *Taittirīya* ritual (*Taitt. Br.*, I. 7. 8) where the Priest as Brahmin, Rājanya, Vaiśya, and lastly, Janya, do the besprinkling. The last one, Janya, stands for the Śūdra in the sense of a man of the 'hostile' tribe as in the *Aitareya Brāhmaṇa*, VIII. 26, as originally he was. In later times the Śūdra always appears.

The king-elect then puts on a silk underwear, a mantle and a turban or diadem.[27] Our *Śatapatha Brāhmaṇa* does not approve of the dressing, and there is that artistic touch in the reason given which was common to the Hindus and the Greeks. "For the limbs being his natural vestments they deprive him of his native bodily form." [28]

Investiture and Announcement

Then follows the Investiture, and Announcement. The priest gives him a strong bow with three arrows with the formula "*Protect ye him in front,*" etc. After the investiture while the king-elect is standing on the ground over the tiger-skin an Announcement is made,—the Āvid formulæ are called out :[29]

---

[26] *Śatapatha Brāhmaṇa*, V. 3. 5. 11-14.

[27] *Ushṇīsha* is taken by some to be turban and by others diadem. The *Rāmāyaṇa* has diadem (*kirīṭa*), *Yuddha Kāṇḍa*, 128. 64.

[28] *Śatapatha Brāhmaṇa*, V. 3. 5. 25.

[29] *Vājasaneyī Saṁhitā*, X. 9 :—

आविर्मर्य्या आवित्तो अग्निर्गृहपतिरावित्त इन्द्रो वृद्धश्रवा आवित्तौ मित्रावरुणौ

धृतव्रतावावित्तः पूषा विश्ववेदा आवित्ते द्यावापृथिवी विश्वशम्भुवावावित्तादितिरुरुशर्मा ॥

"Informed are ye Men! Informed is the house-lord Agni! Informed is the far-famed Indra! Informed are Mitra and Varuṇa, the upholders of the vow! Informed is Pūshan (the lord of wealth)! Informed are Heaven and Earth, all beneficial! Informed is Aditi, of great shelter!"

The author of the *Śatapatha Brāhmaṇa* points out that the announcements are symbolical[30]; Agni symbolising the Brāhmaṇas; Indra, the nobility; Pūshan the world of cattle and so on. In any case, the king-elect is expressly and firstly announced to men, whatever be the real import of the other *āvids*. The *āvids* are made to obtain permission or approval for the consecration, says the *Śatapatha* 'तैरनुमतः सूयते' and approved by them he is consecrated."

[30] *Śatapatha Brāhmaṇa*, V. 3. 5. 31-37.

CHAPTER XXV

Coronation Ceremony of the Brāhmaṇa Period and Its Constitutional Significance (*continued*)

Coronation Oath

After the Āvit-proclamation follows the Indra-ceremony of Sacred *Abhisheka*. (*Śatapatha Br.*, V. 3. 5. 2). The king-elect is unanimously regarded to have taken a vow (*dhṛita-vrata*) before he is seated on the throne.[1] The vow, promise, or oath is again alluded to in the *Taittirīya Br.* (I. 7. 10. 1–6), *satya-sava* "of true sacrifice," *satya-dharmā* "of true (or faithful) conduct," *satyānṛite Varuṇaḥ* "Varuṇa is authority in truth (or oath) and falsehood (or faithlessness)," *satya-rājā* "true king". To what engagement do these repeated expressions allude? The vow or engagement is not cited here. But, it is given in the very Indra-ceremony in the *Aitareya Brāhmaṇa*. Evidently that was universally adopted, as the testimony of later books and practice proves. It is therefore simply alluded to and not repeated in other Brāhmaṇas. The vow which the king-elect took, or, to use modern phraseology, the Coronation Oath, as given in the *Aitareya Brāhmaṇa* is in these terms :[2]

["Let the Kshatriya be sworn through this Great Coronation of the Indra-ritual. He is to repeat with faith :] 'Between the night I am born and the night I die, whatever good I might have done, my heaven, my life and my progeny may I be deprived of, if I oppress (injure) you'!"

The business-like and contractual nature of the oath is noteworthy. There is no reference to any divine agency in

---

[1] निषसाद धृतव्रतः *Vājasaneyī Saṁhitā*, X. 27 ; *Taittirīya Saṁhitā*, I. 8. 16 ; *Taittirīya Brāhmaṇa*, I. 7. 10. 2 ; *Aitarēya Brāhmaṇa*, VIII. 18.

[2] *Aitareya Brāhmaṇa*, VIII. 15.—[एतेनैन्द्रेण महाभिषेकेण क्षत्रियं शापयित्वा अभिषिञ्चेत् स ब्रूयात् सह श्रद्धया] याञ्च रात्रीमजायेहं याञ्च प्रेतास्मि तदुभयमन्तरेणेष्टापूर्त्तं मे लोकं सुकृतमायुः प्रजां वृञ्जीथा यदि ते द्रुह्येयमिति ।

the oath. It is purely human. It is humanly solemn. According to the *Aitareya Brāhmaṇa* the oath was common to all constitutions. It was administered to the Ruler (Kshatriya) whatever the form of polity, whether he was desirous of being consecrated to Sāmrājya, Bhaujya, Svārājya, Vairājya, Pārameshṭhya, Rājya, Māhārājya, Ādhipatya, or Sārva-bhauma (Monarchy).[3] This proves that the promise by the oath was made to the officiating priest as representing the whole society, for the ritual is the same both for republics and monarchical communities.[4] As we shall deal with the history and effect of the Coronation Oath presently we may pass on to the remaining ceremonials and their meaning.

Ascent to the throne

After the Announcement he is asked to ascend the wooden throne[5] (*Ā-sandī*) spread upon with furs, generally with tiger-skin. The formulæ for the occasion are four, and the four estates are asked thereby to protect the king-elect "as the precious treasure".

People as King's Protector

A point of the greatest constitutional import is that the king is to be protected by the four estates of the realm. Protected by the people (in his office) he is to carry on the administration. This principle was one of the accepted

---

[3] स य इच्छेदेवंवित्क्षत्रियमयं सर्वा जितीर्जयेतायं सर्वाल्लोँकान्विन्देतायं सर्वेषां राज्ञा श्रैष्ठ्यमतिष्ठां परमतां गच्छेत साम्राज्यं भौज्यं स्वाराज्यं वैराज्यं पारमेष्ठ्यं राज्यं महाराज्यमाधिपत्यमयं समंतपर्यायी स्यात्सार्वभौमः सार्वायुष आऽन्तादापरार्धात्पृथिव्यै समुद्रपर्यन्ताया एकराडिति तमेतेनैन्द्रेण महाभिषेकेण क्षत्रियं शापयित्वाऽभिषिंचेत् ॥ *Aitareya Brāhmaṇa*, VIII. 15.

[4] The Brahmin is the mouth-piece and representative of the entire society throughout the Epics. As we shall see later, the sanction in the case of the oath being broken, came from the entire community and not only from the Brahmins.

[5] The wooden throne was adhered to for coronation even when thrones of ivory and gold were in general use. See *Mahābhārata* (Kumb.), *Śānti-Parvan*, XXXIX. 2. 4. 13–14. Though of wood ('*khadira*' *catechu*) it was elaborate, as *Brāhmaṇa* descriptions show. The design of the throne of the Bharatas is famous in the rituals.

axioms of Hindu politics: *rāshṭreṇa rājā vyasane parirakshyastathā bhavet.*[6]

"Ascend thou the East....may the spring season, the priesthood protect thee *avatu* (अवतु), that precious treasure. Ascend thou the South....may the Kshatra protect thee, that precious treasure. Ascend thou the West....may the Viś protect thee, that precious treasure. Ascend thou the North ....may the Phala[7] protect thee, that precious treasure."

He is said to 'ascend the quarters'. It means that his installation is all-sided.

Besprinkling by the Priest

Just before he ascends, he steps upon a gold-plate; and through a gold plate perforated with a hundred or nine holes the waters are sprinkled over his head by the priest, with the following sacred text:[8]

सोमस्य त्वा द्युम्नेनाभिषिञ्चाम्यग्नेर्भ्राजसा सूर्यस्य वर्चसा इन्द्रस्येन्द्रियेण । क्षत्राणां क्षत्रपतिरेध्यतिदिद्यून् पाहि ॥ २ ॥

इमं देवा असपत्नꣳ सुवध्वं महते क्षत्राय
महते ज्यैष्ठ्याय महते जानराज्यायेन्द्रस्येन्द्रियाय ॥
इमममुष्य पुत्रममुष्यै पुत्रमस्यै विश एष वो
ऽमी राजा सोमोऽस्माकं ब्राह्मणानाꣳ राजा ॥

"With Soma's glory I sprinkle thee! with Agni's glow! with Sūrya's splendour! with Indra's energy! be thou the sovereign protector of the ruling powers!

"Make him, O gods, to be unrivalled for great rulership, for great superiority, for great national rule, for Indra's energy

---

[6] *Mahābhārata, Śānti-Parvan*, Ch. 130. 32 (Kumb.).

[7] Evidently standing for the *Śūdra*.

[8] These texts occur in the *Vājasaneyī Saṁhitā* (*Śukla Yajur-Veda*), Chapter IX, ver. 40 and Chapter X, vv. 17 and 18. These two chapters (IX and X) of the *Saṁhitā* give mantras for royal consecration from which different ceremonials have been evolved in the *Brāhmaṇas*.

make him, the son of (the man) XX and (of the woman) YY and of the people ZZ. This man, O ye People! is your king, he is Soma, king of us Brāhmaṇas."

'People' (विश्) according to Āpastamba, Baudhāyana and Kātyāyana (*Śrauta Sūtras* quoted by Sāyaṇa) means 'Nation,' *e.g.*, the 'Bharatas,' the 'Kurus,' the 'Pañchālas'. Kātyāyana explains 'the People' by the word Jāti. He speculates that territory was not (originally) fixed (अनवस्थिता 'fluctuating'), hence *viś* (the people) was used. In place of 'the People!' the *Taittirīya Saṁhitā* (I. 8. 10) of the *Kṛishṇa Yajur-Veda* gives 'O Bharatas' [एष वो भरता राजा] which shows that the explanation of the Śrauta-sūtra-kāras is correct. The *Yajur-Veda* or the Veda of Rituals (formulæ) was evidently composed in the land of the Bharata monarchy (Delhi-Agra).

Brahmin and Taxation

Soma is the life-giver of the vegetable kingdom of *Vanaspatis.*[9] Owing to the connexion of the Brahmins with the sacrificial Soma the deity Soma was considered to be their special deity. Here the king is consecrated as king of the whole people including the Brahmins, and the priest expresses this by calling him Soma.[10] The sacerdotalist author of the *Śatapatha*, however, gives a questionable explanation of the closing sentence in the Vedic text above quoted. He says that it means that Soma and not the king was the king of the Brahmins. This is inconsistent with the existence of the indicative 'this,' '*esha*' in the text, the naming of the people or nation and the homage when the Brahmin resigns his privilege in the person of the king.[10] The *Śathapatha* marks the last stage of the Brāhmaṇa period and it seems that the Priest-Brahmins about that time began to assert a claim of freedom from taxes. The *Śathapatha* explains that the meaning of the exception is that the king is to receive his sustenance from all

[9] *Vājasaneyī Saṁhitā*, Ch. IX, v. 39.

[10] See below under 'Homage' where the king is called a Brahmin made mighty through the strength of the whole people. *Cf.* The address to the king by the priest "Brahmin thou art! Savitar thou art! Varuṇa thou art (etc.)" in *Vājasaneyī Saṁhitā*, X. 28, with the 'Soma' here.

others except the Brahmin.[11] In the *Aitareya Brāhmaṇa*, however, the Brahmin is fully subordinate to the king,[12] and so he appears to be in the *Jātakas*. The *Vājasaneyī-Brāhmaṇa Upanishad* which belongs to the school of the *Śathapatha* places the Brahmin under the king. [तस्मात् क्षत्रात्परं नास्ति तस्माद्ब्राह्मणः क्षत्रियमधस्तुपास्ते राजसूये। '*Hence there is none above the Ruler, hence Brahmin sits under Kshatriya in Rājasūya*' (IV. 11).] The *Taittirīya* school does not accept the interpretation of the *Śathapatha*. Bhaṭṭa Bhāskara exlpains the Vedic text as denoting that as a Brahmin must never be without a king, he is supposed to be under Soma for the period before a king is consecrated, and after the king is consecrated, the king becomes his king also. [अस्माकं ब्राह्मणानां सोमो राजा, अधुना अयंचेति। सर्वदा सराजका वयं इत्यभिप्रायः। *Taittirīya Veda* (Mysore, III. pp. 157–58).] The *Aitareya* implies that he becomes the Protector of Brahmins and Protector of Law (VIII. 12).

The claim of the *Śathapatha* author is limited to a freedom from taxation in favour of the Brahmin. Vasishṭha in his *Dharma-Śāstra* (1. 45),[13] on the authority of the comment of the *Śathapatha*, deduces the rule that a Brahmin should not be taxed, and gives a further reason that he pays his taxes by allowing one-sixth of his good deeds to the king! (1. 44). It seems that originally there was a difference of opinion between the Dharma school and the Artha school on the question of exemption claimed for the Vedic Brahmin. The politicians did not admit the claim. The *Mānava Artha-Śāstra* (a work of authority referred to in the *Mahābhārata* also, but not yet

---

[11] *Śatapatha Brāhmaṇa*, V. 4. 2. 3.—तदस्मा ऽ इद ॐ सर्वमाद्यं करोति ब्राह्मणमेवापोद्धरति तस्माद्ब्राह्मणो नाद्यः सोमराजा हि भवति।

[12] *Aitareya Brāhmaṇa*, VII. 29.

[13] राजा तु धर्मेणानुशासन् षष्ठं धनस्य हरेत् ॥ ४२ ॥ "The king when ruling lawfully should take one-sixth of wealth." अन्यत्र ब्राह्मणात् ॥ ४३ ॥ "Except from the Brahmin." इष्टापूर्तस्य तु, षष्ठमंशं भजतीति ह ॥ ४४ ॥ "For he divides with him one-sixth share of his virtuous deeds indeed." ब्राह्मणो वेदमाढ्यं करोति ब्राह्मणो आपद उद्धरति तस्माद्ब्राह्मणो नाद्यः। सोमोऽस्य राजा भवतीति ॥ ४५ ॥ "The Brahmin enriches the Veda, the Brahmin rescues from calamity; hence the Brahmin is not to be taxed. 'Soma becomes his king' (*Śatapatha*) indeed."

discovered) is quoted by Somadeva in his *Nītivākyāmṛita* (C. VII.) which says that even those practising austerities in the forest and living by gleaning corn from the fields pay one-sixth of it to the king. It is the (share) of him who protects them (उञ्छषड्भागप्रदानेन वनस्था अपि तपस्विनो राजानं सम्भावयन्ति । तस्यैव तद्भूयात् यस्तान् गोपायति इति ॥). Final settlement seems to be that the Priest-Brahmin alone was exempted. The *Mahābhārata*[14] (*Śānti.*, lxxvi. 5) makes Brahmins who are not Vedic priests liable to taxation. Manu's Dharma Code also limits the exemption to the Vedic Priest, *Śrotriya* (VII. 133).[15]

The treatment of the passage from the coronation ceremonial by lawyers like Vasishṭha proves that the constitutional bearing of the ceremonials and formulæ was evident to the ancient Hindus. They were regarded as basis of constitutional law by code-writers.

After three steps he ascends the wooden throne and he is addressed as in the *Vājapeya* with these constitutional sentences taken from the *Saṁhitā* :

Vesting of Sovereignty

इयं ते राट् । . . . यन्तासि यमनो ध्रुवोऽसि धरुणः ।

कृष्यै त्वा क्षेमाय त्वा रय्यै त्वा पोषाय त्वा ॥[16]

(1) " To thee this State is given ; (2) thou art the director and regulator, thou art steadfast and bearer (of this state or responsibility); (3) *to thee* (*this State is given*) for agriculture, for well-being, for prosperity, for development ". After the first sentence is pronounced, he is made to sit down.

The theological interpreter emphasises[17] that it is by virtue of the above formula that sovereignty vests in the man. " By that he is endowed with royal authority. " ' To thee this State is given' is the most sacred text uttered at the Hindu coronation. It bore such a mighty solemn consequence as the vesting

---

14 अश्रोत्रियाः सर्वे एते सर्वे चानाहिताग्नयः ।
तान्सर्वान् धार्मिको राजा बलिं विष्टिं च कारयेत् ॥
Mahābhārata, *Śānti-Parvan*, 76. 5.

15 म्रियमाणोऽप्याददीत न राजा श्रोत्रियात्करम् । *Mahābhārata*, VII. 133.

16 *Śatapatha*, V. 2. 1. 25 ; *Śukla Yajur-Veda*, IX. 22.

17 *Ibid.*

of sovereignty in one man. The terse comment of the author of the *Brāhmaṇa* is immensely important in the history of the institution of Hindu kingship. It is this sacred act of delivering the trust that kingship depended upon, and not on any other principle such as that of succession, or inheritance.

The purpose for which 'the State is given' is defined, 'for culture, well-being, prosperity, development' and is generally summed up in the expression: 'for the weal'; as the Commentator explains (साधवे त्वा). It is not a gift; it is a trust, and a trust made sacred by the most sacred rites.

The conception armoured in sacredness is wholly human. The son of XX and YY is made the king of the people ZZ. He is not the son or lieutenant of any God. Nor is he appointed by any superhuman spirit. He is appointed by man, anointed by man. Gods are invoked to aid him, just as they are invoked in any other undertaking. But they do not confer the State. That is done by the human act expressed in the words—'To thee the State is given'.

These sentences are taken from mantra 22, Chapter IX, of the *Saṁhitā*. The original mantra begins with salutations to the "Mother Land" [नमो मात्रे पृथिव्यै नमो मात्रे पृथिव्याः··] and she is pointed out to the king-elect as the State or Sovereignty. The modern editions of the *Śathapatha* give the words साधवे त्वा after पोषाय त्वा with an intervening इति. The *Saṁhitā* shows that these words are not a part of the sacred text. They must have been used by the author of the *Śathapatha* as explanatory.

Now we come to comparatively unimportant and less rigid post-*Abhisheka* ceremonies.

Post-*Abhisheka* Ceremonies, Symbolism denoting Supremacy of Law.

The "vow-holder" steps down from the throne and puts on shoes of boar-skin,[18] and takes a symbolical short drive in a chariot drawn by four horses.[19] This seems to be the origin of the Hindu pageantry of the coronation procession, which assumes gorgeousness in the age when the *Rāmāyaṇa* was composed.

---

18 *Śatapatha Brāhmaṇa*, V. 4. 3. 19.

19 *Ibid.*, V. 4. 4. 23, etc.

The King comes back immediately to the throne which he again ascends while the priest recites : 'Sit thee on the pleasant soft-seated throne !'[20] Then follows an exceedingly queer procedure. The king's person is silently touched on the back with a rod which is the symbolic sceptre of justice,[21] conveying by the action the view of the sacred common law that the king was not above but under the law.[22] The interpretation given of this procedure is an amusing piece of euphemism. The commentator says that it is done to carry the king's person beyond 'judicial destruction' (*daṇḍa-vadha*) !

The Homage

Amongst the post-*abhisheka* ceremonies, the homage and its symbolical acknowledgment are most important both from the ritualistic and constitutional points of view. The set formulæ with fixed epi thets and adjectives and their universal and uniform occurrence in the Śruti literature indicate sacertdotal rigidity and the consequent importance of the function.

The King seated on the throne is surrounded by the Ratnin sitting below, by Brahmins as an estate of the realm, by Brahmins as priests, by nobles, by the Grāmaṇī, and others. The homage to the King is first paid by the Brahmins both as an estate and as priest in the council of the Ratnins. The homage of the estates is preceded by the homage of the King to the Pṛithivī, the Earth, or the Land :—

पृथिवि मातर्मा मा हिं ॐ सीर्मा ऽ अहं त्वाम् ।

"Mother Pṛithivī, injure me not, nor I thee ."

"This is performed, says the interpreter, 'lest She should shake him off '."[23]

---

[20] *Śatapatha Brāhmaṇa*, V. 4. 4. 4.

[21] *Ibid.*, V. 4. 7. अथैनं पृष्ठतस्तूष्णीमेव दन्डैर्घ्नन्ति । त दण्डैर्घ्नन्तो दण्डवधमतिनयन्ति तस्माद्राजा दण्ड्यो यदेनं दण्डवधमतिनयन्ति ॥

[22] Cf. *Manu*, VII.

[23] *Śatapatha Brāhmaṇa*, V. 4. 3. 20.—भेयं नावधून्वीत. According to the author of the *Śatapatha* the country and the king entered into friendly relations for a mother does not injure her son, nor does a son injure his mother,' नहि माता पुत्रं ॐ हिनस्ति न पुत्रो मातरम् ॥ Eggelling, *S.B.E.*, Vol. XLI, p. 143.

In the prologue of the function to the address 'O, Brāhmaṇa' by the King—the reply comes forth interrupting the king :[24] 'Thou art Brāhmaṇa, thou art Varuṇa of true power'. 'Thou art Brāhmaṇa, mighty through the strength of the whole People (*Viś*) !'[25] Five times, five individual Brahmins and priests, the king tries to address by the privileged designation, and in all cases the title of privilege is, so to say, resigned in the sovereign's favour, and the sovereign and the popular representative character of the king ('through the strength of the people') is pointed out. The idea is that the Brahmin may not now be addressed by his privileged designation of superiority. The superiority which is given to the king by the whole nation including the Brahmin makes the Hindu king legally and constitutionally superior to all classes and castes.

"A Brāhmaṇa or a priest then offers the sacrificial sword"[25] to the king, the increaser of the public prosperity.[26] The sword thus received, he passes on as symbol of authority to all the State Officers and the Village Headmen. And he demands their co-operation by quoting gracefully the very words of fealty used by the Brahmin—'*Rule for me therewith*' (*tena me radhya*). It has a double meaning '*serve me therewith*' (*tena me radhya*).[27] In the latter case the second meaning is intended. The command for co-operation is even directed to the *Sajāta*, an individual member of the nation.[28]

The Symbolic Game of Government

The new king does not stop here. To impress that the administration, like a game of dice, is not possible by a single man, he asks the *Ratnins* to a symbolical game of dice. The bet is a cow,[29] brought for the occasion by an ordinary

---

[24] *Vājasaneyī Saṁhitā*, X. 28 ; *Taittirīya Brāhmaṇa*, I. 7. 10.

[25] *Śatapatha Brāhmaṇa*, V. 4. 4. 15.

[26] *Ibid.*, V. 4. 4. 14. *Lit.* "the much worker, better worker, more worker".

[27] A puzzle in which the author of the *Śatapatha* (V. 4. 4. 15–19) lands himself by not realising the pun.

[28] Receiving costly presents in homage and making generous gifts in return which abnormally developed in later times and which Muhammadan monarchs continued, is not known to the rituals even in symbols.

[29] *Śatapatha Brāhmaṇa*, V. 4. 4. 20–25.

member of the community. Thus in this great game of government which the king and his ministers were going to play, there was laid that sacred bet. The bet was the wealth of the most humble member of the community. It was willingly and graciously offered by the humble citizen. It was placed in their trust by a *Sajāta*, 'one born together' with the players, or, as Sāyaṇa explains, 'one of equal birth,' *i.e.*, one of the Nation. There is a constitutionalism put here in physical symbols; there is pathos intermingled with duty. The abstract has been thickly clad in the concrete.

Summary

Now the chief features of the ceremonies[30] comprised in 'Hindu Coronation' are before the reader. In modern language they may be summed up and expressed for the sake of clearness in a few sentences:

(*a*) Hindu kingship was a human institution.

(*b*) Hindu kingship was elective; the electorate being the whole People.

(*c*) Hindu kingship was a contractual engagement.

(*d*) Hindu kingship was an office of State, which had to work in co-operation with other offices of State.

(*e*) Hindu kingship was a trust, the trust being the tending of the country to prosperity and growth.[31]

(*f*) Hindu kingship is expressly not arbitrary.

---

[30] A son of the king-elect once plays a little part in a minor ritual (*Śatapatha*, V. 4. 2. 8). But it is not found in the corresponding place in the *Kṛishna Yajus* ritual.

[31] Soon after—in the Upanishadic period—a new duty is placed on royal administration. The prosperity of the subjects should be not only material, but also moral. When five great theologians went to Aśvapati, King of Kekaya, he said with satisfaction :—

न मे स्तेनो जनपदे न कदर्यो न मद्यपः ।
न नाहिताग्निर्नाविद्वान्न स्वैरी स्वैरिणी कुतः ॥

"In my kingdom there is no thief, no coward, no drunkard, no man without the sacrificial fire set up in his house, no one uneducated, no adulterer, much less an adulteress" (*Chhāndogya Upanishad*, V. 11. 7). Here we have the beginning of that theory which becomes an axiom in later times, that political rule of the king is responsible for the moral condition of the people and that he is responsible for good and bad times.

(*g*) Hindu kingship was not above the law but under it.

(*h*) Hindu kingship was primarily national and secondarily territorial.[32]

This constitutional conception is not undeserving of our philosophic forefathers. The Hindu race did not care solely for the world after. Here, in one instance, we see the Hindus, of flesh and blood, and of sinews and muscles. It is surely not the despicable picture which represents them as an unholy assemblage of spiritual imbeciles, born to 'bow before the blast and plunge in thought again'.

Hereditary Succession not yet established

The Brāhmaṇas do not recognise such a thing as hereditary succession. Each king must be consecrated as such and no reference is made to the previous successions in the rituals. This was due to the elective origin of the Vedic kingship. In fact, as in theory, Hindu kingship had not yet become hereditary in the time of the Brāhmaṇas. The inception of the hereditary principle, however, is discernible. According to the opinion of one school, if the coronation was desired for the life-time of the king-elect, only the first syllable of the *Vyāhṛiti*—'Bhūḥ' भूः was to be pronounced, if it was for two generations, 'bhūr bhuvaḥ' (भूर्भुवः) and if for three generations, 'bhur-bhuvaḥ svaḥ' (भूर्भुवः स्वः) the complete formula was to be repeated.[33] This was the opinion of one school of ritualists as indicated in the *Aitareya Br.* A historical reference to this theory is found in the inscription of Khāravela where coronation for one generation is mentiond,[34] which naturally implies that coronation for generations more than one was possible. The tendency to hereiditary kingship is corroborated further by the occurrence of *rājānaṃ rāja-pitaram* ('king and father of a king') in the *Aitareya Brāhmaṇa*, VIII. 12, while no such

[32] See 'King of the people ZZ,' and the Collection of the Waters, and the Homage to the Land.

[33] *Aitareya Brāhmaṇa*, VIII. 7—

भूरिति य इच्छेदिममेव प्रत्यञ्चमद्यादित्यथ व इच्छेद्द्विपुरुषं
भूर्भुवः इत्यथ य इच्छेत्त्रिपुरुषं वा ऽप्रतिमं वा भूर्भुवः स्वरिति ।

Cf. also '*rājānaṁ rājapitaraṁ*' in VIII. 12.

[34] *J.B.O.R.S.*, III. 41.

adjective to republican *Svarāj* or *Virāj* is added. But the rituals as originally designed were for each generation, and the one generation consecrated became the rule in practice for all ages to come, even when kingship became hereditary.

Ceremony for deposed king

Before we leave this period we have to take note of the sacred ceremony indicating the fact of deposition. Books XIX to XXI of the *Śukla Yajur-Veda* prescribe formulæ of the *Sautrāmaṇi* sacrifice which a dethroned monarch performed. The *Taittirīya Brāhmaṇa* of the *Kṛishṇa Yajur-Veda* similarly recommends the *Śautrāmaṇi* to a deposed monarch.[35] Deposition thus in this period is as much a recognised practice as in the early Vedic times. Its existence in later times is thus sanctioned by previous history.

---

35 सोमो वा एतस्य राज्यमादत्ते ।

यो राजा सन्राज्यो वा सोमेन यजते ।

देवसुवामेतानि हवीँषि भवन्ति ।

एतावन्तो वै देवानाँ सवाः ।

त एवास्मै सवान् प्रयच्छन्ति ।

त एनं पुनस् सुवन्ते राज्याय ।

देवसू राजा भवति ।

—*Taittirīya Brāhmaṇa*, I. 4. 2. See also Sāyaṇa on it (Ānandāśrama ed., I, p. 179).

CHAPTER XXVI

Coronation in Later Times

Leading Principle remains Vedic

In later times all the constitutional principles upon which the ritualistic coronation was based we find being acted upon, with modifications in details to suit changed and changing circumstances. According to the *Mahābhārata*, Yudhishṭhira 'worshipped' his Ministers before his coronation.[1] Here ministers stand for the Vedic Ratnins. At the proposed coronation of Rāma as King-assistant (*Yuvarāja*)—as described in the *Rāmāyaṇa*,[2] according to the practice and ideas current in the days of its composition[3]—we find the Jānapadas and the Pauras[4] present in place of the Grāmaṇī and Sajātas, and the guild of merchants and traders in place of the Vedic 'rathakāras' and 'karmāras'. In the *Mahābhārata* at the royal coronation of Yudhishṭhira we see the Brahmins, the owners of the land, the Vaiśyas and all the respectable Śūdras invited.[5] In the *Rāmāyaṇa*[6] the Brāhmins, Ministers, Knights (Kshatriyas) and members of guilds (which had all castes in them) sprinkle the king with waters brought from the seas and rivers. A new element introduced is the representation of womanhood: unmarried

---

1 'अर्च्चयित्वा सभासदः' *Sabhā-Parvan*, Ch. XIII, 4. 26. 29.

2 *Rāmāyaṇa*, Bk. II, Ch. XIV, v. 52.—

उदतिष्ठत रामस्य समग्रमभिषेचनम् ।
पौरजानपदाश्चापि नैगमश्च कृताञ्जलिः ॥

3 " The cumulative evidence of the above arguments makes it difficult to avoid the conclusion that the kernel of the *Rāmāyaṇa* was composed before 500 B.C., while the more recent portions were probably not added till the second century B.C. and later."—Macdonell, *Sanskrit Literature*, p. 309. The view is in agreement with Jacobi's analysis (*Das Rāmāyaṇa*).

4 See below Chapters XXVII and XXVIII.

5 *Sabhā-Parvan*, XXXIII. 41. 42 (Kumb. ed.), C. XXXVI,

आमन्त्रयध्वं राष्ट्रेषु ब्राह्मणान्भूमिपानथ ।
विशश्च मान्यान्शूद्रांश्च सर्वानानयतेति च ॥

6 *Yuddha Kāṇḍa*, 128. 62 (Bombay), ऋत्विग्भिर्ब्राह्मणैः पूर्वं कन्याभिर्मन्त्रिभिस्तथा । योधैश्चैवाभ्यषिञ्चंस्ते संप्रहृष्टैः सनैगमैः ॥

girls also take part in the besprinkling. In the *Mahābhārata*, all the representatives of the subjects led by Dhaumya and Kṛishṇa consecrate Yudhishṭhira.[7] The emperor receives presents and makes gifts of honour. According to Nīlakaṇṭha (*Nītimayūkha*)[8] the four chief ministers (मुख्यामात्यचतुष्टयम्) Brahmin, Kshatriya, Vaiśya and Śūdra by caste, consecrated the new king. Then the leaders (Mukhyāḥ) of each Varṇa and of the castes lower still (शूद्राश्चावरमुख्याश्च) consecrated him with holy waters (नानातीर्थसमुद्भवैः). Then followed Acclamation by the twice-born (द्विजकोलाहलेन च). The king next sat amongst ministers and representatives of the people, citizens of the Capital, merchants, traders, leaders of the bazar (आपणेश्वरान्) and others who were introduced by the gentleman-usher to the king (प्रतिहारः प्रदर्शयेत्). A procession through the streets of the capital concluded the ceremony.[9] According to the *Brahma-Purāṇa*, quoted in the *Vīramitrodaya-Rājanīti-prakāśa* (p. 46) the king after the ceremony went round the capital on an elephant, re-entered the palace, and offered worship or honour to all the leaders of the Paura (प्रदक्षिणीकृत्य पुरं प्रविश्य च पुरं गृहम्। समस्तान् पौरमुख्यांश्च कृत्वा पूजां विसर्जयेत् ॥). In the Pushya coronation ceremony as laid down in the *Atharvaṇapariśishṭa*,[10] the king after the ceremony allowed audience to Brahmins, and saluted the wives of the leaders of the subjects, Associations or Guilds, whereupon they gave him blessings.

---

[7] *Śānti-Parvan*, C. XLI.

[8] Benares, 1880, pp. 2–3, ततो भद्रासनगतं to शूद्रामात्योऽभिषेचयेत्।

[9] The king's *ushṇīsha* diadem had five crests (*śikhā*); that of the Queen, three, of the Yuvarāja, three; and of the Senāpati, one, *Ibid.*, p. 4.

[10] Cited by Mitra-Miśra in *V.M.R.*, p. 114.—

ततस्तु दर्शनं देयं ब्राह्मणानां नृपेण तु ।
श्रेणीप्रकृतिमुख्यानां स्त्रीजनं च नमस्करेत् ॥
आशिषस्ते हि दास्यन्ति....

२ ‘ हृष्यत्पञ्चालवृद्धोद्धृतकनकमयस्वाभिषेकोदकुम्भो दत्तः श्रीकान्यकुब्जः ’ *Ep. Ind.*, IV, p. 248. See below Ch. XXVII.

This procedure is really the same in essentials as we find in the Brāhmaṇa period, with an extension of the principle of representation. We find the Elders of Pañchāla, *i.e.*, the members of an association similar to or identical with the Paura and Jānapada of Pañchāla, doing the *Abhisheka* of the new king of Kānyakubja in the time of Dharma Pāla, as recorded in his Khālimpur copper-plate.

Coronation Oath

Similarly the Coronation Oath, now called *Pratijñā*, was administered. In the *Mahābhārata*, it is given in terms which correspond to the oath given in *Aitareya Brāhmaṇa*.

The Oath is called by the *Mahābhārata* a *Sruti*, which denotes that the oath was based on Vedic text. As the *Aitareya* enjoins that the oath should be repeated 'with faith' (*saha śraddhayā*), so here it had to be pronounced without any mental reservation :

प्रतिज्ञाञ्चाभिरोहस्व मनसा कर्म्मणा गिरा ।
पालयिष्याम्यहं भौमं ब्रह्म इत्येव चासकृत् ॥
यश्चात्र धर्म्मो नीत्युक्तो दण्डनीतिव्यपाश्रयः ।
तमशङ्कः करिष्यामि स्ववशो न कदाचन ॥[11]

"Mount on the *Pratijñā* (take the oath)[12] from your heart (without any mental reservation), in fact and by word of mouth ;

(*a*) 'I will see to the growth of the Country[13] regarding it as God himself and (this) ever and always ;

(*b*) Whatever law there is here and whatever is dictated by Ethics and whatever is not opposed to politics I will act according to, unhesitatingly. And I will never be arbitrary'."[14]

---

[11] *Śānti-Parvan* (Calcutta), LIX. 106. 107. Kumbakonam ed., LVIII. 115. 116. The reading in the Southern recension is प्रतिज्ञाञ्चाधिरोहस्व. Instead of नीत्युक्तो of Bengal it has इत्युक्तो which does not give a satisfactory meaning.

[12] 'Mount or ascend (on the *Pratijñā*)' is with reference to the symbolic ascent to the throne and to all the quarters. *Pratijñā* literally means, 'acknowledgment', 'affirmation' or 'vow'.

[13] The original word is भौम, *i.e.*, "all that belongs to the country".

[14] The original word is स्ववश. In the *Aitareya* स्वावश्य form of monarchy is mentioned ; the *Mahābhārata* here shows that it denoted autocracy and that it stood discredited in the country.

To the royal oath the people pronounced 'Amen' (एवमस्तु)

Its unique Character

The most remarkable feature about the Hindu Coronation Oath is still retained; there is not a trace of superstitious or mystic element in it. It stands in this respect in unique contrast with the royal oaths of other countries.[15]

Discussion on Rājan and 'history' of Coronation Oath in the *Mahābhārata*

" O Rājan! of the Bharata race! how this title Rājā as at present understood (signifying 'monarch') evolved: please tell me that, Grandfather! Having hands and arms and neck like others; having intelligence and faculties like others; subject to pain and pleasure like others; having back, face and stomach like others; having similar albumen, bone and marrow, similar in flesh and sinews; similar in inhaling and exhaling breath; in body and life similar to others; equally subject to birth and death; an equal in all the attributes which men possess—how should be, one man, rule over men of uncommon intelligence and heroes? How should he alone rule the whole country full of brave, and heroic Hindus (Aryans)? Again, although he is protecting, yet he seeks the satisfaction and pleasure of the community. At the same time, the whole community is pleased by his, the one man's, pleasure, and when the one man is in distress all become distressed. This is a settled principle. I want to hear on this from you, O Chief of the Bharatas. Please expound to me the subject with underlying principles exhaustively, O you the Great Expounder. The reason of this, O Leader of the people! could not be insignificant, for to this one man the whole creation looks for guidance as if he were a God."[16]

---

15 *Cf.* article on Oath in the *Enc. Britt.* (Eleventh ed.).

16 *Śānti-Parvan* (Calcutta), LIX. 5. 12 (Kumbakonam LVIII. 5–8).—

य एष राजन्राजेति शब्दश्चरति भारत ।
कथमेष समुत्पन्नस्तन्मे ब्रूहि पितामह ॥ ५ ॥
तुल्यपाणिभुजग्रीवस्तुल्यबुद्धीन्द्रियात्मकः ।
तुल्यदुःखसुखात्मा च तुल्यपृष्ठमुखोदरः ॥ ६ ॥

(Contd. on p. 226.)

This was the question put by Yudhishṭhira which elicited from Bhīshma a history of kingship and of the Coronation Oath.

The 'not-insignificant' reason was explained by Bhīshma with a professed historical account of the institution of Hindu monarchy. 'There was no monarchy and no monarch,' he related, in early times, and that then the people protected one another by law. As they thus lived, they found in time that mutual co-operation was not sufficiently powerful and law itself began to suffer. These men in consultation with Gods decided to elect a monarch. The gods gave them Virajas who however refused to be king. His three successors followed as 'Protectors' (Rakshayitās), the fourth one 'built an empire and became arbitrary'. Evidently they had not taken any oaths, coming, as it is said, from gods to men. The fifth Protector of divine origin, called Vena proved to be quite 'unlawful' to the people, and he was deposed and executed. Thereupon the men (the wise)[17] elected a man called Pṛithu,

---

तुल्यशुक्रास्थिमज्जा च तुल्यमांसासृगेव च ।
निःश्वासोच्छ्वासतुल्यश्च तुल्यप्राणशरीरवान् ॥ ७ ॥
समानजन्ममरणः समः सर्वैर्गुणैर्नृणाम् ।
विशिष्टबुद्धीञ्शूरांश्च कथमेकोऽधितिष्ठति ॥ ८ ॥
कथमेको महीं कृत्स्नां शूरवीरार्यसंकुलाम् ।
रक्षत्यपि च लोकस्य प्रसादमभिवाञ्छति ॥ ९ ॥
एकस्य तु प्रसादेन कृत्स्नो लोकः प्रसीदति ।
व्याकुले चाकुलः सर्वो भवतीति विनिश्चयः ॥ १० ॥
एतदिच्छाम्यहं श्रोतुं त्वत्तो हि भरतर्षभ ।
कृत्स्नं तन्मे यथातत्त्वं प्रब्रूहि वदतां वर ॥ ११ ॥
नैतत्कारणमत्यल्पं भविष्यति विशांपते ।
यदेकस्मिञ्जगत्सर्वं देववद्याति सन्नतिम् ॥ १२ ॥

[17] *Ṛishis.* In this description there is a tendency to attribute the credit of destroying the pseudo-historical tyrant to Brahma-philosophers and *Ṛishis.* There are clear traces of a subsequent Brahmanisation of the theory in certain places. All the *varṇas*, it is said in the beginning of the chapter, went to the Creator for advice on the appointment and election of a king. Why in subsequent procedure, then, should the *Ṛishis* alone figure prominently? The reply may be given that *Ṛishis* were from, and represented, all the

a descendant of Vena. He promised faithfulness[18] and the above oaths were administered to him. He ruled successfully in accordance with law and his undertaking. The people were pleased with him and he obtained the title Rājā ('Pleaser').[19]

Analysis of the Oath

Such is a pseudo-historical theory devised to explain the Hindu Corontion Oaths by political writers. The germs of the theory go back to the *Śatapatha Brāhmaṇa*[20] which says that Pṛithu Vainya was the first anointed king of the Hindus. The theory implies that the Oath originated with kingship, that it was as old

---

three Aryan *varṇas*. Yet there is no doubt as to a leaning towards Brahmin prominence. In the same book combined action by all the *varṇas* in a similar matter is discussed. The explanation of the fact that the *Mahābhārata*, the *Rāmāyaṇa* and the *Mānava Dharma Śāstra* bear very strong marks of an overstatement of Brahmin claim, attributable to the same period and to almost the same pens and hands, is found in the political history of the 2nd century B.C. At that time a great Brahmin (Pushyamitra) actually ascended the throne of India and brought about a mighty religious and social revolution as against the previous political and religious systems. When the Brahmin ruler crushed the Greek power and saved Hindu civilization, the claims could be made with some justification, and in view of the great success and popularity of the new *régime*, could become current with greater ease than they would have been otherwise. Both the epics clearly state that they were revised (*e.g.*, पुरा वाल्मीकिना कृतम्) *Rāmāyaṇa* (Bk. VI, Ch. 128, 105 and 110) and *Mahābhārata* (Bk. I). Their attacks on Buddhism, and the political data which in the case of the *Rāmāyaṇa* exclusively and in the case of the *Mahābhārata* mostly, belong to the 2nd century B.C., prove that revision to have been made in the early Śuṅga period. Overstatement of Brahmin claim in them therefore should not mislead us. It can be fortunately corrected in the light of inscriptions, the *Jātakas* and other Pāli works and books like the *Artha-Śāstra*, the *Dharma Sūtras*, and the records left by foreign observers.

18 यन्मां भवन्ती वक्ष्यन्ति कार्यमर्थसमन्वितम् ।
तदहं वः करिष्यामि नात्र कार्या विचारणा ॥

"Whatever you gentlemen tell me, proper for me to do in accordance with the Science of Politics, I will do for you without any objection."—*Mahābhārata*, *Śānti-Parvan*, LIX. 102.

19 रञ्जिताश्च प्रजास्सर्वा तेन राजेति शब्दते । *Ibid.*, verse 125.

20 *Śatapatha Brāhmaṇa*, V. 3. 5. 4. Vainya is known even to the *Ṛig-Veda*, VIII. 9. 10. In the *Ṛik* he appears to be a *Ṛishi* and a historical person (II. 112. 15).

as kingship itself. An analysis of the oaths discloses the following position of the Hindu king:—

1. That the trust in his hand—the tending ('I will see to the growth,' '*pālayishyāmi*') of the country—is the foremost solemn obligation of the sovereign.

2. That the country put under his care is to be regarded by him as nothing less than God,[21] which implies sincerity, respect and awe. The relation is far from being patriarchal, theocratic or aristocratic.

3. That he is expressly not to be arbitrary. He is bound by the law, is brought under the law. He undertook to act according to the law established. He was further bound by the rules of Political Science. These two were to regulate his actions in internal administration and foreign relations. And he undertook never to disregard them.

Effect of Coronation Oath in actual life

Nations of antiquity and nations of our own times have devised Coronation Oaths for their kings. But none brings more forcibly to the notice of the new king the all-powerful, the all-sacred position of the Country he is going to rule. To offend against that country was to offend against God Himself. Having once uttered this oath it was impossible to forget it. If a Hindu monarch failed to keep his Coronation Oath he would be *a-satya-pratijña* (असत्यप्रतिज्ञ) and *a-satya-sandha* (असत्यसन्ध), 'false in his vow,' and he would forfeit his title to remain on the throne. That the Coronation Oath was not an empty formality is evidenced by the fact that kings at times said with pride that they were true to their oaths. The Hinduised foreigner Rudradāman was anxious to declare in his inscription that he was *satya-pratijña* (सत्यप्रतिज्ञ), that he never levied takes which were not lawful.[22] The charge of breaking the oath was at times constructively

---

[21] The subjects are called God (Vishṇu) in an Abhisheka text quoted by Chaṇḍeśvara (*RNR.*, Ch. XVI):—

अद्यारभ्य न मे राज्यं राजाऽयं रक्षतु प्रजाः ।
इति[सर्वं]प्रजाविष्णुं साक्षिणं श्रावयेन्मुहुः ॥

[22] *Epigraphia Indica*, VIII, pp. 43, 44.

extended. If the monarch failed to maintain the integrity of the state he was considered guilty of breaking his vow. Bṛihadratha Maurya who was weak as ruler and during whose reign the Greeks made a second attempt at conquering India, was removed from the throne, and was called (*e.g.*, by Bāṇa) '*weak in keeping his Pratijña*' (*Pratijñā-durbala*). If a king, having taken the oath to act according to the law as established, acted unlawfully and committed a crime, he would be considered to have broken faith, and his action would be illegal, for which the people who had installed him would remove him.[23] The *Jātakas*,[24] tradition, literature and history furnish illustrations. In the *Mahābhārata* the plea for the deposition and execution of the tyrant Vena was that he had become unlawful (*vidharmā*); the 'formal' deposition of Nāga-Dasaka of Magadha and his punishment was due to his parricide.[25] King Pālaka of the *Mṛichchhakaṭika* was deposed because he had incarcerated Āryaka without the latter having committed any crime.

Coronation Oath in Middle Ages and later

The oath was deemed to be the essential sacrament down to later Muhammadan times. The ceremonials of coronation as then prevalent are not the same in all details as in the *Brāhmaṇas*. The coronation procession has developed out of the simple chariot drive. The king, as we have seen, holds a Sabhā where the leaders of the community are introduced to him. The modifications are many and considerable. But the Coronation Oath is the oath of the *Aitareya Brāhmaṇa*, and Hindu lawyers[26] did register it in spite of their mediæval ideals

---

[23] See *Mahābhārata, Anuśāsana-Parvan*, LXI :—

अरक्षितारं हर्त्तारं विलोप्तारमनायकम् ।
तं वै राजकलिं हन्युः प्रजाः सन्नह्य निर्घृणम् ॥ ३२ ॥
अहं वो रक्षितेत्युक्त्वा यो न रक्षति भूमिपः ।
स संहत्य निहन्तव्यः श्ववशैवोन्मादातुरः ॥ ३३ ॥

[24] *E.g.*, *Jātaka*, I. 398.

[25] *Mahāvaṁsa* (IV. 4), compiled by a Hindu in Ceylon in the 5th century A.C. who drew upon the old traditions of his own country.

[26] *Rājanīti Vīramitrodaya*, p. 52 (Benares, 1916).
See below, Chapters XXVIII and XXIX.

of kingship. In spite of vicissitudes in fortune, in spite of contact with contrary doctrines, the Hindu race did not forget the Coronation Oath devised by their Vedic forefathers. Thanks to sacerdotalism, the oath has been preserved for history and posterity.

Coronation and Elective Theory in later times

Kingship had become hereditary.[27] Yet the theory that Hindu kingship is elective was never forgotten. This was due to, I think, two factors. On failure of the lines, as Megasthenes[28] has recorded, elections had been actually taking place;[29] and the observance of the coronation ceremonials and rituals kept the theory ever green. Even in Moslem times when Śivaji was installed as King, 'Chhatrapati,' the ceremony took the form of election. The theory was a living force as late as the time of the Pāla kings of Bengal. Gopāla claims the benefit of the principle of election in his inscription. He says that the people joined his hand with sovereignty and put an end to anarchy.[30] In earlier times the theory was, of course, current in the mouths of sovereigns and peoples. In the second century of the Christian era Rudradāman states in his inscription that he had been[31] '*elected* by all the *varṇas* to kingship'.

Age for Coronation

By the inscription of the emperor Khāravela it is evident that Hindu Coronation could not take place before the completion of the twenty-fourth year of the King-elect. One branch of the Jaina literature asserts that Vikrama was crowned in his twety-fifth year. This was the age when ordinarily a Hindu (*e.g.*, Śvetaketu) was supposed to have completed his academic career in the period of Upanishads. The existence of the constitutional law for

---

[27] *Rāmāyaṇa, Ayodhyā Kāṇḍa*, 21. 32; 6. 16.
राज्यं गृहाण भरत पितृपैतामहं ध्रुवम्, 79, 5; 79, 7.

[28] Arrian, *Indika*, VIII.

[29] See the case of Yaśaskara's election on failure of the Utpala dynasty in Kashmir (*R.T.*, V).

[30] मात्स्यन्यायमपोहितुं प्रकृतिभिर्लक्ष्म्याः करं ग्राहितः ॥
—*Ep. Ind.*, IV. 248.

[31] सर्ववर्णैरभिगम्य रक्षणार्थं पतित्वे वृतेन । *Ibid.*, VIII. 43.

coronation at the age of twenty-five which the inscription of Khāravela points out, is confirmed by the *Bṛihaspati Sūtra*, I. 89, *pañcha-viṁśativarshaṃ yāvat krīḍā-vidyāṃ vyasanāt kuryāt ata uttaram arthārjanam*,[32] which agrees almost literally with the record of Khāravela.

Observance of Coronation Law of Constitution

We have historical examples of the fact that the coronation laws were strictly complied with. Even Aśoka's family who had accepted heterodox philosophies could not interfere with the orthodox and sacred coronation laws.[33] He was not crowned for four years after his what we to-day call succession. Evidently he had not completed his twenty-fourth year as in the case of Khāravela. The uncrowned period of his reign in the eye of the Hindu law was a period not to be recognised. If we keep this in view we can understand the provision in Vasishṭha's *Dharma-Sūtra* that interest on loan was not to be calculated for the period between the death of the sovereign and the coronation of the new king.[34] The legal years were counted only by regnal years (*Rājavarsha*).[35] Hence also the Purāṇas do not count the pre-coronation years of Aśoka's reign while they include it in the total for the dynasty.[36] This also shows that a king to be a legal sovereign must receive his royal consecration. The Purāṇas call foreign barbarians of the sixth century '*naiva-mūrdhābhishiktās-te*,' 'unconsecrated heads,' *i.e.*, 'usurpers'.[37] Unless one accepted the responsibility by a solemn engagement he was not lawfully entitled to govern.

---

[32] *Arthārjanam*, 'engagement in commonwealth *or* political life'.

[33] His grandson Daśaratha mentions his own *abhisheka* in his inscriptions.

[34] राजा तु मृतभावेन द्रव्यवृद्धिं विनाशयेत् ।
पुना राजाभिषेकेण द्रव्यमूलं च वर्धते ॥
—*Vāsishṭha Dharma-Sūtra*, II. 49.

[35] राजवर्षंमासः पक्षो दिवसश्च......इति कालः ।
—*Artha-Śāstra*, p. 60 (II. 6. 24).

[36] Jayaswal, *J.B.O.R.S.*, I. (1915), p. 93; Vol. III. 438; V. Smith, *Early History of India* (third ed.), p. 197.

[37] *Vāyu Purāṇa*, Pargiter, *PT.*, p. 56.

The legalism about coronation was so strong that Kālidāsa in drafting Pushyamitra's letter to Agnimitra takes care not to describe Pushyamitra as king.[38] The preparations for coronation by a Rāja-Sūya were still in progress, coronation had not yet taken place. He was therefore not a king *de jure*.

[38] *Mālavikāgnimitra*, Act III (3).

The absence of the royal title in the letter gave occasion to much controversy amongst scholars. The constitutional explanation given above might be the real solution. Kālidāsa assumes that he was not yet crowned.

CHAPTER XXVI (A)

Sacrament of Coronation Oath and Theory of Divine Origin of King

Sacrament of Coronation Oath

With the actual observance of the sacrament of Coronation Oath, it was impossible for a theory of origin other than human to take root in Hindu Politics. Even a usurper, as long as he was a Hindu, had to undergo the sacrament of coronation and when he actually took the oath, his old title of force and conquest disappeared. In the second century A.C., when Hindu society had already undergone a great social change as is evinced by the law-books and controversies of the time,[1] even foreigners sought to legalise their position by the sacred, constitutional ceremonies. Rudradāman based his claim on election and his responsibility on the Coronation Oath. No room for a theory like divine origin existed.

Divine Origin of King

This was demonstrated when an attempt at establishing a theory which was the nearest Hindu approach to the divine theory of kingship miserably failed. The *Mānava-Dharma-Śāstra* which was written under the revolutionary régime of the Brahmin, Pushyamitra[2] preached that the king should

---

[1] *E.g.*, the *Vajrasūchī* of Aśvaghosha :—

गोत्रब्राह्मणमारभ्य ब्राह्मणीनां शूद्रपर्य्यन्तमभिगमनदर्शनात् । अतो जाति-ब्राह्मणो न भवति । इह हि कैवर्त्त-रजक-चण्डाल-कुलेष्वपि ब्राह्मणाः सन्ति...... एकवर्णो, नास्ति चातुर्वर्ण्यम् ॥ etc.

Baudhāyana condemns the Punjab as a place of mixed *varṇas*. In the period of the Upanishads the Punjab was the home of orthodoxy. Baudhāyana's condemnation would refer to the period of the rise of Buddhism in the Punjab—Aśoka to Menander.

[2] His caste is discussed by me in the *Brahmin Empire* (1912), a revised edition of which is published in *J.B.O.R.S.*, 257–65. See Pānini, IV. 8. 117 on *Śuṅga*; Patañjali, VI. 2. 130 on *Brāhmaṇa-rājya;* and Tārānātha, p. 81 on *Brahmānen Koenig*, Pushyamitra. For connection between the *Mānava-dharma-Śāstra* and Pushyamitra see my *Tagore Lectures on Manu and Yājñavalkya*, I. In the time

not be despised because he was only a man; he was a deity in human form.[3] For this theory the author found no direct support in earlier literature. He uses the theory of politicians, which we have already noticed (pp. 86–89), that when the people were dissatisfied with the *Arājaka* system they consulted the Creator who recommended a king. He leaves out the theory about the election of Manu Vaivasvata and takes apparently the story of Vena. He says God created king to save the people from *Arājaka*.[4] But he ignores the further tradition of the deposition of Vena of divine origin because he ruled unlawfully. The Mānava Code twists the import of the coronation ritual invoking the help of gods to the elected king in his new career.[5] The Code says that these gods come into the person of the king and he becomes a great Deity.[6] The king is not to be despised. I think the idea of such a theory was suggested by some discussion as the one in the *Artha-Śāstra*.[7] A man in the pay of the Government was made to say:

"The king's office is that of Indra and Yama, visible inflictor of punishment and bestower of reward. On those who

---

of the Mānava Code the Parthians were neighbours of India but the country of which Mathurā was capital was yet orthodox; the country of the Mlechchha was still beyond India proper. This indicates the period about 150 B.C.

[3] *Mānava-Dharma-Śāstra*, VII. 8.—

बालोऽपि नावमन्तव्यो मनुष्य इति भूमिपः ।
महती देवता ह्येषा नररूपेण तिष्ठति ॥

[4] *Ibid.*, VII. 3.—

अराजके हि लोकेऽस्मिन्सर्वतो विद्रुते भयात् ।
रक्षार्थमस्य सर्वस्य राजानमसृजत्प्रभुः ॥

[5] In this connection see also the text of the *Vājasaneyī Saṁhitā*, X. 16. 17. 28, along with the corresponding Brāhmaṇa passages.

[6] *Mānava-Dharma-Śāstra*, VII. 7.—

सोऽग्निर्भवति वायुश्च सोऽर्कः सोमः स धर्मराट् ।
स कुबेरः स वरुणः स महेन्द्रः प्रभावतः ॥

[7] *Artha-Śāstra*, p. 23.—इन्द्रयमस्थानमेतत् राजानः प्रत्यक्षहेडप्रसादाः । तानवमन्यमानान्दैवोऽपि दण्डः स्पृशति । तस्माद्राजानो नावमन्तव्याः इति क्षुद्रकान्प्रतिषेधयेत् ।

despise them even divine punishment descends. Hence they are not to be *despised.*"

This is urged by the official spy in defence of the new king and was intended to support him, in reply to those who cited the social contract theory of kingship.[8] If there had been a theory of divine origin already current it would have been cited at once. But no divine origin of king is preached in the passage of the *Artha-Śāstra*, nor is any absolutism preached there. The divine punishment mentioned in the hired speech refers to the consequence of sin which in every case is supposed to be visited with divine punishment; and treason was always regarded as a sin. The Government spy is not advancing any theory of absolutism. He is only drawing attention to the position of the king as such resembling that of Indra and Yama, and to the sin which would be caused if the people went against the king. The author of the *Mānava* Code made his king a Divinity itself, to despise which was to be punished with powers of absolutism. And he preached perfect absolutism.[9]

This he had to do as he had to support an abnormal state of affairs opposed to law and tradition, *viz.*, political rule by Brahmin.[10]

The theory of the *Mānava* was never approved or adopted by a single subsequent law-book. By constitutional writers the very theory was converted into a divine theory of the

---

[8] See p. 172 above.

[9] *Mānava-Dharma-Śāstra*, VII. 9–13 :—

एकमेव दहत्यग्निर्नरं दुरुपसर्पिणम् ।
कुलं दहति राजाग्निः सपशुद्रव्यसंचयम् ॥ ९ ॥
कार्यं चावेक्ष्य शक्तिं च देशकालौ च तत्त्वतः ।
कुरुते धर्मसिद्ध्यर्थं विश्वरूपं पुनः पुनः ॥ १० ॥
यस्य प्रसादे पद्मा श्रीर्विजयश्च पराक्रमे ।
मृत्युश्च वसति क्रोधे सर्वतेजोमयो हि सः ॥ ११ ॥
तं यस्तु द्वेष्टि संमोहात्सविनश्यत्यसंशयम् ।
तस्य ह्याशु विनाशाय राजा प्रकुरुते मनः ॥ १२ ॥
तस्माद्धर्मं यमिष्टेषु संव्यवस्येन्नराधिपः ।
अनिष्टं चाप्यनिष्टेषु तं धर्मं न विचालयेत् ॥ १३ ॥

[10] Jayaswal, *Tagore Law Lectures on Manu and Yājñavalkya*, II.

servitude of the king to the subject[11]: that the king was a mere servant or slave of the people and that he was made so by the Creator. Even in the *Mānava* itself, either when it was revised and put in its present form, or originally in its desire to justify the removal of the Mauryas, the theory was superseded by another theory which was inserted immediately below it :—

"The Lord created his own son and made him Law for the protection of the entire living world : it was endowed with Brahmā's own vigour as Law's administration (*Daṇḍa*)."[12]

"Law's administration is the real king, it is the ruling authority (*Daṇḍa, i.e.*, executive authority in polity), it is the surety for the population.[13]

"The king who properly employs it prospers, but if he be selfish, abnormal and deceitful, *Daṇḍa* destroys him.[14] *Daṇḍa* is of great lustre, it cannot be held by despots. It strikes down the king who swerves from law, together with his relatives."[15]

Thus the king is again brought down under law; he is reduced to his human and contractual status. A higher origin to law was attributed. The king was aggregate of only portions of several gods, but Law-and-Sanction was produced by Brahmā himself and it was his own son. He came to rule

---

[11] See Chs. XXXV, and XXXVI below.

[12] *Mānava-Dharma-Śāstra*, VII. 14.—

तदर्थं सर्वभूतानां गोप्तारं धर्ममात्मजम् ।
ब्रह्मतेजोमयं दण्डमसृजत्पूर्वमीश्वरः ॥

[13] *Ibid.*, VII. 17.—

स राजा पुरुषो दण्डः स नेता शासिता च सः ।
चतुर्णामाश्रमाणां च धर्म्मस्य प्रतिभूः स्मृतः ॥

[14] *Ibid.*, VII. 27.—

तं राजा प्रणयन्सम्यक्त्रिवर्गेणाभिवर्धते ।
कामात्मा विषमः क्षुद्रो दण्डेनैव निहन्यते ॥

[15] *Ibid.*, VII. 28.—

दण्डो हि सुमहत्तेजो दुर्धरश्चाकृतात्मभिः ।
धर्माद्विचलितं हन्ति नृपमेव सबान्धवम् ॥

over the king as over the whole world. It was the real sovereign and not the king. In fact the *Mānava* as a code went back to the old position :—

" Only a king who is honest and true to his Coronation Oath and follows the Śāstras, and rules with colleagues (ministers) could wield the *Daṇḍa,* not one who is despotic, greedy, stupid and who rules personally. "[16]

He was not only expected to be true to his ' undertaking,' his contract, *i.e.*, his Coronation Oath[17] it was further enjoined on him that he should work with colleagues and should not rule personally. We shall see its significance when we survey the constitutional position of the Hindu Ministry.

Divine theory of kingly origin and kingly right could have found soil in Hindu India if there had been no live interest and constitutional jealousy in the people to check such pernicious claims and notions. The Hindu theory of kingship was not permitted to degenerate into a divine imposture and profane autocracy. Jugglery in the divine name of the Creator was not possible for the Hindu King as the race never allowed the craft of the Priest to be united in the office of the Ruler. The reason why the sceptre of Hindu sovereign never became the wand of magician, was that the matter of constitutional powers of the king, in fact, lay beyond the province of the ritualist and the priest. It lay in the hands of those ' through whose strength ' the king had become ' mighty ' or vested with the power. It lay in their *Samiti* in the early period. In later times it lay in the equally important machinery—the Paura-and-Jānapada.[18]

---

[16] *Mānava-Dharma-Śāstra,* VII. 30-31.—

सोऽसहायेन मूढेन लुब्धेनाकृतबुद्धिना ।
न शक्यो न्यायतो नेतुं सक्तेन विषयेषु च ॥
शुचिना सत्यसन्धेन यथाशास्त्रानुसारिणा ।
दण्डः प्रणयितुं शक्तः सुसहायेन धीमता ॥

[17] On *Satya-Sandha* as referring to ' Oath ', *cf. Artha-Śāstra,* p. 312. Here it refers to the ' Oath, ' *i.e.*, the Oath of Coronation.

[18] See next Chapter.

CHAPTER XXVII

The Jānapada or the Realm Assembly and The Paura or the Assembly of the Capital City (600 B.C. to 600 A.C.)

The *Samiti* and Territorial Monarchies

Just about the time of the rise of large monarchies we find developed a popular institution of great constitutional importance. The period succeeding the Vedic, from the Mahābhārata War down to the end of the Bṛihadrathas (700 B.C.)[1] —is characterised by states which were co-extensive with their respective nations and lands inhabited by them. We may call that period, the epoch of National States and National Monarchies. The Bharatas,[2] and Pañchālas,[3] for instance, had their own national kings; and so had the Videhas; the nation called Aikshvākas[4] (*Aita. Br.* to Patañjali) had their own king. A little before 600 B.C. we find a new tendency in Indian states to develop what we may call non-national, territorial monarchies. The national basis begins to give way to a propensity for encroachment by one national unit upon others, and of amalgamation. Large states arise which are no more national but merely territorial units. We find, for instance, the old *Aikshvāka janapada*, *i.e.*, Kosala, transforming itself into *Kāśi-Kosala*,[5] and the Magadha state comprised of the territories of Magadha and Aṅga.[6] The process develops very rapidly between 550 B.C. and 300 B.C. The ground for this had already been prepared philosophically. The Buddha, though a born republican, was ambitious to found a one-state empire

---

[1] Jayaswal, *J.B.O.R.S.*, IV, pp. 26–35; 262.

[2] *Cf. Taittirīya Saṁhitā* of *Yajur-Veda*, एष वो भरता राजा, 1. 8. 10.

[3] *Bṛihadāraṇyaka Upanishad*, VI. 2.

[4] *Aitareya Brāhmaṇa*, VII. 13. 16; Patañjali on *Pāṇini*, IV. 2. 104.

[5] *Jaina Sūtra*, '*Āchārāṅga*'; see p. 50 above; *Buddhist India*, pp. 24–25; *Janavasabha Sutta* quoted by Oldenberg, *Buddha* (Eng. trans.), p. 407, f.n.; see काशिकौशल्य as one unit in the *Gopatha Brāhmaṇa*, II. 9.

[6] *Buddhist India*, p. 24; *Gopatha Brāhmaṇa*, II. 9.

of his religion.[7] The *Aitareya Brāhmaṇa* had preached for an empire extending up to the sea.[8] The *Jātakas* are full of the ideal of an all-India Empire (*Sakala-Jambudīpe eka-rajjaṃ*).

In the period of large monarchies or empires, country became more important than the nation (*jana*). In fact, the term *janapada*, which literally and originally meant 'the seat of the nation' and which had been secondarily employed as denoting the nation itself, lost its old significance, and came to mean what we call to-day country,[9] without reference to the racial elements inhabiting it. In the period of large monarchies we never hear of the *Samiti*.[10] This, of course, is natural. The basis of the *Samiti* was the national unit, and the national unit now ceased to be a factor in matters constitutional.

We, however, hear of another institution which probably was an incarnation of the old *Samiti* under changed circumstances.

Rise of the *Jānapada* Assembly

The division of a kingdom in the period between 600 B.C. and 600 A.C. is made into 'the capital' and 'the country'.[11] The former is designated *Pura*[12] or *Nagara*[13] (the City) and occasionally *Durga*[14] (the Fort), and the latter is called *Janapada*, with synonyms in *Rāshṭra* and *Deśa*. The

---

[7] Probably not so much *religion* as *philosophy*. The difference between the two, as Megasthenes describes, was very slight. Aśoka certainly made it a religion and a world-religion.

[8] See below, Ch. XXXVII on Hindu Imperial Systems.

[9] See *Artha-Śāstra*, p. 45, and foot-note at p. 46, जनपदो देश: ।

[10] The *Jātakas* do not know anything about the *Samiti*. There were numerous occasions to mention it if the *Samiti* did actually exist. The *Dharma Sūtras* also do not give any direction, writing on the duties of king, as to his relation with the *Samiti*. Nor does the *Mahābhārata* recollect it.

[11] The *Jātakas* and Pāli Canon have *Janapada* and *Nigama*. *Nigama*, as will be seen, is constitutionally identical with *Nagara*. The *Artha-Śāstra* has *Janapada* and *Durga*; the *Rāmāyaṇa*, *Nagara* (also *Durga*) and *Janapada* (वने वत्स्याम्यहं दुर्गे रामो राजा भविष्यति । II. 79. 12).

[12] पुरं मुख्यनगरम् । *Vīramitrodaya*, p. 11.

[13] *Cf. Artha-Śāstra*, p. 46 f.n. नगरं राजधानी ।

[14] *Cf.* the modern *garh* ('fort') to denote the seat of the ruler; also German *schloss*.

expression *Jānapada*, a derivative from *janapada*, we find occurring in the Pāli Canon, the *Rāmāyāṇa*, the *Mahābhārata* and other books, and in inscriptions. In our day, it has been taken to mean an inhabitant of *Janapada*. Its use as a technical term has been missed. This is due to the fact that the term is generally found in the plural, *e.g.*, *jānapadāḥ* (जानपदाः) which has been translated as 'The people of the *Janapada*'. Modern writers have further made the mistake of regarding *Janapada* as a province which is against all ancient authority. It really means the whole area of a kingdom, minus the capital constitutionally.[15] The technical significance of the *Jānapada* as a collective institution has now been established by Khāravela's inscription of *c.* 170 B.C.[16] Mediæval commentators not knowing that there was a collective institution *Jānapada*, 'corrected' the singular form into the plural *Jānapadāḥ*. A very good example of this is verse 54 (Ch. XIV) of the *Ayodhyā-Kāṇḍa* of the *Rāmāyaṇa*.[17] King Daśaratha is sought to be intimated: "The *Paura*, the *Jānapada*, and the *Naigama* are present respectfully waiting for Rāma's consecration (as Crown Prince)." The verb *upatishṭhati* ('*is waiting*') is in the signular and this requires the subjects in each case to be in the singular. But in the text only the *Naigama* (corporate association of guilds merchant of the capital) is kept in the singular and the word *Jānapada* has been altered into a plural nominative or plural instrumental. The instrumental form is resorted to for a forced grammatical justification ('the *Jānapadas with* the *Naigama*'). The correct reading, in the nominative singular, *Jānapadaścha*, is still found in some MSS. But it is rejected by modern editors as incorrect.[18]

---

15 *Artha-Śāstra*, pp. 45–46, n.

16 Jayaswal, *J.B.O.R.S.*, (1917), III. 451 ; *E.I.*, XX. 71.

17 उपतिष्ठति रामस्य समग्रमभिषेचनम् ।
पौरजानपदाश्चापि नैगमश्च कृताञ्जलिः ॥ II. 14. 54.

Govindarāja in his comment on the variant उपतिष्ठत says: उदोऽनूर्ध्वकर्म्मणि इत्यात्मनेपदम् । उपस्थितमित्यर्थः । ··उपतिष्ठतीति पाठान्तरम् । Four MSS. give the reading उपतिष्ठति in the Kumbakonam edition.

18 See the critical edition of the *Rāmāyaṇa* by Messrs. Krishnāchārya and Vyāsāchārya, I. 68 (MS. "ट"). which is really a valuable edition.

The plural *jānapadāḥ* may equally denote '*the members of the jānapada-institution*' as well as '*the people of janapada*'. The plural form does not exclude the instituional significance. That there was such a body can be established if we find the term used in the singular, not in the sense of one man but in the collective sense, or if we find the plural *jānapadāḥ* in a collective sense. We have instances of both these uses. Moreover, we have evidence of the fact that *jānapadas* as bodies corporate had their own laws and those laws were recognised by the *Dharma-Śāstras*.

There is the unquestionable evidence afforded by the Hāthigumphā inscription of Khāravela, which says that the king granted privileges to the *Jānapada* (on the singular *Jānapadam*). The evidence of the *Rāmāyaṇa* referred to above is equally important. The *Jānapada* was awiting for the consecration of the King-Assistant. They, the *Jānapadas*, according to the *Rāmāyaṇa*, had already come to a unanimous decision in a joint conference with the Pauras and others on the question of this proposed consecration. The resolution was: 'we desire this consecration'.[19]

In the *Mānava-Dharma-Śāstra*, the laws of caste (*Jāti*),[20] of *Jānapada*, and guild (*śreṇi*)[21] are recognised. It is undoubted that the other two institutions of this group were

---

[19] *Rāmāyana, Ayodhyā-Kāṇḍa*, Ch. II, vs. 20–22.—

समेत्य ते मन्त्रयित्वा समतागतबुद्धयः ।
ऊचुश्च मनसा ज्ञात्वा वृद्धं दशरथं नृपम् ॥

.. .. ..

स रामं युवराजानमभिषिञ्चस्व पार्थिव ।
इच्छामो हि महाबाहुं रघुवीरं महाबलम् ॥

See also Daśaratha's speech in reply.—

कथं नु मयि धर्मेण पृथिवीमनुपालति ।
भवन्तो द्रष्टुमिच्छन्ति युवराजं महाबलम् ॥

[20] *Manu*, VIII. 41.—

जातिजानपदान्धर्म्माञ्श्रेणीधर्म्मांश्च धर्म्मवित् ।
समीक्ष्य कुलधर्म्मांश्च स्वधर्म्मं प्रतिपादयेत् ॥

[21] *Śreṇi* literally means 'rows'. Evidently the members sat in rows, and this feature gave the name to the corporate body. Probably *Śreṇi* originally was a general term to signify all those bodies which transacted their business in their 'session' or by assembly system. The *Mahābhārata* in older passages gives *Śreṇibaddhāḥ*

corporate institutions. The Code of *Yājñavalkya* mentions *jānapadas*, *gaṇas*, *śreṇis* and *jātis* (castes) as units which "also must be compelled to follow their own laws".[22] Mandlik with the true insight of the lawyer leaves the word *jānapadāḥ* untranslated and treats it as a technical term like the *gaṇa* and *śreṇi*. These two *smṛiti* passages similarly mention another institution *Kula*. We have already seen that there was a *Kula* form of Government. To find out the identity of *Kula*, let us take parallel passages on the point from the *Artha-Śāstra*. In the chapter dealing with *samaya*[23] or resolutions of corporate institutions (p. 173) Kautilya mentions the *samaya* of *Deśa-saṃgha*, *Jāti-saṃgha*, and *Kula-saṃgha*; *i.e.*, of the country-corporate-association, of caste-corporate-association, and the corporate association of a *Kula*. The *Kula-saṃgha* as we have seen[24] is a technical term of Hindu politics. It means a constitution where *Kula* or family rules, *i.e.*, an aristocratic or oligarchic state. Again at page 407 *Deśa-saṃgha*, *Grāma-saṃgha* and *Jāti-saṃgha* are mentioned. The *Mānava-Dharma-Śāstra*[25] deals

---

rājānaḥ or 'rulers organised in rows', *e.g.*, *Sabhā-Parvan*, XIV. 4 (Kumbakonam ed.):—

राजानः श्रेणिबद्धाश्च तथान्ये क्षत्रिया भुवि ।

These may refer to republican rulers or to a military organization, the *Artha-Śāstra* having *Śreṇi* as a military division. In law-books, general literature, and inscriptions, *Śreṇi* has acquired the technical meaning of guild.

22 *Yājñavalkya*, I. 360 and 361—

व्यवहारान्स्वयं पश्येत्सभ्यैः परिवृतोऽन्वहम् ।
कुलानि जातिः श्रेणीश्च गणाञ्जानपदानपि ॥
स्वधर्माच्चलितान्राजा विनीयस्थापयेत्पथि ।
ग्रामश्रेणिगणानाञ्च सङ्केतः समयक्रिया ॥

—Bṛihaspati quoted in *Vīramitrodaya*, p. 424. See below.

23 देशजातिकुलसंघानां समयस्यानपाकर्म ।

24 See p. 76 above.

25 *Manu*, VIII. 218–21.—

अत ऊर्द्ध्वं प्रवक्ष्यामि धर्म्मं समयभेदिनाम् ॥ १८ ॥
यो ग्रामदेशसङ्घानां कृत्वा सत्येन संविदम् ।
विसंवदेन्नरो लोभात्तं राष्ट्राद्विप्रवासयेत् ॥ १९ ॥

.. .. ..

एवं दण्डविधिं कुर्याद्धार्म्मिकः पृथिवीपतिः ।
ग्रामजातिसमूहेषु समयव्यभिचारिणाम् ॥ २१ ॥

with the 'breakers of *samayas*' (resolutions or laws of corporate assemblies) and mentions the *Gramā-saṃgha* and the *Deśa-saṃgha* which are paraphrased again as *Grāma-samūha*, *Jāti-samūha*, etc. *Deśa*, or the *Jānapada* association is also found in Bṛihaspati[26] where the laws of guild merchant and the laws of *Deśa* are referred to together. In another verse[27] the resolutions of the 'town' and of the 'country' (*Deśa*), 'not being opposed to the laws of the king' are provided for. Manu (VIII. 41), instead of *Jāti-śaṃgha* gives *Jāti* only, and instead of *Deśa-saṃgha*, mentions *Jānapada*. In VIII. 46, in the place of *Jānapada*, *Deśa* is substituted. By *Deśa* in such passages the association *Deśa-saṃgha* or the *Jānapada* is obviously meant. Similarly, when a document registered by the *Deśa-Adhyaksha* is termed by Vyāsa the law-giver a '*Jānapada* document,' the *Adhyaksha* of *Deśa* is the President of the *Deśa* assembly or the *Jānapada*.[28] The above data prove that the *Jānapada* of Manu and Yājñavalkya and the *Deśa-saṁgha* of Manu and Kauṭilya are identical. The corporate association *Jānapada*

---

26 देशस्थित्यानुमानेन नैगमानुमतेन वा ।
क्रियते निर्णयस्तत्र व्यवहारस्तु बाध्यते ॥
—Quoted in *Vīramitrodaya*, p. 120.

27 ग्रामो देशश्च यत्कुर्य्यात्सत्यलेख्यं परस्परम् ।
राजाविरोधिधर्म्मार्थं संवित्पत्रं वदन्ति तत् ॥
—Bṛihaspati quoted in *Vīramitrodaya*, p. 189.

See also *Yājñavalkya*:
निजधर्म्माविरोधेन यस्तु सामयिको भवेत् ।
सोऽपि यत्नेन संरक्ष्यो धर्म्मो राजकृतश्च यः ॥

28 Aparārka (*Yājñavalkya*, II. 92) quotes the verses of Vyāsa on the subject dealing with documentary evidence:—
द्वित्रिलिपिज्ञः स्वकृतेन स्वलेख्येन युक्तिभिः ।
कुर्य्याद्धि सदृशं लेख्यं तस्माज्जानपदं शुभम् ॥
देशाध्यक्षादिना लेख्यं यत्र जानपदं कृतम् ॥

Vyāsa sees danger of successful denial in the case of a document written even in the handwriting of the executant, for a cunning man may write several hands. A *Jānapada* document therefore, 'done', *i.e.*, registered by the Deśa-president or others (*i.e.*, his officers as in the case of government registration by the officer of the king, *Vishṇu*, VII. 3, 'राजाधिकरणे तन्नियुक्तकायस्थकृतं तदध्यक्षकरचिह्नितं राजसाक्षिकं') was a good proof (see p. 260 below).

or *Deśa-saṃgha*, as the name signifies, was a body for the whole country (except as we shall presently see, the capital).

Janapada seals

When the first edition of this work was published the above interpretation of *Jānapada* was adversely criticised. Since then a number of seals found at Nālandā from excavated colleges have confirmed the interpretation as to the corporate character of *Jānapada*. The seals are in Gupta letters and belong to the sixth or seventh century. Every seal is of the corporate body *Jānapada*, *e.g.*, *Purikā-grāma-jānapadasya*.[29] In the period of these seals the general *Jānapada* of the whole country or province, *i.e.*, the *Deśa-saṃgha*, had probably ceased to exist, as the term is here transferred to the *Grāma-saṃgha*. But the corporate character of the term is still there.

The *Jānapada* yet has another synonym in *Rāshṭra*, which is found in later works. In the *Daśakumāra-charita* (Ch. 3) the president of the *Jānapada* is called *Janapada-mahattara*[30] (Lord High President). Further on, the same person is called the *Rāshṭra-mukhya* or the Leader of the Realm (Assembly).

In a manuscript of Mitramiśra's unpublished commentary on Yājñavalkya[31] I find, in connection with the subject of relief which could not be granted or suits which could not be entertained (*anādeya-vyavahāra*), that a suitor who was hostile to the *Paura*, *i.e.*, the City Assembly of the capital (see below), or to the *Rāshṭra* was not to be granted relief. The authority quoted is that of Bṛihaspati. A similar verse is given in the *Vīramitrodaya* (*Vyavahāra*) at page 44, where instead of *Paura*, the reading is *Pura*, capital. The expressions *Pura*

[29] Jayaswal, *Epigraphia Indica*, XX. 71; Hirananda Sāstri, *ibid.*, XXI. 72; see also his forthcoming Memoir (AS) on Nālandā seals.

[30] *Cf. Rāmāyaṇa*, Bk. II, Canto 83, v. 15 : ग्रामघोषमहत्तराः । The Rāma commentary has ग्रामे घोषे च वर्त्तमाना महत्तराः; Govindarāja, महत्तराः प्रधानभूताः । (*ghosha* according to Patañjali and Kātyāyana was a small township with corporate arms and seal, Pt. I, p. 44, *n.*).

[31] *Vīramitrodaya on Yājñavalkya* kindly lent to me by Mr. Govindadāsa of Benares.

and *Rāshṭra* are explained by Mitramiśra as *Paura-Jānapada*. *Rāshṭra* here thus stands for the *Jānapada* body as it does in the *Daśakumāra-charita*.

The *Paura*

Before dealing with the functions of the *Jānapada* it would be convenient to notice the corporate association of the Capital. The Capital Assembly is a twin sister of the *Jānapada* in constitutional matters. The two are almost always mentioned together, and sometimes one stands for both.

Paura does not relate to all the towns in the kingdom as it has been translated by both Indians and Europeans. Earlier Hindu writers understood by the technical *Pura* and *Nagara*, 'the Capital'. *Paura* as a corporate body is mentioned in the singular like *Jānapada* in the inscription of Khāravela *c*. 170 B.C.,[32] who granted privileges to the *Paura*. In the corporate sense it is clearly mentioned again in the *Divyāvadāna* where *Kunāla* is supposed to have entered the *Paura* (used in singular, that is, the *Paura* assembly).[33] Tishyarakshitā addressed her forged letter, according to the *Divyāvadāna*, to the *Pauras*, *i.e.*, on organised body. The author of the *Vīramitrodaya* definitely states that the *Paura*, which occurs along with corporate bodies in the law-books, was 'the body (*samūha*) of the citizens of the capital (*Pura*)'.[34] *Pura* meant the capital (p. 247, *n*. 45). *Samūha* is a well-known constitutional term in Hindu law. Kātyāyana, for instance, defines *pūga*, which according to the accepted interpretation means a 'guild' as the '*samūha of merchants and others*'.[35] Bṛihaspati, the lawyer, describes bodies already known to us to have been assembly ruled organisations,[36] *e.g.*, *pūga*, *gaṇa*, *saṃgha* as *samūhastha vargas* (pp. 251-52 below) or 'bodies incorporated'.[37]

---

[32] *J.B.O.R.S.*, III. 456 ; *E.I.*, XX. 71.

[33] *Divyāvadāna*, p. 410.

[34] पौर: पुरवासिनां समूहः । *Vīramitrodaya*, p. 11.

[35] समूहो वणिजादीनां पूगः संपरिकीर्त्तितः । Cited by Chaṇḍeśvara, *Vivāda R.*, p. 669.

[36] *Cf.* '*Saṁgha* is the *samūha* of the Jainas or Buddhists': आर्हतसौगतानां तु समूहः सङ्घ उच्यते । Kātyāyana in *V. R.*, p. 669.

[37] गणपाषण्डपूगाश्च व्राताश्च श्रेणयस्तथा ।
समूहस्थाश्च ये चान्ये वर्गाख्यास्ते बृहस्पतिः ॥ *Ibid.*

Mitramiśra quotes a text based upon Bhṛigu which calls *grāma, paura, gaṇa* and *śreṇi*, '*vargins*,' *i.e.*, what Bṛihaspati has as '*samūhastha vargas*'[38] (*grāma* here is not the village but the Village Association as Chaṇḍeśvara the lawyer of Mithilā defines: *Grāmo grama-vāsi-samūhaḥ*, p. 179). Chaṇḍeśvara explains *samūhasthāḥ* by '*militāḥ*', 'combined'.[39] Kātyāyana speaks of separate laws of the *samūhas*.[40] *Samūha* which ordinarily means a collection has, thus, a technical, constitutional sense—an organized body.[41]

Amara and Kātya, lexicographers, in giving the meanings of *Prakṛiti* say that the term means amongst others, the *Pauras*, *i.e.*, 'the Associations (*Śreṇayaḥ*) of the *Pauras*'.[42]

In the *Rāmāyaṇa*, the *Paura Jānapada* body is appealed to by Bharata when Rāma refuses to go back to Ayodhya :—

"What do you order His Highness."[43] The body approves of the argument of Rāma, and in reply Bharata speaks, addressing them :—

'Hear please, you my assemblies.'[44] The assembly character thus was prominent.

---

[38] ग्रामपौरगणश्रेण्यश्चातुर्विद्यश्च वर्गिणः. *Vīramitrodaya* (*Vyavahāra*), p. 11.

[39] *Vivāda R.*, p. 653 (समूहस्था मिलिताः).

[40] समूहानां तु यो धर्मस्तेन धर्मेण ते सदा । *Ibid.*, 180.

[41] *Cf.* Mitramiśra's comment on another corporate body (*Sārtha*): मिलितो जनसङ्घः 'associated body of men,' *Vīramitrodaya*, p. 12.

Yājñavalkya provides for punishing those who act contrary to the decision of the '*samūha* well-wishers,' *Ibid.*, p. 179.

Kātyāyana provides for a dispute between *Samūha* and its leader, *V. R.*, p. 184.

[42] अमात्याश्चापि पौराश्च सद्भिः प्रकृतयः स्मृताः । *Kātya.*, quoted by Kshīrasvāmin on Amara, II. 8. 18, राज्याङ्गानि प्रकृतयः पौराणां श्रेणयोऽपि च । *Trivandrum Sanskrit Series*, No. 51, p. 66.

[43] आसीनस्त्वेव भरतः पौरजानपदं जनम् ।
उवाच सर्वतः प्रेक्ष्य किमार्यं नानुशासथ ॥ *Rāmāyaṇa*, *A. K.*, 111. 19.

[44] शृण्वन्तु मे परिषदः मन्त्रिणः शृणुयुस्तथा । *Ibid.*, 24.

Municipal administration of the *Paura*

The *Paura* was a communal association in which was vested the municipal administration of the Capital.[45] Apart from its municipal work it exercised great constitutional powers. Let us first take the Municipal administration of the *Paura*.

It was presided over by a leading citizen, generally a merchant or a banker. The Hindu Mayor was called *Śreshṭhin* or the President. According to the *Rāmāyaṇa*, the *Paura* as well as the *Jānapada* consisted of two sections, the Inner and the Outer bodies.[46] The Inner must have been the

---

[45] *Cf.* मन्दौत्सुक्योऽस्मि नगरगमनं प्रति, *Śakuntalā*, Act I, पुरं मुख्यनगरम्—*Vīramitrodaya*, p. 11. The term for ordinary town or township is ग्राम, *e.g.*, ग्रामपौरगणश्रेण्यश्चातुर्विद्यश्च वर्गिणः। *Ibid.* The *Artha-Śāstra* uses the word नगर and दुर्ग for the capital, and ग्राम for ordinary town. Pānini and Patañjali use नगर and पुर for capital, and ग्राम for ordinary town. *Cf.* Pāṇini, VII. 3. 14 and *Kāśikā* on that; also VI. 2. 100; Patañjali, on the use of ग्राम for town, शाकलं नाम वाहीकग्रामः on Pāṇini, IV. 2. 104. *Śākala* which was the old capital of the Madras ceased to be a नगर or capital under Pushyamitra. It is probably for that reason called a ग्राम, an ordinary town. See also *Artha-Śāstra*, p. 46 f.n. नगरं राजधानी. The commentator commenting on the *nāgarikāḥ* in Vātsyāyana's *Kāma-Sūtra* (Bk. II. Ch. 5) says:

नागरिका इति पाटलिपुत्रिकाः।

On *Durga* as equivalent of *Pura cf.* Nārada—संरक्षेत्समयं राजा दुर्गे जनपदे तथा, *Vīramitrodaya*, p. 425. नगर in Aśoka's inscriptions means a provincial capital as well. Manu, VII. 29, divides the kingdom into दुर्ग and राष्ट्र:

ततो दुर्गं च राष्ट्रं च लोकश्च सचराचरम्।

For दुर्ग and पुर as capital, see Manu, VII. 70:—

धन्वदुर्गं महीदुर्गमब्दुर्गं वार्क्षमेव वा।
नृदुर्गं गिरिदुर्गं वा समाश्रित्य वसेत्पुरम्॥

[46] आशंसते जनः सर्वो राष्ट्रे पुरवरे तथा।
आभ्यन्तरश्च बाह्यश्च पौरजानपदो जनः॥ (*Araṇya-Kāṇḍa.*)

"The whole nation in the *Rāshṭra*, as well as in the best of capitals praises him; likewise the *Paura-Jānapada* body—both the Inner and the Outer—praise him." It should be noticed that the *Paura-Jānapada* is taken as distinct from the people in the realm

executive council which sat permanently. We hear often of the *Paura* and the *Nagara-Vṛiddhas*, or the Elders of the *Paura*. On the analogy of other popular institutions of the country we can say that the *Paura-Vṛiddhas* constituted a Council of Elders which was probably identical with the Inner body of the *Rāmāyaṇa*. An exception is made in the *Dharma-Sūtras* to the general rule of etiquette in the case of a *Paura* ex-member of the Śūdra caste who is entitled to special respect even from a Brahmin.[47] This shows that the *Paura* had a real popular basis representing even the lowest interest.

The *Paura* had a Registrar and a document given by him was regarded as a superior kind of evidence.[48] The Registrar's document was the chief of the *laukika lekhyas* or popular documents as opposed to *rājakīya* or government documents. This shows that *Paura* was not a body appointed by the king.

The non-political functions of the *Paura* which are mentioned in the law books are these :—

---

and the capital. The two bodies, Inner and Outer, are mentioned in the *Mahābhārata* also. See below Ch. XXIII on Taxation. For *jana* in the collective sense, see its use in *Aśoka's Inscriptions*, Pillar Series, VII: जनं धंमयुतं—the body of the men in the *Dharma* Service (Department).

[47] *Gautama-Dharma-Śūtra* (*Śāstra*), VI. 9–11.

A Brahmin who ordinarily is not expected to do any honour to a *Śūdra* has to get up when a *Śūdra* who is an ex-member of the *Paura* came, though he be below eighty. Further, *Sūtra* 15 lays down an exception with regard to etiquette between *Pauras*. Even if the difference in age were of ten years, fellow-*Pauras* were to treat each other as if born on the same day (14–15) :—

ऋत्विक्श्वशुरपितृव्यमातुलानां तु यवीयसां प्रत्युत्थानमनभिवाद्याः ॥ ९ ॥
तथान्यः पूर्वः पौरोऽशीतिकावरः शूद्रोऽप्यपत्यसमेन ॥ १० ॥
अवरोऽप्यार्यः शूद्रेण ॥ ११ ॥
नाम चास्य वर्जयेत् ॥ १२ ॥
भो भवन्निति वयस्यः समानेऽहनि जातः ॥ १४ ॥
दशवर्षवृद्धः पौरः ॥ १५ ॥

[48] *Vasishṭha*, edition by Fuehrer, p. 84.—

चिरकं नाम लिखितं पुराणैः पौरलेखकैः ।

Also *Vishṇu S.*, VII. 3. *Cf.* the survival in the Bengal family title *Pura-Kāyastha*.

(*a*) Administration of Estates: They were authorised by the king to administer, along with government officers, property left by a deceased person[49] (*Vasishṭha*, XVI. 20).

(*b*) Works which contributed to the material strength of the citizens (called *Paushṭika*[50] works) were done by them, and likewise.

(*c*) Works which ensured the peace of the city (*śāntika*),[50] *i.e.*, policing the town. These two classes of work are qualified as being either 'ordinary,' 'extra-ordinary,' or 'discretionary'.

(*d*) Judicial work,[51] which must have been limited to the matter of municipal administration. Criminal authority proper, *i.e.*, in cases of the *Sāhasa*[52] (Violence) class, is expressly excepted from the jurisdiction of the Paura Court. According to an authority quoted by Mitramiśra, probably Bhṛigu, as well as others, the Paura Court was an instituiton recognised by the king.

(*e*) Charge of sacred and public places. The *Paura*, like any township, looked after temples and other sacred places

---

[49] *Vāsishṭha-Dharma-Sūtra* (*Śāstra*), XVI. 19–20.—

प्रहीणद्रव्याणि राजगामीनि भवन्ति ॥ १९ ॥

ततोऽन्यथा राजा मन्त्रिभिः सह नागरैश्च कार्य्याणि कुर्यात् ॥ २० ॥

तथानाथदरिद्राणां संस्कारो यजनक्रिया ।

—Bṛihaspati, *Vīramitrodaya*, p. 425.

Cf. बालद्रव्यं ग्रामवृद्धा वर्धयेयुराव्यवहारप्रापणात् देवद्रव्यञ्च । "Elders of the township should increase property of minors till they attain capacity-at-law. They should do the same with regard to the property of gods."—*Artha-Śāstra*, p. 48.

[50] नित्यं नैमित्तिकं काम्यं शान्तिकं पौष्टिकं तथा ।

पौराणां कर्म्म कुर्य्युस्ते संदिग्धे निर्णयं तथा ॥

—Bṛihaspati in the *Vīramitrodaya*, p. 424.

चाटचौरभये बाधाः सर्वसाधारणाः स्मृताः ।

तत्रोपशमनं कार्य्यं सर्वैर्नैकेन केनचित् ॥ *Ibid.*

[51] See last note, संदिग्धे निर्णयं तथा ।

Also ग्रामपौरगणश्रेण्यश्चातुर्विद्यश्च वर्गिणः ।

कुलानि कुलकाश्चैव नियुक्ता नृपतिस्तथा ॥

—*Vīramitrodaya*, p. 11.

[52] साहसन्यायवर्जानि कुर्युः कार्याणि ते नृणाम् ।

—Bṛihaspati in the *Vīramitrodaya*, p. 40.

of the Capital. They did repairs to those buildings. The buildings named are *sabhā*, *prapā* (place for distribution of water), *taṭāka* (public tank), *ārāma* (rest-house), and *devagṛiha* (temple).[53]

Paura administration of Pāṭaliputra

I propose to identify the description of the municipal government noticed by Megasthenes at Pāṭaliputra, with the *Paura* organisation of Hindu India. Strabo[54] after giving the description of Pāṭaliputra describes its administration. The most important point to mark in that is the phrase 'the City Magistrates' which in the mouth of a Greek will signify popular officers and not officers appointed by the king. The royal officer, Governor of the City, the '*Nāgaraka*' as described in the *Artha-Śāstra* was distinct. These 'city magistrates' had six boards of five members each who looked after

(*a*) industrial matters of the city,

(*b*) foreigners in the city on whose death they administered their properties (forwarded them to their relatives),[55]

(*c*) registration of births and deaths in the city,

(*d*) trade and commerce and manufactures of the city and collection of municipal duty on the sale of articles.

"Such are the functions which these bodies separately discharged. In their collective capacity they have charge both of their special departments and also of matters affecting the general interests, as the keeping of public buildings in repairs, regulation of prices, the care of markets, harbours and temples."

---

53 धर्मकार्य्यमपि संभूय कार्यमित्युक्तं तेनैव—
सभाप्रपादेवगृहतटाकारामसंस्कृतिः ॥

—Bṛihaspati in the *Vīramitrodaya*, p. 425.

Ārāma meant both a 'rest-house' and a 'park-garden'.

54 *Strabo*, Bk. XV. 50 (4–10). Compare the "magistrates of self-governed cities" as opposed to royal officers in *Arrian*, XII.

55 A scholar who does not take so much notice of Hindu authorities as he draws on analogies and comparisons has misunderstood this *Paura* jurisdiction of the Maurya capital as a consular department borrowed from Persia!

It should be noticed that the *Pauras* administered estates in co-operation with the ministry, according to Vasishṭha (XVI. 20).

The 'city magistrates' of Strabo are the *Paura-mukhyas* or the *Paura-vṛiddhas*. The boards of five and the full board of the thirty disclose the same arrangement as the quorums of three, five, ten, twenty and upwards in the *Parishads* of Law, the Buddhist *Saṃgha*, and the *pañchaka*, *daśaka* and *viṃśaka saṃghas* of Patañjali.[56] Bṛihaspati also enjoins committees of five in corporate associations.[57] In the Buddhist *Saṃgha* certain matters could be discussed by small quorums; but matters of greater importance could be discussed and decided by quorums of twenty and upwards only.[58] In the description of the *Paura* of Pāṭaliputra we see that the council decides matters of general interest by the bigger quorum. This collective council of the 'city magistrates' corresponds to what the *Rāmāyaṇa* calls the Inner Body of the *Paura*. The Outer, the general body, must have been composed of a fairly large number, when the Inner alone had thirty members.

Varga

Grāma or Township is called a *vargin* as seen above. *Varga* means an assembly or quorum. In that sense Pāṇini also uses it (V. 1. 60; see *Kāśikā* on it: पञ्चको वर्गः दशको वर्गः). Other corporate associations are called *Vargins* (those who worked by the *Varga* or assembly system). In a law text (Bhṛigu) quoted by Mitramiśra (*Vīramitrodaya*, p. 11) *Paura* and *grāma* as well as *gaṇa* are called *vargins* [*cf.* Kātyayāna quoted by Nīlakaṇṭha:

लिङ्गिनः श्रेणिपूगाश्च वणिग्जातास्तथापरे ।
समूहस्थाश्च ये चान्ये वर्गास्तानब्रवीद्भृगुः ॥]

The *vargas* of Vāsudeva and Akrūra are mentioned in the *Mahābhāshya*, IV. 2. 2. *Varga* in the corporate sense is

---

[56] Patañjali on Pāṇini, V. 1. 58 and 59. In the inscriptions of the seventh century in Nepal, a popular body in charge of pious properties as trustees is called '*Pañchālikas*' (*I.A.*, IX. 171).

[57] द्वौ त्रयः पञ्च वा कार्य्याः समूहहितवादिनः ।
कर्त्तव्यं वचनं तेषां ग्रामश्रेणिगणादिभिः ॥

—*Vīramitrodaya*, p. 427.

[58] *Mahāvagga*, IX. 4. 1. पञ्चसंघा । चतुवग्गो भिक्खुसंघो पञ्चवग्गो भिक्खुसंघो दसवग्गो भिक्खुसंघो वीसतिवग्गो भिक्खुसंघो अतिरेकवीसतिवग्गो भिक्खुसंघो । See also IX. 3. 5. etc.

employed by Gautama in his *Dharma-Śāstra*, Chapter XI, *Sūtras* 20–21:

देशजातिकुलधर्माश्चाम्नायैरविरुद्धाः प्रमाणम् ।
कर्षक-वणिक्-पशुपाल-कुसीदि-कारवः स्वे स्वे वर्गे ॥

"The laws of the cultivators, merchants, cattle-breeders, bankers and artisans should be authority in their own corportations." It should be noticed that cultivators had their own unions in the days of Gautama.

Naigama and its connexion with *Paura*

The *Paura*, according to the *Artha-Śāstra* (p. 89) had gold coins minted at the royal mint. This might have been a constitutional function as exercising check on the royal minting of improper coins or it might have been a purely economic function. Very likely it was the latter.[59] The *Pura* or capital had the association of the City Merchants which was called the *Naigama*.[60] This name was exclusively employed to the Guild of the City Merchants. It is wrong to take it, as it has been done up to this time, as a general term for Guild Merchant. The general term is *Śreṇi* as well as *Pūga*, the difference between the two being not very clear.[61] Now it appears that originally the *Naigama* of the capital was the mother of the *Paura* Association. The *Paura* grew out or around the *Naigama* (p. 254 below). In the *Jātakas* and Pāli Canon *Naigama* (*Negama*) stands for *Paura*.[62] Modern translators

---

[59] Up to recent decades the custom of getting coins minted by merchants was current in this country.

[60] नैगमाः पौरवणिजः, Mitramiśra, *Vīramitrodaya*, p. 120; also नगराणि करवर्जितानि निगमवणिजां स्थानानि, *Praśna-Vyākaraṇa-Sūtra-Vyākhyāna* quoted by Shama Shastry, *Artha-Śāstra*, p. 46 f.n. The law-givers put *naigama* in the list of corporate bodies, *e.g.*,

पाषण्ड-नैगम-श्रेणि-पूग-व्रात-गणादिषु, Nārada quoted in *VR.*, p. 180;

श्रेणि-नैगम-पाषण्ड-गणानामप्ययं विधिः, Yājñavalkya, (*Ibid*)., p. 179.

Pāshaṇḍa here means the Buddhist and Jaina religious associations, their *gaṇas* and *saṃghas*.

[61] Unskilled artisans were combined as *Vrātas*. See Patañjali on Pāṇini, V. 2. 21.

[62] *Jātaka*, I. p. 149—सब्बे नेगमजानपदे; *Kūṭadanta Sutta*, *Dīgha-nikāya*, para. 12, नेगमा च एव जानपदा च ते भवं राजा आमन्तयतं ।

have translated it by 'town'. It really refers to '*the* town' or Capital. Hindu commentators on law books equate *Naigama* with *Paura*.[63] In the Pāli books *Naigama* comes with *Jānapada* as in Sanskrit books *Paura* comes with *Jānapada*. The connection between the City Guild of Merchants and the City Corporation was so intimate that both came to be regarded as identical. This is the reason why the mercantile interest is predominant in the *Paura*.[64] The *Rāmāyaṇa* mentions the *Naigama* always with the *Paura* and treats them as connected though distinct.[65] The *Naigama* had its assembly hall and office—*sabhā*, where it held its meetings as the *Paura-Jānapadas* held theirs in their *sabhās* and on their squares.[66] We find a donor, a nobleman, recording at the *Nigama-Sabhā* his investments with certain guilds, *śreṇis*, of the town Govardhana, the interest to go to certain charities in perpetuity. M. Senart translates the passage in question thus—"all this has been proclaimed (and) registered at the town's hall, at the record office, according to custom".[67] *Naigama* thus was connected with, and probably over, the *Śreṇis* or guilds of the City.

---

[63] Chaṇḍeśvara, *VR.*, pp. 177, 180, नैगमाः पौराः, नैगमः पौरसमूहः ।

[64] *Cf. Śreshṭhin* who is always a rich merchant. See below on the composition of the *Paura*.

[65] *Rāmāyaṇa, Yuddha-Kāṇḍa*, 127, 16.

[66] गुणैः समुदितान् दृष्ट्वा पौराः पाण्डुसुतांस्तदा ।

.. ..

कथयन्तिस्म सम्भूय चत्वरेषु सभासु च ॥

—*Mahābhārata* quoted by Mitramiśra in *VMR.*, p. 40.

[67] Nasik cave inscription, *E.I.*, VIII. 82. Text :—

"गोवर्धन-वाथवासु श्रेणिसुकोलीकनिकाये २००० वृधि पडिकशत..एते च सर्व स्रावित निगमसभाय निबध च फलकवारे चरित्रतोति"

Charitra was recorded in books. See *A.S.*, II. 25. p. 62. *Charitrato* may mean 'as *Charitra* was recorded'; *Śrāvita* according to law books would mean 'attested'. The transaction was 'attested' at the *Nigama Sabhā*, *i.e.*, by registration. Hindu method of attestation included both 'witnessing' and 'hearing'.

'*Negama* coins'

The *Paura* being so pronouncedly mercantile, their getting coins minted at the royal mint we can take as an economic measure. The '*Negama* coins' which are interpreted as coins struck by guilds, are I think, to be interpreted as coins struck at the capital by the state for the association of the City Merchants or the *Paura*.[68] And the coins bearing the name of chief towns, *e.g.*, 'Ujeniya',[69] can be thus explained as being *Paura* coins.[70]

The literal significance of *Nigama*, from which *Naigama* is derived, is in accordance with Pāṇini, III. 3. 119, 'the place (or house) whereinto people resort'. It would have been the meeting-place or the bourse in the Capital where merchants and tradesmen in the Capital met. The body of the people associated with the *Nigama*, the bourse or the guildhall, were called *Naigama*.

---

[68] *Cf. Artha-Śāstra*, p. 89.—सौवर्णिकः पौरजानपदानां रूप्यसुवर्णमावेशनिभिः कारयेत् ।

[69] Cunningham, *A.S.R.*, Vol. XIV. 148.

[70] The *Dojaka* coin bearing the word नेगम (Cunningham, *Coins of Ancient India*, p. 64, pl. III) would signify that the name of the capital was *Dojaka*. See also the Eran coin (*A.S.R.*, Vol. XIV, p. 148; *C.A.I.*, pp. 99–102).

CHAPTER XXVIII

Political Functions of the Jānapada and the Paura

Coinage and *Jānapada*

The *Jānapada* appears to have been concerned with matters mainly constitutional and political. All the references to their work are to such business, with one or two exceptions, *e.g.*, that they got gold coins minted by the royal mint-master.[1] This seems to have been a business of economic nature. Apparently they had to judge as to the number of coins necessary in the country for the purposes of exchange, and probably they exercised some sort of supervision as to weight and purity of the coins, as debasement of coinage by government is found recorded once or twice as a matter of public complaint.

Constitutional business which the *Paura-Jānapada* were supposed to do

In all constitutional matters we find the *Paura* always appearing with *Jānapada*. The *Paura* had thus a double character, as a local self-administration of the capital and a constitutional assembly. The latter function they sometimes discharged, as we shall see, by themselves, especially in provincial capitals. Matters of importance were discussed and decided in a joint parliament of the two bodies, the *Jānapada* and the *Paura*. Their unity then is so complete that the two bodies are regarded as one and referred to as one in the singular. The unity was effected owing to the fact that *Jānapada* had its meeting place and office at the capital itself.[2]

Let us take examples of the business they used to transact. The *Pauras* and the *Jānapadas* meet together along with Brahmins and other leaders of the nation to resolve upon the appointment of a Yuvarāja or king-assistant.[3] They after

---

[1] *Artha-Śāstra*, II. 14 ; 32.

[2] See reference in the *Mṛichchhakaṭika* discussed below (pp. 270–71), and other references indicating their location at capital.

[3] *Rāmāyaṇa*, *Ayodhyā-Kāṇḍa*, II. 19–22.—

ब्राह्मणा बलमुख्याश्च पौरजानपदैः सह ।
समेत्य मन्त्रयित्वा तु समतागतबुद्धयः ॥
ऊचुश्च मनसा ज्ञात्वा वृद्धं दशरथं नृपम् ।
.. ..
स रामं युवराजानमभिषिञ्चस्व पार्थिव ॥
इच्छामो हि महाबाहुं रघुवीरं महाबलम् ।

their deliberations ask the king to consecrate the prince whom, they say, "we want".[4]

They resolve on Nomination of the Crown-Prince

The king is somewhat surprised and asks: "As you desire the Rāghava prince to become protector, a doubt has arisen in my mind which please remove. O you rulers (*Rājānaḥ*, 'kings'), although I am ruling this country in accordance with law, yet how is it, you gentlemen want to see my son appointed as king-assistant, with high powers?" The spokesmen with the members of the *Paura-Jānapada* give their reasons. They say that Rāma was the best of the Ikshvākus on merits; that he was born before Bharata; that be was brave; that he always enquired after the well-being of the *Pauras*; that he took a leading part in the festivities; that he knew the principles of government, etc.; that the country desired him as its lord; and in fine, that not only the people of the kingdom and the capital, but also the

---

[4] *Rāmāyaṇa, Ayodhyā-Kāṇḍā*, II. 26–51.—

ते तमूचुर्महात्मानं पौरजानपदैः सह ।
बहवो नृप कल्याणा गुणाः पुत्रस्य सन्ति ते ।
.. ..
इक्ष्वाकुभ्योऽपि सर्वेभ्यो ह्यतिरिक्तो विशांपते ।
..............बभूव भरताग्रजः ।
.. ..
यदा व्रजति संग्रामं ग्रामार्थे नगरस्य वा ।
गत्वा सौमित्रिसहितो नाविजित्य निवर्त्तते ॥
पौरान्स्वजनवन्नित्यं कुशलं परिपृच्छति ।
.. ..
उत्सवेषु च सर्वेषु पितेव परितुष्यति ।
प्रजापालन संयुक्तो न रागोपहतेन्द्रियः ॥
आशंसते जनः सर्वो राष्ट्रे पुरवरे तथा ।
आभ्यन्तरश्च बाह्यश्च पौरजानपदो जनः ॥ (Kumbakonam)

For *Jana* in the collective sense of a body, compare Aśoka's जनं धम्मयुतं (Pillar Series, VII).

The age of the present *Rāmāyaṇa* should be studied in Jacobi's critical paper on *Rāmāyaṇa* (*Dās Rāmāyaṇa*). It seems that the original edition was composed about 500 B.C., and the revision took place in c. 200 B.C. (*J.B.O.R.S.*, IV. 264).

Paura-Jānapada, both their Inner and Outer bodies, admire the Prince. The king is satisfied with the proposal that they desired to have his eldest son in the office of the Yuvarāja. When the king promises that the desire would be carried out, his reply is acclaimed.[5] And then he makes a speech by which he gives directions to carry out the resolution. This being done, "the *Pauras* who had advised the king, departed, being greatly satisfied".[6] Here it is evident that the expression '*Pauras*' stands for both the *Pauras* and the *Jānapadas*.

They take part in *Abhisheka* as People's Representatives. They can prevent Succession

The *Paura-Jānapada* as one body again wait to take part in the *Abhisheka* (consecration) ceremony.[7] Although the whole body was taken to be present, only the Chiefs or 'Presidents' of the sections were in fact present in person.[8] We find only the *Vriddhas* of the whole of Pañchāla country taking part in the ceremony at Kānyakubja, as Dharma-Pāla's copper-plate records.[9] It is to the

---

[5] *Rāmāyaṇa, Ayodhyā-Kāṇḍā*, III. 2–5.—

अहोऽस्मि परमप्रीतः प्रभावश्चातुलो मम ।
यन्मे ज्येष्ठं प्रियं पुत्रं यौवराज्यस्थमिच्छथ ॥
.. ..
यौवराज्याय रामस्य सर्वमेवोपकल्प्यताम् ।
राज्ञस्तूपरते वाक्ये जनघोषो महानभूत् ॥
शनैस्तस्मिन्प्रशान्ते च जनघोषे नराधिपः ॥
.. ..

[6] *Ibid.*, III. 49.—

ते चापि पौरा नृपतेर्वचस्तच्छ्रुत्वा तदा लाभमिवेष्टमाशु ।
नरेन्द्रमामन्त्र्य गृहाणि गत्वा देवान्समानर्चुरभिप्रहृष्टाः ॥

Ibid., IV. 1.—

गतेष्वथ नृपो भूयः पौरेषु सह मन्त्रिभिः ।
मन्त्रयित्वा ततश्चक्रे निश्चयज्ञः स निश्चयम् ॥

[7] *Ibid.*, XIV. 52.—

उपतिष्ठति रामस्य समग्रमभिषेचनम् ।
पौरजानपदाश्चापि नैगमश्च कृताञ्जलिः ॥

[8] *Ibid.*, XIV. 40.—

पौरजानपदश्रेष्ठाः नैगमाश्च गणैः सह ।

[9] *E.I.*, IV, p. 248.

ladies of the Chiefs of the *Śreṇis* that the king offers salutation after the coronation ceremony.[10]

In other royal ceremonies also, the Alderman of the *Paura*, *Paura-Vṛiddhas*, take part.[11]

Likewise the *Paura-Jānapadas* could interfere with succession and prevent an undesirable prince from coming to the throne.[12]

Depositions

The revolution enacted in the *Mṛichchhakaṭika* throws light on another aspect of the constitutional power of the *Paura-Jānapada*. The reigning king is deposed because of bad administration of law, of which the president of the commercial union had been a victim.[13] The brother of the deposed king who 'established confidence' among the *Pauras*[14] obtained sovereignty. The messenger comes to the *Janapada-Samavāya*, 'corporate association of the *Janapada*' with the news of the revolution,[15] who are shortly after addressed as the *Pauras* and called upon to punish *Saṃsthānaka*. According to the *Mahāvaṃśa* the Ceylonese chronicle, the *Paura* in India could depose and banish the king for illegal acts, and they, mindful of the good of all, could choose another in his place outside the dynasty, by deciding upon it in their meeting.[16] Here again the *Pauras* apparently stand for both the *Pauras* and *Jānapadas*. In the *Daśakumāracharita*[17] the *Pauras* and the *Jānapadas* are said to be friendly to the brothers of the king, it is therefore feared by the speaker that they are bound to succeed the king if the latter dies.

---

10 *V.M.R.*, 114.

11 *Ibid.*, p. 417. In *Deva-pātro* ततोर्चास्नपनस्यान्ते पौरैर्वृद्धपुरःसरैः ।

12 *Mahābhārata*, *Ud.*, Ch. 149, 22–23.

13 See *Trial of Chārudatta*, translated in *C.W.N.*, XVI. ii.—

सार्थवाहविनयदत्तस्य नप्ता सागरदत्तस्य तनयः । Act IX. (छाया)

14 पौरान् समाश्वास्य ।

15 *Mṛichchhakaṭika*, Act X. See also पौरा वावादेध । किं णिमित्तं पादकी जीवावीअदि । which shows that the *Pauras* were present at the place where Chārudatta and Vasantasenā were standing and where the *Janapada-Samavāya* was.

16 *Cf.* *Mahāvaṃśa*, IV. 5–6.

17 Chapter III—

अनुजाः पुनः अतिबह्वः तैरपि घटन्ते पौरजानपदाः ।

Political Discussion in *Paura-Jānapada*

There is a sample of discussion in the assemblies of the *Paura* and the *Jānapada* given in the *Artha-Śāstra*. Spies of the king charged to gauge the political views of the *Pauras* and the *Jānapadas* about the King, would approach (1) the *Tīrtha-Sabhā-Śālā-Samavāya* or the Sectional sub-assembly of the *Paura* in charge of the sacred places and public buildings; (2) the *Pūga-Samavāya* or the sub-assembly in charge of trades and manufactures; and (3) the *Jana-Samavāya* or the Popular Assembly, that is, what the *Mṛichchhakaṭika* calls the *Janapada-Samavāya*. By approaching these assemblies, sectional or permanent councils, the spies ascertained the prevailing feeling of the *Paura* and the *Jānapada*. The spies would broach the subject, for example, in these words:

"We hear that the king is possessed of all the necessary merits. But we do not see those merits, for the man is troubling the *Pauras* and the *Jānapadas* (by demands for) army and taxes."[18]

In the discussion if the members defend and praise the king they were reminded of the Hindu theory of the original contract between the king and the people, the very origin and basis of Kingship:

"Well, (is it not so? that) the Subjects went to Manu, son of Vivasvat, when anarchy prevailed and troubled them. They settled his share in taxes—one-sixth of the crops, (and) one-tenth of merchandise, in cash. That much is the wage of kings for ensuring prosperity."[19]

---

[18] *Artha-Śāstra*, Bk. I, Ch. XIII. 9.—

गूढपुरुषप्रणिधिः कृतमहामात्यापसर्पः पौरजानपदानपसर्पयेत् ।

सत्रिणो द्वन्द्विनस्तीर्थसभाशालापूगजनसमवायेषु विवादं कुर्युः सर्वगुणसम्पन्नश्चायं राजा श्रूयते । न चास्य कश्चित् गुणो दृश्यते यः पौरजानपदान् दण्डकराभ्यां पीडयतीति ।

For the interpretation of दण्डकराभ्यां compare दण्ड in Bk. XIII, Ch. V; 176 (p. 407).

[19] तत्र येऽनुप्रशंसेयुः तानितरस्तं च प्रनितरस्तं च प्रतिषेधयेत् । मात्स्यन्यायाभिभूताः प्रजा मनुं वैवस्वतं राजानं चक्रिरे । धान्यषड्भागं पण्यदशभागं हिरण्यं चास्य भागधेयं प्रकल्पयामासुः । तेन भृता राजानः प्रजानां योगक्षेमवहाः तेषां किल्विषमदण्डकरा हरन्ति । *Ibid.*, p. 23.

For the interpretation of *bhṛila*, *cf.* its meaning in the *Mitāksharā* (Vijñāneśvara).

Appointment of Chief *Mantrin* and *Paura-Jānapada*

The king according to the *Mahābhārata* had to invest only that minister with the jurisdiction of *mantra* or state policy and government (*daṇḍa*), that is, the powers of the Premier (*mantrin*), who has legally earned the confidence of the *Paura-Jānapada*.[20] Resolutions on state policy having been discussed by the cabinet of ministers with the king, had to be submitted to the Rāshṭra, that is, the *Jānapada*, for their opinion (*lit.*, to show दर्शयेत्, through the Rāshṭrīya or the President of the Rāshṭra or *Jānapada*.[21] This was necessary especially because grant of extraordinary taxes, as we shall presently see, was in their hands.

Resolution on State Policy

The tenure of ministers depended, to a considerable extent, on the good-will and confidence of the *Paura-Jānapada*. The minister Chakra-pālita who was the provincial governor of Skanda Gupta in the Western Presidency, records in a public inscription that he gained the confidence of the people and the Nāgaras by his rule in a short time and that he 'coaxed and pleased the *Paura-vargas*' or the association of the *Pauras*.[22] Finally he prays, "May the Capital prosper and be loyal to the *Paura*!"[23]

---

[20] *Mahābhārata* (Kumbakonam ed.), *Śānti-Parvan*, LXXXIII. 45–46 :—

तस्मै मन्त्रः प्रयोक्तव्यो दण्डमाधित्सता नृप ।

पौरजानपदा यस्मिन्विश्वासं धर्मतो गताः ॥

[21] *Ibid.*, LXXXV. 11–12 :—

अष्टानां मन्त्रिणां मध्ये मन्त्रं राजोपधारयेत् ।

ततः संप्रेषयेद्राष्ट्रे राष्ट्रीयाय च दर्शयेत् ॥

[22] विश्रम्भमल्पेन शशास योऽस्मिन्कालेन लोकेषु स नागरेषु ।

योलालयामास च पौरवर्गान्. . ॥

—Junagaḍh Inscription of 457–58 A.C. Fleet, *C.I.I.* (*G.I.*), Vol. III. 60. The reading of Fleet separating न from अल्पे and काले is grammatically impossible.

[23] *Ibid.*, p. 61—नगरमपि च भूयाद्वृद्धिमत्पौरजुष्टम् ।

Paura and Provincial Government

In empires there were presidency capitals. There seems to have been an independent *Paura* body in such a capital. The *Paura* alone in such cases are mentioned. There was no separate *Jānapada* body there and it seems that the latter still sat at the imperial capital representing the whole country. The *Pauras* were prone to take offence at the Ministry's behaviour. The *Pauras* alone of Takshaśilā, the capital of the North (*Uttarāpatha*) in the time of Aśoka, are related to have become 'hostile'. Prince Kunāla was sent by his father, King Aśoka, to pacify them. The *Paura* coming forward told the Prince in their address of welcome: "We are not hostile to Your Highness (the Viceroy) nor are we hostile to King Aśoka, but (we are so to) the rascally Ministers who have come and who are rude to us ('insult us')."[24]

Agitation of the *Paura* of Taxila

We find from Aśoka's inscriptions that the Emperor made an order that the Ministers at Takshaśilā were to go out of office every three years, and new ministers to be sent instead.[25] From other provincial capitals the ministers were changed every five years; but an exception was made in

---

[24] *Divyāvadāna*, pp. 407–08 :—

राज्ञोऽशोकस्योत्तरापथे तक्षशिलानगरं विरुद्धम् । श्रुत्वा च राजा स्वयमेवाभिप्रस्थितः । ततोऽमात्यैरभिहितः । देव कुमारः प्रेष्यतां स संनामयिष्यति । अथ राजा कुनालमाहूय कथयति । वत्स कुनाल गमिष्यसि तक्षशिलानगरं संनामयितुम् । कुनाल उवाच । परं देव गमिष्यामि .. .. .. अनुपूर्वेण तक्षशिलामनुप्राप्तः । श्रुत्वा च तक्षशिलापौरा अर्धत्रिकानि योजनानि मार्गशोभां नगरशोभां च कृत्वा पूर्णकुम्भैः प्रत्युद्गताः । वक्ष्यति च—

श्रुत्वा तक्षशिलापौरा रत्नपूर्णघटादिकान् ।
गृह्य प्रत्युज्जगामाशु बहुमान्या नृपात्मजम् ॥

प्रत्युद्गम्य कृताञ्जलिरुवाच । न वयं कुमारस्य विरुद्धा न राज्ञोऽशोकस्यापि तु दुष्टात्मानोऽमात्या आगत्यास्माकमपमानं कुर्वन्ति । यावत्कुनालो महता सन्मानेन तक्षशिलां प्रवेशितः ।

[25] नगलजनस अकस्मा पलिबोधे व अकस्मा पलिकिलेसे व नो सिया ति एताये च अठाये हकं धंमते पंचसु पंचसु वसेसु निखामयिसामि ए अखखसे अचंड.. सखिनालम्भे होसति एतं अठं जानितु तथा कलंति अथ मम अनुसथीति उजेनिते

the case of the Government at Takshaśilā and that at Ujjayinī. The same records which mention this, namely, the Kalinga Inscriptions called 'Special Edicts' by epigraphists, say that the King insisted on the rule of transfers so that the 'city-body' (*nagara-jana* = *Paura*) might not be suddenly excited and suddenly put to trouble (*Nagala-janasa akasmā palibodhe va akasmā palikilese va no siya ti*). This evidently refers to a sudden excitement of the *Pauras* as in the case of the Takshaśilā agitation described in the *Divyāvadāna*.

Unfortunately we are not in possession of the details of these constitutional 'insults' which entitled the *Pauras* to become hostile and justify their disloyalty. In any case, the *Pauras* were such keen politicians that they would distinguish disloyalty to the Ministers from loyalty to the Crown.

Taxation

The *Paura-Jānapada* are repeatedly mentioned in connexion with taxation. Taxes were fixed by common law. But the king often had the necessity and occasion to apply for an extraordinary taxation. Such taxes assumed the form of '*praṇaya*', 'out-of-affection gifts' or a forced benevolence-tax, and the like.[26] It is evident that proposals for such taxation were first submitted to the *Paura-Jānapada*. According to the *Artha-Śāstra*, the king had "to beg of the *Paura-Jānapada*" these taxes.[27] We have already noticed the discussion of grievance in the *Paura* sub-assemblies and the *Jānapada* sub-assembly about the oppression from the king's taxes. A ruler of a subjugated country, according to Kauṭilya, ran the risk of causing wrath of the *Paura-Jānapada*, and his consequent fall, by raising money and army to be supplied to his suzerain.[28]

पि चु कुमाले एतायेव अठाये निखामयिस..हेदिसं मेव वगं नो च अतिकामयिसति तिंनि वसानि हेमेव तखसिलाते पि अदा अ..ते महामाता निखमिसति.. etc., Dhauli edition, lines 0–25.

I have discussed the significance of the inscription in *J.B.O.R.S.*, Vol. IV. (1918), p. 36.

[26] Jayaswal, *Ind. Ant.*, 1918, p. 50.

[27] *Artha-Śāstra*, Bk. V. Ch. 2 ; 90—

एतेन प्रदेशेन राजा पौरजानपदान् भिक्षेत ।

[28] *Ibid.*, Bk. XIII. Ch. 5 ; 176—

कोशदण्डदानमवस्थाप्य यदुपकुर्व्वाणः पौरजानपदान्कोपयेत् ।
कुपितैस्तैरेनं घातयेत् प्रकृतिभिरुपक्रुष्टमपनयेत् ॥

Disaffection might follow a Regent's threat to realize a war-tax. Secret agents, says the *Artha-Śāstra*, taking service under the Regent, while the enemy king was out with his army in the field, would secretly tell the *Paura-Jānapadas*, as friends, that the Regent had ordered the government to demand taxes the moment the king returned. And when the *Panras* held a general meeting to give their votes on the subject the leaders were to be done away with at night secretly, and the rumour circulated by the agents "this is done because they were opposing the Regent's proposal".[29] This was expected to cause dissension and weakness in the enemy country.

Rudradāman, as he says in his inscription, proposed to his ministers the restoration of the great water-work of the Mauryas, the Sudarśana lake, which proposal was rejected by his Council of Ministers. Thereupon Rudradāman did the repairs from 'his own private purse'. In doing so, he says that he did not trouble the "*Paura-Jānapada jana* (or body)" with a demand of benevolences for the purpose.[30] Just before, he has already said that he realized taxes only so much as was rightfully allowed (by Hindu Law).[31]

---

[29] *Artha-Śāstra*, Bk. XII. Ch. 2 ; 163—

दुर्गेषु चास्य शून्यपालासन्नास्सत्रिणः पौरजानपदेषु मैत्रीनिमित्तमावेदयेयुः । शून्यपालेनोक्ता योधाश्च अधिकरणस्थाश्च कृच्छ्रागतो राजा जीवन्नागमिष्यति, न वा प्रसह्य वित्तमार्जयध्वममित्रांश्च हत इति । बहुलीभूते तीक्ष्णाः पौराञ्चिशास्वाहारयेयुः मुख्यांश्चाभिहन्युः एवं क्रियन्ते ये शून्यपालस्य न शुश्रूषन्ते इति । शून्यपालस्थानेषु च सशोणितानि शस्त्रवित्तबन्धनान्युत्सृजेयुः । ततस्सात्रिणः शून्यपालो घातयति विलोपयति च इत्यावेदयेयुः ।

In the above text वहुलीभूते should be compared with संबहुलं in *Jātaka*, II. 45, and सबहुलेहि in the *Majjhima Nikāya—Gopaka Moggallāna Sutta* where संबहुल denotes holding a meeting to decide a matter by the vote of majority.

[30] *Epigraphia Indica*, Vol. VIII. 44—

अपीडयित्वा करविष्टिप्रणयक्रियाभिः पौरजानपदं जनं स्वस्मात्कोशा (न्) महता धनौघेन अनतिमहता च कालेन....सेतुं....कारितम् । ....अस्मिन्नर्थे महाक्षत्रपस्य मतिसचिवकर्मसचिवैरमात्यगुणसमुद्युक्तैरप्यतिमहत्त्वाद्भेदस्यानुत्साहविमुख-मतिभिः प्रत्याख्यातारंभं, etc.

[31] यथावत्प्राप्तैर्बलिशुल्कभागैः—1. 14.

The Sudarśana lake was a huge irrigation work. The capital being situated on a hill, the people who were most benefited by it were the *Jānapada* people. It would be probably inexplicable why the king should have troubled the *Pauras* unless we accepted that the *Paura-Jānapada* together had to sanction the demand.

Royal Speech to the *Paura-Jānapada*

A sample of an Address from the Throne begging extra taxes from the *Paura-Jānapada* is given in the *Mahābhārata*. I quoted the speech in 1912 but its consitutional character could not be realized before Khāravela's inscription disclosed the corporate *Paura* and *Jānapada*. The passage just before that speech is most important, for it shows the methods to which the Crown resotred, to obtain grants from the *Paura-Jānapada*. The method of securing a majority in the assembly of the *Jānapada* is given, and royal dishonesty in defeating the *Jānapada* is divulged. The very method, at the same time, proves the legal power and authority of the *Paura-Jānapada*.[32]

"To provide for a future distress, kings" (according to our *Mahābhārata* authority) "raise and keep by funds. All the *Paura-Jānapadas* (*i.e.*, all the members) those in session (*saṃśrita*), as well as those taking ease (*upāśrita*), *i.e.*, every one of them should be shown (royal) sympathy, even those who are not rich. Dissension should be created in the Outer (*Bāhya*) body of theirs and then the Middle body to be well (or comfortably) won over (bribed, entertained). The King thus acting, the People will not be excited and disaffected whether they feel (the burden) easy or heavy. Then, before money demand is made, the king going to them and addressing

---

[32] *Mahābhārata*, *Śānti-Parvan*, LXXXVII. 23–25 (Kumbakonam ed.)—

आपदर्थं च निचयान्राजानो हि विचिन्वते ।
राष्ट्रञ्च कोशभूतं स्यात्कोशो वेश्मगतस्तथा ॥
पौरजानपदान्सर्वान्संश्रितोपाश्रितांस्तथा ।
यथाशक्त्यनुकम्पेत सर्वान्स्वल्पधनानपि ॥
बाह्यं जनं भेदयित्वा भोक्तव्यो मध्यमः सुखम् ।
एवं नास्य प्रकुप्यन्ति जनाः सुखितदुःखिताः ॥

by a speech should point out to the Rāshṭra (*Jānapada*) the danger to his country (*e.g.*) as follows :[33]

"Here a danger has arisen. A large enemy army! They forbode our end just as the prospect of coming on fruit to the bamboo.[34] My enemies with the help of *dasyus* (foreign barbarians)[35] want to harm the kingdom—an attempt which, of course, will prove to be their self-destruction. In this serious difficulty and in the nearness of this grim danger, I beg of you money, gentlemen, for your safety. When the crisis is over I will repay, gentlemen, in full. The enemies will not return what they, if they can, carry away by force from here.

---

[33] *Mahābhārata, Śānti-Parvan*, LXXXVII. 26–34 (Kumbakonam ed.)—

प्रागेव तु धनादानमनुभाष्य ततः पुनः ।
सन्निपत्य स्वविषये भयं राष्ट्रे प्रदर्शयेत् ॥

इयमापत्समुत्पन्ना परचक्रभयं महत् ।
अपि चान्ताय कल्पन्ते वेणोरिव फलागमाः ॥

अरयो मे समुत्थाय बहुभिर्दस्युभिः सह ।
इदमात्मवधायैव राष्ट्रमिच्छन्ति बाधितुम् ॥

अस्यामापदि घोरायां संप्राप्ते दारुणे भये ।
परित्राणाय भवतः प्रार्थयिष्ये धनानि वः ॥

प्रतिदास्ये च भवतां सर्वं चाहं भयक्षये ।
नारयः प्रतिदास्यन्ति यद्धरेयुर्बलादितः ॥

कलत्रमादितः कृत्वा सर्वं वो विनशेदिति ।
शरीरपुत्रदारार्थमर्थसञ्चय इष्यते ॥

नन्दामि वः प्रभावेण पुत्राणामिव चोदये ।
यथाशक्त्युपगृह्णामि राष्ट्रस्यापीडया च वः ॥

आपत्स्वेव निवोढव्यं भवद्भिः सङ्गतैरिह ।
न वः प्रियतरं कार्य्यं धनं कस्यांचिदापदि ॥

इति वाचा मधुरया श्लक्ष्णया सोपचारया ।
स्वरश्मीनभ्यवसृजेद्योगमाधाय कालवित् ॥

[34] The prospect is dreaded by the owner of the bamboo clump in our villages as it means the drying up of the whole stock. The bamboo 'fruit' is in appearance like paddy.

[35] *Dasyu* is a technical term both in *Manu* (X. 45) and the *Mahābhārata* (*Śānti-Parvan*, LXV. 13–17) denoting foreign tribes.

From family down to every thing you possess might be destroyed by them. Money is desired only for the sake of person, children and wife. I delight in your prosperity as in the prosperity of my sons. I shall receive what you can spare, without causing pain to the realm and to you. In crisis the honourable assembly (भवद्भिः संगतैः) should bear the burden. You should not value money very much in a crisis."

With such sweet, bland speeches making salutations and showing courtesy (*sopachāro*), kings presented their 'money demands' (*dhanādāna*).

Every *Paura* and every *Jānapada* (that is, every member) was to be humoured by personal attention of the king before the time for the speech and demand arrived.[36] We are already familiar with the Outer body of the *Paura-Jānapadas.* In the *Rāmāyaṇa*, as we have seen, the same term occurs. But what is meant by the Middle body? They here stand for 'the Inner body'. They were to be 'used' and 'given wages' for their dishonourable conduct. They were won over to favour the king's proposal.

It should be noted that the language addressed to the *Paura-Jānapada* is very polite; the pronoun is, *bhavat* 'your honourable self,' *bhavadbhiḥ saṅgataiḥ* 'your honourable Assembly'.[37]

Paura-Jānapada and *Anugrahas* or Privileges

The *Paura-Jānapada* demanded and obtained *anugrahas* or 'privileges'. Khāravela in his inscription says that he granted numerous *anugrahas* in a particular year to the *Paura* and to the *Jānapada*. According to Kauṭilya the *Paura-Jānapada* (leaders) of an enemy country should be advised by secret agents 'to demand *anugrahas* from the king' when there be famine, thefts, and raids by the Aṭavīs (buffers of wild tribes). This is to be read along with

---

[36] *Mahābhārata*, *Śānti-Parvan*, LXV. 26.

[37] That voting prevailed in the *Jānapada* and *Paura* can be gathered from the procedure of contemporory popular institutions which we have already noticed. It is implied here in our text by the directions about creating breach in the Outer body and about winning over the Middle body.

Yājñavalkya, II. 36[38] which enjoins that the king must pay 'to the *Jānapada*' (in the singular) compensation for loss caused by thieves (see also pp. 271–72 below). The *Paura-Jānapada* should couple their demand, according to Kauṭilya with the threat of migration to the enemy's country in case the demand was not allowed.[39]

That the demands for *anugrahas* were mostly of economic character, is shown by the direction of Kauṭilya[40]: that only those *anugrahas* and *parihāras* (fiscal concessions) should be granted which would lead to the strength of the Exchequer and those which weaken it wei to be avoided fcr 'with a small treasury the king oppresses the *Paura-Jānapadas*'. He recommends *parihāra* in famines, and counts the erection of irrigation works as a case where *anugraha* ought to be granted.[41] Aśoka in his Pillar Proclamations says that the Rājūkas or ruling ministers, made independent by him, were to make *anugrahas* to the *Jānapada* body (Ch. XXXI below). Rudradāman calls his restoration of the irrigation lake, Sudarśana, an *anugraha* in favour of the *Paura-Jānapadas*.[42]

---

[38] *Yājñavalkya*, II. 36—

देयं चौर-हृतं द्रव्यं राज्ञा जानपदाय तु ।
अददद्धि समाप्नोति किल्बिषं यस्य तस्य तत् ॥

This verse of Yājñavalkya corresponds to *Manu*, VIII. 40. See Medhātithi's explanation.

Cf. प्रत्याहर्तुमशक्तस्तु धनं चौरैर्हृतं यदि ।
स्वकोशात्तद्धि देयं स्यादशक्तेन महीभृता ॥

—Dvaipāyana in the *Mitāksharā*.

[39] *Artha-Śāstra*, Bk. XIII. Ch. 1; 171 (p. 394)—

दुर्भिक्षस्तेनाटव्युपघातेषु च पौरजानपदानुत्साहयन्तः सत्रिणो ब्रूयुः राजानमनुग्रहं याचामहे निरनुग्रहाः परत्र गच्छाम इति ।

[40] *Ibid.*, Bk. II. Ch. 1. 19 (p. 47)—

अनुग्रहपरिहारौ चैभ्यः कोशवृद्धिकरौ दद्यात् । कोशोपघातिकौ वर्जयेत् । अल्पकोशो हि राजा पौरजानपदानेव ग्रसते ।

[41] *Ibid.*—

निवेशसमकालं यथागतकं वा परिहारं दद्यात् । निवृत्तपरिहारान् पितेवानुगृह्णीयात् । आकर कर्मान्तद्रव्यहस्तिवनव्रजवणिक्पथप्रचारान्वारिस्थलपथपण्यपत्तनानि च निवेशयेत् । सहोदक माहार्योदकं वा सेतुं बन्धयेत् । अन्येषां वा बध्नतां भूमिमार्गवृक्षोपकरणानुग्रहं कुर्यात् ।

[42] *Epigraphia Indica*, VIII. 45—

पुनःसेतुबन्धनैराश्याद् हाहाभूतासु प्रजासु इहाधिष्ठाने पौरजानपदजनानुग्रहार्थं पार्थिवेन etc.

King asks permission of *Naigama-Jānapada* to undertake long sacrifice

The Buddhist books similarly testify to the constitutional practice of the king's approaching the *Jānapada* and the *Naigama* or *Paura* for a 'fresh tax'[43] when he intended to undertake a big sacrifice. The royal speech on that occasion is characteristically polite. The form of demand was this :

"I intend to offer a great sacrifice. Let the gentlemen ('Venerable ones,' Rhys Davids) give their sanction to what will be to me for weal and welfare."[44]

If the *Paura-Jānapada* bodies gave their *anumati* ('sanction') the king was to perform the sacrifice and the country had to pay a tax for that.

Thus the *Paura-Jānapada* were approached and begged by the king to grant extraordinary taxes; and the *Paura-Jānapada* demanded and obtained *anugrahas* or economic privileges from the king. It is not certain but it is very likely that in raising his large armies the king utilised the machinery of the *Paura-Jānapada*. Two references in the *Artha-Śāstra*, noticed above, where taxes are coupled with the *daṇḍa* (army) or rasing of army, suggest this possibility.

Daily business of *Paura-Jānapada* with the King

That the *Paura-Jānapada* had not business of merely occasional or adventitious nature, is proved by the fact that the *Artha-Śāstra* marks out one period in the king's daily time-table to be devoted to the business of the *Paura-Jānapadas*.[45] Daily, therefore, matters went up from them to the king. These must have been of an economic

---

[43] Rhys Davids, *Dīgha Nikāya*, *Kūṭadanta Sutta*, 11 ; *Dialogues of the Buddha*, II. 175.

[44] *Dīgha Nikāya*, *Kūṭadanta Sutta*, 12—

इच्छामहं भो महायञ्ञं यजितुं अनुजानन्तु मे भवन्तो यं मम अस्स दीघरत्तं हिताय सुखायाति ।

[45] *Artha-Śāstra*, Bk. VIII. Ch. 19 ; 16 (p. 37)—

द्वितीयें पौरजानपदानां कार्याणि पश्येत् ।

Cf. Mahābhārata, *Śānti-Parvan*, XL. 19.—

पौरजानपदानां च यानि कार्याणि नित्यशः ।
राजानं समनुज्ञाप्य तानि कार्याणि धर्मतः ॥

and financial nature, and if they had to raise levies for the imperial army, as it seems very probable, the business must have included military matters as well. The daily business before the king suggests a busy time for at least the Inner body of the permanent *Samavāya* of the *Paura-Jānapada*.

Aśoka's new *Dharma* and *Jānapada*

The above matters were not the only concern of the *Paura-Jānapadas*. We find Aśoka, after his piligrimage to Bodh Gaya, discussing his new *Dharma* with the *Jānapada* body.[46] Aśoka proposed to impose a new system on the community and to do away with the old orthodox one. He had to feel his way in proceeding with his intended revolution. He sought countenance from the *Paura-Jānapada* and proclaimed to the public that he had been having the honour of meeting the *Jānapada* (*darśana*) and discussing the *Dharma* with them. They were thus a machinery not only for the restricted purposes of taxation and economic advancement but for all vital interests of the country.

Importance of the *Paura*: *Paura* and Executive work

We find the *Paura* receiving communication from the sovereign to execute measures of moment which properly belonged to the jurisdiction of the executive government or *Daṇḍa*. Tishyarakshitā, queen of Aśoka, sent the letter which she forged under the name of the Emperor and sealed it with his ivory seal, to the *Paura* of Takshaśilā. The story as related in the *Divyāvadāna* may or may not be correct. But the story would not have been detailed in this way if the procedure of sending a royal communication of the nature the missive is said to have embodied, had been unknown at the time the *Divyāvadāna* was compiled. The *Paura* was asked to inflict punishment on the viceregal prince who had been denounced in the letter as

---

[46] Rock Series VIII (Girnar)—

बाह्मणसमणानं दसणे च दाने च थैरानं दसणे च हिरंणपटिविधानो च जानपदस च जनस दसनं धंमानुसस्टी च धंमपरिपुच्छा च..

See below on the mention of the *Jānapada* in Pillar Series IV (Hindu Ministry).

a traitor to the dynasty.[47] The *Pauras* in the *Mṛichhakaṭika* are asked by the people to execute the real culprit Saṃsthānaka who had been treated as innocent by the law-court. The *Pauras*, here probably stands for *Paura-Jānapada* as they are mentioned after the *Janapada-Samavāya*.

The prince-viceroy was supposed to go to their assembly.

King and Governor attend *Paura-Jānapada*

The passage in the *Mahābhārata* implies that the king himself attended the *Paura-Jānapada* assembly. Aśoka received them with great respect.[48]

Paura-Jānapada could make or mar government

The political philosopher Vāmadeva quoted in the *Mahābhārata* sums up the importance of the *Paura* and *Jānapada* by saying that the *Paura-Jānapada* could make or mar the government. If they were satisfied, "the business of the realm would be done by them, if they were not satisfied, they would make government impossible, for they became opposers. The king had therefore to keep them attached by his conduct and by not causing annoyance to them."[49]

As the *Paura* administered relief to the poor and helpless in the capital,[50] the *Jānapada* did the same in their jurisdiction.

---

47 राजा ह्यशोको बलवान् प्रचण्ड आज्ञापयत् तक्षशिलाजनं हि ।
उद्धार्यतां लोचनमस्य शत्रोर्मौर्य्यस्य वंशस्य कलङ्क एषः ॥

—*Divyāvadāna*, p. 410.

The use of the word *jana* should be noticed here and should be compared with जानपद-जन in Aśoka's Inscription (Rock, VIII) and पौरजानपदो जनः in the *Rāmāyaṇa*. The sense is of a collective body.

48 पश्यामि कुनालं··पौरं प्रविष्टः । —*Divyāvadāna*, p. 410.

49 *Mahābhārata* (Kumbakonam ed.), *Śānti-Parvan*, XCIV. 16—

पौरजानपदा यस्य स्वनुरक्ता अपीडिताः ।
राष्ट्रकर्मकरा ह्येते राष्ट्रस्य च विरोधिनः ॥

(The context and grammar show that verse 16 which ought to precede immediately verse 18 has been detached and put in its present position. Verse 17 really reads with verse 15.)

50 तथानाथदरिद्राणां संस्कारो यजनक्रिया ।

—Bṛihaspati, *Vīramitrodaya*, p. 425.

It appears from the view of Vāmadeva that when the *Jānapada* and the *Paura* withdrew from the duty of poor relief the government of the king was in trouble. They could make the government impossible in so many ways: this may be inferred from their various functions which we have noticed. To them, the trouble caused by the non-performance of poor relief, is evidently to be added as a factor of importance. If the *Paura-Jānapadas*, says Vāmadeva, remain kind to beings, having money and grain (for the purpose), the throne will remain firmly rooted.[51]

Compensation bills of *Jānapada* to the Crown

Another method by which the *Paura-Jānapada* made the government of a misbehaving king difficult was that the offended *Paura* and *Jānapada* would make out a bill and present it to the king to make good all the losses sustained in the kingdom by thefts, dacoities, and the like lawlessness. This strange[52] procedure is sanctioned even by the Codes of Hindu Law. We can understand it only if we bear in mind the Hindu theory of taxation. Taxes were paid to the king as his wages, and the wages were wages for protection (see Ch. XXXIII below). The corollary was that if protection which meant both internal and external was not rendered fully, deductions from the wages of the employee would be made by the employer. The refund bills were presented, according to Yājñavalkya, by the *Jānapada*, as it is to them, he enjoins on the king to pay the crown compensation.[53] The passage in the *Artha-Śāstra* which says that the spies were to prompt

---

51 पौरजानपदा यस्य भूतेषु च दयालवः ।
सधना धान्यवन्तश्च दृढमूलः स पार्थिवः ॥

—*Mahābhārata* (Kumbakonam ed.), *Śānti-Parvan*, XCIV. 18.

On the question of the wealth in the hands of the *Paura* and *Jānapada* bodies it should be noticed that corporate bodies not only held money and property but could even legally borrow money as is evidenced by the laws of Bṛihaspati and Kātyāyana (*Vīramitrodaya*, p. 432).

52 Mr. Govinda Das writes, " Even up to very recent times, I understand that in the Rajput States thefts had to be made good by the king's treasury."

53 देयं चौरहृतं द्रव्यं राज्ञा जानपदाय तु ।
अददद्धि समाप्नोति किल्बिषं यस्य तस्य तत् ॥

—*Yājñavalkya*, II. 36. Compare other passages quoted below.

the *Pauras* and *Jānapadas* to ask for concessions if the frontier barbarians committed raids, also indicates the practice of demanding compensations.[54]

Kṛishṇa Dvaipāyana lays down "when the king has failed to recover the property taken away by thieves it should be made good from his own purse (*Svakośāt*) by the impotent holder-of-the-country."[55] *Śvakośa* in the inscription of Rudradāman was the private purse as opposed to the public treasury. This being the sense of Dvaipāyana, the compensation realized (according to the corresponding law of Yājñavalkya) by the *Jānapada* amounted to a personal fine on the king.[56]

Constituency of the *Jānapada*

From the evidence of the *Mahābhārata*, we gather that the members of the *Jānapada* as well as of the *Paura*, were generally rich people. And those who were not rich, were not poor either.

The reference in the *Daśakumāracharita*[57] which represents the king making an illegal request to the president of the *Jānapada* for the oppression of a particular *Grāmaṇī* or the head of the village assembly, associates a *Jānapada* member with the village unit. The *Jānapada*, according to the *Artha-Śāstra*, was composed of villages and towns.[58] It is permissible to assume that the *Jānapada* had similarly its constituents in village corporations and townships of the country.

The *Grāmaṇī* was generally a rich man, a Vaiśya according to a Vedic reference[59] and a Kshatriya according to the Pāli Canon.[60] The members returned to the *Jānapada* were very likely men from the *Grāmaṇī* class.

---

[54] *Artha-Śāstra*, Bk. XIII, Ch. 2; 171 (p. 391).

[55] प्रत्याहर्तुमशक्तस्तु धनं चौरैर्हृतं यदि ।
स्वकोशात्तद्धि देयं स्यादशक्तेन महीभृता ॥
Quoted in the *Mitāksharā* on *Y.*, II. 36.

[56] *Manu*, VIII. 40—दातव्यं सर्ववर्णेभ्यो राज्ञा चौरैर्हृतं धनम् । According to Nandana it means that the king should make good to all the *varṇas* the loss sustained from thieves, etc. The great commentator Medhātithi as well gives the same meaning.

[57] *Daśakumāracharita*, Chapter III.

[58] *Artha-Śāstra*, Bk. II. Ch. 1; 19.

[59] *Maitrāyaṇī Saṁhitā*, I. 6. 5: IV. 3. 8.

[60] See above p. 79, *n*. 2.

The Pāli Sūtra (*Kūṭadanta* of the *Dīgha Nikāya*)[61] which is regarded as almost contemporary in age with the Buddha's time, probably furnishes details of the composition of the *Naigama* or *Paura* and the *Jānapada*. The king invites the Kshatriyas who were '*Negama*' or '*Jānapada*' for the time-being (*anuyuttā negama cheva jānapadā cha*) in the king's country (*Rañño janapade*); likewise those *Negamas* and *Jānapadas* who were officers and councillors (of the *Paura* and *Jānapadas*); *Negama* and *Jānapada* Brahmins who possessed 'larger class of houses'; and finally, *gahapati Negamas* and *Jānapadas* who were of the class of *nechayikas*. The *gahapati* class was composed of ordinary citizens—Vaiśyas and Śūdras, freemen cultivating their land or following their trade, 'the lords of their households'. *Nechayika* probably denoted the richer class of the *Grihapati* members as opposed to the *Mahābhārata's svalpadhanas*, the 'small-wealth' members of the *Paura* and *Jānapada*. This shows that the *Paura* and the *Jānapada* had almost all the classes of the population. The poor but highly intellectual class of Brahmins probably was not there as the qualification required was based on property of some value. The class of Brahmins whom I have described elsewhere as the aristocracy-in-poverty, *i.e.*, those who lived up to the ideal laid down in the *Upanishads* and the *Dharma Sutras*, would not be included in bodies where property qualification was the law. If we keep this point in view we can understand why Brahmins as a class are mentioned in the *Rāmāyaṇa* separately, as joining the conference of the *Paura-Jānapada* to discuss the question of the nomination of Yuvarāja by them.[62] The character of the *Jānapada*, as representing the whole country, is quite clear. They are called the

---

61 *Dīgha Nikāya, Kūṭadanta Sutta*, 12 *et seq.*,

ये भोतो रञ्ञो जनपदे खत्तिया अनुयुत्ता नेगमाचेव जानपदा च....ये भोतो (etc.) अमच्चा पारिसज्जा नेगमा चेव जानपदा च....ये भोतो (etc.) ब्राह्मणमहासाला नेगमा चेव जानपदा च....ये भोतो (etc.) गहपतिनेचयिका नेगमा चेव जानपदा च....

62 ब्राह्मणा जनमुख्याश्च पौरजानपदैः सह ।
समेत्य ते मन्त्रयितुं समतागतबुद्धयः ॥

—*Rāmāyaṇa* (Kumbakonam ed.), *Ayodhyā-Kāṇḍa*, Ch. II. 19–20.

Rāshṭra or the kingdom itself and the *Deśa* or the country itself. The *Pauras* were a fairly large body and presumably the *Jānapadas* were larger in number.

The composition of the *Paura*

We have a clear picture of the *Paura* composition. The description left by Megasthenes,[63] of the City Magistrates or the Executive Bodies of the *Paura* of Pāṭaliputra read in the light of the working system of corporate assemblies of the country, shows that the *Paura* was divided into several sub-assemblies representing different interests of the Capital. The *Paura* was a sort of mother association of different bodies. Patañjali, who uses the word *Saṃgha* in the general sense of a corporate assembly, not limited, as by Pāṇini and also probably by Kātyāyana, to the political *Saṃgha*, mentions as we have seen, *Saṃghas* of 5, of 10, and of 20 men.[64] It may be remembred that Kauṭilya also employs the word *Saṃgha* in the general sense[65] like Patañjali, although the technical sense of Pāṇini is not unknown to either. The significance becomes clear when we refer to the *Mahāvagga* (IX. 4. 1) which lays down that a *Saṃgha* may have a quorum of 5, 10, 20 or upwards. The *Pañchika Saṃgha*, therefore, of Patañjali is the quorum of 5. The boards of 5 members each of Megasthenes were these *Pañchika Saṃghas*.[66] If the boards of 5 each were the *Saṃghas* of 5, then they would represent independent bodies, and their joint meeting would be a meeting of the mother association. This interpretation is supported by the fact that the *Paura* is regarded to have more than one *Mukhya* or *Śreshṭha*, chief or president,[67] and Megasthenes mentions more than one 'City Magistrate'.[68] In the

---

[63] See p. 250 above.

[64] See foot-notes, p. 251 above.

[65] *Artha-Śāstra*, Bk. III. Ch. 14; 66 (p. 185): तेन सङ्घभृता व्याख्याताः। Bk. II. Ch. I; 19 (p. 48): सजातादन्यः सङ्घः। Bk. III Ch. 3; 62 (p. 173): देशजातिकुलसङ्घानाम्।

[66] *Cf.* the *Pañchālika* committees of the Nepal Inscriptions (*I.A.*, IX).

[67] *Rāmāyaṇa*, *Ayodhyā-Kāṇḍa*, Ch. XV. V. 2, मुख्या ये निगमस्य च; Ch. XIV. V. 40, पौरजानपदश्रेष्ठा।

[68] See p. 250 above.

Mudrārākshasa[69] when Chandanadāsa is called by the Chancellor Chāṇakya (Kauṭilya), he is shown great respect and asked whether the people were loyal to the new king. Chandanadāsa thereupon speaks for the whole country ; but he is only the president of the Jewellers' Association (*Maṇikāra-Śreshṭhi*). In the *Daśakumāracharita*, out of the two *Paura-Mukhyas* one is the president of merchants dealing with foreign trade only.[70] In the *Artha-Śāstra* where spies are sent to the *Paura-Jānapadas* to sound their political mind, they go to the "associations" (*samavāyas*) (in the plural) of the *Tīrthas*, of the *Sabhā-Śālas*, of the *Pūga* and of the People.[71] These *Samavāyas* except the last one are evidently identical with the Boards of Megasthenes (as pointed out above) which looked after public buildings and temples, after manufactured articles, after trade and commerce. We have noticed the datum of Gautama which proves that there were Śūdra members also.[72] They were probably returned by the *Jāti-Saṃghas* or the caste assemblies or they might be representing some guild of artisans. The *Pūga* committee must have been mainly composed of the representatives of trade and commerce, apparently middle-class substantial men. The *Paura* was thus composed on the basis of different interests in the Capital.

The *Rāmāyaṇa* gives some details of separate bodies which made up the *Naigama*, probably about 500 B.C. As the *Paura-Jānapada* (with the *Naigama*) appear, taking leading part in the nomination of Rāma as Yuvarāja, so the *Paura*, *Naigama*, or *Jānapada* or probably all of them figure on subsequent occasions when the question of succession to the throne presents itself. In VI. (*Yuddha*) 127. 4, when Rāma is returning to Ayodhyā, the *Śreṇi-mukhyas* ('Leaders of *Śerṇis*') and the '*Gaṇas*' or 'Members of the Parliament' (probably the *Jānapada*) go out to receive him. In verse 16 they are around Bharata along with the Ministers and are mentioned as the *Śreṇi-mukhyas* and the *Naigamas*. The *Naigamas* consecrate

---

69 Act I. For the date of the *Mudrārākshasa* (*c.* 420 A.D.) see Jayaswal, *Indian Antiquary*, 1913, p. 265 ; 1917, p. 275.

70 *Daśakumāracharita*, Ch. III.

71 *Artha-Śāstra*, Bk. I. Ch. 13 ; 9 (p. 22)

72 See *n.* 47, p. 248 above.

Rāma as representatives of Vaiśya and Śūdra elements of the population (C. 128. 62). When Bharata is called from his maternal home on the death of Daśaratha, the *Sreṇis* sanction Bharata's proposed succession which is intimated to him (*Ayodhyā*, C. 79. 4). The "Rāma-Commentary" here explains "*Sreṇayaḥ*" as "*Paurāḥ*" and Govindarāja as "*Naigamāḥ*". Probably '*Śreṇayaḥ*' (*Śreṇis*) has been used in the primary sense, like the *gaṇas* of VI. 127, denoting 'the assemblies', *i.e.*, both the *Paura* and *Jānapada*. Again when Bharata goes to bring back Rāma from exile or hermitage, the "favourites of the *gaṇa*" go with him along with the same associates, the ministers, etc. (81. 12). These favourites or elected rulers of the *gaṇas* (83. 10) are referred to, a little further in connexion with the people of the city,[73] as the *Naigamas* and 'those who confer or together' (*saṃ-matā ye*) in the company of 'all the minsiters'. Immediately following (verse 12 *et. seq.*) are detailed the different bodies or classes of trades and arts who evidently made up the *Naigama*, *viz.*, jewellers, ivory-workers, stucco-workers, goldsmiths, wood-carvers, spice merchants and so forth.[74] They are rounded up with (verse 15) 'Presidents of townships and villages' (*grāma-ghosha-mahattarāḥ*), which the 'Rāma-Commentary'[75] explains as "the Presidents for the time being". As the *Naigama* is detailed by its various trades and arts, the *Jānapada* ('those who think together') is detailed by its component elements—the village and township Presidents. Both these main bodies issue forth from the Capital. The representative assembly of the villages and townships of the realm, as observed above, had their headquarters at the Capital. But the *Naigama* which was similarly at the Capital was the general representative body of different trade-guilds and guilds-merchant of the Capital only, as the commentators imply and the equivalent *Paura* proves.

This conclusion derived from literature is confirmed by certain seals discovered at Basārh, the ruined site of Vaiśāli.

---

[73] *Nāgarikas*, evidently *Pauras*.

[74] Consult Govindarāja on the technical names of trades.

[75] ग्रामे घोषे च वर्त्तमाना महत्तराः । Govindarāja explains *mahattarāḥ* as *pradhāna-bhūtāḥ*, 'made presidents'.

These seals remain learned puzzles in the pages of the reports of the excavation. They become intelligible in the light of the evidence adduced above. One seal bears the legend *Śreshṭhi Nigamasya*, while another reads *Śreshṭhi-Sārthavāha-Kulika-nigama*; again another, *Kulika-Hariḥ* or *Prathama-Kulika-Hariḥ*.[76] The seals ending with *nigama* are the seals of the mother association of *Nigama* or *Paura*. *Kulika* was a judge of the *Paura* as we have already seen[77]; *Prathama-Kulika* would be thus the first judge of the *Paura* Court. '*Śreshṭhin*' 'president' was evidently the General-President. The seal of the '*Śreshṭhi-Śārthavāha-Kulika-nigama*' legend represented the different sections or *Samavāyas* of the *Nigama* through their three chiefs. The separate seals related to the separate entities, the corporations sole, *e.g.*, the judicial seal of the *Kulika* judge.

The 'laws' of *Jānapada* and *Paura*

The laws of *Paura*, alluded to in connexion with the general term *Grāma* or Township, and the laws of *Jānapada*, as we have seen in the last chapter, are recognised in the Codes of Hindu Law. They were really the resolutions of these bodies. They had the force of law. The law courts enforced them against offending members. The resolutions regulated primarily the conduct of the corporate bodies and their business *inter se*. They were called *Samaya*, 'law or resolution agreed upon in an assembly' (*sam* + *ay*). These *Samayas* are called in Manu and Yājñavalkya[78] '*Dharmas*'

---

[76] *A.S.R.*, 1913–14, pp. 139, 140 and 153, seals Nos. 282 B, 320 A, 318 A, and 277 A. For discussion on the seals, see p. 124 *et seq.*

[77] See above, pp. 49–50 and 105.

[78] *Manu*, Ch. VIII. 219–22 :—

अत ऊर्ध्वं प्रवक्ष्यामि धर्मं समयभेदिनाम् ॥
यो ग्रामदेशसङ्घानां कृत्वा सत्येन संविदम् ।
विसंवदेन्नरो लोभात्तं राष्ट्राद्विप्रवासयेत् ॥
निगृह्य दापयेच्चैनं समयव्यभिचारिणम् ।
. . . .
ग्रामजातिसमूहेषु समयव्यभिचारिणाम् ॥

Yājñavalkya *Saṃvid-Vyatikrama prakaraṇa*, Bk. II, ver. 186 :—

निजधर्माविरोधेन यस्तु सामयिको भवेत् ।
सोऽपि यत्नेन संरक्ष्यो धर्मो राजकृतश्च यः ॥

For definition of *Samaya* in other Codes see p. 106 above.

or Laws. We may recall here that according to Āpastamba, the oldest writer on *Dharma* yet discovered, all laws originated in *Samayas.*[79]

Another class of their resolutions was called *Sthiti* ('fixed laws') or *Deśasthiti*[80] (the *sthiti* of the 'country' or 'country-assembly') which were enforceable against everybody. The *Sthiti* was probably the same as the class of their enactments called *Saṃvid*, 'agreement' or 'laws by agreement'. The *Saṃvids*[81] were passed by the *Jānapada* and they were recorded on a roll (*Saṃvitpatra*). They were enacted with the formality of the members taking some special oath. They were binding on the whole kingdom. There is clear evidence of the fact that sometimes *Saṃvids* were against the interest of the king, as some authors of the Codes lay down the exception that those *Saṃvids* only shall be enforced by the Law Courts which are not opposed to the king.[82] The *Samayas* also were put on a roll.[83]

These *Samaya* (*Samayakriya*) and *Saṃvid* enactments were what we call at present 'Statutes'. They were not *leges* which were embodied in the Hindu Common Law. They were administrative statutes of fiscal and political nature.

It is significant that the *Saṃvid* class of acts are mentioned in connection only with the Realm Assembly or the *Jānapada*

---

79 *Apasthamba*, I. 1. 1, अथातः सामयाचारिकान्धर्मान्व्याख्यास्यामः ॥ १ ॥
धर्मज्ञसमयः प्रमाणम् ॥ २ ॥
वेदाश्च ॥ ३ ॥

80 *Vīramitrodaya*, p. 120—
देशस्थित्यानुमानेन नैगमानुमतेन वा ।
क्रियते निर्णयस्तत्र व्यवहारस्तु बाध्यते ॥
—Bṛihaspati.

81 ग्रामो देशश्च यत्कुर्य्यात्सत्यलेख्यं परस्परम् ।
राजाऽविरोधिधर्मार्थं संवित्पत्रं वदन्ति तत् ॥
—Bṛihaspati in *Vīramitrodaya*, p. 169. धर्मार्थं—legal and political rules'.

82 See the above note. Also निजधर्माविरोधेन यस्तु सामयिको भवेत् of Yājñavalkya.

83 यंचैतल्लिखितं पत्रे धर्म्या सा समयक्रिया । —*Vīramitrodaya*, p. 425.

and the Township Assembly. Guilds and conquered *Gaṇas* (republics) and similar bodies could not enact *Saṃvids*. The *Saṃvid* acts were thus the most important of the *Paura-Jānapada* enactments. Probably through them it was also made known to the country to give a particular extra tax, or to desist from doing a thing.

Paura-Jānapada as Hindu Diet

To sum up. We had an organism or a twin organism, the *Paura-Jānapada*, which could depose the king, who nominated the successor to the throne, whose kindly feelings towards a member of the royal family indicated his chance of succession, whose president was apprized by the king of the policy of state decided upon in the council of ministers, who were approached and begged by the king in all humility for a new tax, whose confidence in a minister was regarded an essential qualification for his appointment as chancellor, who were consulted and referred to with profound respect by a king aspiring to introduce a new religion, who demanded and got industrial, commercial and financial privileges for the country, whose wrath meant ruin to provincial governors, who were coaxed and flattered in public proclamations, who could enact statutes even hostile to the king, in fine, who could make possible or impossible the administration of the king—an organism with these constitutional attributes was an institution which we will be justified in calling the Hindu Diet.

The *Paura-Jānapada* were a powerful check on royal authority. At the same time there were also other influences which kept royal responsibility alive and active.

CHAPTER XXIX

Opinion of Thinkers and General Public Opinion

To the constitutional check exercised by the *Paura-Jānapada* we must add the great influence of thinkers and wise men.

Hermits and Recluses

The hermits and recluse thinkers living outside society, in the 'forest',[1] were a political factor in Hindu life. The hermitage was representative of the whole Aryan Society. At the same time it was a repository of past experience in social and political matters and a seat of clear and impartial thinking. The retirements for the people in the third stage were marked out in close neighbourhood of the capital and other towns.[1] Hindu hermits, though in retirement, were not absolutely out of touch with the community and the world of politics. They with their widsom and impartiality could take a correct view of a difficulty in administration and could advise the king thereon, without reserve or fear.

Then there was the floating wisdom of the yet older generation which could speak to the erring with an authority which no temporal power could command. They spoke in the name of morality and they were heard. It was their privilege to communicate their opinion even unasked for. Literature is full of references shewing the influence which the ascetic widsom in Hindu race exercised on current politics. Nārada who must have been as we now know from Pāli documents of early times, a member of the order of the Bhikshus

---

[1] *Artha-Śāstra*, Bk. II. Ch. 2 (p. 49)—

प्रदिष्टाभयस्थावरजङ्गमानि च ब्राह्मणेभ्यो ब्रह्मसोमारण्यानि तपोवनानि च, तपस्विभ्यो गोत्रपराणि प्रयच्छेत् ।

The *Tapovanas* were named after the seven original *gōtras*. The Buddha went to one of such *āśramas* after leaving his home. The *āśramas* named after *gōtra-ṛishis* in the *Rāmāyaṇa* were also such institutions, not that the original *gōtra-ṛishis* were supposed to be still living.

called 'Nāradas', advised Kṛishṇa on his republican difficulties. Coming to later historical times, the Buddha was approached by Ajātaśatru for advice before marching against the Lichchhavis. Viḍūrabha of Kośala once desisted from declaring hostilities against the Śākyas owing to the Buddha's opinion. Alexander found the 'gymnosophists'[2] formidable politicians, and with his usual ferocity towards free ideas could not comfortably bear their existence and had several of them executed. One of them when asked why he urged the leader of a particular state to oppose Alexander, replied because he 'wished him to live with honour or die with honour' (Plutarch, LXIV). Another Sanyāsin is related by Greek writers to

---

[2] *Cf.* McCrindle, *Megasthenes*, pp. 124–26 :—

"God, the supreme king, is never the author of insolent wrong, but is the creator of light, of peace, of life, of water, of the body of man, and of souls and these he receives when death sets them free being in no way subject to evil desire. He alone is the god of my homage, who abhors slaughter and instigates no wars. But Alexander is not god, since he must taste of death, and how can such as he be the world's master, who has not yet reached the further shore of the river Tiberoboas, and has not yet seated himself on a throne of universal dominion?....If his present dominions are not capacious enough for his desire, let him cross the Ganges river, and he will find a region able to sustain men if the country on our side be too narrow to hold him. Know this, however, that what Alexander offers me, and the gift he promises, are all things to me utterly useless....The earth supplies me with everything, even as a mother her child with milk.....Should Alexander cut off my head, he cannot also destroy my soul. My head alone, now silent, will remain, but the soul will go away to its master, leaving the body like a torn garment upon the earth whence also it was taken. I then, becoming spirit, shall ascend to my god....he is judge of all proud wrongdoing; for the groans of the oppressed become the punishments of the oppressors. Let Alexander, then, terrify with these threats those who wish for gold and for wealth and who dread death, for against us these weapons are both alike powerless, since the Bragmanes (=Brāhmaṇas) neither love gold nor fear death."

No wonder that the Greeks should say that 'Dandamis..though old and naked, was the only antagonist in whom he, the conqueror of many nations, had found more than his match'.

The reader need hardly be reminded that the ascetic was quoting the Upanishads. His description of the Brahmin who neither wished for gold nor dreaded death is relevant on what we say below (pp. 282–83).

have given Alexander a lesson in politics by comparing Alexander's empire to a piece of dry hide without a centre of gravity, one edge rising up rebelliously while Alexander stood on the other. The old Daṇḍin (*Dandamis*) of Taxila, when called upon by Onesikratēs to present himself before Alexander, son of Zeus, master of the world, under the threat 'but if you refuse (he) will cut off your head,' 'complacently smiled' and replied that he was as much son of Zeus as Alexander, that he was quite content with India which supported him like a mother; and sarcastically indicated that the people on the Ganges (the army of Nanda) would convince Alexander that he was not yet the master of the world.[3] In the *Artha-Śāstra* the king is told that bad government offends ascetics and recluses.[4] The *Mahābhārata* in its book on politics enjoins upon the king to inform hermits of the affairs of state and to take counsel from one whose experience was large and whose original family was distinguished and who was now selfless.[5]

The learned Brahmin

The tradition came down through the whole course of Hindu history. It was so strong that in the period of Hindu revival it played once more a great rôle. Guru Rāmadāsa was as great a guide to Śivājī as any Nārada to an ancient predecessor of the latter.

With the class of men in hermitage and post-hermitage stages of life, we should count the *Vṛittastha* Brahmin. Nobody can pretend to understand Hindu history without realizing the true social value of the teaching, studying, thinking and sacrificing Brahmin. With a culture of intellect ever developing, from generation to generation, he had grown

---

[3] See the last *n*.

[4] *Artha-Śāstra*, Bk. I. Ch. 4; 1 (p. 9)—
दुष्प्रणीतः (दण्डः) कामक्रोधाभ्यामज्ञानाद्वानप्रस्थपरिव्राजकानपि कोपयति ।

[5] *Mahābhārata* (Kumbakonam ed.), *Śānti-Parvan*, Ch. LXXXVI. vs. 26–28—

आत्मानं सर्वकार्याणि तापसे राष्ट्रमेव च ।
निवेदयेत्प्रयत्नेन तिष्ठेत्प्रह्वश्च सर्वदा ॥
.. .. ..
सर्वार्थत्यागिनं राजा कुले जातं बहुश्रुतम् ।
पूजयेत् तादृशं दृष्ट्वा...............

into a leviathan of brain, who would have eaten up Hindu Society and burst up himself, but for the self-denying ordinance of poverty. He would engage not in what would bring him wealth. The little wealth he required for his sustenance, he would beg of the society he had undertaken to serve. He thus became the true aristocrat of Hindu Society, with the differentia peculiar to him in the whole world; that he was the aristocrat-cum-poverty. By the vow of poverty he secured for him an imperishable intellectual existence rooted in independence of spirit and consciousness of virtuous superiority. The race in which he grew stood loyally by him, nourishing and maintaining that leviathan of brain and virtue.

The Brahmin of poverty living inside society and state, with his little home and his fire-altars, was probably more mindful of current politics than any one else. In the *Jātakas*, the Brahmin versed equally in *Dharma* and *Artha*, Sacred Knowledge and Science of Politics, is a constant figure. Vasishṭha and Vāmadeva in the national epics typify the figures who would turn up at the court and advise the king and point out weaknesses in his administration. It is they that lead the *Paura-Jānapada* deputation in the *Rāmāyaṇa* to the king to announce the national decision about the appointment of Yuvarāja. And the king addresses them and the *Paura-Jānapadas* as 'Rulers' ('Kings'). The Bṛihaspati and Kauṭilya class was not merely concerned with systematizing theories of state; they made the politics of their country an object of their immediate concern. Kauṭilya was a *Śrotriya* or Vedic Brahmin.[6] At the same time Alexander's incoming and the stupid administration of the upstart (Nava) Nanda concerned him more than his Vedic studies. He thought it necessary to overhaul the existing system. The Brahmin emphasised again and again that state was a life on which depended social, individual and spiritual happiness. He

---

6 चाणक्य इति विख्यातः श्रोत्रियः सर्वधर्मवित् ।

Telang's *Mudrārākshasa*, *Upodghāta*, p. 44.

येन शास्त्रं च शस्त्रं च नन्दराजगता च भूः ।

अमर्षणोद्धृतान्याशु तेन शास्त्रमिदं कृतम् ॥

—*Artha-Śāstra* (p. 429).

reminded the people again and again that the bases of civilization of the Race are rooted in polity, that the Sword which protects the people is the womb of civilization.[7] The Brahmin idealised and idolised the country of the Aryas as much politically as religiously.[8]

Public Opinion

The opinion of organised bodies and of ascetics and hermits and *Vṛittastha* Brahmins apart, the administration had to take into consideration the opinion of the general public as well. That there was a real public opinion in the country, is proved by the direction in the *Śānti-Parvan* of the *Mahābhārata*,[9] LXXXIX, 15–16 :

"The King should make secret and trusted agents travel through the kingdom for ascertaining whether his conduct of the previous day has, or has not met with the approbation of the subjects.

"'Ascertain whether my conduct is or is not approved, what action of mine in the country is agreeable and what reputation do I have in the realm.'"

---

[7] *Mahābhārata* (Kumbakonam ed.), *Śānti-Parvan*, Ch. CLXIV. vs. 66–69 :—

असिं धर्मस्य गोप्तारं ददौ सत्कृत्य विष्णवे ॥
विष्णुर्मरीचये प्रादात्मरीचिर्भार्गवाय तम् ।
महर्षिभ्यो ददौ खड्गमृषयो वासवाय च ॥
महेन्द्रो लोकपालेभ्यो लोकपालास्तु पुत्रक ।
मनवे सूर्यपुत्राय ददुः खड्गं सुविस्तरम् ॥
ऊचुश्चैनं तथा वाक्यं मानुषाणां त्वमीश्वरः ।
असिना धर्मगर्भेण पालयस्व प्रजा इति ॥

[8] See, for instance, the interpretation of *Āryāvarta* which Medhātithi gives on Manu, II. 22—

आर्या वर्तन्ते तत्र पुनः पुनरुद्भवन्त्याक्रम्याक्रम्यापि न चिरं तत्र म्लेच्छाः स्थातारो भवन्ति, etc.

[9] अतीव दिवसे वृत्तं प्रशंसन्ति न वा पुनः ।
गुप्तैश्चारैरनुमतैः पृथिवीमनुसारयेत् ॥
जानीत यदि मे वृत्तं प्रशंसन्ति न वा पुनः ।
कच्चिद्रोचेज्जनपदे कच्चिद्राष्ट्रे च मे यश : ॥ (Kumbakonam ed.)

The King's policy and conduct were criticised in the country and the King was anxious to know those criticisms. The ideal is forcefully, though crudely, set forth in the national epic, the *Rāmāyaṇa*, in the alleged reason as to why Rāma parted with his queen. Though personally convinced of her innocence, he separated himself from her in response to the public will.

In the *Bṛihaspati Sūtra* the king is asked to give up the smallest undertaking if there is popular clamour against it.[10] Even the right thing should not be done if the People raise a voice against it.[11]

---

[10] *Brihaspati Sūtra* (Ed. F. W. Thomas) :—

1. 95. जनघोषे सति क्षुद्रकर्म न कुर्यात् ।

[11] *Ibid.*, I. 4.—धर्ममपि लोकाविक्रुष्टं न कुर्यात् ।

CHAPTER XXX

Council of Ministers

Origin

Was the Hindu king a personal ruler? To answer this let us examine the position of the Hindu Council of Ministers. To appreciate the constitutional position of the Council of Ministers it is necessary to recall the previous history of the Council. The Hindu Council of Ministers was a body and an organism which had differentiated and branched off from the old National Assembly of Vedic times. In the *Atharva Veda*, as we have already noticed, the *rājakṛits* are a part of the 'folk-around' the King who invest him with sovereignty.[1] The *rājakṛits* or 'king-makers' appear later as Ratnin High Functionaries (Commander-in-Chief, Treasurer, etc.) whom the king-elect worships before his consecration.[2] In worshipping the Ratnins, he does honour to them both as officers of the state and as representatives of the society. Their approval like the approval of the remaining representatives of the Community was solicited before the election of the would-be king. In other words, they are officers but as part of the community, and not as creatures of the crown. This origin is further borne out by the technical expression applied to denote their collective body.

The Council of Ministers is called the *Parishad*, in the *Artha-Śāstra*[3] and *Parisā* in the *Jātakas*,[4] the *Mahavdstu*[5] and Aśoka's inscriptions.[6] It does not interchange (until late) with other words of similar meaning. Now the *Parishad* was another name for the National Assembly of the Vedic Hindus. In the *Bṛihadāraṇyaka Upanishad* as already pointed out, the *Samiti* is called *Parishad*.[7] The Council of Ministers,

---

[1] See pp. 195–96 above.
[2] See pp. 203–04 above.
[3] *Artha-Śāstra*, Bk. I. Ch. XV.
[4] *J.*, VI, pp. 405 and 431.
[5] *Mahāvastu*, II. 419, 442.
[6] Rock Series III and VI.
[7] See p. 14 above.

thus differentiated from the *Samiti-Parashad*, inherited the same name like the *Parishad* of Law. With that name they likewise inherited and retained the popular tradition and sense of responsibility.

Use of Vedic terms

They never lost their Vedic prestige even in the most powerful days of the Hindu monarch. They had been *rājakṛits* or 'king-makers' and 'kings' (rulers) under popular constitution and they remained 'king-makers' and 'kings' in the Pāli Sūtras, and in the national epic. The Pāli Canon employs 'king-makers' as a synonym for ministers.[8] The *Rāmāyaṇa*[9] in describing the ministers who put their resolution before Bharata, calls them 'king-makers'. In the *Prātimoksha Sūtra* the High Ministers were called 'kings'.[10] Aśoka calls his High Ministers 'reins-holders' (of the state), *i.e.*, 'ruling-ministers'.[11]

Council and King

It is a law and principle of Hindu Constitution that the king cannot act without the approval and co-operation of the Council of Ministers. The law sūtras, the law books and the political treatises are all unanimous on the point. Manu calls a king foolish who would attempt to carry on the administration by himself. He regards such a king as unfit.[12] He lays down that the king must have 'colleagues', *i.e.*, ministers; and that in their midst and along with them he has to consider ordinary and extraordinary matters of state[13]; even ordinary business ought not to be

---

[8] *Dīghanikāya, Mahāgovinda Suttānta*, 32, '*rājakattāro*'.

[9] *Ayodhyā-Kāṇḍa*, Ch. LXXIX. 1. समेत्य राजकर्त्तारो भरतं वाक्यमब्रुवन् ; Commentary स quoted in the Kumbakonam ed. राजकर्त्तारः= मन्त्रिणः ।

[10] राजानो नाम पठव्या राजा पदेसराजा मण्डलिकराजा अंतरभोगिवा अक्कदस्सा महामत्ता ये वा पन छेज्जाभेज्जं अनुसासंति एते राजानो नाम, quoted by Childers, *PD.*, p. 397.

[11] *Rājūka* in Rock Series III; and Pillar Series IV, where the *Rājūka* ministers are entrusted with complete powers of government (*Daṇḍa*). *Cf.* Jayaswal, *J.B.O.R.S.*, IV. 41. See also above Bhaṭṭa-Bhāskara cited under p. 202, *n.* 12.

[12] See p. 233 above; *Manu*, VII. 30–31.

[13] *Manu*, VII. 54–57.

done by one man, not to speak of the conduct of a kingdom.[14] Yājñavalkya is of the same opinion[15] and so are the other law-givers. Kātyāyana ordains that the king should not decide even a law-suit by himself and that he should do it along with the Council.[16] Even Kauṭilya, the greatest advocate of monarchy, has to say that matters of state should be discussed by the Council of Ministers and whatever the majority decides the king should carry out. It should be noted that this rule is enjoined even when there is a body of *Mantrins* or cabinet separate from the *Mantri-Parishad*. The *Artha-Śāstra* says:

"When there is an extraordinary matter the *Mantrins* and the *Mantri-Parishad* should be called together and informed. In the meeting whatever the majority decide to be done, should be done (by the king)."[17]

It is remarkable that the king is not given even the power of vetoing. The *Kauṭilīya* in emphasising the importance of the *Parishad* says that Indra was called 'thousand-eyed', although he had only two eyes, because he had thousand wise

---

[14] *Manu*, VII. 30–31, 55–56—

सोऽसहायेन मूढेन लुब्धेनाकृतबुद्धिना ।
न शक्यो न्यायतो नेतुं सक्तेन विषयेषु च ॥
शुचिना सत्यसन्धेन यथाशास्त्रानुसारिणा ।
दण्डः प्रणयितुं शक्यः सुसहायेन धीमता ॥
अपि यत्सुकरं कर्म तदप्येकेन दुष्करम् ।
विशेषतोऽसहायेन किमु राज्यं महोदयम् ॥
तैः सार्धं चिन्तयेन्नित्यं सामान्यं सन्धिविग्रहम् ।
स्थानं समुदयम् गुप्तिं लब्धप्रशमनानि च ॥

[15] *Yājñavalkya*, Bk. I. 311—

तैः सार्धं चिन्तयेद्राज्यं, etc.

[16] *Vīramitrodaya*, p. 14.—

सप्राड्विवाकः सामात्यः सब्राह्मणपुरोहितः ।
ससभ्यः प्रेक्षको राजा स्वर्गे तिष्ठति धर्मतः ॥

[17] *Artha-Śāstra*, Bk. I. Ch. 15; 11 (p. 29)—

आत्यायिके कार्ये मन्त्रिणो मन्त्रिपरिषदञ्चाहूय ब्रूयात् । तत्र यद्भूयिष्ठाः कार्यसिद्धिकरं वा ब्रूयुस्तत्कुर्यात् ।

See Jayaswal, *Indian Antiquary*, 1913, p. 282.

members in his *Mantra-Parishad* or Council of State who are regarded as his eyes.[18]

The *Śukranītisāra*, which in matters of first principles follows tradition faithfully, prescribes:

"Without the *mantrins* matters of state should never be considered by the king alone, be he an expert in all the sciences and versed in policy. A wise king must always follow the opinion of the members of the Council of *Adhikārins* or ministers with portfolios, of the President (*Sabhya*, p. 303) and Subjects (*Prakritis*, p. 298). He must never follow his own opinion. When the sovereign becomes independent (of his council) he plans for ruin. In time he loses the state and loses the subjects."[19]

The king according to *Manu* (VII. 57), should consult the ministers separately and then "all of them together"—*i.e.*, as Medhātithi explains, in the Council. This is exactly, almost verbally, what Kauṭilya lays down.[20] By thus discussing, the king was to derive benefit. The cleverest of the ministers, who should be a Brahmin, was to be completely depended upon by the king, and entrusted with the execution of all the resolutions.[21] All the business thus was to be left for execution in the hands of a Prime Minister or Chancellor.

The *Bṛihaspati Sūtra* says that even 'a rightful thing (*dharma*) the king should do only on the advice of the wise'.[22]

---

18 *Artha-Śāstra*, Bk. I, Ch. 15 ; 11 (p. 29)—
इन्द्रस्यहि मन्त्रपरिषद्दृषीणां सहस्रं । तच्चक्षुः । तस्मादिमं द्व्यक्षं सहस्राक्षमाहुः ।

19 *ŚNS.*, II, 2–4.—
सर्वविद्यासु कुशली नृपो ह्यपि सुमन्त्रवित् ।
मन्त्रिभिस्तु विना मन्त्रं नैकोऽर्थं चिन्तयेत् क्वचित् ॥ २ ॥
सभ्याधिकारि-प्रकृति-सभासत्सुमते स्थितः ।
सर्वदा स्यान्नृपः प्राज्ञः स्वमते न कदाचन ॥ ३ ॥
प्रभुः स्वातन्त्र्यमापन्नो ह्यनर्थायैव कल्पते ।
भिन्नराष्ट्रो भवेत्सद्यो भिन्नप्रकृतिरेव च ॥ ४ ॥

20 तानेकैकशः पृच्छेत् समस्तांश्च ॥ *A.Ś.*, p. 28.
तेषां स्वं स्वमभिप्रायमुपलभ्य पृथक् पृथक् ।
समस्तानां च कार्येषु विदध्याद्धितमात्मनः ॥ *Manu*, VII. 57.

21 *Manu*, VII. 58–59.

22 धर्ममभि लोकविक्रुष्टं न कुर्यात् । करोति चेदाशास्यैनं बुद्धिमद्भिः ।
Bṛihaspati Sūtra, I. 4–5.

That is, for even a lawful action in administration the king must have the authority of expert ministers.

Gifts by King to be rectified or rejected by Ministry

In this connection we must also notice the very important constitutional law laid down by the Dharma School of law-givers that it was not competent for the king to make gifts even to the Brahmins if the Ministers "opposed" the gifts. The law is as ancient as the time of Āpastamba.[23] (*Circa* 400 B.C.)

With the history of the origin of Hindu Ministry and these laws of the constitution before us we can understand how the Ministry under Chancellor Rādha-Gupta refused to make further gifts to the Buddhist Brotherhood on the order of the Emperor Aśoka.[24] Otherwise we would have fallen into the cheap wisdom of regarding the whole story as a 'myth' and a 'Buddhist fabrication'.

Aśoka in his Rock Series inscriptions, Section VI, says that when he has passed an order with regard to a gift or a proclamation, should a discussion arise in the *Parishad* (Council of Ministers) and they (the ministers) shelve it, he should be informed of it—if there was a division of opinion with regard to his proposal in the *Parishad* or a total rejection, he should at

---

[23] *Apastamba*, II. 10. 26. 1 :—

भृत्यानामनुपरोधेन क्षेत्रं वित्तञ्च ददद्ब्राह्मणेभ्यो यथार्हमनन्ताँल्लोकानभिजयति ॥

For *Bhṛitya* in the sense of minister see *Artha-Śāstra*, p. 320. "मन्त्रिपुरोहितादिभृत्यवर्गम्", and the reference to the *Divyāvadāna* below.

[24] *Divyāvadāna*, p. 430 *et. seq.* I regard the detail of the first gift of Aśoka as given in the *Divyāvadāna* to be substantially true, for it was in the nature of a *Viśvajit Sarvamedha* (सर्वमेध)—fee which a Sārvabhauma Emperor like Aśoka was expected to make (p. 199). The ruler gave away all that belonged to him except the land, *i.e.*, the State as *Mīmāṃsā* says (see Ch. XXXIV below). In other words, he gave away the surplus revenue which he had in his treasury. To an occasional gift like this the ministers would not have objected as that was the right of the Emperor to make. But a repeated procedure of this nature would be objectionable as found by the Ministers of Aśoka.

once be informed of it.[25] That shows that the ministers had been for some time opposing the rulings of the Emperor.

Rudradāman was similarly opposed by his Ministers with regard to his proposal to repair the Sudarśana Lake. Opinion of Rudradāman's Ministers was against the king's proposal for repairing the Sudarśana water-works. They refused to pay for the repairs and the king had to pay from his private purse.[26] Fortunately for Indian History the evidence of Rudradāman's inscription is as clear as any could be. It proves that the constitutional laws were not mere pious wishes, but they were as real as ordinary municipal laws of the law-books. Thanks to the Buddhist works which have preserved the great constitutional datum on the reign of Aśoka in their pathetic lament that the Emperor of the whole of India was deprived of his sovereign authority by the ministers of state.[27] The *Gāthā*[27] quoted by the *Divyāvadāna* is more ancient than the compilation of the *Divyāvadāna*, and the former could not have been composed many centuries after the event. The monks were to gain nothing by an invention of such a story which threw discredit on a great personage of their religious history. They would not have invented a story which would have been a bad precedent in case other monarchs wanting to imitate the munificence of the Maurya Emperor.

---

[25] Jayaswal, *Indian Antiquary*, 1913, p. 242.

[26] See p. 263 above ; *E.I.*, VIII. 44 (insc. lines 16–17).

[27] *Divyāvadāna*, p. 430. Aśoka anxious to complete his intended gift of money to the Kukkuṭārāma monastery says, 'Rādhagupta, I do not mind the loss of money, of government, of authority,'

राजाह । एधगुप्त, नाहं द्रव्यविनाशं न राज्यनाशनं न चाश्रयवियोगं शोचामि ।

* * *

तस्मिंश्च समये कुनालस्य सम्पदिनामपुत्रो युवरज्ये प्रवर्त्तते । तस्यामात्यैरभिहितम् । कुमार, अशोको राजा स्वल्पकालावस्थायी इदम् च द्रव्यं कुर्कुटारामं प्रेष्यते । कोशबलिनश्च राजानो, निवारयितव्यः । यावत् कुमारेण भाण्डागारिकः प्रतिषिद्धः ।

" At that particular time Kunāla's son, Sampadi, was filling the post of Yuvarāja. He was told by the Ministers 'Your Royal Highness, King Aśoka is temporarily in his position but he is sending away the money to the Kurkuṭārāma. King's strength lies in

Number of the members of the Council and the Cabinet

The numerical strength of the Ministry varied from time to time. Bṛihaspati in his book on politics quoted by Kauṭilya gave the number of the council members to be sixteen. The *Artha-Śāstra* of the Mānavas laid down 'that the Council of Ministers should be composed of twelve ministers': *mantriparishadaṃ dvādaśāmātyāṃ*[28] *kurvīteti Mānavāḥ*. Another old authority, Uśānas enjoined in his time twenty, while Kauṭilya would not have any rigid number.[29] Earlier Councils were larger, as one is mentioned

---

treasury. He is to be checked'. The Prince prohibited the Treasurer." (For the position of Yuvarāja as a High Minister, and resolutions going up to him from other members of the Cabinet, see below p. 307.)

*   *   *

अथ राजाशोकः संविग्नोऽमात्यान् पौरांश्च संनिपात्य कथयति । कः साम्प्रतं पृथिव्यामीश्वरः । ततोऽमात्य उत्थायासनाद्येन राजाशोकस्तेनाञ्जलिं प्रणम्योवाच । (p. 431.) देवः पृथिव्यामीश्वरः । अथ राजाशोकः साश्रुदुर्दिननयन-वदनोऽमात्यानुवाच—

दाक्षिण्यादनृतं हि किं कथयथ भ्रष्टाधिराज्या वयम् ।

" Now King Aśoka, very much agitated in mind, called a meeting of the Ministers and the *Pauras*. He asked—' Who at present is the Sovereign of the Country ?' On that the Prime Minister rising from his seat approached the place where King Aśoka was and saluting him respectfully spoke, ' His (= Your) Majesty is the Sovereign of the Country'. Then King Aśoka with tears trickling down his face answered the Ministers : ' Why do you tell an untruth on account of courtesy ? We are deprived of rule ?"

*   *   *

त्यागशूरो नरेन्द्रोऽसौ अशोको मौर्यकुञ्जरः ।
जम्बुद्वीपेश्वरोभूत्वा जातोऽर्द्धामलकेश्वरः ॥
भृत्यैः स भूमिपतिरद्य हृताधिकारो दानं प्रयच्छति किलामलकार्धमेतत् ।

" The liberal king Aśoka, the best of the Mauryas, who was the Emperor of India, became the sovereign of a half-apple (on his plate). That King now deprived of authority by the Ministers, gave away in charity the half-apple."

[28] Kauṭilya, *Artha-Śāstra*, Bk. I, Ch. 15; 11 (p. 29). Read *amātyāṃ* instead of *amātyān* as printed in the *Artha-Śāstra*; it qualifies *mantriparishadaṃ*.

[29] *Ibid.*

in the *Mahābhārata* of thirty-two members (p. 319 below). There has been a tendency towards a smaller body.

We shall revert again to the *Mantri-Parishad*, and to the powers of the Ministers as a body. Let us now note the official designations of different ministers. The number of the Ministry or Cabinet is recommended by Manu (VII. 54) to be seven or eight. The number eight had become nearly fixed when the *Śukranīti* was written, and on its tradition the *Ashṭa-Pradhāna*, or the Ministry of Eight, of Śivāji, was founded. The eight ministers according to 'some' authorities referred to in the *Śukranīti* are the following :—[30]

(1) The *Sumantra* or Minister of Finance.

(2) The *Paṇḍitāmātya* or Minister of Law.

(3) The *Mantrin* or Home Minister.

(4) The *Pradhāna* or President of the Council.

(5) The *Sachiva* or Minister of War.

(6) The *Amātya* or Minister of Revenue and Agriculture.

(7) The *Prāḍvivāka* or Minister of Justice and Chief Justice.

(8) The *Pratinidhi* (Representative : see below).

According to another view two other ministers—

[(9) The *Purōhita* or Minister of Religion.

(10) The *Dūta* or Minister of Diplomacy,[31] should also have seats in the Council]. The exact character of the *Pratinidhi*

---

[30] *Śukranītisāra*, II. 71–72—

अष्टप्रकृतिभिर्युक्तो नृपः कैश्चित्स्मृतः सदा ॥
सुमन्त्रः पण्डितो मन्त्री प्रधानः सचिवस्तथा ।
अमात्यः प्राड्विवाकश्च तथा प्रतिनिधिः स्मृतः ॥

[31] *Ibid.*, II. 84–87—

सर्वदर्शी प्रधानस्तु सेनावित् सचिवस्तथा ॥
मन्त्री तु नीतिकुशलः पण्डितो धर्मतत्त्ववित् ।
लोकशास्त्रनयज्ञस्तु प्राड्विवाकः स्मृतः सदा ॥
देशकालप्रविज्ञाता ह्यमात्य इति कथ्यते ।
आयव्ययप्रविज्ञाता सुमन्त्रः स च कीर्त्तितः ॥

(Contd. on p. 294)

is not clear. He is evidently very important being given precedence over the President of the Council and the *Mantrin.* He was 'to press upon the King the business which must be done whether favourable or unfavourable'. He is certainly not the 'representative' of the King. He might have been the representative of the *Paura-Jānapadas* in the Cabinet or that of the Council in dealing with the King. He is certainly very probably the most important.

इङ्गिताकारचेष्टाज्ञः स्मृतिमान्देशकालवित् ।
षाड्गुण्यमन्त्रविद्वाग्मी वीतभीर्दूत इष्यते ॥
अहितञ्चापि यत्कार्यं सद्यः कर्त्तुं यदोचितम् ।
अकर्त्तुं यद्धितमपि राज्ञः प्रतिनिधिः सदा ।
बोधयेत्कारयेत्कुर्य्याच्च कुर्य्याच्च प्रबोधयेत् ॥
सत्यं वा यदिवासत्यं कार्यजातञ्च यत्किल ।
सर्वेषां राजकृत्येषु प्रधानस्तद्विचिन्तयेत् ॥

et. seq. up to Śl. 106.

Cf. Sivāji's *Ashṭa-Pradhāna.* "The Civil organization of the District was, of course, subordinate to the authorities at head-quarters, two of whom—the *Pant Amātya* and the *Pant Sachiv*, had respectively the charge of what in our time would be called the office of Finance Minister and the General Accountant and Auditor. The district accounts had to be sent to these officers, and were there collated together, and irregularities detected and punished. These officers had power to depute men on their establishments to supervise the working of the district officers. The *Pant Amātya* and the *Sachiv* were, next to the *Peshwā*, the highest civil officers, and they had, besides these revenue duties, military commands. They were both important members of the Board of Administration, called the *Ashṭa Pradhān* or Cabinet of eight heads of departments. The *Peshwā* was Prime Minister, next to the King, and was at the head of both the civil and military administrations, and sat first on the right hand below the throne. The *Senāpati* was in charge of the military administration, and sat first on the left side. *Amātya* and *Sachiv* sat next to the *Peshwā*, while the *Mantri* sat next below the *Sachiv*, and was in charge of the King's private affairs. The *Sumant* was Foreign Secretary, and sat below the *Śenāpati* on the left. Next came *Pandit-rāo*, who had charge of the ecclesiastical department, and below him on the left side sat the Chief Justice (= *Nyāyādhīśa*)."—Ranade, *Rise of Maratha Power*, pp. 125–26.

Yuvarāja and Princes as Ministers

The *Yuvarāja* is not a member of the Cabinet in this enumeration but he is certainly a Minister. He was generally a prince of the blood: uncle, brother, nephew, son, an adopted son, or a grandson.[32] Like other Ministers he was a *Sahāya* or 'Collegue' of the king. The *Yuvarāja* had his seal, and the set formula with which he signed. Under Aśoka, on the authority of the *Divyāvadāna*,[33] Samprati, a grandson, was the *Yuvarāja*, while the son, Kuṇāla was the Presidency Governor at Takshaśilā (the capital of the Northern Presidency).

A prince royal in office was regarded as an officer. Bhaṭṭa-Bhāskara calls him *Kumāra-Adhyaksha* ('Prince Officer in charge of Department') who held the 'reins of government'.[34] In Aśoka's inscriptions despatches to Presidency Governments are addressed to the 'Prince' and High Ministers (*Kumāra* and *Mahāmātras*), the latter being called a *Varga* or Council.[35] Evidently it is such a *Kumāra* whom Bhaṭṭa-Bhāskara, rather his authority, called *niyantā* or 'one who leads' 'by reins' (*rajjubhiḥ*). The Buddhist books[36] make Aśoka governor one time at Takshaśilā and at another at Ujjain (the capital of the Western Presidency). Maurya Princes of the blood royal governed with their Councils in the south; while the conquered province of Kaliṅga was governed only by a Council of *Mahāmātras*.[37] It is significant that Despatches from the Central Government, copies of which are given in the inscriptions, are never addressed to the Prince by name; they are impersonal. The Princes, like the *Mahāmātras* whom we shall presently discuss were probably transferred as the two viceroyalties held by Aśoka indicate. In that case impersonal documents would be quite in form.

---

[32] *Śukranītisāra*, II. 15—

स्वकनिष्ठं पितृव्यं वानुजं वाग्रजसम्भवम् ।
पुत्रं पुत्रीकृतं दत्तं यौवराज्येऽभिषेचयेत् ॥
क्रमादभावे दौहित्रं स्वप्रियं वा नियोजयेत् ।

[33] *Divyāvadāna*, p. 430; see above p. 291.

[34] See above, pp. 200-03, *n*.

[35] See *Separate Edicts of Orissa*; *J.B.O.R.S.*, IV, p. 36.

[36] *Divyāvadāna*, p. 372; *Mahāvaṃśa*, V. 46.

[37] See Jaugaḍa and Dhauli 'Separate' Rock-Inscriptions and Siddhapura Inscription.

The official designations of the Ministers for different portfolios varied from time to time. The *Mānava Dharma-Śāstra* uses the word *Sachiva*, lit., 'helper', 'colleague', as a general term for Ministers[38] as against the *Amātya* (lit., 'those remaining together') of the *Artha-Śāstra*. In the *Rāmāyaṇa Amātya* occurs in the general sense, while *Sachivas* are distinguished from the *Mantrins*.[39]

Designations of Ministers

The Chief Minister is called *Mantrin* (lit., 'Adviser'), *i.e.*, the *Mantrin*, in the *Artha-Śāstra*, whose position is the first amongst the Ministers. Next to him comes in the *Artha-Śāstra* the *Purohita*, then the *Senāpati* and after the *Senāpati* comes the *Yuvarāja*.[40]

The *Mānava Dharma-Śāstra* calls the Prime Minister simply *Amātya*, that is, he was *the Amātya*. In him was vested the administration or *daṇḍa*.[41] He, as especially required by the *Mānava Code* (VII. 58; XII. 100), was to be a Brahmin. In earlier times, in the Pāli Canon, the Prime Minister, *e.g.*, of Ajātaśatru, is styled *Agra-Mahāmātra* 'the Foremost Minister'. In the *Divyāvadāna*, the Chief Minister of Aśoka (Rādha-Gupta) is called *Amātya*. He is evidently the *Mantrin* in the *Sukranīti*. In the Gupta period he is probably called the *Mahādaṇḍanāyaka* (p. 320 below).

The *Mānava Code* does not specifically mention the *Purohita*. But he is very likely included in its 'seven or eight' Ministers. This Minister bears the same designation (*Purohita* or *Purodhas*, lit., 'Leader') throughout, but his functions varied with a tendency to gradual extension. In the *Jātakas* and *Dharma Sūtras*[42] he is expected to be versed both in sacred law and politics. Āpastamba[43] expects him to judge cases where *Prāyaśchitta* or penance was to be inflicted. He was also to

---

[38] *Manu*, VII. 54.

[39] *Yuddha-Kāṇḍa*, 130. 17–20 (Kumbakonam ed.), Govindarāja.

[40] *Artha-Śāstra*, Bk. V, Ch. 2; 91 (p. 245).

[41] *Manu*, VII. 65.

[42] *Jātaka*, Vol. I, p. 437; II, p. 30; *Āpastamba Dh. S.*, II. 5. 10. 13–14.

[43] *Āpastamba Dharma-Sūtra*, II. 5. 10. 13–14, etc.

try Brahmins on hehalf of the king. The *Artha-Śāstra*[44] requires him to be learned in the Veda and its *Aṅgas*, in astrology, and in politics, and that he should also know the Atharvan rites, which were to be performed in cases of national calamities to satisfy the common people. The *Śukranīti*[45] demands a knowledge of the military science and art as well as in the *Purohita*.

The *Mānava* styles the *Minister of Diplomacy* as *Dūta*,[46] who had jurisdiction with regard to peace and war with foreign powers and "who broke up alliances". The *Rāmāyaṇa* (II. 100. 35) knows him by that title and so does the *Śukranīti*. But subsequently he is called *Sāndhi-vigrahika*, in inscriptions of the Gupta period, in Bṛihaspati's law and later. It is curious that this Minister is not found in the list of the *Artha-Śāstra*. Probably the *Mantrin* combined that office in himself. The office was very important in Maurya days.

In the *Mānava Code* the king is his own *Finance Minister*.[47] He himself holds charge of the Finance. He is not directly named in *Manu* but his subordinates are mentioned under the designation which the *Artha-Śāstra* gives to him—*Samāhartṛi*. In the *Artha-Śāstra* there is an allied portfolio of the *Sannidhātṛi* (p. 202 above). Later on the two portfolios coalesce into one. In the *Śukranīti* the Minister of Finance is *Sumantra*. Govindarāja (p. 295 above) gives another designation, *Artha-sañchaya-kṛit*.

The *Senāpati* is evidently the *Minister of War*. He is very important in the government of Chandragupta coming third in precedence, taking his place above the *Yuvarāja*. In the *Śukranīti* he is called '*Sachiva*'. Probably the *Senāpati* was both the military leader in the field and the military member in the Council as is suggested in the *Rāmāyaṇa* (II. 100. 31). But in the time of Kauṭilya the two offices were distinct (p. 302 below) and they remained distinct in later times.

---

[44] *Artha-Śāstra*, Bk. I, Ch. 8; 5 (p. 15).

[45] *Śukranītisāra*, II. 80—नीतिशास्त्रास्त्रव्यूहादिकुशलस्तु पुरोहितः ।

[46] *Manu*, VII. 65-66—दूते सन्धिविपर्ययौ । दूत एव हि सन्धत्ते भिनत्त्येव च संहतान् ।

[47] *Ibid.*, नृपतौ कोशराष्ट्रे च—(65).

In the *Śukranīti* he is a civilian officer, as the eight ministers were transferred from one portfolio to the other and they all occupy equal rank (p. 318 below).

Cabinet

The above five ministers with the *Yuvarāja* in addition, made up the real governing body. The *Yuvarāja* is a post-Vedic development while all others had origin in the Ratnins, except probably the *Dūta* whose functions might have been performed by the *Sūta* as he appears to be rather important in early days.[48] The *Yuvarāja*, it should be marked, occupies the fourth place in the Government of Chandragupta. Then and later he is not the President of the Cabinet or the Council (pp. 299–300), as there are other officers in those posts; evidently no portfolio is given to him. The *Māhābhārata* (XII. 83. 12) calls the cabinet a *gaṇa* and so does the *Śukranīti* (p. 308 below). The *Mahābhārata* says that the king should not be partial to any one member of the *gaṇa*.

An Inner Cabinet

There was a tendency to form a smaller body inside the cabinet. The members of this, what we may call the Inner body, were three or four, according to the *Artha-Śāstra* (p. 28). It was with them that the king constantly conferred. These ministers are called the *Mantrins* in the *Artha-Śāstra* and the *Rāmāyaṇa* and the *Māhabhārata*. In this character the '*mantrins*' mean 'those vested with *mantra* or the policy of state,' as is evident from the expressions *mantradharas* in the *Rāmāyaṇa*[49] and *mantra-grāhas* in the *Māhābhārata*.[50]

The members of 'the mantra-holding' (*mantra-grāha*) body or 'the holders of the reins' of state (pp. 200–03, *n.*) were to be according to the *Mahābhārata* 'at least three' and preferably five.[51] Kauṭilya prescribes it to be three or four' (*A.Ś.*, p. 28). The original view probably was that such holder-of-mantra should be only one as recognised by the king. This was the

---

[48] In the *Mahābhārata*, Sañjaya becomes Minister of Finance.—XIII. 42.

[49] *Ayodhyā-Kāṇḍa*, Canto 100, 16.

[50] *Mahābhārata*, XII. 83. 50.

[51] *Ibid.*, 47. 52. 20–22.

view of that severe theorist, Kaṇika Bhāradvāja[52] (*Artha-Śāstra*, p. 27), and it seems to have been the view of the *Mānava Dharma Code* (VII. 58). Viśālāksha condemned the system of one-minister cabinet (*Artha-Śāstra*, p. 27), and the *Rāmāyaṇa* does the same, according to which (II. 100–18) it should " neither be of one nor too many ". The number three and upwards became fixed, as evidenced by the *Māhābharata* and the quotations in *Nitivākyamṛita*.[53] The uneven number found preference for the same reason as given by Mitramiśra in the case of uneven jury : सङ्ख्यावैषम्यन्तु भूयोऽल्प-विरोधे भूयसां स्यात् 'uneven number is to provide, against difference in opinion, for a majority'.[54]

Aśoka's *rājūka* ministers (pp. 312–13 below) who had the fullest authority to rule over the *prajā* (subjects) and to grant them *anugrahas*, and in whose hands the king left the *prajā* as a mother leaves her child in the hands of a known nurse (Pillar Proclamation IV), and who were declared supreme in the matters of *daṇḍa* (administration) and *abhihāra* (declaring hostilities), seem to be identical with the *mantra-dharas* or *mantra-grāhas*. *Rājūka* signifies the 'ruling minister,' literally it denotes 'the holder of the reins (of Government)' like Bhaṭṭa-Bhāskara's *rajjubhir niyantā*. The number of Aśoka's *Rājūkas* was certainly more than one, they being generally referred to in the plural.

Thus the history of the Cabinet shows a growth in number, and a change—from the authority of one to that of several. The rule of one was always found incompatible with the tradition and the whole social system of the race.

Composition of the "*Mantra-Parishad*" or Council of State

Apart from the cabinet of the *Mantra-dharas* who had the real executive authority, there was, as we have already seen, the *Mantra-parishad* or the *Mantri-parishad*. The *Mantri-parishad* was not solely composed of the *Mantrins*. To the meetings of

---

[52] We ought to recover his work. He is quoted as late as by Govindarāja.

[53] एको मन्त्री न कर्त्तव्यः । एको निरवग्रहश्चरति मुह्यति च कार्यकृच्छ्रेषु । द्वावपि मन्त्रिणौ न कर्त्तव्यौ, तौ संहतौ चरन्तौ भक्ष्यन्तौ गृहीतौ च विनाशयतः । त्रयः पञ्चसप्त वा मन्त्रिणः कार्याः । Ch. X.

[54] *Vīramitrodaya*, p. 35.

this body, the *Mantrins* or 'the holders of Mantra' ministers were called, according to the *Kauṭilīya*. The *Parishad* was composed of (1) these *Mantradharas* (Inner cabinet), (2) other cabinet ministers who held portfolios, (3) ministers without portfolios, and (4) others (see below). The number was generally large, as the numbers 32 of the *Mahābhārata*, 20 and 16 of other authorities, and Kauṭilya's example of Indra's large council show. It thus exceeded the number of the ministers of the cabinet.

Paura-Jānapada and "*Mantri-Parishad*"

We have no definite information as to who composed the class (4). The Council summoned by Aśoka on the ministers refusing to carry out his orders of gifts, consisted of the *Pauras* (Ch. XXVIII), and the *Amātyas*. It seems from other pieces of evidence that the Council had some seats assigned in it to the leaders of the *Paura* and *Jānapada*. The *Mahābhārata* (*Śānti*, Ch. 83) and the *Śukranīti* (II. 3)[55] suggest that. The opinion which the king was bound to follow according to the *Śukranīti* (II. 3), was of (*a*) the *Sabhya*, (*b*) the *Adhikārins*, and (*c*) the *Prakṛitis*, as *sabhāsads* or members sitting in the Council. The *Sabhya* according to the authority quoted by Govindarāja (p. 303 below) was the President of the Council or the *Mantra-Parishad* of Kauṭilya. *Adhikārins* were the heads of *Adhikaraṇas* or Departments, *i.e.*, the Ministers. The remaining one *Prakritis* must necessarily signify the People or Subjects (p. 245 above), meaning thereby their representatives—the chiefs of the *Paura* and *Jānapada* (p. 257 above). In the *Rāmāyaṇa* [*Ayodhyā*, Chs. 81 (12), 82 (1, 4)] the People's representatives and the Ministers meet and hold a *Sabhā* called the 'ruling (*pragrahā*) *Sabhā*' to consider an *atyāyika* ('extra-ordinary,' *cf. A.Ś.*, p. 29) business.

The *Mahābhārata*[56] where it describes the *Sabhā* (XII, 83. verses 1–2) counts these classes :

---

55 सभ्याधिकारि-प्रकृति-सभासत्सुमते स्थितः ।
सर्वदा स्यान्नृप प्राज्ञः स्वमते न कदाचन ॥
—*Śukranītisāra.*

56 सभासदः सहायाश्च सुहृदश्च विशांपते ।
परिच्छदास्तथाऽमात्याः कीदृशाःस्युः पितामह ॥
—*Mahābhārata.*

(1) The *Sahāyas*, by whom it means the 'Ministers (*Amātyas*) colleagues (*Sahāyas*)' or the High Ministers with portfolios (verses 3–4).

(2) The *Parichchada amātyas* who should be very learned, of high birth, natives of the country, deep, wise and loyal. As the name ('Robes') denotes, they were probably ceremonial ministers and dignitaries who had grown out of the king's house-hold. One of them was the *Dauvārika* or Lord Mayor of the Palace occupying a very high position (p. 302 below). They had their *Adhikaraṇas* or Departments (pp. 302–03 below). Out of the above the king chose his '*Mantrins*' (7–8) who are referred to in the *Śukranīti* verse (II. 2), preceding the one quoted above. The subject of Mantrins continues for the rest of the chapter in the *Mahābhārata* and with a small digression is taken up again in Ch. 85, where the list of 32 ministers is given. Out of them the king is to choose 8 ministers as *Mantrins* or the cabinet. Whatever policy they decided upon is to be submitted to the *Rāshṭra* and the President of the *Rāshṭra*, *i.e.*, the *Jānapada*, for opinion.

(3) The *Rāshṭra*. This new element corresponds to the *Prakṛiti* of the *Śukranīti*.[57]

The *Realm* ('*Rāshṭra*') of the *Mahābhārata* and the *People* ('*Prakṛiti*') of the *Śukranīti* are thus identical with the *Paura* in the Council called by Aśoka and the *Prakṛiti-sabhāsads* of the *Rāmāyaṇa* (*Ayodhyā*, 82. 4. 17).

It thus seems that the royal *Parishat* had not only the popular trace in its Vedic name, but a real popular element in it. The "*Mantra*" or *Mantrin Parishat* carried on in some degree the Vedic tradition of the folk assembly.

[57] (It probably corresponds also to the *suhṛid* class of *Sabhāsads* mentioned in the opening verse of Chapter 83, along with the *Sahāya* and *Parichchada* classes. Why the *representatives of the realm* should be called 'friends' is not very clear. The political writers have a classification by which they divide the natural friends and natural enemies of kings. Probably the Realm representatives were considered as the king's 'friends,' for unlike an ambitious relative, they were naturally interested in upholding the king's cause.)

It is better to render the *Mantri-Parishad* as Council of State rather than the Council of Ministers. The form *Mantra-Parishat*, 'Council of State Deliberation' which Kauṭilya applies to the *Mantri-Parishad* of Indra, should be noted in this connexion. Probably the *Mantri-Parishad* there signifies the *Mantra-Parishad*. The tradition of a large *Parishad*, *e.g.*, of 1,000 members, is preserved both in Kauṭilya, and in the *Rāmāyaṇa* (where it stands rather discredited, II. 100). Probably this is a reminiscence of the Vedic *Parishad*.

There was an old grouping called 'the Eighteen *Tīrthas*'. The *Rāmāyaṇa* knows it (II. 100. 36). The *Artha-Śāstra* of Kauṭilya (pp. 21, 22) mentions it and refers to the *tīrthas* as *Mahā-Amātyas*. They were heads of departments of both superior and inferior classes. They contained two offices of the royal household as well. The grouping was old and was fast becoming osbolete. The *Mahābhārata* does not seem to mention it in its book on politics.

"*Tīrthas*"

Tīrthas are defined in a quotation given by Somadeva Sūri[58] as bodies of legal officers and officers in charge of executive works. It seems certain that *Tīrtha* meant the holder of a department, as all the *Tīrthas* mentioned in the *Artha-Śāstra* are in charge of departments. *Tīrtha* literally means a ford to pass through, *i.e.*, a passage. Ministers and heads of departments acquired this name probably because orders passed through them to their respective departments. The *Tīrtha* classification throws light on the significance of the technical officers. They were :—[59]

(1) The *Mantrin*.
(2) The *Purohita*.
(3) The *Senāpati*, the Minister for the Army (see *Nāyaka*, below No. 11).
(4) The *Yuvarāja*.
(5) The *Dauvārika* or the Lord Mayor of the Palace.

---

[58] *Nitivākyāmṛita*, Ch. II. धर्मसमवायिनः कार्यसमवायिनश्च पुरुषाः तीर्थम् ।

[59] *Artha-Śāstra*, Bk. I, Ch. 12 ; 8 (pp. 20–21). *Cf.* also Bk. V, Ch. 2 ; 91 (p. 245).

(6) The *Antarvaṃśika* or the Lord Chamberlain.

(7) The *Praśāstṛi*, evidently the Chief *Praśāstri*, as there were more than one such officers. According to the enumeration of Govindarāja, he was the Minister in charge of Prisons.

(8) The *Samāhartṛi* or the Minister of Revenue.

(9) The *Sannidhātṛi* or the Minister of Treasury.

(10) The *Pradeshṭṛi* whose functions are not clearly known.

(11) The *Nāyaka* or the Generalissimo.

(12) The *Paura* or the Governor of the Capital.

(13) *Vyāvahārika* (lit., 'Judge') or the Chief Justice, according to Govindarāja.

(14) The *Kārmāntika* or the Officer-in-charge of Mines and Manufactories.

(15) The *Mantri-Parishat-adhyaksha* or the President of the Council, *Sabhya* according to Govindarāja.

(16) The *Daṇḍa-pāla* or the Minister-in-charge of the maintenance of the Army.

(17) The *Durga-pāla* or the Minister-in-charge of Home Defences.

(18) The *Antapāla* or *Rāshṭrāntapāla*, *i.e.*, the Minister-in-charge of Frontiers (*Artha-Śāstra*, p. 245).

This list makes it clear that *Senāpati* here is not the Military Commander-in-Chief but the Minister of War. The military leader was the *Nāyaka*. The Lord Chief Justice is called the Judge instead of the *Prāḍvivāka* of later times. The President of the *Mantri-Parishad* is the *Pradhāna* of the *Śukranīti*. He received an allowance from the Civil List (*Artha-Śāstra*, p. 245). Govindarāja commenting on "the Eighteen *Tīrthas*," *Rāmāyaṇa*, II. 100. 36, quotes from an unnamed work on *Nīti-Śāstra* and gives a few different designations in later terminology. In the place of *Praśāstri* which is obscure in the pages of the *Artha-Śāstra*, he gives *Kārāgāra-adhikṛit* which elucidates the former. It should be translated as Inspector-General of Prisons (lit., 'Corrector of Convicts').[60] Against the *Tīrthas* Nos. 8 and 9 of the *Artha-Śāstra*, Govindarāja gives *Artha-sañchaya-kṛit* or the Chancellor of the Exchequer.

[60] The interpretations given by Dr. Shama Sastry are mostly wide off the mark. See his Trans., p. 23.

The *Pradeshṭṛi* who in the Civil List (*Artha-Śāstra*, p. 245), does not occupy a place amongst the *Amātyas*, appears as *Kārya-niyojaka* in Govindarāja and is explained as Despatcher or Director of Royal Orders (राजाज्ञायाः बहिःप्रचारकर्त्ता). Instead of *Vyāvahārika* Govindarāja has the younger term *Prāḍvivāka* (the Pāli Canon knows only *Vohārika*). The *Nāyaka* who appears in the *Artha-Śāstra* as the Highest Military Commander is represented by *Senā-nāyaka*, and the *Paura* by *Nagarādhyaksha*. The *Mantri-Parishad-adhyaksha* corresponds to *Sabhya* (whom Govindarāja incorrectly connects with the building *Sabhā*). Govindarāja's authority has a new officer *Dharmādhyaksha* who is, I think, identical with *Paṇḍita-amātya* of the *Śukranīti*. The order in Govindarāja is slightly altered after No. 8 of our *Artha-Śāstra* list.

Three classes of Ministers

The Ministers were divided into three classes according to the Pāli Canon, the *Rāmāyaṇa* and the *Śukranīti*. In the *Rāmāyaṇa* they are called the Superior, the Intermediaries and the Inferior. The *Śukranīti* has the same division.[61]

Civil List and King's salary

The *Artha-Śāstra* divides the eighteen *Tīrthas* into three classes in the Civil List which fixes the salaries of the permanent officers from the King down to the Historiographer and the Ministerial Establishments. The King's salary according to Āpastamba should not exceed that of the "*Amātyas* and the *Gurus* (religious Preceptors)".[62] This provision becomes clear in the light of the *Artha-Śāstra* Civil List. Kauṭilya says that the King is to get three times the salary of the officers of his equal acquirements (*samāna-vidya*).[63] We may regard the Prime-Minister and the *Senāpati* as *Samānavidya* to the King. The religious chiefs who are placed at the head of the first class of the Civil List are *Ṛitvik* and *Achārya*. These two with the

---

[61] *Ayodhyā-Kāṇḍa*, 100. 25–26—मुख्य, मध्यम, जघन्य । *Śukranīti-sāra*, Ch. II. 109–10.

[62] *Āpastamba Dharma-Sūtra*, II. 9. 25. 10—

गुरूनमात्यांश्च नातिर्जावेत् ।

[63] *Artha-Śāstra*, Bk. V, Ch. 3; 91 (p. 246)—

समानविद्येभ्यस्त्रिगुणवेतनो राजा ।

Purohita are the '*Gurus*' of Āpastamba. The salaries of these three put together or the three highest ministers, namely, *Mantrin*, *Senāpati* and *Yuvarāja* of Kauṭilya's list, should not be exceeded, in the language of Āpastamba, by that of the King. In other words, the two provisions are identical. Now the salary of the *Gurus* and *Amātyas* was 48,000—(silver) *paṇas* a year each.[64] The same salary is allowed to the mother of the King and the consecrated Queen.

The second class of ministers in which occur ministers numbered 5 to 9 of our list were given 24,000 a year. The third class carried the salary of 12,000 a year. The members in this class are those numbered 11 to 18 in our above list. In this class are placed the *Kumāras* and their mothers.

---

[64] The king's salary has been completely missed in the translation of the *Artha-Śāstra* by Dr. Shama Sastry.

CHAPTER XXXI

Council of Ministers *(Continued)*

Government

The duty of the Ministry is summed up in these terms:

Duty of the Ministry

"If the State, the People, the Army, the Exchequer, and lastly Proper Monarchy (*su-nṛipatvam*) do not grow, or the Enemy is not broken through the policy of the Ministers, the Ministers do not justify their existence (lit., 'of what use are they?')."[1]

In connection with 'Proper Monarchy' the preceding verses of the same authority may be quoted. "The Monarch is not controlled, therefore Ministers have to be." "For, if the King could not be kept in check by Ministers, is national prosperity possible by such Ministers?" In the latter case they would cease to be real Ministers and would be no better than ornaments.[2] The *Su-nṛipatva* or 'proper monarchy,' therefore, is a 'controlled monarchy'.

The minister is the *Rāja-Rāshṭra-bhṛit*[3] or 'the bearer of the responsibility of the king and the state'. The king was consequently bound, as observed already, to follow the dictates of the Council, otherwise in the eye of the constitutional law he would cease to be the king.[4] As the *Mahābhārata* put it, he was always '*paratantra*' under the control of others (Ministers)[5] and never *svatantra* (free).

---

[1] *Śukranītisāra*, II. 83—

राज्यं प्रजा बलं कोशः सुनृपत्वं न वर्द्धितम् ।
यन्मन्त्रतोऽरिनाशस्तैर्मन्त्रिभिः किं प्रयोजनम् ॥

[2] *Ibid.*, II. 81, 82—

रोधनं न भवेत्तस्माद्राज्ञस्ते स्युः सुमन्त्रिणः ॥
न बिभेति नृपो येभ्यस्तैःस्यात्किं राज्यवर्द्धनम् ।
यथालङ्कारवस्त्राद्यैः स्त्रियो भूष्यास्तथाहि ते ॥

[3] *Ibid.*, II. 74.

[4] Quotation in *Nītivākyāmṛita*, X.—न खल्वसौ राजा यो मन्त्रिणोऽतिक्रम्य वर्त्तते ।

[5] *Śānti-Parvan* (Kumbakonam ed.), Ch. 325, 139–40.—परतन्त्रः सदा राजा..सन्धि-विग्रहयोगे च कुतो राज्ञः स्वतन्त्रता..मन्त्रे चामात्यसहिते कुतस्तस्य स्वतन्त्रता ॥

Procedure of business in the Ministry

We have seen that extraordinary business was decided; according to the *Artha-Śāstra*, in a full meeting of the Council. This implies that ordinary business went through only ministerial offices. That would have required written notes. There is evidence that written notes as a matter of fact were used. Aśoka in his inscriptions speaks of his oral orders[6] which implies that the orders were generally written orders. The *Artha-Śāstra* also says that the ministers who were not in attendance wrote notes for the king.[7] We have not yet discovered any document which passed through the offices of the ministers. There is, however, on the point a very valuable piece of detail furnished by the *Śukranīti*. The detail evidently belongs to the early centuries of the Christian era as is indicated by the official designation *Dūta*, which is superseded in later (Gupta) times by *Sandhi-Vigrahika*. It is highly important from the constitutional point of view. The procedure it depicts for a matter going through the offices and then reaching the king and becoming a resolution of the ministry, is as follows:

Without a written document no business of State was done. A matter was endorsed first by the Home Minister, the Lord Chief Justice, the Minister of Law, and the Minister of Diplomacy with the fixed style '*This is not opposed to us*,' *i.e.*, their departments had no objection. The Minister of Revenue and Agriculture endorsed with the remark '*The note is all right*,' the Minister of Finance '*Well considered*'; then the President of the Council inscribed in his own hand '*Really proper*'. Next, the *Pratinidhi* wrote '*Fit to be accepted*,' the *Yuvarāja* following, with '*Should be accepted*' in his own hand. The Ecclesiastical Minister endorsed '*This is agreeable to me*'. Every Minister affixed his seal at the end of his note. Finally the King wrote '*Accepted*' and set his seal. He was supposed to be unable to go through the document carefully and the *Yuvarāja* or some one else was to make this endorsement for him

[6] Rock Series, VI.—यं पि चा किछि सुखते आनपयामि हकं दापकं वा सावकं वा etc. (Kalsi).

[7] *Artha-Śāstra*, Bk. I, Ch. 15; 11 (p. 29)—अनासन्नैस्सह पत्रसंप्रेषणेन मन्त्रयेत ।

which was shown to him. After this first stage was over, the minute was signed by all the ministers as the Council (*Gaṇa*) and sealed with the seal of the Council. Finally it was once more presented to the King who 'without delay' wrote '*Seen*' as he had not the 'capacity' to criticise it.[8]

King's 'incapacity' to criticise resolutions of the Ministry

The incapacity referred to here was a constitutional incapacity. We have already seen that the king had no option to veto a measure decided by the majority of the Council (*Artha-Śāstra*). In an ordinary matter for which the king did not call a general Council and which went through the Ministry only, when it had been discussed and finally signed and sealed as a resolution by the Ministry as Council it really became a resolution of the Council and the king was

---

[8] *Śukranītisāra*, II. 362–69—

लेखानुपूर्वं कुर्याद्धि दृष्ट्वा लेख्यं विचार्य च ॥
मन्त्री च प्राड्विवाकश्च पण्डितो दूतसंज्ञकः ।
स्वाविरुद्धं लेख्यमिदं लिखेयुः प्रथमं त्विमे ॥ ३६३ ॥
अमात्यः साधु लिखनमस्त्येनत्प्राग्लिखेदयम् ।
सम्यग्विचारितमिति सुमन्त्री विलिखेत्ततः ॥ ३६४ ॥
सत्यं यथार्थमिति च प्रधानश्च लिखेत्स्वयम् ।
अङ्गीकर्त्तुं योग्यमिति ततः प्रतिनिधिर्लिखेत् ॥ ३६५ ॥
अङ्गीकर्त्तव्यमिति च युवराजो लिखेत्स्वयम् ।
लेख्यं स्वाभिमतं चैतद्धिलिखेच्च पुरोहितः ॥ ३६६ ॥
स्वस्वमुद्राचिन्हितं च लेख्यान्ते कुर्युरेव हि ।
अङ्गीकृतमिति लिखेन्मुद्रयेच्च ततो नृपः ॥ ३६७ ॥
कार्यान्तरस्याकुलत्वात्सम्यग्द्रष्टुं न शक्यते ।
युवराजादिभिर्लेख्यं तदनेन च दर्शितम् ॥ ३६८ ॥
समुद्रं विलिखेयुर्वै सर्वे मन्त्रिगणास्ततः ।
राजा दृष्टमिति लिखेद् द्राक् सम्यग्दर्शनाक्षमः ॥ ३६९ ॥

The set endorsements are all in Sanskrit. This implies that the procedure belongs to the period of the Sanskrit revival which is now to be dated in the light of history of the Śuṅga revolution between 150 B.C. and 100 A.C. (*J.B.O.R.S.*, IV, pp. 257–65).

The *Divyāvadāna* (pp. 404 and 429) also uses the word *gaṇa* to denote the Cabinet or Council of Ministers (*amātya-gaṇa*).

truly, as the *Śukranīti* says, *akshama* or incapable of criticising it. The first submission to the king from the ministers in their individual capacity seems to be an opportunity given to the king to discuss the matter and to make his suggestions.

Resolution with king's fiat was the 'real king'

The document became the resolution of the state with the fiat of the king. And in the eye of the constitutional law that document became 'the king'. To quote the language of the *Sukranīti*:[9] "*The document signed and sealed by the king is the king and not the king himself.*" The officers could not obey any unwritten 'order' of the king. For the signed and sealed order of the king, which as a matter of fact was an order of the Council, being the real king, any one who obeyed an actual order of the king in flesh and blood was regarded in the eye of the constitutional law as obeying an outsider, or, in the language of the *Śukranīti* a 'thief'[10] obeying a 'thief':—

Oral 'orders'

"*A king or an officer who orders or does a business of state without a lekhya* (official document) *are both thieves at all times.*"

As a written *lekhya* became really the order of the Ministry on account of the routine, a king who wanted his personal orders to be observed must take recourse to oral commands and requests. And when an oral command was issued, according to the constitution implied here, the officers had to deal with the command of a thief-in-law, and trouble was a certain consequence to the king. We have, thanks to the inscriptions of Aśkoa, an immortal evidence of this trouble. Aśoka issued orders regarding his proclamations and sermons (*sāvakaṃ*) and gifts (*dāpakaṃ*), and the '*Parisā*' (Council) discussed the 'orders' and 'shelved' them. The angry monarch orders that he should be informed when his oral orders are rejected.[11]

---

[9] *Śukranītisāra*, II. 292—

नृपसंचिन्हितं लेख्यं नृपस्तन्न नृपो नृपः ।

[10] *Ibid.*, II. 291—

अलेख्यमाज्ञापयति ह्यलेख्यं यत्करोति यः ।
राजकृत्यमुभौ चोरौ तौ भृत्यनृपतौ सदा ॥

[11] *Indian Antiquary*, 1913, p. 282.

The essence of the constitution as sketched in the *Śukra-niti* is that the king had actually no power in his own and sole hand. All administrative functions were vested in the Council.[12]

Megasthenes on Ministry's jurisdiction

The account of India left by Megasthenes are to be gleaned from fragments. The fragments as we find them indicate that the actual government did vest in the Cabinet or Council, that the Council was very much respected, and that it had a high character and tradition of wisdom behind it. It deliberated on public affairs and it 'chose' and appointed governors, chiefs of provinces, deputy governors, superintendents (or '*adhyakshas*') of treasury, generals of the army and admirals of the navy, and high officers to superintend agriculture.

(*a*) "The seventh caste consists of the *Councillors* and *Assessors*—of those who deliberate on public affairs. It is the smallest class looking to number, but the most respected, on account of the high character and wisdom of its members."[13]

(*b*) "The seventh class consists of the *Councillors* and *Assessors* of the king. To them belong the highest posts of Government, the tribunals of justice, and the general administration of public affairs."[14]

(*c*) "In point of numbers this is a small class, but it is distinguished by superior wisdom and justice, and hence enjoys the prerogative of choosing governors, chiefs of provinces, deputy governors, superintendents of the treasury, generals of the army, admirals of the navy, controllers and commissioners who superintend agriculture."[15]

This description of the constitutional powers has the direct support in home records. Bhāradvāja, a famous authority on Hindu Politics quoted both in the *Māhābhārata* and in Kauṭilya's *Artha-Śāstra*, sums up the jurisdiction of ministers in these words:

Agreement between Bhāradvāja and Megasthenes

[12] This is supported by the *Mahābhārata*, cited in pp. 304-05 above.

[13] *Epitome of Megasthenes*, Diodorus, II. 41; McCrindle, *Megasthenes*, p. 43.

[14] *Strabo*, XV. 48; McCrindle, *Megasthenes*, p. 85.

[15] *Arrian*, XII; McCrindle, *Megasthenes*, p. 212.

"Between degeneration of the king and the degeneration of the ministers that of the ministers is more serious. (1) Deliberation on the policy of state (*mantra*), (2) realization of the result of that policy, (3) execution of business, (4) the business concerning income and expenditure, (5) army and (6) its leading, (7) providing against enemy and wild tribes (*aṭavī*), (8) maintenance of government, (9) providing against (national) degeneration, (10) protection of the princes and their consecration (coronation) are vested in the 'Ministers'."[16]

(1) *Mantra* of Bhāradvāja corresponds to the '*deliberation on public affairs*' of Megasthenes, (2), (3) and (8) of Bhāradvāja correspond to the 'general administration of public affairs' of Megasthenes, (5), (6) and (7) to 'choosing generals and admirals' of Megasthenes, (8) to Megasthenes' 'choosing governors, chiefs of provinces,' and (4) to 'choosing superintendents of the treasury' and controllers of agriculture.

The 'Assessors' are either the '*Tīrthas*' or the junior ministers (pp. 302–04 above), while the 'Councillors' are the members of the *Maṇtri* Council.

Thus the jurisdiction of the Ministry or Council is fully ascertained. The constitutional law noticed above is borne out by that defined jurisdiction.

Working of the constitution in Aśoka's reign

Under such a constitution if a king had despotic tendencies the result would be a deadlock and a revolution: either the king would be made to mend his ways or the constitution would be subverted and the ministers put in prison or assigned to the executioner. But the ministers had the *Paura*

[16] स्वाम्यमात्यव्यसनयोरमात्यव्यसनं गरीय इति । मन्त्रो मन्त्रफलावाप्तिः कर्मानुष्ठानमायव्ययकर्म दण्डाप्रणयनममित्राटवीप्रतिषेधो राज्यरक्षणं व्यसन-प्रतीकारः कुमाररक्षणमभिषेकश्च कुमाराणामायत्तममात्येषु । Quotation in Kauṭilya, VIII. I. 127, p. 320. This jurisdiction is not controverted by Kauṭilya who says that as the 'Board of Ministers' and the Departments are designed by the king, and he stops degeneration in them, the king is more important. Dr. Shama Sastry has missed the meaning of *āyatta*. Its technical meaning as in law-books, is given here (see p. 320 below).

and the *Jānapada* behind them and the law and tradition of the country to support them.[17] Hindu institutions did not easily change, and constitutional laws once established and made sacred by the Śāstras could not be deviated from with impunity. We have the recorded instance of the pious despotism developed by Aśoka, and what was the result? Was the Ministry overthrown and the constitutional laws set at naught? Or was the despot deprived, if not of his throne, of his sovereignty? There is the combined evidence of Aśoka's inscription and the *Divyāvadāna*, both of which are adverse statements against interest and therefore entitled to perfect credence.

As the inscription referred to is one of the most important documents of the constitutional history of Hindu India I propose to give it here *in extenso*, omitting the last lines which are not relevant. It has remained a puzzle and an object of whimsical treatment by the translators of Aśoka's inscriptions, who never thought that there could be anything else but religious matters, in the 'Edicts' of Aśoka. Early interpreters (to whom India must be thankful for the first interpretations of Aśoka's proclamations) have grasped the letter, not the spirit, of the Proclamation[18] under discussion, *viz.*, that Aśoka made the officers called *Rajjukas* 'independent'. But the circumstances under which the independence in question was granted, and its nature, have been missed. The text is as follows:

देवानं पिये पियदसि लाज हेवं आहा सडुवीसतिवस
अभिसितेन मे इयं धंमलिपि लिखापिता लजूका मे
बहूसु पानसतसहसेसु जनसि आयता तेसं ये अभिहाले वा
दंडे वा अतपतिये मे कटे किं ति लजूका अस्वथ अभीता
कंमानि पवतयेवू जनस जानपदसा हितसुखं उपदहेवू
अनुगहिनेवु चा सुखीयन दुखीयनम् जानिसंति धंमयुतेन च

[17] On the power of the people to depose a king and set up another in his place see *Mahābhārata*, *Āśvamedha-Parvan*, IV. 8–11. See the *History of Kashmir* (*R.T.*, VII. 703), where the Ministry opposes Harsha's succession and thereupon Utkarsha is invited to the throne.

[18] Pillar Proclamations, IV. (Delhi—Sivalak); cf. *Divyāvadāna*, p. 430.

वियोवदिसंति **जनं जानपदं** किंति हिदतं च पालतं च
आलाधयेवू ति लजूका पि लघंति पटिचलिटवे
मं पुलिसानि पि मे छंदंनानि पटिचलिसंति ते पि
चकानि वियोवदिसंति ये न मं लजूका
चघंति आलाधयितवे अथा हि पजं वियताये धातिये निसिजितु
अस्वथे होति वियतधाति चघति मे पजं सुखं पलिहटवे
हेवं ममा लजूका कटा **जानपदस** हितसुखाये येन एते अभीता
अस्वथ संतं **अविमना** कं मानि पवतयेवूति एतेन मे लजूकानं
अभीहाले व दंडे वा अतपतिये कटे इछितविये हि एसा किंति
वियोहालसमता च सिय दंडसमता चा अवहते पि च मे आवुति[19]

It means :

" 'Devānāmpriya' (His Fortunate Majesty) King Priya-darśin (another name of Aśoka) thus says :[20]

" In the year twenty-six (elapsed) of my coronation this document of law was caused by me to be recorded :

" The Rajūkas[21] of mine have jurisdiction over the People who are numerous (hundreds of thousands). Those Rājūkas who are either over (the departments) of *Abhihāra* (War) or *Daṇḍa* (Home Administration) are made (declared) by me to be Protectors by themselves ('of sovereign jurisdiction,' *ātmapatiye*). Why so ? So that the Rājūkas without agitation and with peace of mind (*lit.*, without apprehension) may carry on the business, may administer to the weal and happiness of the nation and the *Jānapada* and may grant them *anugrahas*.

" They shall know as to who are happy and who are in difficulty and distress. They will also get the Nation and the

---

[19] The *āvuti* is :

बंधनबधानं मुनिसानं तीलितदंडानं पतवधानं तिंनि दिवसानि मे योते दिंने नातिका व कानि निभपयिसंति जीविताये तानं नासंतं व निझपयितवे दानं दाहंति पालतिकं उपवासं व कछंति इछा हि मे हेवं निलुधसि पि कालसि पालतं आलाधयेवू ति जनस च वढति विविधे धंमचलने समये दानसविभागेति । Mathia version, *Epigraphia Indica*, II. 253.

[20] 'Thus says'—a style in royal documents to denote '*Proclamations*,' *Artha-Śāstra*, p. 71.

[21] See p. 299 above.

Jānapada advised by the Ecclesiastical Service. Thereby they (the *Rajjukas*) may secure this world and the world beyond.

"If the Rajūkas disregard (*laghanti* = *laṅghanti*) my proclamations, my subordinate officers (*purushas*, cf. *Artha-Śāstra*, p. 245) will promulgate my opinion and orders.[22]

"And they (Rajūkas) will advise the Provinces (*Chakāni*)[23] which wish to serve the Rajūkas, not me.[24] Therefore let me indeed, consign the (Child) Subject to the *viyatā* ('anxious') Nurse. The anxious Nurse becomes tranquil; she wants to defend well my Prājā.[25]

"In this manner my Rajūkas have been made for the good and happiness of the *Jānapada*.

"So that they may with peace of mind, without agitation and without any feeling of hostility (*avimanā*) carry on business. I do make hereby my Rajūkas independent in War and Peace (administration).

"This indeed I desire, *viz*., that the sameness of civil and criminal justice should remain. And though fallen from position (*avaite* = *ava-ṛita*)[26] my prayer[27] is that....(etc.)"

The rule for the maintenance of which the emperor prays here is about allowing religious service to prisoners under sentence of death. It is significant that the king now 'prays' and does not 'command' as in other documents. In the

---

[22] *Chhandaṁ anāni* : cf. *āṇaṁ*, *Jātaka*, I. 398.

[23] Bühler, *Cha kāni*, in the sense of 'some ones'. The corrected reading is indicated by Prof. Rāmāvatāra Śarmā (*Piyadarśi-praśastayaḥ*, p. 33).

[24] ये न मं लाजूकं चघंति अलाधयितवे । (Mathia). Former reading : येन मं लजूका etc. The last word has been taken as *lajūkā*. The Mathia plate (*Epigraphia Indica*, II, p. 250) suggests an *anusvāra*. Without the *anusvāra* the meaning would be slightly changed : "and they will advise the provinces, they the Rājūkas, who do not wish to serve me".

[25] There is a double meaning intended in *Pajaṁ* ('child', 'subjects'); *viyatā* ('anxious', 'separating herself'); and *sukhaṁ palihatave* ('defending', 'snatching away').

[26] *Cf.* the same formation in the *Vājasenyī Saṃhitā*.

[27] *Āvṛitti* in this sense occurs in the Vedic as well as later literature, Monier-William, *Dict.*, 1899, p. 156, *ā-vṛi*.

next regnal year, probably a few months after signing this document, the king composed a retrospect of his reign up to the year of signing this Rajjuka decree. Evidently he then regarded the period of his rule as a past chapter and as distinct from the period of mere reign thereafter.

The passages in the *Divyāvadāna* we have already seen. They clearly say that the Ministers including the *Yuvarāja* deprived the Maurya Emperor of his authority.

The *Jānapada*, as distinct from the *Prajā* and *loka* 'the people' (as in Pillar Proclamations IV and VII) is mentioned here, and it was for their benefit that the Rajūkas wanted independence. The *Jānapada* evidently supported the ministers. The Buddhist monks might well cry at the fate that deprived the Emperor of India of his *aiśvaryya* or sovereign authority. But they do not, as they could not, call the Ministers sinful for that. The Emperor bowed to the authority of the laws of his country. The politicians under the leadership of the polite but firm Rādha-Gupta[28] and the *Pauras* according to the *Divyāvadāna*, listened to the sarcasms of the Emperor—a feature in the Emperor's language even in the inscription—and they let the otherwise great Emperor continue in the enjoyment of his throne and title and preach what they probably considered his 'sublime nonsense'. But the political writers do not seem to have let the license of monkish professions pass unnoticed. 'The *dharma* of the king indeed is the suppression of the evil and the rearing up of the good and not the shaving of the head (becoming a Buddhist monk) or the growing of matted hair.'[29]

A Resolution of the Ministry in Kālidāsa

We are thankful to Kālidāsa for giving in one of his dramas[30] an illustration of the working of the Council of Ministers. The scene is laid in the Śuṅga times. Agnimitra was ruling as a sub-king over the province of Vidiśā in the time of

[28] Probably a descendant of Vishṇu-gupta (Kauṭilya).

[29] राज्ञो हि दुष्टनिग्रहः शिष्टपरिपालनञ्च धर्मो न पुनः शिरोमुण्डनं जटाधारणं वा ।—Quotation in *Nītivākyāmṛita*, Ch. V.

[30] *Mālavikāgnimitra* (M. R. Kāle's ed.), Act V, pp. 903–08; Translation, pp. 59–60 (1922, published by Gopal Narayan & Co., Kalbadevi Road, Bombay).

Pushyamitra. After the successful conclusion of a war with the king of Vidarbha, who had been a supporter of the late Maurya dynasty, the Prime Minister (called here *Amātya* as in Manu's Code) sends a message to the king (Agnimitra): "*We*" (the Council of Ministers) "*have decided what is to be done with regard to Vidarbha*" ('*Vidarbha-gatam anushṭheyam avadhāritam asmābhiḥ*') *I just wish to know Your Majesty's opinion.* Thereupon His Majesty intimates his own view, which the Lord Chamberlain Maudgalya carries to the Council of the Prime Minister. On his return he congratulates the king and announces the reply of the Prime Minister: '*Happy is the insight of His Majesty: such is also the judgment* ('darśanam') *of the Council-of-Ministers* (*Mantri-Parishat*)"; whereupon the king concludes "*Thou, tell the Council of Ministers thus—'please write to General Virasena to act accordingly'*". The General was in command of the Śuṅgan army of occupation. The full text is given below from the edition of Mr. M. R. Kale, with his English translation.

कञ्चुकी—देव कथान्तरेणान्तरितम्। अमात्यो विज्ञापयति। विदर्भगत-मनुष्ठेयमवधारितमस्माभिः। देवस्य तावदभिप्रेतं श्रोतुमिच्छामीति।

राजा—मौद्गल्य तत्रभवतो भ्रात्रियज्ञसेन माधवसेनयोर्द्वयो [*var. lect.* द्वै-]

राज्यमिदानीमवस्थापयितु कामोऽस्मि।

तौ पृथग्वरदाकूले शिष्टामुत्तरदक्षिणो।

नक्तं दिवं विमज्योभौ शीतोष्णकिरणाविव ॥ १३ ॥

कञ्चुकी—देव एवममात्यपरिषदे निवेदयामि।

राजा—(अङ्गुल्या अनुमन्यते।)

(निष्क्रान्तः कञ्चुकी)

प्रथमा—(जनान्तिकम्) भर्तृदारिके दिष्ट्या भर्तृदारकोऽर्धराज्ये प्रतिष्ठां-गमिष्यति।

मालविका—एतत्तावद्बहुमन्तव्यम् यज्जीवित संशयान्मुक्तः॥

(प्रविश्य)

कञ्चुकी—विजययतां देवः। देव अमात्यो विज्ञापयति। कल्याणी देवस्य बुद्धिः। मन्त्रिपरिषदोऽप्येवमेव दर्शनम्। कुतः।

द्विधाविभक्तां श्रियमुद्वहन्तौ

धुरं रथाश्वाविव संग्रहीतुः।

तौ-स्थास्यतस्ते नृपती निदेशे

परस्परावग्रहनिर्विकारी ॥ १४ ॥

राजा—तेन हि मन्त्रिपरिषदं ब्रूहि । सेनापतये वीरसेनाय लिख्यतामेवं क्रियतामिति ।[31]

TRANSLATION :

Chamberlain.—" My lord, the introduction of another matter did not allow me to tell it. The Prime Minister (*Amātya*) begs to say—' *We have decided how matters in connection with Vidarbha are to be settled ; we just wish to know Your Majesty's opinion.*'

King.—Maudgalya, I wish to establish a double monarchy with respect to those honoured cousins, Yajñasena and Mādhavasena.

Let the two govern separately the (territory lying on the Northern and Southern banks of the Varadā, as the moon and the sun rule, dividing between themselves, the night and the day (13).

Chamberlain.—My lord, I shall thus inform the Council of Ministers.

King.—

—(*consents by a motion of his finger*).

(*Exit* Chamberlain.)

First Maiden.—(Aside) Princess, it is a matter for congratulation that the Prince will be established in half of the kingdom.

Mālavikā.—" This should be considered a great thing, in the first place, that he has been rescued from peril to his life.

(*Having entered*)

Chamberlain.—Victory to Your Majesty ! My lord, the (Prime) Minister respectfully says—Happy is Your Majesty's idea ; such is the view of the Ministers also. For,

The two kings possessing royalty divided (equally) between them, and causing no disturbance owing to mutual restraint, will abide by your command, as the two horses bearing the yoke (of a chariot, the weight of which is) equally divided, and harmless, being mutually restrained, follow the will of the charioteer (14).

King.—Tell the Cabinet then to send a despatch to General Viraśena to this effect.

This shows that the constitutional practice in the days of Kālidāsa was that the Council of Ministers was vested with the authority to decide upon the course of action to be taken even in matters of a conquered territory—whether in appointing feudatories or establishing direct Government. The Ministry first decided the matter themselves and then consulted the king's wishes. The practice was well enough established to be enacted on the stage before princes and the public.

---

[31] I am thankful to Mr. B. Upādhyāya for drawing my attention to the correct text. In some editions the text is corrupt and meaningless. Mr. Kāle bases his text on the editions of S. P. Pandit, Appā Śāstri, and S. S. Ayyar.

Junior Ministers or Under-Secretaries

Before we close this brief survey of Hindu Ministry let us note a few more details about their composition. Each minister had two junior ministers or Under-Secretaries.[32] The chief of the three was distinguished by the title *Mahāmātra*' 'Of great measure'. Thus the *Mahā-Sāndhivigrahika*, for instance, of inscriptions is a *Mahāmātra*, the senior minister in charge of foreign affairs, while the simple *Sāndhivigrahika* is a junior minister. In the Gupta inscriptions and seals we have a class designated as *Kumārāmātyas*. Their position in the Gupta period seems to be that of Junior ministers.[33] With regard to the *Daṇḍa-nāyaka* (p. 320 below) class we have in the Gupta inscriptions *Mahā-daṇḍa-nāyaka*, *Daṇḍa-nāyaka* and *Daṇḍanāyaka-Kumārāmātya*.

Transfers

The ministers were transferred from one portfolio to another.[34] The transfers were made every three years, or after every five, seven or ten years.[35] For "authority should not be given in one's

---

[32] *Śukranītisāra*, II. 109–10—

एकस्मिन्नधिकारे तु पुरुषाणां त्रयं सदा ।
नियुञ्जीत प्राज्ञनमं मुख्यमेकं तु तेषु वै ॥
द्वौ दर्शकौ तु तत्कार्ये

[33] There are *Kumārāmātyas* in Nālадā seals as district officers. *Kumārāmātya* ('Prince Minister') originally was a title of the highest distinction, as it appears from Bhāsa (*Pratijñā Yaugandharāyaṇa*, II). *J.B.O.R.S.*, XVII. 399. (The title 'Prince Minister' was conferred on men even who were not princes of the blood.) *Kumārāmātya* thus should be the highest Minister, but in Gupta times his position seems to be that of a junior officer. See also Bhaṭṭa-Bhāskara cited above p. 295 above) who regards *Kumāra-Adhyaksha* as the highest minister.

[34] *Śukranītisāra*, II. 107–13—

परिवर्त्य नृपो ह्येतान्युञ्ज्यादन्योऽन्यकर्मणि ।
नाधिकारं चिरं दद्याद्यस्मैकस्मै सदा नृपः
*   *   *   *
अतः कार्यक्षमं दृष्ट्वा कार्येऽन्ये तं नियोजयेत् ।
तत्कार्ये कुशलं चान्यं तत्पदानुगतं खलु ॥

[35] *Ibid.*, II. 110—

..हायनैस्तन्निवर्त्तयेत् । त्रिभिर्वा पञ्चभिर्वापि सप्तभिर्दशभिश्च वा ॥

hand for a long time. A capable minister should be put in charge of another work (department), and a new competent man should step into his shoes." The rules of three-yearly transfer and of five-yearly transfer are referred to as '*dharma*' or law by Aśoka in his inscriptions at Dhauli and Jaugaḍa (separate proclamations). The whole Council (*Varga*) of Ministers (*Mahāmātras*) went out or rather were 'made to go out', to quote the language of the Emperor, every three or five years. The process is officially called *anusaṃyāna*, that is, 'regular departure', which may be compared with the word '*anugata*' in the above quotation from the *Śukranīti* and with '*anusaṃyāntu*' in the *Rāmāyaṇa*.[36] In the *Rāmāyaṇa* it comes in connection with the '*going out*' of guards to the passes on the route which Bharata was shortly to use.

Caste representation in Ministry

As in other matters, *e.g.*, in the coronation, so in the exercise of the executive power each of the four divisions of the Hindu society was represented. The coronation details given by Nīlakaṇṭha and Mitramiśra show that ministers were taken from all the *Varṇas* up to the last days of Hindu régime. The *Mahābhārata* gives a list of thirty-seven Ministers recruited on the principle of representation from each *varṇa*: four Brahmins, eight Kshatriyas, twenty-one Vaiśyas and three Śūdras, and finally one *Sūta* who was of the mixed caste. The remarkable point is that the largest class (Vaiśya) had the largest number in the Ministry. The Śūdra and the Brahmin are almost equally divided. The real ministry, as it says, was composed of eight members only.[37]

---

[36] *Śukranītisāra*, II. 79. 13; Konow, *A.S.I.*, 1913–14, p. 113—

वने वत्स्याम्यहं दुर्गे रामो राजा भविष्यति ॥ १२ ॥

क्रियतां शिल्पिभिः पन्थाः समानि विषमाणि च ।

रक्षिणश्चानुसंयान्तु पथि दुर्गविचारकाः ॥

'Let the guards go out (after the *Śilpins*) who know the passes on the way.'

[37] *Mahābhārata*, *Śānti*, Ch. 85, 7–11 (Kumb.).

Official designations in Gupta times

The designations of the Ministers in Gupta times changed. We have already seen the *Sāndhivigrahika* superseding the old term *Dūta*. This was evidently necessary to avoid confusion and distinguish the *Minister of Diplomacy* from the *Ambassador*. We do not find *Mantrin* used in the inscriptions of the period. Here again a desire to use an unambiguous expression seems to have operated. For, the minister *Daṇḍanāyaka* or rather *Mahā-Daṇḍanāyaka* appears to have taken its place. In Manu (XI. 100), *Daṇḍanetṛitva* is distinguished from *Senāpatya* and means the leadership of the administration, which in view of Manu's definition of *Amātya's* jurisdiction (*amātye daṇḍa āyattaḥ*. Manu, VII. 56) means the authority of the Prime Minister. *Mahā-Daṇḍanāyaka*, therefore, 'vested *with the leadership of Daṇḍa* (or administration)' would signify the minister in charge of administration or the Prime Minister. This appears to be the more natural interpretation as against the one given by Fleet, *i.e.*, 'the leader of the forces' (*C.I.I.*, III, p. 16 *n.*), for the ministers who bear that title in the inscriptions were civilian officers as proved by their other titles. Further, in that period the military minister seems to be designated *Balādhikṛit* (*Ibid.*, p. 210) and *Mahābalādhikṛit* (p. 109).

The rule of transfer noticed above is illustrated by the occurrence of the ministerial designations in the documents of the period. Harisheṇa, who, as the great inscription of Samudra-Gupta says (Fleet, *C.I.I.*, III. 10), was closely associated with the Emperor and who is described to have gained inspiration for his *Kārya* from that association, was *Mahā-Daṇḍanāyaka*. He had been a Junior Minister of Diplomacy before. But at the time the *Kārya* of Harisheṇa was actually inscribed he was no more *Mahā-Daṇḍanāyaka*. At that time the office was held by another learned gentleman, Tila-Bhaṭṭaka. Past ministers were allowed the courtesy of the employment of their late official designations in official documents, *e.g.*, the father of Harisheṇa who had been *Mahā-Daṇḍanāyaka* in former times is mentioned with that designation in Samudra-Gupta's record.

Charters of grant made by kings in the Gupta period are countersigned by one of the ministers, the *Sāndhivigrahika*.

According to Bṛihaspati a document of gift should obtain the endorsement '*jñātammayā*' or "noted by me" from the office of the *Sāndhi-vigrahika*.[38] Bṛihaspati's law code was a work of the period and this provision is of importance. It shows that the charters which bear the name of that minister or his office were really noted by his department. This procedure throws light on the constitutional position of the ministers in that period. Even a humble gift had to be sanctioned by the ministry and it was sanctioned on their behalf by the *Sāndhi-vigrahika* who apparently had to consider whether the gift was right from the point of view of the foreign department. Donees might be outsiders come in the kingdom, they might be enemy spies; the foreign office, therefore, was the first authority to sanction or to reject the gift which would be passed as a matter of course by the other members of the government. The charters bear the countersignature of the officer or his assistant who passed it last. He is called *Dūtaka* or 'despatcher'. The copper-plate grant made by king Hastin[39] in the year corresponding to 510 A.C. is first sanctioned by *Mahāsāndhi-vigrahika* Vidhudatta and finally passed by the senior minister of the army, *Mahābalādhikṛit*, Nāgasimha who signs as the *Dūtaka*. Another grant made by a contemporary of Hastin[40] is signed by a man who has no official title; it is not countersigned by any minister and it is recorded to have been made on the oral order of the ruler. The charter has no *Dūtaka* either. It is evident that the grant did not pass through the Council as there was no written order of the ruler. It might have been made from the private lands of the donor.

Charters countersigned by Ministers

It is a known fact that Ceylon had numerous institutions in common with India. In fact both had practically the same civilization, and from that point of view Ceylon was a part of India. A Ceylonese friend of mine has often told me that the history of India can never be complete

Illustrations of the practice from Ceylon

---

[38] Quoted by *Vīramitrodaya*, p. 192—

ज्ञातं मयेति लिखितं सन्धिविग्रहलेखकैः ।

[39] *C.I.I.*, III, p. 108.

[40] *Ibid.*, p. 115.

without the history of Ceylon. It must be admitted that it is true. Here we have an illustration. In India while we lost our institutions under stress from outside and decay from within, they lived longer in the island girt by the great sea-moat. As late as the middle of the tenth cenutry A.C. the orders issued by the king are orders of the Council or His Majesty-in-Council (*Sabhā*). All the members of the Council sign the document. See for instance the record of king Abhā-salamevan edited by Dr. Wikramasinghe in *Epigraphia Zeylanica*, Volume II, p. 1, where the whole Council conjointly makes the gift, the grant of privilege :

"Whereas it was decreed by His Majesty-in-Council, we, all of us, namely, Manitila, Kiliyem and Gangulhusu Aga-boyim · · ·and Kavasilangā Gavayim have conjointly with due inaugural ceremonies (*abhishekādi*) granted (the following immunities to the village Itnarugama in the district of · · · · · · · ·" (p. 5).

CHAPTER XXXII

Law and Administration of Justice

King under the Law

Apart from the operation of the Coronation-Oath, the checks and limitations imposed by the *Paura-Jānapada* and the Council, there was the all-powerful Law, the Common, Law of the Hindus, which is declared again and again to be above the king and as the king of kings.[1] In *Manu* the king is made liable to be fined.[2] His powers and obligations are defined in the law-sūtras and law-books as part and parcel of the law (in chapters on Constitutional Law, the *Rājadharma* or 'Laws for Kings'). Even in the palmiest days of Hindu Monarchy, neither in the *Mānava-Dharma-Śāstra* nor in the *Artha-Śāstra*, was the king placed above the law. He could make new laws according to the *Artha-Śāstra*, according to *Manu* he could not do so; but when he could make laws he passed only regulatory laws[3] and not laws substantive or laws making him arbitrary.

The judges in Persia under Cambyses "found a law that the Persian king might do whatever he pleased".[4] But such a finding was impossible to be come to by Hindu judges and lawyers; so much so that even the author of the *Artha-Śāstra* tells his prince that destruction befalls an arbitrary king.[3]

Judiciary and Executive separate

The administration of justice under Hindu monarchy remained always separate from the executive, and generally independent in form and ever independent in spirit. The reason for this was that lawyers were appointed Judges, and lawyers as a rule were from amongst the Brahmins. It was in the pre-classical period (1000 B.C.–500 B.C.) while the Hindu king was

---

1 See the quotation in the *Vyavasthā Darpaṇa*.

2 "Where common man would be fined one Kārshāpaṇa the king shall be fined one-thousand; that is the settled law," VIII. 336—

कार्षापणं भवेद्दण्ड्यो यत्रान्यः प्राकृतो जनः ।
तत्र राजा भवेदण्ड्यः सहस्रमिति धारणा ॥

3 *Artha-Śāstra*, Bk. I, Ch. 3; 3 (p. 11).

4 Rawlinson, *Herodotus*, II, p. 468.

putting or had put on a new garb, that the Brahmin transformed himself from the humble position of the 'Repeater of Songs' ('Brāhmaṇa') into a political estate. The priest-Brahmin became distinct from the Brahmin of politics and ordinary life. The two divisions are clear in the *Śatapatha Brāhmaṇa*. At the coronation ceremony, as we have seen, after the consecration the priest as such does homage to the king, and the Brahmin as an estate of the realm does homage along with the Kshatriyas and others. The class which was midway between the priestly and the non-priestly Brahmins was of the Mahāśāla Brahmins (p. 272 above), the Brahmins of study and action. They mainly devoted their energies to sciences like *dharma*, law, politics and cognate subjects. In the *Jātakas* we have the Purohita politician and Brahmin ministers as embodiments of political wisdom and moral rectitude. To this class belonged the judges. Under the common law the culprit who had committed a crime was to be punished by the king. But under *dharma* law he was also to be punished for the sin implied in the crime.[5] The latter jurisdiction was relegated to the Brahmin. This was because not only he was an expert in the matter, but also because Brahmin culprits were to be dealt with who were to be judged by one who was their equal and who could have no hesitation in punishing them in matters of *dharma* delinquency. The Brahmin for the *dharma* administration was thus absolutely necessary. We find this jurisdiction being exercised by the Purohita in the *Jātakas*. He at the same time heard and decided, sitting along with other officers (probably non-Brahmins), cases of secular law. Law proper and law ecclesiastical in administration tended to unite into one and unite in the hand of the Brahmin judge. And the Brahmin was fairly above the influence of the king.

Sabhā

Then the law-court bore the ancient Vedic name, the *Sabhā*. As the Council of Ministers retained the traces of their independent origin so did the *Sabhā*. The judges were always helped by the community in the administration of justice. They made up the *Sabhā* and were, to quote a modern word, the jury of the court.

---

[5] This is discussed in my *Tagore Lectures*, X.

Their number was odd, to provide for voting (p. 95, *n*. 14, above); and it was enjoined on them to speak according to law. A jury which kept its mouth shut or spoke what is not *Dharma*, was considered immoral.[6]

In the court-scene of the *Mṛichchhakaṭika*, which I regard as the product of the third century A.C.,[7] the jury is mentioned.[8] The function of the jury we find defined in the *Śukranīti* as well as in Bṛihaspati and Nārada[9]; it deserves notice. There the jury is to be composed of 7, 5, or 3,[9] and they are defined as "the examiners of the cause," while the judge, their president, is the "speaker" and the king as carrying out the punishment. In the *Mṛichhakaṭika* the judge says, 'We are authority in deciding the guilt or otherwise. The rest is in the hands of the king'.[10] It was the jury's separate province (*karma proktam pṛithak pṛithak*: Bṛihaspati) to consider the truth or

---

[6] Nārada, Intro., III. 18 (*na sā sabhā yatra na santi vṛiddhā, vṛiddhā na te ye na vadanti dharmam*).

"Either the Judicial Assembly must not be entered at all, or a fair opinion delivered. That man who, either stands mute or delivers an opinion contrary to justice is sinner." Nārada, Intro. III. 10 (Jolly).

[7] In its time the Kushān coin *Nāṇaka* was current.

[8] *Mṛichchhakatika*, Act IX, verse 14—

चिन्तासक्तनिमग्नमन्त्रिसलिलं ।

[9] *Śukranītisāra*, IV. 5. 26–27—

लोकवेदज्ञधर्मज्ञाः सप्त पञ्च त्रयोऽपि वा ।
तत्रोपविष्टा विप्रा स्युः सा यज्ञसदृशी सभा ॥
श्रोतारो वणिजस्तत्र कर्त्तव्याः सुविचक्षणाः ।

* * *

See also *Ibid.*, 14, 17—

यदा विप्रो न विद्वान्स्यात् क्षत्रियं तत्र योजयेत् ।
वैश्यं वा धर्मशास्त्रज्ञं शूद्रं यत्नेन वर्जयेत् ॥
राज्ञा नियोजितव्यास्ते सभ्याः सर्वासु जातिषु ।
वक्ताध्यक्षो नृपः शास्ता सभ्याः कार्यपरीक्षकाः ॥

—*Ibid.*, 40; Bṛihaspati in *Vīramitrodaya*, p. 42. *Cf.* Nārada, Intro., II. 45.—"One condemned by the Judges shall be punished by the king according to law." "Justice is said to depend upon the Jury." Nārada, Intro., III. 6.

[10] आर्य चारुदत्त! निर्णये वयं प्रमाणम् । शेषे तु राजा Act. IX.

otherwise of the cause brought before the court. Thus even when justice was dispensed by royal judges there was a safeguard against the leanings of the judge.

King-in-Council as Judge

We have already seen that the king by himself was not allowed to hear cases.[11] He heard cases sitting in his Council which included the Chief Justice. These were cases which went on appeal to him as the highest court of appeal.[12] This is indicated by the authorities quoted below and still more clearly by the case decided by King Yaśaskara noted in the *Rājataraṅgiṇī* (Ch. VI). The appellant had lost his case in all the lower courts and now he appealed from the judgment of the Justices to King Yaśaskara. He heard it in Council along with the judges of the capital who had already heard the matter. The practice of the king hearing original cases must have been given up very early as there is scanty evidence showing that it was ever done in post-Vedic times.

As the king could not govern by himself personally, so he was not allowed to administer justice, as pointed out above, by himself. This was not only the opinion of the code-writers but also the opinion of the constitutional lawyers who prohibit the king to decide cases by himself.[13]

Justice administered in king's name

In the theory the king always presided over the court, whether he was present there or not.[14] The decree given under the seal of the court was called a document given by the king. When a man was summoned to attend the court

---

[11] Nārada, Intro., I. 35—'प्राड्विवाकमते स्थितः'; Bṛihaspati, I. 24. 'सभ्यशास्त्रमते स्थितः' (*Smṛiti Chandrikā*).

[12] Nārada, Intro., I. 7; Bṛihaspati, I. 29; Yājnavalkya, II. 30.

[13] *Śukranītisāra*, IV. 5. 5–6—

धर्मशास्त्रानुसारेण क्रोधलोभविवर्जितः ।
सप्राड्विवाकः सामात्यः सब्राह्मणपुरोहितः
समाहितमतिः पश्येद्व्यवहारानुक्रमात् ॥
नैकः पश्येच्च कार्याणि वादिनोः शृणुयाद्वचः ।
रहसि च नृपः प्राज्ञः सभ्याश्चैव कदाचन ॥

[14] *Viramitrodaya*, pp. 39–42; *Manu*, VIII. 1. 19.

it was supposed that the king called him. The language of the law-books invariably employs the word 'king' as doing all matters of legal execution, and the commentators explain that the 'king' there means only the officer.

Records kept

Records of cases decided were kept. Such records are mentioned as early as the *Jātakas*. *Viniśchaya-pustaka* is mentioned in Vol. III, p. 292. Even laws of procedure of a monarchy inscribed on gold tablets are referred to in Vol. V, p. 125. That the records were kept in the time of the law-books is evidenced by themselves.[15]

Justice was administered openly ('*narahasi*') not in 'private'[16] and never by one judge.

Proper Justice and fall in litigation

According to the ideal which prevailed in the time of the *Jātakas* right administration of justice resulted in a fall of litigation.[17] Of course the same result would follow equally from an unjust administration. There is however no allusion to such a state of affairs. Constitutionally the latter was impossible in view of the legal sanction.[18]

Sudatta *vs.* Prince Jeta

An incidental reference to actual administration of justice is found in the Pāli Canon. It throws a flood of light on the purity of justice, disclosing a real rule of law.

In the Vinaya Piṭaka, *Chullavagga*, VI. 4. 9, the case of the Anātha-Piṇḍika *versus* Jeta, the Prince Royal, which was decided by the Court of Śrāvastī, the then capital of Oudh, is related to show the great devotion of the Anātha-Piṇḍika to the Śākya Teacher and not to record any extraordinary judicial decision. Sudatta, who was generally called the Anātha-Piṇḍika ("Orphans' co-parcener") on account of his kindness to orphans, was an ordinary citizen—a *gṛihapati*—a leading and rich merchant; Jeta was one of the princes of the blood.

---

15 *E.g.*, see *Vasishtha*, p. 55.

16 *Śukranītisāra*, IV. 5. 6 (see quotation on p. 236 above).

17 *Jātaka*, II, p. 2.

18 *Manu*, VII. 28; Bṛihaspati, II. 28; *cf.* the revolution related in the *Mṛichchhakaṭika*.

The latter had a garden "not too far from the town and not too near, convenient for going and coming .... well-fitted for a retired life." The liberal Anātha-Piṇḍika thought of buying this garden for the use of the Buddha whom he had invited from Rājagṛiha. He went to Prince Jeta and said to him, "Your Highness, let me have your garden to make an *Ārāma* (rest-house) on it." "It is not, O gentleman, for sale, unless it is laid over with crores (of money pieces)." "I take, Your Highness, the garden (at this price)."

"No, gentleman, the garden has not been taken." Then they asked the lords of justice whether the garden was bought (lit., taken) or not. And the lords decided thus: 'Your Highness fixed the price and the garden has been taken.'[19]

On obtaining the decree while the Anātha-Piṇḍika had a part of the garden covered with gold coins, the rest was relinquished by the Prince without further payment.

Here we have a Prince and a private citizen submitting their case to the law-court and the court deciding against a Royal Prince, and the Prince accepting that decision,—all as a matter of course. The case attracted attention not for the principle of offer and acceptance, not as illustrating the independence of the judges, but as observed above, on account of the devotion of the charitable citizen to the Teacher. The

---

[19] Text—Ch. VI. 4. 9—

उपसङ्कमित्वा जेतं कुमारं एतद् अवोचः देहि मे अय्यपुत्त उय्यान आरामं कातुम् ति। अदेय्यो गहपति आरामो अपि कोटिसन्थरेना ति। गहितो अय्यपुत्त आरामो ति। न गहपति गहितो आरामो ति। गहितो न गहितो ति वोहारिके महामत्ते पुच्छिसु। महामत्ता एवम् आहंसु यतो तया अय्यपुत्त अग्घो कतो गहितो आरामो ति।

The above has been translated in the *Sacred Books of the East*, XX, pp. 187–88, by Messrs. Rhys Davids and Oldenberg as follows :—"He went to Jeta the Kumāra, and said to him, 'Sir, let me have your garden to make an *Ārāma* on it'. 'It is not, sir, for sale, even for (a sum so great that the pieces of money would be sufficient to cover it if they were laid side by side.' 'I take, sir, the garden at the price.' 'No, O house-holder, there was no bargain meant.' Then they asked the lords of justice whether a bargain of sale had been made or not. And the lords decided thus: 'The *Ārāma* is taken, sir, at the price which you fixed.'"

legal procedure is described as a mere occurrence of ordinary life. Hence the names of the Hindu Gascoignes have not been mentioned; they in the eyes of their contemporaries, did nothing extraordinary in giving that decision.

Ministers of Law and Justice

The *Prādvivāka* acted in two official capacities. He was the First ('Foremost') Judge and he was the Minister of Justice. We shall note below his functions as the Minister of Justice in comparison with the functions of the Paṇḍita Minister who was the Minister of Law.

It is remarkable that the Minister of Justice and the Minister of Law took precedence over several of their civil colleagues. The premier position in the Council was occupied by the *Pratinidhi*. The *Pradhāna*,[20] who was the President of the Council, came next. After them came the Minister of War or *Sachiva*, and the Foreign Minister or *Mantrin*, who were responsible for peace and war. Next in precedence were the Minister of Law and the Minister of Justice.

Firstly, as the Chief Justice, the *Prāḍvivāka* (lit., the First Judge) presided over the Supreme Court in the capital of the kingdom. Next, as the Minister of Justice he prescribed the law of procedure after ascertaining the opinion of the majority of a jury on the subject and then 'advising' the King accordingly. It is thus described in the *Śukranīti*:

"The *Prāḍvivāka* along with the members of the jury sitting in a meeting may ascertain by majority of opinion the procedure laws, instituted by himself and those come down: where human proof—by witnesses, documents, past and adverse enjoyment—was to be employed, and in which cases divine proof (oaths, ordeals) was to prevail, where interpretation was to be allowed, where a matter was to be proved by direct evidence (प्रत्यक्ष), where inference (अनुमान) and analogy (उपमान) were to be resorted to, where opinion of the community, and where jurisprudence should be followed; and the *Prāḍvivāka*

[20] The officer was alive in Gupta times when in inscriptions we find *Mahā-Pradhāna* (see Fleet, *Gupta Inscriptions*).

then (lit., 'having considered and ascertained these') shall always advise the King."[21]

The Minister of Law, on the other hand, who is elsewhere called the *Dharmādhikārin*, is called the *Paṇḍita* (the Learned Minister) in the *Śukranīti*, and his duties are thus defined:

"The *Paṇḍita*, having considered what ancient and present laws are at present followed by the community, which of them are approved in the codes and which laws now offend against jurisprudence, and which of them are opposed to the community and jurisprudence, shall recommend to the King laws which secure happiness both here and hereafter."[22]

This affords a glimpse into the Hindu method of legal reform. Hindu Law was normally considered traditional and as such could not, in theory, be altered by direct or avowed changes introduced by the State. The law was, however, occasionally altered by direct legislation[23] and more generally by interpretation, and also by new treatises fathered on ancient names, *e.g.*, the *Nārada Smṛiti*. Over and above these there was the agency of the two law ministers. The ministers rejected such laws as having regard to the circumstances of the community and public weal were deemed undesirable to be put into operation. They also took into consideration the popular view with regard to the current laws. This method of legal pruning and regard for the popular opinion resulted in the modification of laws and in effect acted as new

---

21 साक्षिभिर्लिखितैर्भोगैश्छलैर्भूतैश्च मानुषान् ।
स्वेनोत्पादितसम्प्राप्त-व्यवहारान् विचिन्त्य च ॥
दिव्यसंसाधनाद्वापि केषु किं साधनं परम् ।
युक्तिप्रत्यक्षानुमानोपमानैर्लोकशास्त्रतः ॥
बहुसम्मतसंसिद्धान् विनिश्चित्य सभास्थितः ।
ससभ्यः प्राड्विवाकस्तु नृपं संबोधयेत् सदा ॥
—*Śukranīti*, II. 96–98.

22 वर्त्तमानाश्च प्राचीना धर्म्माः के लोकसंश्रिताः ।

23 शास्त्रेषु के समुद्दिष्टा विरुध्यन्ते च केऽधुना ॥
लोकशास्त्रविरुद्धाः के पण्डितस्तान् विचिन्त्य च ।
नृपं संबोधयेत् तैश्च परत्रेह सुखप्रदैः ॥
—*Śukranīti*, II. 99–100.

legislation. It seems that the different treatises on Hindu Law differing from each other and modifying earlier laws, have been the works of Ministers of Law.

Sabhā

The most pronounced feature of Hindu Polity was the dominating position of Law throughout history. It was so when the law was administered by the communal *Sabhā* and it remained so when the law was administered by the royal *Sabhā*. The *Sabhā* had not the same history as the 'Court'. It was not an outcome of the King's household but of the Vedic folk-assembly. History was against a possibility of the *Sabhā* becoming the foot-stool of the throne. When it became the king's right and duty to maintain the administration of justice, he exercised it in accordance with the condition laid down and accepted through the Coronation Oath. He had to administer scrupulously the law of the country. Then, there was the Brahmin agency which always balanced and counterpoised the estate of sword and the estate of wealth. When undue interference was feared, it was laid down that the king must abide by the opinion of the *Prāḍvivāka*.[24]

[24] प्राड्विवाकमते स्थित:——*Nārada*; see p. 295 above. For details on the administration of justice the reader is referred to the author's *Tagore Law Lectures*.

CHAPTER XXXIII

Taxation

Fixed taxes

The Hindu theory of taxation is of immense importance from the constitutional point of view. Taxes had been fixed by Law and the scales had been embodied in the Sacred Common Law. The consequence was that whatever the form of government, the matter of taxation was not an object of the ruler's caprice. No friction could therefore legally arise between the Crown and the People on the question of taxation. The main source of friction and of oppression was thus guarded against.

Legal effect

That the constitutional law of taxation was a living law regulating life, is borne out by pieces of historical evidence. For instance, in the inscription of Queen Balaśrī of the Śātavāhana family, it is proclaimed that *her son levied taxes in accordance with the sacred law*. Other inscriptions point to the same conclusion.[1] Literature has some curious instances proving the inviolability of the taxes fixed by the law. Chandragupta the Great had to raise money, presumably for his intended war with Seleukos. He and his great Chancellor Kauṭilya were at their wit's end to collect a sufficient amount of money; the legal taxes were not productive enough for the purpose. They had to, as is evident from the *Artha-Śāstra*, take recourse to odd methods, which demonstrate the majesty of the law on the one hand and the inconvenience of a rigid legal revenue on the other. Chandragupta asked his people to give him money as a 'token of affection' (*Praṇaya*). He also raised money from temples.[2] Patañjali writing under the reign of Pushyamitra while commenting on Pāṇini, V. 3. 99, humorously remarked that the Mauryas who wanted gold raised it by instituting images of

---

[1] *Archæological Survey Report of Western India*, Vol. IV, p. 108; *Epigraphia Indica*, VIII, p. 60—धर्मोपजितकरविनियोगकरस—1. 5; p. 44, line 14. *Cf.* also "That avaricious king, who foolishly oppresses his subjects by levying taxes not sanctioned by the Śāstras, is said to wrong his own self."—*Mahābhārata*, *Śānti-Parvan*, LXXI, 15.

[2] *Artha-Śāstra*, pp. 241–42.

gods for worship.[3] In the Jaina tradition, Chāṇakya is alleged to have issued eight hundred million debased silver coins called *kārshāpaṇas* to fill the treasury.[4] All these facts indicate a very great urgency, and at the same time a scrupulous respect for the letter of the law.

The revenue raised by taxes was under the control of the Council of Ministers who were also vested with the power of collecting the revenue. As early as the fourth century B.C., as we find from Megasthenes (p. 310 above), the department of the Exchequer was under the Ministry, whose history does not begin there but goes back to the Vedic Ratnins and the Ratnin Treasurer. The evidence of Bhāradvāja (pp. 310 and 311) is also decisive and goes back beyond the fourth century B.C. The Ministry collected revenue and disbursed expenditure according to him.

Taxes as king's wages

Apart from the question of amount and collection of taxes, the taxes themselves were regarded in Hindu politics as wages of the king for the service of administration :

बलिषष्ठेन शुल्केन दण्डेनाथापराधिनाम् ।
शास्त्रानीतेन लिप्सेथा वेतनेन धनागमम् ॥

"The one-sixth *Bali* tax, import and export duties, fines and forfeitures collected from offenders—gathered in accordance with the Śāstras (law and constitution), as your wages (*vetanena*), shall constitute your revenue."[5]

Nārada also ordains :

"Both the customary receipts of a king and what is called the sixth of the produce of the soil, form the royal revenue, the reward for the protection of his subjects."[6]

The theory is as ancient as the *Artha-Śāstra* of Kauṭilya (300 B.C.), or we should say, it is anterior to 300 B.C. for it is quoted in the *Artha-Śāstra*. The taxes were regarded as the

---

[3] Jayaswal, *Indian Antiquary*, 1918, p. 51.

[4] Such silver-coated (copper-core) puch-marked coins of Maurya age have been found from the Maurya level at Pāṭaliputra, and are in the Patna Museum.

[5] *Mahābhārata*, *Śānti-Parvan*, LXXI. 10.

[6] *Nārada*, XVIII. 48 (Jolly).

wages of the king, the wages which were fixed according to the theory mentioned above (p. 259 above) by the original contract between the first King and the People. The broker to that contract, according to the theory, was the Creator himself. It was He who recommended Manu to the People for election.

Divine theory of taxation

The wage-theory was further developed by political scientists and turned into what we may call a divine theory of taxation. I cannot do better than quote that theory in the language of the scientist himself:

स्वभागभृत्या दास्यत्वे प्रजानां च नृपः कृतः ।
ब्रह्मणा स्वामिरूपस्तु पालनार्थं हि सर्वदा ॥

"God has made the King, though master in form, the servant of the People, getting his wages (sustenance) in taxes for the purpose of continuous protection and growth."[7]

In other words, the Master-Servant of the People has his wage or maintenance fixed by divine authority: he was not to take more, for he was not entitled to more. The Subject, really, the Master, was bound to "protect" the king, as promised by the priest on his behalf at the coronation (p. 211 above) by giving him his lawful maintenance, his share (*svabhāga*).

Here we have the arguments (p. 233 above) of the *Mānava-dharma-Śāstra* turned to yield a divine origin of king's servitude. Diamond cuts diamond. In the land of Uśanas and Bhāradvāja, a theory ascribing divine personality to kingship—a potential licence for autocracy—could never be tolerated. It was opposed to the trend of past history. Hence to cut 'Manu' the teacher of men, the Hindu sought out 'Śukra' the Teacher of Gods.

Protection and allegiance

The theory that the taxes were wages for protection was so ingrained in the constitution that even partial failure of protection was deemed to entitle the subject to claim refund of wages in proportion to the loss. And those claims, as we have seen, had to be allowed either in the shape of concessions or actual payment (p. 271 above). The subject thought that the

[7] *Śukranītisāra*, I. 188.

servant-king was not fulfilling his obligation. He thought that the compact was not fully kept and he threatened, as the *Artha-Śāstra* says (XIII. 1, p. 394), to migrate to the enemy country. In other words, the subject threatened to transfer allegiance. The *Mahābhārata* says the same thing when it sanctions the abandonment of that king who fails to protect.[8] He is like a ship which leaks, that is, dangerous to remain with; and he is like the barber who wishes to go to the forest, evidently to become an ascetic. The barber has left his clientele and master, and broken his contract of service. He is fit to be given up and another barber is to be appointed to the household. Similarly the king who failed in his duty was worthless, fit to be given up. The relation between the king and the subject is proved to have ended by the very fact of the former's incapacity. The tie of allegiance is deemed dissolved the moment the king failed to fulfil his duty of protection, and the subject was free to employ another servant-master instead. This was a natural corollary to the theory of taxation and the king's legal position.

Canons of taxation

The canons of taxation settled by constitutional writers agree with the telos for which the Hindu state was created, namely, 'for prosperity, land-culture, wealth and well-being' (p. 215 above).

The mainstay of revenue was the king's fixed *bhāga* or the 'share' of produce of agriculture. His 'share' in merchandise sold in the market was 'one-tenth' or so according

---

8 राजानं प्रथमं विन्देत् ततो भार्यां ततो धनम् ॥ ४२ ॥

* * * *

प्राचेतसेन मनुना श्लोकौ चेमावुदाहृतौ ।
राजधर्मेषु राजेन्द्र ताविहैकमनाः शृणु ॥ ४३ ॥
षडेतान् पुरुषो जह्याद्भिन्नां नावमिवार्णवे ।
अप्रवक्तारमाचार्यमनधीयानमृत्विजम् ॥ ४४ ॥
अरक्षितारं राजानं भार्यां चाप्रियवादिनीम् ।
ग्रामकामं च गोपालं वनकामं च नापितम् ॥ ४५ ॥

—XII. 57 (= 56 Kumbakonam).

The Manu cited here is the author of a work on politics called evidently *Rājadharma*. The work which was probably of a school is quoted by Kauṭilya as the '*Mānavas*'.

to circumstances.[9] There were however some other sources of revenue which are at present called excise and customs (*śulka*). In the regulation of these the king had a somewhat free hand. The later law-books attempted even to regulate these by fixed laws. Yet they could not exhaust the list and a greedy or needy sovereign could find some loop-hole. The Nandas are accused to have taxed hides or furs. Evidently these articles had not been taxed before. There was a vast trade in skins or furs between the Magadha Empire and the Himalayan countries as the *Artha-Śāstra*[10] proves. These imports when taxed by the predecessors of Chandragupta gave rise to accusations of greed. Evidently it was with reference to such occasions and opportunities and the realization of the *bhāga* in general that canons of taxation were evolved and settled.

The general principles of Hindu taxation are:

(1) In taxation the king 'should not by greediness destroy his own foundations as well as those of others.'[11]

(2) Subjects may be taxed in a way that they may remain strong to bear future burdens and, if necessary, heavier ones. "If the calf is permitted to suck it grows strong, O Bhārata, and can bear (heavy weight) and pain." The king should milch taxes keeping the above principle in view. Over-milching is to weaken the calf and consequently harms the milcher himself.[12]

---

[9] *Cf.* Manu, VII. 130–32 ; Gautama, X. 24–27; Vasishṭha, XIX. 26–27 ; Āpastamba, II. 10, 26, 9 ; Vishṇu, III. 22–25 ; Baudhāyana, 1. 10. 18. 1.

[10] XI. 2.

[11] *Mahābhārata*, XII. 87. 18—

नोच्छिद्यादात्मनो मूलं परेषां चापि तृष्णया ।

[12] *Ibid.*, XII. 87. 20–21—

वत्सौपम्येन दोग्धव्यं राष्ट्रमक्षीणबुद्धिना ।
भृतो वत्सो जातबलः पीडां सहति भारत ॥
न कर्म कुरुते वत्सो भृशं दुग्धो युधिष्ठिर ।
राष्ट्रमप्यतिदुग्धं हि न कर्म कुरुते महत् ॥

(3) It is not the heavily-taxed realm which executes great deeds but the moderately taxed one, whose ruler not sacrificing the power of defence, manages administration economically.[13] The subjects oppose that king who is extravagant in administration (' *eating* too much ').[14]

(4) The great principle emphasised is that taxation should be such that it may not be felt by the subject. The ruler should act like a bee which collects honey without causing pain to the plant.[15]

(5) In raising taxes higher it should be done 'little by little when the realm's prosperity is increasing'. The process must be mild so that the realm might not turn restive.[16]

On collection of taxes:

(6) Taxes should be levied "in proper place", "in proper time" and "in proper form".[17] They should never be realised by a painful mode—"milch the cow but do not bore the udders".[18]

---

[13] *Mahābhārata*, XII. 41. 22—

यो राष्ट्रमनुगृह्णाति परिरक्षन् स्वयं नृपः ।
संजातमुपजीवन्स लभेत सुमहत्फलम् ॥

[14] *Ibid.*, XII. 87. 19—

प्रद्विषन्ति परिख्यातं राजानमतिखादिनम् ।

"Eating" (*khad*) is a technical term for taxation even in the Brāhmaṇa period.

[15] *Ibid.*, XII. 88. 4—

मधुदोहं दुहेद्राष्ट्रं भ्रमरा इव पादपम् ।

[16] *Ibid.*, XII. 88. 7–8—

अल्पेनाल्पेनदेयेन वर्धमानं प्रदापयेत् ।
ततो भूयस्ततो भूयः कमवृद्धिं समाचरेत् ॥
दमयन्निव दम्यानि शश्वद्भारं विवर्धयेत् ।
मृदुपूर्वं प्रयत्नेन पाशानभ्यवहारयेत् ॥

[17] *Ibid.*, XII. 88. 12—

न चास्थाने ना चाकाले करांस्तेभ्यो निपातयेत् ।
आनुपूर्व्येण सान्त्वेन यथाकालं यथाविधि ॥

[18] *Ibid.*, XII. 88. 4—

वत्सापेक्षी दुहेच्चैव स्तनांश्च न विकुट्टयेत् ।

On taxing industries:

(7) "Taxes should not be levied without determining the out-turn and the amount of labour necessary for its production."[19] It has to be borne in mind that without proper incentive no body would engage in industry.[20] "What profit (result of production) would keep the producer to the production and produce benefit to the king as well" should be the ruling consideration in deciding upon the amount of taxes to be levied on industries.[21]

(8) In productions of art—materials used, cost incurred, maintenance of the artist required for producing the article, and the condition of the artist have to be taken into account.[22]

In taxing imports:

(9) "Sales (price realised), purchases (capital employed), distance travelled, cost of importing, and the total cost, also the risks incurred by the merchant should be fully considered."[23]

(10) "Imports harmful to the State" and "luxuries" ("fruitless") are be discouraged by taxation.[24]

---

[19] *Mahābhārata*, XII. 87. 16; M. N. Dutt's translation.—

फलं कर्म च संप्रेक्ष्य ततः सर्वं प्रकल्पयेत् ।

[20] *Ibid.*, फलं कर्म च निर्हेतु न कश्चित्संप्रवर्तते ।

[21] *Manu*, VII. 129 —

यथा फलेन युज्येत राजा कर्त्ता च कर्मणाम् ।
तथा वेक्ष्य नृपो राष्ट्रे कल्पयेत् सततं करान् ॥
यथा राजा च कर्त्ता च स्यातां कर्मणि भागिनौ ।
संवेक्ष्य तु तथा राज्ञा प्रणेयाः सततं कराः ॥

[22] *Mahābhārata*, XII. 87. 14—

उत्पत्तिं दानवृत्तिं च शिल्पं संप्रेक्ष्य चासकृत् ।
शिल्पं प्रति करानेवं शिल्पिनः प्रति कारयेत् ॥

[23] *Ibid.*, XII. 87. 13 = Manu, VII. 127—

विक्रयं क्रमयध्वानं भक्तं च सपरिव्ययम् ।
योगक्षेमं च संप्रेक्ष्यवणिजां कारयेत् करान् ॥

[24] *Artha-Śāstra*, II. 21 (p. 112)—

राष्ट्र पीडाकरं भाण्डामुच्छिन्द्यादफलं च यत् ।
महोपकारमुच्छुल्कं कुर्याद्बीजं तु दुर्लभम् ॥

(11) Beneficial imports should be made free of import duties.[25]

(12) Those articles which are rare in the country, and those which would be seed for future production should be allowed in, free.[26]

(13) Certain commodities should not be exported, while their imports are to be encouraged by not being taxed at all. They were, for instance:

- (*a*) weapons and armours,
- (*b*) metals,
- (*c*) military vehicles,
- (*d*) rare things,
- (*e*) grains, and
- (*f*) cattle.[27]

(14) *Principle of countervailing duty was resorted to in certain cases.*

Foreign favourites and private manufactures in wines and liquors were taxed on the principle of 'compensation' with reference to the state manufactures.[28]

Economic considerations are everywhere prominent. Productive power is not to be hampered; profit and not capital is to be taxed; articles which lead to new industries are to be encouraged; exports which cause "artificial" prosperity by driving up prices are to be discouraged; no special protection is granted to ordinary industries; taxes should be gradual, and with reference to capacity, and not in an obnoxious form.

25, 26 *Vide n.* 24.

27 शस्त्र-वर्म-कवच-लोह-रथ-रत्न-धान्य-पशूनामन्यतममनिर्वाह्यम्, etc., *Artha-Śāstra*, II. 21; 39 (p. 111).

28 *Ibid.*, II. 25 (p. 121)—

अराजपण्याः पञ्चकं शतं शुल्कं दद्युः । सुरकामेदकारिष्ट-मधुफलाम्लाम्लशीधूनां च ।
अह्नश्च विक्रयं व्याजीं ज्ञात्वा मानहिरण्ययोः ।
तथा वैधरणं कुर्यादुचितं चानुवर्तयेत् ॥

CHAPTER XXXIV

Economics in Government and Theory of Ownership in Land

Economic enemies

Measures are enjoined in the chapters on taxation for the suppression of certain classes of persons who are regarded as economic enemies.[4] Public women, gambling establishments and gamblers, theatricals, and similar parasites were to be controlled,[1] beggars and burglers to be eradicated,[2] and usurers to be discouraged.[3] Agriculturalists were especially to be protected from the parasites.[4]

Monks and Monasteries were regarded as another economic evil. " No wanderers other than men who have reached the hermit stage, no (*samgha*) corporate community—(*i.e.*, the Buddhist Samgha and the like), other than that of the *Sajātas* (village people), no union formed on mutual compact other than those of merchants, shall be allowed to establish themselves in the country. Nor shall there be Halls (religious) rest-houses and *Vihāras*." [5] Men leaving society and becoming monks before they had provided for their family were legally dealt with. They were arrested and punished. Only those who had passed the age of manhood were allowed to become monks under the orthodox administration.[6]

---

[1] *Mahābhārata*. XII. 88. 14–17.

[2] *Ibid.*, XII. 88. 17 ; 24.

[3] *Ibid.*, XII. 88. 26.

[4] नटनर्तन-गायन-वादक-वाग्जीवन-कुशीलवा वा न कर्मविघ्नं कुर्युः *Artha-Śāstra*, II. 1 (p. 48).

[5] वानप्रस्थादन्यः प्रव्रजितभावः सजातादन्यः सङ्घस्सामुत्थायिकादन्यस्समयानुबन्धो वा नास्य जनपदमुपनिवेशेत। न च तत्रारामविहारार्थाः शालास्स्युः *Ibid.*, II. 1 (p. 48). Compare the *Sajāta* in coronation ceremonies, p. 218 above.

[6] पुत्रदारमप्रतिविधाय प्रव्रजतः पूर्वस्साहसदण्डः; स्त्रियं च प्रव्राजयतः (also those who made women nuns were punished with the highest criminal amercement). लुप्तव्यवायः प्रव्रजेदापृच्छ्य धर्मस्थान्। अन्यथा नियम्येत। *Ibid.*, II. 1 (p. 48).

Law Sūtras also lay down restrictions on leaving one's home.

Economics in government

In the art of government the first lesson taught to the ruler was that on economics depend government and freedom of the country :

(*a*) " कृषि पाशुपाल्ये वणिज्या च वार्ता । ....
तया स्वपक्षं परपक्षं च वशीकरोति कोशदण्डाभ्याम् " । (*A.Ś.*, p. 8.)

(*b*) " अर्थानर्थौ वार्तायाम् " (*Ibid.*, p. 7.)

(*c*) " वार्तया धार्यते सर्वम् " (*M.Bh.*, *Vana*, I. 50.)

(*d*) " वार्ता वै लोक संश्रया " (*Kām.*, IV. 27.)

(*a*) " Agriculture, cattle-culture, and commerce and trade comprise the [Science (*vidyā*)] of *Vārtā*. Success in that leads through Exchequer and Army to the control of one's own state as well as one's enemies. "

(*b*) " In Economics lies politics as well as the reverse of politics."

(*c*) " By economics the whole (body politic) is held."

(*d*) " *Vārtā* is the shelter of society."

Therefore Rulers had to give their best thoughts to Economics. To maintain an economic government was part of their duty. In fact it came first in the division of their duty ; and this position is quite in conformity with the coronation declaration.

'This state to thee (is given) for agriculture, for well-being, for prosperity, for growth' (p. 215 above).

The word '*pālana*' which is employed in classical literature to denote the duty of the king combines two elements : 'seeing to the growth' and protection in general. The second is a corollary from the first which alone is found in the Vedic formula. Hence policy was directed to keep up and develop the *Vārtā* or National Economy.

Policy towards the merchantile element of population

To secure the economic prosperity of the country the merchantile class were treated with particular attention and solicitude.

" The power of production in the merchants should be always encouraged. They make the Realm strong, enhance agriculture, and develop its trade. A wise king should be favourable to them in a studied manner....There is no greater wealth in a kingdom than its merchants."[7]

Again, "the king should always honour those who have earned wealth. He should give them feasts, drinks, and robes of honour. In every realm the wealthy form an estate (*aṅga*—limb)."[8]

State industries

The State at times worked large industries. They were worked by State departments. Both the *Artha-Śāstra* and the *Mānava-Dharma-Śāstra* have Departments of *Ākara* and *Karmānta*, mining and manufacturies. From them the State gained first-hand industrial experience for its economic administration, and at the same time the income of the State was greatly enhanced. It saved the statesmen, partially at any rate, from the necessity of 'begging' 'affection' tax from the people for war preparations and cognate purposes.

Indirect taxation the key-note of the policy

Hindu politicians disliked direct taxation. They had practically no direct tax in their system except the produce-tax. Import duties which were exclusively 'indirect' in their incidence were the next great tax after the produce-tax. Export duties were few and they were more of administrative than revenue levies. Generally those articles which were not encouraged to go out were taxed as exports. The next great source of revenue was the mining industry. The State under Chandragupta and earlier generally nationalized the industry.

Mines

But in the *Mānava Code* (VIII. 39) mining is open to the public. The tax demanded, however, is still heavy. A tax of 50 per cent. is laid down, on

---

7 अजस्रमुपयोक्तव्यं फलं गोमिषु भारत ।
प्रभावयन्ति राष्ट्रं च व्यवहारं कृषिं तथा ॥ ३८ ॥
तस्माद्गोमिषु यत्नेन प्रीतिं कुर्याद्विचक्षणः ।
दयावानप्रमत्तश्च करान् संप्रणयन्मृदून् ॥ ३९ ॥
* * *
नह्यतः सदृशं किञ्चिद्धनमस्ति युधिष्ठिर ॥ ४० ॥
—*Mahābhārata*, XII. 87. 39–40.

8 *Ibid.*, XII. 88. 29–30—
धनिनः पूजयेन्नित्यं पानाच्छादनभोजनैः * * * अङ्गमेतन्महद्राज्ये धनिनो नाम भारत ।

the principle that mine is like treasure-trove which belongs as much to the State as to the person who finds it. A tax for protection, as in any other case, is deemed but lawful, for the king is the protector of both the upper and sub-soil (*adhi-pati*, '*bhumeradhipatir hi saḥ*,' *Manu*, VIII. 39). Medhātithi in explaining the law of the *Mānava Code* says that although no one knows what is there in the land and the government has to do very little guarding thereof yet as there is a likelihood of the whole land being taken away by a strong enemy, the king is entitled to his 'share' for this constructive protection.[9]

Hindu theory on proprietorship in land

This leads us on to the important Hindu theory regarding the proprietorship in land, which is connected with taxation. It is not so connected in Hindu politics in the slightest degree, but in the controversy of the present day raised by Indianist politicians and scholars. Some of these writers have confidently asserted that property in the soil, according to the Hindu view, always vested in the Hindu sovereign. The fact on the other hand is that this is exactly the reverse of the Hindu theory on the subject. The writers unconsciously have read their own feudal law into Hindu jurisprudence. Nothing is so distant from Hindu law as this theory. Numerous instances of gifts and sales of land by private individuals can be given from the earliest literature. Law-books give provisions for sale of land and for acquirement of proprietary right (*svāmya*) by prescription. Inscriptions[10] proving to the hilt private property in the soil are extant. Above all it is expressly and emphatically declared that the king has no property in the soil and this is declared in no less an authority than the very logic of Hindu Law, the *Mīmāṃsā*. I give below the discussion from Colebrooke's essay on *Mīmāṃsā*:

---

[9] Bühler (*S.B.E.*, XX. V, p. 260, *n.*) gives a mutilated passage of Medhātithi and makes bim say what he does not mean. The real portion is left out. अत्रहेतूरक्षणादिति यद्यपि क्षितौ निहतस्य केनचिद-ज्ञानाच्च राजकीयरक्षोपयुज्यते तथापि तस्य बलवतापहारः संभाव्यते अतोऽस्यैव रक्षाया अर्थवत्त्वं एतदर्थमेवाह भूमेरधिपतिर्हि सः ।

[10] *E.g.*, *Indian Antiquary*, 1910, p. 199.

Colebrooke

"A question of considerable interest, as involving the important one concerning property in the soil in India, is discussed in the sixth lecture. At certain sacrifices such as that which is called *Viśvajit*, the votary for whose benefit the ceremony is performed is enjoined to bestow all his property on the officiating priests. It is asked whether a paramount sovereign shall give all the land including pasture ground, highways and the sites of lakes and ponds? an universal monarch the whole earth? and a subordinate prince the entire province over which he rules? To that question the answer is: The monarch has not property in the earth, nor the subordinate prince in the land. By conquest kingly power is obtained, and property in house and field which belonged to the enemy. The maxim of the law, that 'the king is the lord of all excepting sacerdotal wealth,' concerns his authority for correction of the wicked and protection of the good. His kingly power is for government of the realm and extirpation of wrongs; and for that purpose he receives taxes from husbandmen, and levies fines from offenders. But right of property is not thereby vested in him; else he would have property in house and land appertaining to the subjects abiding in his dominions. The earth is not the king's, but is common to all beings enjoying the fruit of their own labour. It belongs, says Jaimini, to all alike;[11] therefore, although a gift of a piece of ground to an individual does take place, the whole land cannot be given by a monarch, nor a province by a subordinate prince but house and field acquired by purchase and similar means, are liable to gift."[12]

---

[11] The text referred to by Colebrooke's authority is न भूमिः स्यात् सर्वान् प्रत्यविशिष्टत्वात् । VI. 7. 3. The previous discussion is as to what a man legally gives when he gives 'all his' (स्वं). The literal meaning of this aphorism is 'Land (of a country) is not transferred (by a king), for it equally belohgs to all'.

[12] *Mis. Essays*, I, pp. 320-21. The comment of Śabara who is the greatest authority on *Mīmāṃsā* agrees with the discussion summarised above by Colebrooke. Śabara on Jaimini. VI. 7. 3 has:—

अत्रैव सर्व्वदाने संशयः। किं भूमि र्देया न इति। का पुनर्भूमिः अत्राभिप्रेता। यदेतन्मृदारब्धं द्रव्यान्तरं पृथिवी-गोलकं न क्षेत्रमात्रं मृत्तिका वा। तत्र किं प्राप्तम्। अविशेषाद्देया प्रभुत्वसम्बन्धेन हि तत्र स्वशब्दो वर्त्तते शक्यते च मानसेन व्यापारेण

The very discussion of the *Mīmāṃsā* proves, for it presupposes, the existence of private property in land. Such private property was deemed inviolable. All possible pretensions by the Crown to such right was denied in the clearest possible terms. And this was quite in consonance with the spirit of Hindu Law which held even the gods subject to law and prescribed punishment for the sovereign, if he was arbibtrary.

Conquest and land

The Hindu lawyer Nilakaṇṭha carries the discussion further and examines the right of the conqueror in these words :

एवं क्षत्रियादेर्जयादिरिति तु युक्तम् ॥ जयेऽपि जितस्य यत्र गृहक्षेत्रद्रव्यादौ स्वत्वमासोत्तत्रैव जेतुरप्युत्पद्यते ॥ जितस्य करग्राहितायां तु जेतुरपि सैव न स्वत्वम् । अतएव सार्वभौमेन सम्पूर्णा पृथ्वी माण्डलिकेन च मण्डलं न देयमित्युक्तं षष्ठे ॥ सम्पूर्णपृथ्वीमण्डलस्य तत्तद्ग्रामक्षेत्रादी स्वत्वं तु तत्तद्भौमिकादीनामेव राज्ञां तु करग्रहणमात्रम् ॥ अतएवेदानीन्तनपारिभाषिक क्षेत्रदानादौ न भूदानसिद्धिः किन्तु-वृत्तिकल्पनमात्रमेव ॥ भौमिकेभ्यः क्रीते तु गृहक्षेत्रादी स्वत्वमप्यस्त्येव ॥

"Similarly conquest and the other (modes) are (available) for a ruler (Kshatriya) and the others. On conquest the ownership of the conqueror arises only in respect of the houses, lands, and personality, etc., of the ruler conquered. Where the latter had a right to taking taxes, the conqueror acquires that much right, and no ownership. Hence '*by an emperor the whole country, and by a provincial ruler the province is not a 'deya'* (a 'subject of gift')' is laid down. in Book VI (of the *P. Mīmāṃsa*). Proprietary right in the whole land with regard to villages and lands, etc., lies in their respective

---

स्वस्य स्वता निर्वर्त्तयितुम् । इति । एवं प्राप्ते ब्रूमः न भूर्मिदेया इति । कुतः । क्षेत्राणाम् ईशितारो मनुष्या दृश्यन्ते न कृत्स्नस्य पृथिवीगोलकस्य इति । आह य इदानीं सार्व्वभौमः स तर्हि दास्यति सोपि न इति ब्रूमः । कुतः । यावता भागेन सार्व्वभौमो भूमेरिष्टे तावता अन्योऽपि न तत्र कश्चिद्विशेषः सार्वभौमत्वेऽस्य त्वेतदधिकं यत् असौ पृथिव्यां सम्भूतानां व्रीह्यादीनां रक्षणेन निर्विष्टस्य कस्यचित् भागस्य ईष्टे न भूमेः तन्निविष्टाश्च ये मनुष्याः तैरन्यत् सर्व्वप्राणिनाम् धारणविक्रमणादि यत् भूमिकृतं तत्रेशित्वं प्रति न कश्चिद्विशेषः । तस्मात् न भूमिर्देया ।

—*Mīmāṃsādarśa*, VI. 7. 3.

land-lords, etc. The king's right is limited to the collection of tax therefrom. Therefore what is technically called at present '*gift of land*', etc. (by the king) does not mean giving away of land, but a mere creation of allowance. If house, land, etc., are bought from the owner (by the king) proprietorship indeed can arise."[13]

Mādhava

The Prime-Minister Mādhava, whose name in legal literature occupies the next place after Vijñāneśvara, is entitled to profound respect in regard what he may have to say on questions of Hindu Law. He discusses the very point in these words:

देया न वा महाभूमिः स्वत्वाद्राजा ददातु ताम् ।
पालनस्यैव राज्यत्वान्न स्वम्भूर्दीयते न सा ॥

यदा सार्वभौमो राजा विश्वजिदादौ सर्वस्वं ददाति तदा गोपथराजमार्गजलाशयाद्यन्विता महाभूमिस्तेन दातव्या । कुतः भूमेस्तदीयधनत्वात् राजा सर्वस्येष्टे ब्राह्मणवर्जमिति स्मृतेः । इति प्राप्ते—

ब्रूमः । दुष्टशिक्षाशिष्टपरिपालनाभ्यां राज्ञ ईशितृत्वं स्मृत्यभिप्रेतमिति न राज्ञो भूमिर्धनम् । किन्तु तस्यां भूमौ स्वकर्मफलं भुञ्जानानां सर्वेषां प्राणिनां साधारणं धनम् । अतोऽसाधारणस्य भूखंडस्य सत्यपि दाने महाभूमेर्दानं नास्ति ॥[14]

"***Mahā-bhūmi*** (the Great Land, Public Land, *cf.* below '***non-public***'): is it or not an object of gift? 'King may give it away, for he possesses it'. *Land is not his property because sovereignty is for protection and growth only. Therefore it is not given.*"

"Doubt may arise in case a *Sārvabhauma* King (Emperor) in ***Viśvajit*** and others 'gives away all he possesses'. In that case (is) the Great Land which contains public roads, ways for cattle, seats of water, etc., to be given away? for in land there is his wealth owing to the text of *Smṛiti*—'King may wish for (the wealth of) all excepting Brahmins.'

"*The reply is that the purport of the Smṛiti is that King's sovereignty is for correcting the wicked and fostering the good. 'Hence land is not king's wealth. On the other hand in that land*

---

[13] *Vyavahāra-mayūkha* (*Dāya-Nirṇaya*).

[14] *Nyāyamālā* by Mādhavāchārya (Ānandāśrama Sanskrit Series), p. 358.

(state land) ***there is the common wealth of all living beings to enjoy the fruit of their labour...Therefore although there can be gift of a piece of*** **non-public (*Asādhāraṇa*) *land there can be no gift of the Great Land.*"**

The *Bhaṭṭadīpikā*

The commentary *Bhaṭṭadīpika* which is an accepted authority in *Mīmāṃsā* has the following exposition on the subject :

सार्वभौमस्यापि न तस्यां स्वत्वम्। जयस्यापि च शत्रुस्वामिकधनगृहक्षेत्रादिविषय एव स्वत्वोत्पादकत्वात्। महापृथिव्यां तु राज्यमात्राधिकारस्यैव जयेन सम्पादनात् राज्यं हि स्वविषयपरिपालनकण्टकोद्धारणरूपं तन्निमित्तकं च तस्य कर्षकेभ्यः करादानं दण्ड्येभ्यश्च दण्डादानं इत्येतावन्मात्रं। न त्वेतावता तस्यां स्वत्वम्। * * * परिक्रयादिलब्धं गृहक्षेत्रादिकं तु देयमेव ॥[15]

"Even a *Sārvabhauma* sovereign has no proprietary right in it (*Mahā-prithivī* = Great Land). For even conquest produces proprietary right only in the personal property, house, fields, etc., of the enemy. In the *Mahā-prithivi* (Great Land) however, as the right is only of government what is acquired by conquest is merely government which is limited to protection and growth of the country and eradication of evil (therefrom) and for that purpose to the realization of taxes from cultivators and of fines from offenders. *In the land there arises no right of any other kind* ····· House, fields, etc., acquired by purchase and the like, may however *become* a subject of gift."

Kātyāyana, the lawyer, deals with the subject in these words[16] :—

---

[15] *Bhaṭṭadīpikā* on *Pūrvamīmāṃsā Darśana* (Mysore ed.), II. 317.

[16] कात्यायनः,

भूस्वामी तु स्मृतो राजा नान्यद्रव्यस्य सर्वदा ।
तत्फलस्य हि षड्भागं प्राप्नुयान्नान्यथैव तु ॥
भूतानां तन्निवासित्वात् स्वामित्वं तेन कीर्त्तितम् ।
तत्क्रियाबलिषड्भागं शुभाशुभनिमित्तजम् ॥ इति ।

अस्यार्थः । राजा, भुवः स्वामी स्मृतः । अन्यद्रव्यस्य, भूमिसम्बद्धद्रव्यस्य, न स्वामी । अन्यथा, भूमिस्वाम्याभावे । भूतानां, प्राणिनाम् । तन्निवासित्वात्, भूनिवासित्वात् । स्वामित्वं, राज्ञ इति शेषः । इत्यतः तत्क्रियाबलिषड्भागं प्राप्नुयात् ।

—*V.M.R.N.*, p. 271.

"When the king is called the *svāmin* (master) of the land and in no case of any other wealth, he only becomes entitled to receive the one-sixth share of the produce from it, not (that he is master) in any other way. The master-ship which is connected with him is on account of population thereof by living beings and is the one-sixth share arising from their acts whether good or bad."

Mitramiśra commenting on this says :—

"Its meaning is (this): king is called the *svāmin* of land, not of other wealth connected with land. '*Not in any other way*' is (laid down) as there is want of mastership in land. 'Living beings' are these having life; 'population thereof' is the habitation of the land; *mastership* that is mastership of the king. Hence he can only receive one-sixth from their acts."

The view of law and *Mimāmsā* in agreement with constitutional theory

This is the traditional view of the law; this is the view of the *Mīmāṃsa* whose verdict in Hindu Law is final. This is in complete agreement with the view of the costitutional writers who have decided that the king is a mere servant getting his wages in taxes. The servant cannot claim as his the very property, to guard which he is appointed and for guarding which he gets his salary. This unanimous view of law and constitution on king's position was not confined to books. It was the common and accepted opinion in the country—so common and accepted that it had

Jātaka

become current coin even in the domain of folk-lore. The *Jātaka*, which we shall quote verbatim below in the next chapter, says (and there it is the speech of a king), *that the king's authority is limited to magisterial duty, that he had nothing more than that, and that he is not the owner of the kingdom.* It is further corroborated by the coronation ceremonial which is the very basis of Hindu

and coronation rites

Kingship and which I have already analysed for the reader. There is not even an atom of suggestion in that chain of formulæ and symbolisms to imagine kingly proprietorship in the land of the realm. The idea is altogether foreign to the whole system.

Inscriptions

Gupta title-deeds inscribed on copper plates and registered at the District Officer's office, whose seals they bear, clearly prove private ownership. In certain cases the king got only the one-sixth 'share'[17] as in any other sale (*e.g.*, of moveables).

Indianists' presentation of the 'Native Law' on the subject

In the face of all this we have in the repeated editions of popular text-books like Dr. Vincent Smith's *Early History of India* confidently stated :—"*The native law of India has always recognised agricultural land as being crown property.*"

"The native law of India" as laid down by its own lawyers of unquestioned and unquestionable authority is the other way. It may be the native law of any other land; it is certainly not the native law of India. It is not fair that a popular text-book should embody such a prejudiced and unwarrantable view dogmatically asserted, and asserted without taking the slightest notice of competent discussions on the subject. Wilks in his *History of Mysore* published as early as 1869 has exhaustively dealt with the subject on materials which were accessible to him[18] and which are accessible to Dr. Vincent Smith. Wilks shows that no foundation exists for attributing the feudal theory to Hindu Law. In the *Introduction to Hindu Polity* the constitutional view of Hindu literature was pointed out. Professors Macdonell and Keith who cannot be accused of any sympathy to matters of Indian history have had to admit in their *Vedic Index*[19] on a survey of all the arguments and materials for the feudal theory that "the evidence is however inadequate to prove what is sought; that the Greek observers are contradictory on the point; that the evidence adduced from the Vedic literature, and the *Mānava-Dharma-Śāstra* and the

---

[17] *Indian Antiquary*, 1910, pp. 199–204 (Plates B and C). Plate A is a conveyance by the Municipal Corporation of a piece of land in town. The vendors are the president and the assembly (called Prakṛitis just as in *Amara*, p. 246 above). In this case the Emperor received "the legal one-sixth share" (*dharma-shaḍ-bhāga*, Plate A, *Indian Antiquary*, 1910, p. 195).

[18] Vol. I, Chapter V, pp. 65–138.

[19] Vol. II, pp. 214–15.

Mahābhārata does not prove the theory; that the evidence so far as it goes of other Aryan peoples does not support the theory of original kingly ownership. Such ownership did not exist so far as can be seen in Anglo-Saxon times, nor in Homeric Greece, nor at Rome." The learned authors, however, pass by Jaimini, totally ignoring him, although they go to South Africa to find analogy for Vedic India.[20]

Artha-Śāstra Commentary's Śloka

While in the second edition (p. 129) no authority was suggested by Dr. Vincent Smith, in the last edition (1914, p. 131 *n.*) from the translation of the *Artha-Śāstra*, Bk. II, Ch. 24 (p. 144), he has quoted a passage given by the translator: 'Those who are well versed in the Śāstras admit that the king is the owner of both land and water, and that the people can exercise their right of ownership over all other things excepting these two.' The passage purports to be the translation of a "couplet of far-reaching political significance" quoted by a commentator of the *Artha-Śāstra*. I have obtained a copy of the manuscript of the commentary which is at the Oriental Government Library, Madras, made under the supervision of the Librarian through the kind agency of Prof. Krishna Swami Aiyangar. The original couplet reads as follows:—

राजा भूमेः पतिर्दृष्टः शास्त्रज्ञैरुदकस्य च ।
ताभ्यामन्यत्र यद्द्रव्यं तत्र साम्यं कुटुम्बिनाम् ॥

A mere reading of this śloka will satisfy those who are familiar with Hindu Law that the translation is not what the śloka says. The natural, unforced meaning of the śloka is: "The king is the protector (*pati*), according to the opinion of the learned in the Śāstras, of the *bhūmi* (land) and water. Excepting these two whatever wealth there may be, his family members have sameness of right therein."

---

[20] Macdonell and Keith, *Vedic Index*, Vol. II, pp. 214–15. The authors also say, "It is not denied that gradually the king came to be vaguely conceived—as the English king still is—as lord of all the land in a proprietorial sense." The authority for this statement is nil, except 'as the English king still is', which is the basis, the original sin, of the theory. The relic of the theory still lingers vaguely.

In effect it is the theory of the *Mīmāṃsa*, and the law and constitution retold. It is retold in connexion with the rights of the family of a ruler. A kingdom is not partible, because according to the Śāstras it is not the property of the king. As the Śāstrakāras have said "*bhūmi 'with seats of water' upon it belongs to the king, only inasmuch as he has to protect it and no more.*" He is only its Protector. Hence of his family members (*kuṭumbinām*) there no copercenary therein. As protector he takes taxes, and as he is the protector of the *bhūmi* 'with seats of water' on it, he is entitled to derive taxes both from land and water. His family members have nothing to do with these taxes or with the sources of these taxes.

To attribute the sense of the translation cited to the śloka is wholly indefensible and unjust. And to attribute the sense to the commentator of the *Artha-Śāstra* is to attribute madness to a Hindu writer of Hindu times. Any one in whose veins ran the culture and tradition of "the Śāstras" could never mean in sound mind what has been fathered on the author of the Śloka.[21]

---

[21] His name and date are not known.

CHAPTER XXXV

Position of the Hindu King

Civil List

To recapitulate the position of the Hindu king. The king had his civil list defined which was called his 'salary' and which had to be fixed with reference to the income of the State and the position of the Monarch and Country.[1] The whole revenue was not his salary. Salaries of the Queen and junior queens, of Queen Dowager and Princes and other members of the royal family were also fixed.

King master of no subject

He had no jurisdiction over individual subjects. He was called master; but it was settled law which people knew like the daily appearance of the sun that he was master of no subject except a criminal. The *Jātaka* which does not deal in philosophy or ideals but facts of every-day life, puts it in these words in reply to the demand of a beautiful wife who was desirous of absolute mastery over subjects :—

"My good lady, to me the inhabitants of the whole realm are no bodies ; I am not their master (*i.e.*, they are their own masters). I am master only of those who offend against the rulers' (laws) and do what is unlawful. For this reason, I am unable to give you mastery and rule over the whole realm."[2]

---

[1] *Artha-Śāstra*, Bk. V. Ch. 2 ; 91 (p. 245)—

दुर्गजनपदशक्त्या भृत्यकर्मसमुदयपादेन स्थापयेत् । कार्यसाधनसहेन वा भृत्यलाभेन शरीरमवेक्षेत । न धर्मार्थौ पीडयेत् । *N.B.*—The term *bhṛitya* includes the king.

समानविद्येभ्यस्त्रिगुणवेतनो राजा । (p. 246).

[2] The *Jātaka*, Vol. I, p. 398—

भद्देमख्यं सकलरट्ठवासिनी न किञ्चि होन्ति नाहं एतेसं सामिको ये पन राजानं कोपेत्वा अकत्तब्बं करोति तेसञ्ञेवाहं सामिको ति इमिना कारणेन न सक्का तुय्हं सकलरट्ठे इस्सरियञ्च आणञ्च दातुं ति ।

The king had evidently a palace jurisdiction of superior nature (*Vaśam* = 'full control') "for the sake of convenience".

King constitutionally a servant

With this defined position, shackled with the checks and limitations we have noticed, subjugated under the great constitutional power of the *Paura-Jānapada*, with a conscience trained to be prone to listen to the public voice, his position really was that of the Servant of State, or rather as our forefathers put it mercilessly, of a drudging '*slave*' (*dāsya*). The epic exhibits as an ideal that a king should even give up his dear wife if asked to do so by his subjects : a popular and somewhat crude way of expressing the king's position, but all the same enshrining the radical demand of Hindu constitution from its king to sink his individuality into his office. With such principles the king was virtually a constitutional slave. Even the Hindu Hobbes, the great monarchist Kauṭilya, would not allow the king to have personal likes or dislikes. "A king has no personal likes : it is the likes of the subjects (that should be followed by him)."[3]

Morally master

This lofty sense of sacrifice made the constitutional slave into the moral master: that 'one man who rules over numerous wise and brave men'. He was born, as says the *Mahābhārata*, for the sake of others, "like the horse or the goat". Hindu kingship is the highest ideal of sacrifice on the part of the individual whose privilege it was to be the king of the Hindus.

Utility

His utility was very great. He saw to the transfer of ministers and ministry and was the co-ordinating spirit in government. Propelled by his high sense of sacrifice, high traditions and high position, morally he stood far higher than the ministers and rulers-ministers. If people found the actual governors bad, he still remained the centre of hope and reform and avoided disruption.[4] Ministers came and went but the king remained.

---

[3] *Artha-Śāstra*, Bk. I, Ch. 19 ; 16 (p. 39)—

प्रजासुखे सुखं राज्ञः प्रजानाञ्च हितेहितम् ।
नात्मप्रियं हितं राज्ञः प्रजानां तु प्रियं हितम् ॥

[4] *Ibid.*, Bk. VIII, Ch. 1 ; 127 (p. 320)—

मन्त्रिपुरोहितादिभृत्यवर्गमध्यक्षप्रचारं पुरुषद्रव्य-प्रकृतिव्यसनप्रतीकारमेधनञ्च राजैव करोति व्यसनिषु वामात्येष्वन्यानव्यसनिनः करोति ।

Even when he was powerless, he was (as Kauṭilya puts it) the Symbol of State.[5] He was the standard of sovereignty to rally loyalty and hold the realm together. He was, in the words of Śukra, the root of the Tree of State:

"King is the root of the Tree of State; the Ministry is its trunk, the military chiefs are branches, the army are the leaves of the tree and the Subjects are its flowers, prosperity of the Country its fruits, and the whole Country the final seed."[6]

But for him the ministry would have tended to become an oligarchy, and the fruits and seeds for future fruits would have fallen in their hands and been misappropriated.

Looking at his utility and at his life of superb sacrifice[7] the Hindu world well put its verdict in the mouth of Bhīshma, the representative of Hindu royalty in Hindu literature:

सर्व-धर्मपरं क्षात्रं लोकश्रेष्ठं सनातनम् ।

'Of all *dharmas* (duties) rulership is the highest in society, for all times.'

---

[5] *Artha-Śāstra*, Bk. V, Ch. 6; 95 (p. 254)—ध्वजमात्रोऽयम् ।

[6] *Śukranītisāra*, V. 12—

राज्यवृक्षस्य नृपतिर्मूलं स्कन्धाश्चमन्त्रिणः ।
शाखाः सेनाधिपाः सेनाः पल्लवाः कुसुमानि च ।
प्रजाः फलानि भूभागा बीजं भूमिः प्रकल्पिता

[7] *Mahābhārata, Śānti-Parvan*, Ch. LXIII. 29—(Kumb. ed. 26).

आत्मत्यागः सर्वभूतानुकम्पा
लोकज्ञानं पालनं मोक्षणञ्च ।
विषण्णानां मोक्षणं पीडितानां
क्षात्रे धर्मे विद्यते पार्थिवानाम् ॥

CHAPTER XXXVI

Character of the Hindu Monarchy

State a Trust

It would be evident from the above discussion of the Mīmāṃsā, from the theory of taxation, from the coronation oath and other points noticed above that the State under Monarchy in the eyes of the Hindu was a Trust. The object of the trust is clearly stated in the *Śruti* text which had to be repeated at every Coronation; "*This State to Thee (is given)*—Thou art the director, regulator, firm bearer (of this responsibility)—*for* (the good of) *agriculture, for well-being, for prosperity, for growth* (of the people), (that is) *for success.*"[1]

The Trust, the State, thus created was for the prosperity of the People. It is this underlying principle which has been expressed in later literature in so many forms, culminating in the fixed maxim that the king is the servant of the people getting his wages. If the object of the trust is not fulfilled, the trustee is "to be shunned like a leaky ship on the sea".[2]

The *telos* of the Hindu monarchical state brings us to the great distinguishing feature of that state. The end of the state was to secure peace and prosperity of the people. Sacerdotal duties were never imposed upon the king. He was never a priest even in the Vedic age. By prosperity was meant, of course, the immediate material prosperity: the state was instituted for *land-culture, wealth,* etc. That prosperity, which was secured by a correct administration and justice, was regarded to bring about moral prosperity in its train as a corollary.

---

[1] The *White Yajur-Veda,* IX. 22—

"This is thy Sovereignty. Thou art the ruler, thou art controller, thou art firm and steadfast.

"Thee for land culture, thee for peace and quiet, thee for wealth, thee for increase of our substance."—R. T. H. Griffith's translation.

[2] *Mahābhārata, Śānti-Parvan,* LVII. 43.

Again, the Hindu Monarchical State was essentially a civil state. Standing armies appear as early as the sixth century B.C. and probably had existed before it for some centuries. At times very large armies, three quarters of a million strong, were maintained.[3] But the State never lapsed into a military polity. The governors of the provinces were civil officers. All the known orders in inscriptions are addressed to civil functionaries. The Commander-in-Chief and all other military chiefs were appointed by the Council of State where the Commander-in-Chief had no place. We do not find the army making and unmaking kings. All the traditions of depositions,—*e.g.*, that of *Nāga-Darśaka*, of *Pālaka* or of the early *Vena*, relate dethronements brought about by the Citizens of the Capital and other constituents of the civil population, not by the army. The king among his several titles—*Narapati* (Protector of the People), *Bhūpati* (Protector of the Country), *Bhaṭṭāraka* (Lord), *Great King* and others—has not got an epithet indicating an official military character, although his personal heroism is often extolled. He as the head of the executive was undoubtedly the head of the army, and in practice he very often led the army and fought, but that was a personal matter. There is no theory which gives him a military halo. He was not the generalissimo of the army by inherent right; that office was quite distinct from that of kingship from Vedic times (pp. 200–203 above).

A Civil State

Likewise, war was to be avoided as far as it was possible, and especially so, for conquest. This was more or less a settled principle of Hindu politics.[4] Militarism as a feature is everywhere absent.

On the other hand the most pronounced feature of the Hindu monarchy, as we have seen, was the paramount position of law in the polity. We have also noticed the prominent reference to law in the coronation oath of the *Mahābhārata*.

---

[3] *E.g.*, in the time of Chandragupta Maurya.

[4] *Manu*, VII. 199; *Mahābhārata*, 69. 23: "Bṛihaspati has laid down that a wise king should always avoid war for acquisition of territory."

The civil character of the Hindu monarchy is reflected in the stress laid on law.

Conquest and Sense of Justice

Laws of war and conquest were incorporated into the Civil Law as one of its limbs. So much so that the question of conquest was often discussed from the point of view of municipal law, the standard being the standard of the morality of law. If a state was conquered its government was to be re-entrusted into the hands of the old ruling house. This was what the *Mānava Dharma-Śāstra*[5] laid down after an experience of a nearly all-India, one-king empire, extending 'from sea to sea' from Madras to the Hindu Kush. It was based on the analogy of the legal theory of '*legitimacy*'. It was not a mere theory which was once preached as a pious opinion and then forgotten. It was largely followed from the fourth to the tenth century A.C. In the Allahabad pillar inscription of the great conqueror Samudra Gupta of the Imperial Gupta Dynasty we find the same principle acted upon. Kālidāsa records the same practice. The earliest Muhammadan writer (851 A.C.) bears witness to it. "The wars they wage with the neighbouring princes are not usually undertaken with a view to possess themselves with the adjoining dominions....When a prince makes himself master of some kingdom, he confers the government upon some person of the royal family" [*Account of the merchant Sulaiman recorded by Abu Zaid*, trans. (1718) by the Abbé Renaudot]. In the age of Hindu Rationalism which formed the palmiest days of Hindu history, the theory existed in the form noticed by the Greek writers with regard to Hindu attitude to foreign politics. Arrian drawing upon Megasthenes records in his *Indika* (IX):

"*Sense of justice, they* (Hindus) *say, prevented any Indian king from attempting conquest beyond the limits of India.*"

Only such a theory would explain the great fact that although Chandragupta's was "the *mightiest throne then existing in the world*" (Rhys Davids) and so it remained under his two successors, and that although the Maurya emperors found their next-door neighbour, the Seleucid

---

[5] *Manu*, VII. 202. Other Law-Codes reiterate the same principle.

empire, weak and crumbling, yet no inclination was exhibited to go beyond the Hindu Kush, the natural frontier of the India of those days.

Longevity a Result of Civil Polity

To this civil and legal character of Hindu Polity, the sociological historian, I venture to think, would mainly ascribe the extraordinary longevity of the Hindu State (p. 366 below), and the absence of a deadly conflict between the People and the Crown.

CHAPTER XXXVII

Imperial Systems

Ādhipatya and *Sārvabhauma*

The *Aitareya Brāhmaṇa* places after the republican group of states the monarchical group which consists of these varieties : (1) Monarchy,[1] (2) Great (or High) Monarchy (*Mahā-rājya*), (3) Over-Lordship (*Ādhipatya*), and (4) Pan-Country-Sovereignty[2] (*Sārvabhauma*).

The High Monarchy is not defined. But the word *mahā*-(mahat) connotes relativity, *e.g.*, superiority between States of the same kind. *Mahā-rājya* probably meant a large monarchy, larger than its neighbours, with certain constitutional features at present not known. *Ādhipatya* in its technical sense evidently signifies an over-lordship embracing protected states ; the *Brāhmaṇa* after the mention of the *Ādhipatya* has "*May I be (sovereign) enveloping neighbours*".[3] *Ādhipatya* thus seems to mean an imperial system in which suzerainty or 'over-protection' (*Ādhipatya*) on states outside its frontiers was exercised by the dominant state. Khāravela who had taken the consecration of *Mahārājya*, was described obviously in consequence of his conquests and *Rājasūya*, as *Adhipati* and *Chakravartin*.[4]

---

[1] The *Rājya* is qualified with *Pārameshṭhya*, apparently to distinguish it as *the* rājya, the rājya superior, *i.e.*, monarchy "सर्वेषां राज्ञां श्रैष्ठ्यमतिष्ठां परमतां गच्छेयम्. It is also possible that *Pārameshṭhya* was some sort of distinct monarchical constitution (*cf*. राजानं राजपितरं परमेष्ठिनं पारमेष्ठ्यम्. *Aitareya Brāhmaṇa*, VIII. 12). I remember having seen a passage in the *Mahābhārata* where some king is styled *Parameshṭhin*. The rare *Svāvaśya* (VIII. 12) if technical, was probably a reminiscence of the discredited '*autocracy*' which the oath in the *Mahābhārata* specifically excludes from Hindu kingship.

[2] *Aitareya Brāhmaṇa*, VIII. 15—

साम्राज्यं भौज्यं स्वाराज्यं वैराज्यं पारमेष्ठ्यं राज्यं माहाराज्यमाधिपत्यमयं समन्तपर्यायी स्यात् ।

[3] *Ibid.*, समन्त पर्यायी स्यात् ।

[4] Jayaswal, *J.B.O.R.S.*, III. 434, 459 ; IV. 376. 396 : *Ep. Ind.*.

The wish to be a *Sārvabhauma* is expressed to become "(the sole) *monarch of the land up to its* (natural) *frontiers, up to the sea, over all human beings*".[5] This is a variety of large monarchy which is based on territory as opposed to nationality (*e.g.*, *Jānarājya* of the *Śatapatha Brāhmaṇa*). It however claims the whole area (*sarva-bhūmi*) within natural boundaries, the country with "natural frontiers". The "natural frontiers" notion is expressed by Kauṭilya in his *chāturanta* sovereignty ('an empire up to the four limits')[6] and he defines it to be the *imperial field* as lying between Cape Comorin and the Himalayas, *i.e.*, the whole of India.[7] The ideal of one-king empire extending up to the seas probably arose in Magadha from where the field for conquest lay open up to the Bay of Bengal. Its non-Āryan population, unlike the Āryan Janas or nations of the Doab, was no moral barrier to the Hindu imperialist.

We have thus two main systems: one is the Suzerainty or *Adhipatya* system and the other is the Pan-Country Monarchy or the *Sārvabhauma.*[8] The latter system was extended and applied even to the Āryan India by the kings of Magadha which shocked the principle of *Jānarājya*. Hindu historians denounced the "one-king," "one-umbrella" sovereignty of *Māhā-Padma* established over the ashes of the houses of Vedic antiquity[9] (see below).

Sāmrājya System

At the same time there was the system called the *Sāmrājya*. This was older than the *Sārvabhauma* and also probably the *Ādhipatya*. This is the favourite of the Vedic literature. It is significant that the *Aitereya Brāhmaṇa* detaches it from the monarchical systems and treats it as distinct. What is still surprising is that the *Brāhmaṇa* places it at the head of the list of non-monarchical systems. We can understand the reason if we

---

[5] *Aitareya Brāhmaṇa*, VIII. 15—
सार्वभौमः सार्वायुष आन्तादापरार्धात् पृथिव्यै समुद्रपर्यन्ताया एकराट्।

[6] *Artha-Śāstra*, III. 1. 58, p. 159.

[7] *Ibid.*, IX. 1, p. 338.

[8] The *Sārvabhauma* does not relate to the 'whole Earth'. See *bhūmi*—country (p. 350 above); *Prithivī*—country, '*deśa*', according to *Artha Śāstra*, p. 338.

[9] See *Purāṇa Text* (Pargiter), p. 25; Jayaswal, *J.B.O.R.S.*, I. 111:

analyse the system. *Sāmrājya* indicates a "collection of states" under one acknowledged super-state. In modern phraseology it was a Federal Imperil system. The federal character distinguished it from the 'one-king' system. According to the *Aitareya Brāhmaṇa* the rulers in the *Prāchī* (East) took the consecration of *Sāmrājya, i.e.*, the *Prāchī* or Magadha had become the imperial seat. The *Sukla Yajurveda* (XV. 12) knows the system as prevalent in another part of India (West). *Prāchī* was under the house of Jarāsandha, called in history, the Bārhadrathas, after his ancestor Bṛihadratha. The *Mahābhārata* says that the position of *Samrāt* was acquired by Jarāsandha. Jarāsandha was the President or *Samrāt* of the Federal Organisation and Śiśupāla, king of the Chedis, was the common generalissimo. In this detail we detect an inter-state basis of originally free nature. In the first book of the *Mahābhārata* we actually find a free election of an emperor by a collection of kings and his consecration to that position.[10] The datum of the *Sabhā-Parvan* also implies that the system had been introduced by the rulers for self-protection,[11] but that Jarāsandha had abused it and reduced other sovereigns to slavery.

In view of our interpretation we can easily imagine how a small king like Janaka of Videha had obtained the position of *Samrāṭ*.[12] Any outstanding personality could be elected leader of the organisation. It seems that owing to the character of the organisation the *Aitereya Brāhmaṇa* classed it with the popular constitutions.

Later History of Monarchical Imperialism

The system which won the day in the post-Bṛihadratha[13] period was the *Sārvabhauma*. The system began to take shape about 700 B.C. when the national states began to give way (page 238 above). The old dynasties, come down from Vedic times, began to dwindle. In the next century, large, non-national monarchies greatly developed. There were about three of these. One, but not yet the foremost, had its

---

10 *Sabhā-Parvan*, Ch. XIX.

11 *Cf. Ādi-Parvan*, Ch. 100. 7.

12 See *ante* p. 189, *n.* 3 ; *Śatapatha Brāhmana*, XI. 3. 1. 2.

13 *C.* 700 B.C. (*J.B.O.R.S.*, IV, p. 26).

seat in Magadha, another in Kosala and the third in Avantī.[14] Competition follows between the three and Magadha finally wins under Nanda-Vardhana.[15] A permanent *Sārvabhauma* is set up about 450 B.C. A century later, the old traditional houses are finally wiped off the tablet of history by the Śūdra Emperor of Magadha (p. 359 above). Literally a 'one-umbrella' empire covering the whol eo fNorthen India except the Punjab was erected: Hindu historians marked it as the beginning of a New Period.

In 600–450 B.C. people began, as it were, to question "Why should the old dynasties be allowed to live on?" And the two first cases of usurpation were enacted—in Avantī and in Magadha. A political thinker actually formulated a theory of usurpation against degenerate houses.[16] The old dynasties seem to have outlived themselves and ceased to perform their function.

Chakravartin

This type of Hindu Imperialism was also known as "*Chakravartin*-system". It has reference to '*the arena where the imperial wheel moved unobstructed*'. The basic idea again is territory. In the place of the old 'up-to-ocean' limit it substituted a new definition—from Cape Comorin to Kashmir.[17] The *Chakravartin* ideal had been in the air certainly as early as 570 B.C. and presumably earlier. The Buddha took it from the phraseology of politics and proclaimed the foundation of the Empire of

[14] First under the *Vītihotras* and then the *Pradyotas*.

[15] Jayaswal, *J.B.O.R.S.*, I. 87. 107.

[16] Bhāradvāja, quoted and refuted by Kauṭilya in *Artha-Śāstra*, V. 6. 95, pp. 253–54. Kauṭilya points out the immorality, the fact that the ministers do really rule, and above all the great danger of punishment by the people.

Bhāradvāja was a ruthless writer. (Kaṇika was his personal name.) He preached, according to the *Mahābhārata*, in Western India, to a Sauvīra king. Govindarāja, *Rāmāyaṇa, Ayodhyā-Kāṇḍa*, 100. 39, calls his a 'crooked policy'.

[17] *Artha-Śāstra*, p. 338 :—देशः पृथिवी । तस्यां हिमयत्समुद्रान्तरमुदीचीनं योजन-सहस्रपरिमाणमतिर्यक् चक्रवर्तिक्षेत्रम् 'Country is the whole land (*i.e.*, India). In it from the Himālaya up to the Ocean—straight north, 1000 yōjanas in measure, is the *Chakravartin*-arena.'

his religion (*Dharma-Chakra*). 'Conquest', 'Conquest', 'nothing but Conquest', and to create oneness by that Conquest, was the breath of the eastern Hindus in 600—500 B.C. The Buddha claimed to be a *Chakravartin*-emperor and the Mahāvira, another great teacher, claimed to be the Conqueror (Jina) of his time. As in the Moghul period the air was surcharged with the idea of founding Badshahis both in religion and in politics, so some two thousand years before people thought nothing but of unifying the continent by conquest in religion and in politics.

The idea of unity was the only element therein which would find approval of the historian. Apart from that element, there was nothing in the system to commend itself to the experience of the country. The system meant development of a tremendous power, but it was a power attained under intoxication. The after-effect was sinking into exhaustion. It never became an approved system. The law-books and political thinkers went back to the ideals of the Federal System and the *Ādhipatya*. They preached that individual states had a right to live.[18]

Centralization

The great feature of the Magadha Imperialism was its centralization. Justice had become royal, even law tended to be royal.[19] The village came under the royal officer. All ships were owned and let by the state. Virtues alone did not come under the focus of the Crown; also vices were brought under the imperial vigilance. Prostitutes were placed under a royal department, gambling was centralised in government buildings or buildings licensed by government, hotels and wine shops were put under an imperial department. Mines were monopolised, or to quote the old phrase, brought 'under one outlet' (*ekamukha*). Some of these measures were beneficial, others injurious.

Centralization was against the genius of the race. The Buddha founded his empire, but the machinery of that empire was self-government, and it flourished. On the other hand

---

18 *Vishṇu*, III. 47–48, "राजा परपुरावासी तु तत्र तत्कुलीनमभिषिञ्चेत् । न राजकुलमुच्छिन्द्यात्.' See also *Manu*, VII. 202

19 *Artha-Śāstra*, p. 150. धर्मश्च व्यवहारश्च चरित्रं राजशासनम् ।

under the Magadhan machinery, the soul of the country was chained round the imperial standard ; and it failed.

An Imperial System of Compromise

The system which was tried next was a compromise. The Gupta system tolerated a few sub-states under it, but in reality it was neither a Federation nor the inferior type, the pure *Ādhipatya*. In essentials it remained a large monarchy. A real federalism with something like equal treatment to other states remained to be revived.

For our purposes of constitutional study the second[20] and the third[21] empires are but mere monarchies. The power of constitutional bodies under them must have varied to some extent according to the periods of peace and war. In periods of war and stress they must have become somewhat weak and in periods of peace they would have grown powerful. The popular forms, at any rate, still lived.

CHAPTER XXXVIII

Revival of Hindu Polity

The period after 700 A.C. is a period of darkness and disruption. Popular institutions decayed and Hindu traditions dwindled. The causes, as observed above, are yet to be investigated.

But when there was a Hindu revival in the time of Śivāji and the Sikhs, the Sikhs as a polity failed. They failed because they could not connect themselves with the Past. They followed a system which prevailed around them and established a polity of one-man's rule; Guru Govinda wanted to remedy it but the attempt brought about 'no man's rule'. It was the "Padshahi", the Moghul form, in success and in defeat, in rise and in fall. But the movement in the Maratha country had a different history. There they looked into past history and drew up a constitution and founded a polity on materials that were easily available to them but the materials which connected them with the Past. They consulted the *Mahābhārata* and the *Śukranīti* and found that king should reign but not rule, that government should be vested in a Ministry of eight ministers. And they founded the *Ashṭapradhāna*.[1] They searched out technical terms from political literature of the country and drew up a *Rājakośa* or Book of State Terms. Yet the system tried was only one portion of Hindu polity, one half of the whole body. They had the *Parishad* but they had not the *Paura-Jānapada*. To their great credit it must however be said that in modern times they were the first to realise that one man's rule was not allowed by the wisdom and experience of their forefathers, that it was foreign to the genius of their Śāstras. Their limitations were the limitations of darkness and ignorance about the constitutional history of the country, a darkness which we have not yet fully removed three centuries after.

Cause of Failure

CHAPTER XXXIX

Conclusion

This is a brief survey, in fact too brief a survey, of a polity which had a free career of at least thirty centuries of history[1]—a career longer than that of all the polities known to history. Babylon probably lived a few centuries longer, but unfortunately Babylon is no more. Against this we have India still existing, and in this respect China—another civil polity—is her only parallel.

The test of a polity is its capacity to live and develop, and its contribution to the culture and happiness of humanity. Hindu polity judged by this test will come out very successfully.

The constitutional progress made by the Hindu has probably not been equalled, much less surpassed by any polity of antiquity. The great privilege of the Hindu at the same time is that he is not yet a fossil; he is still living with a determination which a great historian (Duncker) has characterised as a tenacity which bends but does not break. The Golden Age of his polity lies not in the Past but in the Future. His modern history begins with the seventeenth century when Vaishṇavism preached the equality of all men, when the Śūdra, the helot of the ancient Hindu, preached shoulder to shoulder with the Brahmin (who welcomed and encouraged it), when the God of the Hindu was for the first time worshipped with hymns composed by a Muhammadan,[2] when Rāmadāsa declared that man is free and he cannot be subjected by force,[3] and when

---

[1] Coins have been found which Sir Alexander Cunningham, the most competent critic on Hindu numismatics, has placed about 1000 B.C. The Purāṇas and Khāravela's inscription (*J.B.O.R.S.*, III. pp. 436–37; *Ep. Ind.*, XX. 71) indicate the date of the *Mahābhārata* to have been *c.* 1425 B.C. Megasthenes, 310 B.C., found the Hindus counting 154 kings from the earliest times to Chandragupta.

[2] Rasa-khan's *Savaiyās* have been chanted since then at the evening service in Vaishnava temples. Compare with this the view of Ghalib who would bury the Hindu at Kābā and cremate the Muhammadan at Benares.

[3] नरदेह हा स्वाधीन। सहसा न हे पराधीन॥ *Dāsa-bodha*, I. 10. 25.

the Brahmin accepted the leadership of the Śūdra in attempting to found a State.

The Reformation of the Hindu has come. But a force which is greater still is also coming. This is the pagan thought, the European manhood. What a coincidence that the race which evolved the greatest constitutional principles in antiquity should be placed to-day in contact with the greatest constitutional polity of modern times. The contact is electrifying : it can either kill or rejuvenate the Race.[4] Probabilities however are, as the historian thought, for the latter :

"With this (tenacity) they (the Hindus) have retained a costly possession, that inclination towards the highest intellectual attainments which runs through their whole history. This treasure is still vigorous in the hearts of the best Indians, and appears the more certainly to promise a brighter future."—Duncker, *History of Antiquity* (1852–57), IV. Ch. 10.

Constitutional or social advancement is not a monopoly of any particular race. I am not a believer in the cheap wisdom which preaches that political greatness is inherent in some peoples. It is a superstition which is as baseless as the Spanish superstition of the Blue Blood. There is no such thing as Blue Blood in political and constitutional evolution. Political and constitutional progress is a creation of circumstances and human forces. And even if such Blue Blood be a reality it is certainly present in the veins of the Hindu.

---

[4] There is much unthinking and unreasonable mortification at times witnessed at the thought of being "conquered". But conquest is only a mode of receiving new thoughts and new life. What great modern community was not conquered ? The primitive state of England would have continued much longer but for the advent of the Danes and the Normans. Germany and Italy would have remained a European Rajputana or a Kathiawad but for the French and Austrian domination. India would have become an other Siam, Ceylon or Korea but for the Muhammadan incoming.

APPENDIX A

The Mahābhārata on the Andhaka-Vṛishṇi-Saṃgha

The *Śānti-Parvan* in its Ch. 81 records a discussion on the affairs of the Andhaka-Vṛishni league. It is called an 'ancient history', although it is put in the mouth of Bhīshma, a contemporary. Kṛishṇa puts his difficulties as the Vṛishni-leader before his friend Nārada, and the latter gives his solution. The discussion is important as showing :—

(*a*) that there were two political parties in the joint *Saṃgha or Federal Parliament*, each of which tried to gain the upper hand in political matters;

(*b*) that there were sharp discussions in their parliament or council, and Kṛishṇa was attacked, and he attacked others in return, for Nārada rebukes him for not having a tactful tongue;

(*c*) that at the time to which the history relates Babhru Ugrasena[1] and Kṛishṇa were the elected Presidents;

(*d*) that the republican leaders were mostly related to each other, and that Kṛishṇa was not equal to the influence or intrigue of his relatives. Āhuka on the side of the Vṛishṇis and Akrūra on the side of the Andhakas seem to have led the Federal Diet. (These two, according to the *Sabhā-Parvan*,[2] had contracted a political marriage between their families.)

I give below the text and translation of the discussion.

भीष्म उवाच ॥

अत्राप्युदाहरन्तीममितिहासं पुरातनम् ।
संवादं वासुदेवस्य महर्षेर्नारदस्य च ॥ २ ॥

वासुदेव उवाच ।

नासुहृत् परमं मन्त्रं नारदार्हति वेदितुम् ।
अपण्डितो वाऽपि सुहृत्पण्डितो वाप्यनात्मवान् ॥ ३ ॥

---

[1] उग्रसेनो नामान्धकः । *Mahābhāshya* on P., IV. I. 114; Kielhorn, II, p. 114.

[2] Ch. XIV, 33–34.

स ते सौहृदमास्थाय किंचिद्वक्ष्यामि नारद ।
कृत्स्नां बुद्धिं च ते प्रेक्ष्य संपृच्छे त्रिदिवंङ्गम ॥ ४ ॥
दास्यमैश्वर्यवादेन ज्ञातीनां वै करोम्यहम् ।
अर्धभोक्ताऽस्मि भोगानां वाग्दुरुक्तानि च क्षमे ॥ ५ ॥
अरणीमग्निकामो वा मथ्नाति हृदयं मम ।
वाचा दुरुक्तं देवर्षे तन्मां दहति नित्यदा ॥ ६ ॥
बलं सङ्कर्षणे नित्यं सौकुमार्यं पुनर्गदे ।
रूपेण मत्तः प्रद्युम्नः सोऽसहायोऽस्मि नारद ॥ ७ ॥
अन्ये हि सुमहाभागा बलवन्तो दुरासदाः ।
नित्योत्थानेन संपन्ना नारदान्धकवृष्णयः ॥ ८ ॥
यस्य न स्युर्न वै स स्याद्यस्य स्युः कृत्स्नमेव तत् ।
द्वयोरेनं प्रचरतोर्वृणोम्येकतरं न च ॥ ९ ॥
स्यातां यस्याहुकाक्रूरौ किं नु दुःखतरं ततः ।
यस्य चापि न तौ स्यातां किं नु दुःखतरं ततः ॥ १० ॥
सोऽहं कितवमातेव द्वयोरपि महामुने ।
नैकस्य जयमाशंसे द्वितीयस्य पराजयम् ॥ ११ ॥
ममैवं क्लिश्यमानस्य नारदोभयदर्शनात् ।
वक्तुमर्हसि यच्छ्रेयो ज्ञातीनामात्मनस्तथा ॥ १२ ॥

नारद उवाच ।

आपदो द्विविधाः कृष्ण बाह्याश्चाभ्यन्तराश्च ह ।
प्रादुर्भवन्ति वार्ष्णेय स्वकृता यदि वाऽन्यतः ॥ १३ ॥
सेयमाभ्यन्तरा तुभ्यमापत् कृच्छ्रा स्वकर्मजा ।
अक्रूरभोजप्रभवा सर्वे ह्येते तदन्वयाः ॥ १४ ॥
अर्थहेतोर्हि कामाद्वा वीरवीभत्सया[3]ऽपि वा ।
आत्मना प्राप्तमैश्वर्यमन्यत्र प्रतिपादितम् ॥ १५ ॥
कृतमूलमिदानीं तत् राज-शब्दं सहायवत् ।
न शक्यं पुनरादातुं वान्तमन्नमिव स्वयम् ॥ १६ ॥
बभ्रूग्रसेनतो राज्यं नाप्तुं शक्यं कथंचन ।
ज्ञातिभेदभयात्कृष्ण त्वया चापि विशेषतः ॥ १७ ॥
तच्च सिध्येत्प्रयत्नेन कृत्वा कर्म सुदुष्करम् ।
महाक्षयं व्ययो वा स्याद्विनाशो वा पुनर्भवेत् ॥ १८ ॥
अनायसेन शस्त्रेण मृदुना हृदयच्छिदा ।
जिह्वामुद्धर सर्वेषां परिमृज्यानुमृज्य च ॥ १९ ॥

---

[3] Another reading—वाचावीभत्सया

वासुदेव उवाच ।

अनायसं मुने शस्त्रं मृदु विद्यामहं कथम् ।
येनैषामुद्धरे जिह्वां परिमृज्यानुमृज्य च ॥ २० ॥

नारद उवाच

शक्त्यान्नदानं सततं तितिक्षाऽऽर्जवमार्दवम् ।
यथार्हप्रतिपूजा च शस्त्रमेतदनायसम् ॥ २१ ॥
ज्ञातीनां वक्तुकामानां कटुकानि लघूनि च ।
गिरा त्वं हृदयं वाचं शमयस्व मनांसि च ॥ २२ ॥
नामहापुरुषः कश्चिन्नानात्मा नासहायवान् ।
महतीं धुरमादाय समुद्यम्योरसा वहेत् ॥ २३ ॥
सर्व एव गुरुं भारमनड्वान्महते समे ।
दुर्गे प्रतीतः सुगवो भारं वहति दुर्वहम् ॥ २४ ॥
भेदाद्विनाशः सङ्घानां सङ्घमुख्योऽसि केशव ।
यथा त्वां प्राप्य नोत्सीदेदयं सङ्घस्तथा कुरु ॥ २५ ॥
नान्यत्र बुद्धिक्षान्तिभ्यां नान्यत्रेन्द्रियनिग्रहात् ।
नान्यत्र धनसन्त्यागाद्गुणः प्राज्ञेऽवतिष्ठते ॥ २६ ॥
धन्यं यशस्यमायुष्यं स्वपक्षोद्भावनं सदा ।
ज्ञातीनामविनाशः स्याद्यथा कृष्ण तथा कुरु ॥ २७ ॥
आयत्यां च तदात्वे च न तेऽस्त्यविदितं प्रभो ।
षाड्गुण्यस्य विधानेन यात्रा यानविधौ तथा ॥ २८ ॥
यादवाः कुकुरा भोजाः सर्वे चान्धकवृष्णयः
त्वय्यायत्ता महाबाहो लोका लोकेश्वराश्च ये ॥ २९ ॥

Bhīshma said :—In this connection (on relatives in politics) this *old history* is quoted—this dialogue between Vāsudeva and the great sage Nārada (2).

Vāsudeva said :—

Nārada, matters of State-counsel of vital importance can neither be made known to one who is not a friend, nor to a friend who is not an expert, nor even to an expert if he is not of master mind (3).

As I find the right friendship in thee on which I can depend, I want to speak something to thee, Nārada. In view of thy all-embracing intelligence, I want to put a question to thee, the happy one ! (4).

Rulership (*Aiśvarya*) it is called, but really it is *slavery* to relatives that I am performing. Although I am entitled to the *half of the executive powers*, I have only got to suffer bitter speeches (5).

My heart between cruel words, O Divine Seer, is like the Araṇi (wood) which a man, desirous of producing fire, is twirling. It is consuming me every day (6).

(Although) Samkarshana is always noted for strength and Gaḍa for princely qualities, and Pradhyumna is even handsomer than me, still I am without a following, O Nārada (7).

Other Andhakas and Vrishṇis indeed are endowed with great prosperity and might and are redoubtable. They are, Nārada, always full of (political) energy (*utthāna*) (8).

For him, in whose favour they are, there is everything. If they are not so, then one cannot exist.

As regards Āhuka and Akrūra, if they are in one's favour there is no greater misery for that man. And if they are not in one's favour, there is no greater misery for him either. I cannot elect the party of the either (9–10).

I am between these two, Great Sage, like that mother of two gamblers (gambling against each other) who can neither desire the victory of the one nor the defeat of the other (11).

Now, Nārada, take into consideration my position and also the position of my relatives and tell me please what may be beneficial to both. I am distressed (12).

Nārada replied :

(In a republic) dangers are of two kinds, Kṛishṇa, the external ones and the internal ones, or, those which are created internally and those which arise from elsewhere (13).

It is the internal difficulty which is present in this case. It is the result of (the members') own acts. The following of Akrūra the Bhoja, with all these families from (hope of) material gain, from caprice or from envy of bravery,[4] have transferred the political power (lit. 'rulership') obtained by them to some one else (14–15).

The authority which has taken root already and which is fortified with the title of relatives[5] they cannot take back like vomited food. They can in no way take back government from Babhru Ugrasena for fear of disunion with a relative. And you especially cannot (help them), O Kṛishṇa (16–17).

And if that is even done (Ugrasena is driven out of authority, *i.e.*, presidentship), by doing a bad (illegal) act, there would be fear of serious loss, waste, and there may be even a fear of destruction (18).

Use then a weapon which is not made of steel, which is very mild and yet capable of piercing all hearts, sharpening that weapon again and again, rectify the tongues of relatives (19).

Vāsudeva said :

What am I to understand, O Sage, by that weapon which is not made of steel and is mild, and sharpening which I have to employ in rectifying their tongue (20).

Nārada said :

The weapon which is not made of steel is this : Recognition of merit in others and honouring them, mildness, straightforwardness, toleration, and constant entertainment according to your capacity (21).

Of relatives who are anxious to speak, words which are bitter and light you should not really mind and you should by your reply appease their mind, sentiments and tongue (22).

None but a great man, one of master mind and commanding a following can successfully exert himself in carrying on high political responsibility (23).

Every ox can bear upon him a heavy burden and carry it on plain ground. It is only a noble and experienced animal that can carry a difficult burden through a difficult path (24).

Destruction of *Saṃghas* (republics) lies in disunion. You are the leader of them, O Keśava. As the republic has got you (as president at present), act in the manner that the *saṃgha* should not decline (25).

Nothing but tact and tolerance, nothing but control of one's personal tendencies, nothing but liberality, are the qualities which reside in the wise man for the successful leadership of a republic (26).

Kṛishṇa, elevation of one's Party leads always to long life, glory and wealth. Act in a way that destruction may not befall the relatives (27).

There is nothing, O Lord, in the matter of Future Policy and Present Policy as well as in the Policy of Hostility and in the Art of Invasion, in employing Foreign Policy, which is not known to you (28).

(Prosperity of) all the Andhaka-Vṛishṇis, the Yādavas, Kukuras, and Bhojas—with their people and rulers of people,[6] depend upon you, O you of long arms (29).

---

[6] Īśvara in the meaning of 'ruler' is a techincal term, *e.g.* *Mahābhāshya* on P., VI. 1. 2, Kielhorn, III, p. 7, 'ईश्वर आज्ञापयति। ग्रामाद्ग्रामान्मनुष्या आनीयन्तां प्रागाङ्गं ग्रामेभ्यो ब्रह्मणा आनीयन्तामिति'। *Cf. ibid.*, II. 365. See also *Gautama-Dh. S.*, IX. 63; *J.*, I. 510 '*issariya*,' 'sovereignty'.

APPENDIX B

List of Indian Republics discussed in Part I

1. Agra-śreṇi (Agsinæ)
2. Ambhashṭha (Ambastanoi, Sambastai)
3. Andhaka
4. Andhra
5. Araṭṭa, Arishṭa (Adrestai)
6. Audumbara
7. Avanti (Dvairājya)
8. Ābhīra
9. Ārjunāyana
10. Bhagala
11. Bharga
12. Bhoja
13. Brāhma-gupta
14. Brāhmāṇaka (Janapada) (Brāchmanoi)
15. Buli.
16. Chikkali Nikāya
17. Dakshin-Mallas
18. Dāmani
19. Dāṇḍaki
20. Gandhāra
21. Glauchukāyanaka (Glaukanikoi, Glausai)
22. Gopālava
23. Jālmani
24. Jānaki
25. Kāka
26. Kāmboja
27. Karpaṭa (Kharaparika)
28. Kaṭha (Kathaians)
29. Keralaputa
30. Kauṇḍibrisa
31. Kauṇḍaparatha
32. Kaushṭaki
33. Koliya
34. Kshattriya (Kathroi)
35. Kshudraka (Oxydrakai)
36. Kukura

37. Kuṇinda
38. Kuru
39. Lichchavi
40. Madra
41. Mahārāja (Janapada)
42. Mālava
43. Malla
44. Mauṇḍi Nikāya
45. Moriya
46. Muchukarṇa (Mousikani)
47. Nābhaka and Nābha Paṅkti
48. Nepal Dvairājya
49. Nysa (Akoubhi)
50. Parśva
51. Patala
52. Pāñchāla
53. Pitinika
54. Prārjuna
55. Prasthala (Preshti)
56. Pulinda
57. Pushyamitra
58. Rājanya (Janapada)
59. Rāshṭrika
60. Satvat
61. Śākya
62. Śālaṅkāyana
63. Sanakānīka
64. Satiyaputa
65. Śayaṇḍa
66. Sāpiṇḍī-nikāya
67. Saubhūti (° ta) (Sophytes)
68. Śibi (Janapada) (Siboi); (Mādhyamikeya)
69. Surāshṭra
70. Śūdra (Śudrāyaṇa = Sodrai)
71. Trigartas
72. Uttara-kuru
73. Uttara-madra
74. Utsava-Saṅketa
75. Vasāti (Ossadioi)
76. Vāmaratha

77. Videha
78. Vṛiji
79. Vṛika
80. Vṛishṇi
81. Yaudheya
82. Yona.

APPENDIX C

Additional Notes on Part I (1924)

P. 4—*Artha-Śāstra* (KAUṬILĪYA)—Its authorship and date.

Recently the controversy about the date of this work has revived. Dr. Jolly (*Artha-Śāstra of Kauṭilya*, Lahore, 1923, Intro. pp. 1–47) has pronounced the work to be a piece of forgery of about the third century A.C. (pp. 43, 47) : 'we might abide by the third century as the probable date of the A.,' 'the real author was a theoretician' and Kauṭilya himself a 'fabulous minister' (p. 47).

(i) AUTHORSHIP

To take up the latter thesis first, Jolly's arguments are :

(*a*) 'the traditional accounts of K. do not refer to K. in the capacity of a teacher or author of literary compositions,'

(*b*) 'nor is his name ever mentioned by Megasthenes,'

(*c*) 'nor does the latter writer's description of India bear out the theory that he was a contemporary of K.'

(*d*) 'Patañjali in his *Mahābhāshya* refers to the Mauryas and to the *sabhā* of Chandragupta, he is silent about K.'

(*e*) 'K. is a mere nickname denoting falsehood or hypocrysy, which could hardly have been devised by the renowned minister of Chandragupta himself,'

(*f*) 'nor does the character of the work stamp it the production of a statesman, filled as it is with pedantic classification and puerile distinctions, like all the Śāstras composed by Paṇḍits.

Jolly's Conclusion.—

"The real author" therefore "was a theoretician, no statesman but perhaps an official in a state of medium size" (p. 47). 'The ascription of the work to K. or Chāṇakya was entirely due to the myths current regarding that fabulous minister who was looked upon as the master and creator of the art of polity and as the author of all the floating wisdom on the subject of *Nīti*' (p. 47).

Argument (*a*) is contradicted by the latter portion of the conclusion, admitting that K. is traditionally regarded as the author, ' etc. Such tradition in literature does exist, *e.g.*, Jaina—' Koḍilliyam a false Śāstra ' in the *Nandi-Śūtra* cited by Dr. Shāma Śāstry, *A.Ś.* (1909), *Upodghāta*, IX, and Sanskrit—*Pañcha-tantra*, *Kāmandaka*, Daṇḍin (' revered teacher ') Medātithi, etc.

Argument (*b*) is disposed off by the simple answer: where is the book written by Megasthenes? Find that first, as we cannot build a hypothesis on a book not yet found.

Argument (*c*) evidently refers to a theory started on the supposition that K. knows no large empire but only a small kingdom, as he has the *maṇḍala* or *prakṛiti* theory of neighbours and records the existence of republics and a policy towards them. The supposition is contradicted by fact: K. says that the Imperial tract (*Chakravarti-ksehtra*)[1] lies between the Himalayas and the Ocean, nine[2] thousand yojanas in the straight line (as the crow flies). It is hardly possible to imagine a state without neighbours, a policy towards neighbours will have to be postulated by any statesman however large his empire may be. Then we know that there were a number of neighbours in the South who were reduced in the next reign—*i.e.*, of Bindusāra.[3] When Chandragupta took the north-western provinces from the Greeks, it does not follow that he took the land without its rulers, republics generally, who were existing under the system of Alexander. The *Saṇgha-vṛitta* lays down a policy towards the republics which it assumes to be under the king's sphere of influence, be they in (1) the Punjab, (2) Afghanistan (Kamboja), (3) Western India, or (4) North Bihar. There were therein parties in favour of the suzerain and parties against him (*A. S.*). He was to sow the seed of dissension, patronize some, instal or

---

[1] IX. 1, p. 338.

[2] Śaṇkarārya's reading, *KNS.*, I. 39.

[3] *J.B.O.R.S.*, II. 81.

depose one of the leaders (p. 376). Now we know that in no other than the early Maurya time Afghanistan, the Punjab, Western India and North Bihar at one and the same time were under the sphere of one Indian king. The fact that K. hardly tolerates sub-kings is one which is only compatible with the Maurya times. Under the Śuṅgas the imperial policy changes; it becomes largely feudal (see the local *rājas* in the inscriptions and on coins).

Argument (*d*) Patañjali, it is true, does not refer to Kauṭilya. But Jolly ought to have shown any sūtra of Paṇini or a Vārtika of Kātyāyana or a comment of Patañjali which could be the occasion of a mention of Kauṭilya. If Patañjali does not mention Bindusāra, Aśoka, Rādhagupta or the Buddha; is that a reason to hold that they did not live? Patañjali was not writing history.

Argument (*e*) Names are not devised by the bearers: they are given by parents. It is difficult to get rid of names, and no sensible man cares to change an awkward name, *e.g.*, *Sunaḥśepha*, *Piśuna*, *Fox*. As it has been repeatedly pointed out,[4] *Kauṭilya* was a *gotra* name coming down from generations. The forefather who bore the name *Kuṭila* or *Kauṭili*[4] is answerable to Dr. Jolly and not Kauṭilya Vishṇugupta. *Chāṇakya* (the name derived from the father according to Hindu literature[4]) is mentioned in a painted inscription in the Bijayagaḍh cave (Mirzapur) in Gupta script of the fourth century A.C., a photograph of which has been brought by Rai Saheb M. Ghosh, Curator, Patna Museum. It reads *Chāṇakya-roshaḥ*.

Argument (*f*) If all the Śāstras composed by Paṇḍits have puerile distinctions and pedantic divisions, it is a literary fault of Kauṭilya's country; he could not escape the traditional mannerism in letters. The style of a certain European country is heavy and pedantically detailed in the eyes of other Europeans. That style, be the author a college professor or a statesman lecturing on statecraft, cannot be avoided by the native. To me, the details and theories of the *A.Ś.* are such that no theoretical writer, *i.e.*, the contemptible 'Paṇḍit'

---

[4] *J.B.O.R.S.*, II. 97–80, *n*.

could have written it. This is in fact admitted by Jolly when he says that the writer was probably an official knowing administration. The admission itself contradicts the 'Paṇḍit' 'theoretician' theory. 'The A. deals with internal and external policy and may be designated as an ancient Imperial Gazetteer of India, as a manual of political economy and polity' (Jolly, 1–2). Again, 'the general tendency of the A. is thoroughly realistic and worldly' (Jolly, p. 3). The onus on Dr. Jolly is very heavy to prove that the author is some one other than the named and acknowledged (*e.g.*, by Śankarārya, Bāṇa, Daṇḍin, Kāmandaka and others) author of the work. Forgery is to be proved, not merely asserted, and proved by the party alleging it. It is for the reader to see if Dr. Jolly has discharged that onus. In my opinion he has not.

(ii) DATE

Now let us take the theory of date.

One has to agree when Dr. Jolly, very rightly, says that there is a rare unity of plan and structure pervading the whole work (p. 5). The device beginning with contents and ending with the notes on the system of the work which unifies the whole work, and the cross references in the body of the work leave no doubt that the whole work is by one and the same author. There is also common ground when he shows that the book as we have it (I may add, but for faulty readings and copyist's mistakes) is the same which existed about 400 A.C. (pp. 8, 9 and 12). Thirty quotations in the *Tantrākhyāyikā* and citations in later books prove it. Thus the question in controversy is reduced to this, when was the *A.Ś.* written between 300 B.C. and 400 A.C. This limit is further narrowed down by Jolly's view, rightly held, that Vātsāyana had before him the *A.Ś.* while writing the *S.* and he takes the time of the *K.S.* to be the "fourth century or so," and consequently places the *A.Ś.*, in the third century A.C. (pp. 29, 43).

Arguments for the third century A.C. Date

Arguments of Jolly for the third century date are:

1. That both Kauṭilya and Bhāsa have a verse (नवं शरावं etc.) in common and K. takes it as a quotation, hence he

must have borrowed it from Bhāsa whose date is third century A.C. (p. 10).

2. That K. and Yājñavalkya agree in their laws; that K. therefore converts Y's laws into sūtras (p. 17), and Y's date is the same, *i.e.*, third century A.C. (p. 47).

3. That the *Mahābhāshya* nowhere mentions the A.

4. That the Rājadharma in the *Mahābhārata* and the *Dharma Sūtras* are in an embryonic condition as compared with the A.'s detailed provisions and advanced condition of life (p. 30).

5. That the A. knows the Purāṇas.

6. That one of the Kāmaśastra sections, the Vaiśika, is mentioned by K. (p. 32).

7. That the A. knows technical terms of Sanskrit grammar and is acquainted with Ashṭādhyāyī (p. 32).

8. That astrology and divination are known to it and two plantes are mentioned by name in it.

9. That it knows a book on metallurgy called *Śulba-dhātu Śāstra* (on copper, p. 33).

10. That it knows many technical treatises, *e.g.*, on mining, architecture, finance, jewels, alchemy, etc. "His work is the outcome of a long period of literary activity in the field of polity rather than the production of a creative genius—another reason for not fixing its age-limit too high' (p. 33).

11. That "the minister (R.) in the *Mudrā-Rākshasa* is probably a myth, why should not K. be mythical as well" (p. 34). The Greeks do not mention him. The rise of a new dynasty might have 'given a start to the invention of myths' (p. 34).

12. That K. refers to alchemy which was 'a late growth on the tree of Indian science' (p. 34).

13. That K. mentions *Suraṅga* which is from the Greek term *Syrinx*.

14. That the description of India by Megasthenes and the Aśoka inscriptions do not show such an advanced stage as the A. (p. 31).

e.g., the A. knows State monopoly of mines, superintendents of mint, metal, mineralogy, chemical skill in producing coins, ornaments, etc., while Megasthenes refers to five metals only and Strabo says that Indians are inexperienced in the art of mining and smelting.

15. That the A. mentions written documents, while Megasthenes says that the Indians did not know writing.

16. That Megasthenes does not mention the premia on coins, taxes on gambling, liquors, road-cess, etc., which the A. describes.

17. That the description of Megasthenes agreeing with the A. proves nothing as the A. agrees also with the Chinese pilgirms and Alberuni.

18. That Pātaliputra is nowhere mentioned (p. 43). Geographical horizon of the author indicates that the book was written in the South from where it has been discovered.

19. That the A. gives the opinion of K. by name: this comes under the definition of *apadeśa* of the A. proving that K. could not himself have written the work.

20. That the opinions of others cited are imaginary, the names being taken from the *Mahābhārata* (pp. 31, 44).

Examination of Jolly's Arguments

1. The verse '*Navaṃ śarāvaṃ,*' etc., is a memorial verse used in exhorting soldiers in war. Exhortation to soldiers is as old as history; the verse is based on a primitive belief which is reminded thereby—that the faithless soldiers will go to hell. If we consider the following point, it will be evident that it is not possible for K. to have borrowed from Bhāsa, but that he must have borrowed either from some other book or as he implies, अपीह श्लोकौ भवत:, from floating, current memorial verses. The point is that K. gives two verses and the *Navaṃ ś.* one is the second, reading after the first (X. 3). Without the first it is incomplete. Bhāsa has only the latter one. How could it be said then that K. borrowed from Bhāsa.

2. It is perfectly true that there is a close agreement between Y. and K. in laws. I have discussed the point in my Tagore lectures. Here I shall take up only one datum

which completely disposes of the question of priority. K. uses a term *Yukta* meaning an official, which occurs in Aśoka's inscription as *Yuta*. The latter term none could understand before the publication of A. as the term in literature subsequent to A. has gone out of use altogether. Y. could not understand it as used in the A.: 'युक्त-कर्म चायुक्तस्य' 'an official act of a non-official' (as pointed out by Dr. Shama Sastry in his first edition of the A. Intro., p. x), and he uses *yogya* 'proper' अयोग्यो योग्यकर्मकृत्, II. 235) where K. gives *Yukta*, and *ayogya* 'improper' where K. has *a-yukta*. This can only be explained on the hypothesis that Y. versified the laws of K. and in places could not understand it. Jolly tries to meet this by saying that the demand for statement on oath being unauthorized was 'improper' and therefore the difference is purely nominal. But how could any one explain, even by straining, अयोग्यो योग्यकर्मकृत् 'an incapable man doing a work which should be done by a competent man' on the theory of nominal difference'?

Then, K. uses verses at times; if he was going to borrow from Y. why should he have turned verses into sūtras? The more rational process is to versify sūtras, and Y. followed that. There is no case made out for supposing a reverse process.

As Y. is assigned to the third century A.C., and *Yukta* has so long ceased to have the technical sense that a legal author could not understand it, the date of A. should be some centuries before 200–300 A.C.

3. Occasion for the mention of the A. is to be shown in the *Mahābhāshya* before we can deduce anything from the silence. Many Vedic works are not mentioned by Patañjali, for that reason no one can say that they did not exist. He was not writing a histroy of literature.

4. The Dharma Sūtras deal with Dharma laws, while the A. deals with Artha principles and laws. The subject of the Dharma Śūtras, is not political science but Dharma law. The subject of politics being principle in one and incidental in the other, no comparison can be instituted for the purposes of chronology. I would demur to characterize the M. Bh. Rāja dharma as being in embryonic state; in the theory part

it is more developed than the A. Then, every inferior writer does not change chronology. Some Tagore lectures after those of Dr. Jolly are far inferior; they for that reason could not be placed in a time earlier than his.

5. The oldest Dharma Śūtra knows Purāṇic literature, Āpastamba mentions the *Bhavishya Purāṇa* (II. 24, 6, p. 98). and "Purāṇa" again in II. 9. 23, 3. The *Bhavishya* existed according to Pargiter's researches very early. *Purāṇa* is mentioned as early as the *Chhāndogya Upanishad* (II. 3).

6. The *Vaiśika* book was written by Dattaka at Pāṭaliputra before Vātsyāyana. There is nothing to show that it or any other *Vaiśika* was not written before 300 B.C.

7. Knowledge of Pāṇini does not go against the 300 B.C. date of K. (see *ante*, p. 30 *n.*). Also note the pre-Paṇinean use [*cf.* Macdonell, *HSL*, p. 267 in the A. of *nāma*, *ākhyāta*, *upasarga* and *nipāta* (II. 10)]. In other words, Pāṇini's terms had not become established fully as in the time of Patañjali and later.

8. Divination is as old as the *Atharva Veda*. The origin of astrology has been already shown to be Mesopotamian.[5] The Greeks and Hindus both borrowed from the same source. No argument of chronology can be based on the mention of two planets. The fact that the planets as they appear in Greek astrology and later Indian literature do not find place in the A. is an argument in favour of an early date for the A.

Metallurgy, particularly knowledge of working copper, must have been known in a country where copper coins, silver coins, alloys in coins, "white metal" (or nickel? brought to Alexander in the Punjab), bronze, iron, glass, etc., have been worked for centuries before Alexander and Chandragupta, as proved by the positive evidence of finds (punch-marked coins, utensils at Pāṭaliputra and other places). Rai Sahib M. Ghosh found cast iron in the Maurya stratum at Pāṭaliputra. Cast glass seals were found with Maurya and pre-Maurya lettering by Dr. Spooner and the Rai Sahib at Pāṭaliputra

[5] *J.B.O.R.S.*, 1910, p. 664; *Ind. Ant.*, 1918, p. 112.

(*J.B.O.R.S.*, Sep. 1924). Seven metals are known as early as the *Yajur Veda* (*Vāj. S.*, XVIII. 13, XXIII. 37).

(A positive confirmation of the *A.Ś.* as a contemporary work is found in the cast coins found at the earliest Maurya level (20′ to 19′) which on being analysed have shown the same composition as prescribed in the *A.Ś.*).

9–10. The argument is against the theory of fanciful quotations in the *A.Ś.* If there was a long previous literary activity, the quotations are natural. If before the A., *i.e.*, before Alexander, there were technical treatises, K. could not make every science begin after the Greek invasion. Why the existence of treatises should be a reason to fix the date too low and not 'too high' (a term too ambiguous to meet) is not explained by the learned scholar.

11. It is not proved that 'Rākshasa' is a myth. From unknown to unknown is not a logical step. Further, if one minister is mythical why should all others be mythical? If the Greeks do not mention him, it is K.'s ill-luck. Non-mention by the Greeks, though it may take away the distinguished character of a human being, cannot disprove the very existence of a man. Moreover, where have you got the complete writings of the Greeks (*i.e.*, Megasthenes)? Rise of a new dynasty may give rise to myths, at the same time it *may not*, or may on one point and may not on others.

12. Dr. Jolly knows the Hindu theory that alchemy was born in India before the Christian era.[6] In any case it is not yet proved where the so-called science first made its appearance. In connection with alchemy in later Indian literature we have the mention of Constantinople (Rūma); if we connect the *A.Ś.* with later alchemy we have to come down to Muhammadan times. Jolly therefore has to postulate a probable "Greco-Syriac" origin and to place that hypothetical origin in the first century A.C. But one hypothesis cannot prove another. We must have a proved fact that alchemy is not original to India and that it was borrowed by India from a "Greco-Syriac" original and from nowhere else. The very

---

[6] Alberuni (XVII) gives the name *Vyāḍi* before the Christian era. *Vyāḍi* must have had predecessors.

fact that we have alchemy before A.C. 300. in India shows that we have to give up the theory of Arabian origin and admit that there was an earlier stratum, either Indian or foreign. We cannot go further than that because nothing can be proved at this stage beyond that. *Rūma* and *Barbara* as found in later literature must refer to another and a subsequent importation.

13. Syrinx was employed in sieges in India in Alexander's time. K. living both before and after Alexander's invasion can very well use the term. Besides, some Greeks had been living on the Indian frontier earlier and under the Persians in the Punjab, as Greek letters are found on Persian coins struck in India (see above, p. 124 *ff.*)

14. Aśoka's inscriptions do not undertake to give a gazetteer of the administrative system. Can any one attach the slightest importance to the Greek allegation that Hindus did not know smelting when we have coins, ornaments (*e.g.*, the fine gold ring found at Pāṭaliputra), cast iron, cast glass seals, etc. of the Maurya and pre-Maurya times? The Greeks themselves mention the fine vases carried in front of Chandragupta and gold vine in his palace. If Megasthenes mentions only five metals, his knowledge is poor as in so many other instances (seven castes, writing, etc.). Seven metals are known to the *Y. Veda* alone. In the absence of his original book we cannot say what M. actually said and of which part of India.

15. Megasthenes himself says that there were registers kept on the roads to find out distances and there were milestones. The *Jātakas* mention written tablets; seals, and inscriptions of Aśoka prove writing to have existed and been largely employed in the Maurya times. Could writing suddenly appear with Alexander? Aśoka two generations later publishing his inscriptions all over India and his father Bindusāra writing to the Greek king disprove the utterly untenable assertion.

16. Megasthenes' 'tax on articles sold' would include octroi and general taxes of the A. Besides, Megasthenes' work is not before us.

17. If agreement between Megasthenes and the A. proves nothing, how can disagreement prove anything?

18. The non-mention of Pāṭaliputra proves nil. The trade route to the South for the sake of shell, diamond, gems, pearls, etc., was no doubt important. At the same time the A. mentions Kāśi, Nepāla, Kukura, Lichchhavi, Malla, Kamboja, Kuru, Pāñchāla, Surāshṭra, Madra, etc. His horizon is predominantly northern.

So many MSS. have come out in the South. Did all those authors (Bhāsa, etc.) belong to the South for that reason?

19. The A. being avowedly based on old works, and the Sūtra and Bhāshya being combined in one treatise, every sūtra having original opinion of the author necessarily became *apadeśa*. As Fleet has pointed out and almost every Hindu knows, it is a very ancient and even current practice to give the author's name in his composition in this country. It appears odd to a foreigner, but it is commonplace in this country.

20. As Mahāmahopādhyāya Gaṇapati Śāstri has shown (*A.Ś.* II. Intro.) quotations from Visālāksha and Bṛihaspati are extant in literature. I may add to them by pointing out quotations from Śukra (Uśanas) and Bṛihaspati in the *Ṭīkā* to the *Nītivākyāmṛita* published by Paṇḍit Nāthūrāma Premin of Bombay, and from the *Mānava A.S.* pointed out above (p. 8; *Add. I*).

In the face of these quotations nobody will be heard to say that the authorities in the A. are imaginary.

Jolly has rightly ignored such untenable views as for instance 'that the style of the A. is not archaic' and 'that geographical data prove a late date'.[7]

---

[7] Mention of *Chīna* is innocuous, for *Chīna* which invariably comes along with *Darada* or other Himalayan countries in ancient Sanskrit literature clearly refers to '*Shīna*', the Gilgit tribe still retaining the word and having mulberry tree and silk industry. See the article in *Ency. Brit.* on 'China', and the identification by Sir George Grierson in *LSI.*, X, Part 4, p. 5, *n.* ['but I would suggest that in this (*Manu*, X. 44) and similar passages, they are the great Shiṇ race, still surviving in Gilgit and the vicinity']. It may be

(iii) New Arguments for the Fourth Century B.C. Date

There are pieces of evidence in the A. which are compatible only with the fourth century B.C. date.

(i) The use of *Yukta* which is only known to the Maurya times, and the 'geographical horizon' in laying down the policy towards the republics can only refer to the Maurya times. In the first century B.C. and the first or second century A.C. there was no power, no 'king' (for whom Kauṭilya wrote the Saṃgha-vṛitta policy) who had from Videha to Afghanistan under him.

(ii) Take again the term *Yuga*, meaning five years (II. 20). This is known to the Jyautisha Vedāṅga, and is not known to the literature of the early centuries including the *Mānava Dharma Śāstra*.

(iii) Take also the datum that the rainy season started in *Śrāvaṇa* (*Śrāvaṇa-proshṭhapadaṣeha Varshā*), *i.e.*, in the author's time the rainy season began in Śrāvaṇa, unlike to-day when it begins in the middle of Āshāḍha. Now, season falls back about one day and a half every century :—

---

added that the Chinas were regarded to have been of Kshatriya origin. They spoke a language of Sanskrit base as shown by the *A.Ś.* which says that the silks produced in China-country bore the names *kauśeya* and *chīnapaṭṭa*. Neither *kauśeya* nor *paṭṭa* (Skt. *pattra*) is a Chinese word. All the members of the group where China occurs are Himalayan peoples. *Chīna* alone cannot jump over thousands of miles away into China. In the same chapter (XI. ii) chīna-si furs or skins are mentioned as coming from Bālhava, which according to Bhaṭṭasvāmin is a Himalayan country. Gilgit and Cashmere still produce both skins and silk.

Interchange between *ch* and *sh* (*Shīn* = *Chīn*) is common in Shin, *e.g.*, *push* = *puch*.

Similarly, *ālakanda* of the *A.Ś.* (p. 78) is misunderstood as being connected with Alexandria on a wrong philology. *Alexandria* becomes *alasaddā* as in the *Milinda P.* A coral variety is called *ālakandaka* in the *A.-Ś.* Any root-like thing is *kanda* in Sanskrit A coral-shoot will be called *kanda*. *Ala* means yellow (orpiment, orpiment-colour)—*ālakandaka* = 'root-coral with yellow tinge'. (Recently Prof. Lévi utilized the statement of Pliny on import of coral into India as a proof of a late date of the *A.S.*, but Pliny does not say that coral had been unknown to the Indians before.

"In consequence of this difference the beginning of Varshā, or the rainy season, in the times of Alexander and Aśoka, would have fallen just one month earlier than at present."[8]

(iv) See also (*A.Ś.*, *ibid.*) आषाढ़े मासि नष्टच्छायो मध्याह्नो भवति- This could be written only in the North (Pāṭaliputra) and not in the South.

(v) The political data taking us to the Maurya times, we have further materials to hold that the book could not have been written in the later Maurya times. The position of the Śākyas and Ājīvakas could not be low as in the A. (III. 20),[9] they being grouped together with or as Śūdra monks. Under Aśoka or his successors it was not likely that a law hostile to them would have been promulgated. Again, the sarcasm of Patañjali that the Mauryas were fond of money (gold), finds corroboration in the A. that the Maurya sovereign did institute 'archās' or worships for making money.[10] Now Aśoka could not have done it, he was too conscientious and religious for that. His descendants were also religious. The datum of Patañjali and the A. thus should refer either to Chandragupta or to Bindusāra, and under both sovereigns K. served.

The heterodox Jaina and Buddhist and the orthodox Brahmin literatures assert that Kauṭilya was the minister of Chandragupta. The Buddhist and the Jaina books treat him as having been a rascal, debasing coins and making money, making conquests and killing men, etc. The Purāṇas, on the other hand, show him to be an able minister. How could such contrary and human details be given to a person imaginary? His condemnation and awkward Gotra-name are proof to my mind of his historical existence. If we look into the A. it answers both characterizations of K, the heterodox and orthodox. He would put down the heterodox, and the heterodox would find him a bad man.

(vi) If the Purāṇas turn out to be true in asserting the existence of Chandragupta, why should we not believe them about Kauṭilya? If K. existed, why should we not take the

---

[8] Cunningham, *Indian Eras*, p. 3.

[9] Munich MS., Shama Sāstry's trans., p. 251 *n.*

[10] *Ind. Ant.*, 1918, p. 51.

book to be his, especially when we find the last but one verse in the book, giving the authorship, to have been in the book before Kāmandaka who paraphrases it in his introduction? [Jolly (though without assigning any reason) also takes the Śloka to be contemporary with the composition of the book.][11]

(vii) If the book existed before Vātsyāyana, and Kāmandaka ascribed it to K., the onus is on him who wants to ascribe the authorship to another to prove that and disprove the evidence of the A. itself corroborated as it is by Vāt. and Kām., Daṇḍin and Medhātithi, *Pañcha T.* and *Tantrākhyāikā.*

(viii) There is motive for promulgating a Dharma Śāstra ascribing it to a Ṛishi, but there is no such motive in ascribing a material book to another. Besides, Kauṭilya is not a Ṛishi. Earlier A.Ś. books had Ṛishis as authors. If a Paṇḍit writing the book wanted to foster it on another, he would have ascribed it to some Ṛishi and a name unhated by a large section of the community (Buddhists and Jainas).

(ix) The Purāṇas seem to give a second name of Chandragupta as *Narendra.*[12] There is evidence that not only the name of the author is in the book, but also the name of the king, '*Narendra*' whose monogram or mark '*Narendrāṅka*' is directed in the A. to be put on arms (V. 3, p. 247; see also नरेन्द्राङ्क, II. 10).

(x) Only the empire of the early Mauryas could take note of exports and imports from Mahāvisi (*A.Ś.*, II. 11) = Mahāvṛisha of the Veda),[13] the raisin wine *mṛidvī* of Afghanistan (Arachosia), the weights and measures of the Śibi (II. 19) and Mekalā and Magadha at the same time, of Uttarāpatha and Dakshiṇāpatha simultaneously, and provide punishment (from Pāṭaliputra) for defaming the Gandhāra country. And only a minister very highly placed could have all the fiscal and military information which are contained in the A.

---

11 The first Śloka giving the author's name was in the book before Daṇḍin who gives the identical measure of the book just preceding and says that the work was composed as an abridgement by Vishṇu-gupta for the Maurya, almost quoting the words of the A. as in the śloka and the previous passage.

12 *Ind. Ant.*, 1918, p. 55.

13 M. & K., *V.I.*, II, 142, 346.

Punishments for turning women into nuns, and for monks leaving families unprovided for could be laid down (II. 1) only under the early Maurya rule of the first two emperors. Raising a prince on the unmarried daughter of a king (while even Niyoga is condemned in the Śuṅga times, *e.g.*, in the *M. Dh. S.*), knowledge of the epics different from the ones we have, are all indications of an early and pre-Śuṅgan date.

P. 6—Works of the fourth-fifth cen. A.C. and the date of the Kāmandakīya.

Quotations in the *Rāja-N. Ratnākara* indicate that there was also a *Nāradīya Rāja-nīti*. (See *Introduction* to the *R. N. R.*, 1924, p. v).

Nārada figures as a teacher of political wisdom in the *Mahābhārata* (*Sabhā-Parvan*), and he is not known to Kāmandaka. The Nāradīya thus probably came into existence before the sixth century and after Kāmandaka.

Kāmandaka cannot be put in the eighth century as done by Jolly and Winternitz (Jolly's *A.Ś.*, 46). His general style (*cf.* the *Nārada-Smṛiti*)[14] indicates Gupta times. The known date of Bhavabhūti helps us further. Bhavabhūti as ably shown by MM. Gaṇapati Śāstri (*A.Ś.*, II, Intro., p. 7) knew his work; not only he knew Kāmandaka but his audience also must have known his work as a well-established authority to be able to follow and enjoy the character "Kāmandakī" like the "Buddharakshitā" and "Avalokitā." Kāmandaka must have published his work a few centuries before Bhavabhūti (first half of the eighth century). Its earlier limit probably is the *Tantrākhyāyikā* which does not know it. The interval between the *A.S.*, and Kāmandaka is large, for not only several subjects and topics in the *A.Ś.*, have become in Kām.'s time antiquated enough to be left out, a new group of authorities, unknown to the *A.Ś.*, had intervened.

There is a revival of the tradition of Chandragupta Maurya in Gupta times. Royal parents name their sons after him. Viśākhadatta compares him with Vishṇu in his play written under one of the Chandraguptas of the Gupta dynasty (*I.A.*, 1913, p. 265). Chandraguptan laws in the *Kauṭilīya* are closely

[14] See the monitary system of Nārada (App. 56–60) which extends up to the Punjab and knows Dināra.

reproduced in the *Nārada-Smṛiti*. Chandragupta's *Artha-Śāstra* is verified and adapted in the *Kāmandakīya Nītisāra*. There is an ambition, partly realized, of founding a large empire from Pāṭaliputra like that of Chandragupta Maurya. Kālidāsa, a Gupta poet, says that the country becomes *Rājanvalī*, 'possessed of a just king,' only on account of the Magadhan emperor (*Raghuvaṃśa*).[15] The opening verse of the *Kāmandakīya* suggests the reign of Chandragupta II (*J.B.O.R.S.*, XVIII, 1932, p. 37).

P. 6—Pushkara.

He figures also in the political science dialogue in the *Vishṇudharmottara* (II). Probably he is only an ideal person and no author.

P. 6—14th–18th cen. Digests.

To this class is to be added Vāchaspati Miśra's Rājadharma (See *Intro.* to *R. N. R.*, p. *u*). The commentary on the *Nīti-vākyāmṛita* (the date of which must be earlier than its MS. copied in the 1463, *ibid.*) may be included in the class. The commentator does not restrict himself to the orthodox Dharma Śāstra view. He, trying to give all the original sources of Somadeva, really gives a small Digest of *Artha-Śāstra*.

P. 8—Works in Vernaculars.

Lallu Lal wrote a Hindi book based on the *Hitopadeśa* and the *Pañchatantra* and called it 'Rājanīti'.

P. 16—Village fined.

See *Vasishṭha Dharma Śāstra*, III. 4—

अव्रता ह्यनधीयाना यत्र भैक्षचरा द्विजाः ।
तं ग्रामं दण्डयेद्राजा चोरभक्तप्रदो हि सः ॥

P. 17—न सा सभा ।

It is given also by Nārada (1. 18).

P. 23—*Gaṇa*.

The Vedic use of *gaṇa* is in the sense of 'company of soldiers'—व्रातं व्रातं गणं गणम् (*Ṛ. V.*, III. 26, 6).

P. 39—State-arms of the Republics.

---

[15] To say this he has even to commit an anachronism, making the Magadha monarchy which came into existence only with Vasu (*J.B.O.R.S.*, 1) contemporary with Raghu.

Lañchh itself may be from *Laksh* with what is termed by Grierson as 'spontaneous nasalisation' (*J.R.A.S.*, 1922, p. 381 ff).

For *Aṅka* see 'kṛita-Narendrānkaṃ śastrāvaraṇamāyudh-āgāram praveśayet' in the *A.S.*, V. 3, p. 247.

P. 49—Decisions on rolls (Book of Precedents).

The *Jātaka* also knows such books of precedents. See *J.*, III. 292, wherein the law-court precedents are entered : "*vinicchaye potthakam lekhāpetvā*". Probably Vasishṭha also refers to precedents in XIX. 10.

P. 49—Ashṭa-kulaka.

See *E.I.*, XV. 136, the Ashṭa-kula-adhikaraṇas as town corporation officials, and note in App. D, on Part II.

P. 50—'Lechchhai.'

Riksha would also give both *Lichchha* and *Likkha*, but we get such forms for the Lichchhaviṣ (*cf.* Jaina spelling *Lekkhai*) as point to *likshu*, louse as the origin. Manu's *Nichchhavi* would be a local dialectical variation which is peculiar to Eastern India.

P. 53 *n*[18]—शवति ।

Sav = Skt. *Chyab*, Avestan *Syav*.

P. 67—*Jauhar*.

It is derived from either *Jatu ghara* (the *Mahābhārata* '*Jatugriha*,' 'the house of lac', made to entrap and burn the Pāṇḍavas) as has been suggested, or preferably from *Jama-ghara* 'House of Death'. *Jauhar* is spelt as *Jama-hara* in the 'Kānhaḍa de Prabandha' (a work in Old Rājasthānī), p. 94 (pointed out to me by Dr. Suniti K. Chatterji).

P. 73—'Every man in the community had franchise':—citizens *versus* non-citizens.

From a statement of Patañjali it is clear that in a republic there used to be slaves and artizans to whom the peculiar forms which denoted the citizens of a particular republic did not apply—नैतत्तेषां दासे वा कर्मकरे वा (see above p. 31, *n*). This indicates that the artizans as well as slaves were not franchised. The Mauchikarṇas did not keep any slaves in their state (hence the legend in Megasthenes that there were no slaves in India).

Pp. 73–74 *n.*—*Kauninda* and *Kanet*.

Sir G. Grierson is also of the opinion that the *Kanets* should not be identified with the *Kunindas* (*L.S.I.*, Vol. IX, p. 6, *n.*). The form *Kanet* is correct which was personally ascertained by me at Sipri (Simla).

P. 78—Vāhīkan physique.

On the physique of the Vāhīkas we may note that the *Mahābhārata* in abusing their heterodoxy (probably they had then become Mahāyānist Buddhists) quotes a parody of a song of the Vāhīkas which shows that their women were large-bodied and that mutton was their favourite food. "When shall I next sing the song of the Vāhīkas in this Śākala town, when shall I again, dressed in fine garments in the company of fair-complexioned large-sized women eat much mutton, pork, beef and the flesh of fowls, asses and camels? *They who eat not mutton live in vain.*" "So do the inhabitants, drunk with wine, sing. How can religion be found among such people?"

At the time when the *Karṇa-Parvan* (Ch. XLIV) was written, evidently they had become heterodox, probably Buddhists, as it says, 'the Vāhīkas who never perform sacrifices, whose religion has been destroyed,' 'they are without the Veda and without knowledge'. They are orthodox in the *Satapatha Br.* (I. 7. 3. 8, Grierson, *L.S.I*, 4 *n.* 8), in the Upanishads which describe Śvetaketu going into the Punjab for religious tournament, and also evidently in Pāṇini.

P. 82—Madra Country.

In mediæval Indian tradition the Punjab, especially the northern part, was always called Madra-deśa. Guru Govinda Siṃha in his "Vichitra Nāṭaka" says that he was brought from Patna, where he was born, to Madra-deśa or the Punjab.

P. 95—Śalāka :

'Pin' probably does not convey the full sense of 'Śalāka'. *Cf.* Aksha-Śalāka, the Hindu dice. The Śalāka was a small oblong piece which could come easily within the fist.

P. 149—Yaudheya coin legends : *Bhagavato Svāmina* (*ḥ*) : *Brahmaṇya-devasya* (*C.C.I.M.*, 181–82, *C.A.I.*, p. 78) seems to be the correct legend. *Brahmaṇya* is not the name of the Yaudheya king (Rapson, *J.R.A.S.*, 1903, 291), but the name of the god who in some coins is shown with six heads—Kārttikeya (as recognized by Rapson himself).

P. 152—Mālava Coins.

The variety of coins bearing single names and generally no legend of the Mālava *Gaṇa* found at the same place, are attributed to the Mālavas (*C.C.I.M.*, 163, 174–177). Probably they represent the power which superseded the Mālavas. The names are so many puzzles—*e.g.*, *Maraja*, *Jamapaya*, *Paya*, *Magaja*. They seem to be abbreviations—*Maraja* = *Mahā-rāja*; *cf.* 'Mahārāya' (p. 177). *Jama* and *Yama* appear again and again (pp. 174, 176, *Jama-paya*, then *Paya* only). *Mapojaya*, *Mapaya* and *Magaja* (pp. 175, 176) are probably *Mahā*-(*Mahārāja*) *jaya*, *Mā*. (*Mahā-rāja*) *Paya*, and *Ma*. (Mahārāja) *Gaja*. Similarly, *Magajaśa* = *Ma*. (*Mahā*°). *Gaja* (*Gajaśa*), *Gajava* = Gaja-pa ; *Mā go* (read *ga*) *java* = *Ma*. *Gajapa* ; *Mapaka* = *Ma*. *Paka* ; *Mā*. (read *ma*) śapa = *Ma*. *Sarpa* ; *Magachha* = *Ma*. *Gachha* ; *Majupa* = *Ma*. *Jupa* (*Yūpa*) *Bhapamyana* (plate XX, 24) I read as *Bhampāyana*.

P. 153—Freedom in preference to home.

Cf. Manu, VII, 212.

"Let a king, without hesitation, quit for his own sake even a country, salubrious, fertile and causing an increase of cattle" (Bühler).

P. 155 *n*.—*Sanākanīkas*. A 'Mahārāja' *Sanakānīka* as a feudatory of Chandragupta II has left an inscription in the Udayagiri *Vaishṇava* cave temple (Bhilsa, Gwalior) dated GS. 82 (401–2 A.C.). He is the son of a 'Mahārāja' and the grandson of a Mahārāja. *GI.*, p. 25.

P. 181—Ethnology of the republicans.

See R. Chanda, *Indo-Aryan Races* (Rajshahi, 1916), pp. 24, 25, 240, 241.

APPENDIX D

Additional Notes on Part II (1924)

P. 247—*Śreshṭhin* or President of the Town.

Divisional capitals or seats of Governments (*adhishṭhānas*) had their *Śreshṭhins* under the Guptas. *E.I.*, XV, 130, gives the *Nagara-Śreshṭhin* of *Koṭi* in the Province of Bengal under Kumāra Gupta. He is given the honorific '*ārya*' before his name (p. 142), and is associated with the district officer in the administration of the district.

Cf. also Rhys Davids, *Buddhist India*, pp. 96–97, for *Jeṭṭhakā*, *pamukhā*, taken as Aldermen or Presidents, and *Mahā-seṭṭhi* as the Chief Alderman over the Aldermen of the guilds.

P. 293—*Pratinidhi*: whether a Representative of the People?

Pp. 299–300—Council of State and Representative of the People—

District administration in Gupta times and Local Representatives—

A sidelight is thrown by the Gupta system of District administration. The Damodarpur copper-plates, discovered in the district of Dinajpur, Bengal (*E.I.*, XV, pp. 113–145), prove that the District Officer [*Vishaya-pati* or *Vishaya āyuktaka*, appointed by the Governor (*uparika*) of the Province of Bengal (Puṇḍravardhana *bhukti*), the latter holding his appointment from the Emperor direct] made settlements of land in conjunction with the President of the town (*Nagara-Shresṭhin*), the President of the merchants, the senior (*Prathama*) *Kulika* (town judge), the senior city Registrar (*Prathama Kāyastha*). We thus find the Government District Officer co-operating (*samvyavaharati*) with the local representatives in an administerial act of the District.

'The governmental authority of the district' (*adhishṭhān-ādhikaraṇa*) is expressly mentioned as vested in the government official along with the popular officials of the city corporation

—*e.g.*, *Niyuktaka-kumārāmātya-Vetravarmaṇi adhishṭhānādhikaraṇam cha Nagara-Sreshṭhi*° (*etc.*).—*puroge samvyavaharati* (p. 133).

Similarly in the Government of the State it is very probable that the process was repeated.

P. 276—*Mahattarāḥ*.

See *I.A.*, X. 213 and *E.I.*, XV, p. 136, on *Mahattaras*. In the Damodarpur plate (*E.I.*, XV, 36) the *Mahattara and other Ashṭa-kula-adhikaraṇas* deal with settlement of land and report to the Governor. *Cp.* this with *ibid.*, p. 133, where the same function is performed by the President (*Śreshṭhin*), Kulika, Registrar, etc., along with the Government District Officer. The Mahattara is there reporting from some interior town.

Bibliography

(with Abbreviations used)

Account of the Merchant Sulaiman recorded by Abu Zaid.	Translated by Abbé Renaudot.
A., *Artha-Śāstra* *A.S.*, *AŚ.*, Kauṭilīya	The *Artha-Śāstra* of Kauṭilya, ed. by R. Shama Sastry, 1909, Mysore. Govt. Oriental Library Series, Bib. Sanskrita No. 37.
	Its translation by Dr. Shama Sastry, Bangalore, 1915, Same series, No. 37, Part II.
Abhidhāna-Rājendra ..	Jaina Prakrita Kosha Ed. Rutlam, 1919.
Adhyaksha-prachāra, notes on	Notes on that section of *A.Ś.* by Dr. I. J. S. Taraporewala.
Aggañña S. Aggañña Suttanta	See *Dīgha Nikāya*.
Agni-Purāṇa ..	Bengal Recension.
Ait. Br., *Aitareya*, *Aitareya Br.*, *Aitereya Brāhmaṇa*	Ānandāśrama ed.
Alberuni ..	Author of *Alberuni's India*.
Alberuni's India ..	By Alberuni : Trans. by Sachau in two volumes, (Eng. Trans.) Trübner, 1888.
Altindisches Leben ..	By Zimmer, Berlin, 1879.
Amara-kosha ..	By Amarasiṁha. Ed. in Trivandrum Sanskrit Series Nos. XXXVIII, XLIII, LI, LII, by T. Gaṇapati Sāstrī with the commentary *Tīkāsarvasva* of Vandyaghaṭīya Sarvānanda.
Amara-simha ..	Author of the *Amara-kosha*.
Ambaṭṭha Sutta ..	See *D.N.;* translation of, in *Dialogues of the Buddha*, Vol. I.
Ambaṭṭha Suttanta ..	See *D.N.* Translation in *Dialogues of the Buddha*, Pt. I.
Anabasis	By Arrian.
G.P.	*Gaṇa-Pāṭha* of Pāṇini.
Ancient India as described by Classical Writers, or *Ancient India* as described in Classical Literature	By Mc Crindle.

Aṅguttara Nikāya	..	Ed. by the Pāli Text Society.
Anuś. P. *Anuśāsana Parvan*	..	See *M.Bh.*
Aprārka	..	Commentator on *Yājñavalkya-Smṛiti.* Ed. by Hari Nārāyana Apte, 1903.
A.S.R. *Archæological Survey Report*	..	By Cunningham.
Arrian	..	Author of *Anabasis and Indika.* See Megasthenes and IIA.
Asahāya	..	Commentator of *Nārada Smṛiti.*
Aśvaghosha	..	Author of *Vajrasūchī* Ed. by Weber in *Indische Studien.*
A.V. *Atharva Veda*	..	Ed. by Whitney.
Aṭṭhakathā		Commentary on the *Tripiṭaka,* by Buddhaghoṣa; extracts from, translated, in *J.A.S.B.*, VII (1838).
Avadāna-Śataka	..	Ed. by Speyer, in two volumes, Petrograd, 1902.
Ayodhyā K. Ayodhyā Kāṇḍa	..	*Rāmāyaṇa.*
Āchārāṅga Sutta or *Ayāraṅga Sutta*		(*a*) Ed. by Jacobi, 1882. (*b*) Ed. Asiatic Society of Bengal when not otherwise specified.
Apastambīya Dharma-Sūtra, *Āpastamba Dh. S.*		Ed. Georg Bühler, Bombay Sanskrit Series, No. XLIV (with Haradatta's commentary).
Aśvalāyana Gṛihya Sūtra	..	Ed. Ānandāśrama Series, Poona.
Āryadeva	..	Author of *Chatuś-śatikā*; fragments of, in *J.A.S.B.*, 1911.
Bāla., Bāla Kāṇḍa	..	See *Rāmāyaṇa.*
Bālama-Bhaṭṭī	..	Commentary on Mitāksharā, Chowkhambhā Series.
Bāṇa	..	Author of *Harsha-charita.*
Baudhāyana Dh. S. *Baudhāyana Dharma-Sūtra*	..	Ānandāśrama Ed. in the *Smṛiti-Samuchchaya.*
Bhāṭṭadīpikā	..	Commentary on the *Pūrva-Mīmāmsa Darśana* by Khaṇḍadeva. Ed. by Mahādeva Sastri and L. Srinivāsāchārya, Mysore, 1911.

Bhāgavata *Bhāgavata Purāṇa*	Bengal Recension.
Bhaṭṭojī-Dīkshita ..	Author of *Siddhānta Kaumudī*.
Bloomfield ..	Translator of the hymns of *A. V.* in *S.B.E.*, Vol. XLII.
Bṛ. Ar. U.p., *Brihadāraṇyakopanishad*	Nirṇaya-Sāgara Edition.
Bṛihaspati ..	Translated by Jolly in *S.B.E.*, Vol. XXXIII.
Bṛihaspati Sūtra ..	Ed. by Dr. F. W. Thomas (Le Muséon, pp. 131–166).
Bṛ. S., *Bṛihat Saṃhitā* ..	By Varāhamihira, ed. by Kern. Asiatic Society.
Buddhische Kunst in Indien	By Grünwedel.
Buddha	By Oldenberg.
B.I. Buddhist India ..	By Rhys Davids.
C. C. I. M., *Catalogue of Coins in the Indian Museum*	By Vincent A. Smith.
Chaṇḍeśvara ..	Author of *R. N. R.* and *V. R.*
Chāṇakya ..	Same as the author of *AŚ.* (the son of Chaṇaka).
Chatuś-śatikā ..	By Aryadeva, Ed., Haraprasāda Shāstri (ASB).
Chullavagga ..	Vinaya Texts, Vol. II. Translation of, by Oldenberg and Rhys Davids, in *SBE.*, Vols. XVII and XX.
Childers ..	Author of the *Pāli-English Dictionary*.
C. A. I., *Coins of Ancient India*	By Cunnigham, London, 1891.
Corpus Inscriptionum Indicorum III, *C. I. I. III.*	By Fleet for the *Corpus Inscriptionum*.
Cunningham ..	Author of *C. A. I.* and *A. S. R.*, Report of the Archæological Survey of Western India, Indian Eras.
Curtius ..	See *I. I. A.*, Megasthenes.
Chh. Up., *Chhāndogya Up.* *Chhāndogya-Upanishad*	Nirṇaya-Sāgara Edition.

Daṇḍin ..	Author of the *Daśakumāra Charita*.
Daśakumāracharita ..	By Daṇḍin; Ed. with various reading by Nārāyaṇa Bāl Krishṇa Godbole (eighth Ed.), Bombay, 1917.
Das Rāmāyaṇa ..	By Dr. H. Jacobi.
Dāsabodha ..	By Rāmadāsa, Poona Ed.
Dialogues of the Buddha ..	By Rhys Davids, Sacred Books of the Buddhists Series, 2 Parts.
D.N., *Dīghā-Nikāya*	Pd. by the Pāli Text Society (in three volumes).
Diodorus ..	See *I. I. A.*, Megasthenes.
Divyāvadāna	Ed. by Cowell and Neil, Cambridge.
Early History of India ..	By Vincent A. Smith.
Enc. Britt., *Encyclopedia Brittanica*	Eleventh Edn.
Ep. Ind., *EI.*, *Epigraphia Indica* ..	*Epigraphia Indica*.
Epigraphia Zeylanica ..	Ed. by Wickramsinghe (Archæological Survey, Ceylon).
Epitome of Megasthenes ..	By Diodorus, see Megasthenes.
Fleet ..	Author of *Gupta Inscriptions*.
Gautama ..	Author of *Gautama Dh. Ś.*
Gautama Dh. Ś., *Gautama Dharma-Śāstra*	Ed. by Stenzler.
Geschichte des Tāranātha	Trans. by Scheifner.
Grierson ..	Author of *Linguitic Survey of India*.
Gopatha Brāhmaṇa ..	Ed. Bibliotheca Indica.
G.I., *Gupta Inscriptions*	Edited by Fleet.
Govindrāja ..	Commentator on *Rāmāyaṅa*.
G.R.M. *Gaṇa-Ratna-Mahodadhi*	By Vardhamāna; Ed. by Bhīmasena, Allahabad, 1898.
Grünwedel ..	Author of *Buddhische Kunst in Indies*, translated into English by Burgess.
Harsha-charita ..	By Bāṇa.
Haradatta ..	Commentator of *Āpastambha Dh. Ś.*
Herodotus ..	By Rawlinson.

History of Antiquity	..	In four volumes by Prof. Max Duncker, translation of, by Abbot.
History of Mysore	..	By Wilks, 2nd. Ed., 1869.
H. I. L., History of Indian Literature.		By Weber, translated by Zacharæ (Trübner).
History of Sanskrit Literature, Sanskrit Literature		By Macdonell, 1899.
Ind. Ant., I. A., Indian Antiquary		
I.C., Indian Coins	..	By Prof. Rapson.
Indika	..	By Arrian.
Indische Alterthumskunde, Ind. Alt.		By Lassen.
Indo-Aryans		By Rājendra Lall Mitra.
Indo-Aryan Races	..	Ramāprasād Chanda.
J., Jātakas	..	Ed. by Fausbjoll, Kopenhagen, in six volumes.
Journal Asiatique		
J.A.S.B., Journal of the Asiatic Society of Bengal	..	(Calcutta).
J.B.O.R.S., JBORS, J. BORS. Journal of the Bihar and Orissa Research Society.		Patna, 1915 to 1924.
J.R.A.S. Journal of the Royal Asiatic Society.		London.
Jaimini	..	Author of the *Mīmāṃsā-Darśanam.*
Jolly, J.	..	(*a*) Ed. *AŚ.* Punjab Sanskrit Series' No. 4, Vol. I, Lahore, 1923. (*b*) Ed. *Nārada-Smṛiti.* (Bib. Ind.). (*c*) Translation of (*b*) in *SBE.*, Vol. VII.
K. Kauṭilya		Kauṭilya, author of the *AŚ.*, full name—Vishṇugupta Kauṭilya. See *AŚ.*
Kalpa Sūtra	..	See Translation of, by Jacobi, in *S.B.E.*, Vol. XIII.

K P.. *Karṇa Parva*	See *M.Bh.*
Kaṭha Upanishad ..	Bom. Ed.
Kālidāsa ..	Author of *Raghuvaṁśa*, *Śakuntalā* and *Mālavikāgnimitra*.
Kāmandaka ..	Author of *K. N. S.*
Kāmandakīya, *Kāmandakīya Nītisāra*, *K. N. S.*	The *Nītisāra* of Kāmandaka with the commentary *Jayamaṅgala* of Śaṅkarārya, ed. by T. Gaṇapati Sāstrī, Trivandrum, 1912 ; Trivandrum Sanskrit Series, No. XIV.
Kāma-Sūtra *Kāma S.*, *K S.* ..	By Vātsyāyana Ed. (*a*) Nirṇayasāgara (*b*) Chaukhāmbā Sanskrit Series, Benares.
Kaśikā ..	By Paṇdits Vāmana and Jayāditya, Ed. by Bāla Śāstrī, Benares, 1898.
Kātyāyana ..	Quoted by Chaṇḍeśvara, Mitra-Miśra and Nīlakaṇṭha.
Kātyāyana ..	Author of the *Vārttikas*.
Kṛishṇa Dvaipāyana	Quoted in *Mitākshardā*.
Kṛishṇa Yajurveda ..	Mysore edition.
Kāṭhaka Saṃhitā ..	Kāṭhaka Recension of *TS*.
Kullūka ..	Author of a commentary on *Mānava-Dharma Śūtra*.
L. V., *Lalita-vistara* ..	Bib. Ind. Asiatic Society, Ed.
Lassen ..	Author of *Indische Alterthumskunde*.
Lévi ..	Author of *Le Nepal*—in three volumes.
Life of Appollonius ..	By Philostratus
Life of the Buddha ..	By Rockhill (Trübner).
L. S. I. *Linguistic Survey of India*	By Grierson.
M. and K. Macdonell and Keith	Authors of the *Vedic Index*.
Māhābhārata, *M. Bh.*	Bengal Recension (when not specified otherwise), Kumbakonum (when so specified) edited by T. R. Vyāsāchārya, 1908.
M.G. *Mahā-Govinda Sutta*	See D. N., Vol. II.
Macdonell ..	Author of the *History of the Sanskri Literature* and the joint author of *V.I.*

M.P.S., Mahāparinibbāna Suttanta	See D. N. Translation in *S.B.E.*, Vol. XI. and *Dialogues of the Buddha*, Pt. II.
Mahāvagga ..	Ed. by Oldenberg; Translation of, by Rhys Davids and Oldenberg in *S.B.E.*, Vols. XIII and XVII.
Mahā-Bhāshya Kielhorn ..	By Patañjali, Ed. by Kielhorn.
M. N., Majjhima Nikāya	Ed. by the Pāli Text Society.
M. V., Mahāvastu ..	Ed. by Sénart in three volumes.
Mādhava ..	Author of *Nyāyamālā*.
Mārkaṇḍeya P., Mārkaṇḍeya Purāṇa	Bengal Edition.
M. Manu Dh. Ś.; Mānava; Mānava Dharma Śāstra	Ed. by (*a*) J. Jolly (*b*) Ed. by Māṇḍalik.
Mahāvaṃsa ..	Ed. by Geiger.
Mālavikāgnimitra ..	By Kālidāsa.
Maitrāyaṇī, M. S.	Ed. by Schröder.
Māitrāyaṇī Samhitā	
Mc Crindle	Author of *I.I.A.*, Ptolemy, *Ancient India as described in Classical Literature* and Megasthenes.
Mitāksharā ..	By Vijñāneśvara.
Megasthenes Ancient India as described by Megasthenes	Mc Crindle.
Milinda-Pañho ..	Translated by Rhys Davids in *S.B.E.*, Vols. XXXV and XXXVI.
Mitra-Miśra ..	Author of the Commentary *Vīramitrodaya*, on *Yājñavalkyasmriti* (unpublished) a manuscript of in the possession of Mr. Govindadāsa of Benares, author of *V. M. R. S. V. M.*
Mīmāṃsā-Darśanam, P. Mimansā ..	By Jaimiui with the Commentary of Śabarasvāmī (*Bib. Ind.*).
Mṛichchhakaṭika ..	By Śūdraka; Ed. by Kāsīnātha Pāṇḍurang Parab, with the commentary of Prithvīdhara, Bombay, 1900.
Modern Review ..	Monthly, Calcutta.

Monier-Williams .. Author of the '*Sanskrit-English Dictionary*'.

Moribus et Populis Germaniæ .. By Tacitus.

Mudrā-Rākshasa .. By Viśākha-datta, ed. by K. T. Telang, Bombay.

Nāgeśa .. Author of the *Pradīpodyota on Māhā-Bhāshya* by Nāgeśa (Asiatic Society, Calcutta.

Nārada .. Translated by Jolly in *S.B.E.*, Vol. XXXI. II, Quotatoins in Digest.

Nāmaliṅgānuśāsana .. *Amarakosha.*

Nārada-Smṛiti (text) .. Ed. by Jolly with passages from the commentary of *Asahāya* (Asiatic Society, Calcutta).

Nepal .. By Lévi.

Nirukta .. By Yāska.

Nīlakaṇṭha .. Author of *Vyavahāra-Mayūkha*, Ed. by Mandlik with English Translation, 1880.

Nītivākyāmṛita .. By Somadeva,
(*a*) Ed. by Gopālanārāyaṇajanata, Bombay.
(*b*) Ed. by Nāthurāma Premī, Bombay, 1923.

Nyāyamālā .. By Mādhavāchārya, Ed. Ānandāśrama Series.

Oldenberg .. Author of *Buddha*. Translated into English by William Hoey.

Oldenberg .. Editor of *Vin*.

Pañcha Tantra .. Calcutta Ed.

Patañjali .. Author of the *Māhā-Bhāshya.*

Pargiter .. Author of the Purāṇa-Text, and article in *J.R.A.S.*

P.E. Dictionary, Pāli-English Dictionary Childers.

Pāṇini .. Author of *Sanskrit Grammar.*

Parāshara Gṛihya-Sūtra Hathwa ed. with the commentaries of Karka, Jayarāma, etc., Lazarus, Benares.

Pradīpaddyota .. See Nāgeśa.

Philostratus .. Author of *Life of Appllonius.*

Proc. A. S. B. Procedure of Asiatic Society of Bengal

Praśna-Vyākaraṇa-Sūtra-Vyākhyāna — Quoted by Shamashastry in *A.-Ś.*, p. 46, F.N.

Pratāp Chandra Ray — Translator of *M. Bh.*

Priyadarśi-Praśastayaḥ — By Rāmāvatāra Śarma, Patna, 1915.

P.T., Purāṇa Texts of the Dynasties of the Kali Age, or Purāṇa Texts or Pargiter's Texts — By Pargiter, Oxford, 1913.

Raghu-Vaṃśa .. By Kālidāsa.

Ranade .. Author of *Rise of the Maratha Power.*

R N. R. N. R., Ratnākara Rāja-Nīti-Ratnākara, — By Chaṇḍeśvara, Ed. by K. P. Jayaswal, Bihar and Orissa Reserach Society, 1924.

Rapson .. Author of *I.C.*, Ed. Grundriss Series.

Rāja-Nīti-Mayūkha .. By Nīlakaṇṭha, Kāśī-Saṃskṛita Yantrālaya, 1880.

R. Mitra, Rajendra Lala Mitra — Author of *Indo-Aryans.*

Rāma .. Commentator on *Rāmāyaṇa.*

Rāmāyaṇa .. The *Rāmāyaṇa* of Vālmikī with the commentary (Tilaka) of Rāma, ed. (*a*) by Kāśīnāth Pāṇdurang Parab, Bombay, 1888; (*b*) by Messrs. Krishnāchārya and Vyāsāchārya.

Rāmadāsa .. Author of *Dāsabhodha.*

Report of the Archæological Survey of India — Cunningham and others.

Rhys Davids .. Author of *B.I.* and *Dialogues of the Buddha.*

Rise of the Maratha Power — By Ranade.

Rock Series and Proclamations — See *Ep. Ind.*, Vol. II.

Rockhill .. Author of the *Life of Buddha.*

Romantic Legend of Śākya Buddha. — By Beal (Trübner).

Roth	.. Joint Author of *St. Petersburgh Dictionary*.
Ṛ. V., *Rig-Veda*	.. Ed. by Max Müller (with the commentary of *Sāyana*).
Śakuntalā	.. By Kālidāsa.
Śaṅkarārya	.. The commentator on *K.N.S.*
Śat. Br., *Śatapatha*, *Śatapatha Br.*, *Śatapatha Brāhmana*,	Asiatic Society ed., the Translation of, in *S. B. E.* Series.
Sabara	.. Commentator on *Jaimini*. See *Mīmāṃsā Darśanam*.
Ś., *Śānti*, *Śānti P.*	.. See *M.Bh.*
Ś. P., *Śāntiparvan*	.. See *M.Bh.*
Ś. N. S. *Sukra-Nīti-Sāra*	.. Ed. by Jīvānanda Vidyāsāgara Bhaṭṭāchārya, 1890.
Strabo	.. *See Ancient India as described in Classical Literature*, Megasthenes.
Sabhāparvan, *S. P.*	.. See *M.Bh.*
Sāmaññaphala Sutta	.. See *Dīgha Nikāya*, Vol. I.
S B E., *Sacred Books of the East*	Ed. Max Müller, Clarendon Press. Oxford.
Saint Petersburg Dictionary, *St. Petersburg Dictionary*.	.. By Roth and Böhtlingk.
Sanskrit Grammar of Pāṇini, *Pāṇini*, *P.*	.. *Ashṭādhyāyi* by Pāṇini.
Siddhānta Kaumudī	.. By Bhattoji Dīkshita.
Tacitus	.. Author of *Moribus Populis Germaniæ*.
Tagore Lectures	.. By K. P. Jayaswal.
Taitt, Br., *T. Brāhmaṇa*, *Taittirīya Br.* *Taittirīya-Brāhmana*	Mysore ed., with the commentary of Bhaṭṭa Bhāskara.

T.S. *Taittirīya Saṃhitā*	..	Mysore ed., with the commentary of Bhaṭṭa Bhāskara Miśra.
Ud. P. *Udyoga Parvan*	..	See *M.Bh.*
Vajrasūchi	..	By Aśvaghosha.
Vāmadeva	..	Quoted in *M.Bh.*
V. Mihira. Varāhamihira		Author of *Bṛ. S.*
Vardhamāna	..	Author of *Gaṇa-Ratna-Mahodadhi*; Ed by Bhīmasena, Allahabad, 1898.
Vasishth Dh. Ś, *Dharm-Śāstra.*	..	Ed. by Fuehrer.
Vājasaneyi-Saṃhitā	..	Ed. Bombay.
Vārttikas	..	On Pāṇini by Kātyāyana.
V., Vātsyāyana	..	Author of *Kāma Ś.*
Vāyu P. *Vāyu Purāṇa,* *P.T.*		Bengal Recension : See Pargiter's Text.
V.I. *Vedic Index*		By Arthur Anthony Macdonell and Arthur Berriedale Keith, London, 1912.
Vijñāneśvara	..	Author of *Mītākshara*, Bombay Ed.
Vinaya, Vin., *Vinaya Texts*	..	Ed. by Oldenberg.
V. Smith	..	Author of *C. E. I. M.* and *Early History*
Vincent A. Smith		*of India.*
Vishṇu Purāṇa, *Vishṇu P.*		Bengal Edition.
Vishṇu Purāna	..	Translation of, by Wilson and Hall.
V.M. *Vīra-Mitrodaya*	..	By Mitra Miśra, Ed. by Jivānanda Vidyāsāgara Bhaṭṭāchārya, 1875.
V.M.R.N. *Vīra-Mitrodaya*		By Mitra Miśra; Ed. Chaukhambā Sanskrit Series, 1916.
Vyavahāra-Mayūkha	..	By Nīlakaṇtha, Ed. by Mandalik.
Vyāsa	..	Quoted by Aparārka.
Walsh	..	On Kongu Administration in *I.A.*, 1906.
Weber	..	Author of *H.I.L.*
White Yajur-Veda, *W. Yajur Veda,* *White Yajurveda.*		Mādhyandina Śākhā, Nirnaya-Sāgara Ed.

Yājñavalkya, *Yājñavalkya Smṛiti* .. (*a*) See Aparārka, (*b*) Ed. by Mandalik together with English translation, (*c*) Ed. by Wāsudev Laxman Shāstri Pansīkar with the commentary on *Mitāksharā* of Vijñāneśvara (2nd), Bombay, 1918.

Yāska .. Author of *Nirukta*.

Yuddha K., *Yuddha*, *Yuddha Kāṇḍa*. See *Rāmāyaṇa*.

Zimmer .. Author of *Altindisches Leben*.

INDEX

A—*Contd.*

A—*Contd.*

B

B—*Contd.*

C

C—*Contd.*

C—*Contd.*

C—*Contd.*

D

D—*Contd.*

E

E—*Contd.*

F

G

G—*Contd.*

H

H—*Contd.*

I

I—*Contd.*

J

J—*Contd.*

K

K—*Contd.*

K—*Contd.*

K—*Contd.*

L

L—*Contd.*

M

M—*Contd.*

M—*Contd.*

M—*Contd.*

N

P—*Contd.*

P—*Contd.*

P—*Contd.*

Q

R

R—*Contd.*

R—*Contd.*

R—*Contd.*

S

S—*Contd.*

S—*Contd.*

S—*Contd.*

T

V—*Contd.*

W

X

Y

Y—*Contd.*

Z

ERRATA

Page	Note	Line	For	Read
5	8	1, 3	मनुष्यवतो	मनुष्यवती
5	8	6	लब्धपरिरक्षणे	लब्धपरिरक्षणी
5	8	6	रक्षितविवर्धने	रक्षितविवर्धनी
13		12	समितोरियानः	समितीरियानः
14	9	3	अभिभूरहमागमविराड-प्रतिवास्याः	अभिभूरहमागम् विराडप्रतिवास्याः
16		10	संग्रामे संयन्ते समयकामः	संग्रामे संयत्ते समयकामः
16	18	1	भामणीरेषां	ग्रामणीरेषां
16	19	1	शत्रुभिः	शत्रुभिः
18	1	3	संगछा	संगच्छा
18	1	8	यद्रवो	यद्वो
18	1	8	यद्रवड्वमिह	यद्वद्धमिह
18	1	9	तद्रव	तद्व
19		3	वदेयुस्तहि	वदेयुस्तद्ध
19	2	1	सद्भिर्वा	सद्भिर्वा
20	6	2	नदनशोला	नदनशीला
20	7	1	यद्रग्रामे	यद्ग्रामे
20	7	2	धर्माणि	धर्मणि
21		2	व	च
24	3	2	विरुद्धराज्आणि	विरुद्धरज्जणि
25		15	संघोद्घौ	संघोद्घौ
25	7	1	भविस्सामोति	भविस्सामीति
27	15	1	*tini*	*tiṇi*
28	19	2	महाकप्रफिणस्य	महाकपूफिणस्य
28	19	2	प्राभृतमुपनौतम्	प्राभृतमुपनीतम्
28	19	3	गणाधोनाः	गणाधीनाः
28	19	3	केचिद्राजाधोना	केचिद्राजाधीना
29	21	1	लोगम्नि	लोगम्मि
29	21	1	मल्लपूरादी	मल्लपूरादि
29	21	2	कुप्पावयणम्मी	कुप्पावयणम्मि
29	21	2	ओसन्नगोयाणं	ओसन्नगीयाणं
29	21	5	कूप्रवचने	कुप्रवचने

Page	Note	Line	For	Read
31	4	2	आयुधजीविसंघस्तद्दाचिनः	अयुधजीविसंघस्तद्वाचिनः
31	4	2	प्रातिपदिकाद्ब्राह्मण	प्रातिपदिकाद्‌ब्राह्मण
31	4	4	क्षौद्रक्यः क्षौद्रक्यो	क्षौद्रक्यः। क्षौद्रक्यौ
31	4	4	मालव्यौः। मालव्य	मालव्यौ। मालव्याः
31	5	1	१६७	१६८
32	5	11	लुक्तास्मिश्चाल्लुग्	लुक्तस्मिंश्चाग्लुग्
32	6	1	वृकाट्टिण्यण्	वृकट्टेण्यण्
32	8	1	कौण्डीपरथदण्डको	कौण्डोपरथदाण्डकी
32	8	2	कौष्टुकिर्जाल्मानिश्च	कौष्टकिर्जालमानिंश्च
33	9	1	पर्श्वादियोधेयादिभ्या-मणञौ	पर्श्वादियौधेयादिभ्या-मणञौ
35	18	4	तद्व्याख्यातारः	तद्‌व्याख्यातारः
36	24	1	वुञ्	वुञ्
38	37	3	अन्धकवृष्ण्य	अन्धकवृष्णय
39	43	2	संघंः	संघः
40	44	1	प्राड्विवाकादि	प्राड्‌विवाकादि
40	50	2	कर्त्तव्य	कर्त्तव्यम्
41	52	2	क	कः
48	16	1	सत्तसहससानि	सत्तसहस्सानि
55	18	1	कम्बोजेष्येव	कम्बोजेष्वेव
55	18	1	काम्बोजाः	कम्बोजाः
64	27	1	क्षुद्रकौर्जितम्	क्षुद्रकैर्जितम्
65	29	10	ञ्प्राधेनवत्	आधेनवम्
65	*	1	९	२
65	*	5	गोत्राहुञ्न	गोत्राद्वुञ्न
65	*	8	कोसलोया	कोसलीया
66	*	20	यथावाध्येत	यथाबाध्येत
66	*	21	वाधत	बाधत
69	47	2	वदन्तः	वदन्त
69	47	3	योक्ते	योक्त्रे
79	2	1	कुलपुत्तस्म	कुलपुत्तस्स
79	2	2	ग्वत्तियस्स	खत्तियस्स
79	3	2	वापिअंजे	वापिअंभे
81	9	1	विहान्..गच्छीत	विद्वान्..गच्छति

Page	Note	Line	For	Read
81	9	2	ज्येष्ठयाय	ज्यैष्ठयाय
81	11	1	स्वराडस्युदाची	स्वराडस्युदीची
83	18	1	वैराज्यां	वैराज्यं
87	34	16	नरव्याध्र	नरव्याघ्र
87	34	18	राजसोत्त	राजसीत्त
87	34	23	धर्मस्तेषामनोनशत्	धर्मस्तेषामनीनशत्
87	34	31	कृशन्	कृशान्
87	34	36	९	१९
89	36	2	इक्स्वागकुलाणि	इक्खागकुलाणि
93	8	2	भिक्त्ववे वग्गकम्म	भिक्खवे वग्गकम्मं
102	3	1	पच्चेकाभिपच्च	पच्चेकाधिपच्चं
103	7	2	वासुदेवार्जुंनाभ्यां	वासुदेवार्जुनाभ्यां
103	9	2	माद्रौ	माद्री
103	9	3	वार्ज्यौ	वार्जी
105	2	3	कुलिकास्मार्थमुख्याश्च	कुलिकास्सार्थमुख्याश्च
108		6	विजिगोषन्ते	विजिगीषन्ते
109		1	भ्रातृन्	भ्रतॄन्
109		4	माहाबाहो	महाबाहो
109		12	भूयसो	भूयसी
109		20	कुलवृद्धैः रुपेक्षिता	कुलवृद्धैरुपेक्षिताः
121		9	इधाराजविसयाह्मि	इध राजविसयम्हि
127		14	ह्रदाः	ह्रदाः
135		31	ह्दिालाजविशवबि	ह्दिालाजविशवषि
172	10	1	समयं	समग्रं
173	13	1	मात्स्यन्यायाभिभूताः	मात्स्यन्यायाभिभूताः
173	14	5	षष्ठ	षष्ठं
193		13	धारया	धारय
194		21	वृणती	वृणतां
196	11	1	विश्यामि	षिश्यामि
196	11	2	वर्वसासिश्चब्रापो	वर्चसासिश्चब्रापो
197	12	2	अपरद्धं	अपरुद्धं
197	13	2	सांयिधानः	संविधानः
197	15	2	देवोमैर्त्या	देवोमर्त्यां
197	15	3	सुष्टुतिमां	सुष्टुतिमा

Page	Note	Line	For	Read
198	15	7	विलम्	बिलम्
201	9	2	परिवृत्का	परिव्रक्त्या
205	20	1	धुरोडाशेन	पुरोडाशेन
208	29	2	अग्निर्गृहपतिंराविंत्त	अग्निर्गृहपतिरावित्त
211	3	1	सर्वाल्लो ँकान्विन्देतायं	सर्वाँल्लोकान्विन्देतायं
211	3	2	राज्ञा	राज्ञां
214	13	3	वष्ठमंशं	षष्ठमंशं
217	21	1	त	तं
220	33	2	व	य
221	35	3	देवस्त्रुवामेतानि	देवसुवामेतानि
227	18	1	भवन्ती	भवन्तो
228		31	takes	taxes
241	19	9	द्रष्ठुमिच्छन्ति	द्रष्टुमिच्छन्ति
243	28	11	तदध्यक्षकरचिह्नितं	तदध्यक्षकरचिह्नितं
245	37	1	श्रोणयस्तथा	श्रेणयस्तथा
247	45	3	विंद्यश्च	विंद्याश्च
249	49	6	वर्धयेयु....	वर्धयेयु....
249	51	2	ग्रौमपौर....विंद्यश्च	ग्राम....विंद्याश्च
254	68	12	....मावेशनिभिः	....मावेशनीभिः
257	5	2	अहोऽस्थि	अहोऽस्मि
257	6	5	गतेष्यथ	गतेष्वथ
258	11	1	पौरैवृद्धपुरःसरैः	पौरैर्वृद्धपुरस्सरैः
259	19	1	Omit प्रणितरस्तं च	
260	20	3	दण्डमाधित्सता नृपा	दण्डमाधित्सता नृप
262	27	2	भिक्षते	भिक्षेत
265	33	18	कार्य	कार्यं
267	41	3	आकर कर्मान्त..पतननि	आकरकर्मान्त..पत्तनानि
267	41	4	मभ्रतां	बभ्रतां
267	42	2	इहादिष्ठाने	इहाधिष्ठाने
271	51	1	पोरजानपदा	पौरजानपदा
272	56	1	सर्ववर्णोभ्यो..चौरैर्हृतं	सर्ववर्णेभ्यो..चौरैर्हृतं
284	9	1	अतीव दिवसे	अतीतदिवसे
287	10	1	अकदस्मा	अक्स्वदस्सा
288	16	2	सप्राडविवाकः	सप्राडविवाकः

Page	Note	Line	For	Read
288	17	2	मन्त्रिपरिषदश्वाह्वय	मन्त्रिपरिषदश्चाहूय
289	19	5	स्यान्नृपः	स्यान्नृपः
289	22	1	कुर्यातू	कुर्यात्
291	27	4	एधगुप्त	राधगुप्त
291	27	6	युवरज्ये	युवराज्ये
291	27	7	कुर्कुंटारामं	कुर्कुटारामं
297	45	1	नीतिशस्त्रास्त्र··	नीतिशास्त्रास्त्र..
299	53	1	एको मन्त्रौ	एको मन्त्री
299	53	2	भक्ष्यन्तौं	भक्षयन्तौ
300	55	2	स्यान्नृप	स्यान्नृपः
300	56	2	विशांपते	विशांपतेः
304	63	2	..वेतनी	..वेतनो
308	8	5	लिखनमत्स्येनत्प्राग्लि-खेदयम्	लिखनमत्स्येतत्प्राग्लिखेदनम्
308	8	6	विर्लिखेत्ततः	विलिखेत्ततः
309	10	3	चोरौ तौ मृत्यन्नृपतौ	चौरौ तौ मृत्यन्नृपती
313		2	पलिचलिटेव	पलिहटेवेति
314	24	1	अलाधयितबे	आलाधयितवे
316		21	आत्रियंज्ञसेन माधवसेन	आत्रोर्यज्ञसेनमाधवसेन
316		23	शिष्टामुत्तरदक्षिणो	शिष्टामुत्तरदक्षिणे
316		24	विमज्योभौ	विभज्योभौ
316		28	प्रतिष्टां-गमिष्यति	प्रतिष्ठां गमिष्यति
316		31	प्रविष्टय	प्रविश्य
316		37	परस्पर..विंकारी	परस्पर..विकारौ
318	34	2	ह्येतान्युभयादन्यो..	ह्येतान्युभयादयो..
318	34	5	कार्यऽन्ये	कार्येऽन्ये
318	34	6	कुंशल	कुशलं
318	35	2	सप्तभिर्दशभिश्च	सप्तभिर्दशभिश्च
323	2	4	कार्षापणं भवेद्दण्ड्यौ	कार्षापणो भवेद्दण्ड्यः
325	8	2	चिन्तासक्तनिमग्र..	चिन्तासक्तानिमग्न..
326	13	4	पश्यैच्च	पश्येच्च
327	16	1	236	326
330	21	1	सीाक्षभिर्लिखितै..	साक्षिभिर्लिखितै..

Page	Note	Line	For	Read
334		11	क्तः	कृतः
336	11	2	नीच्छिद्यादात्मनो	नोच्छिद्यादात्मनो
336	11	2	तृष्टणया	तृष्णया
337	16	4	दमयन्निर्व	दमयन्निव
337	17	2	ना	न
338	21	3	तथा वेक्ष्य	तथाऽवेक्ष्य
338	23	2	क्रमयध्वानं	क्रयमध्वानं
338	24	2	भाण्डामुच्छिन्द्यादफलं	भाण्डमुच्छिन्द्यादफलं
339	28	3	अङ्कश्च	अह्नश्च
340	5	1	सङ्घस्मामुत्थायकादन्य- स्ममयानुबन्धो	सङ्घस्सामुत्थायकादन्य- स्समयानुबन्धो
340	6	1	पूर्वस्माहसदण्डः	पूर्वस्साहसदण्डः
340	6	1	प्रव्राजयतः	प्रव्राजयतः
340	6	3	प्रव्रजेदात्रुश्च्य धर्मस्वान्	प्रव्रजेदाक्रन्दयधर्मस्थान्
345		13	स्वत्वमासोत्तत्रैव	सत्वमासीत्तत्रैव
345		13	सेव	सैव
345		15	तत्तद्ग्रामक्षेत्रादी	तत्तद्ग्रामक्षेत्रादौ
345		17	गृहक्षेत्रादी	गृहक्षेत्रादौ
345	12	7	भूर्मिदेया	भूमिर्देया
345	12	10	भूमेरिष्टे	भूमेरीष्टे
346		16	स्मृतैः	स्मृतेः
347	16	7	भूमिस्वाम्याभावे	भूमिस्वाम्यभावे
352	2	2	सकलरट्ठवासिनी	सकलरट्ठवासिनो
352	2	2	सामिकी	सामिको
352	2	3	करोति	करोन्ति
352	2	4	इस्मरियम्ब	इस्सरियम्ब
359	3	1	समन्तपर्यायी स्यात्	समन्तपर्यायी स्याम्
362	17	1	हिमयत्समुद्रान्त . .	हिमवत्समुद्रान्त . .
362	17	2	सहस्रपरिमाण . .	सहस्रपरिमाण . .
370		4	अर्धभोक्ताऽस्मि	अर्धभोक्तापि
371		20	षाड्गुण्यत्य	षड्गुण्यस्य
390		5	मध्यह्नो	मध्याह्नो